PINK TRIANGLE

THE FEUDS AND PRIVATE LIVES OF

TENNESSEE WILLIAMS, GORE VIDAL, TRUMAN CAPOTE,

AND MEMBERS OF THEIR ENTOURAGES

OTHER BOOKS BY DARWIN PORTER

PINK
TRIANGLE

THE FEUDS AND PRIVATE LIVES OF

TENNESSEE WILLIAMS, **GORE VIDAL,** **TRUMAN CAPOTE,**

AND MEMBERS OF THEIR ENTOURAGES

Darwin Porter & Danforth Prince

PINK TRIANGLE

THE FEUDS AND PRIVATE LIVES OF TENNESSEE WILLIAMS, GORE VIDAL, TRUMAN CAPOTE, & MEMBERS OF THEIR ENTOURAGES

Darwin Porter and Danforth Prince

Manufactured in the United States of America

ISBN 978-1-936003-37-2

Special thanks to the Stanley Mills Haggart Collection,
the Woody Parrish-Martin Collection, the H. Lee Phillips Collection,
and Elsa Maxwell Cafe Society.

Cover designs by Richard Leeds (Bigwigdesign.com)
Videography and Publicity Trailers by Piotr Kajstura

Distributed in North America, the U.K., and Australia
through National Book Network (www.NBNbooks.com)

1 2 3 4 5 6 7 8 9 10

THIS BOOK IS DEDICATED

TO THESE WITNESSES OF THE TRIO WE'VE DEFINED AS
"THE PINK TRIANGLE:"

FRANK MERLO & STANLEY MILLS HAGGART

Frank Merlo

Stanley Mills Haggart

CONTENTS

AWARD-WINNING ENTERTAINMENT
ABOUT HOW AMERICA INTERPRETS ITS CELEBRITIES

WWW.BLOODMOONPRODUCTIONS.COM

Introduction

In the aftermath of World War II, during the latter half of "The American Century," when literacy was higher and where more people discussed contemporary books and theater than they do today, three men, each a homosexual, rose from obscurity to positions of spectacular literary fame.

Collectively, they changed America's tastes in entertainment, expanded the boundaries of censorship, and redefined "The Golden Age of Postwar American Literature."

They paid a high price for their success. Their ferociously competitive personalities and private lives—frequently referenced in the tabloids, in literary journals, and on TV—eventually became more widely reviewed than their writings.

There were many witnesses to the sometimes bitchy dynamics of this infamous trio. Their habit of pulling other famous people into their slugfests invariably drew explosive media coverage and rivers of gossip among insiders on Broadway, in Hollywood, and among the jaded *cognoscenti* worldwide.

Darwin Porter, the senior co-author of this anthology of scandal, began recording its information when—as the youthful Bureau Chief for *The Miami Herald* in Tennessee Williams' home town of Key West—he began asking questions, taking notes, and dreaming of the day when his overview of the "Lavender Literati" could become public.

With the publication of this book, Blood Moon has made history's first attempt to compile an overview of this brilliant trio into a coherent whole. The Triangle it illuminates is Pink, its references are literate and sexy, its gossip is captivating, and its meat is raw, juicy, and bloody, indeed. For more about how it was compiled, please refer to the Acknowledgments and Authors' Bio sections at the back.

With this book, we proudly present, as a documentation of another, more literate era, The Pink Triangle, and through it, an insight into the awesome personal histories of Tennessee Williams, Truman Capote, and Gore Vidal.

Happy reading, with best wishes
Danforth Prince

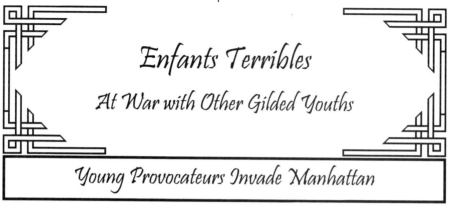

Chapter One

Enfants Terribles

At War with Other Gilded Youths

Young Provocateurs Invade Manhattan

Enfants Terribles: (Left to right): **Tennessee Williams, Gore Vidal,** and **Truman Capote**

It was right before Christmas in December of 1945.

The streets of Manhattan were filled with Santas, often with a pillow stuffed into their red suits. The Salvation Army was out in full force.

The El rumbled along Third Avenue, and double-decker buses, called "Queen Marys," rolled along Fifth Avenue. The *Twentieth Century Limited* pulled into old Penn Station every night as movie stars stepped off to be greeted by photographers and reporters—Paulette Goddard, Gene Tierney, Cary Grant, Joan Crawford, Rosalind Russell, Myrna Loy, and a newcomer, Ava Gardner.

Author John Cheever remembered "When the city of New York was still filled with a river light, when you heard the Benny Goodman quartet from a radio in the corner stationery store, and when almost everybody wore a hat."

In midtown, servicemen were having one final blast before returning home. That was the Christmas that New York, and the rest of America, celebrated the end of World War II. Surrender had come with the dropping of the atomic bomb

(Left to right) Gore, Truman, & Tennessee
The only known photo of "The Unholy Trio."

on Nagasaki, which led to the final collapse of the empire of Japan.

That December in New York had been blustery, cold, and gray, but there was optimism in the air. For the first time since the war, shapely women were seen wearing nylons. Sugar was no longer rationed. New Yorkers were buying cars fresh from the factories of Detroit, and used car lots were glutted with models from the late 1930s.

On Broadway, drama was flourishing, including a wildly successful "memory play," *The Glass Menagerie.* It had been written by Tennessee Williams.

His future friend, Gore Vidal, had already written two novels, and his third, and most controversial, was on the way. Truman Capote was still struggling with his first novel, *Other Voices, Other Rooms,* a book that would propel him into international fame and notoriety.

On the heterosexual front—"I was only a latent homosexual"—Norman Mailer was contemplating *The Naked and the Dead,* his 1948 novel about World War II. Violent clashes with the three gay writers lay in his future. In the meantime, Mailer proclaimed, "New York is the center of the universe, the only place for an artist to be. Of course, there is still Hollywood for those who want to be the next Lana Turner."

"It's a great time to be alive," said Marlene Dietrich before boarding a train that would take her to Chicago and then westward to California. Once there, she hoped to pick up the pieces of an almost abandoned career. It had been interrupted by the war, when she had entertained Allied troops and had spoken out against Hitler and her Fatherland.

Just as Gore and Truman were enjoying the first taste of their oncoming fame, Tennessee, flush with Broadway success, found the New York brew too heady and was planning to flee. But, first, he paid a call on "the woman I wrote all my plays for her to star in."

Before leaving to spend most of December in residence at Hotel Pontchartrain in New Orleans, Tennessee had stopped off for a "little bourbon and branchwater" at the home of Tallulah Bankhead. He was accompanied by a young marine he'd just picked up on the sidewalk, and whose name he could

Bourbon and Branchwater with Tallulah Bankhead

not remember.

Ever since the summer of 1937, Tennessee had been a defender of Tallulah when she was under attack from his fellow Southerners. "I do not consider the alleged perversions and promiscuity of the star, Tallulah Bankhead, to be filth, but a robust natural life, boiling up to the surface."

He told Tallulah that "Broadway seems like some revolting sickness," even though he was enjoying his first success there. "It's centered around eating, then vomiting, and ultimately shitting—all at once. One's ego becomes so sickly bloated with it."

Tallulah Bankhead

"Would that I, a mere mortal woman, was suffering through such a triumph," she said. "The wolf is always at my door, *dahling*."

Tennessee confessed that one of his major reasons for leaving New York involved his wish to overcome his sex addiction. "I can't get any work done here. All I have to do is walk out on the streets around Times Square. Soldiers, sailors, marines, like this gentleman sitting here with us, and Air Force pilots, are returning home in droves, one horny bunch. I haven't had so much sex since I departed wartime San Francisco, where I met countless young men, who'd left their wives or girlfriends back home, before shipping out to the Pacific theater—and perhaps death."

Gore and Truman Encounter a Bisexual & Bigamous Femme Fatale

Anaïs Nin

It was inevitable that the three most famous homosexual writers in America—Tennessee Williams, Gore Vidal, and Truman Capote—would eventually meet in postwar America. Years later, after the 1940s had long ago been buried, they would communicate with each other mainly through their attorneys, threatening lawsuits.

But early friendships were possible among this "Unholy Trio," as each of them wandered, young and most often alone, down the lonely sidewalks of New York and through its cold canyons.

First came the historic meeting of 20-year-old Gore and 21-year-old Truman, who looked like he was twelve and spoke like a strangled child.

In Greenwich Village, Gore Vidal and Truman Capote were heading for the same party, where they would meet for the first time. The party would already be underway before they arrived. Fellow guests included an array of mostly struggling poets, novelists, playwrights, actors, and actresses, plus a flotsam and jetsam of people who lived on the periphery of the arts world in post-war America.

The meeting between Truman and Gore occurred in the skylit bohemian apartment of Anaïs Nin, a fifth floor walkup on West 13th Street.

She had already met and befriended a handsome young Gore Vidal, who was serving his final days in the military. Throughout most of them, he'd been stationed in the Aleutian Islands.

Anaïs, the party's host, was already an underground legend of her own making. Unable to get her novels published in the 1940s, she had arranged to have them printed herself. At the time of her party, Gore had promised to get her novels republished by E.P. Dutton, where he was its youngest editor.

In *The Erotic Life of Anaïs Nin*, author Noël Riley Fitch defined her as "the ultimate *femme fatale*, a passionate and mysterious woman, world famous for her steamy love affairs and extravagant sexual exploits, most notably her simultaneous affairs with Henry and June Miller, and her bicoastal bigamous marriages."

She was continuing to work on her endless diary, which she'd begun as a young girl and which her former lover, Henry Miller, had proclaimed would one day take its place alongside the writings of Marcel Proust.

At that point in her life, she viewed herself as an Earth Mother to a growing number of homosexual artists, including the young poet James Merrill.

Gore spent most of the party talking to Merrill, whom he'd first seduced when he met him as an undergraduate at Amherst. He later likened himself to "an older warrior to his unpublished Ephebe."

The night of their first meeting, he'd gone to bed with Merrill, the son of Charles Merrill, co-founder of the brokerage house, Merrill Lynch.

James had published his first book at the age of sixteen. His wealthy father had paid the printing costs.

Author Christopher Bram defined Merrill as "pale, lean, and an aloof young man, cool and cryptic, full of courteous formality, suggesting that in some photos he looks like a suave extraterrestrial."

Gore later suggested that Anaïs praised Merrill's poems only because he wrote favorable critiques of her own prose.

At Anaïs's party, Gore would later disappear into the night with Merrill to repeat a seduction that had begun at Amherst.

In 1977, Merrill would win the Pulitzer Prize for Poetry. Later on, Gore would mock him for selling so few books.

"I'd rather have one perfect reader instead," Merrill told him. "Why dynamite a pond in order to catch that single silver carp?"

In later years, especially during the 1970s, Gore, with a tinge of jealousy, watched as Merrill became one of the most celebrated poets of his generation.

Gore met another noted American poet at the party, Robert Duncan, and his lover, the expressionist painter Robert De Niro, Sr., father of the famed actor, Robert De Niro, Jr.

Duncan was a pivotal figure in Gore's life, giving him some of the courage to write his gay novel, *The City and the Pillar.* In 1944, Duncan had written the landmark essay, *The Homosexual in Society,* comparing the plight of gay people to that of African Americans and Jews. It became a pioneering treatise on the plight of homosexuals in American society.

In the 1950s, Duncan's mature works were consumed by the Beat Generation, who adopted him as a cultural hero. He also became a shamanic figure in artistic circles, especially in San Francisco, in a movement hailed as the "San Francisco Renaissance."

When Gore complained to him about the hardships he'd experienced in the military, Duncan chided him. "You should have done what I did. When I was drafted in 1941, I declared myself a homosexual. There was no way the Army wanted me to share the shower with all those innocent young men from the Grain Belt of America."

At the party, the other soon-to-be famous writer, a young Capote, had never heard of Merrill or Duncan, although he'd heard a lot about Gore.

Anaïs had never met Capote, who arrived on the arm of her friend, Leo Lerman, the writer and critic, who in the words of Anaïs, talked and looked like Oscar Wilde. At the time, Truman was using Lerman as his role model.

"Leo parries with quick *repartée*," wrote Anaïs. "He is a man of the world who practices a magician's *tour de force* in conversation, a skillful social performance, a weather vane, a mask, a pirouette, and all you remember is the fantasy, the tale, the laughter."

She remembered Truman as a "small, slender young man, with hair over his eyes, extending the softest and most boneless hand. He seemed fragile and easily wounded."

She had been impressed with Truman's short story, *Miriam,* which had been published in *Mademoiselle* in its edition of June, 1945. It was the story of a sinister little girl who moves in with an older widow, gradually taking over her life.

Truman was not immediately introduced to Gore, until he had pirouetted around the room, showing off his black cape and his large black hat that evoked the popular concept of the headgear of a witch.

Anaïs must have wondered if Truman had adopted her own dress code. She often ap-

James Merrill

5

Anaïs Nin and a very young **Gore Vidal**: It began as a harmless flirtation and ended as one of the most venomous literary feuds of the 20th Century.

peared in an Elizabethan hat like that worn by Sir Walter Raleigh, and she, too, wore capes around Manhattan, brightening many a gray day in Greenwich Village with her capes in tones of chartreuse, magenta, cerise, marigold orange, emerald green, or sapphire.

Truman came up to Gore. "How does it feel to be an *onn-font-tarribull [enfant terrible]?*" he asked.

Gore chose not to answer, but to ask a question instead. "Did you know that in Italian, *capote* means 'condom?'"

Thus, one of the famous literary feuds in American letters was launched, although it didn't heat up right away.

"Almost from the beginning," Anaïs later said, "Gore and Truman sized each other up as future rivals. After all, there could be only one *enfant terrible.* Gore was almost a historian, dealing in facts, whereas Truman came from the Southern school of *raconteur,* meaning he never wanted a fact to get in the way of a good story. Gore camouflaged his homosexuality, whereas Truman used it to draw attention to himself. The more flamboyant he was, the more onlookers he attracted."

The painter, Paul Cadmus, was at the party, observing both Truman and Gore. "Gore was formal and stiff, with military posture. Truman was the opposite. I always liked the little devil. He didn't give a fuck what people thought of his high-pitched voice or anything else, including his outrageous opinions about anything. He was brave and gutsy."

"At a time when all of America was afraid of J. Edgar Hoover, this Southern Magnolia (i.e., Capote) denouncd him at Anaïs' party as a 'killer fruit,' a certain kind of queer who has Freon refrigerating his bloodstream," Cadmus said.

[The F.B.I director may have had a spy at Anaïs' gathering. Just weeks later, Hoover would order his assistant and lover, Clyde Tolson, to set up a file on Truman. He would later demand that the F.B.I establish equivalent files on both Gore and Tennessee.]

Before the party ended, Cadmus had

Leo Lerman:
Literary critic and literary lion

asked both Truman and Gore to pose in the nude for him. Truman accepted, but Gore rejected the idea.

The New York-born artist was notorious for his paintings and drawings of nude male figures, which combined eroticism and a style he referred to as "magic realism."

In 1934, he painted *The Fleet's In* for the Public Works Art Project of the WPA. It became one of the most controversial paintings of the Depression era, featuring carousing sailors, female prostitutes, and a homosexual couple. Such a public outcry arose that it was placed in mothballs and not allowed to be exhibited until the more tolerant year of 1981.

It is not known if Truman ever showed up to pose for Cadmus as an erotic nude model.

Gore was awed to see that within 15 minutes, Truman had most of the party-goers clustered around him as he told a most outrageous story:

Truman claimed that he'd been informed by the British actress Elsa Lanchester that "Noël Coward eats shit. Certain young boys are recruited in London to deposit their loads, and they're put on a strict diet one week before they perform that service. When they're squatted in position over Coward's face, they are instructed to very slowly begin their bowel movement, allowing Coward time to taste and savor."

"Truman didn't stop there," Gore later recalled. "He also claimed that that beautiful man, Tyrone Power, also ate shit."

What made that story believable was that this in-the-

Paul Cadmus

know group was already aware that Power and Coward at one time had been lovers. The accusation of shit eating, as relayed by Truman, originated with Elsa Lanchester, who was married to Charles Laughton, another alleged shit-eater. As bizarre as it seems, handsome Ty had seduced toad-like Laughton.

In reference to this incident, when Gore published his memoir, *Palimpsest,* in 1993, he claimed that to his horror, he later heard from several people that "*I* had been transformed into the source of this truly sick invention that will be grist to the satanic mills of Capotes yet unborn."

When Truman got around to actu-

The Fleet's In was so controversial that the painting was suppressed for decades.

ally talking to Gore, and not performing for the rest of the guests, he found they had certain similarities. "Both of our mothers were named Nina, and both of them were alcoholics," Truman said. "We were both unloved as children. Both of us were amusing and bright, and fond of our own sex…at least in bed. And both of us were so terribly, terribly young, filled with such hopes and dreams that life had not destroyed for us, or made us cynical."

"I wanted to be the firecracker of American writers. And Gore wanted that for himself. He also wanted to be President of the United States and the American version in letters of W. Somerset Maugham. Regrettably, he never found his literary voice except for his vinegary essays. His copy, unlike mine, lacked my sensitivity."

During her "after-party analysis" with Gore, Anaïs claimed that "Truman wants to become one of my loved ones. But I'm already surrounded by enough childlike men, and I can't take on another person. Truman reminds me of a Venus's flytrap. I once saw one along the coast of South Carolina. Truman is exotic like that flower, but also devouring. He will feed on you, but give nothing in return."

Gore met the following night with his closest friend at the time, interior designer Stanley Mills Haggart. Gore told him: "Capote gives homosexuality a bad name, and Anaïs does the same for self-love."

An Ex-Con from San Quentin On Parole at the Everard Baths

Truman and Gore were not physically attracted to each other, but they began to "date" after the party at the apartment of Anaïs Nin. These dates were not romantic, at least not with each other. When they set out to explore underground New York, it was with the understanding that if either of them were able

Truman Capote was accused of "spreading the most vile gossip" about **Noël Coward** *(left)*, **Tyrone Power** *(center)*, and **Charles Laughton** *(right)*. However, some latter-day biographers have suggested that his shocking revelations may indeed have been true.

to pick up a trick, they'd be free to run off into the night with the object of their desire, with no questions asked the next day.

On their first date, Gore invited Truman to join him at the infamous Astor Bar at 7th Avenue and 45th Street, near Times Square. "Wear a red tie," Gore instructed. "That will signal your sexual preference to the initiated."

Gore later wrote that the Astor Bar was "the city's most exciting place for meeting soldiers, sailors, and Marines on the prowl. No woman ever dared intrude into these male mysteries. After all, we had—all of us except Truman—won the great Imperial War, and, thanks to us, the whole world was briefly American."

Since 1910, the Astor Bar had become legendary as a pickup spot at the "Crossroads of the World." On its rooftop, beginning in 1940, Frank Sinatra had made early appearances with the Tommy Dorsey Band.

During the War, with so many U.S. military men in town, the Astor Bar experienced its greatest fame, welcoming thousands upon thousands of gay patrons in uniform—with the expectation that they be discreet, based on the standards of the time.

At the Astor, hundreds of men would be sardined, packed six deep around the long oval-shaped black bar within whose center bartenders ruled the sea of men on the make for each other.

A love object did not emerge for either Gore or Truman that night at the Astor Bar.

"The competition was too great," Truman later recalled. "All the queens from Manhattan, the Outer Boroughs, and New Jersey, too, were making off with all the 'seafood' that night."

After a quick hamburger at a joint on Times Square pushing papaya juice, Truman and Gore journeyed to the notorious Everard Baths, a place aptly nicknamed "Everhard," which was said to operate because of frequent payoffs to the police.

From 1888 to 1985, these baths, housed in a former church, were the gay mecca of New York. Many great artists such as actor Emyln Williams, composer Ned Rorem, and even Truman himself, have written about their experiences cruising these baths. Other patrons have included Rock Hudson, Alfred Lunt, Lorenz Hart, Rudolf Nureyev, Dana Andrews, Montgomery Clift, Leonard Bernstein, Zachary Scott, and Dan Dailey.

In a memoir, Gore had nothing but fond memories of the Everard, even though it was mildewed, grungy, and dingy. "Military men often spent the night there because it was hard to get a hotel room in New York right after the war. This was sex at its rawest made most exciting. Newly invented penicillin had removed fears of venereal disease. Most of the boys knew that they would soon be home for good, and married, and that this was a last chance to do what they were designed to do with each other."

Gore once published a paperback original under the

nom de plume of "Katharine Everhard." Although it was a straight romantic novel, the pseudonym was an inside gay joke.

Truman and Gore rented a cubicle and changed into the skimpy, knee-length white cotton robes offered as part of the entrance fee.

In *The Gay Metropolis,* author Charles Kaiser wrote: "You usually wore the robe loose with your cock hanging out. I guess you could have sex with as many as a dozen people. There were group scenes. There was a very impressive steam-bath room down in the lower level, as well as a swimming pool and a big sort of cathedral-like sauna room. It was very steamy and you could hardly see. You could stumble into multiple combinations."

Like two voyeurs, Gore and Truman trolled the hallways, visiting the steam room, but finding nothing particularly appealing.

On the way back to their cubicle, they spotted an open door three down from their own cramped quarters. A well-built young man had just entered and had taken off his robe, lying nude on the bed with only a dim light illuminating his muscled body.

Both Gore and Truman surveyed what they called "a Greek God."

The Everard Baths, NYC

FINAL **DAILY NEWS**

9 DIE IN W. SIDE BATHHOUSE FIRE

Fear More Bodies in Rubble

Sprinklers Set for Use On June 1

"Adonis" accepted their request to enter. Both of the gay men came into the cubicle and fastened the latch on the door behind them.

Gore later told Stanley Haggart, his friend, what happened. "Truman and I devoured this handsome bit of man-flesh. But it led to our first major feud. I did a lot of the work myself, and we took turns sharing the riches. But at the last minute, Truman popped down on him and drained him dry to the last drop, although it rightfully belonged to me."

After their communal sex, the young man was invited out to dinner at a restaurant in Greenwich Village.

He told Gore and Truman that he was an actor named Frank McCowan, and that he'd appeared in five movies—"Just small parts." He claimed that Alan Ladd had discovered him, and he bragged that Ladd would be arriving in New York to spend four days in the city with him.

"The implication was clear that Ladd and he were lovers," Gore claimed.

After Frank and Gore said goodnight to Truman, Gore learned that his newly minted friend had less than fifty dollars to live on for four nights. That's why he was sleeping at the Everard, because it had the cheapest bed in town. Until Ladd flew in, four days hence, Gore invited Frank to live with him at his apartment.

"I'll stay with you if you'll give me all the sex I demand," Frank said.

Gore gleefully agreed to those terms.

As he told Stanley, "The next morning, I got to enjoy the taste treat that Truman had greedily swallowed for himself."

During the next four days, Gore and Frank bonded and would become longtime friends, seeing each other infrequently during Gore's trips to Hollywood.

He learned a lot about Frank during their time together in Manhattan. When he was only thirteen, he'd stolen a revolver and was later arrested with it. A judge sentenced him to the California Youth Authority's Preston School of Industry Reformatory at Ione, California.

A very inventive young teenager, he plotted his escape and pulled it off one night when there was a delay in the change of guards. He went on a rampage, robbing three jewelry stores before making his escape in a stolen Ford. He drove the car north toward Oregon, where he was arrested.

This spree involved crossing a state line, which elevated the caper to a federal offense. Frank was eventually recaptured and sentenced to three years in the penitentiary at Springfield, Missouri.

When he finished his sentence there, he was transferred to San Quentin on other charges that had been lodged against him during his rampage. He would be an inmate at San Quentin until he was paroled shortly before his twenty-first birthday.

He told Gore that in 1943, he'd gone horseback riding in the Hollywood Hills. There, he met Alan Ladd, who was just becoming famous as a movie star, after having appeared as the laconic gunman in *This Gun for Hire* (1942), co-starring with Veronica Lake. A closeted homosexual, Ladd was married to his agent at the time, Susan Carol Ladd.

The next time Gore heard of Frank, he'd changed his name to Rory Calhoun, and was seen escorting Lana Turner to a premiere. Frank (Rory) had been cast in movies which included *That Hagen Girl (1947)* alongside Shirley Temple and Ronald Reagan.

A bisexual, Rory would also become known for seducing his leading ladies, appearing in two movies with Marilyn Monroe, *How to Marry a Millionaire* and *River of No Return.*

By 1948, he'd married Lita Baron, and had become the father of three daughters. When she sued him for divorce in 1970, she named Betty Grable and Susan Hayward as two of 79 women with whom her husband had engaged in adulterous relationships.

At a Hollywood party after his divorce, Gore met up with Calhoun once again. Speaking of his divorce, he confided, "Heck, Lita didn't even include half of them. For the sake of my masculine image, I'm glad she didn't name my alltime favorite squeeze, Guy Madison."

At that point in his life, Calhoun had delivered his most famous line: "The trouble with Hollywood is that there aren't enough good cocksuckers."

Gore, with Truman, Savor
The Taste of Their First Mandingo

Anaïs Nin, in *Volume Four* (1944-47) of her famous diary, claimed that "Gore has a prejudice against Negroes." In later years, the very liberal author would vehemently deny such an accusation.

In a memoir, he did admit that when he was growing up, his contact with African Americans was limited to servants. "The Gores were Reconstruction Southerners, and they got on well with our dusky cousinage in master-servant relationships, but they did not believe in equality."

As the decades went by, Gore's assertions became more indiscreet and ironic. "Half the mulattoes in Mississippi are related to the Gore family," which included, of course, Al Gore, the former Vice President.

Anaïs had told Stanley Haggart that both Gore and Truman had been shocked at her party when she'd introduced them to two guests she indentified in her diary as "Rita, a Negro girl, and Don, a Negro guitar player."

Two views of former jailbird **Rory Calhoun**, who climbed the lavender ladder to success, seducing some of the biggest stars, both male and female, in Hollywood

"He was the first movie star we ever seduced," Truman said. "Gore and I shared him, although I got the best of Rory back when he was still named Frank."

This surprised Stanley, who decided that both of these young writers needed greater exposure to the art world in New York. Stanley enjoyed friendships with many of the leading black artists of the late 1940s and 50s, especially dancers and singers. He would later be the art director for projects that featured Louis Armstrong, Lena Horne, and Alvin Ailey.

He decided to invite both Gore and Truman to his multiracial parties and to a gala where elegantly dressed blacks and whites mingled as equals.

Stanley's parties in New York rivaled those of Anaïs Nin in bringing key players in the arts world together. He invited Gore and Truman to a party he was giving for

Martha Graham, the dancer and choreographer.

At that party, Gore was introduced to a rising young novelist, James Baldwin, who was African American.

Truman and Gore also met the rather flamboyant and eccentric Richard Bruce Nugent, a writer, painter, and key figure in the "Harlem renaissance." In 1926, he'd published "Smoke, Lilies, and Jade," a short story that was the first publication by an African American to openly depict homosexuality.

Nugent had once lived in Harlem in an apartment complex nicknamed "Niggerati Manor," in which he'd decorated the walls with murals depicting homoerotic scenes.

Stanley also introduced Gore and Truman to Langston Hughes, an early innovator of the then-new literary art form known as jazz poetry. A poet, dramatist, and novelist, he was the leader of the Harlem Renaissance, an era which flourished *[his words]* "when the Negro was in vogue."

Hughes was rather closeted, but exhibited a strong sexual attraction to his fellow black men, including writing beautiful poems to a male lover.

The press dubbed the appearance of **Lana Turner** *(left)* and **Rory Calhoun** *(right)* at a Hollywood premiere as "Blonde and Ebony."

Rory would generate additional headlines appearing with yet another blonde in Hollywood through appearances with Marilyn Monroe in *How to Marry a Millionaire* and *River of No Return.*

Gore and Truman also met Zora Neale Hurston, an American folklorist, anthropologist, and author best known for her novel, published in 1937, *Their Eyes Were Watching God.* Like Truman, she had grown up in Alabama.

Hurston told Truman that she was writing a novel *[Seraph on the Suwanee, eventually published in 1948]* about "white trash women."

Sadly, Truman watched her decline into obscurity. In 1948, she was accused of molesting a ten-year-old boy. Although the case was dismissed and viewed as a false accusation, it seriously damaged her reputation. She ended up broke and in ill health, dying in a welfare home. The year of her death (1960) she was buried in an unmarked grave.

Stanley also took Gore and Truman to the annual black tie drag ball, an event inaugurated in the 1920s by Phil Black, Harlem's most famous female impersonator. Josephine Baker, Billie Holiday, and Eartha Kitt were among the famous entertainers who'd attended this annual event in the past.

The setting was the dazzling Savoy Ballroom, with its crystal chandeliers and elegant marble staircase. The highlight of the event was when fashionably dressed drag artists vied for the title of "Queen of the Ball."

Drag artist **Phil Black** in the 1920s.

At the ball, Stanley's longtime friend, Phil Black, wearing a pink satin gown, came up to him and executed a pirouette. In reference to the gown, he said, "I made it myself, *dahling.*"

Stanley introduced him to Gore and to Truman. Black ignored Truman, turning his full attention to Gore. "You're cute, honey," Black said, reaching out to fondle Gore's crotch.

Gore withdrew in horror, which Truman found "oh, so amusing."

When Black departed, Gore turned to Stanley, saying, "This queen is outrageous. No one has ever done that to me before."

Ordering champagne, Stanley sat with Gore and Truman watching the excitement reflected on their faces. The audience was mesmerizing, even to the jaded eye. Many men wore tuxedos, escorting as their dates other men clad in gowns and high heels. "The patrons were multiracial and multisexual," Stanley said.

What caught the attention of both Gore and Truman was when Stanley introduced them to a stage performer known only as "Mandingo."

He had originated in Martinique, and was the offspring of a Creole woman and a Frenchman from Toulouse who had settled on that island into a life as a planter.

Mandingo never liked to be called a Negro or referred to as black, preferring to identify his complexion as *"café au lait."* He showed up at the ball wearing a sequined jockstrap. A performer at private parties and at exhibitions he was known for the size of his penis, which was nine inches when flaccid, rising to 13½ inches when erect. He also hustled on the side, renting his body to both straight women and homosexual men.

By the second bottle of champagne, Stanley became more daring, deciding that the time had come for Gore and Truman to cross the color line sexually. He proposed to Gore and Truman that he could arrange separate "dates" for them to be entertained by Mandingo. At first, they resisted, but curiosity and daring eventually won out. As the evening progressed, they became more relaxed.

"It was a big step for both of them to consider. It defied everything they'd been taught as teenagers," Stanley said. "Not only miscegenation, but homosexual miscegenation, which was illegal in every state of the union."

During the coming weeks, and on separate occasions, both Gore and Truman engaged in sexual interludes with Mandingo, who charged each of them $50 for his services.

Later, in the afterglow of seduction, Gore confided to Stanley, "For once, and perhaps never again, I completely lowered my inhibition. I learned what animal passion really means. I want to cage that beast within myself and never let him out again."

In contrast, Truman claimed, "I lived out my boyhood fantasy of being raped by a wild savage. The experience nearly put me in the hospital."

Unlike Gore, Truman was so inspired by the experience that he wrote another one of his short stories, which he showed to Stanley. It was entitled *Black Mischief and Dark Desires.* Both men decided that no publisher at the time would touch it, so Truman destroyed it.

Whether it was true or not, Truman always claimed that Tennessee's short story, *Desire and the Black Masseur,* was lifted directly from his experience with Mandingo which he'd relayed to the playwright.

James Baldwin

For Truman, his experience in breaking down the color barrier led him to travel with Stanley to Port-au-Prince, capital of Haiti, in 1948. Here, he would find inspiration for his Broadway play, *House of Flowers.*

Perhaps to convince Anaïs that he had no prejudice against the American Negro, Gore showed up at her next party with his date for the evening, James Baldwin.

Before going out in public with Baldwin, Gore told Stanley that the writer is "as black as they come. He was born in a hospital in Harlem. He's got a wide mouth, eyes as big as Joan Crawford's, with heavy lids as droopy as those of Robert Mitchum. Call it a sandwich mouth and frog eyes. In the homophobic black world, he's already been gang raped by hoodlums from Harlem."

Gore later told Stanley that Baldwin was "a cross between Martin Luther King, Jr. and Bette Davis in *A Stolen Life.*"

At the party, Baldwin pointedly informed Gore, Anaïs, and Stanley, "I don't want to be known as a Negro Novelist, and I certainly don't want to be called a homosexual Negro Novelist."

"All of us live with the poisonous fear of what others think of us," Stanley said.

Gore later tried to get his editor at E.P. Dutton to purchase the rights to Baldwin's first novel, *Go Tell It on the Mountain.* The editor rejected the idea telling Gore, as a means of explanation, "I'm from Virginia."

The brief fling between Baldwin and Gore quickly died. Stanley said, "Don't call it love. Gore was trying to prove something to his friends, especially Anaïs."

What's Love Got to Do With It?

Before the friendship between Gore and Truman withered, they met every Thursday at one o'clock for lunch in the Oak Room of the Plaza. As biographer

Gerald Clarke noted: "They niggled at their friends during the first course, devoured their enemies during the second, and savored their own glorious futures over coffee and dessert."

Gore was struggling with his sexuality, even defining Anaïs Nin to friends such as Stanley Haggart as "my mistress."

Truman had no such qualms. "I didn't feel as if I were imprisoned in the wrong body," he told Gore. "I didn't want to be a transsexual. I just felt things would be easier for me if I were a girl. But I've always had a marked homosexual preference, and I never had any guilt about it."

Even though pretending a surface friendship with Gore, Truman undermined him behind his back.

Marella Agnelli, the Italian socialite Truman would befriend in later years, figured it out: "Capote despises the people he talks about. Using, using all the time. He builds up friends privately and knocks them down publicly."

When he met Bennett Cerf, publisher of Random House, at a party, Truman lashed into Gore. "From what I've seen, his writing is lifeless. There are those who say he might be another Hemingway. But really, my dear, let's come to our senses."

"Gore told me that while serving in the Aleutians, he suffered frostbite. He's still not melted down yet."

"I will give Gore credit for one achievement though," Truman told Cerf. "He delivers the best known impression ever of Eleanor Roosevelt."

He leaned in close to Cerf. "Gore has connections with the upper crust. He told me a secret that must go no farther than your ear to my ear. Gore claims that Mrs. Roosevelt is having an affair with Katharine Hepburn."

[Actually, it was Truman, not Gore, who spread that rumor.]

Cerf had his own impressions of both Truman and Gore. He defined them as "a pair of gilded youths who thought they'd soon win Pulitzer Prizes followed by the Nobel Prize for Literature before either of them turned thirty. Judged by their work, Truman from the beginning found his voice in writing *Other Voices, Other Rooms*. Vidal is still struggling to find his voice. Incidentally, from what I've seen, Vidal's novels are unreadable."

"Speaking of voices," Cerf said, "one of his schoolteachers in Alabama said Truman's voice was identical to what it was in the fourth grade."

During a private luncheon with his mentor, Leo Lerman, Truman confided secrets Gore had told him in confidence. "Gore confessed to me that he does not like women, with the possible exception of Anaïs Nin. I'm sure he'll turn on her at one point. He finds women silly and giggly or else strident dykes. He also told me that he's incapable of ever loving anyone except some boyhood friend of his who died in the war."

"Another thing, Gore's got this crazy obsession about the death of Amelia Earhart. Whether it's true or not, he claims that his father financed that ill-fated around-the-world trip of hers. There's more, although I hesitated to reveal it. What the hell...I will. Gore does a great imitation of Winston Churchill. He claims he found the wartime speeches of Sir Winston 'raucously funny,' although he has it from an authentic source that the prime minister has a big dick."

The rich and famous in New York began to invite Truman to their parties. "He told the most delicious stories about everybody," said socialite and party-giver Elsa Maxwell. "God knows what he said about me behind my back."

"I remember one night Truman showed up at this party wearing some outrageous cape," Maxwell recalled. "He had this large sapphire ring on. I don't know if it were real or fake. When people admired it, he claimed it was a gift from John Steinbeck. At another party, I heard gossip that Truman claimed the ring was a love token from Ernest Hemingway. The more heterosexual the writer, the greater Truman's claim that these authors were mad for the boy."

These lies infuriated Gore, who ultimately doubted every word Truman uttered, including "the dots over the i's and the crosses over the t's."

Stanley Haggart sounded a different note: "Truman lived in the world of the *demimonde* and was often privy to some occurrences going on behind locked doors among celebrities—closeted homosexual encounters among movie stars, adulterous affairs with many actors and actresses, and betrayals, including embarrassments we'd all like to forget. As a rough estimation, I'd say that half of what Truman told was fabricated. But much of it was true."

"Anaïs and Gore would later dismiss Truman's claim that he had a brief affair with James Dean before he became famous," Stanley said. "But I knew that boast was true, because it occurred secretly in my Manhattan apartment."

Gore was not alone in defining Truman as a liar. Another famous post-war novelist, Calder Willingham, began to size up Truman. He found him "attractive, clever, an excellent talker, but insincere, extremely mannered, snobbish even. He tries too hard to be charming. Also, he uses his homosexuality as a comedy, playing the role of the effeminate buffoon, making people laugh to call attention to himself. In any gathering, he wants to be at the center."

"Both writers seemed obsessed with each other," Stanley recalled. "When you were with Gore, he talked incessantly about Truman, mostly attacking what a fake he was. When you were with Truman, he spread vile gossip about Gore, some of it true."

As time drifted by, Truman began to confront Gore with some of his shortcomings. If Truman met a young man who had gone to bed with Gore, Truman wanted to know all the details. One night at a drunken party, which Stanley attended with Gore, Truman came up to them.

In his high-pitched, drunken voice, he confronted Gore. "I hear from many sources that you're just the *lay lousé.*"

"At last, Truman, you've got it right," Gore admitted, to Stanley's astonishment.

Later that night, Gore confessed a fuller review of his point of view to Stanley. "I pick up these poor young guys in the Times Square area and take them back to those Dreiserian hotels in the area, very seedy. They provide momentary pleasure for me, but I give them little in return. It's only fair that they walk away from my rented bed with a ten-dollar bill as opposed to the street rate of five dollars."

When Titans Clash

Gore (G. I. Joe) Confronts a Southern Pit Viper

It was publisher Bennett Cerf who revealed what finally destroyed any pretense of a real friendship between Gore Vidal and Truman Capote. "Blame it on *Life* magazine," Cerf claimed.

Right before Truman published his first novel, *Other Voices, Other Rooms,* at the age of 23, in 1947, *Life* published a photo essay entitled—"Young U.S. Writers: A Refreshing Group of Newcomers to the Literary Scene Is Ready to Tackle Almost Anything."

The editors plastered a full-page spread about Truman as the cover story's lead. He was photographed amid the Victorian bric-a-brac of Leo Lerman's living room. Beautifully dressed, hair artfully arranged, he was smoking a long cigarette. *Life* defined him as "esoteric, New Orleans-born Truman Capote."

Since nothing Truman had written till then had been published, *Life* was obviously not awarding literary prizes. Truman was positioned as the featured writer only because his flamboyant picture generated the most attention. Gore would later describe it as "looking waxy, as if from under a Victorian glass bell."

In the subsequent pages, smaller pictures were run of Jean Stafford, Calder Willingham, Thomas Heggen, and an unflattering likeness of Gore, with a caption identifying him as "a writer of poetry and Hemingway-esque fiction."

When the *Life* article was published, Truman, in his exaggerated way, announced, "I'm the darling of the Gods. I'm the toast of New York, the only real city in America. I define a city as a place where you can buy a canary at three o'clock in the morning."

With bitterness in his voice, Gore told a reporter, "Mr. Capote has launched himself as a celebrity, hardly as a writer."

When Truman heard that, he shot back, "The *Life* article claimed that Mr. Vidal is twenty years old. Take it from me, she's twenty-five if she's a day."

Bennett Cerf said, "Truman never forgave Gore for publishing *Williwaw,* his G.I. Joe novel written when he was only nineteen. It was a young soldier's novel. The ending was like a cinematic rainbow and very influenced by Stephen Crane's *The Red Badge of Courage* (1895).

Gore wrote: *"The sky was blue and clear now and the sun shone on the white mountains. They walked back to the ship."*

Chapter Two

Tennessee in Provincetown

An Affair to Remember

Dancer from the Dance — The Canadian Draft-Dodger

A young **Tennessee Williams**, modeling nude on the sand dunes of Cape Cod

In 1940, just before the United States entered World War II, Tennessee Williams set out to visit the artists' colony and gay mecca of Provincetown at the tip of Cape Cod.

In his two-tone saddle shoes, a gift from his shoe salesman father, he would define his age at 26 if anyone were impolite enough to ask.

Actually, the Mississippi-born author was almost thirty.

After his arrival, he headed for the fishermen's quarter, inhabited mostly at the time by the Portuguese. It was a cloudy day, and his vision was impaired as his left eye was weakened by a cataract.

In a three-piece, ill-fitting dress suit, he was searching for a room to rent. He paused from time to time to inhale smoke from his cigarette, held in a long ebony holder.

Occasionally, he would stop to look out over the sea, across which had come the first of the Portuguese fishermen from the remote Azores in the 1850s, hoping to catch even bigger Moby Dicks than those available in the off-shore waters of their home islands.

He spotted a ROOM FOR RENT sign on a small cottage overlooking the wharf. It was owned by a Portuguese fisherman and his wife, who lived downstairs. Climbing the rickety staircase, he found a small, cramped little room with a window overlooking the sea. Later, he would write of the "lonely sand dunes, sea-gulls, and blue ocean, an excellent catharsis for a sin-sick soul such as mine."

"P-Town," as it was affectionately known, had long been a retreat for artists, writers, and various "queer folk." Preceding Tennessee had been a long list of the bohemian *literati*, including novelist Edna Ferber, whom Noël Coward always insisted was a man in disguise. "The other Edna," Edna St. Vincent Millay, had also visited the sand dunes of Provincetown. At one time, you could even have seen Gertrude Stein wandering these lonely, windswept dunes.

The diarist, Anaïs Nin, had also visited during "one of her frequent lesbian periods," according to author Henry Miller, her lover, confidant, and muse.

Tennessee had wandered the town for only a few hours before he pronounced it "the frolicsome tip of the Cape."

Not as sophisticated in 1940 as he later became, Tennessee was still imbued with mores imbedded in him in his early years growing up in Mississippi before his family moved to St. Louis. At first, he found the "behavior of the beach crowd shocking." At the time, he compared himself to "an old auntie," suggesting that "I had to leave my glasses in my bedroom if I planned to go to the beach."

But he readily adapted and soon was aping the mores of the "natives," and perhaps outdistancing some of them.

"P-Town was a place back then—perhaps even today—where one took one's pleasure as

"Last night, you made me know what is meant by beautiful pain," dancer **Kip Kiernan** (photo above) told Tennessee Williams after their first night of love-making.

Le Dieu bleu (The Blue God) With the "Callipygian Ass"

The painter, **Jackson Pollock** *(photo above)*, often hung out with Tennessee Williams in the bars of Provincetown during the months before World War II. He confided to the aspiring playwright that his mistress, the heiress Peggy Guggenheim, was insatiable. "She even wakes me up in the middle of the night, demanding more."

Peggy Guggenheim, a multi-millionairess, is pictured above against the backdrop of the Grand Canal in Venice with two favorite pets. Her other pets included a string of young artists from whom she purchased paintings. Many of these painters later became world famous.

She often had sex with these artists. She once told Truman Capote, "It's smart business to buy a painting from a struggling artist that one day will be worth $5 million."

one found it," he told author Darwin Porter in Key West. "What I like about the place was that it was unnecessary to disguise one's eccentricities. P-Town offered liberation to those of us who harbored souls that had suffered repression somewhere else in America, as I did in St. Louis. Considering some of the secret passions that resided in the hearts of many of the summer residents, homosexuality was viewed as one of the lesser evils."

"The Gay Colony"—*[it wasn't called that then]*—was tolerated by the supposedly straight Portuguese fishermen and sailors in town," Tennessee said. "We queer ones provided a quick and easy way for them to supplement their meager incomes. Not bad. Two dollars in exchange for a blow-job. Two dollars was the going rate, until some vicious queen arrived from Brooklyn Heights that summer. He started giving these robust men three dollars. We practically lynched the flamboyant dandy for causing immediate inflation after dark."

Tennessee quickly became the third member of a notorious trio who included Jesse Steele and the heiress, Peggy Guggenheim, who was having a torrid affair at the time with the artist, Jackson Pollock. Tennessee soon discovered Pollock's "drip paintings."

Steele was a landscape painter. *[Peggy, a noted art collector and connoisseur had claimed he had no talent.]* He was the scion of a wealthy auto-manufacturing family from Detroit, who sent him monthly checks to stay out of Michigan.

He was known as a "mincer," dressing flamboyantly in pink and lavender. In spite of his effeminate manner and slight lisp, he was a favorite with the fishermen at the port, a scattering of beach boys, New England boat builders, and itinerant sailors, some of whom he shared with Tennessee.

Steele's parties were "all the rage," that summer, attended frequently by Tennessee, Peggy, and Pollock.

The town's foremost sexual predators—Tennessee, Steele, and Peggy—bonded. All three of them shared a mutual belief. "A small stipend discreetly slipped to your man of choice for the night will guarantee a much more reliable erection," Steele asserted, with a great degree of accuracy.

Frequently, Tennessee and Steele would argue and not speak for days. But eventually, the wounds would heal, and they'd be seen biking down the main street of town together in their eternal search for young men.

"Tennessee, with a few drinks in him, would criticize my profligate ways," Steele said. "Actually, he indulged in far more daring and dangerous sex than I did. At one point, his behavior became so outrageous that the couple with whom he was boarding kicked him out. He was bringing back some of the better-developed teenage sons of the local families. He was bragging about a steady diet of fifteen- or sixteen-year old semen, which he told me was good for the skin. He was kind in his assessment of the age of these boys. I saw many of them. Fourteen, if they were a day. His only requirement was that a young boy should have reached puberty. As for myself, I preferred more mature and manly men, those with a lot of experience."

One night, Tennessee was invited to a cook-out on the beach. His first view of Kip Kiernan was of his "callipygian ass," as he'd later recall. "He was bending over a pot, stirring clam chowder. It was an ass like I'd never seen before. Even without seeing his face, I had fallen in love."

"When he turned around to greet me, I stared into his lettuce green eyes and took in the glory of his shirtless body. I knew at once that a great bronze statue of Ancient Greece had come back to life. But with a little boy's face."

"Kip, My Sweet Bird of Youth"

After knowing each other only a night and the following day, Kip Kiernan and Joseph Hazen invited Tennessee to move with them into the two-story shack they rented on Captain Jack's Wharf. Both men were dancers, having studied in Manhattan at the Madame Duval Ballet School.

For the first three nights, Tennessee slept on a cot beside Hazen downstairs, while Kip occupied the small bedroom upstairs. But by that weekend, Kip had invited Tennessee upstairs to sleep with him.

As it turned out, Kip had selected the name of Kiernan from one he'd found within the telephone book. He was actually Bernard Dubowsky, who had fled from his native Canada during World War II as a means of escaping the draft. If discovered and convicted, he could be jailed. He was of Russian Jewish descent, descended from Alexander Kipnis, the great Ukrainian opera singer. His nickname of "Kip" had derived from "Kipnis."

At the age of twenty-two, Kip was tall and handsome, with high-slanting cheekbones that evoked the Russian dancer Vaslav Nijinsky. To support himself, he posed as a nude model at the Hans Hofmann Art School in the center of Provincetown. If requested by one of the photographers at the school, Kip would pose privately with a full erection.

After their first night together, Kip presented Tennessee with a photograph of himself posing in imitation of Nijinksy during a performance of *Le Dieu bleu* (*The Blue God*), a one-act ballet composed by Jean Cocteau and choreographed by Michel Fokine.

Produced by Nijinsky's lover, the theatrical impresario Sergei Diaghilev, the ballet, first staged in Paris in 1912, was a failure. The ballet had been presented three times in Paris that year, and three times in London the following year, but was never staged again. Yet Kip had found inspiration in the doomed ballet's legend.

Until the photograph was stolen from his wallet in 1960, Tennessee carried it around with him wherever he went.

From Cape Cod, Tennessee wrote his friend and fellow author, Donald Windham, about the joys of having Kim as a lover. "When I lie on top of him, I feel like I am polishing the Statue of Liberty or something. He is so enormous."

He confessed to waking up throughout the night five or six times to make love to Kip.

Kip became devoted to Tennessee, but the young man lived in fear that he would be deported as an undesirable alien because he was a practicing homosexual.

Biographer David Kaplan, an author who would later direct some of Tennessee's plays, said, "Tenn gave his heart unguardedly for perhaps the only time in his life."

"Nobody ever loved me before so completely as did Kip," Tennessee later recalled.

When Kip complained at being awakened repeatedly during the night for love-making, Tennessee blamed him. "It's your fault for being so beautiful."

Tennessee had met Paul Bigelow, one of the guiding lights of the influential New York Theater Guild, who would become one of the major forces in his private life and career. He came to visit Tennessee and found the playwright planning to move with Kip to New York at the end of the summer.

Tennessee later criticized Bigelow for defining his affair with Kip as "purely physical." He even gave a motive for Bigelow's harsh appraisal. "Either consciously or unconsciously, Bigelow desires Kip for himself."

Tennessee had confided to Bigelow that his relationship with Kip "was an intense and strange kind of love affair."

As an afterthought, Bigelow later claimed, "All of Tennessee's love affairs were intense and strange."

Tennessee's idyllic summer on the Cape came to an abrupt end one hot afternoon in August of 1940. He was enjoying the beach with Pollock, who had escaped from Peggy Guggenheim's constant sexual demands because the heiress had returned to New York to meet with her attorneys.

Kip asked Tennessee to ride on the handlebars of his bicycle back into town. It was while riding on the bike that Kip broke the news that Tennessee would later call "one of the saddest moments of my life."

"It's all over between us," Kip whispered into Tennessee's ear. "I'm going back to a girlfriend I left in New York. You and I will never be physical again. Being a homosexual violates me in a way that is unacceptable to who I am."

Tennessee remembered turning around to look deeply into the "Slavic blue eyes" of his former lover. Originally, he'd written that Kip's eyes were "lettuce green."

When Tennessee saw Kip off to New York, he kissed him goodbye for a final time. Later, he wrote to his friends that "some stupid little girl has persuaded Kip to resist the homosexual world."

Broken-hearted, Tennessee recorded in is journal, "No bug-house for me, baby. Somewhere, when the heart mends, there is another rare and beautiful stranger waiting for me."

Later, he wrote that his break with Kip was "only an incident in a long cumulation of tensions and difficulties, actual and psychic, and the result was a sort of temporary obliteration of everything solid in me. All I thought about was my own immediate preservation through change, escape, travel, new scenes, new people."

He decided to flee from Provincetown for Mexico and adventure.

Before leaving, he wrote Kip in New York on August 22. "I hereby formally bequeath to you the female vagina, whose vortex will inevitably receive you with or without my permission."

In New York, Kip resumed his study of ballet and married Robin Gregory, a ceremony that made him an American citizen.

During the next few months, he experienced a series of blackouts, which finally forced him into a doctor's office. After an extensive examination, the physician issued Kip his death notice. "Young man, you have inoperable brain cancer."

At the age of twenty-five, he knew he had only weeks to live. He contacted two or three of Tennessee's friends, who managed to reach the elusive playwright. On hearing the news, Tennessee rushed to St. Clare's Hospital in Manhattan.

There, he met Kip's wife, who granted him unlimited visitation rights. By the time he'd reached Kip's bed, the dancer had grown blind, but he was still vaguely coherent.

Tennessee would later write of "the transparent beauty of those who are about to die. Never has the doomed looked as beautiful as Kim. Forget about Greta Garbo in *Camille*. Never has love seemed that ephemeral. He was like one of those breakable glass animals in my first Broadway play, *The Glass Menagerie*. He was the *The Sweet Bird of Youth* in my much later play."

Three days later, Kip drifted into a death coma. Tennessee was sitting at his bedside at the moment of death. "His hand reached up into the air searching for mine," Tennessee later wrote in his journal. "I clasped it and held onto it as he slowly slipped from me and from the world around him, a world, he'd inhabited for such a short time."

Kip died on May 22, 1944.

Chapter Three

A Portrait of the Artist

As a Young Man

Tennessee Confronts the Uber-Divas:
Tallulah Bankhead, Joan Crawford, & Miriam Hopkins

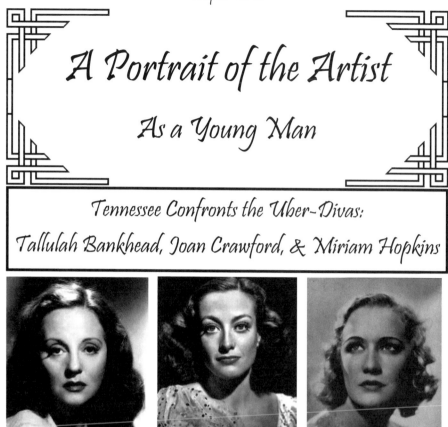

| Bankhead | Crawford | Hopkins |

"He's got a very odd name. Calls himself Tennessee

Williams. He's written some one-act plays that are very different from what's out there."

That was Molly Day Thacher, speaking to her husband, the actor and director, Elia Kazan. *[She would later urge him to direct the stage version of* A Streetcar Named Desire (1947)]

She was a kind of literary scout, a reader going through countless plays, hoping to find properties for the Group Theater. Through producer Harold Clurman, she managed to get Tennessee a special prize of $100 for some of his one-act plays collectively entitled *American Blues*.

She sent him a check for the prize money and a note of encouragement to his address in California. At the time, he was putting in a sixty-hour week, working for Clark's Bootery in Culver City as a clerk and salesman, which paid only $12.50 a week.

Thacher even got the emerging playwright a literary agent, Audrey Wood, who would become "his mother, his older sister, and his guiding light," throughout his heyday on Broadway. Along with her husband, William Liebling, she ran the Liebling-Wood Agency at 30 Rockefeller Center.

Tennessee's literary agent, **Audrey Wood**, with **William Liebling**, her husband and business partner.

Bored with California, Tennessee wanted to try his chances in New York. Money was a problem until Wood advanced him the price of a Greyhound bus ticket as an advance on a piece of short fiction, "The Field of Blue Children," which had been sold to *Story Magazine.*

Tennessee arrived in Manhattan at the Port Authority Bus Terminal. Unshaven and in rumpled clothes, he made his way to the RCA Building at Rockefeller Center. There, he spotted Liebling, who was a casting director auditioning thirty hopeful chorus girls, each showing off her legs. As Tennessee remembered them, they were "chattering like birds high on locoweed."

He was introduced to Audrey Wood, "a tiny little thing, with very bright eyes. She was witty, bouncing around the room with a certain exuberance. She had hair so bright red it could only have come from a bottle. In all, she reminds me of a porcelain china doll."

For shelter, he found lodgings in an apartment hotel way up on West 108th Street, which charged $4.50 a week for mostly out-of-work actors and various artists who arrived daily at the Greyhound Bus Station.

Since he had less than ten dollars in his pocket, Tennessee was rescued when Wood persuaded actor Hume Cronyn into taking an option of $50 a month on nine one-act plays by Tennessee.

In a touch of irony, Cronyn would later marry actress Jessica Tandy, who would star on Broadway as Blanche DuBois in *A Streetcar Named Desire.*

There was almost no off-Broadway in those days, and no producer wanted to invest time and money on one-act plays by this unknown Southern writer. Some of these producers considered the plays "the work of a degenerate."

Eventually, Cronyn's option expired and Tennessee's money dwindled. He

A Struggling Playwright by Day, Tennessee Suffers from "Deviate Satyriasis" at Night

returned to his family residence in a suburb of St. Louis, where he occupied a bed in the attic. There, he began to work on a long play entitled *Something Wild in the Country.*

"I am writing furiously with seven wild-cats under my skin," he claimed in a memoir.

The play focused on the social and sexual decadence of a small Southern town. A drifter, Val Xavier, arrives in a snakeskin jacket. Here, he finds employment in the shop of the store's dying owner and his sexually frustrated wife, Myra. In addition, Xavier gets involved with a local seer and a religious fanatic.

"On the day of my worst depression," Tennessee recalled, news arrived from Wood. The Dramatists Guild had awarded him a grant of $1,000 from the Rockefeller Foundation. More good news was on the way about his long play, which he'd retitled *Battle of Angels.* The Theater Guild had taken an option on it, which would pay him $100 a month as long as the contract was in effect.

He was aboard the next Greyhound bus pulling out of St. Louis. He arrived in New York in January of 1940 with high hopes.

This time, he lodged on the tenth floor of a dingy and cramped room at the local branch of the YMCA on West 63rd Street. During the day, he worked on *Battle of Angels* on his portable typewriter.

At night, he cruised the Times Square area in search of sailors and G.I.'s. As his brother, Dakin Williams, in Key West told Darwin Porter, "Tennessee admitted to me that he cruised Times Square at night, often for hours at a time. No love was involved, only the thrill of pursuit and temporary pleasures with the momentary object of his desires, meaning those young men who agreed to come back with him to the Y, often because they had been unlucky finding a girl for the night."

Tennessee himself admitted in print to this "deviant satyriasis which was a round-the-calendar thing, as opposed to animals which have seasons for it."

In spite of his support from Wood and Thacher, Tennessee felt New York was a lonely place, and he wanted to be back in the Taos desert or in a cottage overlooking the Pacific. As he recorded in his journal: "Most people in New York are involved in their own lives. I need somebody to envelop me, embrace me, pull me by sheer force out of this neurotic shell of fear I've built around myself."

Finding New York too distracting, Tennessee left on a Greyhound for Boston, where he took a boat to Provincetown. Once there, he settled in to rewrite and polish *Battle of Angels,* hoping for a Broadway opening in the late autumn of 1940.

He wrote his mother, Edwina Dakin Williams, that "Miriam Hopkins, Tallula (sic) Bankhead, and even Katharine Cornell were reading *Battle of Angels.*" Tennessee expressed his belief that Bankhead "would be damned good as Myra, not a little short on tenderness but imbued with plenty of richness and drama."

After writing that, he received word from Wood that another internationally famous actress was also intrigued by the role of Myra.

Tennessee Meets "The Gorgeous Hussy," (Aka, "Mildred Pierce")

Joan Crawford

In New York, Joan Crawford heard that a young playwright had written a strong role for a woman of a certain age in a play called *Battle of Angels*. Crawford knew that both Miriam Hopkins and Tallulah Bankhead, two failed candidates (like herself) for the role of Scarlett O'Hara, were considering making bids for the female lead.

Crawford contacted Wood, who arranged for the playwright to return from Provincetown to meet the actress at "21" for lunch the following week.

Slightly nervous and feeling inadequate, Tennessee arrived at the chic restaurant wearing a black suit borrowed from a Baptist preacher from Kansas City who stayed at the YMCA to cruise young men.

Tennessee wanted to show Crawford great respect, but he'd read F. Scott Fitzgerald's description of her, and, based on that, he seriously doubted if she could play Myra.

Fitzgerald had written of Crawford's "monolithic fierceness. She can't change her emotions in the middle of a scene without going through a sort of Jekyll and Hyde contortion of the face. Also, you can never give her such a stage direction as 'telling a lie,' because if you did, she would practically give a representation of Benedict Arnold selling West Point to the British."

Before meeting Crawford, Tennessee had seen virtually every movie she'd ever made, finding her for the most part tough, gutsy, and fiercely competitive on screen. He suspected she was like that in real life, too.

In later years, he claimed, "I'm glad I met Miss Crawford before her adopted daughter turned her image into a *chiaroscuro* of camp."

He was referring, of course, to the "lynch biography," *Mommie Dearest*, penned by her disenchanted adopted daughter, Christina Crawford.

"I liked Joan Crawford," he later said, "and feared we shared certain things in common—notably a shady background and a tendency to sleep with one man too many. She had worked her way to the top, and I was on my way there, too. She was a rival of such stars as Garbo and Norma Shearer. All of these stars were fading at the box office, and Joan wanted to test her talent on the Broadway stage. She thought my play might do it for her."

"At 21, Joan knew that her days as a big MGM star were numbered," Tennessee later claimed. "Beneath the perfect grooming, the expensive clothing,

28

and the glamorous façade lurked a woman who lived in fear. I mean, she'd been born in 1904, or so I'd heard, and it was already 1940. New crops of the young and beautiful were arriving in Hollywood to fuck her longtime beau, Clark Gable."

"Joan had no trouble with my homosexuality," Tennessee said. "In Hollywood, she was known as 'Cranberry' to the gay set, including the likes of William Haines and director Edmund Goulding."

"Our luncheon went well until we actually started to talk about her starring in *Battle of Angels,*" he said. "She wanted me to rewrite the play, turning the main character of Val Xavier into a *femme fatale* in a snakeskin jacket."

"I can see myself arriving in this nothing town and exciting the local men to mayhem and violence," Crawford said. "My death at the end can come from a posse of jealous women who can't stand the competition of a real woman."

Tennessee was prepared to make all sorts of changes to the text of his play, but none this drastic. He had to tell her he couldn't do it.

"There is a pivotal scene where a painting of Val as Jesus Christ is displayed," he told her.

"Oh, hell, boy, get me rewrite," she said. By this time in the course of their luncheon, she was tanked up on vodka. "That's easy to change. Fuck Christ. Paint me as the embodiment of Mary Magdalene, which would be more interesting than Christ. He's done to death."

After their ill-fated sojourn at "21," he always regretted that he could not have revised his play into a suitable vehicle for her, because he admired her, although knowing she was not a great actress. "On screen, Joan personified both the dreams and disappointments of millions of American women."

In spite of her hopes, Crawford never got a chance to play a Tennessee Williams character. She felt she would have been ideal cast as Alexandra del Lago in *Sweet Bird of Youth.*

Crawford said that the closest she came to a Williams character was in her role of Eva Phillips in the 1955 *Queen Bee,* in which she was cast as an imperious, domineering diva presiding over a dysfunctional family in a Georgia mansion. She told the press, "*Queen Bee* owes so much to Tennessee Williams that we should pay him royalties. I felt like Carte Blanche DuBois."

Tallulah, Outraged: "Me, A Southern Lady, Appearing in Such Filth?"

Tennessee heard that Tallulah was starring in a play in the town of Dennis on Cape Cod. Since he'd written *Battle of Angels* specifically for her to play Myra, the female lead, he sent her his first draft of the play. After two weeks, when he hadn't received any word from her, he decided to bicycle to Dennis, a distance of forty miles from Provincetown.

There as part of a summer tour, Tallulah was starring in Arthur W. Pinero's *The Second Mrs. Tanqueray,* which had had its premiere in London in 1893. She had been cast as Paula Tanqueray, a woman who'd been the mistress of several men. "Type casting, *dah-ling,*" Tallulah had told the press.

Backstage, Tennessee was introduced to Colin Keith-Johnson, a distinguished British actor cast as her long-suffering husband. He was handsome, tall, and blonde, with the physique of an athlete. Only later, Tennessee learned that the married actor was also playing Tallulah's husband off the stage as well as on it.

Tallulah herself was emerging from her own failed marriage to actor John Emery, who was unfairly called "a John Barrymore clone" by harsh critics.

At this point in his young life, Tennessee was not used to visiting actresses in their dressing rooms, especially an actress as uninhibited as Tallulah. He'd later see the vaginas of such stars as Vivien Leigh and Elizabeth Taylor, but at this point, he blushed when he discovered Tallulah sitting nude in front of her dressing room mirror, making emergency repairs to her face. "As you can plainly see, dahling," she said to him, "my breasts, contrary to rumor, are not altogether fallen. Come in."

"It's an honor to meet the great Tallulah Bankhead," he said. "I'm Tennessee Williams."

"I understand you were born in Mississippi," she said. "As you know, I'm from Alabama. Our Southern culture probably forms a bond between us."

"I hope so," he said. "I wrote the role of Myra hoping you could play her on stage. You'd be devastating in the part."

"You do write with a certain sensitivity," she said. "Perhaps we'll work together some day in one of your future plays. But I consider *Battle of Angels* degenerate filth. You must remember this: I am a lady, although not as chaste as Helen Hayes. There is no escaping the fact, young man, that you have written a dirty play."

Tennessee tried to defend himself in front of such a formidable presence. "I had hoped that you'd see my play as a mixture of super religiosity and hysterical sensuality spinning around the central character of the drifter, Val Xavier. My play is dedicated to D.H. Lawrence, who inspired some of the themes, mixing Freudian motifs with Christian symbolism and Dionysian myth."

"Oh, please, dahling, all that symbolism is hard to take before I've had my first bourbon of the afternoon," she said. "If you want to write plays, you must learn that on stage, religion and sex do not mix."

"But I read that you wanted to appear as Sadie Thompson in W. Somerset Maugham's *Rain,*" he said. "A prostitute deported to the South Seas, who attracts the attentions of a zealous reverend mired in his own lasciviousness."

"Oh, *dah-ling,* it's vulgar to speak of one's past indiscretions," she said.

There was a knock on her door, a voice announcing himself as Leonard Bernstein.

"Just a minute," dahling," she called out. She whispered to Tennessee. "I will not star in your play. I read yesterday that Miriam Hopkins is considering it.

We both lost out on the role of Scarlett O'Hara. Maybe she'll make a comeback as your Myra."

"In the meantime, I don't want you to think your bike ride down here was a total waste. I want you to meet this musician, Mr. Bernstein. I had him last night. Perhaps you'll get lucky tonight." She turned toward the door, "Come in, Leonard."

It was Tallulah herself who brought the flamboyant soon-to-be musical giant of the 20th century together with the flamboyant playwright who would both shock, delight, and dazzle audiences in the 1940s and 50s.

"Glitter and Be Gay" from Candide
With Music by Leonard Bernstein

The Peacock & His Pleasures

As Tallulah had predicted, Leonard Bernstein and Tennessee were intrigued with each other. The composer/conductor invited Tennessee to drive back with him to Tanglewood, where he was the assistant to the great Russian conductor, Serge Koussevitzky.

On the way there, Tennessee learned how Tallulah had met Bernstein. On a hot summer afternoon, she'd seen him in rehearsal, "shimmying" his way through *The Rio Grande,* a composition by Constant Lambert. Because the auditorium was so hot, he'd removed his shirt. Tallulah had been so impressed with his "rippling back muscles" that she invited him to dinner.

Tanglewood was the name of the Tappan Family Estate, a mile southwest of Lenox, a town in the Berkshire mountains of Western Massachusetts. The Tappan family had donated 210 acres of meadowland on the

"Supreme egotist! Pinko faggot! Great talent!" All of these names were used to describe composer and conductor **Leonard Bernstein.**

"We fought over the 'rights' to bed dancer John Kriza," Gore Vidal later claimed.

31

north shore of Lake Mahkeenac to the Boston Symphony Orchestra.

Tennessee would record in his journal what Bernstein told him about the young musicians at Tanglewood. "We never sleep, at least not much. We are forever playing music or playing with each other, love and music. Love and music. It's so exciting to be alive."

At Tanglewood, Tennessee, to his dismay, found that Bernstein shared a bed in a dormitory with six other conducting students. "Whenever we get lucky, one of us hangs this miniature replica of a harp on the door, which means 'keep out' until one of us completes our conquest inside."

Later, Bernstein put those much admired back muscles to work as he plunged into Tennessee's much used butt. Tennessee later recalled, "I will always remember his words before he took the dive, 'A peacock must take his pleasure,' I heard."

In time, Bernstein would become notorious for his kissing of both men and women, especially men. Tennessee once commented on his kiss. "It was like an assault by a sort of combination of sandpaper and sea anemones!"

[That quote is sometimes attributed to theatrical director Jonathan Miller.]

Although seemingly dedicated to music, Bernstein shocked Tennessee by telling him, "I would gladly give up music to become a film star."

[On three different occasions in his future, Bernstein would be signed to star in a Hollywood film, but each of the deals fell through because of lack of funding.]

After Bernstein's stint at Tanglewood, both Tennessee and Tallulah would be added to his list of A-list seductions. Other names on that list included a young Marlon Brando, composer Aaron Copland, Farley Granger, dancer Harold Lang, Rudolf Nureyev, Jerome Robbins, composer Ned Rorem, and *(surprise!)* Lana Turner.

For the sake of heterosexual appearances, Bernstein in Hollywood had taken Turner out on three highly publicized dates. She later told Ava Gardner, "Bernstein is not that successful with women. He told me he would be more inspired in bed if I had asked Tyrone Power to join us in a *ménage à trois.*"

Although Bernstein and Tennessee would soon become disenchanted with each other's personalities, each remained in awe of the other's talents.

At the end of World War II, Tennessee campaigned for Bernstein to write the incidental music for the theatrical production of *The Glass Menagerie.*

But by the time they met in Mexico City a few years later, the bloom on their friendship had withered.

Tennessee revealed in his memoirs that in Mexico City, he and Bernstein were invited to a luncheon by a "pair of very effete American queens." Within those memoirs, he complained about how embarrassed he'd been by the composer's treatment of their hosts.

Bernstein told the men, "When the revolution comes, you two will be stood up against a wall and shot. *[You're]* totally worthless to society."

Tennessee noted that Bernstein was going through a period known as his "radical chic."

"I wonder if he is not as true a revolutionary as I am," Tennessee wrote. "The difference between us is that I am not interested in shooting piss-elegant queens or anyone else. I am only interested in the discovery of a new social system—certainly not communist, but an enlightened form of socialism."

He later referred to Bernstein as "a total egotist. When not getting all the attention, he sits in a chair with closed eyes, pretending to be asleep."

Bernstein's opinion of Tennessee was expressed as part of a laconic postscript in a letter sent to his former lover, Aaron Copland. "Tennessee Williams is here in Mexico City—*que fastidio, [translation: "What a pain!"]*

Bernstein would enjoy a more enduring friendship with Gore Vidal.

[Gore and Leonard Bernstein were attracted to the same type of man, including the short, stocky, blue-eyed dancer, Harold Lang, who had starred in the Jerome Robbin's ballet, Fancy Free. *It was about three World War II sailors "on the town," as the movie musical based on it would later be entitled. The 1949 film would co-star Gene Kelly and Frank Sinatra.*

At Gore's home in Ravello, Italy, the composer and author talked of past conquests, including Lang. "I will say that Harold's was one of the seven—or whatever number it is—wonders of our time," Bernstein told Gore, who agreed.

Through a mutual friend, Bernstein and Gore had attended a homosexual orgy in the upper rooms of the American Embassy in Rome. Eight grade-A Roman hustlers had been hired as the evening's entertainment.

When Gore was in Hollywood for the filming of his play, The Best Man *(1964), he and Bernstein shared adjoining bungalows at the Beverly Hills Hotel.*

Gore later wrote: "As Lenny was eager for sex, I arranged for two would-be actors to join us for the evening. At some point, Lenny vanished into his own quarters wearing only a towel and a happy smile."

He disappeared for such a long time that Gore feared he might have been murdered by the hustler. He opened the connecting door between their two suites, finding the young man sitting nude with an equally nude Bernstein on his bed. "In the afterglow of sex, Lennie was lecturing the actor on the art of performing. Lenny was a born pedant."

By the time Bernstein paid a final visit to Gore's vacation retreat at Ravello in 1987, there were no more orgies. Gore later claimed, "We spent a lot of time bad-mouthing President Ronald Reagan. For amusement, and over sundowners on my terrace overlooking the Amalfi Drive, we speculated on the exact measurements of Reagan's dick. We combined our sources of information, ranging from Susan

Leonard Bernstein *(left)* with fellow composer, **Aaron Copland**. "He wasn't my prettiest lover, but we made beautiful music together in bed," Bernstein claimed.

Hayward to Lana Turner. Doris Day wasn't talking."

Gore went to his grave without revealing their ultimate conclusion about the presidential penis.

Both men left the comparisons of such measurements to Truman Capote, who billed himself as "the world's expert on the size of presidential dicks, beginning with John F. Kennedy and extending to Lyndon B. Johnson and on to Richard M. Nixon."

Boston Is Outraged by Battle of Angels

At long last, and after many a struggle, *Battle of Angels* was set to open in Boston on December 30, 1940, at the Wilbur Theatre, with hopes of taking it to Broadway after a two-week run.

Designated as its director, Margaret Webster, who knew nothing about life in a Southern town, was an unusual choice. "I'd been to Washington, but never crossed into Virginia and points south," she said.

The New York-born actress, producer, and director held a dual citizenship. She was the daughter of two famous actors, Ben Webster and Dame May Whitty. Ben Webster had already scored his greatest triumph, directing Paul Robeson in *Othello (1943),* with José Ferrer cast as Iago. It had played for 296 performances, by far the longest run of any Shakespearean production in the history of Broadway till then.

When Tennessee met Margaret Webster, she was involved in a longtime romantic relationship with Eva Le Gallienne, one of the most celebrated actresses of the American theater.

Webster later recalled meeting the playwright: "He was a short, sturdy, young man with crew-cut hair, pebble-thick glasses, and an even thicker Southern accent, dressed in shabby corduroy jacket and muddy riding boots."

Webster introduced him to Miriam Hopkins, who had been assigned to star in the play's leading role of Myra, the character's name later changed to Lady Torrance.

After having great success as a film star in the 1930s, Savannah-born Hopkins had scored a number of triumphs at Paramount, especially during the pre-Code era. Her other successes had included three films with Ernst Lubitsch and *The Old Maid* (1939) with her arch-enemy, Bette Davis.

Based on the outfit he was wearing, Hopkins mistakenly assumed that Tennessee was

| Margaret Webster | Eva Le Gallienne |

Miriam Hopkins in
The Old Maid (1939)

fresh from riding horseback. He had to assure her, "I will never be Tom Mix. I can't ride a horse."

Although known as a difficult actress to work with, she was imbued with Southern charm and graciousness, and even invited him to a champagne-infused supper later that evening. He knew she was "between husbands," having divorced the famous director Anatole Litvak in 1939.

After having been teamed with Davis once again in *Old Acquaintance* (1943), Hopkins seemed to have bowed out of films. "I didn't desert them," she told Tennessee. "No offers were coming in, and that's why I've turned to the stage."

Arriving at her hotel suite in Boston, Tennessee feared that she might be intent on seduction. She told him that her favorite line in his play was when Val Xavier is told that all the women in this southern town were suffering from "sexual malnutrition."

"That line could describe my current state of affairs, or I should say 'lack of affairs,'" Hopkins said.

She amused him with stories of Hollywood in the 1930s. "When I can't sleep, I don't count sheep," she said. "I count lovers. And by the time I reach thirty-eight or thirty-nine, I'm asleep. I usually start with actors—Fredric March, Robert Montgomery, Bing Crosby, Maurice Chevalier (he couldn't get it up), Gary Cooper, Franchot Tone, John Gilbert; or else directors—King Vidor or Ernst Lubitsch."

She expressed how embarrassing it had been for her in Boston: "This year, *The Harvard Lampoon* picked me as 'the least desirable companion on a desert island.'"

Hopkins was no dumb blonde Hollywood actress. She was sharp and insightful, shocking Tennessee when she surmised that "You are actually Myra. And the character you write about, Val Xavier, is the kind of man who makes you swoon, makes you feel helpless, erotic, in love."

"You've nailed me," he admitted to her.

After the champagne was consumed, Hopkins finally got around to revealing the purpose of their late night supper. She wanted her part greatly enlarged at the expense of the other performers, notably actress Doris Dudley. She also lobbied for a rewrite. "At the end of the play, when I'm shot, I want the character of Val Xavier to carry me up the stairs. That way, I will remain the center of attention on stage, even though dead."

He would later claim that there was a glittering, hot-tempered ferocity to her that would make her ideal in the role. "She has a great Southern pride, typical of her native Georgia, and a feeling of superiority over others. She is one high-spirited blonde with the subtlety of a wrestler in a to-the-death match."

She did ask him a question which he never answered: "How can a play or a motion picture reflect real life when it is created by people who lead artificial lives?"

Even before he left her suite, he knew he was going to reject all of her ideas for script changes. The problem involved summoning enough courage to tell her the next day.

When forced to deliver the bad news to her, she attacked him on a sexual level. "I bet you're a premature ejaculator, a real fast starter and a lousy finisher."

"At lease she didn't call me a faggot," he later said. "But in front of cast and crew, Miriam made me feel like two cents—and two inches."

Hopkins and Tennessee did not nurture a grudge and by the time the play opened, they were defending each other artistically. He said, "Miriam could have been an Amanda to rival even Laurette Taylor in *The Glass Menagerie.* What I liked about her was her love of literature and her ability to recite by heart the poems of Lord Byron, Rossetti, and William Cullen Bryant's 'Thanatopsis.'"

Opening night was disastrous. Many in the audience of tuxedos and expensive gowns thought they were going to see a play about angels. As part of the scenery, an artist had created a backdrop depicting Val Xavier as Jesus Christ. There was a rumbling the audience and cries of "blasphemy."

Before the play ended, half of the audience had walked out. Those who remained for the final curtain were nearly asphyxiated. The script called for a building to catch on fire. Smoke pots had been placed about and lit, but too many were added. Both the cast and the audience went into coughing fits.

The next morning, critics were harsh. The New York critic for *Variety* (who was in Boston for the event), defined *Battle of Angels* as "sordid and amateurish." Tennessee said that the Boston audience "received my play like the outbreak of the Bubonic plague."

The Boston City Council was deluged with phone calls, mostly from people who had not seen the play. There were protests that *Battle of Angels* should be forcibly closed.

Members of Boston's City Council met with Webster and Tennessee, demanding the removal of some of the scenes and lines in the play as a condition for letting its short run continue.

In anger, Hopkins called her own press conference, denouncing the members of Boston's City Council. "I suggest that these blue-nosed city fathers be flung into the Boston Harbor like the tea at the historic Boston Tea Party."

At the play's run, the Theater Guild in New York notified Tennessee that it was dropping its option on *Battle of Angels.* "It cannot be brought to Broadway," Tennessee was told. "It is not dramatically successful."

He entered into a months-long depression, and for a time was almost suicidal. "But," as he later recalled, "I did not self-destruct easily." He predicted that he would live to see *Battle of Angels* open on Broadway.

In the years to come, he would brush the dust off *Battle of Angels,* and continue to rewrite it, hoping for a "kind of perfection" he never obtained, at least not critically.

Brando Says No,
But Orpheus Descends on Broadway Anyway

In 1957, Tennessee finally presented *Battle of Angels* on Broadway in the form of a rewritten adaptation, *Orpheus Descending.* He had reworked the play, reshaping the plot, characters, and dialogue.

The play still dealt with passion and repression and was replete with lush, poetic dialogue and imagery. It was a modern retelling of the ancient Greek legend of Orpheus, searching the Underworld in an attempt to resuscitate his lover, Euridice.

In Manhattan, Tennessee went to the apartment of Marlon Brando, urging him to accept the role of Val Xavier on the stage, since the male role had not only been enlarged, but vastly improved. He assured the actor that *Orpheus Descending* would bring him even greater acclaim than his role of Stanley Kowalski in *A Streetcar Named Desire* (1947).

"I like some of the lines," Brando said, "particularly when Val classifies people into three types—'the buyers, the bought, and those who don't belong to no place at all.'"

"But this boy Val never takes a stand," Brando continued. "I don't really know what he's for or against. Well, you can't act in a vacuum."

Eventually, Robert Loggia was assigned the role, but after Loggia was dismissed during the play's previews in Philadelphia, it was taken over by Cliff Robertson.

Tennessee later claimed that he thought Robertson was "too clean cut and American to capture the undeniable animal erotic energy and appeal of Val. Brando could have pulled it off."

Maureen Stapleton, whom Tennessee often described as "my favorite actress," starred in the Broadway version as Lady, although in the play's eventual reworking into a movie, *[entitled The Fugitive Kind],* she'd be reduced to playing the very minor role of Vee Talbot, the wife of the local sheriff. As Stapleton ruefully observed, "Sometimes the acceptance of a lesser role, regardless of how humiliating, is the question of a paycheck."

Before the play opened for its very brief run, Tennessee told *The New York Times,* "It is still the tale of a wild-spirited boy who wanders into a conventional community of the South and creates the

Cliff Robertson

commotion of a fox in a chicken coop. But beneath the surface it is a play about unanswered questions that haunt the hearts of people, as well as the acceptance of prescribed answers that are not answers at all."

As he left the theater, Tennessee was greeted with catcalls and boos. "I just booed right back," he said.

Critics sharpened their knives for their assault on him. *The New Yorker* ignored the play's poetry, labeling it as "cornpone melodrama." Other reviews weren't much better.

A depressed Tennessee told the press, "I feel I am no longer acceptable to the theater public. Maybe they've had too much of a certain dish, and don't want to eat any more from my plate."

"The Critics Want a Quart of My Blood"

—Tennessee Williams

It took two decades, but finally, *Battle of Angels* reached the screen with a new title—*The Fugitive Kind*. At long last, Tennessee got his wish. Marlon Brando signed to appear as Val ("Snakeskin") Xavier, the guitar-playing drifter.

Anna Magnani was cast as Lady, with Joanne Woodward appearing as the second female lead, that of Carol Cutrere, an alcoholic nymphomaniac.

Sidney Lumet signed on as the film's director, although he would later face critical attacks, the *Chicago Reader* claiming, "He is completely baffled by the Gothic South and doesn't quite know what to do with the overlay of Greek myth either."

Anthony Franciosa, the husband of Shelley Winters, Brando's former girlfriend, had agreed to star as Val for $75,000. But Lumet went after Brando when he heard that his bank account was bare, drained not only by his divorce from Anna Kashfi but from the financial failure of his film studio, Pennebaker.

Lumet showed up on Brando's doorstep with an offer of one million dollars. Without hesitation, Brando said, "Sign me up," although he still felt the character of Val Xavier was "a playwright's failure."

He was also concerned that Anna Magnani, in a stronger role, "will wipe my ass off the screen."

The Fugitive Kind was not shot in the South, but in Milton, New York, a small town eighty miles north of Manhattan.

Both Lumet and Tennessee feared the meeting of Brando with Magnani, Tennessee likening it to "two hydrogen bombs going off at the same time."

Both Tennessee and Lumet were unaware that a younger and sexier Brando had seduced a younger and sexier Magnani on her home turf in Rome years before.

In a private agreement with Lumet, Tennessee agreed to act as a referee between Brando and Magnani. At first, she was enthusiastic. "When I work with

Marlon, it is like working with a strange animal about to pounce. It's a wonderful experience to see him so realistic. So completely *all* man."

Brando had a different view about her, confiding to Tennessee, "When I encountered *La Lupa [her nickname]*, I discovered that she had turned into an Italian Tallulah Bankhead, an older creature and one even more sexually aggressive than before. She is that kind of woman, like Tallulah, who makes me flinch. Nothing but a sexual predator and a caricature of the actress she used to be. She once possessed a certain raw beauty. She has now reached the borderline of old and ugly."

Armed with this information, Tennessee tried to discourage Magnani in any fantasy she might have had about pursuing Brando to bed him. At that point, she had not told him of her long-ago adventure with him in Rome.

In his autobiography, Brando confessed what happened when he accepted Magnani's invitation to visit her in her suite during rehearsals for *The Fugitive Kind*.

"She started kissing me with great passion," he wrote. "I tried to be responsive, because I knew she was worried about growing older and losing her beauty. As a matter of kindness, I felt I had to return her kisses. But once she got her arms around me, she wouldn't let go. I started to pull away, but she held me tight and bit my lip, which really hurt."

[He also wrote: *"With her teeth gnawing at my lower lip, the two of us locked in an embrace, I was reminded of one of those fatal mating rituals of insects that end when the female administers the coup de grace. We rocked back and forth as she tried to lead me to the bed. My eyes were wide open, and as I looked at her eyeball-to-eyeball, I saw that she was in a frenzy, Attila the Hun in full attack. Finally, the pain got so intense that I grabbed her nose and squeezed it as hard as I could, as if I were squeezing a lemon, to push her away. It startled her, and I made my escape."]*

The next day, Brando informed Tennessee that, "I will never work with Magnani ever again unless I have a rock in my fist."

After filming wrapped, Tennessee told the press, "Marlon and Anna engaged in a clash of egos never before known in the history of cinema."

When *The Fugitive Kind* officially opened in April of 1960, it played to nearly empty houses across the country. Exhibitors reported that audiences often left in disgust before "THE END" flashed across the screen.

Lumet, Brando, and Tennessee were "burned alive" *[the playwright's words]* by the critics. "They wanted not only to behead me, but drink a quart of my tainted blood."

Brando was also attacked. Critic Clancy Sigal wrote: "Watching Brando imitating Judy Holliday's impersonation of him in *Bells Are Ringing* is, at its most serious, like seeing a scratchy old film of Duse or Bernhardt; surely someone is kidding someone."

Time Out claimed that "despite the film's stellar credentials, just about everything is wrong in this adaptation of the Tennessee Williams play. Lumet's direction is either ponderous or pretentious, and he failed to crack the problem of the florid stage dialogue and the dangerously weak role of Brando."

In an angry flash, Brando phoned Tennessee. "I told you the role of Val Xavier was weak. If only you would have listened to me." Then, abruptly, he put down the phone.

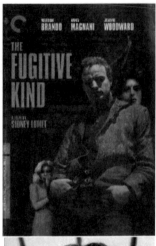

In Key West, Tallulah Bankhead had just finished a road tour in a play called *Crazy October.* She was staying in the home of its playwright, James Leo Herlihy. Darwin Porter, then the chief of the Key West bureau of *The Miami Herald,* invited Tallulah and Herlihy to a showing of the film in a dingy theater along Duval Street.

To the trio's surprise, they found Tennessee and his longtime lover, Frank Merlo, sitting directly behind them.

Tallulah sat patiently through the film adaptation of a play she'd rejected twenty years before. At the end of the screening, she stood up, and in a bellowing voice loud enough to be heard in the back row, she said, "Tennessee *dah-ling*, they've made an absolutely dreadful film out of a perfectly awful play."

Regrettably, this final failure marked what Tennessee called his "funeral rites. There went my once fashionable reputation. Never again would I be the darling of the critics. From then on, the mere mention of my name would bring only the most savage of attacks, those that tore at a human heart. I had to be a tough old bird to continue to write plays at this point in my life."

In her native Rome, a younger **Anna Magnani** had known the loving embrace of a sexually fired-up **Marlon Brando**. But when it came time to star together in *The Fugitive Kind,* "Magnani was a hungry tigress devouring her very young," in Brando's words.

Chapter Four

The Saga of Lana Turner and "The Celluloid Brassiere"

Tennessee & Lana Face Two Faux Clark Gables— James Craig & John Hodiak

> *"I think that is one of the funniest but most embarrassing things that ever happened to me, that I should be expected to produce a suitable vehicle for this actress. I feel like an obstetrician required to successfully deliver a mastodon from a beaver."*
>
> —Tennessee describing his MGM assignment
> to write a screenplay for **Lana Turner** *(photo above)*

In time, Hollywood would turn out some memorable films based on the plays of Tennessee Williams. But fame, riches, and glory did not come for him overnight.

When he first moved to Los Angeles in 1939, Tennessee was desperate for money. The only job he could find was as a feather picker on a squab ranch outside the city limits.

"My time of dread was when a group of young men, most of them boys, actually, came over three times a week to commit mayhem in a place known as 'The Killing Shed.' Here, they would murder the squabs by slitting their throats with sharp knives. The poor birds would frantically twitch as these killers would hold them by their legs over a bucket to bleed them."

The slain squabs were then delivered to the feather pickers, who included Tennessee among a group of mostly Mexican co-workers. Tennessee said that after he picked the feathers off a dead squab, he would then drop a feather in a milk bottle with his name on it. He would be paid—"very very little money it was"—based on the number of squabs he'd picked that hot, sweaty, smelly day.

In the future, if his host ever served him squab, he'd leave the table.

When he plucked the last feathers of his last squab, he returned to New York. The only job open was a $16-a-week position as an usher at the old Strand Theater on Broadway. "They did nothing but show *Casablanca* day and night. I learned all of Bogie's dialogue, then Bergman's role. I never tired of Dooley Wilson playing that oldie, 'As Time Goes By.'"

"Then it came like an electric shock or else a bolt of lightning," he recalled. "Audrey Wood got in touch to inform me that she'd just 'sold' me to MGM in Hollywood. I'd get 250 big ones a month, or so I thought, until she informed me that the $250 was per week. I was overjoyed. Never in my life had I been paid that kind of dough."

As the job was originally described to him in New York, he'd been assigned the task of reading a romantic novel, *The Sun Is My Undoing.* He was to write a scenario for its adaptation to the screen.

He arrived by train in Los Angeles, getting off at Union Station with David Greggory, a friend of his from New York. Both of them set out to look for a place to live, finding a cheap two-room apartment in the "honky tonk" section of Santa Monica, overlooking the Pacific Ocean.

"The wallpaper was stained, and the decoration consisted of a plaster model of Mae West—nude, of course," Tennessee said.

His half-gypsy landlady, "Jezebel" Ringo, became a literary inspiration for him. In the morning, she fed him red tomatoes from her garden patch outside and also fed him Red propaganda from *The Daily Worker.* In the afternoon, she lolled about on a raggedy old mattress in the garden beside her tomato patch.

Young Tennessee in Tinseltown: Plucking Squabs & and Cruising the Palisades

At night, she was visited by a series of military young men, often two at a time, whom she serviced in her apartment. Her nocturnal pastimes inspired Tennessee later in life to use as the basis for his character of Maxine Faulk in *The Night of the Iguana.* The role was interpreted on Broadway by a red-wigged Bette Davis and later, on the big screen, by Ava Gardner. The Maxine character first appeared in Tennessee's writing in a short story "The Mattress by the Tomato Patch."

The other apartments were filled with women of a rather dubious character," Tennessee said. "Jezebel offered me a reduction in rent if I'd inspect the halls right before dawn and remove all the used condoms," Tennessee said. "Because of the wartime blackout, the halls were very active at night with enough sailors to man a warship. The bedrooms were often occupied, so much of the work went on in the hallways."

Sometimes, when there were a lot of ships in port, Jezebel or the working girls in the apartments could not service all the young men.

Opportunistic Tennessee invested his first paycheck and bought plenty of liquor. The "overflow" in the hallways were invited inside his apartment for plenty of liquor and sex.

"As one sailor told me, 'I'm so horny, I could fuck a snake.' That was the attitude of most of these soldiers and sailors. They didn't care what legs opened for them at night. It was a heady time during the blackout in Los Angeles. I dreaded when the lights would be turned on again."

On some nights, Tennessee trolled the plateau of the Pacific Palisades of Santa Monica, that high promontory that overlooked the ocean. He pedaled a bike along "a route of little arbors and bosky retreats in a park planted with royal palms. The sounds of sex in various combinations filled the night air."

"Everything was blacked out in fear of an air raid on Los Angeles from Japan," said Tennessee. "The Palisades were infested with young sailors, soldiers, and marines, each of them looking for a good time, and not caring too much where they got it."

He couldn't always see clearly the man of his desire, so he developed a technique. He'd approach a young man who looked promising and would offer him a cigarette. As he lit a match, he would check out the man's looks. He recalled many memorable encounters, particularly one with a gay marine. In his journal, he made the claim that "I screwed him seven times in one night." But on most occasions, Tennessee was "the fuckee, not the fucker."

Tennessee Williams, writing at his desk in 1942.

Snubbed by Kate Hepburn,
Tennessee Collaborates With a Pregnant Lana

The first Monday after his arrival in Los Angeles, when he reported for the first time to the MGM factory, he learned that one of its chief honchos, Pandro S. Berman, had reassigned him. His new job was to adapt a novel by Judith Kelly, *Marriage Is a Private Affair,* into a vehicle for Lana Turner's comeback after an eighteen-month absence from the screen.

At the time, he had no respect for her talent—in fact, he claimed "she couldn't act her way out of her form-fitting cashmeres." He wrote to friends that he had been assigned "to embroider a celluloid brassiere for Lana Turner."

He was told that it had not been decided by Louis B. Mayer, but if the lead male role was strong enough, it might be a star vehicle for Clark Gable, if he could be temporarily relieved of his duties to the U.S. military. To Tennessee, that seemed like a remote possibility.

He was to fashion a story about an impulsive wartime marriage between a handsome pilot and a glamorous society girl, and the adjustments they had to make. A dazzling wardrobe of 20 gowns, including a fantasy satin wedding dress, was being created by the designer, Irene. When Tennessee heard that, he said, "MGM doesn't want a movie script. They're putting on a fashion show starring Lana as the model."

For the third lead, Tennessee was instructed to write a non-dancing role for Gene Kelly, who wanted to try his luck performing in a drama instead of a musical.

There was pressure on MGM to get *Marriage Is a Private Affair* before the cameras. Surpassed only by Betty Grable, Lana was the second most popular pinup girl for G.I.'s. Letters were pouring in to MGM asking when Lana would be appearing in her next picture. Louis B. Mayer announced that *Marriage* would be shown in "all the theaters of war around the world."

Tennessee was also asked to write a small prologue that Lana would deliver at the beginning of the film, a sort of morale booster for the troops. He jokingly told friends, "In it, I'm going to suggest that both Lana and I will be waiting to service the returning troops. I'll meet them on the piers of San Francisco."

Each day Tennessee struggled with the script, not finding it "my kind of story." He grew so frustrated trying to write it that he once said, "I can *almost* hope that Lana will die in childbirth." *[The star was pregnant at the time.]*

Late one morning, the lesbian film editor, Jane Loring, showed up unannounced at his little office. She told him that she was assisting Berman in producing *Marriage.* She'd come to check on the script to see if he were progressing properly. "Pandro wants me to help you invent some sexy situations that will pass the blue-nosed censors of the Hays audience."

Loring wore white flannel pants, a beret, and large sunglasses—very mannish attire. "She did not conceal the fact that she was a lesbian, but didn't hide it either," Tennessee later said. "I'd heard rumors that she was the lover of Katharine Hepburn. My suspicion was confirmed when she invited me to lunch in the commissary with Hepburn herself."

In the commissary, Hepburn arrived thirty minutes late and was introduced to Tennessee. "Back then I think she regarded me as a little minnow in a fast-flowing stream. They spent most of the luncheon talking to each other about difficult plights of women in film."

When the subject of Lana Turner came up, Hepburn flashed anger.

"That god damn bottle of bleach practically threw herself at Spencer when they made that movie," Hepburn said.

Katharine Hepburn

She was referring to the 1941 release of *Dr. Jekyll and Mr. Hyde,* starring Spencer Tracy, Ingrid Bergman, and Lana.

The irony of Hepburn's snub of Tennessee was that he would one day create two of her most memorable roles—that of Violet Venable in *Suddenly Last Summer* and that of Amanda in the television version of *The Glass Menagerie.*

He chose not to mention her brilliant portrayals in his memoirs, referring to Hepburn only once, and not in a very flattering way. "Has anyone ever understood the gallantry and charm of old ladies, in and out of the theater, as well as Giraudoux in *The Madwoman of Chaillot?"* he wrote. "Kate Hepburn was just not old enough or mad enough to suggest the charisma of their lunacy."

On another hot afternoon, Tennessee got to meet the love goddess herself, Lana Turner, who called on him at his office. She was obviously very pregnant.

Instead of discussing the script with him, she poured out her marriage woes. "I should say her 'lack of marriage' woes," he said.

In July of 1942, she'd married a handsome, unemployed young man of whom she knew little. As she explained to Tennessee, she didn't know that he had been previously married.

She suggested that, "My personal situation might be an interesting plot device to enliven *Marriage Is a Private Affair."*

She explained that Stephen Crane's divorce from his first wife, Carol Kurtz, had not become final at the time of her marriage, and as a means of avoiding charges of bigamy, she was going to have to seek an annulment. "That seems like a respectable way out of the mess," he told her.

"No, it's more complicated than that," she said. "I don't know if I want to remarry Steve just to legitimize my unborn child. When I told that to Steve, he went crazy. That night, he drove his car over the cliff above where I was living, hoping his car would crash into my house on the way down. But the thick underbrush on the hill brought his car to a halt. Perhaps you could also work that actual event into a plot device for *Marriage.* In other words, an event torn from the pages of real life. And two nights ago, he tried to overdose on sleeping pills and had to be rushed to Cedars of Lebanon in critical condition."

"For god's sake, Lana," he said. "Marry the man if he's any good in bed."

"Oh, it's not that," she said. "He's a great lover."

"Finding a man who's great in the sack is its own reward," he said. "Based on my experience, such a creature is a rare commodity."

"That may be true," she said. "But life is so complicated. Right now, I'm trying to get Frank Sinatra to marry me as soon as I have my child. If he has to wait around for me to remarry Steve, have the child, and whatever, he might divorce Nancy and marry not me, but Marilyn Maxwell. Nancy's a brunette, and Frank told me he's starved for blondes."

Honeymooners:
Stephen Crane and **Lana Turner**

She told Tennessee that because of a lot of expenses, "I am flat broke and the bills are piling up." She asked him if she could take home some pages from the *Marriage* script to read.

The next day, she called, complaining that she was "dumbfounded by a lot of the dialogue. It's so poetic. My character is not a poet. Can't you make her speak like a regular woman?"

He later claimed in his memoirs that he had avoided "any language that was at all eclectic or multisyllabic. But the dialogue was beyond the young lady's comprehension."

When he wrote his play, *Small Craft Warnings,* later in his life, Tennessee would have his character of Quentin, an elderly writer, comment about his experience in Hollywood. "They found me too literate on my first assignment, converting an epic into a vehicle for the producer's doxy, a grammar school dropout."

Tennessee was obliquely referring to producer Pandro S. Berman and to Lana. *[Synonyms for doxy include bimbo, floozy, hoochie, hussy, minx, slut, tramp, trollop, wench, and whore.]*

A "Faux" Clark Gable With a "Beer Can" Penis That's Much Discussed by Lana and Tallulah

Two weeks later, there was another knock on Tennessee's office door. In walked John Hodiak, the son of Ukrainian immigrants who was being promoted by MGM as "another Clark Gable." Quiet spoken and likeable, he was ruggedly masculine and handsome in his rough kind of way. "To me, he was the stuff of a wet dream," Tennessee later confided.

Hodiak had just learned big casting news: Clark Gable had turned down the lead role in *Marriage*, and that role had subsequently been assigned to the handsome heartthrob, James Craig. *[Ironically, MGM had billed Craig as "another Clark Gable," too.]*

James Craig

Hodiak told Tennessee that he'd be assuming the role of Lt. Tom West that would have been played by Gene Kelly. The purpose of Hodiak's invitation to lunch became all too clear over a chicken club sandwich. He wanted his role expanded at the expense of Craig's part as Captain Miles Lancing.

Over lunch, Tennessee later said, "I found John marriage material. With him in my bed at night, I would abandon cruising forever,"

He'd seen Hodiak and Tallulah Bankhead in their 1944 film, *Lifeboat,* directed by Alfred Hitchcock. "I just assumed that Tallulah had already sunk her greedy claws into this walking streak of sex," Tennessee said.

"When John excused himself to go to the men's room, I shamelessly followed him, pretending I had to go, too," Tennessee claimed. "I stood beside him at the urinal. What he hauled out was an economy size penis the size of a Budweiser can. And it was still flaccid. By that time, I was hopelessly in love, and I made my intentions very obvious. He continued to exhibit for me, even with a few extra shakes at the end, but he turned down my invitation, even an offer for a quickie in my office with the door locked."

"I liked John a lot, but he was not a desperate sailor on a brief shore leave," Tennessee claimed. "From what I heard, he had all the poontang he could handle. In a 1944 picture he made with Anne Baxter, called *Sunday Dinner for a Soldier,* he fell for her. They later got married. But that didn't stop him from seducing Gene Tierney when he played Major Joppolo in *A Bell for Adano* (1945). That is, when Miss Tierney was not entertaining John F. Kennedy."

"Later, to my horror, I learned that Lana had seduced John when they made *Marriage Is a Private Affair,*" Tennessee said. "Unlike me, Lana always got her man except for Tyrone Power, who finally fled from her clutches. But I understand he really preferred boys."

"I was very sorry to hear that John had been labeled as 'box office poison' by exhibitors in the late 1940s," Tennessee said. "The era of rugged masculinity was on the way out to make room for Henry Willson's pretty boys of the 1950s—Robert Wagner, Troy Donahue, Rock Hudson, Tony Curtis, Tab Hunter, and the ilk."

"When John died of a heart attack at the age of 41, I think Hollywood lost a special actor. There was

John Hodiak

nothing phony about him. He was all man, and how many of those are left?"

After weeks of work, Tennessee was called upon by Berman to produce the script he'd created for Lana. He'd completed no more than twelve pages. The star "hated it," and Berman told Tennessee "the part you've attempted to write is too fey for a woman like Lana. You are fired. But since you're under contract, I'm punishing you by giving you a six-week suspension without pay. When you come back, I'll give

John Hodiak with Lana Turner

you a new assignment so simple even a child could write it."

In the aftermath of Tennessee's firing, Ring Lardner, Jr. *[a screen writer who, later, was famously accused of being a Communist sympathizer during McCarthy's Red Scare of the 1950s]* was assigned the task of adapting *Marriage* for the screen, since nothing Tennessee wrote was usable. But even such a well known and talented screenwriter as Lardner was also removed from the project, the final screen credits going to David Hertz and Lenore J. Coffee.

[Lana Turner agreed to remarry Stephen Crane, although the marriage was doomed almost from the beginning. Cheryl Christine Crane, the only child she'd ever have, was born on July 25, 1943.

Marriage Is a Private Affair was released in 1944, starring Lana, James Craig, and John Hodiak. That same year, Lana divorced Crane.]

Reinstated by the studio after his six-week suspension, Tennessee returned to his office at MGM. Back on the job, he contemplated writing a ballad for a movie short, *Billy the Kid,* with gay composer Aaron Copland and gay choreographer Eugene Loring. In a letter to his close friend, fellow author Donald Windham, he claimed that he found Loring "so cute, all five feet three inches of him."

Nothing of any merit ever materialized from Tennessee's arduous work on *Billy the Kid,* despite his best intentions and the many hours he spent fretting about it. The 1938 ballet, written by Copland and choreographed by Loring, became one of the most popular of its era, widely known for its development of an American ballet idiom and its skillful incorporation of American folk songs.

During Tennessee's "flirtation" with the project, he spent more time making love to Loring than on his ballad to the western outlaw.

Chapter Five

Sybaritic Isherwood

Encounters Tennessee's Amused Malice

Sally Bowles, "Big Boy," and The Man in the Green Tights

Christopher Isherwood *(left)* and **Liza Minnelli** *(right)* interpreting a character he created, cabaret entertainer Sally Bowles

"I want to meet the man who created the character of

Sally Bowles," Tennessee Williams told friends of the author, Christopher Isherwood. And so a meeting between these two gay writers came about at the celebrity-studded Brown Derby restaurant in Hollywood.

Tennessee had read and been enthralled with Isherwood's novels, *Mr. Norris Changes Trains* (1935) and *Goodbye to Berlin* (1939).

Born in England, Isherwood at the time was labeled "an angry pacifist, a worldly spiritualist, and an ascetic sybarite." He was considering becoming an American citizen, which he did in 1946.

By the end of World War II, Isherwood was the most celebrated gay writer in America. What Tennessee didn't tell him was that he wanted to assume that role for himself.

Isherwood sized up the emerging competition, referring to Tennessee as "a strange boy, small, plump, muscular, with a slight cast in one eye—and full of an amused malice."

Isherwood, who had been in Hollywood since 1939, was also appraised by Tennessee. "I was amazed at how short he was. I found him a ruggedly handsome blue-eyed Englishman with the build of a bantam boxer. He spoke in a thin, rather reedy voice. I ruled out romance. He wasn't my type."

"I am a lonely man wandering in a foreign country," Isherwood told Tennessee. "I no longer have a country. I am a citizen of love."

Christopher Isherwood

Sensing a kindred spirit, Tennessee immediately became confidential, discussing his sex life. "I have these uncontrollable sexual urges," he confessed. "I cruise for young men day and night. This obsession interferes with my work. My libido is a painful burden to carry."

Isherwood responded with confessions of his own. "For a while, I flirted with the idea of becoming a monk. That is, until I fell in love with this blonde-haired soldier. Celibacy went out the window the first night he fucked me."

He even explained why he went to Berlin in 1931, where he met a little cocotte, Jean Ross, who became the inspiration of his fictional character, Sally Bowles. She would later become immortalized on the screen by Liza Minnelli in *Cabaret* (1972).

[The director of Cabaret, *Bob Fosse, sent the film's Fred Ebb-John Kander script, based on the 1955 play,* I Am a Camera, *first to Julie Andrews. But her agent wouldn't even let her read it, rushing the script of* Mary Poppins *to her instead.]*

"I didn't find Englishmen very sexy, but I was powerfully attracted to working class German men," Isherwood said. "I went to Berlin seeking love and found it in the arms of a handsome, muscled, blonde-haired, blue-eyed, sixteen-year-old boy, Heinz Needermeyer. When Hitler and the Nazis took over in 1933, I fled from Germany with Heinz at my side. We wandered through Europe in a kind of limbo, living in seedy hotels often filled with prostitutes and drunkards."

Tennessee's Libido: "A Painful Burden"

"When the British blocked me from bringing Heinz into London, we went to Paris, where he was arrested in 1937 for not having identity papers. The French deported him back to Germany, where he was arrested by the Gestapo for draft dodging. After serving six horrible months in prison, he was then forced to become a Nazi soldier. Life without my Heinz was devastating for me."

LOUD, LOUTISH, and BIG
Big Boy Williams, with one of his movie posters

By the end of the lunch, the two authors, Tennessee and Isherwood, had bonded, leading to a life-long friendship. But their date at the Brown Derby ended in a most unconventional way. Throughout their meal, they had been hawkeyed by a Western character actor, Guinn ("Big Boy") Williams. He had been dining with Errol Flynn, with whom he'd starred as a "sidekick" in movies.

Perhaps goaded by Flynn, who was a prankster, Big Boy rose from the table, an impressive 6' 2" of Texas manhood. He headed toward the table where Isherwood and Tennessee were seated.

Both writers were astonished when he pulled out a pocket knife from his pants and

Errol Flynn

proceeded to slice off the tongues of their ties. The men were more astonished than frightened. "Do you collect ties?" Isherwood asked.

Big Boy grabbed his crotch. "You two faggots suck on this."

"We can't unless you whip it out," Tennessee quipped.

Big Boy stormed toward the door, cursing under his breath. The *maître d'* confronted him on his way out, asking him never to set foot in the Brown Derby again.

"That was the only tie I owned," Tennessee lamented to Isherwood.

"I'll buy you another one."

Suddenly, as they looked up, it was Flynn himself who stood before them, looking "even handsomer than he did on the screen," Tennessee recalled.

"Welcome to Hollywood, boys," he said. "Sorry about Big Boy. It was just a little joke I conjured up to amuse myself on this hot, boring afternoon. No hard feelings." He stuck out his hand.

Both writers shook his hand, Tennessee holding it for an extra long time.

Deliberately provocative, Tennessee said, "Is the rumor true that when you were fitted into those green tights to play Robin Hood, Warners insisted you wear a heavy duty jock strap so as not to give the men in the audience penis envy?"

"There are many rumors spread about me which are lies," he said. "But you nailed me on that one."

He fingered each of what remained of their ties. "You guys are good sports, and I'll make it up to you by paying for your lunch."

"I think we have a right to demand more trib-ute than that," Tennessee said, eying Flynn's ample crotch.

The actor winked at him. "Yes, I could do more to make you guys forgive me. Give me a rain check."

Sexual Santa Monica:

During the War, Seafood Wasn't Restricted to Fish Restaurants

That night, Tennessee invited Isherwood, his newly found friend, to go cruising with him along the blacked-out Pacific Palisades.

Isherwood later commented on that experi-ence: "Tennessee could be quite courageous in approaching a sailor. He would single out his vic-tim for the evening and just go up to him and make his pitch. Perhaps it was because of the war when most sexual restraints were removed, especially by those who thought they were going to die tomorrow. But during the time we knew each other in Hollywood, Tennessee often got his man, turning his apartment into a USO."

"During the war years and beyond, Ten-nessee was constantly trying to find some fulfill-ment in the body of another man," Isherwood said. "I don't think he ever found what he was searching for during those hazy, drunkard, Dionysian nights he spent wandering, search-ing, forever on the move, seeking the next ex-

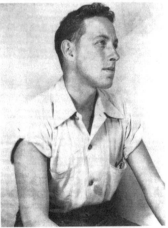

In this photo from 1938, before he went to Hollywood, **Tennessee** ap-pears like a serious writer, which he was. For fun, he cruised the Pa-cific Palisades in a search for the type of "seafood" depicted above.

52

perience, even courting violence. So many of these young men were away from their homes, their mothers, their girlfriends, and they sought someone to love them wherever they could find it."

Two days after their Brown Derby luncheon, Isherwood showed up at Tennessee's apartment. He later said, "I had seen nothing like this since I visited a cheap abortionist in the slums of Berlin in 1932."

"It was a dingy apartment where I found Tennessee sitting before a typewriter and wearing a yachting cap amidst a litter of dirty coffee cups, crumpled bed linen, and old newspapers. I learned that he works until he's tired, eats only when he feels like it, and sleeps when he can no longer stay awake. He also told me he spent two or three hours every day on the beach."

That night, when Isherwood and Tennessee went to a little fish house on the Santa Monica pier, Tennessee confessed why he'd been so drawn to the character of Sally Bowles. "She knows the difference between being fucked and being well fucked."

Gore Vidal: "In the Bedroom, I'm Like Picasso"

When Gore Vidal first met Christopher Isherwood in a Paris hotel room in 1948, Gore was in his underwear and in bed. "We checked each other out for about an hour," Gore later recalled, "and decided to become friends—not lovers."

When Gore finally put on his pants, they walked to *Les Deux Magots*, the legendary café on the Left Bank. Jean-Paul Sartre and his mistress, Simone de Beauvoir, sat at an adjoining table.

Isherwood would remember Gore as "a big husky boy with fair hair and a funny, rather attractive face—sometimes he reminds me of a teddy bear, sometimes a duck. He's typical American prep school. His conversation is all about love, which he doesn't believe in—or rather, he believes it's tragic. He is very jealous of Truman Capote and talks about him all the time. What I respect about him is his courage, though it's mingled with a desire for self-advertisement."

Even at this early stage in his life, Gore claimed he didn't believe there was such a thing as a homosexual. "We are all bisexuals," he proclaimed. He admitted that only hours before their meeting, he'd had sex with a Parisian hustler who had once worked in a bordello in Algiers before moving to France.

"And the night before that, I made love to a young Juliette Greco lookalike in my hotel room," Gore confessed to Isherwood. "She compared my love-making to Picasso's, and I was flattered...at first. 'Oh,' I said to her, 'I'm a genius in the boudoir, too.'"

"Not at all," Gore quoted her as telling him. "Like Picasso, you're a very bad lover. Just in and out and back to work." After she said that, the girl stormed out of Gore's bedroom.

"At least Picasso and I have something in common," Gore told Isherwood.

That autumn in Paris, after Isherwood got to know Gore, he wrote: "Gore feels that life is too damn much trouble. Being with him depressed me, because he exudes despair and a cynical misery. He's got a grudge against society which is really based on his own lack of talent and creative joy."

When Isherwood, back in America, confided these concerns to Tennessee, the playwright responded, "Oh, Gore is just trying to defend himself against pain."

Bette Davis, a Homophobe, Meets the Chicken Hawk

After Paris, Gore and Isherwood saw each other only infrequently, although they wrote letters. March of 1955 found them both in Hollywood working side by side in office cubicles, turning out film scripts—Gore for Bette Davis, Isherwood for Lana Turner (as Tennessee had done before him, rather unsuccessfully).

Gore was adapting a teleplay, *The Catered Affair*, for the big screen. On his first day, he had met the play's original author, Paddy Chayefsky. "He seemed very neurotic," Gore recalled. "He told me he was haunted by a feeling of horror and unreality."

"I deal with it by lighting one cigarette after another and sitting down to eat a large chocolate cake in one sitting," Chayefsky confided. "I call it 'chocolate by death,' or perhaps it should be called 'death by chocolate.'"

In the adjoining office, Isherwood was writing a screenplay for Lana Turner. The script was vaguely related to the life of Diane de Poitiers (1499-1566), the French noblewoman and courtier at the courts of Kings François I and his son, Henri II. As the "favorite" of Henri II, and a woman who reputedly retained her sexual allure and beauty through witchcraft, she became notorious throughout France.

In 1956, the Lana film was released as *Diane* by MGM. François I was played by Pedro Armendáriz, and a young and very handsome Roger Moore starred as the future king, Henri II.

Bette Davis in
The Catered Affair

[Isherwood invited Tennessee to a screening of the film. After sitting through it, Tennessee did not have a comment until Isherwood asked him for his opinion. "I think Lana never looked lovelier," Tennessee said.]

Gore confessed that he could not live on the meager royalties generated by his novels. That had led him to accept the job as a scriptwriter. At the end of their lunch in the MGM commissary, the two writers went for a walk around the studio lot.

They paused to sit down for a while beside the train under whose wheels Anna Karenina

(Greta Garbo) had made her last dive, committing suicide.

Isherwood was despondent over his own career, urging Gore, "Don't become a hack like me." He also spoke of the difficulty he was having with the censors at the Breen Office. "They say I condone adultery. They want adultery to be punished by stoning, and they also think that homosexuals should be burned alive."

In spite of his career problems, Gore claimed that he was "feeding my libido in Hollywood. Before six o'clock in the afternoon, all the hustlers along The Strip charge only ten dollars. I prefer sex in the afternoon anyway, so that suits me just fine."

During their time at MGM, Gore and Isherwood lunched together almost every day, sometimes with a guest.

On one occasion, they dined "with a young Jewish producer. *[Neither writer identified him.]* The producer took exception with Gore comparing the plight of the Jews during the Holocaust with that of homosexuals rounded up by the Nazis.

"There was a difference," Gore said. "The Jews wore yellow stars and the gay men had to wear pink triangles. But regardless of their badges, the end result was the same: the gas chamber."

"The two persecuted groups should be allies," Isherwood said. "Hitler killed six hundred thousand homosexuals."

"But Hitler killed six million Jews," the producer protested.

"What are you?" Isherwood asked. "In real estate?"

At one point, Bette Davis dropped by Gore's office to see how work was progressing on *The Catered Affair.* She joined both Gore and Isherwood for lunch.

"I was surprised that over lunch, she brought up the subject of homosexuality and shared her views with us," Gore said. "For such a supposedly sophisticated woman, her point of view shocked me."

HISTORICAL DRAMA:
Lana Turner, as Diane de Poitiers, getting kissed by **Roger Moore** as Henri II

"For the life of me, I can't understand how anyone could be attracted sexually to a person of the same sex," she told the startled writers. "It completely baffles me."

[Throughout the life of Bette Davis, she never wavered from that position and always refused to support any gay causes. In private, she often made flippant homophobic remarks.]

Gore challenged her view, pointing out that at this stage in her film career her largest fan base consisted of gay men.

"That's true," Davis responded, "and I'm aware of that. I also know that I'm the one actress most female impersonators select to imitate." The more she talked, the less homophobic she sounded, although at no point did she back down from her original comments.

"The homosexual community is the most appreciative in backing the arts," Davis said. "They are knowledgeable and loving of the arts. They make the average male look stupid. They show their good taste in their support of my own efforts on the screen. Most of my fan mail today is from gay men. Even so, I still can't understand why they want to sleep with each other. For the life of me, I will never condone that."

"Don't get me wrong," Davis said. "I believe in equal rights for all—no matter the race, religion, or sexual orientation. At this point in my life, I'm also opposed to age discrimination, especially that dished out to fading movie queens."

Through Isherwood, Gore met far more tolerant movie queens with far more sophisticated views about homosexuality.

But first, at his cliffside home in Malibu, Isherwood introduced Gore to his teenaged lover, Don Bachardy, whom the older writer had met on the beach when he was eighteen. Friends said Bachardy at the time looked no more than sixteen, if that. Gore referred to Bachardy as "thin, blonde, chicken-hawk handsome, an unformed neophyte who gradually discovered his passion for painting."

At one party, Isherwood introduced Gore to Marlene Dietrich, who had been a great admirer of his Berlin novels. "Dietrich ruled the night from one corner of the room, Claudette Colbert on the opposite side."

Gore had heard rumors that both Dietrich and Colbert had been lovers in the 1930s, and that there was a famous photograph showing Colbert sitting between Dietrich's legs as they slid down a chute.

But their relationship had grown sour. When she spoke of Colbert to Gore,

Homosexuals, each forced into wearing a pink triangle,
during their internment during WWII in a concentration camp, before being sent to the ovens.

Dietrich seemed to hold the Paris-born actress in contempt, referring to her as "that ugly French shopgirl."

Gore did not share Dietrich's feelings and was delighted to meet Colbert later in the evening. Bachardy told them that in gay circles in Hollywood, Colbert was called "Uncle Claude. She lives deep in the closet."

On the screen in such classics as *It Happened One Night* with Clark Gable, Gore had found Colbert the personification of gaiety and sophistication, who, when the script called for it, could also be provocative. "She stood before me showing only the left side of her face, which she considered her more beautiful," Gore said.

Claudette Colbert *(right)*, caught between **Marlene Dietrich's** legendary legs

During the years to come, he always challenged people who labeled Colbert as a lesbian. She'd been married twice—once to Norman Foster, who later married Sally Blane, Loretta Young's sister, and later to Dr. Joel Pressman—but Colbert always maintained a separate residence.

"Colbert should be called a bisexual," Gore said. "I mean, Maurice Chevalier, Gary Cooper, Leslie Howard, Fred MacMurray, and Preston Sturges weren't exactly females the last time I got their peckers hard."

After they finished their respective scripts for Bette Davis and Lana Turner, Gore and Isherwood were assigned two new screen treatments. Isherwood's job involved writing a screenplay about Buddha entitled *The Wayfarer*. It was never filmed.

In contrast, Gore's script, based on the trial of Albert Dreyfus, was released in 1958. It starred José Ferrer. *The New York Times* warned that the audience "is likely to feel more frustrated by political obfuscation and courtroom wrangling than poor Captain Dreyfus was. Ferrer's Dreyfus is a sad sack, a silent and colorless man who takes his unjust conviction with but one outburst protest and then endures his Devils Island torment lying down."

Unusual for Gore, he maintained a friendship with Isherwood until the older writer died.

In 1984, on the occasion of Isherwood's eightieth birthday, Gore visited him in Malibu. He later wrote Paul Bowles in Tangier, claiming that Isherwood had decided to emulate Tithonus.

[In Greek mythology, Tithonus, of the royal house of Troy, was kidnapped by Eos to become her lover. She asked Zeus to make Tithonus immortal, but she forgot to ask for his eternal youth. He did live forever, "but when loathsome old age pressed full upon him, he could not move nor lift his limbs."]

In his report to Bowles, Gore claimed that Isherwood "looks amazingly healthy, preserved in alcohol, so life-like."

But when Gore visited later that year, he painted a different portrait. "Chris is dying. He is small, shrunken, all beak, like a newly hatched eagle."

Fresh from a trip to London, Gore complained about the fecklessness of the English. "It's just like the grasshopper and the ant, and *they* are hopeless grasshoppers."

Isherwood's last words to Gore were, "So, what is wrong with grasshoppers?" Then he dropped off into a deep sleep.

On January 4, 1986, Isherwood died, suffering from prostate cancer. His body was donated to the UCLA Medical School.

In 1966, Gore reported that he was shocked when the first volume of Isherwood's diaries were published. "He was very censorious of me, even when writing about the days when I thought we were having such convivial times together. You never know what friends really think of you until they publish their god damn diaries, Anaïs Nin being the best example of that."

Nude Photographs & A Nantucket Party for "Testicular Aficionados"

It was a hot day in late May of 1947 at Random House in New York City. Christopher Isherwood had just called on its publisher, Bennett Cerf. As Isherwood was being shown out by an assistant editor, a mannish-looking woman with short cropped hair, Isherwood asked if Random House had discovered any exciting new writers. "It's always good to be aware of tomorrow's competition," Isherwood told the editor.

"There is one novelist we're very excited about," the editor said. "Truman Capote of New Orleans, who used to dance on a showboat on the Mississippi and also painted roses on glass. His novel, *Other Voices, Other Rooms,* can only be compared to Proust."

As if on cue, Truman himself suddenly appeared in the hallway. As Isherwood remembered him, "He was like a sort of cuddly little Koala bear. His hand was raised high. Was I to kiss it?"

That was the beginning of a beautiful, sometimes tumultuous friendship that would last until Truman's death.

In later years, Gore Vidal would proclaim that Truman's most famous character, Holly Golightly, in *Breakfast at Tiffany's*, "was merely a redrawing of the character of Sally Bowles in Isherwood's *Berlin Stories*."

As Isherwood later noted, "Fuck a comparison to Marcel Proust. This was a living, breathing character that stepped right out of the pages of Ronald Firbank. He was like a rare orchid growing in a hothouse in New Orleans, perhaps a man-eating plant that would later appear in Katharine Hepburn's garden in Tennessee's *Suddenly Last Summer*."

"Truman seemed to throw a spell of enchantment over me, no doubt something he picked up at a Witch's Sabbath."

"Long after the editor left, we stood and talked and I did something I'd never done before. For myself and my lover, William Caskey, I accepted an invitation to visit Truman and his lover, Newton Arvin, at their cottage on Nantucket that July."

Isherwood's lover at the time, William Caskey, was a good-looking photographer in his mid-twenties who had been born in Kentucky. Isherwood had met him near the end of the war, and they had begun a serious affair. In Isherwood's memoir (1943-1951), the writer claimed that Caskey "was the most uninhibited homosexual; he seemed very tough yet very female. He loved getting into drag. He loved straight men. But he despised queens and didn't think of himself as one. He wanted to fuck straight men, not be fucked by them. He proclaimed his homosexuality loudly and shamelessly and never cared whom he shocked."

Truman's lover, Professor Newton Arvin, also surprised Caskey and Isherwood when they arrived at Truman's rented cottage in the village of Siasconset. "We were expecting some muscle-bound character rescued from some seedy gym in Brooklyn."

Arvin was a middle-aged professor and critic, who had lost his job at Smith College when his homosexuality had been exposed. Newton was shy and retiring, preferring not to join in all the gay chatter and meals. He was spending most of his days and nights writing the biography of Herman Melville.

"You're just as Virginia Woolf said you would be," Truman once told Isherwood. "An appreciative, merry little bird."

Actually, Truman was more intrigued by the pronouncement of another British writer, W. Somerset Maugham. The novelist had written "the future of the English novel lies in Isherwood's pen."

But Truman and Caskey were intrigued by each other. "Isherwood's lover is completely uninhibited," Truman said. "If such a thing were possible, he is even more shocking than I am."

"You are so tiny," Caskey said to Truman. "Do you also have a small dick?"

"A studly six inches," Truman shot back. "Just ask Newton. He knows every inch intimately."

Newton would later describe Truman's penis in a letter: "One peppermint-stick, beautifully pink and white, wonderfully straight, deliciously sweet. About a hand's length. Of great intrinsic and also sentimental value to owner."

Isherwood was amazed that "Truman wasn't the purple orchid I thought he'd be. He has strong arms and legs and is a good swimmer. He liked to bike around the island or go horseback riding. He has a sturdy body bronzed by the sun."

That summer, Jared French, a photographer, snapped nude pictures of both Caskey and Isherwood, which they did not like.

"We looked like two hippos mating," Isherwood later said. One of those photographs later appeared in Devid Leddick's book, *Naked Men: Pioneering Nudes 1935-1955.*

Truman introduced Isherwood to the critic, Leo Lerman. He found Isherwood "quite delightful, with strange eyes and a delight in malice and in hurting himself."

Truman entertained Lerman and other members of the Nantucket gay colony in the late afternoon. Mornings were reserved for writing *Other Voices, Other Rooms.* He complained to Isherwood that "the last pages are draining my blood. The final chapter is obdurate."

"Finally, while we were still staying with him, Truman raced down the stairs one afternoon," Isherwood said. "The last paragraph of that obdurate chapter had been completed."

"It's over," he shouted in an almost hysterical voice. "With its publication, I'm going to become famous. Two hundred years from now, the world will be talking about *Other Voices, Other Rooms.*"

"Right in front of us," Isherwood said, "he danced a jig of joy, evoking Hitler's high stepping at the fall of France."

In talking to friends, Isherwood later said, "Truman is completely outrageous. You never know from night to night what the entertainment will be. Friends dropped in from cottages nearby to be entertained by Truman. One night he put on an exhibit for testicular aficionados."

He announced that a hustler would be arriving "with the world's largest set of balls."

After dinner and

Newton Arvin *(left)*, and **Truman Capote**

60

too many Manhattans and martinis, Truman answered the doorbell. A very young, very muscular, and rather handsome young man walked into the room. Introduced as Tony, he wore tight-fitting blue jeans and a form-fitting T-shirt, standing about five feet ten and weighing some 150 pounds. He pulled off his T-shirt to reveal broad shoulders and a ripply stomach.

"He stared at us almost defiantly, with the kind of blue eyes possessed by the Nazi soldiers who sent Jews to the gas chamber," Isherwood later said.

"Slowly, very slowly, Tony unzipped his fly, revealing that he wore no underwear," Isherwood said. "Gradually, he began to strip, lowering his jeans until his pubic hair burst into bloom. First he exposed a 'hose-like penis.' He saved the biggest show for last. He peeled down his jeans to his knees, exposing testicles that were like baseballs. No, larger than baseballs. They were gigantic. Almost a deformity. The image of the supreme male. Hitler would have abducted him and would have used him in one of his breeding camps."

For the finale of the evening, Truman announced that Tony could later be found nude and lying spread-eagled on a bed in the guest room at the top of the stairwell. "All visitors are welcome, and the door will remain open until three o'clock," Truman said. "That's when Tony has to return home to his Portuguese wife and three children, all of them boys, as could be predicted. Tony's been a father since he was fifteen years old. Those testicles actually started producing sperm, or so I was told, when Tony was only nine years old."

***

Years would come and go; lovers would change, sometimes with the season, but Truman and Isherwood remained steadfast in their friendship. Sometimes there would be disagreements, but they would smooth things over because they genuinely liked each other.

They were not always appreciative of each other's work. With friends, they often delivered private critiques. But unlike Gore and Truman, they did not deliver these insults face to face, only behind each other's back.

When Isherwood finally got a copy of *Other Voices, Other Rooms*, he had reservations. "Unlike what I'd been told, Proust can snooze peacefully in his grave—nothing to fear from Truman. The novel seems to be mere skillful embroidery, unrelated to Truman and therefore lacking in essential interest."

Over the years, Isherwood recalled some bizarre encounters with Truman. One such occurrence took place in the airport lounge of the Los Angeles airport as all of them were awaiting a plane to fly them to New York. Isherwood was traveling with his lover, Don Bachardy, and Truman was with William Paley, president of CBS.

The airport was fogged, and all flights were delayed. "Just call us the fog queens," Truman said.

As the hours wore on, he announced, "I have this premonition of a disaster in the air. I've had these premonitions before. All of them come true."

Paley stood up and faced him with anger. "God damn it, you're getting on that fucking plane with us tonight whether you like it or not. If it's going down, you'll go down with us for alarming us like this."

Obeying Paley like a stern father, Truman boarded the flight. Paley and Truman were seated in adjacent first-class seats, with Isherwood and Bachardy riding together in coach. At midnight, during the flight, Truman came back to visit Isherwood and his young lover. He scooted into the seat with them, sitting on their laps and throwing his arm around their necks.

"Are you bunnies scared?" he asked.

***

[At the time of Truman's death in August of 1984, he'd lost most of his friends. Isherwood still remained loyal, however, and even attended the funeral services at Westwood Mortuary in Los Angeles.

It was later revealed that the aging Isherwood snoozed through most of the memorial service, finding the eulogies too long.

Actor Robert Blake, who had played Perry in the movie version of In Cold Blood, gave a speech that Isherwood found "too egomaniacal, having little to do with Truman's life."

Also delivering a long, rambling eulogy was a surprise speaker, bandleader Artie Shaw, former husband of Ava Gardner and Lana Turner. His punch line was, "Truman died of everything. He died of life, from living a full one."

When Shaw returned to his seat, Bachardy nudged Isherwood, who stumbled to the podium. He gave the shortest eulogy of all. "There was one wonderful thing about Truman," he said. "He could always make me laugh." Then, as if remembering some long ago joke of Truman's, Isherwood laughed loudly before Bachardy gracefully ushered him back to his seat.]

Chapter Six

Clark Gable—
A Potential Stepfather for Gore?

Mom Delivers a Tall Order for the King of Hollywood—
"Make a Man Out of My Pansy Son"

Nina Vidal *(above, left)* and **Clark Gable**

"I fell in love with Clark Gable when I went to see him in *A Free Soul* in 1931," Nina Vidal said, "the movie he made with Norma Shearer. I found him impossibly handsome and dangerous. When he shoved Shearer back onto the couch and commanded, 'Take it and like it,' I was enchanted. He was a new kind of man in a rapidly changing world. During the war, I learned that Hitler wanted to bring him caged, live, and nude to Berlin."

Eugene Luther Gore Vidal (born October 3, 1925; died
July 31, 2012) was born in the Cadet Hospital of the United States Military Academy at West Point. He was the only child of Eugene Luther Vidal (1895-1969) and Nina Gore (1903-1978). Gore's grandfather was the blind Senator from Oklahoma, Thomas Pryor Gore (1870-1949).

Gore's father, Eugene, a first lieutenant, was an aeronautics instructor at West Point. His mother, Nina, a socialite, married him in 1922, divorcing him in

1935.

[Nina followed this with two more marriages, one to a wealthy stockbroker, Hugh D. Auchincloss, nicknamed "Hughdie." Nina was married to him from 1935 to 1941. In 1942, Auchincloss became the second husband of Janet Lee Bouvier, the mother of First Lady Jacqueline Kennedy, through Janet's previous marriage to Jack Bouvier.

Nina's final marriage was to Army Air Forces Major General Robert Olds, who had produced four children from a previous marriage, but who died in 1943 after only ten months of marriage to Nina.

Gore was the only child produced by his biological parents. The four half-siblings from his parents' later marriages included Vance Vidal, Valerie Vidal, Thomas (Tommy) Gore Auchincloss, and Nini Gore Auchincloss. He also had four stepbrothers from his mother's third marriage to Olds.]

The mother-son relationship of Nina and Gore seemed torn from the pages of Philip Wylie's bestselling indictment of the American way of life, *Generation of*

Eugene Vidal *(left)* and **Nina**

College football hero **Eugene Vidal** *(left photo)* and *(right)* on his wedding day to **Nina**.

"Erectile Dysfunctions, and Too Many Testicles"
—*Gore discussing his father and "the kike hater" (his stepfather)*

64

Vipers [published in 1942] , a much-talked about condemnation of "momism."

After reading it, Gore commented: "I thought Wylie was writing about my own mother, the unrealness, the infantile unreasonableness, the child wife, the psychotic personality of a woman who cannot reason logically, the bridge fiend, the murderess (symbolically speaking), the habitual *divorcée*, the serial adulteress, the sex experimentalist, the quarreler, the castrator, the nagger, the pathological liar, the puerile bitch, the raging hyena—all those endearing identities I know as Mom."

Young **Gore**, 1936

"After reading *Generation of Vipers,* I was filled with a splenetic outrage against Nina. As I listened to her high-octane twaddle, I never knew if she hated me more than I hated her. The life she led was one of orgiastic claptrap, overwrought emotion, florid excess, and niggling demands."

Gore had an entirely different relationship with his father, Eugene.

In an interview in 2008 with *The Independent,* Gore proclaimed that Eugene "was like a film star. He was the most famous college athlete in the history of the United States. A quarterback at West Point, he competed in the decathlon in the Antwerp Olympic Games of 1920, finishing in seventh position. He was also an assistant track coach in charge of the modern pentathlon and decathlon squads at the Summer Olympic Games in Paris in 1924. In the forty-three years that I knew him, we never quarreled once, and we never agreed on anything."

At the peak of her beauty, Nina met Eugene at a football game in 1921, when he was twenty-six and she was a virginal eighteen. It was love at first sight, at least on his part.

She later characterized her feeling for him as "a mere infatuation."

In spite of misgivings, she married him in 1923 at St. Margaret's Episcopal Church in Washington, D.C., which was decorated with pink roses and illuminated by soft, scented candles.

On the way to their honeymoon bed, she told him she'd been an unwanted child. "The only reason I was born was that rats chewed up my mother's douche bag," Nina told him.

Before he stripped down for her first sight of a fully nude male, he, too, had a revelation. "I have three balls!" he told her.

She was not unduly alarmed, since she wasn't exactly sure how many testicles a man usually had. She later told her son, Gore, "All three of his balls were of equal size. He was a virtual sperm factory."

After only a few months into the marriage, Nina realized she'd become an alcoholic. "After a party we'd give, I'd go around the room drinking up what was left in the liquor glasses," she said.

The Vidals (Eugene & Nina) Fly (Separately) with Amelia Earhart & Charles Lindbergh

After the birth of Gore in 1925, Eugene rarely visited his wife's separate bedroom.

Airlines consumed most of his time, that and his affair with Amelia Earhart, who was the most famous woman aviator of all time. According to biographer Susan Butler, "Vidal became the great love of Amelia Earhart's life."

Along with the world's most fabled male aviator, Charles Lindbergh, Eugene worked with Earhart in the founding of Ludington Line *[which eventually, after mergers, became Eastern Airlines]* and Transcontinental Air Transport *[which eventually seguéd into TWA]* and Northeast Airlines.

Nina soon learned of her husband's affair with Earhart, but didn't seem unduly concerned. "Those two can go fly a kite as far as I'm concerned," she told her friends.

Young Gore was amazed when he was introduced to Earhart, finding her "the most thrilling woman I'd ever met." Later, he said, "In time, I knew Elizabeth Taylor. But Amelia was a far bigger name than Elizabeth. Once we walked down Fifth Avenue in Manhattan. When we turned around, we found 500 people following us. Even at the age of ten, I was impressed."

He was so impressed that he urged his father to divorce Nina and marry Earhart. "Amelia was delighted with the idea," Gore said, "but my father only blushed."

At a party at the Vidal home, Eugene introduced Nina to both Earhart and Lindbergh, whom she found "extremely handsome—devastatingly so."

Gore noticed that his mother spent the entire night talking just to Lindbergh.

"He was America's hero, and, like Nina, I, too, developed a crush on this dashing airman," Gore said.

The next weekend, when Eugene was out of town, Gore came home early and at first thought he was in the house alone until he heard a noise coming from upstairs.

He went to investigate. Nina was supposed to be out shopping, so he opened the door to her bedroom.

"The world's most famous aviator rose up suddenly from the bed," Gore recalled. "I got to see an impressive closeup of *The Spirit of St.*

Eugene Vidal *(left)* with **Amelia Earhart**

Louis in all the glory of its raging manhood. His erection was like the rest of his body, long and lean."

"Nina screamed for me to get out, and I left," Gore said. "They stayed in the bedroom for another hour, so I guess they finished their business in spite of *coitus interruptus.*"

When Gore learned that Lindbergh had seduced Nina, he again pressed his father to divorce his mother and marry Earhart, whom he liked and admired greatly.

"Although I love her, I have no intention of marrying a boy," Eugene said.

Gore was shocked by his father's rather bizarre answer. He had once felt that Earhart was rather mannish and was perhaps a lesbian, but

Charles Lindbergh,

the aviator and Eugene seemed to have a torrid sex life together. Gore was later told that Earhart's marriage to George P. Putnam "was in name only."

She did have a physical resemblance to Lindbergh, who was known as "Lucky Lindy" in the press.

Earhart was dubbed "Lady Lindy."

[Eugene was portrayed by the actor Ewan McGregor in the 2009 film Amelia.*]*

"Although Eugene told me he didn't want to actually marry a boy *[a reference to Amelia],* I learned years later he was not averse to having sex with one. Much later in life, an occasional man as well."

Two Boys in Love amid the Winter Winds of South Dakota

As a teenager growing up in Madison, South Dakota, Eugene might have followed a different sexual path. "I might never have existed if he'd continued his early pattern," Gore said.

He was referring to the love affair between his father, Eugene, and Robert McAlmon, the author, poet, and publisher, who became a stellar member of the literati.

"Eugene, who was fifteen, and Bob, who was fourteen, were inseparable," said Margaret Vidal, Gore's aunt. "They even took turns sleeping over at each other's houses. We didn't understand different types of love in those days, and were pleased that the boys were so close. Even so, it was rather clear that Bob liked Gene *too much!* Occasionally, they got into a fight. One time, Bob accused Eugene of paying too much attention to the strikingly handsome president of his fraternity."

After South Dakota, both men went their separate ways. In New York, McAlmon became a publisher, printing poetry by Ezra Pound, Marianne Moore,

67

and Kay Boyle. He collaborated with William Carlos Williams on *Contact Review.* McAlmon also typed and edited the handwritten manuscript of *Ulysses* by James Joyce before its eventual publication in 1922.

Later, McAlmon moved to Paris, where he married the wealthy lesbian English writer, Annie Winifred Ellerman, who wrote under the pen name of "Bryher."

Her father was the shipowner and financier John Ellerman, who at the time of his death in 1933 was the richest Englishman who had ever lived.

Gore got to meet Bryher in Paris, and learned fascinating things about her life there in the 1920s. In Paris, she had been an unconventional figure, lending money to struggling writers like James Joyce and Edith Sitwell. She also financed Shakespeare and Company, Sylvia Beach's bookshop on the Left Bank. Bryher's writings brought Sergei Eisenstein to the attention of the British public.

Gore learned that she'd written a series of historical novels, most of which were set in Britain. The one he chose to read was *The Coin of Carthage* (1963), which he later inspired him to write his own historical novels, especially *Julian,* published in 1964.

Robert McAlmon in Nice in 1929 and *(lower photo)*, in 1928

In Paris, McAlmon also became a close friend of Ernest Hemingway until one night in a café he drunkenly referred to him as "my fellow fag."

Along with Kay Boyle, McAlmon wrote *Being Geniuses Together (1920-1930),* which previewed their relationships not only with Hemingway, but with Gertrude Stein, James Joyce, John Dos Passos, F. Scott Fitzgerald, T.S. Eliot, Djuana Barnes, Ford Maddox Ford, Katherine Mansfield, and Alice B. Toklas (Gertrude's lover).

Gore met Boyle later in her life when her literary reputation had faded. She confirmed that "Bob never got over his love for your father. His picture in a football uniform is always at his bedside."

"She was very bitter at getting blacklisted, along with her husband, by Senator Joseph McCarthy and that snake, Roy Cohn," Gore said.

"Other than that," she told Gore, "I have few regrets. People with full sex lives don't have regrets."

She presented Gore with a copy of McAlmon's novel: *Village: As It Happened Through a Fifteen Year Period* (1924). "The character of Eugene Collins written about in the novel is your father."

That night, Gore read the novel in one sitting. He later said, "It was clear that McAlmon was in love with Eugene. It was most curious to encounter one's father as a boy of fifteen as seen through the eyes of a boy of fourteen who is in love with him."

At the time he wrote his own novel of homosexual love, *The City and the Pillar,* Gore had not read McAlmon's novel. "My tale of Bob Ford and Jim Willard in *The City and the Pillar* paralleled the real story of Eugene and McAlmon. If nothing else, the very ordinariness of the story makes it a good deal more universal than I realized. McAlmon must have been intrigued that the son of 'Eugene Collins' had written a variation on his *Village* novel without having ever heard of the book or its author."

Gore learned of his father's affair with yet another man through a coincidence. In the mid-1940s, he was introduced to the designer, Stanley Mills Haggart, who for the rest of the decade, became his best friend.

Gore learned that for a brief period in the late 1920s, when both Eugene and Stanley were working as extras in films, they roomed together and became lovers. When Eugene returned to the East Coast, Stanley went on to become intimately involved with Randolph Scott during that actor's pre-Cary Grant days.

Back East, Eugene entered politics long before his son ran for Congress, representing a district in New York State. After his election in November of 1932, Franklin D. Roosevelt summoned Eugene to Warm Springs, Georgia, where he met the left-leaning Vice President, Henry A. Wallace. The President-elect asked Eugene if he would assume the position of Director of Air Commerce. *[In a country such as France or England, that would represent the equivalent of Minister of Aviation.]* Eugene accepted the post, serving in that capacity throughout FDR's turbulent first term in office.

Eugene paid several visits to the home of Orville Wright, the last surviving brother of the team that invented the airplane. Orville died in 1948.

At one point Eugene told his son that the Wright Brothers, both lifelong bachelors, had been lovers during the 19th century. Or, as Gore obscurely wrote in his memoirs, they were involved in "uranism."

Only the hippest of gay people knew that he intended that as a descriptive term for male homosexuality. *[Uranism derived from the word "Uranian," a 19th century term that referred to people "of the third sex—that is, someone with a female psyche in a male body.]*

One gay newspaper claimed that "Vidal could have written with more clarity, saying that Wilbur and Orville liked to suck each other's cocks."

***

Eugene Vidal stands between **the president, FDR** *(left)* and his vice-president, **Henry Wallace**. Later, Eugene made the cover of *Time,* owned by Henry Luce, his wife's lover.

It seemed inevitable that Eugene would try to interest his son in becoming a pilot.

Near the end of his term working in aviation commerce for the government, Eugene became interested in developing a low-cost "flivver plane" that most middle class households could afford as a mode of transportation equivalent to the family car. He told the press that, "It will be so simple to operate that even a ten-year-old can do it."

To prove that, he brought his ten-year-old son to pilot a prototype Hammond Y-1. Pathé newsreel cameras recorded the event for presentation in theaters across America.

"I was the cutest looking boy in the history of the world," Gore later said. "For a while, at least, I became the most famous kid in America. I expected a movie contract to arrive at any minute. Move your ass, Freddie Bartholomew. Alas, the film contract never arrived on my doorstep. So much for that dream. Eugene's dream of the flivver plane in every household didn't come true either."

Nina on Gore: "The Best Reason to Abort!"

Three years after the birth of her son, Nina had grown tired of motherhood.

By 1928, she was pursuing her dream of becoming a Broadway actress, a goal inspired by Tallulah Bankhead, who had become a close friend. "I'm sure my mother and Tallulah bumped pussies on occasion," Gore later claimed.

Nina did manage a one-week engagement in a minor role in a road show production of *Sign of the Leopard* at Washington's National Theater. But her dreams of stardom didn't lead her into acting. As her father, Senator Gore, said, "She wanted the fame and glory, but wasn't prepared to do the hard work to get there."

"I found the best way to get along with Nina was never to see her," Gore recalled.

With each passing year, Gore's hatred of Nina seemed to grow. He admitted in a memoir that at the age of eleven, he started mysteriously to vomit in her presence.

"My mother, Nina Gore Vidal, was just atrocious," he wrote. "Everybody who knew her hated her. It was the race Anglo-Irish. They are more vicious than most. She was a shit. A drunken shit."

He later was relieved that for some eight years, beginning at age ten and ending at age 18, he was sent away to boys' schools "far away from the repulsive presence of my drunkard whore of a mother. Reunions were rare."

When she did see her son, she denounced him, claiming that she'd devoted her life to "undeserving husbands, lovers, and children. I could have become a celebrated actress, perhaps a challenge to Joan Crawford and Barbara Stanwyck. I could have played the same roles they starred in."

"I noticed you left out Garbo," he said sarcastically. She threw her glass of Scotch at him, narrowly missing his head.

"I despised Nina, but loved my grandfather, Thomas Pryor Gore (1870-1949)," Gore said. "I once posed for a photo standing by his side. I was ten years old, the same age he was when he had been blinded by two separate accidents. His left eye was made of glass, and I used to play with it as he shaved."

He was first elected to the U.S. Senate in 1907 from Oklahoma. He served until he was defeated in the summer of 1936, when FDR was running for a second term. He used to tell Gore, "If there was any race other than the human race, I'd join it."

Through his grandfather's blood line, Gore was distantly related to Al Gore, the former U.S. Vice President under Bill Clinton.

Outside their home, or inside it on some occasions when a spouse was away, both Eugene and Nina pursued other affairs. Gore referred to Nina's string of male lovers as "a scandalous field of operations."

Since Eugene was away with Earhart, flying around the country, Nina felt free to bring her casual lovers back to the Vidal home. Gore soon learned that these pickups weren't decorous social visits, when Nina took their hands to lead them upstairs to her bedroom. The Vidals had a black nurse to look after Gore, since his parents were gone most of the day and night. "Mrs. Goodman—that was her name—caught Nina smuggling a black taxi driver up to her bedroom. The poor woman, a Bible-thumping Baptist from Alabama, was shocked by what she called 'the Devil's Lust.'"

Most of Nina's affairs were with anonymous men she randomly encountered. But on

Ten-year-old **Gore** at the controls of a prototype for the experimental Hammond Y-1, with his father

The blind Senator from Oklahoma, **Thomas Pryor Gore**, with the grandson, **Gore Vidal**, who read to him.

a few occasions, her affairs were with famous men.

Gore arrived home one afternoon to hear Nina sitting with Henry Luce in the living room. As the founder of both *Time* and *Life,* he was one of the most influential private citizens in America, a major player in what he called "The American Century."

At the time Nina met Luce, he was married to his first wife, Elizabeth Hotz, and had not yet married Clare Booth Luce, whose fame at one point almost equaled his own.

Gore overheard Luce tell Nina that "my wife doesn't understand me. There is no love between us any more. I need a woman in my life. Will you go to bed with me?"

Gore didn't hear his mother's answer, but he did hear both of them ascending the steps to her bedroom. She remained locked away with the publisher for two hours. He later learned that Luce made repeated return visits to seduce his mother.

At one point, Gore dared confront her. He told Nina, "It would be a good career move if you got a divorce and married Henry Luce."

"Fuck you, you little son of a bitch," she shouted at him, slapping his face. Then she paused, as if realizing that if Gore were a son of a bitch, then she was the bitch.

At one point, Gore was introduced to Luce. He didn't remember what they said, but he did recall "his long fingers covered with orange fur like a caterpillar."

Nina and Eugene: Wife Swapping With the Whitneys

At a lavish party in Washington, D.C., during the early 1930s, Eugene and Nina met a powerhouse couple, John ("Jock") Hay Whitney, the wealthy publisher of *The New York Herald Tribune,* and his beautiful socialite wife, Mary Elizabeth Altemus Whitney, known as "Liz" to her friends. She was the champion horsewoman of America and its most prominent breeder of thoroughbreds. *Time* magazine defined her as "a spir-

Nina made it a point to socialize with (and sleep with) the A-list: *(photo above)* **Henry Luce**

ited devil-may-care rider and a blue-ribbon champion of the horseshow circuit."

She had married Jock in 1930. For his bride, he purchased the Llangollen Estate, a sprawling historic property in Southern Virginia at the foot of the Blue Ridge Mountains.

No one knows exactly what happened at that Washington party, but Jock secretly made arrangements to set up a rendezvous with Nina. Likewise, Eugene and Liz exchanged phone numbers for what became a series of love-in-the-afternoon sessions.

Both of the Whitneys launched these adulterous affairs at the beginning of their marriage, a pattern that would continue throughout the remainder of their decade-long union.

On one occasion, Eugene took Gore to visit Liz on her Virginia estate. She was throwing a lavish "wild hunt ball" at which Prince Aly Khan, her close friend, was the guest of honor. Neither Jock nor Nina were among the invited guests.

Gore bonded with Liz, finding her "funny, amusing, with chiseled features including a gorgeous nose. She was very rich and uneducated," he later said. He remembered the "little dirt marks in the wrinkles around her neck, as she emerged from working in the stables all day. In the moccasins she always wore during the day, she looked like an Indian princess with flashing black eyes."

"She was certainly eccentric," Gore said, "a sort of Auntie Mame character. She brought her favorite horse right into her vast living room. Guests had to avoid stepping in a pile of horseshit. She had at least three dozen dogs running about. She took me on a tour of a vast freezer filled with her favorite dogs of yesteryear. When they died, she put their bodies in deep freeze."

These eccentricities did not turn off Gore, who urged Eugene to divorce Nina and marry Liz if she could free herself from Jock.

In the months to come, both Jock and Liz talked not with each other, but privately with friends about getting divorces which would free them to marry Nina and Eugene, respectively. Washington society just assumed that divorces were inevitable.

At one point, Liz dropped in on her friend, President Franklin D. Roosevelt, unannounced. Although mired in the enormous burden of trying to get America out of its worst depression, he agreed to see her. She confessed to FDR that she wanted to divorce Jock and marry Eugene. FDR recommended a good divorce lawyer to her, although she later attacked FDR for giving her bad advice.

Unknown to Nina at the time, Jock was a serial seducer of famous actresses, including Paulette Goddard, Joan Bennett, and even the regal Joan Crawford. At one point, he proposed marriage to Tallulah Bankhead, pending his divorce from Liz. Tallulah used to tell her lovers, including Burgess Meredith, "For God's sake, don't come inside me. I'm engaged to Jock Whitney."

When Nina divorced Eugene in 1935, she thought Jock would marry her immediately. But he seemed reluctant to do so. At that point, he had tired of her, and she went instead in search of another potential husband, providing he was rich.

Liz was still deeply in love with Eugene and wanted to marry him, but he

Jock Whitney (in 1942)
and his then-wife, **Liz**

never proposed, even after his divorce from Nina was finalized.

[Jock and Liz would not divorce until 1940. Two years later, he would marry Betsey Cushing Roosevelt, the ex-wife of James Roosevelt, son of FDR. Liz herself would marry three more times. Her fourth marriage, in 1960, to Col. Clyce J. Tippet was her most successful, lasting until her death in 1988.]

When Liz read that David O. Selznick was conducting a nationwide search for an unknown to play Scarlett O'Hara in the upcoming movie adaptation of Margaret Mitchell's *Gone With the Wind* (1939), she prevailed upon Eugene to take her to Hollywood. "I feel I am destined to play Scarlett. I've lived in Virginia long enough to develop a Southern cornpone accent."

But within a week of settling into Hollywood, Liz heard the bad news. Jock had learned of her dream, and had called Selznick and nixed the idea. "Everybody I fuck wants to play Scarlett. Just as I'm about to have an orgasm, Joan Bennett, Joan Crawford, Tallulah Bankhead, or Paulette Goddard demand that I call you and get them cast as Scarlett. But there is no way in hell I'm going to let you cast Liz Whitney as Scarlett. NO WAY!"

Selznick had to placate Jock because he'd invested $870,000 into the making of *Gone With the Wind,* and he was chairman of the board of Selznick's production company. Jock had also put up half the option money for Mitchell's novel.

There was more bad news for Liz to face: Her beloved Eugene had met a beautiful woman, Katherine Roberts *[nicknamed "Kit"]*. A Powers model, she was only six years older than Gore. The slim, dark-haired beauty was the daughter of Owen Roberts, a multi-millionaire, with a seat on the New York Stock Exchange and a "priceless" art collection. Katherine had spent much of her life living with her parents in Peking in a palace with twenty servants.

Eugene married Katherine right before Christmas of 1939. The news shocked Liz. "She went ballistic," Gore recalled. "She made threatening phone calls to my father and came up with various blackmail schemes. She felt Eugene belonged to her. He told me that at one point, she called him in the middle of the night and threatened she was going to have Kit murdered.

"Two hit men are on the way," Liz shouted before slamming down the phone.

When Gore met his new stepmother, he found her "young and attractive, evoking Katharine Hepburn in looks. She seemed madly in love with Eugene, in spite of the difference in their ages. Because of Nina, the word 'mother' would send me up the walls. Also, Kit didn't seem to want to be my mother, as I was practically the same age as she was. We were awkward and tense around each other."

Even though Jock did not marry Gore's mother, he and Gore continued to encounter each other over the years, often showing up at the same parties in Washington. In the 1950s, Dwight D. Eisenhower appointed Jock as the U.S. Ambassador to the United Kingdom.

On the occasions that Gore and Jock met, they avoided talk of politics, as Jock was a staunch Republican and Gore a liberal Democrat.

Jock had never lost his interest in show business, and Gore always brought him up to date on the inside gossip.

In the 1930s, Jock used to invest in Broadway shows. That had led to his involvement in half of what Gore dubbed "The Odd Couple of Show Business," Jock Whitney and Fred Astaire.

Astaire and the publisher had initially been drawn together because of their mutual passion for horse racing. Astaire placed bets through bookmakers and even cabled London with wagers on English races.

A deep, intimate relationship formed between these two widely diverse personalities. Jock was an early backer of Astaire, investing in two of his Broadway stage vehicles, *The Band Wagon* in 1930 and *The Gay Divorce* in 1932. Jock even arranged Astaire's first contract with RKO in 1933, using his influence with the producer, Merion C. Cooper, a close friend of Jock's.

During their early days together, Astaire had even taught Jock how to dance the Charleston and the Black Bottom. As Astaire once told Gore, "I much preferred Jock as my dancing partner instead of Ginger Rogers."

In Hollywood in later years, Gore and his longtime companion, Howard Austen, once attended a party at Astaire's home. They were astonished at the number of pictures of Jock on display, including some taken of him during his years at Yale.

After leaving the party, Gore remarked, "I'm sorry that Fred's love for Jock has gone unrequited…at least I think it has. But who knows? For Fred's sake, I'm glad Randolph Scott was more accommodating."

Later that night, when Austen and Gore joined Christopher Isherwood for a drink, Austen told him they'd been to a party at the home of Fred Astaire. Isherwood looked as if he had not heard that correctly.

"How in hell did you come to know Astaire?" Isherwood asked.

Fred Astaire
in *You'll Never Get Rich* (1941)

75

"Jock Whitney introduced us," Gore said. "When I first came to Hollywood, he called Fred and told him to— quote— 'take me under his wing.'"

"I'm afraid Astaire did a little more that that," Gore continued. "It's one of the best kept secrets in Hollywood, but Fred on occasion has gotten into trouble with the police. He has this thing for little boys. As I was just young enough at the time to pass his physical, he went for me. I had sex with ol' skin and bones. He's definitely not my type—tiny dick, bony ass—but I endured it because he's a big time movie star."

"You're a god damn starfucker, now admit it!" Isherwood demanded.

"As you know, it's called 'climbing the lavender ladder' in Hollywood," Gore said.

***

"Of all that wife swapping and bed jumping, and all those marriages in the 1930s, there was at least one endurable one, and that was my father's marriage to Kit," Gore said. "Because of the wide difference in their ages, I thought their marriage was doomed from the beginning. But Kit was still around in 1969 when Eugene came down with cancer. She was a good caretaker right until the end, looking after Eugene with a stoic but sinking heart."

"I came to the hospital to see him," Gore said. "I encountered his doctor in the hall. I saw on his face that it was hopeless."

"There is nothing else that any of us can do for Mr. Vidal," the doctor said. "I advised him to have a double martini. That was my way of saying, 'It's all over, so you might as well get drunk.'"

Stepfathers: What's Love Got to Do With It?

In 1935, after Nina divorced Eugene, she married a wealthy second husband, the stockbroker Hugh D. Auchincloss, the marriage lasting until 1941. The year after he divorced Nina, Auchincloss, nicknamed "Hughdie," married Janet Lee Bouvier, mother of Jackie and Lee Bouvier.

Gore was never that close to his stepfather, although he made him the model for the tedious general in his play, *Visit to a Small Planet.*

"One of my most vivid memories is that Hughdie knew the original Jewish name of every movie star who changed his name—for example, Jacob Julius Garfinkle for John Garfield; Issur Danielovitch for Kirk Douglas; and Asa Yoelson for Al Jolson.

Nina spoke very frankly to her son about sex. "Hughdie has a real problem: a complete inability to maintain an erection. His doctor says it's because of excessive masturbation when he was a boy. Let that be a lesson to you, young man."

"My greatest sex education as a teenager was when I discovered

Hughdie's collection of pornography," Gore said. "He had the most complete set of pornographic books, slides, films, and manuals I would ever see—pederasty (obviously his favorite subject), sado-masochism, bondage, dominance, submission, homosexuality, bisexuality, transsexuality, bestiality, and a great interest in scatology, a subject unfamiliar to me at the time."

"He was a bit absent minded at times," Gore said. "Once, he took me swimming. It was a mixed crowd of about fifty people. He walked out completely nude. He'd forgotten to put on his bathing suit."

Gore claimed that Nina married Hughdie strictly for financial reasons. "He wanted her to bring glamor into his life. She told him that she didn't care for him *that way,* so it would be a *mariage blanc.* He agreed to those terms, signing a prenuptial agreement that provided her a fixed income for life."

Gore did not care for Hughdie, writing that he was "large, cumbersome, stammering—simply neither plausible nor decorative. I would much have preferred Jock Whitney's money instead."

Nina had met her third and final husband, Major General Robert Olds, on the set of *Test Pilot,* where he was a technical advisor. *[Released in 1938 and directed by Victor Fleming, it starred Clark Gable as a daredevil pilot, his wife, as played by Myrna Loy, and his best friend, as played by Spencer Tracy. It also featured Lionel Barrymore and some of the most cutting-edge racing aircraft of its day.]* But Nina was too busy to pay Olds any attention at the time, because of her aggressive pursuit of Clark Gable.

Unlike Hughdie, Olds was rather handsome and an Air Force brigadier general, having achieved fame as a Flying Fortress pilot. When he married Nina, he was in charge of the Ferry Command, a large air transportation network, whose assignment involved the delivery of bombers to Britain.

The forty-four year old military man already had four grown sons.

When Nina married Olds in June of 1942, she did not invite Gore to the wedding. The marriage lasted only ten months before Olds died of a heart attack.

Gore would remember Olds and his military friends. "He denounced President Jew Franklin D. Rosenfeld who got us into the war on the wrong side."

"We ought to be fighting the Commies, not a man like Adolf Hitler," Olds told Gore. "FDR is not only a kike, but sick in the head—and not just from polio, but from syphilis. Eleanor has moved her lesbian lover into the White House."

After she buried Olds, Nina told Gore, "Of my three husbands, I loved Robert the most. But I've had more passionate sex with my extramarital af-

Hugh Auchincloss, stepfather (based on separate marriages) to both Gore Vidal and Jacqueline Bouvier

fairs."

"Of my three husbands, the first had three balls, the second had two balls, and the third had one ball," she said. "I dare not take a chance on a fourth husband."

The King of Hollywood Inspires
"Twinges of a Sexual Urge Beyond Belief"

On MGM's set, during pre-production of *Test Pilot,* Fleming spoke to Eugene Vidal, asking him to contact a group of skilled pilots he knew who might serve as technical advisers and also perform some daring feats in the sky for his cameras.

Eugene agreed to contact some pilots, especially recommending Paul Mantz, a noted air-racing pilot.

Mantz and Eugene had become close friends in 1937 when he had tutored Amelia Earhart in long distance flying and navigation. He had accompanied her as co-pilot on her aborted first attempt at an around-the-world flight.

At that point, Eugene was still engaged in a sporadic romantic liaison with Earhart. She would later disappear on July 2 of that year during her ill-fated attempt to make a circumnavigational flight of the globe in a Lockheed Model 10 Electra whose costs were paid for, in part, by Purdue University.

Earhart had wanted Mantz to be her co-pilot, but he had bowed out. Eventually, the aviatrix selected Fred Noonan. Earhart and Noonan disappeared somewhere over the Central Pacific Ocean during the final leg of their attempted around-the world flight. As Mantz told Eugene, "There but for the grace of God go I."

Initially, Eugene had invested his private money to defray some of the costs that Earhart incurred during her preparations for this historic flight.

Howard Hughes, who had directed and produced the classic aviation film, *Hell's Angels* (1930), was among Mantz's first clients. He also worked on the 1932 film *Air Mail.* He had been financially involved in the formation of Paul Mantz's Air Services, a charter company jokingly christened "The Honeymoon Express," because it carried so many lovers aboard chartered flights to secret rendezvous points. Mantz had developed a number of friends among the stars of Hollywood, notably Clark Gable, James Cagney, and Errol Flynn.

Mantz was eventually hired by Fleming as pilot for some of the avant-garde flight scenes filmed during the making of *Test Pilot,* and Mantz called Eugene to thank him. He had a favor to ask, explaining that he was trying to interest his son, Gore, in becoming a pilot. "Could you let him visit the set on a few occasions? I would appreciate it very much."

Mantz arrived to retrieve Gore, where he was staying with Nina in a bungalow in back of the Beverly Hills Hotel. At the bungalow, the pilot found not only

Eugene's son but a beautifully dressed and made up Nina, who wanted to go along too. She was very frank in her reason for wanting to visit the set:

"Ever since 1930, I'd had this crazed ambition to meet Clark Gable and to see for myself if he is as handsome on the screen as off."

Mantz agreed that she could accompany him to the set, but warned both Gore and Nina that they had to stay in the background and not interfere with production.

When Gable was resting between takes, Nina approached him and introduced herself. He invited her to take the chair beside him, even thought it was clearly marked for Myrna Loy, then the unofficial "Queen of Hollywood." Nina had heard that Loy had a reputation as a lesbian, so she didn't think she'd present any competition for Gable's attention.

Nina had been made aware that Gable's marriage to socialite Ria Langham existed in name only. To judge from her photographs, Langham "was old enough to be Clark's mother."

Nina's closest friend in Hollywood was Dolores Stein, the beautiful wife of Jules Stein, the reigning talent scout and casting entrepreneur. "Dolores was up on all the gossip, real inside stuff," Nina told her son. She'd become aware that Gable had seduced practically every female star at MGM, including Marion Davies, Mary Astor, Loretta Young (she'd given birth to his child), Lupe Velez, Norma Shearer, and especially Joan Crawford. Early in his career, as a young actor trying to break into pictures, he'd also "serviced" some of the gay set, including director George Cukor and actors William Haines, Rod LaRocque, and among others, Johnny Mack Brown.

Gable was once defined as "Jack Dempsey in a tuxedo." Crawford claimed that being near him gave her "twinges of a sexual urge beyond belief." Nina echoed Crawford's enthusiasm, and so did Gore himself, even at his young age. "I wanted Clark to be my daddy, and all gay men will know what I mean by that."

Nina had not been completely informed. Unknown to her, Gable was having an affair with a beautiful actress, Virginia Grey, who had been cast in the minor role of Sarah in *Test Pilot*.

With Grey, Gable would become involved in

Gore's mink-clad mother, now **Nina Olds**, harshly appraises him in uniform at the USO in 1944. "With my son in uniform, the Nazis and Japs are sure to win," she said.

Nina told her son, Gore, "Of my three husbands, I loved **Major General Robert Olds** *(photo above)* the best. But my outside lovers were more passionate."

his longest-running relationship, which lasted between marriages and during marriages. Grey never married. As she once told a reporter, "If I couldn't have Gable, I didn't want any other man."

Nina was also unaware of a major development occurring in Gable's love life. Unknown to most of Hollywood, he had begun an affair with Carole Lombard at the time. Ironically, Gable had first met Lombard at a party hosted by Jock Whitney.

Although swearing that Lombard was the great love of his life, Gable continued to cheat on her. In fact, when she died in 1942 in an airplane crash, she was rushing back to Hollywood after a tour selling War Bonds to rescue her man from the arms of Lana Turner, who had been his co-star in *Honky Tonk* (1941) and *Somewhere I'll Find You* (1942).

On the set of *Test Pilot,* Nina met veteran actor Lionel Barrymore. Again, Stein hadn't filled her in on yet another secret in Gable's promiscuous life. As a young actor, he had let Barrymore perform fellatio on him in his dressing room during Gable's early days at the studio. After Gable became a star (and consequently refused Barrymore's request for more sex), a friendship between the two men had survived.

Nina flirted with Gable, but according to Gore, she had to wait three days before he invited her for an afternoon session in his dressing room. Her big chance with Gable came when he invited Nina, along with Gore, to drive with him to the Air Corps Base at March Field in Riverside.

It was during that time that both Nina and Gore got to know Gable a lot better. In the back seat during the 65-mile eastward drive from Los Angeles, Gore was "all ears" as to what was being said in the front.

The actor was aware that he had become the front runner to play Rhett Butler in *Gone With the Wind.* "Six million eyes would be trained on me, and most of them will want me to fail."

He explained to them that almost every member of the American public had already decided that he was the actor to play Rhett on the screen. "Thousands of fans want me. Others want Errol Flynn, Gary Cooper, Ronald Colman, Basil Rathbone, Warner Baxter, and, would you believe, a moronic choice of Humphrey Bogart." Gable went on to tell Nina and her son that he'd learned that Selznick had gone to John Gilbert's widow and had told her, "We have buried the actor who should have been Rhett Butler.'"

Spencer Tracy *(left),* **Myrna Loy,** and **Clark Gable** in *Test Pilot*

On the set, Gore was mesmerized at what went on behind the scenes during the making of a movie. In the future, he would spend much of his life on movie sets, battling actors over lines in their scripts.

On the set of *Test Pilot,* Gore witnessed his first actor/writer fight, hearing Gable in a bitter argument with Waldemar Young, who was one of four writers working on the screenplay. *[Much of the script had been written by director Howard Hawks, who was assisted by Vincent Lawrence and John Lee Mahin.]*

Gable accused Young of writing "fag dialogue between Spence and myself. What red-blooded pilot recites poetry and quotes from the classics? And that death scene when I'm supposed to hold Spence in my arms and say, 'I love you, Gunner?' Why don't you have us end up doing a sixty-nine on the screen? You might as well. We're obviously playing fuck buddies. *[Gable had been cast as Jim Lane, the reckless test pilot, and Tracy was playing Gunner Morris, the grease monkey "who constantly fusses over him."]*

"You've also butched up Myrna," Gable continued. "She knows more about baseball than I do. When I start to fall for Myrna, you have Tracy throwing a jealous fit. I'm going to Fleming, to tell him I won't play some of these queer scenes."

Even after it was rewritten, Gable hated playing the death scene where he holds a dying Tracy in his arms. He always jokingly referred to Tracy as "The Wisconsin Ham." Deciding that Tracy was unnecessarily drawing out his death scene, Gable finally dropped Tracy's head with a thud on the ground. "Die, goddamn it, Spencer. I wish to Christ you would." Then he stormed off the set.

Clark Gable with the doomed **Carole Lombard**

In Riverside, Gore was assigned a room of his own, as was Nina. But he soon learned that she was slipping into Gable's bedroom late at night, leaving in the morning before breakfast.

"Nina and Clark found they had something more in common than sex," Gore said. "Both of them were heavy drinkers, downing the booze during the golden hours of the day and at twilight and midnight."

As her relationship with Gable deepened, Nina at one point asked Gable "if you can make a man out

Fred Noonan with the doomed **Amelia Earhart** in 1937

of my pansy son?"

That meant inviting Gore along for some of his macho activities, such as hunting and fishing, which Gable called "taking to the hills."

Gable agreed to let Gore go with him. For the young boy, that meant rising at four o'clock in the morning and helping make breakfast "for a lot of smelly men. It also meant getting poison ivy and being chased by a black bear."

Gable also gave Gore lessons in marksmanship, skeet shooting, and fly casting. Later, the movie star told Nina, "I don't really think this boy is cut out to be an outdoorsman, but I'll keep trying. I just hope he doesn't grow up to be a fag like most of the guys in this town. I should know."

For a brief time, Gore and Nina were invited to stay at Gable's secret hideaway in North Hollywood. He'd rented a house which used to be owned by the famous silent screen star, Alice Terry, and her director husband, Rex Ingram.

It was while staying at this house that Gore was invited to fly to Catalina with Gable aboard a B-17 flown by Paul Mantz. Tracy had turned down the invitation, telling Gable, "I'm on the wagon and all of you guys will get stinking drunk."

Gable's friend from MGM, "pretty boy" Robert Taylor, was invited to go along instead.

Taylor—who was married at the time to the bisexual actress, Barbara Stanwyck—often accompanied Gable on his hunting trips. George Cukor once commented on this arrangement. "Clark Gable was fucking Lana Turner; Robert Taylor was fucking Lana Turner; and Clark Gable was fucking Robert Taylor. Hollywood...don't you love it?"

It was in a small motel on Catalina Island, through paper-thin walls, that Gore was introduced to Hollywood seductions. He and Mantz were assigned one bedroom, Taylor and Gable the other, with a shared bathroom between the two bedrooms. One night when Gore got up at around 2am to urinate, he heard noises coming from Gable's room. The door to his bedroom had been left slightly ajar.

"I listened to the noises coming from inside," Gore later told Mantz. "It was Gable's voice I heard, so I assume it was Taylor doing the sucking. Taylor was sucking Clark's dick.

"Get used to it, kid," Mantz told him. "Don't forget I run the Hollywood Express and could write a book about what goes on. You won't believe some of the combinations of lovers I fly to secret hideaways. Remember one thing, kid. To become a *bona fide* member of the Hollywood community, you've got to be a pervert."

"Well, I met Spencer Tracy last week," Gore said. "He's not a pervert, and he's involved with Katharine Hepburn."

"Let me tell you about those two: He's a closeted homosexual—just ask his best friend, George Cukor—and she's a lesbian. They love each other. In case you don't know the expression yet, it's called 'a platonic relationship.'"

Later, when Gore told others what he'd heard that night in Gable's room, he said "The only thing that pissed me off about Taylor and Gable getting it on is they didn't invite me to join them. Those were two good-looking guys."

***

Upon their return to Gable's lodgings in North Hollywood, when Gore was lounging with Gable beside a pool, the young boy told him his secret dream. "I want to become a movie star."

He even told Gable about the three young actors who were his greatest inspiration: "When I went to see Mickey Rooney appear as Puck in *A Midsummer Night's Dream* (1935), he became my role model. I

Paul Mantz, "flying illicit lovers"

was just ten at the time, and Mickey could have been fourteen, although he looked nine. Seeing him cavort around on the screen, I just knew what I wanted to become."

Years later, when describing this Hollywood role model to Tennessee Williams, the playwright said: "Mickey Rooney was the best actor in the history of movies. You sure aim high, Gore. What talent that little kid had. Amazing."

Gable was somewhat surprised at Gore's other role models: They included the identical twins, Bobby and Billy Mauch, as they appeared with Errol Flynn in *The Prince and the Pauper* (1937).

"The boys were four years older than me, and the two most beautiful boys I'd ever seen. They looked so much alike, even their own mother couldn't tell which one was Billy and which one was Bobby."

Later, he wrote that when he first saw Billy and Bobby on the screen, he didn't want to be Puck or even Mickey Rooney any more. "I wanted to be myself. *Twice.* I think a palpable duplicate of oneself would be the ideal companion."

Gore confessed one night to Tennessee on his porch in Key West that for years, he kept a studio still of Billy and Bobby. "I masturbated to it every night."

"I thought Billy and Bobby Mauch were cute as a pair of bug's ears, and I wished I were either one of them, if not two of *me.*"

The Mauch twins never again managed to replicate their original success, although they did go on to star in three films based on the Penrod stories by Booth Tarkington. "Then they vanished, except in my psyche," Gore wrote.

Actually, Billy continued to play minor roles in a number of films. Late in 1950, Gore met Billy for the first time, although he was disappointed that "he didn't look as glorious as he did in *The Prince and the Pauper.*"

"He told me that he was working in a film called *Bedtime for Bonzo* that starred Ronald Reagan and a chimpanzee." Gore said. "Its female star, Diana Lynn, became my future girl friend."

"Ronald Reagan?" asked Gore. "That has-been actor and FBI informant?"

83

The Nina/Gable affair continued on and off until the end of World War II, interrupted for long periods of time during his marriage to Lombard.

In 1944, near the end of his stint in the Army, Gore was granted a two-week leave. He journeyed to Hollywood to find Nina back again in a bungalow at the Beverly Hills Hotel. Hugh D. Auchincloss, her former husband, was picking up the tab. His son, Tommy Auchincloss, was in residence as well,

Nina was invited to a Hollywood party, and she asked Gore to be her escort. As he remembered it, "I was the only man in uniform at the gathering. Frank Sinatra came up to me."

"I'm getting a lot of bad publicity because I'm not in uniform," Sinatra told him.

"It's no damn fun, I can assure you," Gore told him.

He later admitted, "I was shameless that night. I waited until Sinatra had to take a leak. The *voyeur* in me won out. I followed him to the toilet, wanting to see for myself if all those rumors were true. I think he sensed what I was up to. Instead of beating me up, he put on a show for me. The rumors were true."

Nina and Gore also met Marlene Dietrich that night. The screen goddess seemed aware that Nina was having an affair with Gable. She was very dismissive of him. "Oh, he is just a gigolo, or was. When he got his start in Hollywood, he would go for anything with a hole and a promise of a couple of dollars."

Two days later, Gable, also on leave from the Army, paid an afternoon visit to Nina at her bungalow on the grounds of the Beverly Hills Hotel. This time, instead of asking him to make a man out of Gore, she wanted him to teach Tommy Auchincloss how to swim in the hotel's pool.

As Gore and Nina watched from *chaises longues*, Tommy and Gable were having a lot of fun. At one point, Tommy rode Gable's back, with his legs wrapped around the actor's neck. It was at this inappropriate moment that Tommy decided to take the leak of all leaks. When Gable felt the warm, golden stream cascading down his back, he tossed Tommy into what might have been his watery grave if Gore hadn't jumped into the pool to rescue him.

Gable's final words to Tommy were, "Sink or swim, pisser!"

"That was the last we ever saw of Clark," Gore said. "I think he decided that my mother's vagina just wasn't worth putting up with her brood. He never came back, which explains why Clark never became my stepfather. It was such an inglorious ending to Nina's romance with 'The King' that I decided to leave it out of my memoirs."

The Decline and Fall of

The Mauch twins in
The Prince & the Pauper.

Nina Vidal

At the end of his Army career, Gore produced his first novel, *Williwaw* (1946), which earned a certain amount of praise, even an endorsement from Eleanor Roosevelt, who later became his friend and political ally.

In a critical study, Bernard F. Dick wrote: "*Williwaw* was a sort of elegiac *Story of G.I. Joe,* somewhere between a hymn to the survivor and a threnody *[A poem or song of mourning or lamentation]* for the misbegotten."

Williwaw was named for the sudden winds that roar down from the Alaskan and Siberian mainland, affecting ships with their fitful rage. It was based on Gore's experience in the military when he was stationed in the storm-tossed Bering Sea offshore from the Aleutian Islands.

Four of his next five novels failed: *In a Yellow Wood* (1947); *The Season of Comfort* (1949); *A Search for the King* (1950); and *Dark Green, Bright Red* (1950). His notorious homosexual novel, *The City and the Pillar* (1948), however, was a bestseller.

Gore claimed that Nina was "thrilled at the failure of those novels." As for the one defined as a commercial success, Nina asserted that more than any of his other works, *The City and the Pillar* subjected her to disgrace.

"Gore isn't really a novelist," she told her friends. "He's only a journalist. He had only that one book in him, and now, of course, he's finished."

She visited him only infrequently, showing up at his country home, Edgewater, his house on the Hudson. "She arrived through the kitchen door," he said. "with this young man, who was a pilot for Pan American. "Right in front of him, and me as well, she announced, 'He's got the biggest cock I've ever seen.'"

Then she disappeared upstairs with him to the guest bedroom.

Years would go by before Nina and Gore got together again, and letters were rare.

Gore met his mother again at the wedding of her daughter *[Gore's half sister]*, Nini Gore Vidal Auchincloss. The groom was Newton Steers, and the wedding in 1957 was attended by both Gore and Senator John F. Kennedy, Nina's stepbrother-in-law.

Gore recalled his mother as being "uncommonly sober at the event. She also ran into a lot of her oldtime Washington gents who remembered affairs with her twenty years earlier, when she was a reigning beauty. At the wedding, she looked rather puffy."

That same year, Gore invited Nina to spend Christmas in London with Howard Austen and him. Austen was his closest friend and companion. Gore and Austen had rented a large flat in London with three servants.

In London, Gore discovered that her condition had worsened. In addition to alcohol, she had become a morphine addict.

"Like Capote, she was also a liar, and I detest liars," Gore said.

Few things about her son impressed her, except for a visit from actor

Robert Morley, wanting to appear as the lead in the 1960 film, based on Gore's play, *Visit to a Small Planet*.

She complained to the servants that Gore's relationship with his "Jew boyfriend" had destroyed her social status. "I am shamed by Austen's presence in this flat."

When he could no longer tolerate her attacks on Austen, his most loyal friend over the years, he sent Nina packing. In the aftermath of her visit, she wrote him "the most savage letter I have ever received in a lifetime of receiving the most vicious of letters. It was so violent I had to burn it right away."

"I answered her letter. In it, I told her that I never planned to see her as long as I lived. During the remaining twenty years of her life, I kept my promise."

When Gore appeared on the cover of *Time* magazine in 1976, Nina wrote him a letter asking for money. In response, without any accompanying letter, he sent her a check for $8,000.

After she'd cashed the check, she wrote a "rebuttal" to *Time's* largely flattering portrait of her son.

"I never saw the complete letter," Gore said. "But I was told it was written with a serpent's pen. *Time's* editors published only a small part of it under the subhead of 'A Mother's Love.'"

Nina Gore Vidal Auchincloss Olds died in 1978, after suffering a painful bout with cancer. Gore did not attend the funeral. Neither did his half sister, Nini Gore Auchincloss. When her daughter had been involved with her first husband in a custody battle, the mother appeared in court to testify that Nini, her daughter, "is an unfit mother."

Tommy Auchincloss, her son, handled the funeral arrangements. She was cremated and her ashes placed in Tommy's attic, where they rested for a decade.

He finally followed through on her request to scatter her ashes on the mountain near San Francisco where the ashes of General Olds had previously been scattered, but Tommy discovered that he'd thrown the ashes to the wind 400 miles off course, onto the wrong mountain.

The last words from Nina's lips, Gore learned, had been a lie. On her deathbed at Sloan Kettering Institute in Manhattan, she told Tommy that Gore had come to the hospital and apologized to her for the way he'd treated her.

"I forgave him for all his evil deeds," she confessed before dying.

"It was her fantasy," Gore said. "I never went to see her."

During the last brutal winter (1944-45) of World War II, **Gore** mans the wheel of an *F.S. 35* as it heads in for a perilous landing in the remote Aleutian Islands.

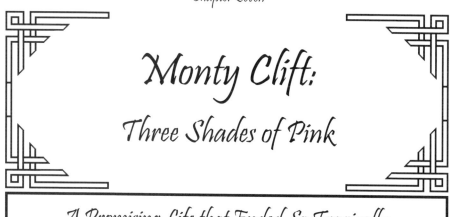

Chapter Seven

Monty Clift:
Three Shades of Pink

A Promising Life that Ended So Tragically

A doomed love affair both on and off the screen, **Montgomery Clift** and **Elizabeth Taylor** confront reality in George Stevens' *A Place in the Sun* (1951). Clift's brilliant performance and that of plain girl Shelley Winters re-created Theodore Dreiser's novel, *An American Tragedy* in a cinematic remake.

With one of those boyfriends who pass quickly into

the night, Tennessee first met Montgomery Clift on April 27, 1942, when he attended the premiere of an experimental, well-reviewed play, *Mexican Mural,* at the Brooks Atkinson Theatre in Manhattan. The production had been funded by the wealthy bisexual torch singer, Libby Holman. She had developed an intense, decade-plus obsession over the beautiful homosexual young actor.

"Monty brought a tragic stature and a great delicacy to the stage in his role," Tennessee recalled. "It was one of my most memorable nights in the theater. I thought a new Broadway star had been born."

Backstage, Tennessee was also introduced to two women who would increasingly assume major roles in Monty's life.

"I came face to face with the black widow spider herself," Tennessee said, a reference to Holman.

She had once been charged with the murder of her 20-year-old millionaire husband, Zachary Smith Reynolds, heir to a tobacco fortune. Murder charges *[based to some degree on pressure the Reynolds family exerted to suppress a subsequent scandal]* were eventually dropped.

Libby Holman

"I remember her standing there before me in a Mainbocher dress, with black, oily hair," recalled Tennessee, "smelling of the perfume, Jungle Gardenia. It was known at the time that she was attracted to young gay men with sexual inadequacies, and to such women as the actress Jeanne Eagels and the DuPont heiress, Louise d'Andelot Carpenter. And later, to my dear friend, the author, Jane Bowles."

At the time of their inaugural meeting, Tennessee remembered that "Standing next to Holman was Monty's acting coach, Mira Rostova, a Russian *émigré* with a little face out of a Kathe Kollwitz drawing."

"When it comes to acting, what I tell an actor is always right," Rostova told Tennessee. "I am never wrong."

Tennessee did not really get to know Monty until he was cast as the lead in *You Touched Me!*, a play that Tennessee had co-authored with his longtime friend, Donald Windham. Their plot was adapted from a story by D.H. Lawrence.

[You Touched Me! tells the story of a retired and now drunken sea captain, his austere sister, his daughter, and a young man he had taken from an orphanage some years before. That boy has grown up to become a Canadian pilot.

Coming home on leave, he recognizes that the daughter will soon be like her spinster aunt. A love story develops between them, as he tries to free her, wanting her to run away with him. In that effort, the sea captain aids and abets, knowing that whereas he has been defeated by life, he does not want that despair to descend on his daughter.]

That wonderful old character actor, Edmund Gwenn, was cast as the

Clift: Powerful, Sensitive, Magnetic, & Tragically Flawed

drunken captain. Monty was cast as Hadrian, a Canadian flier who comes home from the war to woo the spinsterish young Marianne Stewart.

The director was Guthrie McClintic, who was engaged in the most famous "lavender marriage" in the theater world. He was married to the great Katharine Cornell, who was a lesbian. Previously, he'd been married to Estelle Winwood, Tallulah Bankhead's best friend. She later claimed, "Guthrie spent all the days of our marriage 'auditioning' handsome young actors, but never got around to me."

During the run of *You Touched Me!*, McClintic fell in love with Monty, devoting all his attention to him and virtually ignoring the other members of the cast. "He was practically salivating over this young boy," Gwenn claimed. "I thought it was amusing. Guthrie was one of the most professional men in the business, except when Monty was around. He sure went crazy over the boy, who seemed rather indifferent to him."

When McClintic met Tennessee, he proclaimed that "Monty is the most promising young actor on Broadway."

Tennessee later told Windham, "Perhaps Monty's greatest acting challenge was to pretend passion with Guthrie."

"I want to play Hadrian as incandescent, mysterious," Monty told Tennessee." Deeply devoted to his self-image as a Method actor, he annoyed the rest of the cast because he kept changing his blocking on stage.

Years later, Tennessee told his friend, author Dotson Rader, that he was "beguiled by the very feminine beauty of Monty. He was the loveliest man in the world then, and he was considered the finest young American actor until he threw it all away. I think Marlon Brando broke his heart. I was mesmerized by his eyes. They were like a wounded bird's. People say he liked to go into the back rooms of gay bars and pass out and anybody could fuck him."

A lavender and very theatrical marriage: **Guthrie McClintick** and **Katharine Cornell**

Tennessee found Monty "up-jittery, overly enthusiastic. I visited him backstage in his dressing room. He was in his underwear. Such a hirsute creature. His next play should be called *The Hairy Ape*."

"At first, he didn't like me," Tennessee continued,

Tennessee Williams and **Donald Windham** in Rome in 1948

"because I was open about my homosexuality, and he was in the closet. But he eventually warmed to me because he respected the arts, especially theater. After seeing *The Glass Menagerie,* he became convinced that I was an important new voice in the theater. Actually, we were both aware that *You Touched Me! [which opened on September 25, 1945]* was only produced to capitalize off my success with *Menagerie,* which had opened in April of 1945, just two blocks to the north. It had become the hottest ticket in town."

[For the most part, You Touched Me! *was negatively reviewed and suffered unfavorable comparisons to* The Glass Menagerie. *Lewis Nichols, writing in* The New York Times, *claimed that the play "is not an improvement nor an advancement for Tennessee Williams; in fact, it represents a step down." Nichols attacked the play for being "verbose and filled with lofty and long speeches. It needs editing as well as cohesion. Finally, it does not have the warm acting which glossed over the imperfections of* The Glass Menagerie, *for the members of its cast play in several styles. It is, in short, a disappointment."]*

One strange night, Clift arrived drunk and drugged at Tennessee's apartment at one o'clock in the morning. He had an unusual demand. "I want you to take me to the inner circle of hell. Once there, I want to experience depravity, debauchery, degradation, the three Ds. I've been a puritan too long, so very disciplined, but now I want to release my inner demons, my darkest desires."

"That's a pretty tall order for me to fulfill," Tennessee said, "But come on in."

As Tennessee later told Windham, "In bed, I found Monty passive, tender, not very aggressive. At the time I was a raging sex maniac, so I took advantage of him, even though he is not my physical type. He had a great embarrassment over his small penis, but I was never known as a Size Queen. His feeling of inadequacy was one of the secret tragedies of his life."

"Monty and I ended up admiring each other's talents, not necessarily our sexual prowess," Tennessee said.

"In private," Tennessee continued, "Monty would sometimes display a delicate femininity, but on stage in his role as the R.A.F. pilot he personified virility rather like 'The Gentleman Caller' in *The Glass Menagerie.* He exuded male sensuality without the vulgar display of it—say, Brando's portrayal of Stanley Kowalski in *A Streetcar Named Desire.*"

One night over dinner, Monty confided to Tennessee that he'd escaped the draft because of "this dysentery I can't get rid of. Some bug in Mexico that lives forever in me. Actually, I was scared shitless of going to war and getting my face blown off. As an actor, I say everything with my face, more than with my body."

"It was ironic that he said that," Tennessee said. "Later, he'd have that horrible automobile accident when his face had to be almost totally rebuilt. He ended up with some plastic mask created by doctors, as anyone who has seen the closing reels of *Suddenly Last Summer* can testify."

Monty's performance in *You Touched Me!* would have a great impact on his film career. Director Howard Hawks came to see it, and decided that he would be ideal cast as the foster son of John Wayne in *Red River,* released in 1948.

"I saw Monty after he'd shot the movie for Hawks," Tennessee recalled. "He told me that Wayne had denounced him as a fag. But one drunken night Wayne grabbed him and kissed him, sticking his tongue down Monty's throat. Fortunately, John Ireland, who played a minor role in that film, was more delectable."

"It was the mating of two opposites," Monty said. "I was called Princess Tiny Meat, and John Ireland is known to have the largest cock in Hollywood."

In the early 1950s, after he'd co-starred in *A Place in the Sun* with Elizabeth Taylor, Monty optioned *You Touched Me!* for the screen. Both Tennessee and Windham were surprised, eventually learning that Monty had wanted to function as both the producer and the star in whatever film adaptation of *You Touched Me!* was eventually crafted. As part of his plan to expand his career into that of a Hollywood producer, Monty joined with his best friend and fellow actor, Kevin McCarthy, brother of the famous author, Mary McCarthy, to write the screen play.

During their struggles with the script, Tennessee visited Monty at his apartment. "I was shocked, and few things ever shock me. Both Kevin and Monty were sitting nude on the living room floor eating raw meat with blood running down their chins. I thought they were cannibals."

"Monty explained that raw meat made him more creative, and that he had persuaded Kevin to try it," Tennessee said. "Kevin was presumably straight, but it was obvious that Monty was madly in love with him. I also learned that whenever Kevin came to visit Monty, his host insisted that Kevin remove all his clothing."

"I read some of their screenplay," Tennessee said, "and I was kind in my remarks. It was awful. They had such lines as, 'Would you like to stroke my pussy?'"

The McCarthy/Clift screenplay version of *You Touched Me!* was sent to every major studio in Hollywood, including 20th Century Fox and MGM, but no producer went for it.

In later years, Tennessee saw less and less of Monty, as both Gore and Truman assumed larger roles in the actor's life.

Tennessee did meet with him in 1955 to see if Monty wanted to play the closeted homosexual character of Brick in *Cat on a Hot Tin Roof* on Broadway. Monty turned it down, the role going to Ben Gazzara instead.

When Paul Newman interpreted Brick on the screen opposite Elizabeth Taylor, Tennessee met with Monty one night in a small tavern in the Manhattan's theater district. "I

Two views of **Montgomery Clift** in *Red River*. *Upper photo*: with **Joanne Dru**. *Lower photo*: with **John Wayne**.

noticed that many critics are calling Newman 'the new Montgomery Clift' for his performance as Brick. All that acclaim and adulation could have been yours."

"What are you trying to do to me? Monty asked. "Increase my liquor consumption and pill popping over my regrets in life?"

Tennessee, from afar, heard of Monty's journey into self-destruction—his car accident, his reliance on drugs, his struggles during his involvement in the filming of Tennessee's play, *Suddenly Last Summer.*

As both men moved into the 1960s, Tennessee was more sympathetic than Gore and others about Monty's drug usage. "I was taking drugs myself," Tennessee confessed. "Much the same stuff that Monty consumed—Doriden, Luminol, Seconal, Nembutal, Phenobarbital. Of course, mixed with liquor, these drugs can become poisonous, lethal even, driving Monty to that land romantically called 'The Far Frontier.'"

In 1965, one of Tennessee's closest friends, novelist Carson McCullers, called him to tell him that her *Reflections in a Golden Eye* was to be filmed. Elizabeth Taylor, the star, wanted Monty to make a sort of comeback, cast as a homosexual army officer. A starting date had not been announced.

Originally, when the novel was optioned for the screen, Tennessee was first queried to see if he'd like to write the film script.

It was with sadness to Tennessee that Monty never got to star with Taylor, his *A Place in the Sun* costar of long ago, in the McCullers drama. Monty died before filming began.

It was a bittersweet memory for Tennessee when he recalled his last time with Monty.

Accompanied by Julie Harris, Tennessee had a reunion with Monty in the studio of Caedmon Records. Harris and Monty were there to record an audio version of *The Glass Menagerie.* Monty told Tennessee that except for the McCullers project, he had not been offered a part on the screen or stage in four years—"Just two spaghetti Westerns to be shot in Italy."

Later, from a VIP position in the control booth, Tennessee listened to Monty emote during his portrayal of "The Gentleman Caller."

"I wept when I heard that tender, beautiful voice," Tennessee said. "In just a few months, Monty would be dead, but he brought my character to life again."

"In his Passage to Hell, Monty lived in a dark closet where no moonlight ever penetrated," Tennessee said. "He did not hear the music of the wind."

Burnt out far too early in life, Monty, born in Omaha, Nebraska, in 1920, died on July 13, 1966

Dana Wynter and **Kevin McCarthy** flee together in terror in this scene from *Invasion of the Body Snatchers* (1956).

92

Montgomery **Clift** before his debilitating car accident.

in Manhattan. Marlon Brando replaced him in the lead role of *Reflections in a Golden Eye.*

Tennessee said that he would have liked to see Monty interpret the role of the tormented, gay army major instead of Brando. "Monty's inner demons included his struggle with his own sexual identity growing up in a less tolerant age. He would have brought an extra personal dimension to the character."

Film critic David Thomson wrote, "We know now how far Clift was destroyed by drink, drugs, and neurosis; and we recognize the neurosis being intensified by his gay yearning that had to lurk within a heterosexual image. And Clift was beautiful—which is the way movie stars are expected to be. Does his torture bear out the secret permission by which viewers can aspire to same-sex fantasies?"

Sodomy, Incest, and Cannibalism; Voluptuous Liz; Monty Looks for Love in the Arms of the Wrong Men; Suddenly Last Summer Is Publicly Condemned as "The Work of Degenerates"

[It was May 12, 1956 when Elizabeth Taylor, married at the time to British actor, Michael Wilding, decided to throw a dinner party. She would regret that decision for the rest of her life.

She invited, among others, Rock Hudson, her co-star in Giant *(1956), but her guest of honor was Montgomery Clift, who was filming* Raintree County *(released in 1957) with her at the time.*

At MGM, Dory Schary, the chief, had told Benny Thau, his assistant, "I don't want Monty to become another Jimmy Dean style auto casualty, so we'd better get a full-time driver for our druggie star."

On the evening Elizabeth telephoned Monty, he'd sent his chauffeur home for the night, planning to turn in early. He refused her invitation at first, asserting that he was too tired.

But she kept calling until he relented, although he claimed that the road to her house was too dangerous to drive at night. He'd also taken sleeping pills, but wasn't sure of how many.

To entice Monty, Elizabeth had also invited his best friend, Kevin McCarthy, who at the time was shooting a movie called Invasion of the Body Snatchers (1956), that became a cult classic.

At the party, Monty drank "piss-warm pussy pink rosé," and grew sleepy as the hours passed. Finally, claiming he was dead tired, he headed out the door. In his own car, McCarthy set out first, leading the way down the "murderous cork-twisted road" that eventually funneled into Sunset Boulevard.

As he headed down the mountain, Monty drove dangerously and at one point lost control. His car careened off the road, crashing violently downhill.

Hudson and Elizabeth were the first to reach the scene of the accident, after McCarthy summoned them by pounding on her door.

Hudson managed to tear away the smashed-in door to the car. Elizabeth crawled inside to rescue Monty, who was bleeding profusely. "A tooth was hanging on his lip by a few shreds of flesh, and he asked me to pull it off because it was cutting his tongue," she recalled. She reached inside his throat and removed two more teeth. His face had been virtually destroyed and was a bloody mass of pulp, evoking a horror movie.

In the ambulance, she claimed that his head had swollen until it was almost the size of his shoulders. "That beautiful face of his looked like a giant red soccer ball."

Monty survived to endure a massive surgical reconstruction of his face.

As author Ellis Amburn wrote: "When he recovered, he was scarcely recognizable as Montgomery Clift, appearing pinched and withered. The famous gullwing eyebrows were now shaggy thickets; the left side of his face was almost paralyzed; the once heroic jawline was soft and mushy, and his eyes looked dead."

A few years later, it was this new face, the artificial-looking creation of "the beauty butchers," as he called them, that confronted the crew on the set of Suddenly Last Summer (1959), where he met Gore Vidal, its scriptwriter.]

***

One hot dull afternoon, Gore was struggling to write a historical novel, *Julian*, when an unexpected call came in from producer Sam Spiegel, a man known for quickly getting to the point. "Will you adapt Tennessee Williams' one-act play, *Suddenly Last Summer,* for the screen?"

The play was originally paired with *Something Un-*

In the hours that followed Elizabeth Taylor's dinner party, the shattered state of **Montgomery Clift's car** in the image above mirrored the shattered wreck of his face.

spoken as part of a 1958 off-Broadway double bill collectively entitled *The Garden District.*

In the wake of *A Streetcar Named Desire* (1951) and *Cat on a Hot Tin Roof* (1958), *Suddenly Last Summer* was the third of Tennessee's plays adapted for the screen that dealt with homosexuality.

"Homosexuality was the love that dare not speak its name on the screen," Gore said.

After talking for an hour with Spiegel, Gore agreed to take the job, providing that Tennessee would not be allowed to interfere and that Bette Davis would be cast in the lead role of the evil matriarch, Violet Venable.

Within two weeks, Gore was flying to Miami to meet with Spiegel and Tennessee. Once there, he learned that previously, Spiegel had offered Tennessee the job of adapting his own play for the screen, but that Tennessee had rejected the idea.

On the other hand, Gore was intrigued by "the balls on Spiegel. Most producers wouldn't touch this controversial play. It dramatized both late 1950s cultural repression and the incipient countercurrents that would radically change sexual politics in the 1960s."

It was in Miami that Gore learned that Spiegel had already cast the film. "Your Miss Bette Davis can't do it, but we've got somebody even better: Katharine Hepburn herself."

Gore was disappointed but moved ahead anyway. The other female star would be Elizabeth Taylor, the biggest box office draw in America at the time. She was insisting that Montgomery Clift be given the male lead, although no company would insure him. His reputation for alcohol and drugs had more or less ruined his name in Hollywood. "To get Liz, I'm willing to take a risk, although I have two secret weapons," Siegel said.

"What might those be?" Gore asked.

"Both Peter O'Toole and Laurence Harvey are standing by if Clift fucks up," Spiegel told him.

Back in Manhattan, Gore called Monty, mainly to see what condition he was in. Spiegel had asked Gore to be a secret spy reporting back to him about Monty.

Norman Mailer had previously adapted his 1955 novel, *The Deer Park,* into a play. He called and asked both Gore and Monty to join him and his wife, Adele, at their apartment on Perry Street in Greenwich Village.

With others, Gore and Monty took over the reading of the script. Halfway through it, Monty, who had been drinking

Publicists at MGM deliberately chose this provocative photo of **Elizabeth Taylor** eyeing a man's crotch to publicize *Suddenly Last Summer*

95

heavily, began to slur his words. Within fifteen minutes, he passed out on the floor. At that point, Gore began to read both his own part and that of Monty too.

The next day, Spiegel called Gore to inquire about the state of Monty's health. Gore decided to lie. "He's in wonderful shape. Did a great reading of Mailer's script."

Later, Mailer said, "Regrettably, except in sophisticated circles, homosexuality isn't acceptable in any disguise in most of society. Monty has great guilt over his sexual preference. As an extremely sensitive man, he suffers more than most. But his struggle against his own urges seems to be destroying him. He's always miserable. He drinks all the time, not wanting to grow up and face life as who he really is. He has my deepest sympathy."

Half way through the writing of his screenplay of *Suddenly Last Summer,* Gore received an urgent call from Tennessee. "I was awake all night before making this call," the playwright said. "But I want—actually, I'm demanding— that I be listed as co-author of the film script, although I don't plan to submit one page of dialogue."

"Why this sudden change of heart?" Gore asked.

"These are crazy times," Tennessee said. "In this mixed-up world of emerging sexual liberation, I think, baby, that *Suddenly* might be a shoo-in for an Oscar for Best Script. As you know, I'm not exactly opposed to accepting an occasional literary prize."

After an hour of argument, Gore caved in, later writing, "The Bird *[his nickname for Tennessee]* was ravenous for prizes."

After the film opened to scathing reviews, Tennessee expressed regret at being listed as the co-author. When the reviewers attacked the subject matter—sodomy, incest, and cannibalism—Tennessee told reporters, "Blame it on Gore. He's always had a perverted mind."

During the shoot, Gore became very protective of Monty. "Between drinks and painkillers, he could work only in the mornings. Even under the influence, he was better than most actors."

During the first week of shooting, Joseph Mankiewicz, the film's director, had been respectful of Monty, even inviting him, along with Gore and some members of the cast, to a lavish dinner. Monty showed up drugged. Halfway through the dinner, he started throwing pieces of food at his fellow diners.

Eating with his hands, he made outrageous and provocative remarks. At one point, he said, "Let's go around the table. I want to know the size of every man's penis. As for the ladies, I need to know the largest object you've ever inserted into your vagina."

"Joe came to hate Monty," Gore said.

Even the artful (and lavish) use of makeup in this photo from *Suddenly Last Summer* couldn't fully conceal the ravages, post-accident, to **Montgomery Clift**'s face.

"One day, he made Monty repeat, over and over again, a scene where he must hold a document in a shaking hand. The result, when we heard the tape, sounded like a forest fire."

For Monty, some of the scenes had to be shot in multiple takes, as he could effectively deliver only one or two lines at a time.

"Since I knew Joe was plotting to fire Monty, I moved in with him," Gore said. "I was hoping to cut down on his intake of drugs and alcohol. Night after night, I had to undress him. What happened was inevitable. Late one night, I woke up to find him going down on me. I was not that attracted to Monty's body, but I reciprocated in my way."

"That love-making—and I hate to use the term—went on night after night. For some reason, Monty found comfort in my arms. He seemed desperate to be loved, and he wasn't getting his usual support from Elizabeth, who was deeply involved in her own turmoils and romantic problems."

Tennessee had called with suggestions for the script, although he'd agreed not to. The playwright was adamant that Sebastian Venable, Violet's gay son, should never show his face on the screen. "There is no actor in Hollywood who could convincingly portray Sebastian," Tennessee claimed. "Just show a man in a white suit running from the little boys who plan to cannibalize him. Sebastian's facial absence from the screen will only make his presence more strongly felt."

Hoping for greater box office, Mankiewicz wanted Gore to rewrite the ending to make it more gruesome and dramatic. "I will not depict the ghastly death of Sebastian, devoured by the flesh-eaters, but I want the plot to call for him to be chased, bludgeoned, and stripped by a group of angry young boys who are intent on eating pieces of his flesh," Mankiewicz said.

When Tennessee saw the final cut, he said, "That scene is the ultimate parody of a blow-job."

"In spite of all my efforts," Gore said, "Monty walked through the picture, giving a strangulated and neurasthenic performance. He spent a great deal of time on screen repeating the words of others, reformulating them in the form of a question."

Gore knew that Hepburn's character of Violet Venable was based on Edwina Williams, Tennessee's mother, who had encouraged doctors to perform a lobotomy on his sexually frustrated sister, Rose Isabel Williams.

The Queen of High Camp: Katharine Hepburn

Most of *Suddenly's* interior scenes were filmed at Shepperton Studios in Surrey, England, although the dreadful cannibalistic scene in the fictional "Cabeza de Lobo" was shot on the Balearic island of Majorca off the Mediterranean coast of Spain.

Several biographies have suggested that until she made *Suddenly Last Summer*, Hepburn was not aware of what homosexual men did in bed together and that Gore had to explain it to her. That, of course, is a laughable assertion about a woman who had spent decades in Hollywood among homosexuals. As a lesbian herself, she was deeply involved in a platonic relationship with another closeted homosexual actor, Spencer Tracy. Her best friend was George Cukor, the gay director, and her best female friend and lover was Laura Harding, the American Express heiress.

On the set one sultry afternoon, when London was experiencing a rare heat wave, a jittery Hepburn confronted Gore and Elizabeth, who were sitting in directors' chairs, discussing the next scene.

"Mr. Vidal, I talked it over with Spence last night, and he and I decided I can't go on with this film. Your script is just too vile. Give the role to that poor, wretched Mildred Dunnock. She'll play any part, no matter how demented. With all its flesh-eaters, lesbian nurses, sadistic nuns, it's all so *Grand Guignol*," Hepburn said. "No movie-goer will sit through this muck. The characters you and Mr. Williams have created are perverted. I do not understand perversion—never have, never will. I'm far too mentally healthy to be appearing in such demented trash."

"Miss Hepburn," Gore said with *gravitas.* "You understand perversion to your toenails. You'll give one of the most electrifying performances of your life. Forget Dunnock. Do you want us to give the role to Bette Davis? You'll probably get nominated for an Oscar."

"Perhaps you're right," Hepburn said before walking away.

She went ahead and finished the film as Gore had written it. In fact, she worked even harder to improve the demented and perverted quality of Violet Venable's character.

That same day, a reporter encountered Elizabeth and asked her what she thought about appearing in such a controversial film. "I've always wanted to appear on screen with Venus's-flytraps," she said. That was a reference to the re-creation of a carnivorous garden as a set within the movie.

As a kind of gag, her husband, Eddie Fisher, appeared uncredited as a street urchin begging Elizabeth for food. Frank Merlo, the lover of Tennessee Williams, also made an uncredited appearance, as did Gore. Gore and Merlo can be seen among the audience in a wraparound balcony observing Monty in his role as a surgeon performing an operation in a "surgical theater" below.

Mercedes McCambridge, cast as Elizabeth's greedy mother, recalled what an unhappy time filming *Suddenly* was for everybody: "Monty was coming apart right on the set, but Elizabeth could not provide her usual help because of her own misery. I read constantly in the papers about how much she loved Eddie Fisher. London was an inferno that summer. She and I walked off the sound stage to get some fresh air. Outside, she was in tears. 'My life is a shambles,' she admitted. 'I made a horrible mistake. I married Eddie and I don't love him. At times, I can't even stand him.' I could not believe my ears. Once we went inside, Eddie was there. She made a spectacle of showing her affection for him."

"Whereas working with Joan Crawford is a nightmare, working with Elizabeth Taylor is merely a disturbing experience," McCambridge said. "On the set she sounded like a fishwife, calling people 'assholes' or 'schmuck.' I thought she was completely outrageous. She was tender to Monty, but by the end of the shoot, she wasn't speaking to Hepburn. Elizabeth told me that Hepburn came on to her in her dressing room one afternoon—and she was rejected. That's why Hepburn was so bitter. A lot of those old dragon stars of the 1930s were dykes—not just Hepburn, but Garbo and Dietrich, too. Might I have the honor of adding Joan Crawford to that list—I should know!"

Tennessee arrived on the set and spent time with Elizabeth. He told her, "I was with Monty last night. He's washing down his codeine pills with brandy. But who am I to cast stones? He told me that after the accident, he has become impotent and the only way he can achieve sexual satisfaction is to peform fellatio on a man or else be penetrated by one."

"Thank you, Tennessee, you're a darling, but I really don't know what I can do with this personal data about Monty," Elizabeth said.

When Truman Capote saw the movie, he claimed that Elizabeth's final dramatic monologue was "the best scene she'd ever performed before or likely ever again. She should win the Oscar."

Mankiewicz defined her long, concluding monologue as "an aria from a tragic opera of madness and death."

After she shot that scene, Elizabeth became hysterical and couldn't stop crying for hours.

***

Throughout the filming, Hepburn had been consistently furious with Mankiewicz for his brutal treatment of the tormented Monty. She was also furious for his treatment of herself as well, interpreting his behavior as condescending.

On the last day of Hepburn's appearance before the camera, the tension between Mankiewicz and Hepburn was obvious to the entire crew. By ten o'clock, she and the director were screaming at each other. But once the camera was turned on her, the star became her carefully controlled, professional self, giving an awesome interpretation of her particular manifestation of evil.

By five o'clock that afternoon, Mankiewicz defined the experience as a wrap. Then Hepburn walked over to him. "Are you absolutely sure that that is all you'll need from me on this film?"

"I am absolutely sure," he told her. "You're free to go."

"Fine, she said. Then in front of everybody, including Elizabeth, she spat in his face, turned her back to him, and stormed off the set.

Wiping the spit off his face, Mankiewicz, in front of Elizabeth said, "Miss Hepburn is the most experienced amateur actress in the world. Her performances, though remarkably effective, are fake."

In contrast, Truman Capote found that "Hepburn is the Queen of High Camp as she stands in that fantasy New Orleans garden filled with insectivorous growths. Monty looks as if he is going to expire at any minute. Although I detest the film's scriptwriter, Gore Vidal, I have to admit *Suddenly Last Summer* marks the end of the 1950s. The public is obviously eager for a more candid expression of sex."

The National Legion of Decency, affiliated with the Catholic Church, relaxed its draconian Production Code rules for *Suddenly.* "Since the film illustrates the horrors of the homosexual lifestyle, it can be considered moral in theme even though it deals with sexual perversions," the organization announced.

In spite of their difficulties during the shoot, Mankiewicz later said, "Her role as Cathy was the best performance Elizabeth ever gave on the screen."

Time claimed that watching *Suddenly* was like being crushed in the "clammy coils of a giant snake." The critic for *Variety* made the claim that, "It's the most bizarre film ever made by a major studio."

Inadvertently, film critic Bosley Crowther increased attendance in droves when he wrote that the movie was about "the world of degenerates obsessed with rape, incest, homosexuality, and cannibalism." By "degenerates," he was referring, of course, to Gore and Tennessee.

"We could not have asked for better advertising," Gore said, in response.

"It stretched my credulity to believe such a 'hip' doll as our Liz wouldn't know at once in the film that she was 'being used for something evil,'" Tennessee said.

In contrast to Tennessee's objections to Elizabeth and her performance, he referred to Hepburn as "a playwright's dream. She makes my dialogue sound better than it is. She invests every scene with the intuition of an artist born to act."

The New York Times shrieked that *Suddenly Last Summer* "was a celebration of sodomy, incest, cannibalism, and Elizabeth Taylor at her most voluptuous."

Ultimately, she came to prefer *Suddenly* as her favorite film—"emotionally draining, but also emotionally stimulating."

In spite of the critics, and in spite of the doom-predicting Hedda Hopper, *Suddenly* became the fourth highest grossing movie of 1960, earning nearly $6 million in domestic ticket sales alone.

Far from emerging as a flop, as some in Hollywood had predicted, *Suddenly* kept Elizabeth in the ranks of Hollywood's Top Ten box office stars, a list that was dominated at the time by Rock Hudson and Doris Day in the wake of their highly successful *Pillow Talk* (1959).

Elizabeth told her secretary, Dick Hanley, "I think I will win this time, if for no

Film diva **Katharine Hepburn** objected to appearing in "such vile, perverted trash as *Suddenly Last Summer,*" yet delivered one of her greatest screen portraits.

other reason than the Academy overlooked my performance as *Maggie the Cat*. It's time they made up for that oversight."

"Don't get your hopes up," Hanley warned her. "Hepburn is running against you. That old dyke wouldn't listen to reason and run as Best Supporting Actress. That way, you both might take home Oscars."

At the presentation of the Oscars, Elizabeth once again had her hopes crushed. She and Hepburn cancelled each other out in the Best Actress category, the award going to Simone Signoret for her star part in *Room at the Top*.

Privately, Gore told friends, "Actually, Hepburn should have won. In spite of her objections, it was per-

Katharine Hepburn as Violet Venable wanders through her cannibalistic New Orleans garden, plotting a frontal lobotomy for Elizabeth Taylor. "By the time I tried to get out of my contract, it was too late," she claimed.

haps her greatest movie role. She even made me forget my original dream casting of Bette Davis."

But later, even Gore criticized the movie. "It was not helped by those overweight ushers from the Roxy Theater on Fire Island pretending to be small, ravenous boys."

Finally, as the years went by, Mankiewicz himself attacked the play, appraising *Suddenly Last Summer* as "badly constructed, based on the most elementary Freudian psychology."

Monty's Place in the Sun Grows Dimmer

Truman Capote first met Montgomery Clift in the early 1950s in Manhattan when he was living in a $40-a-month walk-up at 209 East 61st Street.

"I had seen him emote with Elizabeth Taylor in *A Place in the Sun,* and I thought he looked absolutely divine," Truman said.

"The elegant man I saw on the screen was not the actor I encountered in the flesh," Truman recalled. "At the time, Monty was living with this Italian named Dino, an unemployed airline pilot who was an absolute moron. Monty had been reared within a cultured background. Perhaps as a rebellion against that uptight environment, he was chasing after trashy men. He told me, 'If the dick is big enough, the class doesn't matter.'"

Since the earliest stages of his life and career, Truman had been intrigued by this kind of intimate inside gossip. "It's the Southern storyteller in me," he always said, if caught up in the delivery of a non-factual account.

As he sat drinking with Monty, he gently probed him to learn of his early relationship with Marlon Brando. At one point in the 1940s, they had been hailed as the two greatest actors on Broadway.

Before the night was over, Truman learned that Monty had met Brando backstage near the end of his 1944 run in *I Remember Mama,* a play that marked the debut of the theater-going public's interest in him.

Because of his baby face and almost poetic beauty and sensitivity, Monty looked even younger that the more masculine and well-built Brando.

Both men hailed from Nebraska, and often, they were up for the same roles, particularly in their future when Monty was offered the star part in *On the Waterfront* (1954) before Brando.

Monty admitted to Truman that he'd had an affair with Brando shortly after they met. "Perhaps it was more of a fling than an affair," Monty said. "Don't call it love. I think both of us, as competitors, were mainly checking each other out. How better to do that than having sex with your rival? It was just too intense. Our relationship was destined to burn itself out quickly."

Director Elia Kazan told Truman, "Both Monty and Marlon are often compared in the press, but their acting styles are quite different. Of course, both can play deeply troubled young men. Monty is more intellectual in his approach to a role. Marlon acts more out of instinct. Monty is soft, even fragile, in his characterization. Marlon is more brutish, as exemplified by his portrayal of Stanley Kowalski in *A Streetcar Named Desire.* Monty is far more uptight than Marlon. He once told me that he felt that Monty walked like he had a Mixmaster up his ass."

Monty admitted that on his first date with Brando, both of them, in the middle of the night, had pulled off their clothes and had run through the deserted canyons of Lower Manhattan's Financial District. "We were chased by a military policeman. We never could go back to our clothing. We made it to my apartment wrapped in a newspaper dress."

"For a few weeks, we were seen everywhere together in New York," Monty said. "I fell big for Marlon. He was in love with himself. We were both crazy—two real lunatics. We did stupid things, like run out in front of traffic to see if cars could brake fast enough. We'd go to an expensive restaurant, then run out without paying the bill."

The gay actor, Tom Ewell, who would later star with Marilyn Monroe in *The Seven Year Itch,* remembered seeing Monty Clift and Brando at a gay party in Greenwich Village. He told Truman, "Monty sat in Marlon's lap, fondling him and kissing him throughout the entire party."

"What happened to you two?" Truman asked Monty.

"I went to Hollywood before Marlon," he answered. "We found others. But it was a hell of a lot of fun while it lasted."

"Ultimately, what was Marlon to you?" Truman asked.

Monty's answer was enigmatic, "A mother substitute—that's all!"

Truman rarely saw Monty in Manhattan, but became intimately involved with him when he flew to Rome to work on a movie called *Stazione Termini*

[(1953), released in America that same year as Indiscretion of an American Wife.*]*

David O. Selznick had cast his wife, Jennifer Jones, as the adulterous American in the lead, with Monty playing her Italian lover. Its director was Vittorio De Sica.

Originally, Selznick had hired the novelist, Carson McCullers, to work on the movie script. McCullers struggled with the dialogue, but a few weeks later, Selznick flew into Rome—"gal-

Greedy, dirty hands reach out to grab **Elizabeth Taylor** in the final reel of *Suddenly Last Summer.* Traumatized, she flees, but her gay cousin, Sebastian, is devoured by these flesh-eaters.

loping into town and trampling over people like a herd of stampeding animals." He decided to fire McCullers and rewrite the script himself.

When he ran into trouble, he called Truman and asked him to fly to Rome to work on the script.

His bank account depleted, Truman took the job. Once in Rome, he discovered that filming had already begun. At times, he had to work at a ferocious speed, writing lines as the actors stood on the sound stage, waiting to recite them before the cameras.

In Rome, he became intimate with Monty, and they moved in with each other. Amid the confusion, both men found comfort in each other's arms. Truman learned that Jennifer Jones had developed a crush on Clift. "When she found out that Monty was gay, she became hysterical," Truman said. "She ran to her dressing room and stuffed a mink jacket down her portable toilet."

On January 7, 1953, from an address at 33 Via Margutta in Rome, Truman wrote his friend, Andrew Lyndon, in New York. Lyndon's companion, Harold Halma, had been the photographer who had snapped the notorious picture of a young Truman lying seductively on a *chaise longue*—the photo used on the jacket of his first novel, *Other Voices, Other Rooms.* According to Truman:

"I got started on a great feud with Monty Clift. For six weeks, we really loathed each other—but then (this is for your eyes alone!), we suddenly started a sort of mild flirtation, which snowballed along until it reached very tropic climates indeed. Nothing too serious, but it has been rather fun, and anyway, he is really awfully sweet and I like him a lot."

Truman later recalled that "Even though Monty is a terrible mess, I adore him. He is always high on something and at times becomes almost impossible for De Sica to direct."

Over pillow talk, the voyeur in Truman elicited all sorts of very personal details from Monty about his sex life.

Monty told Truman that he had been taught how to masturbate when he was thirteen years old, in the attic of his family's home, by his older brother.

103

He also said that he turned down the role of the gigolo in *Sunset Blvd.* because of its young man/older woman love affair. "I don't think I could be convincing making love to a woman twice my age."

[Truman avoided reminding Monty that he was involved at the time in a torrid romance with Libby Holman.]

Truman was startled to learn that Monty had had an affair with playwright Thornton Wilder.

Monty also claimed that he'd gotten involved with Steve McQueen when that then-unknown actor was working in Greenwich Village as a TV repairman.

"Steve—he called himself Steven back then—did more than repair TVs," Monty said. "He became more or less my boy. One night, he tended bar for me at a party I threw. There, he got to meet his dream girl, Elizabeth Taylor, whom I call Bessie Mae."

Monty also told Truman that he'd seduced Paul Newman when he was working as a temporary fill-in for Ralph Meeker, who otherwise held the star role in Broadway's 1953 version of *Picnic.*

"After a few weeks with Paul, he escaped my clutches because at the time, I was going through an S&M period. He told me that I liked it rough, whereas he was more vanilla. He claimed that when I kiss, I don't do it with love, but to give someone a bloody lip. We were not meant to be. Besides, Paul is too deep into the closet."

Newman would later tell his closest friend, Gore Vidal, "In a relationship, Monty just didn't know what the limits were. All relationships, even the closest ones, have limits."

Truman had only minor regrets when, at the end of filming, Monty had to leave Rome. He wrote to his friend, Lyndon: "Monty's leaving next week—going to Hawaii to film *From Here to Eternity (1953)*. So I guess everything will cool down. Just as well. It's all been too nerve-wracking."

Back in America, and during the years to come, Truman saw Monty less and less. He recalled a final encounter with him in 1964, when they dined together at the Colony Restaurant in Manhattan. "He had only one drink, but he must have popped a lot of pills when he went to the men's room."

"He wanted to go Christmas shopping with me, and I took him along," Truman said. "We stopped in this Italian shop that specialized in exquisite and very expensive sweaters," Truman said. "From one of the counters, Monty picked up sixteen sweaters and took this huge bundle out onto the street where it was pouring rain. He threw all of them into the gutter."

The salesman handled it gracefully, asking for Monty's

Montgomery Clift emoting with "Selznick's woman," **Jennifer Jones**

address so he could send him the bill.

"Then in a taxi on the way to his home, Monty went berserk," Truman claimed. "He insisted on getting into the front seat with the driver, where he tried to take control of the wheel in busy traffic. He nearly wrecked the car, and the driver tried to throw him out until I promised to give him a hundred dollar bill if he'd take Monty home."

"Monty was delivered, kicking and screaming, to his home, where his houseman finally took over," Truman said. "While I called his doctor, Monty's houseman carried him up the steps to his bedroom."

"Monty needed constant care, and I didn't know what to do," Truman said. "I finally called Elizabeth Taylor, who was staying at The Regency. She agreed to take care of him, so I had him delivered to her. She'd once been in love with him. But a person can become such a mess that he becomes impossible to love."

"That was the last time I ever saw Monty," Truman recalled. "He died a few months later. Such a waste of a brilliant theatrical talent. He was Hell bent on self-destruction. I, too, was following the road to self-destruction, but I was taking a different detour."

Tennessee and Donald Windham: Lost Friendships

Author Donald Windham, the longtime friend of Tennessee Williams, met the playwright in 1940. "He immediately made a pass at me," Windham claimed. "I was not flattered. I soon learned that he made a pass at nearly every man he met."

Windham was nineteen; Tennessee twenty-eight, though claiming he was much younger.

A bond was formed. (Windham already had a live-in lover.) "Tenn was a wandering gypsy in those days. but he wrote me from the road, his first letter written from Lake George, New York, on May 15, 1940. He'd gone there 'to check out the swimming and the beautiful boys.'"

Tennessee's last letter to Windham was written on February 5, 1965, while Tennessee was residing in New York.

By 1975, Tennessee and Windham had long ago drifted apart. The origin of their rift derived from their co-authorship of the play *You Touched Me!*. Windham had discovered that Tennessee was being listed in several sources as its sole author. Other fights and betrayals contributed to the destruction of their once close bond.

In 1975, Windham wanted to publish the first ever collection of Tennessee's letters, an anthology eventually managed through Holt, Rinehart, and Winston in New York.

This began a series of misunderstandings, denunciations, and threats of lawsuits.

After long years of separation, Tennessee had been approached by Windham, and he casually granted permission for him to publish the personal letters he'd written to him, mostly when they were poor and struggling.

Later, however, Tennessee had a change of heart and began a public campaign to discredit Windham. He telephoned columnist Liz Smith of the *New York Daily News* and pretended outrage, claiming that Windham "is trying to ruin me." Then he threatened legal action to prevent publication.

At one point, Tennessee accused Windham of "stealing my copyright."

As for their previous agreement, Tennessee maintained that Windham had gotten him drunk and tricked him into signing.

Tennessee really didn't have a case, and his threatened action eventually faded. Soon, however, other implications bubbled to the surface.

When Gore Vidal met with Windham in California, Gore said, "What Tennessee said about me in those letters is actionable. At least they show he used to be able to write. But they also show that he had a murderous streak in him as far back as the Forties."

In November of 1977, Robert Brustein, after reading the published correspondence, delivered a devastating denunciation of Tennessee in *The New York Times Book Review*. Windham himself called the critique "a nightmare come true."

Subsequently, Tennessee denounced Brustein as "ruthless. I'm too old to be afraid of him. He is despicable beneath contempt."

Tennessee had other published comments to make about Windham, citing his "petty resentments and embittered false pride rubbed sore by too little achievement in too long a career." He had other epithets as well: Windham was "pernicious, lacking in decency, self-serving, self-deluded, arrogant, derailed, jealous, a squirrel, a scavenger, a peddler, a failed writer, a false friend, around only when he needed something."

In April of 1985, Windham had some final thoughts about his long lost friend.

In the wake of Tennessee's death, Windham wrote: "There has been scarcely a day in the last forty years that I have not thought of him. And there seems little chance that I will cease to think of him now."

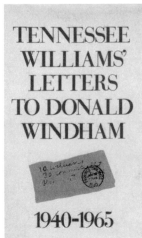

TENNESSEE WILLIAMS' LETTERS TO DONALD WINDHAM

1940-1965

Tennessee's letters to Donald Windham were written during the most creative period (1940-1965) of the playwright's life. Rich in anecdote and gossip, they display a young author eager for life, though occasionally filled with "blue devil moods of despair."

But when the letters were published in 1976, Tennessee attacked Windham viciously, claiming "an invasion of my privacy."

He told author Darwin Porter, "When I agreed to this, it was with the intention that Donald would publish the letters in a limited edition of five hundred copies, perhaps at some small publishing house. To my horror, they were issued by Holt, Rinehart, & Winston, hardly the small little press I had in mind. I feel betrayed."

Chapter Eight

Tennessee's Glass Menagerie

"An Act of Compulsion—Not Love"

An Alcoholic Stage Diva & The Texas Tornado

Two views of the emotionally tormented actress who "launched" the avant-garde's appreciation of Tennessee Williams, **Laurette Taylor**

The stage director and producer, Margo Jones,

was the first to realize the future greatness of Tennessee Williams. He called her "The Texas Tornado."

As early as 1945, she was producing his *Stairs to the Roof,* a "fantasy" about the International Shoe Company, for which he'd worked, at the Pasadena Playhouse.

[The subtitle of the play, based on earlier stories, is A Prayer for the Wild of Heart That Are Kept in Cages; *it combines romance and fantasy with a* Deus Ex Machina *ending.* Stairs to the Roof *was based on early stories that Ten-*

nessee wrote in the mid-1930s, including one entitled The Swan.

The play was written after he recovered from a nervous breakdown arising from his employment in that large shoe factory. He admitted that the play was a bit "didactic," but, even so, considered it suitable for the screen, believing that Burgess Meredith would be ideal as the male lead.

Six years after the play was written, he wrote some program notes for the Pasadena Playhouse: "When I look back at Stairs to the Roof, I see its faults, and very plainly, but still I do not feel apologetic about this play. Unskilled and awkward as I was at this initial period playwrighting, I certainly had a moral earnestness which I cannot boast of today, and I think that moral earnestness is a good thing for any time. I wish I still had the idealistic passion of (protagonist) Benjamin Murphy. You may smile as I

The theatrical producer and "Texas tornado," **Margo Jones**, was as extraordinary in her way as Laurette Taylor, Glass Menagerie's female lead, was in hers.

do at the sometimes sophomoric aspect of his excitement, but I hope you will respect, as I do, the purity of his feeling and the honest concern which he had in his heart for the basic problem of mankind, which is to dignify our lives with a certain freedom."]

Jones, the lesbian dynamo of the theater, had inherited a Texas oil well and used its profits to pursue her passion for the performing arts.

This big, rawboned woman fitted more into West Texas than Fifth Avenue. Their first meeting in a Manhattan brownstone was a disaster. This Amazon frightened Tennessee so much, he excused himself, ostensibly to go to the bathroom. Actually, he fled into the streets. "She scared the daylights out of me," he recalled. "When I hit the streets, I actually ran."

Instead of trying to make a deal with Margo, he took a job ushering at Manhattan's Strand Theater in which he wore a uniform that looked like that of a Prussian general.

Months later, in the bright sunlight of Los Angeles, Margo didn't look so intimidating, and he dined with her at the Brown Derby, with the suggestion that she might present You Touched Me! at the Pasadena Playhouse. [Written in

A Peeping Tom at Harvard;

Rosalind Russell Gets Dykey;

How Decapitation Ended One of Tennessee's Hot Affairs

conjunction with Donald Windham, this was the play that prompted Lewis Nichols at The New York Times to write: "Every playwright is entitled to a slight fall from grace occasionally. "You Touched Me!" is Mr. Williams's.].

At the time of their Derby luncheon, Tennessee, otherwise fretting over a suitable cinematic vehicle for Lana Turner at MGM, was working on a play called *The Gentleman Caller.*

In Key West, Tennessee recalled to Darwin Porter the most memorable part of that dinner. "Rosalind Russell arrived late and joined us for dinner. Ten minutes into the conversation, I realized that Margo and Rosalind were lovers. Whereas Rosalind on the screen might appear to be in love with Cary Grant, off screen, her secret passion was for Margo. That love affair had a certain irony. At the time, Rosalind was married to Frederick Brisson, the producer. He was in love with Cary Grant. Hollywood love affairs get very complicated."

As he came to know Margo, Tennessee bonded with her, claiming "she had the energy of Niagara Falls and an enthusiasm which is either irresistible or overwhelming."

Eventually, he became fascinated by Margo, who had spent a year in India and written a book on Hindu philosophy. She'd traveled around the world and had directed plays for seven years in Houston.

She'd used the profits from her oil well to launch herself into regional theater, introducing the theater-in-the-round concept to audiences in Dallas. In time, she would stage 85 plays in Dallas, 57 of which were new.

Later, it was Tennessee who brought Margo into the Broadway production of *The Glass Menagerie,* where she served as assistant producer to Eddie Dowling.

She would later direct Tennessee's *Summer and Smoke,* a flop when it opened for the first time in 1948, but highly regarded years later. Geraldine Page would be Oscar-nominated for her film performance in *Summer and Smoke (1961).* Margo also directed the original Broadway version of Maxwell Anderson's *Joan of Lorraine* 1946) starring Ingrid Bergman, who would repeat her performance as *Joan of Arc* (1948), a film for which she was Oscar-nominated.

Night after night, Margo and Tennessee worked to bring *You Touched Me!* to

Tennessee Williams, playwright wannabe, in 1939

"Yes, I have tricks in my pocket. I have things up my sleeve. But I am the opposite of a stage magician. He gives you the illusion that has the appearance of truth. I give you truth in the pleasant disguise of illusion."

—Tom Winfield in the opening soliloquy of
The Glass Menagerie

Pasadena. Somewhere in her booze-soaked mind, Margo came up with the idea she wanted to marry Tennessee.

When his father, Cornelius Williams, came to Los Angeles to visit his son, he was introduced to Margo. "She was bored and drank a quart of liquor and performed a half-clothed wild dance around the room." When she left, Cornelius warned his son about the "dangers of marrying a drunkard woman. Of course, I've been known to have a few drinks myself."

In 1944, Tennessee wrote Margo that he was finishing *The Gentleman Caller* "as an act of compulsion, not love. Just some weird necessity to get my sister on paper."

[He was referring to Rose Isabel Williams. As a young girl, she had sunk into madness, throwing violent fits and talking explicitly about sex with her puritanical mother, Edwina. She was threatening to murder her father for his rape of her.

Although lobotomies were relatively rare at the time, such a procedure was recommended for Rose.

Her skull would be opened, as a brain surgeon would sever the nerve fibers between the thalamus and the frontal lobes.

Tennessee would later use the real-life drama on the stage in Suddenly Last Summer, *when Katharine Hepburn (as Violet Venable) urged Doctor Montgomery Clift to perform a lobotomy on Elizabeth Taylor.*

For the rest of his life, Tennessee would be haunted by Rose's dangerous operation. "I always felt that somehow, I failed Rose. Perhaps I could have stopped it if I had been there when Edwina and those butchers were making that ghastly decision to cut open Rose's head. It's true Rose had sexual fantasies. But that's all they were—fantasies. I've had sexual fantasies. Who hasn't?"]

After his departure from his employment at MGM in Los Angeles, Tennessee finished writing *The Gentleman Caller* in the dormitory of some law school students at Harvard University. At some point, he changed the title of this "memory play" to *The Glass Menagerie.*

In the summer of 1944, he'd met a Harvard Law student, William Cannastra, on the beach at Provincetown. When classes began at Harvard, Cannastra illegally slipped Tennessee into his dormitory, finding a closet-like room for the young playwright, where they could have sex without attracting undue attention.

"He was one wild boy," Tennessee recalled, "but with a lot of male flash and charm if you could see beyond his eccentricities."

Most evenings, Cannastra made a meticulous, somewhat obsessive tour of the Harvard campus. A peeping Tom, he had carefully plotted X-locations on a map, marking spots where he was likely to see window shades left up, providing a peep show for him.

He was especially fond of watching young men seduce coeds. If the men attracted him sufficiently, Cannastra would later approach them and offer to perform fellatio on them.

Right before December, when Tennessee had relocated to Manhattan, Cannastra visited him over the holidays. The trip ended violently and tragically.

The Harvard student was drinking heavily. One drunken night, he boarded a subway in the Times Square area. He was leaning out the window to wave goodbye to a sailor he'd only recently seduced. The train rushed forward, and the student's head collided with a steel column, decapitating him.

"It was a ghastly end to a summer romance," Tennessee later said.

Tennessee, Accompanied by "The Gentleman Caller," from The Glass Menagerie, Seeks Flesh on the Hoof

Tennessee's agent, Audrey Wood, had secured investors and a producer for *The Glass Menagerie,* which was to go into rehearsals in Chicago. Margo Jones had already signed on as associate director.

The new producer, Eddie Dowling, was an actor, screenwriter, playwright, director, songwriter, and composer. When he met Tennessee, he told him, "I am a Renaissance man."

"Perhaps his background prepared him to become a producer," Tennessee said rather facetiously. "He was number 14 in a family of 17 children. He dropped out of school when he was eight years old to become a cabin boy on a Mississippi showboat. Later, he became a music hall singer in Brooklyn. At one time, he owned a small sausage factory in Los Angeles."

He also confided a deep dark secret to Tennessee. His name wasn't Eddie, but "Narcissus."

Wood had been impressed with Dowling as producer of plays by such authors as Philip Barry and a young William Saroyan.

Together, Margo and Dowling set out to cast *The Glass Menagerie.* It was Margo who suggested the great actress, Laurette Taylor, who was in retirement. Born in 1883 in New York City to Irish parents, she had once been a major star on the American stage and in films. But in 1944, she was a recluse, mired in alcoholism.

When Tennessee first met her in a Chicago hotel room, he discovered that she was drunk. "Not only that, she was a larger-than-life personality, a woman of mercurial moods and great eccentricities, taking refuge from life and its unbearable realities by escaping into romantic daydreams."

In Hollywood in the 1920s, she'd had a torrid af-

Eddie Dowling
Paramount

fair with screen heartthrob John Gilbert. Greta Garbo had lured him away. Laurette had distinguished herself in such plays as *Peg O' My Heart* *[wherein she emoted as the romantic lead in almost 1300 performances, beginning in 1912, endearing her to millions]* and *Outward Bound.*

"I had great sympathy for her," Tennessee said. "Far, far, from that lonely hotel, she knew the squalid life, what it

Eddie Dowling with **Laurette Taylor** in the original stage version of *The Glass Menagerie.*

was to be cut off from the world and love during her days of purgatory."

In New York, Dowling had delivered a copy of the script of *The Glass Menagerie* to her apartment. She spent all night reading it, and was in Dowling's office when it opened the next morning. "At last I've found the role of Amanda that I have been waiting for all my life. I can play that nagging, down-at-heel, ex-Southern Belle. I know her to my toenails."

Wandering the streets of Chicago at night, Tennessee found many lovers enrolled at the University of Chicago. He would pick them up, take then to his hotel room, read Hart Crane to them, and then make love to them for most of the night. "These young men, for the most part, were emotionally petulant, but sexual dynamos," he later said. "They were also very fickle. If you dared fall in love with one of them, it was like a fox's teeth biting into your heart."

Even as preparations for the production of the play were underway, Tennessee, in a hotel room, continued to polish the characters of *Menagerie. [They included the family's toxic matriarch, Amanda Wingfield, whose husband worked for the telephone company "and fell in love with long distance," leaving her to raise her two children under harsh financial conditions.*

Her son, Tom Wingfield, is really an autobiographical version of Tennessee himself. He worked at a shoe warehouse, but aspired to be a poet. His sister, Laura, has a limp, owing to a childhood illness. She also had an inferiority complex and was isolated from the outside world, preferring her menagerie of glass figurines, a unicorn being her favorite.

The Gentleman Caller is Jim O'Connor. A popular athlete during his school days, he works as a shipping clerk at the same shoe warehouse as Tom. Tom invites Jim home for dinner as a possible beau for Laura, not knowing that he already has a girlfriend.]

From the beginning, Dowling made it clear that he wanted to play the role of Tom.

As Laura, he cast Julie Haydon.

Tennessee was unhappy with the choice of Haydon, who had had an undistinguished film career in the 1930s, ending with *A Family Affair* (1937), the movie that launched the Andy Hardy series that made a big star out of Mickey Rooney.

[In 1944, the drama critic, George Jean Nathan, would review both the play and Haydon's performance in it. In 1955, Haydon married him. Throughout her life, Haydon maintained her link to The Glass Menagerie, *in spite of Tennessee's objections. In later revivials, as she aged, she assumed the role of Amanda once in a performance off off-Broadway. She lived to the age of 84, and* The New York Times, *as she had predicted, headlined her demise as "A STAR IN GLASS MENAGERIE DIES"*

The casting of Anthony Ross as the Gentleman Caller pleased Tennessee immensely. This was the first and only important role for Ross, who went on to make some undistinguished films at 20th Century Fox and some appearances in television productions before dying in 1955 at the age of 46 of a heart attack.]

Laurette nicknamed Ross and Tennessee as "Big Bum" and "Little Bum," respectively.

"Every night in Chicago, Tony and I went cruising together for rough trade," Tennessee admitted. "I scored more than he did because he'd get too drunk to pick anyone up. Finally, I felt sorry for him and began to purchase flesh on the hoof for him to enjoy if he were sober enough."

"He always pulled himself together the following day at rehearsals. His performance was extraordinary, considering how tormented he was. Or maybe it was that inner turmoil that made him such a good actor."

Julie Haydon
She married her reviewer

"It wasn't a different man for me every night," Tennessee said. "Sometimes, I focused on just one man, however brief the affair. I temporarily fell in love with this young Irish actor who was appearing in Chicago in a play called *Winged Victory.* He was remarkably handsome and perhaps more gifted offstage than on. I stayed at the Hotel Sherman, located within the Loop of Chicago. In my single room, this Irishman made the nightingales sing and sing. When I introduced him to Tony, he was very jealous of my catch."

"Alas, this son of Ireland deserted me for another, but I managed to hook up with another handsome student from the University of Chicago. A tall blonde, he and I used to go swimming in the nude at the Y, where he attracted a lot of envious eyes from the other

Anthony Ross
"Big Bum" to Tennessee's
"Little Bum"

male bathers. With this blonde, the nightingales continued to sing their hearts out. The student would explode with a crescendo, sleep for thirty minutes, and then the music would start all over again."

During the day, Tennessee attended rehearsals, noting, to his dismay, that Dowling and Laurette were not compatible. She denounced his lack of talent as an actor and, as a director, she appraised him as inarticulate. "Talking to him is like wading through molasses," she told Tennessee.

Firing back, he said that Laurette's Southern accent was acquired "years ago from some long ago black domestic."

As Laura, Haydon never impressed Tennessee. He called her "bright-eyed attentiveness a symptom of lunacy."

Tennessee was eventually introduced to the financial backer of the play, a shady Chicago entrepreneur, Louis J. Singer, whose main business involved running seedy hotels catering to prostitutes, drunkards, and drug addicts.

The Glass Menagerie had its Chicago premiere the day after Christmas in 1944. The initial opening was lackluster. The critic, George Jean Nathan, defined it as "less a play than a palette of sub-Chekhovian pastels brushed up into a charming resemblance of one."

Laurette Taylor got the best reviews.

In an act of malice, Nathan sent a bottle of liquor backstage to Taylor, knowing that she was on the wagon as an alcoholic struggling to recover. Tennessee never forgave him for this "wanton cruelty."

During the next two weeks, the play was presented to half-full theaters. But two critics, Claudia Cassidy and Ashton Stevens, championed it, writing about it almost daily. Cassidy called it "a rare evening in the theater." Ticket sales rose, and even the mayor of Chicago urged his citizens to go and see it.

A ham actor desperate for applause, Dowling seemed to resent all the acclaim going to Laurette and Tennessee. At one point, he told the press, "I rescued the young playwright from the bottom of a rain barrel." Tennessee, of course, resented Dowling for taking credit for nearly all of his success. He especially objected to Dowling's claim, "The poor, wilted manuscript arrived on my doorstep, and I struggled to rescue it from a dark oblivion."

Word reached people in show business, who stopped in to see it during their sojourns in Chicago, and Tennessee found himself greeting Katharine Hepburn, who one day would appear on TV as Amanda; Helen Hayes, who would play Amanda in London; Gregory Peck *["He gave me an erection," Tennessee claimed]*, and such stellar lights as Maxwell Anderson, playwright Mary Chase, Guthrie McClintic, Ruth Gordon, Raymond Massey, and Luther Adler.

After the run of *The Glass Menagerie* in Chicago, Tennessee packed his lone suitcase and headed for the uncertainties of Broadway, where both the critics and the theater-going public, in his estimation, "had fang-like teeth."

J. Edgar Hoover Warns President Harry S Truman:
"Tennessee Williams Is a Degenerate"

In Manhattan, on the afternoon before the opening of *The Glass Menagerie* on Broadway, Laurette Taylor seemed to be coming unglued. She kept excusing herself to go to the toilet to vomit. Tennessee himself was in such a nervous state that he later revealed, "I had to have sex every other hour to steady my nerves."

The play opened in Broadway's Playhouse Theater on March 31, 1945. "Even my nemesis, critic George Jean Nathan, arrived in town to see it again. I expected a blistering attack."

Actually, Nathan wrote that "*The Glass Menagerie* provides by long odds the most imaginative evening that the stage has offered in this season."

Tennessee's most treasured review came from Arthur Miller, who said: "The play in one stroke lifted lyricism to its highest level in our theater's history."

At the end of the play, the audience shouted AUTHOR! AUTHOR! From his fourth row seat, Tennessee rose to take a bow. He bowed to the actors, "thereby presenting a view of my posterior for the world to see."

Backstage, he congratulated Laurette. The play had opened on the day before Easter Sunday. She told him, "Jesus Christ will rise tomorrow—but I shan't."

The Glass Menagerie was swamped with awards, including the Drama Critics Circle Award for Best Play. But the Pulitzer Prize eluded Tennessee, that coveted award going to Mary Chase for her comedy, *Harvey,* a blockbusting, long-running play that opened on Broadway in November of 1944 about a kind and gentle man with an invisible friend who resembled a giant rabbit. *[In 1950, it was made into a movie starring James Stewart.]*

Dowling seemed to resent the many awards the play received, telling Audrey Wood, "It doesn't seem dignified somehow." She reminded him that he was benefitting financially from all the acclaim.

To its playwright, after years of struggle, *The Glass Menagerie* brought fame, adulation, and financial independence.

Summing it up, Tennessee said, "For the first

Two views of the most terrifying (and most deeply closeted) homophobe in the history of law enforcement, **J. Edgar Hoover**

time in my life, I've truly become Tennessee Williams."

Months later, when he was traveling with his newly minted friend, Gore Vidal, the young novelist found the older playwright "coldly realistic."

"Baby," Tennessee said to Gore. "The playwright's working career is a short one. There's always somebody new to take your place."

Before the year ended, the original cast gave a command performance of *The Glass Menagerie* in Washington. First Lady Bess Truman invited the cast to the White House for tea.

Hearing this, F.B.I Director J. Edgar Hoover telephoned the President, warning him that "Tennessee Williams is a degenerate and should not be honored at the White House."

After he put down the phone, Truman told his aides, "To hell with that. The biggest degenerate in Washington is Hoover himself."

Actually, Hoover need not have sounded an alarm. The night before, Tennessee had picked up a sailor in the Greyhound bus station in Washington, D.C., and consequently, slept through the tea at the White House. That night, when the play was actually presented, he appeared at the Presidential Box to apologize profusely to Mrs. Truman for not showing up.

A shy, frumpy and reluctant style-setter for the postwar Presidential administration of her husband, First Lady **Bess Truman** invited the cast of *The Glass Menagerie* to the White House for tea.

[In the years to come, on the stage and on radio and in films, Tennessee would see many actresses play Amanda, including Fay Bainter, Anne Pitoniak, Jessica Tandy, Julie Harris, and Judith Ivey, among many others. But his favorite remained Laurette Taylor.

The Glass Menagerie was revived on Broadway in 1956, with Helen Hayes cast as Amanda. Critics found her performance "acceptable but lacking the magic of Laurette Taylor." Maureen Stapleton, one of Tennessee's favorite actresses, met the same fate when she played Amanda on Broadway in 1965.

Helen Hayes as Amanda in *The Glass Menagerie*

Maureen Stapleton as Amanda in *The Glass Menagerie*

Even in the 21st Century, The Glass Menagerie would continue its tradition of Broadway revivals. In 2005, a production starring Jessica Lange and Christian Slater drew mixed to negative reviews. In 2013, the American Repertory Theater staged another production, starring the Tony Award-winning actress, Cherry Jones, as Amanda, and Zachary Quinto as her son, Tom.]

***

The date was December 7, 1946, and Tennessee was living in New Orleans on St. Peter Street when he heard a friend shouting up the air shaft, "It's just come over the radio. Laurette Taylor is dead."

Judy Holliday shouldered, disastrously, the task of interpreting the title role of a play based on a biography of Laurette Taylor, written by Taylor's daughter, Marguerite Courtney.

He was so stunned with the news that he couldn't respond.

After two minutes of silence, his friend called up again. As Tennessee later revealed, the friend shouted up an appalling one-liner: "I knew you'd be disappointed."

Tennessee was more than disappointed. He was heart-broken. He wrote a posthumous tribute to her, praising "the great warmth of her heart. There was a radiance about her art which I can compare only to the greatest lines of poetry, and which gave me the same shock of revelation as if the air about us had been momentarily broken through by light from some clear space beyond us."

[At the time of her death, Laurette Taylor was too prominent an icon not to be celebrated by the entertainment community. In 1955, her daughter, Marguerite Courtney, published a widely respected , psychologically complex biographical tribute to her mother which modern-day reviewers define as one of the first books ever written from the point of view of the child of an alcoholic. In 1960, after a laborious search to find an actress who could capture the essence of the mercurial Taylor (Vivien Leigh was considered), Judy Holliday was cast in a show directed by José Quintero. When Holliday became ill and had to leave the show, which had been rancorously divided during rehearsals based on bickering between its creative team and its management, it closed without ever opening on Broadway.]

Still "holding a special place in my heart for Laurette," Tennessee journeyed to Philadelphia to attend a performance of Judy Holliday playing Laurette during the period the play was still being fine-tuned for the Broadway opening that never happened.

He met and talked with *Laurette's* director, José Quintero, who told him that, "Judy is dying. She's got to leave the show. We're closing in Philadelphia. I don't plan to take it to Broadway with another star."

After Tennessee praised Judy's performance, she left to enter the hospital for throat surgery.

On June 7, 1956, after years of fighting the disease, she died from breast cancer two weeks before her 44th birthday.

Tennessee later said, "I'm sorry the world didn't get to see Judy Holliday as Laurette. She was wonderful in bringing Laurette back to life. Both Laurette and Judy died far too soon. The most sensitive moths fly too close to the flame. The dragonflies live forever."

"I Have No Affection for Aging Southern Belles"

—Helen Hayes

While *The Glass Menagerie* played in Chicago, Helen Hayes was also starring there in a play entitled *Harriet.* She and Laurette Taylor had long been friends. Hayes often met with Tennessee and Laurette after their respective shows. He would take them to one of the State Street bars for a relaxing drink, limiting Laurette to just two cocktails because of her alcoholism.

In ill health, Laurette's voice often failed her. Sometimes, Hayes arrived at Laurette's hotel suite with an electric steam kettle to which she'd add decongestants in an attempt to help restore Laurette's ailing throat. "I often stayed the night, leaving in the early morning after making sure Laurette could breathe properly. To save her vocal cords, she didn't speak during the day."

Laurette sensed that she might not be around by the time *The Glass Menagerie* opened in London. "She made me promise that if something happened to her, I would play Amanda on the stage in London," Hayes said. "I promised her that I would, although I didn't like the role of Amanda. She reminded me of all those aging Southern belles I had known during my youth in Washington. I also didn't want to follow Laurette in a role she'd brilliantly made her own."

When Laurette, as she herself had predicted, had died prematurely, Hayes signed to interpret the role of Amanda during *The Glass Menagerie's* stint in London. John Gielgud signed on as its director, although, in Hayes' view, he seemed contemptuous of American plays.

"All during rehearsals, Gielgud kept warning me that he doubted if *The Glass Menagerie* would find an audience in Britain. I had been told that he was given to throwing fits on opening night. He lived up to his billing. He became so hysterical I couldn't understand what he was screaming about. I was told by Tennessee that

No Southern Belle: **Helen Hayes**

118

homosexuals call a man like Gielgud 'a queen.'"

Tennessee also gave a bad review to Gielgud. "He's a *prima donna*, nervous and high-handed, rather snobbish. He surrounds himself with an entourage of middle-aged fags who still think they look young and pretty."

But Tennessee kept his contempt for Gielgud concealed. Gielgud even gave an A-list party for Tennessee at the Savoy. Tennessee spent most of the night in gay chatter with Noël Coward.

He virtually ignored guests Vivien Leigh and Laurence Olivier. "Had I known that Vivien would become in a few short years the greatest Blanche DuBois of them all *[in* A Streetcar Named Desire], I would have paid her more attention."

"Gore was also in London and was invited to the party," Tennessee said. "Gore told me later that Gielgud begged him to let him suck his dick."

After Laurette Taylor's "definitive Amanda," Tennessee was disappointed in Hayes' interpretation. "Helen told me my character was a nutbag. She was so diminutive, so sweet voiced, but could be a witch when crossed. I never cared for her in the movies or on the screen, even though she was hailed as 'The First Lady of the American Theater.' Give me Ethel Barrymore any day."

To Tennessee, Hayes expressed her personal philosophy of life:

"I've always been concerned with the whole of life, not the fragments. I prefer the positive to the negative."

"I've read a copy of your play, *Battle of Angels,*" she said, "Degeneracy has always been a part of life. But do we really need to dramatize it on the stage? Furthermore, I resent the promiscuity among actors. When I made *The White Sister* (1933) with Clark Gable, and *A Farewell to Arms* (1932) with Gary Cooper, both men propositioned me. I, of course, turned them down. "

He shocked her with his response: "If only Gable and Cooper had propositioned me, I would never have let either of them out of my bed."

Before the *The Glass Menagerie's* opening night in London's West End, Tennessee, with Gore, fled to Paris, where they went carousing with the novelist, Carson McCullers. The evening before he was scheduled to take a train back to London, Tennessee, with Gore, picked up two hustlers near Place Pigalle. After a drunken orgy, Tennessee passed out and didn't wake up until it was too late to reach his opening night in London.

However, his mother, Edwina Williams, and his brother, Dakin Williams, did show up for the premiere.

After the play, Edwina went backstage to congratulate Hayes. She introduced the star to her other son. "I want everybody to see that I have one son who is a gentleman."

Based on her understanding that the role of Amanda had been inspired by Edwina, Hayes didn't like Tennessee's mother very much. "She was everything I disliked in an aging Southern Belle," Hayes later said.

John Gielgud

119

As predicted by Gielgud, British critics lacerated the play, although most of them praised the performance of Hayes. One headline was typical—"BAD PLAY WELL ACTED"

Years later, Hayes told Darwin Porter that she was much better in the role during her three-week run of *The Glass Menagerie* at New York City Center in 1956. "I forgot about Laurette's interpretation of Amanda and made it my own."

Even *The New York Times'* theater critic, Brooks Atkinson, liked it better. He'd panned the 1945 opening, but after Hayes' performance eleven years later, he wrote that *The Glass Menagerie* was Tennessee's finest achievement.

"He also said I was at the peak of my career," Hayes said. "But I knew that once an actress hits her peak, there is nowhere to go but down. By 1960, both Tennessee and I had 'peaked,' so to speak. Our greatest years and theatrical achievements were behind us."

Jane Wyman Plays a Club-Footed Wallflower, And Reagan Makes Off with Doris Day

A new saga in the very dysfunctional life of the Wingfield family began when Charles Feldman and Jerry Wald, as producers, set out to bring *The Glass Menagerie* to the screen. They envisioned it as a 1950 release directed by Irving Rapper.

Casting was a major issue. Tennessee rarely got his wish when it came to stars for screen adaptations of his plays. Originally, he'd wanted Teresa Wright for the role of Laura. "Her sad eyes and the aching vulnerability in her voice would make her ideal as Laura," he told Feldman.

But by the time Tennessee reached Hollywood, he had changed his mind, telling Feldman, "Only Judy Garland can capture the poignancy of Laura."

The producer had his own ideas. "I'm pitching the role of Amanda to Ethel Barrymore and the part of Laura to Jeanne Crain."

Over the next few weeks, Feldman ran into roadblocks and kept calling Tennessee to announce changes in his vision for the cast. In the first of these, he announced, "I think Gene Tierney should play Laura, with Montgomery Clift in the role of The Gentleman Caller." Tennessee at least liked the idea of Clift.

Two days later, Feldman called again with another change: "How about Marlon Brando as The Gentleman Caller, and Tallulah Bankhead as Amanda?"

"As much as I adore Tallulah, don't you think she's a bit strong to play a gentle Southern belle?"

Before Feldman called again, he'd spoken to Brando. "Marlon said he'll never work with Tallulah again unless the Earth is attacked by Martians."

[In 1947, Tallulah and Brando had starred together, with frequent outbursts of spleen, rage and fury, in the Jean Cocteau play, The Eagle Has Two Heads.*]*

A week later, Feldman called again. "I've come up with the best idea of all: Miriam Hopkins, that Savannah magnolia, as Amanda, with Ralph Meeker playing The Gentleman Caller. He's less than lovable to work with, but brazenly masculine for the role."

Although it had been pre-arranged that the film would be distributed by Warner Brothers, there were rumblings from Louis B. Mayer at MGM. He had called Audrey Wood, claiming he owned the rights to *The Glass Menagerie* because Tennessee, while on salary at MGM, "wrote the play on our dime. By giving this to Warner's, he's biting the hand that fed the little faggot. I'm finding it harder and harder to cast Greer Garson. But she'd be great as Amanda. I also resent Williams' criticism of my judgment at MGM."

[Tennessee had told the press that he had been dropped by MGM "in retaliation for my unwillingness to undertake another stupid assignment after I fucked up on Marriage Is a Private Affair *for Lana Turner."]*

Mayer's threat of a lawsuit did not materialize, and eventually, to his humiliation, he lived to see his own daughter, Irene Mayer Selznick, produce Tennessee's second film, *A Streetcar Named Desire,* for Warner Brothers, not MGM.

Tennessee was surprised once again when Feldman called to tell him that he'd just signed the British star, Gertrude Lawrence, to play Amanda. Tennessee knew her as a singer, dancer, and musical comedy performer. *The Glass Menagerie* would be Lawrence's only film in which she worked at an American studio with an otherwise all-American cast.

Since, contractually, Feldman had the power of casting, Tennessee relented, but nevertheless threw in a dig, "Is Lawrence bringing Daphne du Maurier to Hollywood with her?"

[Both Tennessee and Feldman knew that Lawrence and the world-famed novelist were lesbian lovers.]

When Tennessee actually met Lawrence, he was provocative: "In London, Noël Coward told me that he lost his virginity to you when he was just thirteen years old. According to Noël, the two of you did it on a train."

"That story is absolutely true," she answered. "I fear I scared off the boy from women for life."

With some reluctance, Tennessee accepted a screenwriting credit with Peter Berneis, the play's adapter.

Tennessee shuddered when he learned the details of the movie's final casting. The role of Amanda went to Jane Wyman, the former Mrs. Ronald Reagan, who had won an Oscar as Best Actress for her portrait of a deaf-mute, Belinda MacDonald, in *Johnny Belinda* (1948), a film that dealt with the till-then-taboo subject of rape.

Tennessee feared that Wyman was too old for the part, but the co-producer, Jerry Wald, assured him she'd be terrific. "Jane, of course, isn't fresh anymore. But unlike her in the past, she studies a character for weeks and throws herself into the part."

It was the director, Irving Rapper, who called Tennessee to tell him that the pivotal character of Tom Wingfield would be played by Arthur Kennedy, and the part of The Gentleman Caller would be given to Kirk Douglas, then in the first flush of his stardom.

Visiting the set, Tennessee met with Wyman, later defining her as "a strong, cold, and determined bitch."

He remembered her divorced husband, Reagan, dropping by the set to give Wyman a poodle for her birthday.

"I later met John F. Kennedy before he became President," Tennessee said. "I thought he was much too good looking and sophisticated to get elected. As for Reagan, there is no way in hell that I could believe this untalented actor would ever become president. It was inconceivable. I guess I don't know how to pick them in politics."

Reagan invited Tennessee to join Wyman and him in the commissary.

As he remembered it, Reagan and Wyman talked about which boarding school would be the right choice for their daughter, Maureen. "They decided on Palos Chadwick School at Palos Verdes. That's where Joan Crawford sent her daughter, Christina, instead of smothering her. I'm sure Joan would have decided on

Jane Wyman lovingly surveys her glass menagerie in the cinematic adaptation of Tennessee Williams' stage play. In the center is her beloved unicorn.

In private, Wyman collected glass animals, and even lent some of her favorites to the studio for the film. *Time* magazine found that with her blonde wig..."and her childlike smile, she gives the part of the girl half her age an almost equally poignant sincerity."

death-by-strangulation if she knew that Christina would write that horrid little memoir, *Mommie Dearest, [published in 1978]* about her adoptive mother. Maureen never wrote a *Daddy Dearest* book about Reagan, but that other daughter of his, Patti Davis, came close, or so I'd heard. I never read crap like that."

After Reagan told Wyman and Tennessee goodbye, he headed out the door. Ten minutes later, Tennessee left the commissary with the intention of beginning his afternoon walk. "Reagan was waiting to be picked up by someone. This blonde suddenly pulled up in her car. I strained my one good eye. The face was unmistakable. That blonde taking Reagan away, no doubt, for a session of love in the afternoon, was none other than perky little Doris Day."

The filmed version of *The Glass Menagerie* did not do well at the box office. Even Kirk Douglas expressed his disappointment. "Unfortunately, the movie was not well directed," he said, "and Gertrude Lawrence's vanity had to be appeased. She insisted on a flashback, where she was young and glamorous, so no one would think she was the old lady that she actually was. The elements didn't mesh; the movie just didn't come off."

Years later, Douglas would recommend that moviegoers wanting to see *The Glass Menagerie* should, in lieu of the version he was in, catch the one Paul Newman directed, starring his wife, Joanne Woodward.

Tennessee himself later claimed, "I detested the film. As I predicted, Lawrence was a dismal error in casting. The film version was a dishonest adaptation of my play. I would soon get used to that in Hollywood's other attempts to film one of my dramas."

Bosley Crowther of *The New York Times* agreed with Tennessee about the miscasting of Lawrence. He called her "a farcically exaggerated shrew with the zeal of a burlesque comedian to see her diffident daughter wed. Her Southern accent has an occasional Cockney strain."

Tennessee would also be disappointed with other filmed versions too, notably a 1966 TV premiere of *The Glass Menagerie,* starring Shirley Booth as Amanda, with Pat Hingle and Hal Holbrook as the two male leads. He retained his low opinion, even after actress Barbara Loden as Laura won raves for her "transcendent performance," and some reviewers called the film "one of the greatest broadcasts in the history of television." Booth was nominated for an Emmy.

"Whatever it was, it was not my play," a disheartened Tennessee said.

Although reluctant at first to take on the role of Amanda, Katharine Hepburn agreed to play the role in a 1973 version for television, along with fellow cast members Sam Waterson, Joana Miles, and Michael Moriarty. The teleplay marked Hepburn's first appearance in a made-for TV movie.

Dancer/actor George Murphy, **Ronald Reagan**'s best friend, urged him, "Dump Nancy Davis and marry **Doris Day** instead." *(The photogenic duo are pictured above in a publicity still for one of Reagan's favorite movies,* The Winning Team, *released in 1952).*

Reagan, who admitted that he had "Leading Lady-itis," later told Murphy, "I can't marry Doris now because I've knocked up Nancy."

Hepburn feared her sharp New England accent was wrong for that "Steel Magnolia" she was playing. She was right. Many critics noted how Hepburn's Southern drawl came and went. She also infuriated Tennessee by rewriting much of Amanda's dialogue "to make it right for me."

He forgave Hepburn when she told him that his character of Amanda "was the most tenderly observed, the most accessible woman you've ever created."

For yet another film, Paul Newman directed his wife, Joanne Woodward, in a 1987 film version of *The Glass Menagerie.* Woodward joined the long list of actresses who had attempted the role of Amanda. In his critique of that rendering, Desson Howe (known after 2003 as Desson Thompson), in *The Wash-*

ington Post criticized the acting and found much of the dialogue "time consuming, inflated, dated, and theatrical. The film's few good moments happen when mouths are firmly shut. Woodward is a disappointment, speaking in a low, squeaky voice—a kind of laryngitic falsetto. Newman emphasizes the artificiality of the theater and distances you from the play."

The critic for *Variety* found it "a reverent record of the Williams play that one watches with a kind of distant dreaminess rather than an intense emotional involvement. There are brilliant performances well defined by Newman's direction."

Kirk Douglas, with kindness and courtliness, emotes with **Jane Wyman** in their film adaptation of *The Glass Menagerie,* which he detested.

In Tennessee's ultimate summation, he said, "Nothing ever equaled that night of March 31, 1945, when Laurette Taylor as Amanda came out and cast a glow over the theater."

DESIRE—The Party Girl (Marilyn Monroe) & Tennessee Share a Notorious Playboy

Charles Feldman had not only produced *The Glass Menagerie,* but he arranged with Audrey Wood for the acquisition of the film rights to Tennessee's *A Streetcar Named Desire.*

Therefore, with the intention of introducing Tennessee—Broadway's hottest new playwright—to the movers and shakers of the West Coast's entertainment industry, Feldman decided to "throw a big blowout" at Ciro's, where Tennessee would meet *tout* Hollywood—directors, producers, A-list stars, gossip columnists, and studio chiefs.

The producer even convinced Wood to fly across the country to attend the party.

At the time, Tennessee was engaged in a torrid affair with a hot young Sicilian lover, Frank Merlo. On Sunset Strip, Tennessee took Frank to rent white dinner jackets for both of them, even though the invitation read "black tie."

The rentals turned out to be a mistake. At the door, Tennessee and Frank found that their names weren't on the guest list. Just as the doorman was rejecting them, Feldman arrived with a beautiful blonde starlet on his arm.

It turned out that Feldman had not included the guest of honor on the list for the doorman. He quickly ushered Frank and Tennessee inside without introducing them to the starlet, who uttered a brief "hi," in a sexy, rather breathy voice.

Once inside, Feldman, with Tennessee on his arm, made the rounds. Frank was left at the bar. Tennessee met the top guests, including both Hedda Hopper and Louella Parsons, who would write about him in their gossip columns.

Even though she was fully aware that Tennessee was gay, like her son, William Hopper, Hedda cattily asked Tennessee, "Which of our beautiful stars would you most like to date?"

"Ethel Barrymore is my favorite dame," he answered. "I like the motherly type."

Then Louella approached him. "I understand *Streetcar* is a dirty play and will have to be cleaned up for the movies."

"I based the character of Blanche DuBois on myself, and my impulses were never dirty," he said. "If anything, I'm like a character in the Bible. Mary Magdalene comes to mind."

"Is it true your agent is going to ask one million dollars for the film rights to *Streetcar,* which would be an all time high?" Parsons asked.

"Audrey Wood is here tonight," he answered. "You must ask her. I'm a poet and an artist, and never concern myself with money matters unless I don't have any."

Moving on, Tennessee was introduced to such producers as Samuel Goldwyn, David O. Selznick, and Jack Warner. "I also got to shake hands with many of the men I'd had wet dreams about—Clark Gable, Errol Flynn, Gary Cooper, Glenn Ford, and sexy Robert Stack."

Tennessee was delighted to be associated with an iconoclastic, avant

Two versions of Amanda, *The Glass Menagerie's* toxic Southern matron: **Hepburn,** "Inflexible and authoritarian"

and **Joanne Woodward,** with her "laryngitic falsetto"

garde producer like Feldman. He told people "Charles has more balls than any other producer in Hollywood."

John Wayne came up to Tennessee. "I just heard that Feldman, my agent, has bought the rights to that play Brando did on Broadway. Is it true it's about incest and homosexuality?"

"Not at all," Tennessee said. "It's about the enemy of the delicate everywhere."

"I think I'll skip it," Wayne said, sauntering off.

Feldman also introduced Tennessee to some of his clients, including Charles Boyer and Irene Dunne.

When Tennessee broke loose and wandered about on his own, he ran into

Perhaps **Gertrude Lawrence** (shown here with **Noël Coward**) was better suited to Mayfair drawing rooms than to the sweaty rigors of motherhood in St. Louis.

confusion. Because of his white dinner jacket, many of the guests sitting at tables thought he was the bar waiter. They called him over and placed their drink orders with him.

"Not knowing what else to do, I took down their orders and returned with their drinks," he said. "Nearly every table, except that of George Sanders, gave me a dollar tip, which was good money for the time. Before the night ended, I had made at least twenty-five dollars."

Near the end of the party, Feldman introduced Tennessee to the blonde starlet he'd seen at the door. He said she'd changed her name to Marilyn Monroe because it looked better on the marquee.

"In a town of phonies, she was refreshingly honest," Tennessee said.

She congratulated him on his success.

"My agent had a hard time peddling my play, *A Streetcar Named Desire,*" he told her. "I thought I'd have to fly to Hollywood to land on a few casting couches."

Of course he was joking, but she seemed to take him seriously. "I've been on a few of those myself. But I've never been kept. I keep myself. Hollywood is just an overcrowded, overworked brothel, a merry-go-round with beds for the horses."

"Darryl F. Zanuck told me that studio men like it when a starlet responds to their propositions,"

Arthur Kennedy as Tom, **Gertrude Lawrence** as Amanda in *The Glass Menagerie*

she said. "If they find you fuckable, they think movie audiences might, too."

"Well, you'll have to show me who I have to fuck out here to sell more scripts," he said.

"Forgive me for asking, but are you good at fellatio?"

"A first-rate sword swallower," he said.

"Good. Fellatio is the preferred form of sex, since it avoids birth control. Of course, some men won't go for it and demand it the old-fashioned way. I've only recently arrived in Hollywood, but already I've had three abortions."

"You sound overbooked," he said. "If you can't handle the demand, perhaps you'll throw some hunks my way."

"I'll see what I can do," she promised. "Actually, I think some of the men I date have homoerotic impulses. That's a word I recently learned. On my dates with them, they spend most of the night grilling me about the sexual performances of their male friends. They want to know everything, including penis size."

"I think I'm going to have a hell of a lot of fun out here," he told her.

"You've got to be careful," she cautioned. "Two months ago, I was invited to this party where I was told that I would meet some producers. When I got there, I found four actors waiting to gang rape me. I'll tell you who they are in case they try to trick you, too—Bruce Cabot, Steve Cochran, Lawrence Tierney, and his brother, Scott Brady."

Before leaving, Marilyn turned to him. "Loved talking to you, Mr. Williams, but I've got to work the room. Do you write plays with characters I could play?"

Charles Feldman
"Plugging Marilyn"

"I'm afraid not," he said. "I failed writing a script for another blonde actress, Lana Turner, and I fear I'd do the same for you."

"In that case, I'd better wiggle my ass elsewhere," she said.

[Time would prove him wrong. For the 1956 film version of Baby Doll, *co-produced by Williams and adapted from his one-act play,* 27 Wagons of Cotton, *Marilyn discovered a role she wanted to play, the title role of Baby Doll Meighan, a role eventually snared by Carroll Baker.]*

***

Marilyn Monroe to Tennessee:
"Are you good at fellatio?"

127

At Ciro's, Feldman also introduced Tennessee to the notorious playboy, Pat DiCicco.

DiCicco was already a well-known name to Tennessee. He'd been famously implicated in the 1935 murder of his first wife, the screen actress, Thelma Todd.

During the war years, he'd married the heiress Gloria Vanderbilt, which ended in disaster. He called her "Fatsy Roo" and frequently beat her, sometimes holding her head and banging it against the walls.

He'd once been the lover of the aviator/movie producer Howard Hughes. When that sexual relationship waned, DiCicco became Hughes' pimp, rounding up a harem of beautiful wannabe starlets willing to sleep with the eccentric billionaire.

Before the party ended, DiCicco whispered an invitation to Tennessee and pressed a note into his hand. "Ditch your boyfriend tomorrow afternoon and come by my apartment. The details are in the note. You and I have a date with destiny."

The hustler was tall, dark, and handsome, with a lot of male flash, and Tennessee was tempted. Before the party ended, Marilyn was leaving with Feldman, but she stopped to wish Tennessee good luck in Hollywood.

She whispered to DiCicco, "See you at ten tomorrow night, sugar man."

It was obvious to Tennessee that Marilyn was not only seducing Feldman, but engaged in an affair with DiCicco, too. Tennessee was convinced that there were others—"so many, many others," he would later say.

The following day, Tennessee made up some excuse to ditch Frank Merlo and took a taxi to the address DiCicco had written down for him. He arrived exactly at two o'clock. DiCicco was waiting with two bottles of champagne cooling in an ice bucket.

He answered the door completely nude. "He had a body worth viewing," Tennessee recalled. "Very impressive, indeed. In plain sight, I could see why he had attracted an heiress, America's so-called 'poor little rich girl,' as well a billionaire who liked to make around-the-world flights."

In the late 1960s, at the home of his Key West friend, Danny Stirrup, Tennessee talked to Darwin Porter about DiCicco:

"Pat had obviously heard that I was going to be a successful playwright on Broadway, with more money coming in from movie sales of my plays. Although he was in incredibly good shape, he wasn't getting any younger, and his notorious reputation was working against him. The bad publicity he'd received during his marriages to Todd and the Vanderbilt woman was very damaging. He was looking for another gig—mainly, me."

"Every gay man in America should have had sex with Pat DiCicco," Tennessee said. "If the Nobel Prize committee in Stockholm gave awards to hustlers, the prize would have gone to him. He was amazingly skillful, an instrument of the greatest pleasure to a man and, of this I'm certain, to a woman as well. It wasn't just the size of his proud possession, but his technique in making use of it."

"Of course, it was all so mechanical. He was a machine making love, hitting all the right spots. That machine was well lubricated, at least from a technical point of view. For sheer love making, it was the best sex of my life. But something was missing, and that was an almost total lack of passion. There was not one spontaneous emotion. It was as if every move had been carefully choreographed. But who says a whore has to love you?"

"I had to say no to a permanent arrangement with Pat, which pissed him off seriously. He would mark the first in a series of young actors and hustlers who bedded me during my fifteen-year reign as America's leading playwright. You would not believe the A-list movie stars who offered themselves to me. Many of the big names will surprise you, especially those with reputations as Lady Killers. You know who they are. I don't have to name them."

"Personally, I don't believe there is such a thing as a straight actor. At least I never met one. Even the most heterosexual of actors seem willing to drop their trousers for you if they want a certain role. These actors in their conceit seem to think that your lips on their genitals entitle them to a choice role, such as Brick in *Cat on a Hot Tin Roof,* or Stanley Kowalski in one of the many revivals of *A Streetcar Named Desire.* Think Marlon Brando and Paul Newman."

[When Tennessee returned to New York, he encountered a fellow playwright, Arthur Miller, one night in the theater district. At the time of their first

Overview of a Gigolo: Three views of Pat DiCicco.

Left: with **Thelma Todd** shortly before her suspicious death in 1935.

Center: Studly and alone, waiting for his next conquest, male or female

Right: with **Gloria Vanderbilt**. "If you've got the dough, bitch, I'm for sale."

Inserts: billionaire **Howard Hughes** *(left)*, and **Tennessee** *(right)*, who "Drained Pat to the last drop."

meeting, Tennessee had already met Marilyn Monroe, but Miller was years away from making the blonde goddess his wife.

The two writers spoke of Hollywood, Miller calling it "a place of sexual grat-ification but also one of danger. I find the sexuality liberating but also cloying."

Miller spoke with a certain literary flourish that was hard to decipher. "Hol-lywood is a contradictory mixture of certain scents. A sexual damp, I call it, the moisture in the creases of a woman's flesh, combined with a challenging sea-salt smell, the exciting sea air surrounding a voyage on the water and the dead ozone inside a sound stage."

"Whatever you're saying, I agree with it," Tennessee said. "Hollywood is all that, if not more so."]

Chapter Nine

Gore Meets the Glorious Bird

Rome—City of Beautiful Men—For Sale, CHEAP

Two views of **Tennessee Williams** *(the left-hand figure in each of the two photos above)* with **Gore Vidal.** "We traveled and cruised together before the bright rose of spring turned into winter's faded flower," Tennessee said.

Flush with hits on Broadway, with both of his plays,

The Glass Menagerie and *A Streetcar Named Desire* firmly entrenched as successes, Tennessee headed for Europe. For the first time in his life, he had enough money to live comfortably.

He'd met Greta Garbo when she came to see *A Streetcar Named Desire.* For his trip to Paris, she'd recommended that he stay at the supremely upscale George V. Once at the hotel, in the city's posh 8th Arrondissement, he felt out of place. "I never hated a hotel quite so much in a life filled with rented hotel rooms."

He checked out and headed for a seedy hotel off Place Pigalle. "It was teeming with hustlers and prostitutes, a real hot-bed hotel, and I felt right at home," he recalled.

From there, he could walk several blocks up the street to a notorious club called Madame Arthur. "Love was for sale at Madame Arthur," Tennessee said. "Men came here who wanted to seduce drag queens, but there were a lot of young hustlers there, too. Some of them had been hired by Nazi generals staying at the Ritz Hotel during the Occupation. On one Saturday night, I spotted at least a dozen Louis Jourdan lookalikes, and that actor had only recently

Gore, with **Tennessee**, in Rome, in a used Jeep, before setting out for a sexual tour of Southern Italy.

been voted the handsomest man in the world."

On this visit, Paris and Tennessee did not successfully mix, especially when he became ill. He checked into the American Hospital at Neuilly, where in later years, Rock Hudson would be diagnosed with AIDS. A doctor told Tennessee he was suffering from both hepatitis and mononucleosis. As strange as it seemed, he had never heard of either disorder.

Fleeing from Paris, he left the city by train to sunny Italy to recover from his illnesses. He was deposited at Rome's Stazione Termini, where he took a taxi to the Hotel Ambassador along the Via Veneto.

"I was in possession of what back then was called the God Almighty Dollar, and I had quite a few of them," he said.

A newspaper man from the *Brooklyn Eagle* had told him, "The Eternal City crawls with pickpockets and mendicant whores of all three sexes."

"As I walked the streets of Rome in those days, I rarely saw a man who did not have a slight erection," Tennessee later wrote. Along the Via Veneto at night, he noticed young men caressing their genitals as they strolled along, hoping to attract customers.

Post-war Rome was still forbidden territory for most Americans, except for members of the homosexual community, who flocked there in droves. "Roman men are known for their beauty, and they were available for the price of a simple meal in a trattoria or even a used jacket," Tennessee said. "Many of the best of them could be found on the Spanish Steps, posing without their shirts. Ostensibly, they were available for artists seeking nude models, or for something more intimate. It was a glorious time—in many respects, the happiest days of my life, especially after I met Salvatore Crocetti" *[Crocetti was identi-*

A Year Devoted to Sensual Pursuits in Europe

fied as Rafaello in Tennessee's memoirs.]

One night, as Tennessee was cruising the Via Veneto, he spotted a remarkably attractive boy at Doney's, a café frequented by the American expatriates. "He smiled at me, and I smiled back. I gave the doorman at the Ambassador a large tip to let me slip him into the lobby. Salvatore wore a tattered jacket and strings held his shoes together on his feet. But beneath the rags was a golden Neapolitan seventeen-year-old, as I found out later that night."

Salvatore turned out to be so skilled in bed that the next day, Tennessee purchased him a new wardrobe and moved him into the Ambassador. Later, they found a two-room apartment off the Via Veneto on Via Aurora, overlooking the Villa Borghese Gardens.

Salvatore spoke no English. If the two men had to communicate something important, they used an Italian-English dictionary.

[In years to come, Salvatore would inspire the young hustler depicted in the closing scene of The Roman Spring of Mrs. Stone. *In the movie, Vivien Leigh, as Mrs. Stone, tosses her key out the window to the young man in tattered clothing.]*

At Doney's Café, Tennessee also met a brooding Orson Welles, sitting by himself. He introduced himself to the famous actor, and they chatted for about an hour. Welles told Tennessee that he was in Rome working on a film script inspired by the life of Cagliostro. Welles just assumed that Tennessee knew who Cagliostro was.

Tennessee did not.

[The life of Alessandro Cagliostro (1743-1795, an Italian adventurer, mystic, con artist, and oculist, is shrouded in rumor, propaganda, and mysticism. In the 1780s court of the French king, Louis XVI, he

Orson Welles in a role inspired by the 18th century rake, con artist, and mystic, Allesandro Cagliostro

was implicated in the notorious, murky, and politically loaded "Affair of the Diamond Necklace" whirling around the head of Marie Antoinette. Her reputation (and that of the monarchy itself), was tarnished by vengeful accusations that claimed (incorrectly) that she had participated in a crime to defraud the crown jewelers of the cost of the most expensive diamond necklace in Europe.]

Welles ended up portraying Cagliostro in the 1949 movie, Black

Orson Welles with his wife, **Rita Hayworth** in *Lady from Shanghai.*

Magic.]

Tennessee decided to throw a party for Rome's American expatriates in his Via Aurora apartment. Since Welles was "connected," Tennessee asked him to invite several key American expatriates, friends of his, as guests.

"At the time, I thought that Orson was the only *bona fide* male American heterosexual in Rome," Tennessee said. "I found out differently. His previous conquests were legendary, and I heard about them when I lived in Hollywood. He freely admitted that he'd been a patron of prostitutes in brothels from Singapore to Shanghai. He was also reported to have seduced a string of entertainers, including Lucille Ball, Marlene Dietrich, Dolores Del Rio, and Judy Garland. He also didn't mind crossing the color line. He bedded both Lena Horne and Eartha Kitt…the list was long. Of course, he was known mainly for his marriage to the goddess Rita Hayworth."

At Tennessee's party, a drunken Welles made a number of revelations to Tennessee, all of which surprised him.

Welles told him that on his first visit to Rome as a young man, "A gypsy taught me to walk with a live chicken between my legs." Tennessee was too polite to ask why he needed to do that.

Welles had some homosexual liaisons to confess. "When I became an actor and a young director, I was the Lillie Langtry of the homosexual set. Everyone wanted me. Whenever I directed a picture, I always tried to seduce my actors. I make them fall in love with me before I cast them."

When Welles was introduced to Salvatore, he told Tennessee, "The Italians believe that any young boy is meat for a quick seduction, and it will have no effect on him and his masculinity as a grown man. Salvatore here will probably settle down with a little wife and have twelve children."

The distinguished guests began to arrive, led by "the American social duenna of Italy," Sir Harold Acton. The social historian would later write about the guests in his published diaries. He found Tennessee "a pudgy, taciturn, moustached little man without any obvious distinction."

He met Gore Vidal at the party. Acton found him "aggressively handsome in a clean-limbed sophomore style, with success written all over him."

Gore was taken over to meet the host. Tennessee had heard of him. His homosexual novel, *The City and the Pillar,* had just reached number five on *The New York Times'* bestseller list, a literary success he would not know for a long time.

At the age of twenty-two, Gore found the 37 year-old Tennessee "ancient."

Tennessee later said, "Unlike Capote, I got on with Gore, but only by the strenuous effort it took to overlook his conceit. He had studied ballet, I learned, and he constantly did pirouettes. He flexes his legs and then prances about. The rest of the time, he compares himself to Balzac and attacks Truman Capote. Gore is good-looking, with a keen patrician humor."

Tennessee told Gore that he'd come to Rome to "partake of *dolce far niente*" [*loosely translated as "sweet indolence"*].

Gore soon learned that Tennessee had "indifference to place, art, and his-

tory. He seldom read a book, and the only history he knew was his own. He depends on a romantic genius to get him through life. Above all, he's a survivor."

Gore was not impressed with Salvatore except sexually. "He was just another Italian kid renting his ass," Gore later said. "When I learned that Tennessee was seeing him only every other night, I booked him for those other three or four nights a week. I felt I could learn more about Tennessee by experiencing what he liked first hand in young men."

Gore and Tennessee hung out with the A-list of postwar Europe's avant-garde, including the composer, **Samuel Barber** *(right)*, depicted here with his longtime companion, **Gian-Carlo Menotti** *(left)*.

As Gore had his first drink with Tennessee, one of many to come in their future, he told the playwright, "I've encountered you before. Once I was walking up Fifth Avenue and I spotted you trailing me. You were obviously cruising me. I remember your blue bow tie with its white polka dots. Actually, I was cruising some other guy that afternoon, a hot marine. I turned around and gave you such a scowl that you fled."

Gore had shown up at the party on the arm of two A-list guests, both of them invited by Welles. One was Samuel Barber, the American composer, one of the most celebrated of the 20th Century. He was without his companion, Gian Carlo Menotti, the famous conductor, whom he had met at school.

The other guest with Gore was Frederic Prokosch, the controversial American writer known for his novels, poetry, memoirs, and criticism.

[Frederic Prokosch (1906-1989), whose novels The Asiatics *and* The Seven Who Fled *received widespread attention in the 1930s, remains one of the most mysterious figures on the American literary landscape. Born in Wisconsin, he spent most of his adult life in Europe, more or less wandering. He defined his life as a hopeless riddle: "I have spent my life alone, utterly alone," he claimed. "My real life has transpired in darkness, secrecy, fleeting contacts, and incommunicable delights, any number of strange picaresque escapades and even crimes. My life has been subversive, anarchic, vicious, and capricious."*

In 1983, he would publish his notorious Voices: A Memoir, *a self-proclaimed record of his encounters with some of the century's leading artists and writers. But in 2010, the book made headlines when it was shown to be almost wholly fictitious and part of an enormous hoax.]*

"There were a lot of egos at my party, but I don't think any topped Prokosch," Tennessee said.

In a corner of the room, where he held court, Prokosch told the other guests, "My most ardent fans are Thomas Mann, André Gide, Sinclair Lewis,

Albert Camus, Thornton Wilder, Dylan Thomas, Anthony Burgess, W. Somerset Maugham, T.S. Eliot, and Lawrence Durrell."

"Gore became a friend of this weird gentleman, Mr. Prokosch," Tennessee later said. "In those days and for the rest of his days, Gore liked to picture himself an intellectual. I did not. I was a poet of the heart."

As dawn came up over the legendary seven hills of Rome, Tennessee invited Gore to go for a ride in "the grandfather of all Jeeps. It sounds like a pair of fire engines in a fit of passion."

"I purchased it from a G.I. after seducing him," Tennessee said. "It has a defective muffler."

He and Gore were later seen racing around the fountains of St. Peter's in the pre-dawn Roman ritual of sobering up. As Tennessee claimed, "An American could get away with a whole lot in 1948 in Rome."

An Artsy, Alienated Expatriate: **Frederic Prokosch** in 1938

As he recklessly drove the Jeep, he told Gore, "I'm *molto umbriaco.*"

"What in hell is that?" Gore asked.

"Americans call it shitface drunk," Tennessee said.

On the Trail of "The Wickedest Man in the World"

One hot afternoon in Rome, Tennessee's new friend, Gore Vidal, invited the playwright to accompany him to the Convent of the Blue Nuns in Rome. "What is this?" Tennessee asked. "Get thee to a nunnery?"

The invitation involved meeting the widely acclaimed George Santayana, who had retreated to the convent with the "Blue Nuns" *[at 6 Via Santa Stefano Rotundo, on the Celian Hill, in Rome]* for peace, contemplating, thinking, and writing. Gore had to explain to Tennessee that Santayana was a world famous philosopher, essayist, poet, and novelist, a towering figure. Tennessee had heard of his famous line, however—"Those who cannot remember the past are condemned to repeat it."

Santayana was not at all familiar with the works of these Americans. He was more at home conversing with figures he'd met during his stint teaching at Harvard, including Robert Frost, Gertrude Stein, T.S. Eliot, and Walter Lippman.

At the convent, Santayana received Gore and Tennessee in a mauve-gray vest from 1890 and a Byronic shirt open at the neck. He was eighty-five years old.

During his time with Gore and Tennessee, he presented them with copies of his famous 1935 novel, *The Last Puritan,* which had become an unexpected bestseller. He told them that his book was a *bildungsroman [a novel centering on the personal growth of the protagonist.]*

During the course of his talk, Santayana revealed that he was a classical pragmatist committed to metaphysical naturalism. "I believe that human cognition, cultural practices, and social institutions have evolved so as to harmonize with the conditions present in their environment. Their value may be adjusted by the extent to which they facilitate human happiness."

George Santayana at the age of 81

"A lot of that went over my head," Tennessee later said, "but Gore at least pretended he knew what Santayana was talking about."

Even though Tennessee had not "tuned in" to Santayana, he felt his meeting with the philosopher was worth noting in his *Memoirs:*

"When we met Santayana, he was an octogenarian, semi-invalid, and a saintly old gentleman. He had warm brown eyes of infinite understanding and a delicate humor, and he seemed to accept his condition without the least bit of self-pity or chagrin. It made me, this meeting, a little more at ease with mankind and certainly less apprehensive about how the close of a creative life might be. His gentleness of presence, his innate kindness, reminded me very strongly of my grandfather."

***

After all that spiritual uplifting, Tennessee decided it was time he returned to a life of decadence. He invited Gore to join him in his old battered army Jeep for a tour of Southern Italy—the Amalfi Coast, Capri, and Sicily—"to meet the golden boys of the Mediterranean."

In Rome, both writers had been told that they might have to compete with "hordes of German women" flocking at the time to Southern Italy for sex, since millions of their own young men had been killed in World War II while fighting for the Nazis.

On their southbound trip in the Jeep, Gore noted Tennessee's work habits:

"He worked every morning on whatever was at hand," Gore said. "If there was no play to be finished or new dialogue to be sent round to a theater, he would open a portable file and take out the draft of a story already written, which he would begin to rewrite it."

When Gore once discovered him revising a short story that had already been printed, he asked why.

"Well, obviously, it's not finished," Tennessee answered, returning to his typing.

Perhaps Gore's most astonishing statement about Tennessee was that his "puritanical guilt drove him to relentless self-punishment. He was—and is—guilt ridden. Although he tells you that he believes in no afterlife, he still is too much the puritan not to believe in sin. At some deep level, he truly believes that the homosexualist is wrong and the heterosexual is right. Given this all-pervading sense of guilt, he is drawn in both life and work to the idea of expiation of death."

On the Amalfi Coast, Gore, along with Tennessee, paid his first visit to the little village of Ravello, which in time would become Gore's residence.

"We walked in the footsteps of D.H. Lawrence, André Gide, and Bocaccio," Gore said. "I vowed to return to Ravello."

That night, they descended on the taverns of Amalfi, where Gore determined that "many of the penises of these young Amalfi boys, when flaccid, evoke a piece of okra."

After Ravello, Tennessee drove Gore to the little fishing village of Positano, which he would visit several more times in his future without Gore.

After World War II, the village had been discovered by troops stationed in nearby Salerno *[less than 30 miles away]*, under the command of General Mark Clark.

Then, Gore and Tennessee took a ferryboat to Capri. An aging British homosexual in Positano had told them that Capri "had the tastiest young men."

Following in the footsteps of such artists as D.H. Lawrence and Noël Coward, they arrived on the island which the early Greeks had dismissed as "a haven of wild boars." Later in life, Tennessee would use the island as a setting for *The Milk Train Doesn't Stop Here Anymore.*

Capri also had a reputation as "the Island of the Sirens," a temptation to Ulysses. Tennessee became fascinated with one of the legends of the spectacularly debauched Tiberius (born 42 BC, died 37 CE), who had retired to the island after fleeing from the tortures, pain, and degradations he had inflicted on Rome since he had ascended to the status of Emperor in 14 CE. He and Gore visited the ruins of the Villa Jovis, one of several palaces the Emperor had constructed there. Gore told him that when Tiberius tired of a young boy or a young girl, he tossed them off the cliffs to their deaths on the rocks below, instructing his Centurions to hack their bodies, living or dead, to pieces.

"That depraved emperor knew how to get rid of a lover who no longer amused him," Tennessee said to Gore. "We might follow his example."

Then Gore urged Tennessee to drive his Jeep further south until they reached the departure point of a car ferry which would haul their vehicle across the Strait of Messina to the eastern coast of Sicily. From there, they would drive to the fishing village of Cefalù, once a Norman stronghold with a cathedral dating from 1131, 44 miles east of Palermo.

Gore had been reading extensively about Aleister Crowley (1875-1947), an early 20th century English occultist, mystic, ceremonial magician, and poet. The popular press of the day had dubbed him "The Wickedest Man in the World," and "The Great Beast 666."

Gore had been tempted to follow his controversial *The City and the Pillar* with an even more daring book. With an interim, working title of *The Beast of the Apocalypse,* it would have been based on the flamboyantly notorious life and legacy of Crowley and the cultish commune he had established in a small stone-sided house ("The Abbey of Thelema") in the hills above Cefalù,

Extracurriculars: Truman and Gore investigated the murky legacy of the most notorious occultist of the mid-20th Century, **Aleister Crowley** *(depicted above)*, sometimes referred to as "The Beast of the Apocalypse."

There, Crowley had built up an ostentatiously bizarre cult devoted to a creed of "Do What Thou Wilt." In time, and in the future, Crowley's writings would influence such diverse writers, musicians, and entertainers as Marilyn Manson, Ozzy Osbourne, Kenneth Anger, and Dr. Timothy Leary of LSD fame.

[Thelema, the religion developed by Crowley, was based on a mystical experience that he and his wife, Rose Edith, had shared in Egypt in 1904. According to Crowley, a spiritual being defining itself as Aiwass dictated a text known as The Book of the Law *(aka, Liber AL vel Legis), which outlined the principles of Thelema. An adherent of Thelema is a Thelemite.*

As Crowley developed his core of acolytes from his base in Cefalù, he wrote about and widely publicized his "Holy Books of Thelema," as reviewed, worldwide, by a raft of scandalized tabloid journalists. Thelema blended ideas from the Quabala, alchemy, tarot divination, yoga, astrology, sexual disciplines which included the Tantra, and various forms of occult mysticism that some clergymen and journalists, outraged, defined as Satanism. In 1923, universal hatred throughout the U.K. was intensified when London's Sunday Express *published the allegation that a 23-year-old Oxford undergraduate, a recent convert named Raoul Loveday, had died from drinking the blood of a sacrificed cat during one of the Thelema community's ritualized worship services. (More likely, later medics have surmised, was acute enteric fever derived from polluted water from a nearby spring.)*

*In May 2009, after protracted courtroom tussles that were widely reviewed in the mainstream and tabloid press, Thelema was recognized by the British legal system as a religion, as it has both a "Holy Book" (*The Book of the Law*) and a deity (Nuit, invoked mainly during rites of initiation) as defined by Crowley and by his later disciples.]*

Crowley was also an insatiable bisexual and drug experimentalist who staged orgies—many associated with mystical rites and a pervasive sense of the occult—the scope and breadth of which had not been seen in Italy since the days of the Roman Empire.

In Cefalù, Tennessee and Gore located and visited the ruined Abbey of Thelema, a small stone house whose interior was adorned, during Crowley's tenure, with cultish murals later highlighted in a film by Kenneth Anger and described in some of Marilyn Manson's lyrics. It had been abandoned since Benito Mussolini had ordered Crowley out of Italy in 1923.

Through a translator, Tennessee and Gore interviewed an aging fisherman who told them that during Crowley's tenure in Cefalù, boys and girls aged 12 to 16, rounded up from villages along the northern coast of Sicily, were involved in "deflowerings." He had been one of those virginal boys.

"He called me Sweet Flesh and buried his face between what he called 'the scented valley between down-covered hillocks.' He said the greatest treasure that could be given to a man's hot prick is the virgin arse of a tender boy."

"He was my tormentor, and the more I screamed and cried and thrust about, the more his monstrous assault on my buttocks continued. When it was over, I was bleeding."

The fisherman also claimed that Crowley "had planted his seed" in many of the women of Cefalù, and that some of their descendants defined Crowley as their ancestor.

"There were lessons that Crowley taught all of us, both boys and girls," the fisherman said. "That is, to rejoice when others inflict physical pain upon us, and to view such suffering as a celebration of life."

When Gore returned to New York, he found no publisher willing to distribute a graphic novel depicting the sexual (some said Satanic) contexts incited by Crowley.

[In 1908, W. Somerset Maugham had already used Crowley as a model for a character in his novel, The Magician, which film producer Rex Ingram had turned into a silent screen picture with the same title in 1926.]

Back in Rome, Tennessee sold his Jeep and told Salvatore goodbye. He and Gore had heard that Truman Capote had arrived in Paris and was virtually the toast of the town. "We've got to go there at once and put a stop to that!" Gore commanded Tennessee.

Tennessee was only too willing to go along. "After Paris, we can go on to England. After all these Mediterranean dark-haired boys and olive-skinned bodies, I'm famished for blondes."

Both of them would use that line when they worked on *Suddenly Last Summer* (1959), which originated as a one-act play by Tennessee that would later be made into a movie adapted for the screen by Gore.

Gore, in Paris, 1948

A Visit to a Male Brothel
Established with the Participation of Marcel Proust

When the pleasures of Rome faded for them, Gore and Tennessee made their way to Paris. They stayed briefly at the Hotel du Pont Royal, where they encountered Jean-Paul Sartre and his mistress, Simone de Beauvoir, in the bar.

Gore tried to strike up a conversation with them, but "these French Gods ignored us."

When they heard of the Left Bank's Hotel de l'Université, Gore and Tennessee moved in. "This hotel seemed to prefer young bachelors of a certain kind," Tennessee said. "I especially liked the hotel because its staff didn't mind if we returned with gentlemen callers at night."

In Paris, Gore began to refer to Tennessee as "The Glorious Bird," which he soonafter shortened to "Bird."

"A lot of people asked me why I called him that," Gore said. "The image of the bird figures in much of his work—the bird in flight, in poetry, in life. The bird is time, death. Tennessee once asked me, 'Have you ever seen the skeleton of a bird? If you have, you will know how completely they are still flying.'"

Gore and Tennessee were seen together so often that the Parisians they met just assumed they were lovers. "That was not the case," Tennessee said. "Gore and I liked boys of the same type, and we frequently traded them back and forth. We went out cruising together, but one night, we came back without catching any game. I was a bit drunk and suggested to Gore that we make it together in the sack."

Gore turned to Tennessee and looked startled. "Don't be macabre," he warned.

Except for a brief fling with playwright William Inge, Tennessee had an aversion to sex with other writers. "It was most disturbing to him to think that the head beside you on the pillow might be thinking, too," Gore claimed. "The Bird had a gift for selecting bodies attached to heads usually filled with the bright confetti of lunacy."

The highlight of their trip to Paris occurred on a hot summer afternoon in July, when Gore invited Tennessee to accompany him to a male brothel originally financed and subsidized (and frequently patron-

The greatest aesthete of the *Belle Époque*,
Marcel Proust

ized) by Marcel Proust. Known as the Hotel de Saumon, it was located between Les Halles and rue Réaumur. It was still decorated with some of Proust's furnishings, which Oscar Wilde on a visit had defined as "hideous."

Gore and Tennessee were introduced to an old bald Algerian named Said. In Gore's words, "He looked like an evil Djinn from *Arabian Nights.*" As a young boy during Proust's heyday, Said had worked as a prostitute in the brothel. Gore was eager to interview him about Proust's sexual preferences.

Said claimed that the fabled French writer always came in wearing a fur coat, even on a hot summer night. He never removed that coat even when he took a boy to one of the rooms upstairs.

"I always kept three caged rats," Said told them. "Anticipating a visit from Monsieur Proust, I made sure they were very hungry. Proust would insist that the boy he hired stick his hand into the cage containing the ravenous rat. Invariably, the boy's hand would get bitten. Proust would then go into rapture, as if experiencing some sort of orgasm."

Later, through a peephole, Tennessee and Gore observed about eight young blue collar youths, sitting around smoking, drinking beer, or reading newspapers. The ethnic range of male flesh was widely varied: There was usually at least one blonde from Scandinavia; a Slavic type; a young man from Senegal; two or three boys from North Africa; and the rest from throughout the French provinces.

Gore and Tennessee spent a lot of time walking around Paris, which looked shoddy after its long wartime occupation, during which no repairs had been made.

"One afternoon as we sat drinking at La Coupole, I gave Tennessee a copy of my first play, *A Search for the King,*" Gore said.

After making an ostentatious show of reading it, Tennessee announced, "This is the worst play I've ever read."

"Our friendship survived that attack," Gore said. "But he had mortally wounded me."

"As for Capote, I followed his lying trail like a truth squad," Gore said. "I heard the lies he was spreading and followed up on them, telling people the truth. Unlike Josef Goebbels, most people hate a liar, and I did much to destroy Capote's reputation."

London's Literati Entertain Two Gay American Writers

Midway through June of 1948, the literati of London seemed eager to welcome two emerging writers, Tennessee Williams and Gore Vidal. Tennessee arrived in time to attend rehearsals of *The Glass Menagerie,* where John Gielgud was directing Helen Hayes in the role of Amanda.

Gore and Tennessee arrived in the British capital separately. In London, Gore lodged at the Hyde Park Corner Apartments as a guest of the aristocratic

Edward Montague. Like Oscar Wilde, Montague had gone to prison for eighteen months because of his affair with a young boy.

Shortly after Tennessee arrived in town, he attended a party in Montague's flat. "I noticed a lot of rough trade belonging either to Gore or to Montague," Tennessee recalled years later in Key West. "Since there was so much of it, I stole only one of their young men that night."

At various parties, Tennessee and Gore met the literary elite, including Noël Coward, Graham Greene, V.S. Pritchett, and E.M. Forster.

Forster had read the play, *A Streetcar Named Desire,* and had high praise for Tennessee, who had never read anything by Forster.

In contrast, according to Gore, "Forster virtually ignored me, and I had read all of his books."

Tennessee was not impressed. "Forster looked like an old river rat to me."

At party's end, Forster invited both Gore and Tennessee to visit him at Cambridge, where he promised to show them the sights of that university town.

Shortly before the prearranged day of their tour, at the last minute, Tennessee bowed out, claiming, "I cannot abide old men with urine stains on their trousers."

Consequently, Gore traveled alone from London to Cambridge, where Forster later invited him back to his rooms. There, he showed Gore his unpublished novel, *Maurice.*

E. M. Forster

[Written beginning in 1913, with multiple adaptations during the author's lifetime, Forster intended to never publish it while his mother was alive, fearing the pain that the resulting scandal would cause her. Although it was shown to friends, including Christopher Isherwood and Gore Vidal, it was eventually published after Forster's death in 1971, based on the approval of the board of fellows of King's College at Cambridge, which had inherited the rights to his books.

Although they were reluctant to grant their permission to film Maurice—*not because of the novel's homoerotic theme, but because literary critics had defined it as one of Forster's lesser achievements—the aesthetic success of Ismail Merchant's previous adaptation of one of Forster's other works,* Room with a View, *eventually won them over.*

In 1987, Maurice *became a celebrated and internationally famous Merchant & Ivory film starring James Wilby, Rupert Graves, and Hugh Grant.]*

At another London *soirée,* Gore and Tennessee met the wealthy aristocrat, Sir Henry Channon. American by birth and known as "Chips" to his friends, he had married an heiress to the Guinness fortune.

Noël Coward | **V.S. Pritchett**

Unlike Forster, Channon praised Gore, having been enthralled by his novel, *The City and the Pillar.* He kept an elaborate diary in which he recorded his impressions of both Tennessee and Gore. He defined Tennessee as "a terrific Rodinesque character of force and vitality, and a great writer of poetic prose."

Actually, he was more attracted to Gore. "He wears his hair like a Nazi, *en brosse;* he is very dark," Channon later wrote.

"To look like a Nazi was to rank high in Sir Henry's rating," Gore later claimed. "He was a member of that pro-German set in England, the group that had been entranced by Hitler's envoy, Joachim von Ribbentrop, when he was Berlin's ambassador to the Court of St. James's. I had the Nordic looks, the requisite blonde hair."

Both Gore and Tennessee were invited to Channon's country estate at Kelveden, near Plymouth. They were introduced to Channon's companion, Peter Coates, although Gore suspected that Sir Henry was more sexually aroused by the British playwright Terence Rattigan.

Graham Greene

Gore later remembered Channon's dining room as evoking the setting within one of King Ludvig's Bavarian castles. "He amused us by telling us about the long letters he used to receive from Marcel Proust."

"I burned them, although I realize now I should have saved them for posterity's sake," Channon claimed.

Tennessee grew bored and wanted to leave the house party early. The following morning, as he and Gore were getting into a limousine to take them back to London, Channon had to break free from saying goodbye. He rushed over to greet the arriving Queen

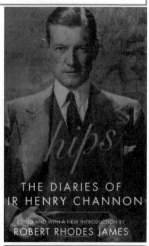

THE DIARIES OF SIR HENRY CHANNON

EDITED AND WITH A NEW INTRODUCTION BY
ROBERT RHODES JAMES

Sir Henry Channon

of Spain.

Back in London, Gore and Tennessee continued to be introduced to the British aristocracy, including Judy Montagu, an intimate friend of Princess Margaret. She was the daughter of Edwin Montagu, who had been a member of the Cabinet of Prime Minister Herbert Henry Asquith [*Liberal Prime Minister of the United Kingdom from 1908 to 1916*].

Judy told him she was going to marry the American journalist, Joseph Alsop.

"I find that odd," Gore told her. "I know him. "He's in love with this ex-sailor from Brooklyn, Frank Merlo."

[*Ironically, this was the same Frank Merlo who would later become the most enduring of all of Tennessee's love affairs.*]

Both Gore and Tennessee came to realize that, "We've lingered too long at the party," in Tennessee's words. "It's time to return to renew our careers in New York."

Each would return separately to America.

Before his departure from London, Gore told his new admirers, "I'm going back to lead the American people into the new Sodom, out of their pillar-marked wilderness."

Confronting General Eisenhower
in a New York City Gay Bar

Back in New York, although Tennessee and Gore pursued separate interests, their friendship continued. They met two or three times a week over drinks at The Blue Parrot on Lexington Avenue. In his memoir, *Palimpsest*, Gore referred to this meeting place as "a faggot bar."

General Dwight D. Eisenhower, home from liberating Europe from Nazi tyranny, maintained his offices upstairs, over the bar.

One night at The Blue Parrot, Gore introduced his "stepsister-in-law," the film actress, Ella Raines, to Tennessee.

Under contract to director Howard Hawks, and actor-producer Charles Boyer, she complained that, "I'm just playing second fiddle to male stars—nothing else."

Raines surveyed all the military men hanging out in the gay bar, along with their dozens of male admirers. She said, "It's just like being in an officers' club."

On several occasions, Tennessee and Gore were in the bar for pre-dinner drinks when the general came down from upstairs, accompanied by two or three of his aides.

Upon seeing him for the first time, Tennessee whispered to Gore, "Does the general know this is a gay bar?"

Gore told him that Eisenhower had spent much of his life having drinks in an all-male setting. "He probably doesn't think The Blue Parrot is anything out of the ordinary. After all, every man in here but you is so very discreet."

Tennessee was amazed at the intricate personal knowledge Gore had of American political and military figures. *[In 1996, Gore would write a very short (only 95 pages) book,* The American Presidency, *that revealed a number of secrets about American presidents, including how George Washington acquired his fortune; how Andrew Jackson broke 93 treaties with the Indians, and how Lincoln became a dictator.]*

"Ike sleeps in the nude," Gore revealed to Tennessee. "When he gets up in the morning, his personal aide actually puts his boxer shorts on him, and also his wristwatch."

Gore also told him that during the war, when Eisenhower was stationed in England, he'd had an affair with his personal driver, Kay Summersby.

Salutes from the Supreme Commander, future U.S. President, **Dwight D. Eisenhower**

"Well, I wouldn't call it a real affair. Kay knows my mother, Nina. She told Nina that 'Ike's stick didn't shift too well.'"

"Do you mean that one of history's most famous generals is impotent?" Tennessee asked.

"Exactly," Gore said.

"Poor Mamie," Tennessee said. "How dreadful."

Because he was seen so frequently at The Blue Parrot, word got around that Eisenhower was secretly bisexual.

But when he ran for president against the Democratic candidate, Adlai Stevenson, it was the former governor of Illinois who would be outed as a homosexual.

Gore later told Tennessee that close friends of Stevenson referred to him as "Adeline," and that police officers in both Illinois and Maryland had told FBI agents that Stevenson had been arrested for homosexual offenses, and that the records for those arrests had later been expunged.

Tennessee had been mistaken in thinking that Eisenhower might be gay friendly. Once he was installed as President, he became a major homophobe. When he moved into the Oval Office in 1953, to the dismay of both Gore and Tennessee, he signed an executive order listing "sexual perversion" as sufficient grounds for dismissal or exclusion from employment in any capacity by the Federal government.

Throughout his administration, ending in 1961, State Department officials appeared annually in Congress, proudly reporting the number of homosexuals they'd fired during the previous year.

During the Cold War, the State Department fired more homosexuals than communists, in spite of the Red Scare of Senator Joseph McCarthy of Wisconsin, who was later revealed to be a homosexual himself.

Gore was delighted to read *The Washington Post's* comment: "Just as the ancient Aztecs or Mayans used to sacrifice virgins, annually, to propitiate the gods and to gain favors from them, the State Department sacrifices homosexuals, annually, to propitiate the House Appropriations Committee, and to gain money from them."

One night at The Blue Parrot, Gore revealed his secret ambition to Tennessee.

"I want to become the third gay president of the United States. Eleanor Roosevelt has already promised she'll back me."

"The third?" asked an astonished Tennessee. "Who were the first and second?"

"You should read more American history," Gore said. "The first was a lifelong bachelor, James Buchanan, the president before Lincoln. His lover was William Rufus King, who had been Franklin Pierce's Vice President. Congressmen ridiculed them as 'Miss Nancy and Aunt Fancy," or sometimes just "President and Mrs. Buchanan.'"

"The other was Abraham Lincoln. In 1837, Lincoln was 28. In Springfield, Illinois, he met 23-year-old Joshua Speed. Speed invited this tall stranger to share his bed, and Lincoln did so for the next four years until he decided he'd better get married for appearances sake. Lincoln's law partner, William Herndon, claimed that Lincoln loved Speed 'more than anyone dead or living.'"

"Well, Gore, count on my support if you want to run for President one day, providing you don't name Truman Capote as your vice presidential running mate," Tennessee said.

"The country may be ready for me," Gore said, "but not Capote. Once he speaks, and America hears that voice, the election will be lost."

Twilight Time for the Wounded Bird

Throughout the 1960s, mired in drink and drugs, Tennessee did not see a lot of Gore. When they eventually met again in Manhattan, Tennessee confessed, "I slept through the Sixties."

"Well, you didn't miss a thing, baby," Gore said. "If you missed the sixties, Bird, God knows what you're going to do with the seventies."

"I'll tell you exactly what I'm going to do in this new decade," Tennessee said. "I'm going to overcome the bitter, queenie attacks of the critics. Once again, I plan to achieve the kind of success I had in the late 40s and 50s. I feel that success is within my reach. I know it will come again."

"You'll defy F. Scott Fitzgerald then," Gore said. "He said there are no second acts in American lives."

"I'll give Fitzgerald the finger," Tennessee said. "In fact, I plan to write a long play about Zelda and him. I'm calling it *Clothes for a Summer Hotel.*"

In 1970, Gore published an article about Tennessee in *Esquire.*

Tennessee told his friend, Stanley Mills Haggart, "According to the Gospel of Gore Vidal, I'm a bit mad. He also suggests I'm a communist when, in fact, I am merely an old-fashioned anarchist."

In 1976, Gore reviewed Tennessee's autobiography, entitled *Memoirs*. Shortly after his review was published, he ran into Tennessee in the lobby of a Broadway theater. Tennessee's cloudy blue eyes zeroed in on Gore.

"When your review appeared, my *Memoirs* was number five on the non-fiction bestseller list of *The New York Times*. Within two weeks of your review, I'd completely fallen off the list."

Later, Gore claimed "After that encounter, I never saw the Bird, or at least very much of him, in his final years. The barbiturate Nembutal and vodka are a lethal combination, and they did his brain no good. But the writing was often still marvelous; also, more adventurous than before."

"Unfortunately, he'd lost interest in people; he doesn't read a newspaper, doesn't read a book, doesn't know what country he's in. He's a romantic writer who is essentially working out of his own past, and that kind of writer has just so many cards."

In Gore's final summation of Tennessee, delivered after the playwright's death in 1983, he said: "The best of his plays are as permanent as anything can be in the Age of Kleenex."

Tennessee Williams

Chapter Ten

Tennessee Confronts Truman's "Forked Tongue"

(Truman is) "A Sodomite's Delight, A Monster Unleased from Vaginal Portals" — *Tennessee Williams*

Three views of **Truman Capote**,
a young man of contradictions and seemingly multiple personalities

In the closely knit circle of gay authors who thrived in the

late 1940s, it seemed inevitable that Tennessee would eventually meet the rising young novelist, Truman Capote.

"When I first met Truman," Tennessee recalled, "I thought he was rather cute, very slim, with a little boy's ass—a sodomite's delight. From the beginning, I knew his impulse, and his personal style, involved being catty. At first, his remarks were relatively harmless, but, as he aged, they became more malicious."

"Right away, he told me he'd been born in New Orleans, which has a certain kind of glamor attached to it. I soon learned that Truman liked to take liberties with the truth. He was actually born in Huntsville, Alabama, which has no glamour whatsoever." *[Editors note: Actually, Truman had been born in New Orleans, moving when he was four to Monroeville, Alabama.]*

If Tennessee's memory was correct, he first met Truman at a small dinner party at the home of Andrew Lyndon and his companion, photographer Harold Halma, before they had a serious rift in their relationship and separated.

When Truman went into the kitchen of their small apartment to get a drink, he heard Tennessee tell his host, "Baby, I think your little friend is charming."

Yet as the decades passed, Tennessee would reverse that opinion on countless occasions.

Carson McCullers, one of Tennessee's closest friends, had attempted to turn him against Truman even before they actually met. *[In Tennessee's view, Carson was "spitefully jealous" of Truman for the success of his first novel,* Other Voices, Other Rooms.*]* She accused him of "stealing my style and getting acclaim he does not deserve. He is a derivative artist raiding my literary pantry."

Carson McCullers

Tennessee wrote back, "Aren't you allowing yourself to judge this little boy a bit too astringently?" he asked. "I see him as an opportunist and a careerist and a derivative writer whose tiny feet have attempted to lift the ten league boots of Carson McCullers and succeeded only in tripping him up absurdly. But surely, he is not one of the bad boys. His little face, as photographed by Cecil Beaton against a vast panorama of white roses, has a look of prenatal sorrow, as if he were still in the womb and already suspected how cold the world is beyond the vaginal portals."

Carson wrote back: "I wonder how Truman missed being the flower girl at the

Clark Gable (as Rhett Butler) woos **Vivien Leigh** (as Scarlett O'Hara) in *Gone With the Wind* (1939)

Casting Crisis: Scarlett and Rhett are Considered for the Roles of Blanche DuBois & Stanley Kowalski

recent wedding of Rita Hayworth to Prince Aly Khan?"

In the vanguard of what later evolved into a major flood of North American visitors to war-ravaged Europe, all three members of the "Pink Triangle"—Gore Vidal, Tennessee Williams, and Truman Capote—toured Italy, France, and England in late 1948 and '49. They either hooked up with each other, or, in the case of Truman and Gore, tried to avoid each other whenever possible.

In Paris, during dinner with Tennessee in a Left Bank bistro, Truman said to him, "Now that you're enjoying the catastrophe of success, I noticed that the press does not discuss your sexuality except for some vague allusions. With me, it's different. They all but call me 'Faggot of the Year.'"

"There's enough bad press out there to guarantee that I won't be voted Father of the Year at the Elks Club," Tennessee said.

The following night, Tennessee did something impish by inviting both Truman and Gore to attend a *boîte [nightclub]* with him on Paris' Left Bank.

Truman had once worked as a professional dancer, or so he said," Tennessee recalled. "As for Gore, he readily admitted, 'I'm no Ann Miller.'"

The nightclub had imported a group of black musicians from New Orleans. Truman asked Gore to dance to the sound of "Bongo, Bongo, Bongo, I Don't Want to Leave the Congo." Gore rejected his offer, and consequently, Truman monopolized the dance floor by himself.

"The rest of the night was spent with Gore and Truman shooting verbal daggers at each other's contributions to literature, or lack thereof—mostly the latter," Tennessee said.

Tennessee was traveling at the time with his new lover, Frank Merlo, a former hustler who, oddly enough, specialized in seducing successful authors. Truman was traveling with Jack Dunphy, who had danced as a chorus boy in the Broadway hit, *Oklahoma!*.

The two writers and their newly acquired lovers agreed to reunite, later, in Rome.

In the aftermath of that night out together in Paris, Tennessee wrote a let-

Frank Merlo *(left)* with **Tennessee Williams**   **Truman Capote** *(left)* with **Jack Dunphy**

ter to his literary agent, Audrey Wood, in which he was rather contemptuous of the many American writers passing through Rome, including "Truman and his paramour." Tennessee collectively referred to these writers as "the spiteful sisterhood."

After rendezvousing in Rome, the four of them agreed to drive south to Naples where they would take a ferry to the offshore island of Ischia, known for its spa treatments.

At a café table at the departure point for the ferryboat headed to Ischia, Truman related a story he'd heard about the Texas-born producer, Margo Jones, who had labored to bring Tennessee's latest play, *Summer and Smoke,* to the stage.

In front of Tennessee, Truman recited a provocative story: "On the night before the play's opening, Margo assembled the cast for a macabre pep talk. To the assembled cast, she said, 'This is the play of a dying man. 'You've got to give it all you've got.'"

His words incensed the hypochondriacal Tennessee. Rising abruptly, in fury, from a seat at a small table, he turned it over, spilling the drinks that had rested upon it onto Truman's lap. Then Tennessee and Frank stormed out of the café, but not before announcing that they would not go to Ischia with Truman and Dunphy.

Truman later claimed, "I didn't realize that I was touching the nerve nearest to Tennessee's heart. I didn't think what I said would upset him. After all, every day he got up, he announced to us, '*Ah'm a dyin' man!*'"

In a March, 1949, letter to Audrey Wood, Tennessee wrote, "I am not sure how much of Capote I can take. He is completely disarming; and then all at once, out shoots the forked tongue. And the sting is all but mortal."

A few days later, Tennessee, who had remained behind in Naples, finally decided to forgive Truman, and consequently, he and Frank sailed to Ischia to join the novelist and Dunphy.

The traveling couples hooked up again in London. Truman found Tennessee very depressed over the bad reviews generated by the British press in the wake of the London opening of *The Glass Menagerie,* starring Helen Hayes. Truman tried to cheer him up. "Good God, who cares what anyone in England thinks?"

Both Tennessee and Truman had booked tickets for themselves and their companions to sail back to New York aboard the *Queen Mary,* sailing from Southampton, for the Port of New York. Before he went aboard, Tennessee posted a letter to his friend, Donald Windham. "Please stop referring to Capote as a child. He is more of a sweetly vicious old lady."

Truman and Tennessee were the two new celebrities aboard, joining more legendary icons—Clark Gable, Spencer Tracy, and Charles Boyer—all of whom were onboard and returning to New York after stints or sojourns in Europe.

"Truman was an amusing shipboard companion," said Tennessee. "But at times, his pranks became tiresome. One night, he switched around all the shoes his fellow passengers had set out in the corridors to be shined. And throughout most of the trip, he told amusing stories about being chased by an alcoholic Episcopalian bishop."

"Truman finally got rid of him by suggesting that he might acquire his bishop's ring after he was defrocked," Tennessee said.

During the crossing, one night over dinner, Tennessee and Truman discussed their "first time" sexual experiences.

Truman confessed that he had been repeatedly seduced at the age of twelve when he was enrolled in the St. John's Military Academy in Ossining, New York.

"When the lights in the dormitory went out at night, the younger, beautiful boys such as myself were forced into the beds of the bigger, stronger boys. My first one was Bill, and he took sex very, very seriously. It took him only about twenty minutes to recover before he wanted more. He told me to 'grin and bear it,' not knowing how much I enjoyed his attacks."

Truman had told Windham the story of his early seduction, but with a variation. "I seduced all the boys in grammar school before I was ten and then went to bed with all the other boys in my high school."

Tennessee responded to Truman that he'd lost his virginity to Bette Reitz, a fellow student at the University of Iowa. "I was twenty-six at the time. I had previously ejaculated with males, but never had sex with them. Actually, I never masturbated until I was twenty-five years old."

"Tennessee, I love you dearly," Truman said. "But I think you're taking poetic license. There's no way in hell you could have held out that long."

HOLLYWOOD'S RELENTLESS HETEROSEXUALIZATION OF BISEXUAL MOVIE STARS

Shown above, **Charles Boyer**, with **Hedy Lamarr** in *Algiers*

Before the end of their transatlantic crossing, Truman and Tennessee, either separately or together, had dinner with the three big-name movie stars who were on board.

Gable sought out Tennessee for a special encounter. "I didn't know if Rhett Butler planned to rape me or not, perhaps like he did when he carried Scarlett O'Hara up those steps and she woke up the next morning with a smile on her face."

"In the years to come, even as he aged as a matinee idol, I avidly read about the women he'd seduced—Ava Gardner, Shelley Winters, Mamie Van Doren, Hedy Lamarr, Grace Kelly,

and **Spencer Tracy**, shown here with **Katharine Hepburn**

Yvonne De Carlo, even Nancy Davis (Reagan) and Marilyn Monroe. When I accepted that dinner invitation, I wondered if my name would one day be added to that list. No such luck."

"Clark had seen *A Streetcar Named Desire* on Broadway, with Brando, and he felt it was inevitable that a movie version would be made. He asked me if I could rewrite the role of Stanley Kowalski as a somewhat older character. He dream was to reteam with Vivien Leigh, who had co-starred with him as Scarlett O'Hara in *Gone With the Wind* (1939)."

"Just think of the publicity—Rhett and Scarlett return to the screen again, but this time as Stanley Kowalski and Blanche DuBois," Gable said.

"I told him I'd think it over, but I never did," Tennessee said. "Clark just wasn't my ideal Stanley. I felt only Marlon Brando could bring Stanley to the screen, although the suggestion of Vivien as an aging Blanche DuBois would be perfect, or so I felt."

Both Truman and Tennessee dined one night on board the *Queen Mary* with Charles Boyer. Neither writer found him sexy, although they thought the opinion of Bette Davis a bit harsh. When she co-starred with Boyer in the 1940 *All This and Heaven Too,* she'd said, "Terribly serious about his looks…a wig, a corset, lifts in his shoes, and so on. When he took all that off, he must have looked like the Pillsbury Doughboy."

Truman seemed to know details about the private lives of every celebrity. He told Tennessee, "Boyer likes to keep it discreet in Hollywood, but when he travels abroad, he heads for a port on the Mediterranean. He likes young boys with olive skins."

Two nights before reaching New York, Tennessee and Truman dined with Spencer Tracy, who was involved in a platonic relationship with Katharine Hepburn. He had already seduced, among others, Joan Bennett, Ingrid Bergman, Nancy Davis (Reagan), Judy Garland, and Loretta Young. Joan Crawford had filed a bad report on him after he seduced her. She said, "Spence was a very disturbed man. He was a mean drunk and a bastard."

Truman told Tennessee that he had it "on good authority" that Tracy was also bisexual like Boyer. "One of the reasons he drinks so much is he's ashamed of his homosexuality, which mainly manifests itself when he gets stinking drunk."

"After dinner," Truman said, "I fully expected Spencer to invite me to his cabin for the night, but he didn't."

Later, Truman heard that one of the waiters was seen leaving Tracy's cabin at three o'clock in the morning. Over breakfast the next morning, Truman described the incident to Tennessee. "The waiter served us Beef Wellington last night. But Spencer obviously preferred pork in the early morning hours."

After they docked at the Port of New York, during his appearances on the party circuit, Truman spread the word that he'd had sex with Tennessee. "Onboard, he cruised me from deck to deck and followed me back to my cabin, where he forced his way in and raped me."

Tennessee, of course, denied it. "I never had sex with Truman. He's very effeminate, and I prefer masculine young men. As for rape, that's physically impossible in his case. If he saw a man with an erection, he would immediately surrender the rosebud without protest."

"Truman is a mythologist," Tennessee continued, " a good story teller. Like many Southerners, he loves to fabricate for the sake of the story. I love him too much to accuse him of being a liar."

And What, Mr. Merlo, Do You Do for Mr. Williams?

With the arrival of the 1950s, Tennessee and Truman remained "friendly rivals." Truman once explained to Donald Windham what that meant: "Whereas Gore and I, to each other's face, denounce one another, Tennessee and I only stab each other in the back. To Tenn's face, I have nothing but praise for him. But just let him leave the room—and then he gets the dagger as only I can plunge it."

To others, Tennessee and Truman were each brutally critical of the other's writings. When Tennessee read *Other Voices, Other Rooms,* he asserted, "One third of it is brilliant. The rest falls flat and is terribly derivative of William Faulkner and Carson McCullers."

In October of 1950, Truman wrote his friend, Andrew Lyndon, asking him if he'd read Tennessee's first novel, *The Roman Spring of Mrs. Stone* (1950). "*Multo volgare,* to put it mildly," Truman wrote. "Tennessee is a bad writer."

Even though he'd once seduced him, Truman never managed to say anything good about Frank Merlo, Tennessee's longtime lover.

In another letter to Lyndon, written from Tangier, Morocco, Truman said: "Tenn and that loathesome *(sic)* Merlo boy are on their way to Hollywood—Perhaps Frankie will get in the movies, because I understand all the old Lon Chaney movies are going to be remade, and by hiring him, they'd save on makeup."

In September of 1952, Truman wrote Lyndon again from Tangier. "Two weeks ago, Frankie Merlo descended without warning *sans* Tennesee *(sic),* who is off sucking cock in Germany. I thought Frankie would never stop talking and never leave. Finally, I convinced him to get on a train."

Truman turned to playwrighting with the opening of *The Grass Harp* in 1952. Tennessee flew into a jealous rage, sensing that Truman "is moving in on my territory."

He wrote to Maria St. Just, one of his best friends. "I've only seen one notice of *The Grass Harp, The Times,* which was a rave. I, of course, am insanely jealous. How I do hate myself for it."

Tennessee attended the opening night on Broadway, and later described, in writing, his reaction to Donald Windham. He mocked Truman's fascination with celebrities.

"Before the opening at the Martin Beck, Truman was on the sidewalk across the street, together with the bummier *(sic)* spectators, delightfully watching the celebrities enter, and pointed them out to us after he saw us and called us over to him—'Oh, there's the Countess so-and-so, etc.'"

Writing in *The New York Times,* Brooks Atkinson interpreted *The Grass Harp* as a play with "dramatic strength and timely wisdom." But, in Truman's opinion, other reviews were "sadistic. These attacks managed to shut down the play after only thirty-six performances."

During a subsequent trip to Italy, with Frank, in the summer of 1953, Tennessee wrote once again to Carson McCullers. "I understand that Miss Capote is in Europe, in Italy, but we have not yet collided. She is now reported to be at the fashionable resort of Portofino, which is now much smarter than Capri."

That letter was composed in July, and by August, Tennessee and Frank were together in Portofino, being entertained by Truman and his lover, Jack Dunphy.

When Tennessee discovered that Truman had purchased a female dog, he wrote, "Now there is more than one bitch in residence."

Noël Coward showed up, followed by John Gielgud, each of them guests at the vacation home, in the hills above Portofino, of Rex Harrison and his wife, Lilli Palmer.

In Portofino, Truman had rented an apartment on the top floor of an old house overlooking the harbor. He invited Greta Garbo to come and visit him. He later relayed to Tennessee: "I tried to convince her to star in one of your dramas, but she told me that she does not play *'fallen vomen.'"*

Truman was in his element that summer, mixing with high society, which he would woo for many years to come "until they tossed me out on my bum."

Tennessee later remembered an encounter he had one night over drinks with Jack Dunphy. "I'm new to the homosexual world," Dunphy said. "I guess I'm expected to go to bed with everyone. But I don't have affairs. I just go to bed with people. That's all."

One night, Frank and Tennessee were invited to a rather chic party at the home of the Harrisons. Lilli Palmer approached Frank and said, magisterially, "And, Mr. Merlo, exactly what is it you do for Mr. Williams? A social secretary, no doubt?"

Completely unphased and utterly without hesitation, Merlo responded in his nasal, rapid-fire New Jersey accent: "Sometimes I suck his cock, sometimes he sucks my cock, sometimes I fuck him in the ass, sometimes he fucks me in the ass."

Lilli Palmer with **Rex Harrison** on the cover of the December, 1950, edition of *Life* magazine

"He's A Liar, A Monster, A Cold-Blooded Murderer"

—Tennessee Describing Truman

By the 1970s, Tennessee came to realize that "all the nuts and bolts that kept Truman's head together were coming loose."

At the time, Tennessee was seeing a lot of author Dotson Rader, who later wrote an intimate memoir, *Tennessee: Cry of the Heart,* about their experiences together.

In Manhattan, as described by Rader, Truman began to invite him, with Tennessee, to some of the most bizarre bars and private gatherings in the history of New York. They flourished in that decade, disappearing with the advent of AIDS in the early 80s.

According to Rader, the first invitation from Truman was to "The Toilet," a notorious "scat bar" in a loft in a battered industrial building near the waterfront in the western sector of Greenwich Village.

In the rear of the bar was a huge urinal where young men would strip naked and lie down. Other men would come to the urinal and spray them with their "golden shower." After a few minutes there, Rader and Tennessee fled in horror.

Another invitation, and this one was extended to Norman Mailer as well, was to a bar catering to gay African Americans, who did not welcome white men who acted inappropriately in their midst. Some of the white intruders who didn't were beaten up, in some cases, according to Rader, because they enjoyed it. Truman told Mailer, "Surviving inside is a test of one's manhood and jungle skills."

Yet a third invitation was extended to Club Forty-Eight, the most notorious private club in Manhattan, drawing a mixed clientele of gays and straights.

Through an arrangement with a funeral home, a recently deceased corpse—either male or female—was smuggled into the club for necrophiles to assault sexually. The unfortunate deceased was placed naked on a steel table, where it was ritualistically defiled by any number of patrons before dawn, at which time the body was covered with semen.

As a sexual sophisticate, Tennessee had long ago heard of the bizarre and shadowy erotic phenomenon known as necrophilia. "Most forms of human sexuality do not offend me," he said. "But I always found it disgusting to make love to a dead body. In my lifetime, I have had many partners who may have been dead in bed, but at least their hearts were still beating."

In 1976, Tennessee picked up a copy of *Esquire.* In the magazine was a short story entitled "Unspoiled Monsters," part of Truman's unfinished novel which he'd entitled *Answered Prayers.*

Tennessee practically shouted "libel" when he read the section that dealt with a "Mr. Wallace," who was identified as "the most acclaimed playwright in America."

The narrator of the story in *Esquire* was P.B. Jones, a voice representing Truman himself. As the story relates, Jones hires himself out as a hustler, and gets a call from Mr. Wallace, who wants him to come over and walk his English Bulldog, a pet residing in "the playwright's" suite at the Plaza Hotel.

Inside Wallace's suite at The Plaza, Jones discovers that it's littered with dog feces, since Mr. Wallace is usually too drunk to walk the dog. Shortly after his arrival, Jones slips on one deposit and slides, headfirst, into a second.

Responding to Jones' embarrassment, Mr. Wallace, in a cornpone Southern accent, says, "*Heh, heh, that's just mah dawg.*"

In the story, Truman described Mr. Wallace as a "chunky, booze-puffed runt with a mustache glued above laconic lips." At one point in the narrative, the bulldog sexually assaults Jones.

Evoking Tennessee himself, the story's Mr. Wallace also wears horn-rimmed glasses, carries pencils in his vest pockets, and drinks undiluted scotch from a glass stained with toothpaste. His speech is a "way-down-yonder voice as mushy as sweet potato pie."

In the story, Truman also satirizes Tennessee's hypochondria, prompting Wallace to declare: "I'm a dying man. Dying of cancer. Blood. Throat. Lungs. Tongue. Stomach. Brain. Asshole."

The character of Wallace, the playwright, also laments "six failures in a row—four on Broadway, two off. The critics are killing me out of envy and ignorance. What do they care about the cancer eating my brain?"

The scene ends with a cigar-smoking Mr. Wallace instructing P.J. to "roll over and spread your cheeks."

"Sorry," Jones answers, "but I don't catch. Pitch, yes. Catch, no."

Mr. Wallace then suggests that he needs to extinguish his lit cigar in Jones' rosebud.

At that point in the story, Jones says, "Boy, did I beat it out of there."

Biographer Ronald Hayman accurately observed: "Capote was writing with merciless accuracy, aiming his satirical darts at Tennessee's most repulsive traits and exposing the squalid messiness of his daily life in luxury hotels. Mr. Wallace is a man who has lost control over his daily routine and, having nothing else to live for, uses his wealth to indulge his persecution complex, his egocentricity, his self-pity, and his streak of cruelty. The prodigious energy that had once been channeled into writing was being wastefully and self-destructively diffused."

In reference to the story, in a letter to Truman, which was never mailed, Tennessee wrote: "Dear Truman, what a generous nature you do seem to have!"

During the limited number of years that remained for the both of them, they kept up a certain politeness. But James Kirkwood, author of the Broadway musical, *A Chorus Line,* noted the jealousy and the barely concealed animosity between them during Truman's visit to Key West in the late 1970s. He invited both of them to Louie's Backyard, an open air restaurant overlooking the ocean.

"Tennessee had always been King of Key West, at least since Hemingway left," Kirkwood said. "But on this visit to Key West, Truman was getting all the attention, much to Tennessee's annoyance. People were used to seeing Tennessee all the time. But this little Truman Capote, that was something different. His outrageous, drunken remarks made far better copy than any of Tennessee's utterances."

Truman's friend, John Malcolm Brinnin, the poet, critic, biographer, and historian, had a ringside view of Truman's disenchanted observations about Tennessee:

"*[Truman's]* slightly detached air of amused tolerance toward Tennessee was the norm, but this would often change to a kind of vindictive outrage out of all proportion to its causes. Truman assumed that his own sophistication and social grace were of an order beyond the reach of his friend. The latter showed itself in tongue lashings evoked by some newly uncovered evidence of Tennessee's 'tackiness,' in dealing with people; some new report of his abrupt abandonment of a friend or lover. Tennessee was never out of Truman's purview, or beyond the reach of his contumely."

Brinnan recalled that in March of 1981 in Key West, Tennessee called him aside. "Is Truman trying to commit suicide in public?" Tennessee asked.

"What now?" Brinnin inquired.

"They've hauled him off another stage, smashed out of his skull. This time in San Francisco."

[Truman had accepted an invitation to fly to San Francisco to give a talk before Authors and Artists in the Herbst Auditorium. His sponsor, Maria Theresa Caen, said, "He came out clearly disoriented. He lost his place and then he couldn't find it. Then he turned back another page and started to read an earlier passage, and lost his place again. He was sad and hopeless. The plug had to be pulled on Truman. It was announced that the audience had to be cleared out because of a bomb threat. The people knew that was a lie, just an attempt to save face for Truman."]

As time went by, with continued resentment, Truman expressed more outrage at how quickly Tennessee had tired of his latest lover. He called Brinnin, claiming, "Tennessee has done it again. Remember little Andrew, that nice, quiet kid? He's just been dumped like some trussed-up body you'd find in the East River. Meanwhile, the fiend is on the loose, scot-free to do it all over again. And he will. The man's a killer."

Tennessee's last encounter with Truman was in February of 1982, when the Mayor of New York presented Tennessee with a medallion of honor for his contributions to

Truman named **John Malcolm Brinnin** *(above, right)* as his most learned friend. From time to time, Truman used him like a father confessor, pouring out his woes.

Despondent over the failure of *House of Flowers* in 1954, he wrote that, "Nothing seems to be going right for me—I seem to be a welter of unsolvable problems, literary and otherwise."

the Broadway Theater. Coming face to face with Truman, Tennessee had not forgiven him for the cruel portrait in *Esquire*, which had published chapters from his unfinished novel, *Answered Prayers*.

Tennessee asked Truman when he expected they would meet again.

"In Paradise," Truman said.

Tennessee would die in 1983, Truman within two years.

An Enfant Terrible, Deep in December

As Truman neared the end of his life, his dependence on drugs clouded his judgment. More and more, he made public appearances at readings or on TV when he was clearly under the influence of drink and drugs. His addictions had begun when he was only a teenager, stealing sleeping pills from the medicine cabinet of his mother, Nina Capote.

By the arrival of the drug-hazy 1960s, he was already deeply addicted to mood-altering drugs consumed with large amounts of alcohol, notably Russian vodka.

By the time he researched *In Cold Blood,* he was clearly an alcoholic, although he had pulled himself together enough to write what many critics hailed as his masterpiece.

Throughout the late 1970s, he was unable to function on most days. "My candle burns at both ends, it will not last the night," he was fond of saying, quoting one of his favorite poems from childhood.

At times, Truman tried to cure his addiction as he did in 1977 when he had himself committed to the Smithers Clinic in Manhattan, a place known as "The Devil's Island" of alcohol dependency rehabilitation centers. Author John Cheever had told him, "The place is grim, glum, and gloomy. If you survive it, you'll come out sober."

Truman's most notorious TV appearance occurred during the summer of 1978, when he appeared on Stanley Siegel's controversial talk show. In its immediate aftermath, he generated a headline: "DRUNK AND DOPED, CAPOTE VISITS TV TALK SHOW" shouted the *New York Post.*

The Post also published a savage cartoon, depicting him with droopy eyes enveloped by piles of discarded liquor bottles and used hypodermic needles, along with a book entitled *Breakfast at the Bowery.* John Cashman, in *Newsday,* wrote, "A talented man of considerable literary stature was making a fool of himself in front of 250,000 viewers."

To recover from his embarrassment, Capote spent that night at Studio 54 with owner Steve Rubell and Liza Minnelli, who was not in great shape herself. In the next few days, Truman announced to friends, "I'm going to kill myself as soon as I work up the courage. I'll hire someone to kill me *In Cold Blood.*"

He told Jack Dunphy, "I've been at a long, long party. But the party's over. It's time to leave after this never-ending farewell I call my life."

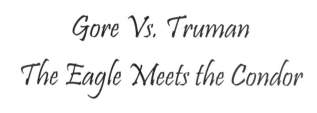

Chapter Eleven

Gore Vs. Truman
The Eagle Meets the Condor

Existential Anguish: Capote's "Love Affairs" with
André Gide and Albert Camus

Belles Lettres: (Left) **André Gide** *and (right)* **Albert Camus**

"After the war, everybody was waiting for the next Hemingway or Fitzgerald to appear," Gore Vidal said. "That's why a new novel by one of us was an event. The effete Truman Capote was definitely the dark horse in the race."

Biographer Gerald Clarke wrote: "Gore was terribly anxious to be number one. If Truman thought of himself as a condor waiting to pounce on literary fame, Gore believed that he was a golden eagle who, if he could not find fame first, would quickly snatch it away."

Truman more or less echoed that sentiment. "Gore was very anxious to be the number one American writer. He was afraid that maybe I was going to do him out of that honor."

Writer and critic Glenway Wescott defined Gore as "lunatic competitive. When I told him I found Truman extremely talented, he blew up. 'How can you call anybody talented who's written only one book at twenty-three? I've written three novels and I'm only twenty-two.'"

"When I mentioned this to Truman, he stamped his feet like Rumpelstiltskin." Westcott said.

"Miss Vidal has no talent—*None! None! NONE!*" Capote shouted.

Tennessee was one of the first to learn of the competition between the two writers. "Gore is infected with that awful competitive spirit and seems to be continually haunted over the successes and achievements of other writers—namely, Truman Capote," Tennessee said. "He is positively

When a very young **Gore Vidal** *(left)* met an only slightly older **Truman Capote** *(right)*, their smiles were not to last. In fact, within a short time, they began a literary feud that Gore eventually won.

obsessed with poor little Truman Capote. You would think they were running neck and neck for some fabulous gold prize."

Both Truman and Gore found themselves in the post-war Paris of 1948, where the boys were cheap and the food not only cheap but terrific. It was a time for Gore to discover what a liar Truman was. Before the summer was over, Gore would proclaim, "Truman made lying an art form—a minor art form."

From the Right Bank to the Left Bank, at various parties, Truman uttered some startling name-dropping news. He spread the world that both Albert Camus and André Gide were in love with him.

Truman confided to Tennessee that "Camus comes to my room every night. He is madly in love with me." Tennessee reported this to Gore.

"Could you imagine Camus wanting to hold that dwarfish body of Capote's in his loving arms?" Gore asked.

"My imagination has unlimited possibilities," Tennessee said, jokingly. "For all you know, Camus has sworn eternal devotion to *me.*"

Gore was very skeptical. He'd actually been with Truman when both of them had met Camus at a party thrown by the French publishing house, Gallimard.

"From what I gathered, Camus was fucking beautiful actresses that summer," Gore said. "There were stories about how, in his native Algeria, he'd

(Truman is) "*An Amusing Pet to the Ruling Class*"

—*Gore Vidal*

162

plowed a few boy asses in his day, but Truman's butt wasn't one of them."

"If Truman were having sex with Camus, he might have caught TB before the end of that summer," Gore claimed.

[Albert Camus, the world-renowned existentialist and author of The Rebel, The Stranger, *and* The Myth of Sisyphus *contracted tuberculosis in 1948 and went into seclusion for two years to recover from the disease.*

A French-Algerian born into a pied-noir family in 1913, he became the second youngest recipient of the Nobel Prize for Literature (in 1957) after Rudyard Kipling.

On January 4, 1960, he died in a car accident near Sens, France. In his coat pocket was an unused train ticket. He had planned to travel by train with his wife and children to Paris, but made a last minute decision to drive to Paris with his publisher instead. He left an unfinished novel, The First Man *(aka* Le premier homme; *not published until 1995), which he was writing before he died. It was an autobiographical work about his childhood in Algeria.]*

When not discussing the sexual prowess of Camus as it applied to his (non-existent) affair with him, Truman spread the word around Paris that the great André Gide was also in love with him.

Truman showed everyone who wanted to see it—even those who didn't want to view the object—a gold and amethyst ring, asserting that it was "a love token from André."

[Born in 1869, the fabled French author had won the Nobel Prize for Literature ten years before Camus.

Like Camus, Gide, too, had spent time in North Africa, mostly in Algeria. He admitted that one of the attractions of that country was its "coven of beautiful boys," available for rent at extremely reasonable prices.

In 1895, Gide had indulged his passion for Algeria with his traveling companion, Oscar Wilde. Long before Gore wrote his homosexual novel, The City and the Pillar, *Gide had published* Corydon *(1924), in which he defended pederasty. The book received widespread condemnation.]*

"Before my eyes, Truman turned himself into a gemlike flame with the aged Gide as a suicidal moth," Gore claimed.

When Gore met Gide, he asked about his

Both **Oscar Wilde** *(upper photo)* and **André Gide** *(lower photo)* caused uproars in conservative circles on either side of the English Channel as regards their respective attitudes about *L'Amour Interdit* (a.k.a. "The love that dare not speak its name.")

Capote was quick to claim comparisons, no matter how far-fetched, between himself and the *enfants terribles* (especially Gide) of an earlier age.

relationship with Truman.

"Who?" Gide asked. "I've never met him."

In the following year, August of 1949, Gore and Truman found themselves in the same place together, the port city of Tangier on the northern coast of Morocco.

To his friend, John Malcolm Brinnin, Truman wrote:

"Gore Vidal has been here—*has,* I'm overjoyed to say. When I think *I'm* paranoid, I listen to him and feel better at once. He dropped in on a Sunday morning to find me *déshabillé* over coffee. He pushes in, hopped up and crazy-eyed. 'Truman,' he says. 'They're out to get us!' He starts off on his totally incomprehensible routine about 'them' and how we have to 'stand pat' and 'close ranks.' 'What in hell are you talking about?' says I. 'I think you've come to the wrong door. If you don't mind, I'd like to close it.'"

Years later, when he was no longer speaking to Gore, Truman made a confession to Jack Knowles, his neighbor on Long Island. Truman claimed that in the late 1940s, he'd been in love with Gore, who had spurned his overtures.

When Gore heard that, he said, "That is one of the biggest lies Truman ever told, one of his gold-plated, spur-of-the-moment inventions."

By the early 1950s, the feud between Gore and Truman had intensified. Gore mocked Truman's attempts to break into what he called "Capote's jet-setters."

"Truman mistook the rich who like publicity for the ruling class, and he made himself far too much at home with them, only to find that he was to them no more than an amusing pet," Gore claimed. "A pet who could be dispensed with when he later published lurid gossip about them."

[Gore was referring to the chapters of Truman's unfinished novel, Answered Prayers, *which* Esquire *ran in installments.]*

Encounters between the two of them were rare in the years to come. They did see each other at a party at the home of critic Leo Lerman.

Lerman maintained a surface friendship with Gore, but denounced Gore's homosexual novel, *The City and the Pillar,* to Truman.

"I loathe Gore's book," he told Truman. It makes all things dirty. The meretricious—soap operas, slick fiction—always blacken whole areas—like locusts—and this is because in these works, there are always some echoes of truth. If they were totally false, they would have no effect on anyone, but their partial truths make them so monstrous, so insidious."

"Hearing this from Leo was like a rhapsody to my ears," Truman said.

Behind his back, Lerman was also critical of Truman. He felt that his sheltered life showed up in his writing. "I wonder whether he doesn't need at least the terror of living in so dreadful a world as the army for at least a little time. I think he needs some experience in a wider life than any he seems to have known. When I tried to tell him that if he got into a sex scandal, no one save avant-garde publications would publish him, he said that I really had the most morbid approach to life. Truman lacks almost all education. He's very Southern Belle, that Truman, at times."

At Lerman's apartment, Gore and Truman clashed head to head, each critical of the other's published work.

"At least I have a style," Truman told him.

"Of course you do," Gore said. "You stole it from Carson McCullers, along with a bit of Eudora Welty."

"Better than stealing from the *Daily News,*" Truman shot back.

Tennessee, who was also at the party, overheard this exchange. He rolled his eyes. "Please! Please! You are making your mother ill."

Truman and Gore saw each other for the last time at a party at Drue Heinz's house in Manhattan. "Without my glasses, I mistook him for a small ottoman and sat on him," Gore said.

Truman charged that Gore "is so cold and so distant. No one is close to him anymore, unlike myself, who has thousands of devoted friends and countless admirers. There's not a week that goes by but what I receive at least two gay marriage proposals, even though there is no such thing as gay marriage."

Throughout the 1970s, Gore and Truman continued to make hostile remarks about each other, both privately and as part of media appearances. Appearing on *The David Susskind Show,* Truman said, "Of course, I'm always sad about Gore Vidal, very sad that he has to breathe every day."

Truman maliciously planted fake items about Gore with gossip columnists. Gore was mailed a quote attributed to him that appeared in the Canadian *Sunday Telegraph.* The article quoted Gore as saying, "I am resented because of my genius, my sex, and my beauty."

Of course, Gore was far too clever to make such a silly remark.

To counterattack, Gore told the press, "If Truman Capote had not existed in his present form, another would have to be run up on the old sewing machine because that sort of *persona* must be, for the whole nation, the stereotype of what a fag is."

Andreas Brown, literary archivist, said, "People feared Capote, no doubt about it. Perhaps everyone but Gore Vidal. He was perhaps the only person who did not fear Capote and in fact relished doing public battle with him. They were real enemies."

How Gore Vidal—According to Truman Capote— Was Forcibly Ejected from The White House

The year 1975 marked a turning point in the feud between Gore and Truman. Long past their prime, both writers had dreamed of movie stardom. Whenever a role loomed as possible for them, both went for it like a shark sensing blood in the water.

Such a role arose during the casting of Neil Simon's farce, *Murder By Death.*

Gore wanted the role, but producers expressed their belief that "Truman will bring more camp to it."

When Truman was cast, he said, "Gore must be dying of envy—hopefully—or else turning green with jealousy."

Truman interjected his own personality, with very little interpretive acting, into a character which had assembled the world's greatest detectives to solve a murder he'd carefully plotted. In addition to Truman, the other members of the cast included such luminaries as David Niven, Elsa Lanchester, Peter Falk, Alec Guinness, Peter Sellers, Maggie Smith, Nancy Walker, and James Coco.

With the understanding that he'd have to report for work to a movie studio in Burbank every morning at 6:30AM, Truman was paid $10,000 a week for an eight-week gig.

To the press, he defined himself as an actor. "I am what Billie Holiday is to Jazz, what Mae West is to tits, what Seconal is to sleeping pills, and what King Kong is to penises. Truman Capote is the great god Thespis! Eat your heart out, Gore Vidal! The role is mine."

Robert F. Kennedy: The Attorney General was not amused.

"It has been reported that the two men he most hated were Jimmy Hoffa and me."
—Gore Vidal

Months later, after Gore had schlepped to a movie theater to see *Murder By Death,* he told a columnist, "And now we know why Capote never became a movie star. The *Harvard Lampoon* will surely award him as the worst performance of this or any other year. What a ham! And the bitch looked on screen exactly like he looks in person. The dog's dinner. No, no. No self-respecting dog would touch that plate of maggot-ridden rotting flesh."

Perhaps in retaliation, Truman arranged an interview between himself and one of the editors at *Playgirl,* a publication noted for its nude male centerfolds. He had never seen the magazine before, until one afternoon he visited Liberace in his outrageously decorated home in Las Vegas.

The entertainer revealed to him that he was a devotee of its centerfolds. "What I do is take a thousand dollar bill and split it in half," Liberace said. "I then send one half to the centerfold of the month, telling him that if he wants to claim the other half, he needs to come to Vegas and spend some time in my elegant boudoir. I have almost never been turned down."

In the interview with *Playgirl,* Truman described an incident that had allegedly happened at the White House in 1961 when Jackie Kennedy had invited Gore to a party honoring her sister, Lee Bouvier (Radziwill).

A ham actor, **Truman Capote,** confronts the world's greatest detectives

166

The September-October, 1975 edition of *Play-girl* showcased a headline on its front cover: OUTRAGEOUS INTERVIEW WITH TRUMAN CAPOTE. Its subhead trumpeted: GORE VIDAL...BOBBY THREW HIM OUT OF THE WHITE HOUSE.

In the article, Truman claimed that this was the only time that Gore had ever been invited to the White House. According to Truman, he not only got drunk, "but insulted Jackie's mother. Bobby Kennedy and Arthur Schlesinger, I believe it was, and one of the guards just picked Gore up and carried him to the door and threw him out into Pennsylvania Avenue. That's when he began to write all those cruel pieces about the Kennedys."

"Before I pay good money for a hustler, I see what I'm getting in the *Playgirl* centerfold!" **Liberace** claimed.

As his source for this information, Truman listed his close friend, Lee Radziwill.

The fireworks were yet to come in a retaliatory blast from Gore at that ill-starred bash in Camelot.

As best as the "RFK vs. Gore" story can be pieced together, Jackie had invited Gore to the White House, mainly because of his status as the stepson of Hugh Auchincloss, who also had been the stepfather to both Lee and Jackie. At the party, Gore sustained an extended chat with Janet Auchincloss, mother of Jackie and Lee, although there is no evidence that Gore insulted the matriarch.

Witnesses said that Gore made several visits to the well-stocked bar, and became noticeably drunk before he had confrontations with both Lem Billings and Robert Kennedy.

Gore had long been fascinated by the intimate relationship between JFK and LeMoyne Billings. "He was not only Jack's lifelong slave, but had been in love with him ever since he'd gone down on him in the shower back in 1933 at Choate. Jackie once told me she'd love to spend a weekend with her husband without Lem tagging along. Because of his bad back, Jack was even helped into his jockey shorts by Lem, who also put on his black socks in the morning."

Gore later claimed that "Lem had challenged me for not attending meetings of the Council on the Arts. I told him that I didn't believe the government should involve itself in the arts."

In print, Gore referred to Lem as "the principal fag at court, who wanted to eliminate any potentially controversial figure from the scene. In Lem's view, here was room for only one queer in residence at the White House. He always wanted to be near the only man he ever loved."

Gore admitted that he and Lem had "exchanged words, none of them pleasant. I detested the little creep. In fact, I ended our dialogue by telling him, 'Why don't you go and suck a cock? Not mine. The President's.' The fag stormed away in a huff."

Later, Gore was crouched next to Jackie, who was sitting in an armchair. As he rose to his feet, rather unsteadily at this point, he balanced himself by placing his hand on her shoulder.

Bobby saw that and rushed over to Gore, asking him to remove his hand from the First Lady.

As Bobby turned to leave, Gore shouted at him. "Don't ever do anything like that again. I've always thought you were an impertinent son of a bitch."

"What do you mean, buddy boy?" RFK asked. "You're a nobody! Why don't you go fuck yourself?"

"Fuck off, yourself!"

The Attorney General not only walked away, disentangling himself from further confrontation, but asked Arthur Schlesinger and George Plimpton to drive Gore home because he was obviously too drunk to do it himself.

In brief, Gore wasn't "thrown" onto Pennsylvania Avenue, but escorted and driven away from the White House grounds.

Although many aspects of the incident were disputed, both sides agreed that RFK and Gore had engaged in a verbal fight.

Within the pages of his memoir, *Palimpsest,* Gore got even with RFK. "Between Bobby's primitive religion and his family's ardent struggle ever upward from the Irish bog, he was more than usually skewed, not least by his own homosexual impulses, which Rudolf Nureyev once told me, were very much in the air on at least one occasion when they were together. 'We did share a young soldier once,' he said. '*American soldier.'* Anyone who has eleven children must be trying to prove—disprove?—something other than the ability to surpass his father as an incontinent breeder."

At his home at Ravello, along Italy's Amalfi Coast, Gore received a copy of the *Playgirl* interview and was angry and shocked at the inaccuracies. He decided not to sue, having been burned in his libel suit against right winger William F. Buckley. "My experience with Buckley made me sensitive to the misuse of libel laws to discourage free speech." But in Amsterdam, when confronted with row upon row of copies of *Playgirl* displayed in a local kiosk, he decided to sue Truman for libel. Shortly thereafter, he filed a million dollar lawsuit.

The press went wild. Not since Oscar Wilde threatened the Marquess of Queensberry with slander had such a lawsuit generated so much publicity. At the age of 53, Gore was suing Truman, aged 54. The press referred to them as "a pair of razor-tongued salon fighters aboil with malice."

To bolster his defense in the libel case, Truman wanted to drag Lee Radziwill into the fray, citing her as the source of the story. He wanted her as an eyewitness that the story about Gore's explusion was true after all.

Lem Billings

168

Lee, however, denied that she had been the source of the story, and made it clear that she didn't want to become involved. When Jackie heard about the lawsuit, and Lee's possible involvement, she pronounced that "this whole mess is just too damn ridiculous." She saw it as a "frivolous squabble" between two authors she'd once befriended, but had now distanced herself from. "Both Gore and Truman have become too hot for me to handle."

Lee's lawyers warned that if she admitted to being the source of the story, that Gore could instruct his lawyers to amend their complaint, naming her as a codefendant. If Gore had won such a case, Lee would have been liable for untold damages, whatever the court decided, plus legal fees. The case had already cost Truman $80,000, money he could ill afford.

Desperately wanting her help, Truman telephoned Lee repeatedly in 1979. His desperate calls were not returned.

Truman then telephoned columnist Liz Smith and asked her to intervene. Somewhat reluctantly, Smith phoned Lee, a woman she had met but didn't know too well.

During her dialogue with Smith, Lee was dismissive of Truman. Reportedly, Lee told Smith, "All this notoriety is too much for me. I am tired of Truman riding on my coattails. Liz, what difference does the suit make? Truman and Vidal are just a couple of fags."

When Smith told Truman what Lee had said, he went ballistic: "Riding on her coattails?" he said, mockingly. "Who in the fuck is she kidding? She rode on my coattails. I even talked David Susskind into casting her in Laura. And you know how that turned out. Gene Tierney, Lee was not."

"If the lovely, divine, and sensitive Princess Radziwill has such a low opinion of homosexuals, then why did she have me for a confidant for the last twenty years?" he asked.

To her frequent escort at the time, Newton Cope, a middle-aged widower who had married the late heiress, Dolly MacMasters, Lee said, "Now I'm in hot water. The little worm [a reference to Truman] is threatening to sue me."

Cope said, "What can you expect from a has-been writer who is all washed up and fighting for any kind of publicity on the way down?"

Forced to respond, Lee delivered a sworn statement to Gore's lawyers. "I do not recall ever discussing with Truman Capote the incident of that evening, which I understand is the subject of a lawsuit."

When Truman heard that Lee had acquiesced to Gore's lawyers, he said, "She's a treacherous lady, and that's the truth of it. She's treacherous to absolutely everyone."

***

The lawsuit seemed to have no end, dragging on for years.

Hoping to score points, Truman, in June of 1979, allowed *New York* magazine to publish the strong anti-Vidal depositions he had submitted to his lawyers as part of the legal proceedings.

In *New York* magazine, Truman said, "Gore Vidal wants to be all things to all men. I mean, he wants to be Caesar and Cleopatra at the same time—and he isn't."

Upon publication of that article, Truman was gleeful. "Right now my depositions are rolling down the chutes, along with Gore's career. When people read my dialogues, they'll know he's Captain Queeg in *The Caine Mutiny.*This will explode and destroy his career, giving me the greatest single revenge in literary history. It will be humiliating for him. I love it! I love it! I love it! When he dies, *they'll write on his tombstone, 'HERE LIES GORE VIDAL: HE MESSED AROUND WITH T.C.'*"

Contrary to Truman's hope, *New York* magazine's publication of his depositions had no noticeable effect on Gore's literary career. The publicity they garnered only strengthened Gore's resolve to continue with his lawsuit, which dragged on until the autumn of 1983, less than a year before Truman's death, when Truman's lawyers assured Gore's attorney that he had no money left to pay for any damages. Gore's career was not affected by the depositions and he continued his lawsuit for more tortuous years. In the autumn of 1983, the case was finally settled out of court when Truman agreed to write a letter of apology:

"Dear Gore,
I apologize for any distress, inconvenience, or expense which may have been caused you as a result of the interview with me published in the September, 1975, issue of Playgirl. *As you know, I was not present at the event about which I quoted in that interview, and I understand from your representative that what I am reported as saying does not accurately set forth what occurred. I can assure you that the article was not an accurate transcription of what I said, especially with regard to any remarks which might cast aspersions upon your character or behavior, and that I will avoid discussing the subject in the future.*
Best, Truman Capote."

The only legal ruling that ever came down from the bench had occurred in August of 1979, when a judge denied Truman's request for summary dismissal. The same judge also denied Gore's request for summary judgment.

But in a preliminary ruling, as part of a statement indicating that the law would probably rule in Gore's favor, the judge was quoted as saying, "Mr. Capote's statements were, as a matter of law, libelous *per se*, and Mr. Vidal's attorneys had demonstrated actual malice."

On August 24, 1984, a bulletin came over Gore's television that Truman Capote was found dead in Bel Air at the home of Joanne Carson, ex-wife of TV host Johnny Carson.

Later that day, in response to Truman's death, Gore told the press, "I've always been an atheist, but tonight, I know there is a God."

Chapter Twelve

The City and the Pillar
The Novel Made Gore Vidal Notorious

Jimmie Trimble, Whose Sweat Smelled Like Honey
—An Unfinished Life—

"Homosexuality was practiced quite widely in my adolescence. In schools, in camps, in the Army. Some stayed with it and some didn't. I fell in love with Jimmy Trimble, and wrote *The City and the Pillar.*"

—*Gore Vidal*

What would become Gore Vidal's most controversial novel,

The City and the Pillar, grew out of a luncheon he shared with his senior editor at E.P. Dutton, John Tebbel. The editor was not aware at the time that Gore was a homosexual.

Tebbel had been unimpressed with Gore's second novel, *In a Yellow Wood,* finding it "boringly flat, not nearly as taut, as focused, as compelling as his first novel, *Williwaw.*"

The two men began to talk about a possible third novel. "You need to do something really good."

Somehow, the conversation focused on homosexuality, which in the wake of World War II had become increasingly evident on the streets of New York. "This is a dark, shadowy world that most people know nothing about except for a few locker room jokes," Tebbel said. "Perhaps you should explore the subject in a novel. Such a book would attract a lot of attention."

Gore seemed to agree. "I'm bored with playing it safe. I want to take risks, to try something no American has done before."

"You could be objective about it," Tebbel said, "a bit impersonal, approaching it from the sociological standpoint, but with a literary overlay."

Jimmie Trimble

"I hope you're not leading me into a trap," Gore said. "Let's face it: To most mainstream publishers and most critics, homosexuality is an anathema."

"That certainly has always been true, but I've heard that homosexuality blossomed during the war, when millions of young men, on both sides, were thrown together in crotch-to-crotch encounters night after night."

"Give me some time to think about this," Gore said. "Many people might get the idea I'm a homosexual, and as you well know, I don't like fags."

Whereas *The City and the Pillar,* Gore's third novel, grew out of that luncheon, its origins began in the 1930s when Gore met "the only man I have ever loved."

His name was Jimmie Trimble. The two boys met at St. Albans, an all-boys prep school near the Washington Cathedral.

As Gore remembered, "Jimmie had pale blue eyes; mine were pale brown. He had the hunter-athlete's farsightedness; I had the writer-reader's myopic vision. He was blonde with curly hair. His sweat smelled of honey, like that of Alexander the Great."

Their affair began when he followed Jimmie into the shower room one afternoon after he'd played a baseball game. "In those days, boys at St. Albans fell into two categories: Those with pubic hair and those with just a little peach fuzz. I wanted to see what Jimmie possessed. He not only had pubic hair, but a large, rather fat, uncut penis. When he caught me looking at it, he smiled with

"My Dream Life Ended That Day on the Sands of Iwo Jima"

—Gore Vidal

172

a very come-hither look. I knew I'd found my man."

On a hot sunny afternoon, on a rock overlooking the Potomac River, Gore and Jimmie made love. "I discovered the type of sex I'd been looking for all my life. "I'd made love to a girl named Rosalind Rust. It did nothing for me."

Jimmie was also dating a girl, an aspiring actress named Chris White.

"I later became very close friends to Joanne Woodward," Gore said. "Ironically, in the early part of the 1950s, this Chris White woman was getting roles that Joanne desired for herself."

Gore brought his new lover home to meet Nina, his mother, who was married at the time to Hugh Auchincloss. Jimmie later told his own family, "They have silk sheets, and the butler asks you at night what you want for breakfast." He had never experienced such luxury before.

The two handsome men began to date, going to hear Benny Goodman at the Capitol Theater and secretly holding hands in the dark. "I preferred classical music, but Jimmie could listen for hours to Billie Holiday records. He also loved swing music that was so popular during the war, and he even played the saxophone. In contrast, I was non-musical."

Jimmie gave Gore a portrait of himself, which had been painted in 1937, depicting him holding a model sailboat. Gore would keep that picture by his bedside until the end of his life.

Jimmie had to undergo surgery to enlarge his urethra, and Gore hovered over his bedside like a Florence Nightingale until he recovered.

"Once again, on the baseball field, "Jimmie overflowed with animal energy, not to mention magnetism for both sexes," Gore said.

As Fred Kaplan, Gore's biographer, wrote, "Jimmie was Gore's alter ego, a twin who would be the playmate of his soul, a completion of the incomplete, the perfect fit that makes two comrades into one friendship."

After graduation, the two young men separated. Nina sent Gore to the wilderness of New Mexico to the Los Alamos Ranch School. It specialized in turning "sickly boys into healthy men."

In marked contrast, Jimmie had been offered a contract to play professional baseball with the Washington Senators, which also included a scholarship to college. That would have kept him out of World War II.

The last time Gore saw Jimmie was right before Christmas of 1942 at a dance, when he told Gore that he'd enlisted in the Marines and was going to be sent to the Pacific. On seeing him again, Gore longed to return to the woods above the Potomac River, where they'd first made love.

Eager to reunite physically with each other, the two young men went to the toilet, where in a cubicle, they made love again,

Unrequited: Miss **Rosalind Rust**

"standing up, belly to belly," as Gore wrote in his memoirs.

Gore always wondered if Jimmie found another lover in the Marines. "I learned from his mother that he'd written home for a copy of Walt Whitman's *Leaves of Grass.* Did some more poetic male friend advise him to read these homosexual poems?"

By 1944, Jimmie was in the Marines, Gore in the Army. "We were worlds apart, but I thought of him every day and especially at night. Our futures were uncertain. For Jimmy, there would be no future."

On February 2, 1945, on the Sands of Iwo Jima, Jimmie joined 6,821 other American Marines, mostly teenagers, who died storming the beaches.

Gore later learned that Jimmie had been shot by a Japanese soldier and was later bayoneted almost eighteen times, even though he was already dead.

Gore later wrote, "Those Marine landings were a mindless slaughter of our own. The waste of young American lives was appalling. When I went to see John Wayne's *Sands of Iwo Jima (1949),* I cried all the way through it."

Living at the time in low-cost Guatemala, his retreat from the world, Gore finished *The City and the Pillar.* He dedicated it to "J.T."

Gore never recovered from Jimmie's death, and wrote about his slain Marine in his memoirs. Jimmie also appears in disguise in other novels written by Gore.

Gore's memory of Jimmie Trimble was still going strong in 1970 when he wrote a screenplay, *Jim Now,* based on his 1949 novel. Franco Rossellini expressed interest in shooting a low-budget movie adaptation in Rome, but financing was difficult. In Hollywood, Gore shopped the script from studio to studio, getting only negative reactions to its homosexual theme.

"Death, summer, youth—the triad contrives to haunt me every day of my life."

He often lamented "a few scraps of bone and cartilage scattered among the volcanic rocks of Iwo Jima that Jimmie left behind."

In 1971, Gore experimented with a hallucinogenic drug. "Jimmie arrived in bed wearing blue pajamas. I could actually feel his body."

In later years, Gore recalled his youthful romance with Jimmie as "the unfinished business of my life."

Avant-Garde Catfights with a Literary Poseur
—Anaïs Nin vs. Gore Vidal

Anaïs Nin, Gore's mentor, was the first person to whom he showed his first draft of *The City and the Pillar.* She was horrified, mainly at the portrait of herself, whom she recognized in the character of Marie Verlaine, an aging *femme fatale.*

"She is a woman who has seen two wars, who has lines around her eyes, and who cannot find satisfying sexual relationships," Anaïs said. "You have written an aggressive hostile caricature of me, a brutal parody of a woman. I have been betrayed by someone I trusted. I can never forgive this."

She also objected to the idea, as expressed in Gore's novel, that a sophisticated woman, such as Marie Verlaine, might ever have been attracted "to such a colorless clod of a boy as Jim."

"Perhaps she was right," Gore later said. "Jim was so unlike those plumed, serpentine Mexican beach boys that she had fancied."

"You have written a novel without illusion, without feeling, and without poetry," she charged. "Everything in your eyes is diminished and uglied. To see only ugliness, that is what people do when they do not love. You live without faith, and that will make your world gray and bitter."

Bigamous **Anaïs Nin** with her second husband, **Rupert Poole**, at a "come as your madness" party

Ironically, Anaïs objected to "the promiscuity of homosexuals." Gore found that surprising and hypocritical, "but I did not bring up her own powerful sexual appetites."

Her biographer, Deirdre Bair, put it this way: "Anaïs had a continuing procession of young boys who came and went from Greenwich Village with interchangeable ease, and she cast herself in the role of Colette's Léa, instructing whichever youth was her *Chéri* of the moment."

Her relationship with Gore would continue, but her reaction to *The City and the Pillar* marked the beginning of one of the most famous literary feuds of the 20th Century. She would seek her own form of revenge in *Volume Four (1944-1947)* of her diary through an unflattering portrait of him. When she wrote her novel, *Solar Barque*, Gore, in disguised form, would appear as an impotent homosexual. *[Solar Barque, originally published in 1958, would re-emerge a year later as Seduction of the Minotaur.]*

"Disgusting Perversions"
Which Evolve into a New York Times Bestseller

Gore already had two novels on the market, *Williwaw* and *In a Yellow Wood,* and consequently, Dutton delayed the release of his *The City and the Pillar* (written in 1946) until January of 1948 because it didn't want to glut the market with Vidal novels. Dutton editors were also concerned by the homosexual theme, and some were troubled that the novel might harm Gore's promising career as a novelist, as indeed, it did. *[Partly because of the negative reviews it received, Gore would wait for another twenty years before he returned to a gay theme in* Myra Breckinridge, *his novel about camp, gender, and the movies.]*

"If you hold it much longer, I'll be scooped," Gore protested.

[Indeed, during Dutton's deliberately calibrated delay, two other widely discussed gay-themed novels were published, mitigating to some degree the novelty of Gore's City and the Pillar. *They included* The Gallery, *by John Horne Burns, and* End as a Man, *by Calder Willingham.]*

The Gallery, published in 1946, depicted life in Allied-occupied North Africa and Naples in 1944, as seen through the experience of homosexual military personnel. It included a "lurid" account of a gay bar in wartime Naples frequented by soldiers of various nationalities.

Rather jealous of Burns, Gore sought him out and reported, "He was a difficult man who drank too much, loved music, detested all other writers, and wanted to be great. He was also certain that to be a great writer, it was necessary to be homosexual. When I disagreed, he named a half-dozen celebrated contemporaries. 'A Pleiad,' he roared delightedly, 'of pederasts.'"

"But what about Faulkner?" Gore asked. "And Hemingway?"

Burns was disdainful of Gore's question. "Who said they were *any* good?" he asked.

Calder Willingham, born in Atlanta, burst onto the scene with his novel, *End as a Man (1947),* a withering indictment of the macho culture of military academies. The story also focused on sex and suggested homosexuality, which led to the New York Society for the Suppression of Vice to file obscenity charges against its publisher, Vanguard Press.

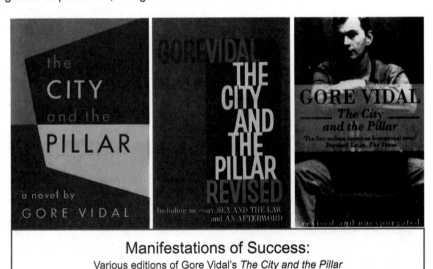

Manifestations of Success:
Various editions of Gore Vidal's *The City and the Pillar*

Pressing on, Willingham turned the book into a play at New York's Actors Studio, where it was an off-Broadway success, featuring a very young James Dean and introducing actor George Peppard, who would later star as the dashing romantic hero in Truman Capote's *Breakfast at Tiffany's.* Both Truman and Tennessee saw the play together and met both Dean and Peppard. They were particularly fascinated by Dean.

Willingham would also go on to achieve success as a screenwriter, credited for screenplays of *The Graduate* (1967), which co-starred both Dustin Hoffman and Anne Bancroft.

Condemned before its release, *The City and the Pillar* is today an American classic.

It was the first book by an accepted American author to define his protagonist as strong, athletic, relatively well-adjusted, and masculine, and the first to portray overt homosexuality as a natural behavior. Harmless, even "vanilla," by today's standards, *The City and the Pillar* tells the story of handsome Jim Willard, a coming-of-age drama of a tennis player who discovers his homosexuality. He falls for his best friend, Bob Ford. Eventually, Bob gets married. The end of their relationship unfolds in the bed of Bob's hotel room. In the novel's original version, an infuriated Jim, spurred on and antagonized by Bob, murders him. In Gore's revised version, released in 1965, he rapes him instead.

Tennessee told Gore, "You spoiled it with that revised ending. You didn't know what a good book you had."

Christopher Isherwood, traveling at the time in South America, was also put off by the ending. He thought the novel suggested that homosexuality brings tragedy, defeat, and death. "Many men live together for years and make homes and share their lives and their work, just as heterosexuals do," Isherwood claimed.

"The gay revolution began as a literary revolution," wrote Christopher Bram in his book, *Eminent Outlaws, The Gay Writers Who Changed America.* "Vidal was the godfather of gay literature, in spite of himself—a fairy godfather. He would cringe at this description. He continued to insist that there is no such

Two views of **John Horne Burns** and *(left backdrop)*, the cover of his novel, *The Gallery.*

177

thing as a homosexual person, only homosexual acts."

The City and the Pillar drew almost a completely negative response. The New York Times Book Review dismissed it as "disgusting" and "gauche."

Orville Prescott of The New York Times said he was so horrified by Gore's book that he would neither review nor ever read another novel by him. Gore accused anti-gay critics of blocking his career.

The New Yorker found the novel "unadorned tabloid writing, the kind of dreary information that accumulates on a metropolitan police blotter."

Despite their condemnations, The City and the Pillar rose quickly to the bestseller list, eventually selling 30,000 copies in hardcover.

The release of The City and the Pillar had been immediately preceded by the January, 1948, publication of The Kinsey Report a major scientific study revealing that male homosexuality was more frequently practiced than most Americans had ever realized. Adding to that month's abundance of gay-favorable (or gay-indulgent) reading material, the publication of The Kinsey Report was followed a week later by the release of Truman Capote's Other Voices, Other Rooms.

Gore met and was interviewed by Alfred C. Kinsey, author of Sexual Behavior in the Human Male. "After many serious talks, Kinsey told me that I was not homosexual, doubtless because I never sucked cock or got fucked. Even so, I was setting world records for encounters with anonymous youths, nicely matching busy Jack Kennedy's girl-a-day routine."

Based on countless testimonies associated with Gore's sexual conquests, his statement about his sexual practices to Kinsey appear to be completely untrue.

"I traveled with Gore," Tennessee later said, when he read the statement. "Gore performed fellatio and allowed himself to be sodomized. Yet he was suggesting that he was exclusively a passive partner in fellatio and an active partner in sodomy. That was merely his fantasy, hardly the truth."

Seven subsequent novels by Gore were not reviewed by The New York Times. Mimicking the policies of "The Old Gray Lady," both Time and Newsweek seemed to pretend that Gore did not exist as an entity in American letters.

Since his novels were not selling, in 1954, Gore was forced to turn to work writing scripts for live television drama, at which he distinguished himself. He also became the last contract writer employed by MGM, right before it fired all scriptwriters because of dire economic necessity.

Gore would also follow Tennessee into scriptwriting, scoring hits with Visit to a Small Planet and The Best Man.

SEXUAL REVOLUTION
Alfred Kinsey, conducting one of his infamous interviews

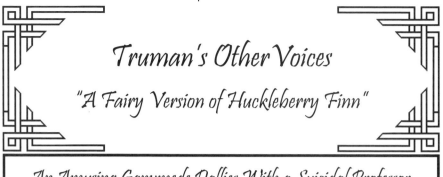

Chapter Thirteen

Truman's Other Voices

"A Fairy Version of Huckleberry Finn"

An Amusing Ganymede Dallies With a Suicidal Professor

Developing a persona: Male Lolito and *Enfant Terrible, Truman Capote*

Truman Capote's first novel, *Other Voices, Other*

Rooms, was published in 1948 by Random House. Its book jacket, showcasing a photograph by Harold Halma, depicts a young, sloe-eyed Truman lying supine on a sofa facing the camera with an emphasis on his petulant mouth, baby bangs, and seductive, come-hither gaze.

One reviewer advised American housewives to keep their husbands away from this tantalizing boy. Another warned "Something evil and awful this way comes."

The novel was dedicated to Newton Arvin, a literary luminary whose name was for the most part unknown to the average American.

Truman's agonizing saga with Arvin began at Yaddo, a creative community near Saratoga Springs, New York,

[The school was founded in 1900 by the very wealthy financier Spencer

Trask, an early financial backer of Thomas Edison and later, Chairman of The New York Times, and his wife Katrina, herself a poet, in the wake of the premature deaths of each of their four children. Yaddo is a financially self-sustaining artists' community located on what originated as the Trask family's 400-acre estate in Saratoga Springs, New York. Its mission is to nurture the creative process by providing an opportunity for artists to work without interruption in a supportive and creatively stimulating environment. Prior to Truman's arrival, it had previously attracted such authors as the stately but still beautiful at fifty-six, Katherine Anne Porter.]

Truman allowed time at Yaddo for summer romances. One of them was with Howard Doughty. Bearing an uncanny resemblance to the Hollywood actor, James Stewart, Doughty, when not in temporary residence at Yaddo, was an English instructor at the prestigious Smith College, located about 120 miles away, in Northampton, Massachusetts.

Doughty's bloodlines stretched back to Cotton Mather (1663-1728), the Puritan minister whose fire and brimstone sermons and pamphlets profoundly affected the punitive moral climate of America's English colonies. *[Mather is often remembered for his role in the Salem witch trials.]*

Tall and dark, with dashing good looks, Doughty spoke in a Brahmin accent. Truman later claimed, "Howard and I just got together for sex. He was very attractive, but I was not in love with him."

The Scarlet Professor:
Two Views of **Newton Arvin**

After the first flush of his affair with Truman, Doughty wrote to his friend and lover, Newton Arvin, a scholarly professor at Smith, that "The child *[i.e., Truman]* really has an uncanny talent—almost frightening. Of course, so far, his main literary accomplishment has been getting canned as a messenger boy for *The New Yorker,* but his short stories are just amazing."

It was inevitable that Doughty would eventually introduce Truman to Arvin. As biographer Gerald Clarke wrote: "Truman entered the lives of both Arvin

Truman's Image as a Seductive, Underaged Lolito Brings Him Overnight Fame

and Doughty, hurtling toward them like a shooting star, stunning them, dazing them, dazzlingly them altogether."

Soon, Truman was sleeping with both men, until Doughty left Yaddo for another commitment. If there was jealousy, the two older men covered it up rather well.

Truman and Arvin made love almost every day, although Truman admitted, "He's not my type at all—bald, wears glasses, is middle aged, very shy, has frequent depressions, anemic, psychologically damaged. Once he swallowed sixteen Seconals in an attempt to commit suicide, but was rescued."

Newton Arvin *(left)* with Howard Doughty, two of Truman's early lovers.

Based on Truman's fanciful self-image as Ganymede, Arvin had assigned him that nickname.

Arvin described his involvement with Truman in a letter to Doughty: "This naughty Ganymede has made me come alive again. And I want to live."

After a week of sexual contact with Truman every night at Yaddo, Arvin told his friend, Granville Hicks, "I'm experiencing psychological euphoria."

Leo Lerman, a friend to both men, claimed that Truman was not attracted so much to Arvin for his physicality, but for his vast knowledge. Truman, in fact, called Arvin "my Harvard" and the older man quickly became a *[spectacularly erudite]* father figure to him.

Truman, pensive, all ears, soaking up data from the academes "like a sponge"

After dark, Arvin sometimes spent an hour or so reading Truman passages from the *Iliad.* Arvin soon learned that Truman was not well educated. In Manhattan, during time away from Yaddo, he went to Radio City Music Hall to see *Great Expectations,* a David Lear movie released in 1946, adapted from the tale by Charles Dickens.

Truman returned to Yaddo in a rage. "Lean has stolen the plot of *Other Voices,*" he screamed. Arvin patiently explained that *Great Expectations* was a Victorian-era plot from the 19th-century pen of Charles Dickens.

Beginning on June 14, 1946, Arvin wrote that he was "encircled by the magic ring of love." Arvin's biographer, Barry Werth, claimed that the professor interpreted "in Capote's Southern Gothicism a darkness and beauty as rich and poetic as that of Nathaniel Hawthorne."

In a love letter to Truman, Arvin wrote that, "We are drinking the water of Truth, and what we are making between us is purely beautiful."

Doughty compared the "marriage of Truman and Arvin to Faustus and Helena." As a literary scholar, Arvin was well aware of what an uncomfortable reference that was. After all, Helena was the Devil's gift to Faustus, who in return had to surrender his soul.

During another brief respite from Yaddo, Truman met with Doughty, telling him, "Newton is like a lozenge that you keep turning to the light and the most beautiful colors emerge."

The love affair between Arvin and Truman endured until 1949, even though both men slept with others on the side. From a base in New York, Truman would travel by train to Northampton, Massachusetts, to stay with Professor Arvin on weekends.

As the years passed, Arvin continued to define Truman as a "dear child," even though he had evolved into an internationally established writer who no longer needed him. Truman continued to love and respect Arvin, but was delighted to have "escaped from the mothball world that envelops him."

Truman was not jealous, but delighted when Arvin, in 1951, won the National Book Award for his biography of Herman Melville. But Truman detested *Moby Dick,* loudly and somewhat insensitively asserting, "Who wants to read a novel about chasing after a big whale?"

Instead of to an upfront-and-personal lover, Arvin turned to pornography as a sexual outlet, amassing a large collection of gay erotica which, by today's standards, would be interpreted as safe and rather vanilla. But at the time, possession of such material was illegal in Massachusetts.

In September of 1960, without a lot of support from Smith College, he was arrested and charged with being "a lewd and lascivious person in speech and behavior," even though he was the exact opposite of that. He suffered a nervous breakdown and was admitted to the Northampton State (Psychiatric) Hospital, an overcrowded hellhole—nicknamed "Dippy Hall"—with the dubious honor as the third state institution for the insane built in the state of Massachusetts.

From Europe, Truman wrote to Arvin, lending his support and offering money. Lillian Hellman initially offered her support too, until Arvin, to avoid a jail sentence, gave the police the names of more than a dozen other Smith College faculty members who collected gay erotica.

"He panicked and ratted, poor bastard," Hellman said.

Because he had betrayed and informed upon his friends, Arvin was spared a term in jail. In March of 1963, Truman heard that Arvin was dying of cancer and came to see his long ago lover.

As he was leaving the hospital after an hour-long visit, Arvin took Truman's hand and said, "I've grown up at last."

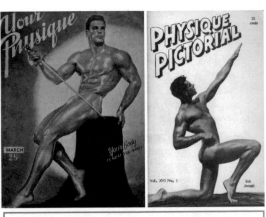

Newton Arvin was tossed into both jail and a mental asylum for lewdness, after the discovery of "Men's Physique" magazines in his home.

Succès de Scandale: "It Makes the Flesh Crawl"

Ironically, because of all the advance publicity, including a spread in *Life* magazine, Truman Capote was already a celebrated novelist before Random House published his first novel, *Other Voices, Other Rooms,* in 1948. Publisher Bennett Cerf gave Truman an advance of $1,200.

Other Voices, Other Rooms was released about a week after Gore Vidal's more blatantly homosexual *The City and the Pillar.* Truman's prose was remarkably different from Gore's, which was more trimmed and succinct, in some ways evoking the style of Hemingway. In noteworthy contrast, Truman wrote in a style best defined as High Southern Rhetoric, each sentence poetically and painstakingly crafted as in: "*He listened content and untroubled to the remote singing-saw noise of night insects.*"

Semi-autobiographic, *Other Voices, Other Rooms,* tells the story of a precocious thirteen-year-old, Joel Knox, who is sent to live in a small hamlet in a backwater of Alabama called Skully's Landing. Truman shared many of Joel's characteristics. Both the character and the author who created him were more or less abandoned children who lived, or had lived, in big houses in rural Alabama. Both of them were delicate and pretty, ostracized because they were effeminate.

In *Other Voices,* Truman used Harper Lee as his role model for the tomboy Idabel. In turn, she used him as inspiration for her character of Dill in *To Kill a Mockingbird.*

Truman's widely anticipated novel immediately hit *The New York Times* Bestseller list, selling 26,000 copies, which was four thousand short of what Gore's *The City and the Pillar* sold.

Even though it was firmly perched on the list of America's top-selling books, Truman was disappointed. "I wanted to sell more copies than Margaret Mitchell's *Gone With the Wind,*" he said.

Although Truman would not write overtly about homosexuality until three decades later, the other characters in *Other Voices* were gaudy, grotesque, and peripherally effeminate, especially Randolph, who once appears at a window dressed as a lovely lady from the court of Louis XVI.

Randolph mourns the loss of his great love, a Mexican boxer. He wears a seersucker kimono with butterfly sleeves and tooled leather sandals revealing painted toenails. His sunflower yellow curls fall over his forehead, and his hair is sprinkled with the scent of lemon cologne.

The book drew mixed reviews, the harshest attacks coming from New York City. Except for a few missiles, reviewers in the hinterlands were more praise-

---

"*The brain may take advice, but not the heart, and love, having no geography, knows no boundaries.*"

—Randolph, in *Other Voices, Other Rooms*

worthy. Perhaps the sharpest criticism came from a magazine that defined *Other Voices, Other Rooms* as "the fairy version of *Huckleberry Finn.*"

One Alabama newspaper tersely asserted, "Capote has produced a basket of rotting apples evoking so-called Southern Decadence, which, incidentally, does not exist except in the minds of Tennessee Williams, Carson McCullers, and William Faulkner."

The prestigious *Library Journal* warned libraries not to stock it.

Saturday Review claimed that "Mr. Capote has concocted a witch's brew which boils and boils to no avail."

Critic Diana Trilling, in *The Nation,* defined Truman's much-vaunted first novel as "an apology for homosexuality."

Other Voices, Other Rooms "made our flesh crawl" according to the editors and critics at the offices of *Time* magazine.

In marked contrast to their New York City competitors, the *Chicago Tribune* claimed "*Other Voices, Other Rooms* is a short novel which is as dazzling a phenomenon as has burst on the literary scene in the last ten years."

The *Indianapolis Times* found it "a book of extraordinary literary virtuosity—the kind of thing that makes most other fictional writing seem pedestrian and uninspired."

In *Harper's Magazine,* Jacques Barzun stated that "Truman Capote is destined for the higher places of literary creation."

Newsweek found it "a deep murky well of Freudian symbols."

Writing about it in *Partisan Review,* Elizabeth Hardwick intoned, "It's a minor imitation of a talented minor writer, Carson McCullers."

As a mature man, looking back years later, Truman wrote: "*Other Voices, Other Rooms* was an attempt to exorcise demons, an unconscious, altogether intuitive attempt, for I was not aware, except for a few incidents and descriptions, of its being in any serious degree autobiographical. Rereading it now, I find such self-deception unpardonable."

Ganymede Sells! Provocative images of Truman move from the back cover to the full-center front of subsequent editions

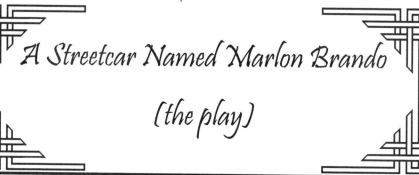

Chapter Fourteen

A Streetcar Named Marlon Brando

(the play)

Close Encounters with Marlon's "Noble Tool"

Ready to rape: **Marlon Brando** as Stanley Kowalski in *A Streetcar Named Desire*.

"The playwright" [Tennessee Williams] and

the actor *[Marlon Brando]* were destined to meet," said heiress Peggy Guggenheim, a frequent summer visitor to Provincetown at the tip of Cape Cod. "Tennessee was born in Mississippi in 1911 and Marlon was born in Omaha, Nebraska in 1924. What an odd couple. But each artist needed the other. Tennessee supplied Marlon with the words; Marlon supplied the emotional intensity needed to bring those words into a memorable reality in the theater. Forget all those memoirs about them meeting at the time of the casting for *A Streetcar Named Desire*. They knew each other—rather intimately, I suspect—long before Marlon ever took a ride on that *Streetcar*."

Sidney Shaw, a homosexual lyricist linked to the Katherine Dunham dance troupe, was the first to turn Brando on to the glories of summertime P-town. Planning to spend a few weeks at the Cape, Brando arrived with only eighty dollars. "Bronze, blonde, and muscled, he was addicted to wearing jeans so tight you could tell that he was uncut," claimed summer resident Jesse Steele, one of the first to meet Brando.

The son of a rich auto manufacturer in Detroit, the flamboyant Steele fancied himself a landscape painter. His gay parties were all the rage in 1945, attended not only by Guggenheim, but by her lover *du jour,* Jackson Pollock, and invariably by Tennessee himself. Steele, dressed in pink and lavender, introduced Tennessee to Brando.

Marlon Brando as Stanley

"I first met Marlon his very first day in town," Steele claimed. "I'm not exactly saying that he was in town hustling. Well, not exactly. But if you wanted to give him a free dinner—and a big one at that—free lodgings in your home, and free drinks, he wasn't opposed to accepting gratuities. All of us had Marlon that summer—or rather, what he called 'my noble tool.' He was passed from one queen's mouth to another like Southern fried chicken at the communal table of a boarding house."

Dame May Whitty

That summer, Brando was often seen escorting Dame May Whitty around town. In 1945, she was appearing at the Provincetown Playhouse, repeating her performance in *Night Must Fall,* in which she'd scored a hit both in London's West End and on Broadway. Based on her co-starring with Robert Montgomery in the 1937 film version, she'd won an Oscar.

It was Dame May who introduced Brando to his benefactor for the summer,

Broadway Falls in Love with a Sweaty Red T-Shirt and Too-Tight Jeans

Clayton Snow, known as "the Queen of P-town."

A jealous rival and gossipy competitor, Steele detested "Claytina," his nickname for Snow, who he alleged "looked like Eleanor Roosevelt in 1934."

Snow was a bartender at Central House, a battered dive next door to the playhouse. Dame May and Brando came every night after her performance for her "nip of gin."

The actress arranged for a homeless Brando to move into Snow's two-room cottage on a lane called Pumpkin Hollow. In the days that followed, Snow announced to half of P-town that, "I've had Marlon. In exchange for one rough-trade blow job a day, I'm giving him room and board. I told him that he'd have to hustle his own drinks and spending money from the other queens."

Steele said that Brando didn't confine his sexual charms exclusively to Snow. "He made out like a bandit with a lot of young women that summer, mostly actresses or dancers. He liked women with dark skin. Marlon looked upon sex as a giant smörgåsbord, and he wanted a taste from every platter."

Established in 1933, The Flagship was the most popular restaurant in P-town, having been patronized in the past by Gertrude Stein and Anaïs Nin. Tennessee that summer was a regular patron. He appeared almost nightly with his lover, Pancho Rodriguez y Gonzalez, a strikingly handsome young desk clerk he'd first met at La Fonda de Taos in New Mexico, and with whom he later lived with in New Orleans.

That night, Brando was invited to join Tennessee's table by James Bidwell, an acquaintance of the playwright's. Tennessee's *The Glass Menagerie* had opened in New York around Easter of 1945. Brando had seen the play and had high praise for both Laurette Taylor's performance as Amanda and for Tennessee's writing.

At the time of this historic meeting, Tennessee was struggling with a play he called *The Poker Night. [Its title was later changed to* A Streetcar Named Desire.*]*

Before the meal ended, Brando presented a drunken, cackling Tennessee with a piece of silver jewelry handmade by his lover (Wally Cox) in New York. Tennessee slipped the silver bracelet onto his wrist and dangled it in front of the other diners at his table. "Then he moved in on Marlon with the inner radar he seemed to possess," said Bidwell. "For Tennessee, it was love at first sight."

"Does that mean we're engaged?" Tennessee said flirtatiously to Brando.

Seated beside Tennessee, Pancho stared at the new boy in town with a barely controlled fury. He had refused to speak to Brando when introduced by Bidwell.

"Oh, that blonde hair," Tennessee proclaimed not

Pancho Rodruiguez

187

only to Brando but to the table at large, as he took in the actor's sensitive, poetic face, devoting equal attention to the muscles encased like sausage in a white T-shirt. Referring to Brando, he said, rapturously. "They sent a Viking god directly from the shores of Valhalla."

"Marlon Brando," he repeated the words, dangling his bracelet. "Soon, all the world will know of you. As I told John van Druten after sitting through his *I Remember Mama*, I didn't remember Mama at all. But who could forget Marlon Brando and that fabulous erection you were showing on stage?"

Much to Pancho's rage and regret, Brando continued to show up at The Flagship, where he would "bum meals off Tennessee," according to Pancho. Increasingly isolated, Pancho would sit beside his lover nightly, being virtually ignored, as Tennessee amused Brando with stories of the theater.

Occasionally, Tennessee would look over at Pancho and make some comment as if he weren't there. "Pancho fears he will lose me to the seductions that fame will bring. When one becomes famous, one must share oneself with the world, like it or not. When you become famous, Marlon, and I'm sure you will, you will understand the great burden that fame imposes on a life. Your own life will never be yours again."

Pancho here prefers a one-to-one relationship," Tennessee said to Brando. "But at night, my heart is a lonely hunter. I have never endorsed the idea of sexual exclusivity. One must venture forth each night onto the lonely beaches to find greater tenderness and a rawer and immediate emotion that one can encounter in more stable relationships."

At that point, according to Steele, Pancho "stormed out of the café. Then, when Tennessee suggested that I, too, should leave him alone to talk theater with Marlon, I made my exit like Lynn Fontanne at her final curtain call."

On other nights in front of Brando, Steele, and other members of Provincetown's gay colony, Tennessee amused his listeners. "It was important to him

Pancho Rodriguez, depicted in the left-hand photo with **Tennessee**, his lover, feared competition from "the shirtless one," **Marlon Brando** (*right*).

that everybody be an audience," Steele said. "Most of us had already heard his stories, everyone except Brando. He took in every word that Tennessee said, viewing it as Holy Writ."

Neither Steele nor anyone else knew on what night Tennessee invited Brando for a walk along a deserted beach. It probably occurred the weekend that Pancho traveled alone to Boston, Tennessee refusing to go with him. The playwright invited Brando for a moonlit walk to one of the Peaked Hill "dune shacks," informing him that Eugene O'Neill had once occupied one of those shanties.

Years later, in Key West, over "pillow talk" with his long-time lover, Frank Merlo, Tennessee revealed details of that long-ago experience with Brando.

"I think you and I might find a bit of comfort with each other," Tennessee said to Brando. "perhaps you can find solace for your pain by suckling on my breasts."

Brando erroneously told Tennessee that he was straight.

"Yes," Tennessee said, "don't you find that the land here, especially the weather at night, all gray and foggy with strange lights, evokes a stage setting? As for being heterosexual, that is a lofty ambition not achieved by all of us. On many a dark night, when the heart feels desolate, you might need my nurturing. All you have to do is lie back on the warm sands, perhaps with the ocean water cleansing your feet. I'll transport you to a sublime shore in a far and distant land. Your heterosexuality will not be compromised in any way, and I'll even pay you. I know you're short of money, and I'll give you five dollars, and that's my highest price ever."

"I don't do it for the money," Brando said. He rejected Tennessee's offer of fellatio, at least on that night, but, according to Merlo, "Tenn got his man about two weeks later." To Merlo, Tennessee remembered seducing a slightly drunken Brando as "the tide lapped under the wharf and the hungry seagulls screeched overhead."

"I managed to extract two offerings from that magnificent tool before I would remove that treasure from my mouth," Tennessee said. "By the time Marlon's cannon shot off for the final time, the early streaks of dawn were in the sky."

Tennessee told Darwin Porter, "Briefly, at least, I entertained a vision of myself becoming Mrs. Marlon Brando, living in some rose-covered cottage with him on the Cape. There, in our cozy nest by the sea, we'd settle in and enjoy everlasting happiness until the end of time. Although Marlon that summer temporarily turned his splendid body over to me, it was a vessel I was to possess only briefly. He was destined to share his magnificence with others. *So many others.*"

***

Deep within the "blonde bombshell" period of her life, Shelley Winters met Marlon Brando at the Actors Studio in Manhattan, where he was taking acting classes with Elia Kazan.

From the first day he met her, Brando was drawn to this actress, who Frank

Sinatra once defined as "this bowlegged bitch of a Brooklyn blonde."

Brando began to meet her backstage after her nightly appearance in the hit musical *Oklahoma!* at Broadway's St. James Theatre, where she'd replaced Vivian Allen as Ado Annie.

One night, he invited her back to his apartment during one of the worst blizzards to hit New York during the 1940s. In her beaver coat and felt-lined galoshes, she braved the chill to climb five flights of stars to the rundown apartment the actor shared with his lover, Wally Cox.

In the apartment, he introduced her to his pet raccoon, which she'd accuse of releasing eighteen separate farts during her time there. After an awful dinner, he took her to his bed, which was in the kitchen, where he shared some body heat, and a lot more. She later gave him a good review, calling him "sexual lightning."

In her beaver coat, over breakfast, she casually mentioned that Mary Martin, the reigning musical star of Broadway, had visited the cast backstage after attending a performance of *Oklahoma!*

"She told me she'd heard of this play by Tennessee Williams called *A Streetcar Named Desire,* and she thinks it'll be bigger than *The Glass Menagerie.* She wants to play the lead role of Blanche DuBois against a brutish character, Stanley Kowalski. From what I hear, it's a part with your name on it."

"I don't do musicals," he answered.

"It's heavy drama, baby," Shelley said. "Martin wants to show the world she's also a great dramatic actress. Bette Davis has even threatened to star in it and put some life back into a stalled career. I know Pauline Lord and Fay Bainter want it. But for my money, I'm voting for that steel magnolia, Margaret Sullavan."

"Who's up for the Kowalski part?" he asked.

"Kazan is going to direct it, and I hear he wants a real big name like John Garfield, He told me the role calls for 'a quintessential semi-Simian actor of undiluted virility.'"

Two views of **Shelley Winters**, inset photo: raccoon.
Right figure in right-hand photo: **Marlon**

190

"Fancy words for 'a brute.'"

"Burt Lancaster has also been suggested," she said. "But I hear it for a fact that Irene Mayer Selznick, who's producing the show, doesn't want either Garfield or Lancaster. She's after Monty Clift." The remark about Monty was not true. Shelley tossed in his name just to provoke Brando into a jealous fury. "Fuck that!" was his response. From that moment, she knew he was going to pursue the role. He told her that when he'd first encountered Tennessee, "That must have been the play he was working on in Provincetown. Perhaps he's written me into the role of Kowalski."

From the stairwell, as she was leaving, Shelley called back to Brando. "You passed the kitchen bed audition last night. I'm ready for a repeat tonight. Meet me backstage tonight at *Oklahoma!* I think this is going to be the beginning of a big love affair. But you've got to get rid of that goddamn stinking raccoon first!"

Even before *Streetcar* went into rehearsal, rumor was rampant on Broadway that it would become the hit of 1947, the second in the till-then brief career of Tennessee.

In its simplest form, *Streetcar* was the story of a neurotic and aristocratic Southern belle, Blanche DuBois. She's lost Belle Reve, her family's estate, and with her illusions still fragile but intact, arrives in New Orleans, having been run out of her hometown because of her profligate ways. She seeks refuge with her sister, Stella, and her brutal brother-in-law, Stanley Kowalski.

From her sixteen million dollar fortune, producer Irene Selznick invested only $25,000 to launch *Streetcar* on Broadway. For the rest of the $100,000 budget, she got Cary Grant and Jock Whitney to invest.

She did not ask her father, Louis B. Mayer, to invest "because Dad likes only happy endings." Also ignored as a potential "angel" was her estranged husband, David O. Selznick, who was carrying on a torrid affair at the time with the beautiful actress, Jennifer Jones, whom he would eventually marry.

As various actresses were being considered for the role of Blanche, a call came in from the Canadian actor, Hume Cronyn. He had been married to the British actress, Jessica Tandy, since 1942. He was only too aware that her career in Hollywood was going nowhere. He invited both Kazan and Tennessee to see a one-act play, *Portrait of a Madonna,* at the Actors Lab in Los Angeles. The protagonist of this play was an early version of Blanche DuBois. Irene joined them to see the production.

Whereas Tennessee and Kazan were immediately enthusiastic about Tandy's performance, Irene wasn't so sure. She was still holding out for a bigger name star. "We need a Vivien Leigh type, but I bet we can't get her. Margaret Sullavan can do it."

Mary Martin had almost convinced Irene she could play Blanche. For a while, Irene considered casting Gregory Peck as Stanley opposite Martin.

But finally, after much debate, Tennessee and Kazan got Irene to offer Tandy the role of Blanche DuBois, which she accepted. The search was then on for an actor to play Stanley. Irene suggested Van Heflin, but both of her associates refused. "He's earnest and dependable—and that's it," Kazan said.

Then Irene put forth the name of Edmond O'Brien. "A face permanently fixed in a troubled squint and with a voice that sounds as if it brings only bad news," was Kazan's assessment.

Then Brando's name was put forth by Kazan. "He's too young," Tennessee objected. "He looks like a boy. I envision Stanley as a thirty-year-old Polack."

Kazan had just finished making *Gentleman's Agreement,* starring Gregory Peck and John Garfield. *Gentleman's Agreement* would win the Best Picture Oscar for 1947. Kazan affectionately called Garfield "Julie," and he told both Irene

Irene Mayer Selznick

Mayer Selznick and Tennessee that the young actor would be ideal for the blue collar role of Stanley Kowalski in *A Streetcar Named Desire.* Kazan and Garfield had worked together in New York as members of the experimental Group Theater, spearheaded by Lee Strasberg, Cheryl Crawford, and Harold Clurman.

Though Tennessee wasn't certain, Irene approved Kazan's suggestion. based on the terms of their contracts they had the power to overrule a playwright as regards casting decisions.

[Tough, cynical, sexually appealing, and edgy, both on and off the screen, and well-suited for the execution of rebellious, working-class characters, New York bad boy Garfield (1913-1952), after growing up in abject poverty in New York City during the Depression, had burst into stardom like a meteor, emoting with Lana Turner in The Postman Always Rings Twice, *and opposite man-eating Joan Crawford in* Humoresque, *both films released in 1946. During the peak of the "Red Scare," he denied Communist affiliation and refused to implicate his friends and associates, effectively ending his film career. His early death at the age of 39, in part because of stress from his battles with right-wing government watchdogs who included Senator Joseph McCarthy, led to his evaluation as a intensely realistic predecessor of such Method actors as Montgomery Clift, Marlon Brando, and James Dean.]*

Arriving in New York fresh from his hit in the film, *Body and Soul* (1947), in which he had played a dim-witted boxer, Garfield was cocky and demanding.

On an otherwise deserted stage, Garfield did a first read-through of *A Streetcar Named Desire*, with Kazan playing the parts of both Blanche and Stella. In Garfield's judgment, "The male role is very secondary," he told both Kazan and Tennessee. "This Stanley character is a mere prop for Blanche's histrionics."

He did not reject the part, but instead issued a series of demands that included an ultimatum that Tennessee would rewrite the play, making Stanley's part the focus of the drama and expanding his role. He also wanted a guarantee that he could leave the play after only four months and that, in the event that the play was adapted into a film, he would have the first right of refusal at the screen version of Stanley.

Tennessee utterly rejected Garfield's request for a rewrite, and Irene categorically refused Garfield's other demands.

Although out of the running himself, Brando was eager to learn any news he could about how casting for *Streetcar* was going. Karl Malden himself told Brando that he'd been assigned the role of Mitch, Stanley's sidekick. Brando had also learned that the relatively unknown actress, Kim Hunter, had been cast as Stanley's brutalized wife, Stella.

At the Actors Studio, Brando confronted his teacher, Kazan. He had heard that Garfield "all but had the part of Stanley, and informed Kazan, "I think Garfield would be perfect as Stanley."

John Garfield

Later, Kazan remembered that Marlon was "stunned" when he told him that Garfield was out and Burt Lancaster was flying into New York to read for the part.

"A circus acrobat?" Brando said. "I'm sure that's the kind of background Tennessee had in mind when writing the character of Stanley."

Defensively, Kazan read a newspaper clipping he was carrying with him. It was by Sheilah Graham, the popular Hollywood columnist and former mistress of the novelist, F. Scott Fitzgerald.

Gushing with praise after seeing Lancaster emote in *The Killers*, a film adapted from a short story by Ernest Hemingway, Graham wrote: "Masculinity was oozing from *[Lancaster's]* every pore. He was thirty-two but looked twenty-two, and what a physique! I could see the muscles rippling up and down beneath his open shirt. It was a pleasure being with a future star at the beginning. He is always so friendly, so eager to please."

"Sounds to me like you want to turn *Streetcar* into a male burlesque show," Brando said.

"Eat your heart out!" Kazan told him.

"I was told that Burt, while in the circus, posed for the meat magazines," Brando said. "You know, in those homoerotic Greco-Roman stances. And there are a lot of candid frontal nude shots of him in circulation. Maybe you could acquire one of them and run a nude billboard of Burt outside the theater. Surely that would guarantee you business for *Streetcar.*"

Kazan remembered losing his patience and actually slapping Brando. "Fortunately, he didn't hit me back. 'Don't let your jealousy overwhelm you,' I told him."

"I've got a great body too!" Brando protested. "I work out all the time."

"Your body's fine for Stanley," Kazan said. "I've told you before, you're just too young. What I didn't tell you, and I'll tell you now that I'm mad at you, you don't have the role in you. The part of Stanley Kowalski is just too big for your limitations as an actor."

"You're a rude, stupid man," Brando said. "I'm dropping out of your class—you're a rotten teacher anyway. Someday I'll be the biggest star on Broadway. You'll come begging to me. Just you wait and see."

* * *

What happened next has become part of Broadway legend and lore. Even today, the scenario is a bit hazy, and all the eye-witnesses are dead, leaving only sketchy reports. "No one," Kazan recalled years later, "was exactly in the loop about that strange and long-ago week that Marlon and Burt Lancaster spent together in New York."

Collaborators:
Tennessee Williams with **Elia Kazan**

Lancaster arrived in New York with his agent, Harold Hecht, a former dancer for the Martha Graham Company and the son of a Brooklyn iron contractor. Lancaster, whose career was soaring, was clearly Hecht's newest meal ticket, and he was ferocious in his attempt to make a big star out of his newly acquired client. The role of Stanley Kowalski in *Streetcar* was only one of several offers Lancaster was considering. Most of the excitement over him was generated for movie roles, not coming from the Broadway stage, except in the case of Kazan and Irene Selznick. Hollywood producers, not just Sheilah Graham, saw his star potential.

Accompanied by Hecht, "guarding him like a box of gold from Fort Knox" in Irene's words, Burt arrived at her grandly furnished Fifth Avenue apartment. She was impressed with the actor's good looks, physique, and male charm. But she later told Tennessee and Kazan that she perceived that Lancaster was more interested in securing the movie contract to play Stanley than he was in appearing on Broadway.

During her first meeting with Lancaster and Hecht, she told them of her triumph earlier in the day. She claimed that "I fished out Tennessee's best line from his wastepaper basket: *'I have always depended on the kindness of strangers.'*"

"I just wish that Williams had put a line or two that good in the mouth of Kowalski," Lancaster told her.

Over drinks, Lancaster agreed to appear at the New Amsterdam Roof Theatre *[on 42nd Street at Broadway]* the following morning for a read-through of *Streetcar*. Once again, as he had with Garfield, Kazan assumed the reading roles of both Blanche and Stella. At the rehearsal hall, perhaps to show off his manly physique, Lancaster insisted on removing his shirt.

Just before the reading, Tennessee slipped into the darkened theater and, without announcing himself, took a seat near the back row. He continued to conceal himself during Lancaster's first "blind read" of the play. It was the only time that Lancaster would appear as Stanley Kowalski in front of anyone.

Tennessee was very impressed with the reading and even more so with Lancaster's physical presence, the style of which he had envisioned for whatever actor would play the role of Stanley.

But because both Kazan and Irene had asked him not to interfere in casting, he quietly sneaked out of the theater and did not introduce himself to Lancaster, the male star of his future movie, *The Rose Tattoo,* with Anna Magnani.

Within forty-eight hours, Hecht called Kazan to tell him that Burt would not be available for an appearance on Broadway, because he had to return to Hollywood to make a film for producer Hal Wallis. Hecht went on to tell Kazan that he wanted "Burt to be your first choice for Stanley when the film version is made."

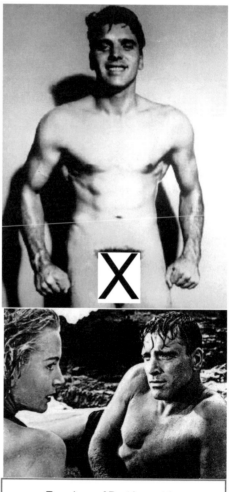

Despondent over not being able to cast the right actor in the role of Stanley, Kazan met with Irene once more to reconsider Brando. In spite of their temporary split, the director finally concluded that Brando "would be a more multi-dimensional Stanley than either Garfield or Lancaster, once he finds himself in the role, which will take weeks, of course."

Irene and Kazan finally decided to send Brando on a trip to Provincetown where Tennessee was applying his final polishing to *Streetcar.* "If Tennessee approves of Marlon in the role, he'll be our Stanley," Kazan said, "but only if our favorite homosexual says yes. One look at Marlon, and I bet Tennessee will get a hard-on." At the time, Kazan was not aware that his playwright not only knew Brando, but that he had already been sexually intimate with him.

On a windy, blustery New York day, Kazan encountered Brando at the Actors Studio where he'd returned in spite of his threat to abandon his studies there. "I've called Tennessee," Kazan told him. "He's waiting for you

Two views of **Burt Lancaster**
lower photo: With **Deborah Kerr** in
From Here to Eternity

on the Cape. He wants to hear you read for the part of Stanley. If he goes for you, you've got the part. Of course, we can always have your blonde hair dyed brown."

"How am I going to get there?" Brando asked. "I'm broke."

"I'll lend you twenty," Kazan said, reaching into his pocket.

Years later, Kazan recalled that moment in the history of the theater with a touch of melodramatic nostalgia. "Marlon headed for the Cape to meet Tennessee. It was to be a date with destiny!"

Inviting Marlon for a Midnight Romp on the Beach

With the twenty dollars in his pocket that Kazan had given him, Brando devoured all the food he could eat. "I was starving," he recalled. "Hadn't eaten a square meal in two days. Just peanut butter without any bread."

With the money he had left over, he bought groceries for Celia Webb, his girl friend from Colombia, and her son. Stashing the young boy with a friend, Celia joined Brando on the trip to Provincetown to read for Tennessee. Since neither of them at this point had any money, Brando stuck out his thumb, hitchhiking along the way and bumming food wherever they could find it. Celia and Brando arrived in P-Town three days late. "In a tizzy," Tennessee had given up all hope of his "star" ever showing up. Kazan had warned him how undependable the actor was.

It turned out that Brando and Celia had to hitch rides with at least eight different drivers before finally reaching the tip of Cape Cod.

In Tennessee's battered cottage, Brando recalled that, "The toilet was overflowing with shit. That shit was swimming onto the tile floor—no one had mopped it up. I dug my bare hand into the toilet and pulled out what looked like a human fetus before delivery. Before I got there, Tennessee's motley crew had been using the bushes. Even the lights were out. Tennessee said they had been 'plunged into everlasting darkness.' I even fixed the God damn electricity using copper pennies in the fuse box."

Sharing the Provincetown house with Tennessee were two strong-willed dames from Texas, producer Margo Jones and her estranged companion, Joanna Albus. The two women had come to the Cape to meet with Tennessee about mounting a production in Texas of *Summer and Smoke.*

Nicknamed "The Texas Tornado" by Tennessee, Jones had spent a period of her life directing plays on Broadway before heading back to the Southwest, landing in Dallas where she'd launched a repertory group named Theatre '47. Tennessee referred to Joanna as "the Tornado's sidekick." Later, Joanna would become assistant stage manager during *Streetcar's* stint on Broadway.

Early gossip in P-Town linked Tennessee romantically with Margo until Joanna arrived on the scene to "set these gay boys straight." In Key West, Tennessee once said, "I have never been especially attracted to lesbians, although there has been a notable exception here and there."

Also sharing the cottage was Pancho Rodriguez, Tennessee's notoriously jealous Mexican lover. At first Pancho threatened to leave P-Town and travel to New Orleans if Brando spent the night. He was just as jealous of Brando as he'd been on the first night they'd met years before. Tennessee prevailed upon Pancho to stay, and he did, although he refused to stick around for Brando's reading.

As he had before, Brando bonded with Tennessee, finding him "a pristine soul who suffered from a deep-seated neurosis, a sensitive, gentle man destined to destroy himself."

In his autobiography, Brando noted, but only casually, that the playwright was a homosexual, "but not effeminate or outwardly aggressive about it. There was something eating at his insides that ultimately propelled him to his death."

Margo Jones

Tennessee later recalled that "all of us were drunk when Brando read for the part of Stanley." Taking the role he secretly coveted for himself, Tennessee played Blanche. He didn't need a script.

"The reading lasted less than two minutes," Margo recalled. "We just knew that Brando was destined to be Stanley. I let out a Texas whoop like I do at the rodeo."

At first Tennessee didn't say anything after hearing Brando read. His face looked as if he had disappointed Tennessee, who just sat there in a wicker peacock chair intently studying Brando as he sucked smoke through a hygienic cigarette holder full of absorbent crystals. "The part is yours!" Tennessee finally said.

Leaving the women to prepare the beds for the night, Tennessee invited Brando for a midnight stroll on the same beach where he'd seduced him some time before. Pancho had gone to the bars in P-Town, and the playwright didn't expect him to return to the cottage any time soon.

Tennessee later recalled that neither Brando nor he said a word. "No mention was made of *Streetcar*. In the moonlight, I had never seen a man of such extraordinary beauty."

The myth about Tennessee never making a pass at his actors has been perpetuated, often in biographies, for decades. The playwright's longtime lover, Frank Merlo, Pancho's eventual replacement, claimed that the statement was true in a technical sense. "But we're splitting hairs here. Tenn never made a pass at actors. They made passes at him. Or, rather, they made themselves available to him. On the beach that night—Tenn told me this himself—he didn't have to grope Brando. Brando whipped it out for Tenn. What gay man worth his salt wouldn't have taken advantage of that? Tenn was only human. And Brando was his sexual fantasy. In Tenn's mixed-up head, Brando and Stanley Kowalski had meshed into the same erotic image. Theirs was hardly a love affair, like Tenn and me. Brando was rough trade to Tenn. He didn't mind servicing the stud."

Tennessee was less than candid in his memoirs, claiming (inaccurately) that he kept the relationship businesslike between Brando and himself. "I have never played around with actors," Tennessee falsely claimed. "It is a point of morality with me. And anyhow Brando was not the type to get a part that way."

Perhaps that was true, but it didn't take into account that Brando had seduced playwrights before, often very famous ones.

Back in his cottage at one o'clock in the morning, Tennessee noted that Pancho still hadn't returned from the bars. Brando claimed he was starving. No great chef, Tennessee went into the kitchen and made him a ham sandwich. The ham was dry, the bread stale. He also poured Brando a glass of milk. In one gulp, he finished the milk and then requested the whole quart, which he proceeded to finish off. "Pure Stanley," Tennessee said.

He kissed Brando on the lips and headed for his own bunk bed. He noted that Celia was asleep under a quilt in a corner of the living room, where Brando went to join her for the night.

The next morning, Tennessee said that Pancho had not returned from his bar crawl of the night before, but Brando didn't seem unduly concerned. Tennessee lent Brando twenty dollars so he could buy bus tickets back to New York. Leaving the cottage, Brando told Celia that "Tennessee is a very easy touch."

On the Greyhound bus heading back to New York, Brando never spoke to Celia. He was lost in a world of his own. "I didn't have anything to say to her because my mind was completely occupied with how to play Stanley. I feared the part was too big for me. A sense of terror, unlike any I'd known before, came over me. I was shaking and sweating a lot. Celia tried to comfort me, but no one could. A demon was taking over inside me and squeezing my guts."

With Brando out the door, Tennessee called Kazan in New York. "I want Brando to be Stanley Kowalski. He's far better than Garfield could ever be."

When Kazan put down the phone, he called Irene Selznick. "That son of a bitch of a faggot up there on the Cape is riding a crush on Brando."

Back in his cottage, Tennessee wrote a letter to his literary agent, Audrey Wood, calling Brando a "God-sent Stanley." He seemed delighted to cast the role eight years younger than he had written it. In the letter, he praised Brando for delivering "the best reading I have ever heard," and that coming from an actor already notorious for his bad readings in which he mumbled, sometimes incoherently. In his letter, Tennessee noted "the physical appeal and sensuality of Brando, at least as much as Burt Lancaster."

Back in New York for the rehearsals of *Streetcar,* Brando is credited with causing the final break between Tennessee and Pancho. During one particularly violent and jealous argument over Brando, Pancho grabbed Tennessee's typewriter and tossed it out of the hotel window, seriously injuring a pedestrian below—in fact, almost killing him.

That was all too much for Tennessee. He bought Pancho a one-way ticket to New Orleans and gave him a thousand dollars "to jump-start another life for yourself."

Pancho had calmed down after the typewriter incident. Pleading and even crying before Tennessee, he begged him to let him stay. "It's over," a somewhat callous Tennessee said. "Time to end what should never have begun in the first place."

On the way out the door, Pancho said, "I hope you and Brando will be very happy together. He's your fantasy both on stage and off."

According to Frank Merlo, Tennessee, post-Pancho, "made himself available" to Brando on several occasions during rehearsals and during the long run of *Streetcar*. Brando was not interested. As reported by Frank, Tennessee told him, "The last time I enjoyed Brando was that night on the beach at the Cape. It is a memory I'll always treasure. If he had wanted to come and live with me, I would have asked Pancho to leave much sooner. But alas, my relationship with Brando never got beyond a blow-job. In my already broken heart, I knew even then that it is a hopeless pursuit every time we go after the unobtainable."

* * *

Tennessee was inside Manhattan's New Amsterdam Theatre on October 5, 1947, to watch Brando begin rehearsals. Despite the success of his reading in Provincetown, Brando was not fitting into the role of Stanley Kowalski. Privately, both Tennessee and Kazan recognized that.

On the third day of rehearsals, right in front of both Kazan and Tennessee, Brando virtually fired himself. He shocked Tennessee when he said, "I can't play this character."

Kazan remembered Brando "all swearing and trembling with grief and anxiety."

He turned his face to Kazan, but his words were actually meant for Tennessee, who was hovering nearby with a pained look on his face.

"I hate Stanley Kowalski," Brando shouted. "He never doubts himself. His ego is so strong. He's always right—or at least thinks he's right—and he's never been afraid. He's the complete opposite of all the things I am."

"You're wonderful in the part because you don't have to be like Stanley," Tennessee assured him. "You only have to act like Stanley. This role could be the defining moment of your theatrical career before it has even started."

Slowly Kazan lured Brando back into the rehearsal hall, putting his arm around him to offer him a kind of macho comfort. "Just think of Stanley as a complete hedonist," Kazan said. "The type of guy who sucks on a cigar all day because he can't suck on a teat. He conquers with his penis like you conquer dame after dame with what you call your noble tool."

During the first week of rehearsals, Tennessee showed up for a assembled gathering on the rooftop terrace of the New Amsterdam, where Florenz Ziegfeld, in the 1920s, had staged midnight musical revues. He circulated among the cast members, speaking to each of them individually. "I'm dying of pancreatic cancer," Tennessee claimed. Brando and Jessica Tandy, along with Karl Malden and Kim Hunter, were stunned at the news and didn't know what to say, other than muttering their condolences.

Kazan was already aware that Tennessee "was the world's most hysterical hypochondriac." He went over and embraced Tennessee. "Don't worry," he told the playwright. "You're a tough old bird and will live to be a hundred years old—maybe more. Now, let's get on with the rehearsals of this poetic tragedy."

As a playwright, Tennessee had originally intended that sympathy generated by the play be directed toward Blanche. But as he sat with Kazan during the weeks of rehearsals, he clearly saw that Brando was altering his original intention. Instead of advising Kazan to restrain him, Tennessee proclaimed, "The boy is a genius! Let's see what he can do. He's a Lawrencian fantasy of the earthy proletarian male." He paused. "A regular midnight cowboy."

Years later in Key West, Tennessee would share his early reaction with his neighbor, novelist James Leo Herlihy. The writer so liked the expression, *Midnight Cowboy*, that he wrote a novel about it, which was made into the Oscar-winning Best Picture of 1969.

Robert Lewis, one of the founders of Actors' Studio, showed up one afternoon and sat with Tennessee to watch Brando emote with Jessica Tandy. Then, in an analysis very tuned into the studio's penchant for unearthing the raw motivation behind an actor's success at interpreting a role, he said, "Marlon is playing against Dodie, not Tandy as Blanche."

He had to explain to Tennessee that "Dodie" was the nickname of Brando's mother, Dorothy Brando.

"In your creation of Stanley, Marlon has found the same heavy drinking, the coquettish sexual flirtations, the lost hopes and dreams that he'd experienced with his own mother. He is seeing Dodie up there on that stage—not Tandy. In the rape scene, he finally fulfilled his incestuous wish to deflower his own mother."

Tennessee was stunned by such an interpretation, not knowing if it were accurate or not.

Lewis dismissed talk of how Brando was slowly and cerebrally "discovering Stanley" as he got deeper and deeper into the role, and offered a far earthier and more pragmatic analysis: "Marlon used his portrayal of Stanley as an excuse to pick up a lot of blue-collar New Jersey truck drivers and give them blow-jobs. That's how he imbued himself with the semen of Stanley."

Kazan was not completely aware of the details associated with Brando's nocturnal adventures during rehearsals for *Streetcar*. Often, on the morning of a scheduled rehearsal, his star actor showed up late. "On some occasions Marlon looked like the shit had been beaten out of him," Kazan recalled. "Which it probably had. All of the cast knew that Marlon was fucking every woman in sight and, for a change of pace, picking up rough trade along the waterfront."

Brando invited Shelley Winters and one of his best friends, Carlo Fiore, to attend a rehearsal of *Streetcar*. They sat in the darkened theater with Tennessee between them. Fiore told Tennessee, "Marlon has put that pelvis-thrust forward slouch of his to good use and turned the petulant pout into a snarl. His T-shirt discloses the heavily muscled torso of a truck driver. He mumbles like a moron. He scratches his asshole, digging in deep to get at the itch."

Lucinda Ballard had worked on costumes for *The Glass Menagerie,* and Tennessee wanted to use her again on *Streetcar.* She met with Tennessee to discuss Brando's wardrobe. "His skin-tight jeans are tapered to show the muscles in his thighs, and to showcase his genitals. During fittings, Marlon insisted on wearing no underwear. He claimed he wanted the jeans to fit like a second skin."

Before the opening, Kazan went to Tennessee, saying, "I think Irene was right. Tandy is too strong an actress to play a weak, vulnerable soul like Blanche."

Consequently, as part of an effort to make her more vulnerable *[and as part of a controversial psychological technique sometimes associated with method acting as espoused during its confrontational early years]*, Kazan ordered Brando, Kim Hunter, and Karl Malden to subject her to touch of emotional sadism.

After she was restrained with ropes, the actors made fun of her in the most cruel and potentially destructive say. She was attacked for her "small tits," her "pus-laden vagina," her utter "lack of talent," even her "cunty smell."

When Tennessee came into the theater and discovered this, he ordered all of them to stop tormenting Tandy. "Are you out of your mind?" Tennessee asked Kazan. "There are limits as to how far you can go in tormenting an actor."

Brando detested Tandy, simultaneous with having an offstage affair with the actress who played "Stella," his onstage wife, Blanche's sister, as interpreted by Kim Hunter.

"Tennessee told me that the only reason Stella, an aristocratic Southern dame, stays with Stanley is because of the way he fucks her," Brando told Kazan.

Tennessee followed the cast and his play to out-of-town tryouts, where he and Kazan listened to Tandy's increasingly strident complaints. "If Brando feels bored or tired, he acts bored or tired. If he feels like a homosexual, he becomes one on stage."

One night in New Haven, Tennessee watched in horror as Brando played Stanley "as a swish." Later, Tennessee berated him for his outrageous performance. Tandy also denounced him, defining him as "the most unprofessional actor I've ever worked with."

She complained to both Kazan and Tennessee that, based on his occasional boredom with both the play and his role, Brando was shifting the emphasis of the play almost nightly. As a performer, she never knew what to expect from him. She had good reasons to complain. Once, in New Haven, during her delivery of one of Blanche's most poignant speeches, the audience snickered. She turned around and, to her horror, caught Brando clownishly puffing away at a cigarette which he had inserted into one of his nostrils.

201

After she complained that Brando was "destroying the integrity" of *Streetcar,* Tennessee attended a performance. After watching some of Brando's alterations, Tennessee proclaimed to Tandy that "Marlon is adding a new dimension to *Streetcar.*"

With a growing sense of despair, Tandy endured night after night, living in dread of what Brando might do at that evening's performance. An acting career loomed in her future, making her wonder if she'd survive opening night playing opposite an actor she called "Broadway's bad boy."

Tryouts in New Haven preceded the troupe's migration to Boston, where Kazan told Tennessee "the blue bloods will object to the raw, animal sex of the play." But contrary to those predictions, *Streetcar* was well received. The cast continued with its optimistic streak as *Streetcar* opened to rave reviews in Philadelphia.

Kazan also warned Tennessee that the early success of the show "will have New York critics sharpening their knives for us. New York critics didn't always follow the praise that came 'from hicks in the boondocks.' I told the cast in Philadelphia that *Streetcar* could be compared to oysters. 'Remember,' I cautioned them, 'not everybody likes oysters.'"

Kazan exhibited increasing bouts of bizarre behavior before the play's opening in New York City. Tennessee interpreted his director as "a bit of a homophobe," as did other members of the cast. But as time went by, the playwright noticed Kazan showing more and more interest in the subject. Tennessee once speculated that he felt that the womanizing Kazan was a closeted homosexual.

"Just show me a womanizer," he said, "from Errol Flynn to Howard Hughes, on down, and I bet you'll find a lavender streak in there somewhere."

One night after a performance, Kazan approached Brando backstage. "I want to know what takes place when two faggots sleep together. I mean, I can picture it in my mind, but I don't quite get the logistics."

In response, on a dare, Brando invited Kazan to share a hotel room with him with two beds. "I'll have a homosexual encounter in my bed, and you can show up with your lady of the evening. We'll watch you and you can watch us."

Brando selected a young actor, Sandy Campbell, who just happened to be the lover of Donald Windham, Tennessee's best friend.

To Brando's surprise, Kazan showed up with Kim Hunter, whom Brando had already seduced.

Sandy later told Tennessee and his lover, Frank Merlo, "Brando and I put on a great show for them. I wanted to perform my best, throwing more gusto into the sex than I usually did. We really went at it. Earlier, Marlon had suggested that we go at it like two animals in heat, getting into every conceivable position that we could think of. I called it our gymnastic romp. As far as I could tell, Kazan seduced Kim in a rather boring, old-fashioned missionary position."

Sandy Campbell is the only source of this amazing story. At first his claim might be met with a degree of skepticism, but not after 1988 when Knopf published *Elia Kazan: A Life,* the director's memoirs. In this autobiography, Kazan admitted that he once extended an invitation to Tennessee for "a double date." The memoir went on to describe how, while Kazan occupied a twin bed with "a young lady" (name unknown), Kazan watched Tennessee and "a Mexican jungle cat" (a reference to Pancho Rodriguez) make love. Kazan's critique of Pancho's lovemaking? "In a word, rambunctious."

After a year's run of *Streetcar* on Broadway Kazan could admit that homosexual love "was no longer a mystery to me."

Truman's Fantasy Encounter with Brando

Author Truman Capote, Brando's future nemesis, during the rehearsals of *Streetcar* was on his way backstage to search for his friend, Tennessee Williams, who was running late for an agreed-upon luncheon date. As he was to later recall, "I stopped in my tracks when I encountered a young man asleep."

"It was a winter afternoon," Truman said. "I found the place deserted except for this brawny young man stretched out atop a table on the stage under the gloomy glare of stage lights. He was sleeping soundly. He wore a white T-shirt and denim trousers that did little to conceal the outline of his genitals. He had a squat gymnasium physique and weightlifter's arms. It was definitely a Charles Atlas chest but he had a copy of Freud resting on the chest of that perfect body. I took him for a stagehand, one who definitely moonlighted for pay with the queens of Broadway."

"I looked closely at his face hoping to wake him up gently and perhaps arrange a rendezvous with him later where I would personally audition him," Truman continued. "It was as if a stranger's head had been attached to the brawny body, as in certain counterfeit photographs. For this face was so very untough, superimposing, as it did, an almost angelic refinement and gentleness upon hard-jawed good looks: Taut skin, a broad, high forehead, wide-apart eyes, an aquiline nose, full lips with a relaxed, sensual expression."

"Finally, I realized it was Marlon Brando!" Truman said. "He didn't have the least suggestion of the unpoetic Stanley Kowalski. It was therefore rather an experience to observe, later that afternoon, with what chameleon ease he acquired the character's cruel and gaudy colors. Superbly, like a guileful salamander, he slithered into the part. His own *persona* evaporated."

Truman remembered how Brando, lying on that table, opened only one eye at first to see what stranger had invaded his lair. "He looked at me as if I were green and a four-headed monster who'd just gotten off the ship from Mars," Truman said. "It was obvious to me that from the first, Marlon was fascinated by me. Perhaps he'd never met anyone like me. I am, after all, unique. Sometimes I have this peculiar effect on men."

The historic fact that Truman met Brando is true, and the details, as noted above, have been reported in numerous biographies. But the choreography of the meeting that's outlined above didn't involve Brando and Truman, but, rather, Brando and Sandy Campbell.

The young actor had told his friend, Truman, about how he'd first met Brando. Truman put a spin on the incident, eliminated Sandy from its context altogether, and substituted himself instead, as he so often did in many other incidents.

In reality, after *Streetcar* had opened on Broadway, Truman was taken backstage by Tennessee and introduced to Brando in a way that was a lot more conventional than in Truman's more elaborate and romanticized version, as noted above.

From the moment they first met, Truman set about to ingratiate himself with Brando. On one drunken

Truman Capote was determined to seduce Marlon Brando. "I just couldn't bear it to think Tennessee had had him--and I had not. He fell into my trap."

In the photo, **Brando** as Stanley Kowalski is calling for Stella (Kim Hunter). "From what I heard, he got her in bed when the curtain went down," Truman claimed.

night in Key West, Truman later claimed that, "Tennessee got him first, but I wanted to be next in line. After getting to know Marlon a bit better, I realized to my regret that the line stretched around the block. I had to persevere. I couldn't let Tennessee have one up on me."

Streetcar On Broadway:

Raw Sexual Passion in a "Fetid Swamp,"

And a Tongue Kiss from Cary Grant

The opening of *A Streetcar Named Desire* made theatrical history as the curtain went up at the Ethel Barrymore Theatre on December 3, 1947. The word had been out there for months that this was going to be "the play" to see that winter. For days in advance, lines had formed around the block, as theatergoers eagerly sought to buy tickets. Scalpers were having a field day, hawking tickets for fifty dollars each.

"Sex sells," said theater *doyenne* Jean Dalrymple, who was one of the distinguished guests on opening night. She joined a wide array of VIPs that also included a well-dressed Marlon Brando, Sr. and his sober wife, Dodie, as well as Tennessee's mother, Edwina Dakin Williams, and the playwright's rather jealous brother, Dakin.

Even David O. Selznick showed up, although Irene had specifically asked him not to. She had suggested that her estranged husband "and your trollop,"—an unkind reference to his mistress, Jennifer Jones—go elsewhere that evening. During the early conceptualization of the production, Selznick had aggressively promoted Jones for the role of Blanche DuBois, casting that was simply unthinkable to Irene.

"We had been told that *Streetcar* was filled with more raw sexual passion than anything that had ever been presented on Broadway," Dalrymple claimed. "The word was also out on Brando. Gossip had it that after *Streetcar* he was going to be the hottest actor on Broadway."

"From the moment Brando walked out on the stage, all eyes were riveted on him," Dalrymple said. "In his sweaty, tight-fitting red T-shirt, and in those even tighter jeans that were very revealing, he was like an animal in heat. It was an exciting moment in the theater."

"You could almost hear the women in the audience swoon as if they had suddenly found the rapist of their dreams," Dalrymple said. "Brando was a savage, but what a sexy one! He was violent, crude, and totally mesmerizing. I don't recall having seen such utter rapture in a drama, and, believe me, I've seen the greatest performances of anybody of my generation—all the greats, from John Barrymore to Katharine Cornell. When the curtain went down that night, it was more than a new star had been born. We were actually devastated, as if a quart of our blood had been drained from us. I knew that after Brando's performance that night in *Streetcar,* that acting, and Broadway itself,

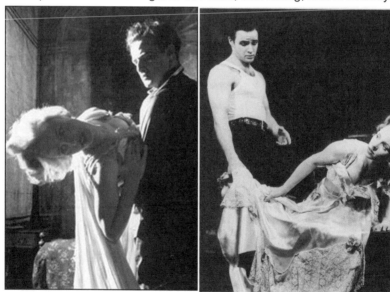

Brando as Stanley Kowalski taunts **Jessica Tandy** as Blanche DuBois

had changed for all time."

Sitting in the front row, along with Irene and Tennessee, were such famous faces as Monty Clift, Edward G. Robinson, Paul Muni, and Cary Grant.

Robert Lewis was also in the audience that night. He would later reflect on that memorable evening in the theater. "Marlon paved the way that night for other actors to come. You just name them, beginning with Marlon's understudy, Ralph Meeker, who in time also played Stanley. The parade of Marlon Brando clones continued: Rip Torn, Paul Newman, Steve McQueen, and most definitely James Dean."

When the final curtain fell that opening night, it was Brando's mother, Dodie, who was first on her feet to launch applause for her son that lasted thirty minutes. "Backstage, Jessica was furious," Kim Hunter recalled. "She knew that all that clapping was for Marlon and not for her star part."

One of the investors, Cary Grant, was the first to rush backstage to greet Brando with a theatrical tongue kiss. "I'm going to get my money back from the show," he proclaimed. "I see a future in Hollywood for you. Irene knows how to get in touch with me. When you get to Hollywood, I want to show you around. You'll find no better tour guide."

It might be hard for modern theater audiences to understand the fuss associated with *Streetcar* in 1947. Of course, the world people inhabited then was a far and different place. As one critic put it, "*A Streetcar Named Desire* was awful and sublime. Only once in a generation do you see such a thing in the theater."

"During the forties and fifties, the anti-fag battalions were everywhere on the march," Gore Vidal claimed. "From 1945 to 1961, *Time* attacked with unusual ferocity everything produced or published by Tennessee Williams. 'Fetid swamp' was the phrase most often used to describe his work. But, in *Time,* all things will come to pass. The Bird is now a beloved institution."

The harshest attack came from Mary McCarthy, the novelist and astringent

Kim Hunter as Stella with **Brando** as Stanley | **Cary Grant**

206

critic. She wrote "the work of Tennessee Williams reeks of literary ambition as the apartment reeks of cheap perfume." She also claimed that his taste inclined more to "the jagged scene, the jungle motifs, ('then they come together with low, animal noises'), the tourist Mexican, clarinet music, suicide, homosexuality, rape, and insanity. His work creates in the end the very effect of painful falsity which is imparted to the Kowalski household by Blanche's pink lampshades and couch covers."

After the opening night performance, Tennessee invited his mother Edwina and his brother Dakin to join him for a party at "21." Director George Cukor was the official host, but behind the scenes, Irene was picking up the hefty tab. On the way there, Edwina told Tennessee that before the curtain she had met the Brandos, as he would later recall.

"They looked very respectable to me," she said. "I don't know how they could have produced a wild thing for a son. And, frankly, if you really want to know my opinion, I think Dakin is far handsomer than Brando."

"Speaking of wild things," Dakin chimed in, "at this fancy party, they just might be asking how a God-fearing woman like you could have produced Tom here."

"Tom," she said, gently reaching for her son's hand, "for the life of me, I don't know why you insist on writing about Southern decadence when there are so many more spiritually uplifting subjects about the South that you could write about. You just give Yankees ammunition to use against us. I mean, even if Blanche and Stanley weren't blood-related, it's still incest!"

"Mother, dearest, I'm writing about fallen women, who exist in every part of America, not just the South," Tennessee said. "You know that's true. I learned about fallen women only after I left home. With you as a mother to Rose, Dakin, and me, I grew up in the home of a Southern lady."

Despite the approbation and spectacular gaucherie of his mother, Tennessee's "hot ticket" on Broadway brought royalties

SIBLING RIVALRIES IN FAMILY HELL

Upper photo, left to right: **Rose Williams** with her mother, **Edwina** and her brother, baby **Tennessee**

Lower photo: **Edwina** with her oldest child, (Tennessee's "more respectable" brother), **Dakin Williams.**

and awards, notably the Drama Critics Circle Prize for best play of the year, followed by the Pulitzer Prize.

"No More Bad Vomen Roles for Me"

—Greta Garbo

Brando Poses Nude for Cecil Beaton

After *Streetcar* opened and perhaps to impress Brando, Truman Capote showed up backstage one night with the photographer, Cecil Beaton on one arm, and with Greta Garbo on the other. Kim Hunter and Jessica Tandy were part of the "audience" at this moment in theatrical history, although they remained out of the loop, except as eyewitnesses to later report what occurred.

After congratulating Brando on his brilliant performance, Garbo told him that she was here tonight because she'd promised Tennessee that she'd go to see the play since he wanted her to star as Blanche DuBois in the eventual film version of the work. If Garbo were aware that she was speaking in the presence of Tandy, who wanted to appear in the film version herself, she didn't seem to have any sensitivity to that.

"I must turn Tennessee down," Garbo told the private audience standing and listening, in utter awe of her. "Blanche DuBois is difficult, much too unsympathetic. I'm an honest and clear-cut woman. I see things with lucidity. I could never play such a complicated woman. I couldn't bear to tell lies and see things around the corner instead of straight-on. Besides, who would believe me as an aging Southern belle on the verge of madness? I couldn't play Scarlett O'Hara either."

At the door to his dressing room, Garbo impulsively kissed Brando on both cheeks as a parting gesture. She reached for a rose held in the hand of Cecil Beaton and handed it to Brando with a certain passion. She seductively kissed the rose before passing it to him. "That will put the dew on it," she said before adjusting her gray highwayman hat and departing into the night.

Beaton remained behind to make a request of Brando, asking him if, over the weekend, he'd pose for a series of photographs for *Vanity Fair.* "Normally, Marlon would turn down such a request from what I'd heard about him," Truman recalled. "But I think he was charmed by Cecil. He must have known that Cecil was primarily homosexual. I'm sure Marlon had heard that Cecil regularly fucked Garbo. For some reason, that held enormous intrigue for Marlon, as I was later to find out. I think Marlon wanted to learn what this mysterious Cecil was all about. In other words, what did a primarily gay photographer have that would make Garbo, who was primarily a lesbian, want to go to bed with him? I fear Marlon never learned the answer to that riddle. But he did agree to the photographic session. I invited myself to attend. This, I just knew, was going to be the best show in town."

The next day Brando encountered Tennessee and reported on his exchange with Garbo, telling the playwright that the actress had turned down the film role of Blanche DuBois.

"It's just as well," Tennessee said. "I got carried away when I offered her the role of Blanche. Garbo is wrong for Blanche." He looked at Brando as if he were a judge at the Spanish Inquisition. "Have you ever seen a drag queen impersonate Garbo?"

Brando said that he had not.

"That's because she is unique," Tennessee said. "Almost impossible to capture in an impersonation. Actually, she's a hermaphrodite, with the cold quality of a mermaid. Definitely not Blanche." As an afterthought, Tennessee added, "I could play Blanche better than Garbo, as you al-

Cecil Beaton with the camera-shy über-star, **Greta Garbo**

ready know from my reading with you that night back on the Cape."

Inviting Brando for a drink, Tennessee told him that when he'd first gone to see Garbo about the role of Blanche, he'd gotten so nervous that he actually pitched a different story idea to her. "I told her all about a film script I was working on. It's called *The Pink Bedroom* and it's about this actress and her lover, who's also her theatrical agent and promoter. For an hour, I babbled on about the script with frequent interruptions of *'Vonderful!'* from Garbo. But when I finally shut up, Garbo, in what appeared to be a complete change of heart, imperiously rose to her big feet to dismiss me. 'Give it to Joan Crawford,' she told me, and then I was out the door."

Truman attended Brando's photo shoot with Cecil Beaton the following week. Brando showed up wearing his dirty T-shirt and tight jeans from *Streetcar*. According to Truman, at one point, Beaton snapped at least a hundred photographs of Brando. After Cecil was satisfied he'd had enough of those, he asked Brando if he would remain behind and pose "for some figure studies," as Truman later quoted Cecil.

"Cecil was well aware that Marlon did not wear underwear under his jeans," Truman said. "Everybody along Broadway had heard that fascinating tidbit."

With absolutely no embarrassment, Brando pulled off his shirt and unfastened his jeans. In a minute, he was stark naked for Beaton's camera. "I decided then and there that this handsome young man could be had," Truman said.

Years later in Key West, Truman became a bit coy, especially when discussing what happened after the photo shoot. "Both Cecil and I had Marlon that night in the same bed," Truman claimed. "He was strictly rough trade, but we managed to coax two loads from him—one for Cecil who got the first eruption, the next for Yours Truly."

After that, Truman drunkenly claimed—in front of Tennessee, Frank Merlo, and novelist James Leo Herlihy—that he "serviced" Brando frequently during the weeks to come. Truman not only lied on occasion about many of his involvements, but exaggerated those that really took place. He was also known for altering the facts to make a good story even better.

Ironically, however, both Tennessee and later Elia Kazan felt that Truman told the truth in this case. "Even so, I think Truman highly exaggerated the extent of his romantic friendship with Marlon," Tennessee said after Truman left Key West. "Truman might have fallen down once or twice on bent nylon and given Marlon a blow-job, or even two or three. But I'm sure that the so-called love affair between Marlon and Truman took place only in the wee one's churning brain."

There is no way at this point of determining if Truman told the truth.

The nude shots of Brando became the talk of gossipy underground Broadway. They have never been published, at least not for public consumption. Brando later denied having posed for the nude shots.

Apparently, the pictures were not part of the vast repertoire of photographs and diary entries that Beaton left behind at his death.

There is speculation that Beaton in the 1950s sold the nude pictures to a very rich and very devoted fan of Brando's, where they may reside to this day, waiting for some future heir to some estate to sell them to the highest bidder as a collector's item.

Chapter Fifteen

The Most Beautiful Man on Earth

A Florida Cracker "Homme Fatale"

"The World's Most Expensive Male Prostitute"

—Christopher Isherwood

Two views of **Dennis Fouts**, whose postwar All-American looks and charm drove Gay Europe wild

Son of a baker, a Jacksonville, Florida cracker, Denham Fouts, nicknamed "Denny," fled from home as a teenager. In Washington, D.C., he worked as a stock boy for only a short time before one of the executives at Safeway promoted him to "The Best Kept Boy in the World," a title that would follow him for the rest of his short life.

His first patron claimed "Denny was thin as a hieroglyph, with dark hair, light brown eyes, and a cleft chin." He also possessed something that Denny defined as "my impressive money-maker."

In time, this extraordinary youth would provide literary inspiration for characters created by Truman Capote, Gore Vidal, Christopher Isherwood, and

Gavin Lambert, among others.

Stifled by the boredom of Washington, Denny escaped on a train to New York to continue his career as a kept boy. He found that his body and sex appeal were all that was needed to launch himself in an even bigger city than Washington. At Manhattan's Astor Bar, he met the writer and critic, Glenway Wescott, who later said, "He was absolutely enchanting and ridiculously good looking."

Later, Wescott claimed "the only thing I like about Denny was that he had the most delicious body odor. I once swiped one of his handkerchiefs after he'd wiped his sweaty brow."

Wescott was one of his early sponsors, introducing him to George Platt Lynes, the American photographer whose pictures had appeared in such magazines as *Vogue* and *Harper's Bazaar.* He also photographed many movie stars and was known for his pictures of nude males. Denny posed in the buff for him, and copies of those photos were shopped around to some of the wealthiest homosexuals in the world, some of whom subsequently sought out Denny's sexual charms.

The novelist and critic, **Glenway Wescott** (1901-1987), linked "beer, piss, and sex" together. When he seduced a young man, such as Fouts, he defined it as "an act of darkness."

Born in 1914, Denny was in his early 20s when he descended on Paris for a series of conquests, often with famous men.

One of his early sponsors was Swiss-Canadian Brion Gysin, the famous painter, writer, sound poet, and performance artist. Among other achievements, he invented the "Dreamachine," a flicker device designed as an art object and "mystical stimulant" whose patterns of light were intended for viewing with one's eyes closed. The flicker device used alpha waves in the 8-16 Hz range to produce a change in consciousness in receptive viewers.

Gysin also collaborated with his close friend, William Burroughs, before he became world famous after the publication of *The Naked Lunch.*

As Ted Morgan, the biographer of William Bur-

The poet and painter, **Brion Gysin**, invited Denny Fouts to Morocco, where they would drop acid before visiting the tomb of the Merinides kings in the ancient city of Fez. "I'm a saint," Gysin told the young man. "But occasionally, I float down to earth to be a king."

"Denny Fouts was Pursued by Kings and by Adolf Hitler"

—Truman Capote

212

roughs, wrote: "Gysin was a tall, broad-shouldered man with thick sandy hair and the ruddy, bony, narrow-eyed face of a Swiss mountaineer, cold and imperious. He had a glacial geniality."

As a joke, Gysin contributed a recipe for marijuana fudge to a cookbook being compiled by Alice B. Toklas. It was included in her cookbook and became known all over the world as Alice B. Toklas's brownies, the most famous recipe to ever emerge from the hippie era.

In Paris, Denny introduced his new lover, Gysin, to his newly minted friends, the composer Paul Bowles and his author wife, Jane Bowles, both of whom indulged in homosexuality on the side.

Paul Bowles later reported that Denny had just returned from Tibet after Gysin and Denny visited the Bowles couple in their hotel room in Paris' 8th *arrondissement.* "In Tibet, Denny had practiced archery and had brought back some huge bows with him," Paul said. "The arrows were made with built-in tampons of cotton, to be soaked in ether before use and ignited. To demonstrate his prowess with the difficult bow, he began to shoot arrows from our hotel window down into the evening traffic of the Champs-Élysées. Fortunately, there were no repercussions."

The Harlem singer, Jimmy Daniels, was also introduced to Denny at a Left Bank night club. "Denny's skin looked as if it just had been scrubbed. It seemed to have no pores at all. It was so smooth. He was just adorable, so very fuckable."

While in Paris, Denny also became the

Truman Capote told Tennessee, "Your friend, **Paul Bowles** *(right figure in photo above),* has finally got around to seducing Denny Fouts. Who hasn't? Paul seems to have put on fat and is filled with remorse that his lesbian **Jane** *(left figure in photo above)* is being committed to a mental hospital in Málaga. Paul is still plagiarizing the writings of his Arab boy lover and passing them off as his own."

The strikingly handsome French actor, **Jean Marais** *(photo above),* numbered among his lovers both the celebrated author Jean Cocteau and Denny Fouts. Cocteau introduced the young Marais to Tennessee when he was considering casting him as Stanley Kowalski in the Paris production of *A Streetcar Named Desire.*

Cocteau told Tennessee, "When I fell in love with Jean, I was searching for a beautiful effigy of my young self, and he was an actor in search of an author."

lover of Jean Marais, the French actor and director more famously associated with Jean Cocteau. Cocteau, in fact, had considered (but later rejected) Marais as the lead, Stanley Kowalski, in the French-language production of Tennessee's *A Streetcar Named Desire,* in Paris.

At the time of his affair with Denny, Marais was yet to make his reputation. He would later star in 100 roles in French films and on television, notably in Cocteau's *La Belle et la Bête* (1946) (aka *Beauty and the Beast)* and *Orphée* (1949). In the 1950s, Marais, the star of many swashbuckling pictures, became known as "the French Errol Flynn."

Marais and Denny made a striking couple on the Parisian nightscape. Once, they were photographed together emerging from a theater off the Champs-Élysées.

Before the outbreak of World War II, a story spread among *tout Paris* that Adolf Hitler had seen this photograph of Marais and Denny and had sent an offer through his propaganda minister, Josef Goebbels, for Denny to visit him in Berlin.

Denny turned down the offer. "Who in his right mind would trade the muscular arms of the gorgeous Jean Marais for the embrace of a beast like Hitler?"

Years later, Truman told Tennessee and anyone else who knew Danny that if the handsome young man had yielded to Hitler's romantic overtures, "there would have been no World War II."

Almost no one believed such a ridiculous assertion. Gore never believed that an overture had ever come in from Hitler at all. When Gore got to know Denny years later, he asked him about Truman's claim.

"Denny produced a 1938 letter from Goebbels, inviting him to Berlin as the personal guest of the Führer," Gore said. "Not only that, but Goebbels was holding out a contract with UFA that would have made Denny a star in German films, with his voice dubbed in German, of course."

"For once in his life, it seemed that Truman was telling the truth," Gore said. "Ever since the 1920s, there had been rumors of Hitler's closeted homosexuality, even a book or two written about it."

Paul Bowles eventually introduced Denny to another artist who

Did **Adolf Hitler** become mesmerized by a photo of Denny Fouts and have Josef Goebbels invite him to Berlin? The jury is still out on that one. Dr. Lothar Machtan, professor of modern history at Bremen University, was the author of *Hidden Hitler,* published in 2001. In it, he documents "the homosexual milieu in which the young Hitler lived and thrived from his early years in Vienna and through the beginning of his poltical career in Munich."

Machtan also documents a succession of homosexual men among Hitler's most intimate friends. "His homosexual past was his Achilles Heel. It threatened him politically and left him open to blackmail by his most intimate former associates. The assassination of Ernst Röhm sent a chilling message to all with knowledge about the Führer's past life."

214

became his lover and sponsor, Gavin Lambert. The British-born author was a screenwriter, novelist, and biographer.

Lambert and Denny had a torrid affair. Lambert was ten years younger than Denny when they met and was more his sexual type since he was only a teenager. Although he slept with older men, Denny actually preferred young boys.

Denny never lived to know that Lambert would one day become famous, first as a screenwriter, personal assistant, and lover to the Hollywood film director, Nicholas Ray. With Ray, he co-wrote the film script for *Bitter Victory* in 1947. The director had previously sampled the youthful charms of James Dean, Natalie Wood, and Sal Mineo, each of whom he'd seduced during the filming of *Rebel Without a Cause* (1955).

Lambert would also adapt for the screen Tennessee's novella, *The Roman Spring of Mrs. Stone (1961),* starring Vivien Leigh and Warren Beatty.

Denny appears in Lambert's *roman à clef, Norman's Letter.*

As Denny's circle of admirers enlarged, an invitation to visit England came in from one of the richest men in England, Evan Morgan, 2nd Viscount Tredegar, who was born into what the Duke of Bedford described as "the oddest family I ever met. His father owned the largest yacht in the world, and his mother built bird nests big enough to sit in to hatch eggs."

The eccentric Viscount was a Welsh poet and author who devoted a great deal of his time to his kangaroos, whom he had taught to box at his private zoo. When Denny arrived in the aftermath of his invitation, it was "love at first sight" on the viscount's part.

Soon, Denny, appearing nude except for a fig leaf, became a featured attraction at the Viscount's notorious weekend house parties, which drew such distinguished guests as Aldous Huxley, H.G. Wells, and the painter Augustus John.

The most notorious guest was Aleister Crowley, noted in the British tabloids as "the world's wickedest man." He had been known for arriving

The **Viscount Tredegar** *(photo above, depicting him at a garden party he hosted in 1935),* was Fouts most bizarre lover. The parrot he carried around with him had been trained to crawl up his leg and stick his head out of the Viscount's fly.

He dressed like Shelley; he seduced page boys at the Royal Court at Windsor; he ordered frequent working class rent boys delivered to his bedroom every week; and he kept rabbits in his bed.

It was estimated that he seduced more men than any other "old sod" in England.

Virginia Wolff described him as "a little red absurdity with a beak of a nose, no chin, and with the general likeness of a callow but student bantam cock that has run to seed."

He was constantly in search of newer, darker sensations and fatally attracted to dangerous people.

with an entourage of six young boys willing to sacrifice their virginity. When Crowley spotted Denny, he told his host, "I've got to have him all night. I will release him only in the morning. Before the rooster crows, I want to have performed every known sexual act—and some unknown ones—on this beautiful American."

[Later, Evan Morgan's private eccentricities were revealed in a book, Not Behind Lace Curtains: The Hidden World of Evan, Viscount Tredegar, *by William Cross. The book exposed not only his homosexuality, but his flirtations with the occult and with the "Black Masses," inspired by Crowley and his teachings.*

Paul of Greece is depicted in the *left photo* as a teenage prince, and in the *right photo*, as King of the Hellenes (ruled 1947-1964).

Denny Fouts gave His Highness "the greatest sex of my life."

Cross estimated that when Morgan came of age, the Welsh estate his family had owned since the 14th century was bringing in what's estimated as today's equivalent of £65,000 a day, or £24 million a year.]

Denny soon fled that bizarre world and returned to Paris, where an invitation was waiting from Prince Paul of Greece. He included air tickets to Athens, where he wanted to cruise the Aegean Sea "with this American beauty."

The prince functioned as titular head of Greece from 1947 until his death in 1964. The third son of King Constantine of Greece, Paul—a handsome, dashing figure in his own right—had been trained as a naval officer. During that Aegean cruise, however, he spent more time in bed with Denny than he did directing his crew.

The prince had been born in 1901 and was not as young as Denny usually preferred.

After that cruise, the two lovers may have as many as three subsequent rendezvous, but details are lacking. During World War II, when Greece was under Nazi occupation, Prince Paul lived in exile in London and Cairo.

Peter Watson, "the Oleomargarine King of England," was among Denny's last lovers before the outbreak of World War II. "I could not be in the same room with Denny without getting an erection," Watson told friends. During the course of their affair, he became so enthralled with Denny that he presented him with a large Picasso painting called *Girl Reading* (1934). Denny once lent the painting to Manhattan's Museum of Modern Art, but later sold it to the Samuel Marx Collection.

Watson also introduced Denny to Cyril Connolly, the British journalist and critic, who also fell in love with him. With Watson's money, Connolly had

216

founded *Horizon* magazine in 1939. Connolly later told his patron, "Denny comes in dripping with all that Deep South charm, enough to make you drop your trousers and bend over for him. But he's got a very nasty temper if provoked. I hear very dark stories about him, some of which must be true. His behavior is erratic, and I understand that some of his past deeds, especially when in residence with Evan Morgan, our Viscount friend, were bloody dangerous."

As France was about to be invaded by Nazi Germany, Watson shipped Denny off to Hollywood. "I could not stand the idea of that beautiful porcelain skin being damaged by one of Hitler's bombs."

Denny Discovers New Lovers In Both Truman & Gore. Ultimately, Opium Wins The Battle For His Affections

In Hollywood in 1940, Denny became involved in an affair with Christopher Isherwood, who had maintained a long-time, widely publicized desire for involvement (some say possession) of the best of both German and American youth. With oceans of pain and regret, he'd been forced to sever ties with his German lover in Nazi-occupied France. Later, he found the object of his obsession for the ideal American male in the flesh of Denham Fouts.

In addition to "hot sex," Denny also would inspire Isherwood's *Down There on a Visit* (1962), which contains the novella *Paul,* whose titular character was based on Denny.

After the war, Denny returned to Paris, where Watson paid the rent on Denny's apartment in rue du Bac and even gave him a large painting by Tchelitchev to decorate it.

Watson introduced Denny to Michael Wishart. "I was warned by Jean Cocteau, of all people, that Fouts was a bad influence and an opium addict. Imagine Cocteau warning someone against an opium addict. I was besotted with Denny," Wishart later confessed. "It's true he was an opium addict. Perhaps Cocteau was right in warning me. I, too, became an opium addict."

Wishart was an English painter who specialized in neo-romantic landscapes and hidden faces captured in bravura swatches of oil. After an exhibition of his paintings in 1956, art critic David Sylvester wrote of Wishart's "sensibility that is at once shamelessly romantic and deeply sophisticated, and which endows the wide open spaces of the great outdoors with a sort of hothouse preciosity . . . he is one

Another Denny Fouts devotee, **Christopher Isherwood,** flashes his boyish smile in 1932.

of the select band of English romantic painters who are truly painters."

Wishart's affair with Denny was written about in his autobiography, *High Diver,* published in 1977. "Denny wore nothing but cream-colored flannel trousers and had the torso of an athlete," Wishart said. "Along with his beautiful shoulders and golden forearms ran snow white mice with startling pink eyes, which he stroked gently with the back of his hands."

After the war, Denny had picked up this eccentricity of having white mice run up and down his arms.

In that wardrobe, shirtless, Denny made frequent appearances with Wishart, who often wore "a full Bonnie Prince Charlie kilt with a lot of écru lace and half my grandmother's pearls and rubies."

[By 1988, Wishart's passion for Denny had long ago been buried upon the young man's death in Rome. In its place, he "conceived a searing passion for Michael Jackson. He wrote to friends, "How I am to live apart from Michael is an appalling quandary."]

While still in Paris, Denny received an advance copy of Truman Capote's first novel, *Other Voices, Other Rooms.* He was especially intrigued by the provocative photograph on its back cover. Truman looked like the type of young boy he preferred sexually. Denny, by then a figure of myth and legend within international homosexual circles, sent Truman a blank check with just one word written as a notation on the bottom—COME—which of course, had a double meaning.

Denny's reputation had preceded him, and Truman was eager to meet him. When he arrived in Paris, he headed at once for Denny's shoddy, heavily curtained apartment on rue du Bac, where the young novelist soon discovered that Denny was addicted to opium.

Even so, he and Truman became lovers. When not making love, Truman spent hours in bed reading stories to Denny, and listening to fascinating tales of his romantic escapades.

"Even though a druggie, Denny looked fifteen years younger," Truman later said, "Actually, he was thirty-four. He radiated health, youth, and an unspoiled innocence, although he was none of those things. He was beyond being good looking. He was the single most charming looking person I've ever seen. Had Denny known Oscar Wilde, he would have been the inspiration for Dorian Gray."

One of Denny's closest friends, John B. L. Goodwin, warned Truman that "Denny invents himself. If people don't know his background, he makes it up."

Truman didn't quite agree with that. "Denny had led a fascinating life. He didn't have to make up romantic adventures with men. He'd actually experienced them."

Alarmed by Denny's large-scale consumption of opium, Truman eventually fled from the scene, promising Denny he would meet him in Rome, but having no intention of keeping that commitment.

"How could I say I never planned to see him again?" Truman asked. "It wasn't just the drugs and chaos, but the funereal halo of waste and failure that hovered over him. The shadow of such failure seemed somehow to threaten my own impending triumph."

It could be argued that Truman saw a foreshadowing of his own drug-addicted future reflected in Denny's dissipation.

Denny would appear as a character in Truman's unfinished novel, *Answered Prayers* upon which he was working—or not working, as the case may be—during his final opium-sodden days. Denny's Paris is evoked by line in the book: "When I think of Paris, it seems to me as romantic as a flooded *pissoir*, as tempting as a strangled nude floating on the Seine."

In the novel, Denny's answered prayers "lead eventually to nightmares of emptiness and abandonment, lived out at "Father Flanagan's All Night Nigger Queen's Kosher Café" a kind of Shangri-La for those who have lost hope."

***

Following in Truman's footsteps, Gore made his own literary pilgrimage to Paris. The first person he wanted to meet was Denny. John Lehmann, the English publisher, escorted Gore to Denny's rue du Bac apartment.

Gore sat on the edge of Denny's bed and smoked from the pipe offered him. "The opium made me deathly ill, and I never tried it again," he later said.

More of a historian than the ever-gossipy Truman, Gore wanted to verify some of the more outrageous stories spread about Denny, mostly by Truman. After verifying the authenticity of letter that Goebbels had written to Denny from Berlin in 1938, Gore then asked about Denny's alleged affair with the King of Greece.

Denny showed Gore a crumpled telegram from a stack of papers on the floor beside his bed. The letterhead was definitely from King Paul. It read:

"My Dear Denham,
So thrilled to hear from you. I am much better than papers report. Hope you can come to Athens.
Love,
Paul."

King Paul was the cousin of Prince Philip, Duke of Edinburgh. At the time of that communication with Denny, the king was suffering from typhoid fever and was too ill to attend the 1947 marriage of Philip to Princess Elizabeth.

In Paris, Gore made six different visits to Denny's apartment, always finding him lying nude on the bed, usually smoking his opium pipe. "His body appeared in fabulous shape," Gore claimed. "He was still slender and boyish, a southern Penrod who still spoke with a North Florida cracker accent. His dissipation was not reflected in his asymmetrical face, which was like a ghost who would soon be dead of a malformed heart."

Gore later claimed that during his visits, Denny was in no condition to have sex. But to Tennessee and privately to gay friends, he relayed a different story.

"Denny was impotent, but I went to his apartment several times and sodomized him. It was such a thrill to rape the young man called the 'most beautiful boy in the world.' His body still could offer sexual satisfaction."

The experience left such an impact on Gore that he used Denny as inspiration for his short story, "Pages from an Abandoned Journal," which later appeared as a subsection of his *A Thirsty Evil: Seven Short Stories,* published in 1956.

Gore paid his final visit to Denham just before he left Paris. Later, he said, "It is a pity that he himself never wrote a memoir. What a story he'd have to tell."

When Peter Watson quit paying the rent on Denny's apartment in the rue du Bac, Denny went to Rome, where he found cheaper lodgings at the Pensione Foggetti.

Gore *(photo above)*: "By the time I finally got around to Denny, he'd been had by every rich man on two continents, and was a bit used up. About all I could do at that point was to tell him to turn over and take it like a man."

Denny's last and final lover was Anthony Watson-Gandy, a writer and translator. "Denny spent his last days dissolute, lying in bed like a corpse, sheet to his chin, a cigarette between his lips turning to ash. I had to remove that cigarette before it burned his lips."

At the age of thirty-four, Denny died on December 16, 1948 of heart failure and was buried in the First Zone, 11th Row, of Rome's Protestant Cemetery.

Amazingly, according to his lover, his body "still looked like that of a Greek god."

A rumor persists that his corpse was violated at the funeral parlor in Rome to which it was sent. Placed nude on a marble slab for "viewing, fondling, or the release of semen," that perfect body was violated in death as it was in life, fulfilling some necrophiliac fantasy of a member, or members, of Rome's gay community who never got to enjoy the pleasures of his flesh when Denny was alive.

Chapter Sixteen

Tennessee's Rocky Ride on "The Little Horse"

Frank Merlo and the Playwright: The Keeper and the Kept

Called "The Little Horse," **Frank Merlo**, a second-generation Sicilian, was Tennessee's long-time lover throughout his most productive years.

The last photograph taken of him *(on the right)* was by his friend, Stanley Mills Haggart, in Key West, who said, "I didn't know at the time that the bare chest I was photographing was already consumed by lung cancer."

Born in New Jersey in 1922, Frank Merlo was twenty-five

years old on the summer night in Provincetown when he first met Tennessee Williams.

He came from a large brood of first generation Sicilian immigrants. His out-spoken mother was tormented by the size of her unruly tribe. When she got into violent arguments with her son, she'd climb a large tree in the Merlo back-yard. After one particularly bitter fight with her son, she scaled the tree and re-fused to come down. After pleading, then shouting at her, the volatile Frank chopped down the tree with her in it. Fortunately, she wasn't injured.

Thoughout his fifteen or so years as the lover of Tennessee, he would dis-play a frequently violent temper. Tennessee preferred their arguments to be oral, Frank resorting on many occasions to violence.

In spite of Truman Capote having bitchily compared him to Lon Chaney, Frank was muscular and attractive, standing one inch shorter than Tennessee. The playwright took in his large brown eyes and equine face, nicknaming him "The Little Horse." Many of Tennessee's friends thought that was a reference to Frank's endowment, which as the young man himself admitted, "just grows and grows with no end in sight."

Late in 1947, Frank had completed a six-year tour of duty in World War II, serving as a pharmacist's mate in the U.S. Navy.

[Two famous homosexual men had each discovered Frank's charms before Tennessee:

Joseph Alsop lived deep in the closet. At the time he met Frank, he was one of the most famous journalists and syndicated newspaper columnists in Amer-ica.

A few years after his affair with Frank, he would be pursued by Senator Joseph McCarthy, who was launching a campaign to remove "perverts" from federal employment, even though he was a secret homosexual himself.

John La Touche

Young Frankie

Joseph Alsop

Frankie Shines in the Limelight
While Concealed in the Shadows

In 1957, in Moscow, the KGB secretly took pictures of Alsop having sex in his hotel room with another man who just happened to be a Soviet agent. The KGB sent copies of these incriminating photographs to every major newspaper in America, exposing Alsop's sexual life.

In 1967, Gore Vidal published a novel, Washington, D.C., in which his character of a gay journalist was based on Alsop.

By the time Frank arrived in Provincetown, he had evolved into a role as the lover of the lyricist John La Touche. His rousing "Ballad for Americans" had been performed in 1940 as the theme song at the National Republican Convention and the convention of the American Communist Party, and eventually recorded by such artists as Paul Robeson and Bing Crosby. La Touche had also written the lyrics for a widely popular song ("Taking a Chance on Love") incorporated into the 1940 Broadway musical Cabin in the Sky, later adapted into a movie (1943) co-starring, among others, Lena Horne.

Years after the end of his romance with Frank, La Touche became an intimate friend of Gore's. It was at Gore's elegant home, Edgewater, built in 1820 on a peninsula jutting into the Hudson River (in Barrytown, Dutchess County, north of Rhinebeck) that La Touche wrote the lyrics for "Lazy Afternoon."

"Both of us wrote during the day and made love at night," Gore told Tennessee. Gore described La Touche as "a hard-drinking Irishman. He was always broke and pretended to be a communist. That let to him getting blacklisted in the 1950s."

At his home in Vermont, La Touche died of a sudden heart attack at the age of forty-one. He had completed revisions on his two-act opera, The Ballad of

Frank Merlo *(photo above, left)* always accompanied Tennessee to the beach every day in Key West. "It was imperative that Tenn take a swim every day." **Tennessee painted a portrait** *(above, right)* of Frank early in their relationship.

Baby Doe. *He was also working on his lyrics for* Candide *with music by Leonard Bernstein, which would be produced in December, just months after his death in August of 1956. He was survived by his longtime partner, Kenward Elmslic, the poet.]*

On a balmy Cape Cod evening, Tennessee, accompanied by Frank, went for a stroll on the beach. Tennessee was tiring of his Mexican lover, Pancho Rodriguez, and La Touche was getting bored with Frank.

In the moonlight, Frank took out a package of cigarettes and asked Tennessee if he had a light.

"As a matter of fact, I don't but I can light your fire in another way," Tennessee promised.

Thus enabled and accompanied with an equivalent roster of corny lines, Tennessee Williams and Frank Merlo began one of the most infamous romances in the theatrical/literary world.

Within fifteen minutes, the playwright and the former sailor were making love on the sands.

Tennessee later recalled, "It was a fantastic hour that I spent with Frankie that night. It was right on the dunes, although I don't regard sand as a reliable bed on which to worship The Little God. However, he was given such devoted service that he must still be smiling."

After they parted, with no commitment to see each other again, Tennessee was walking back to the cottage he shared with Pancho. Suddenly, the headlights of an oncoming car blinded him. Pancho was at the wheel, shouting in Spanish. To avoid being hit, Tennessee jumped into the marsh grass. He later claimed that Pancho had intended to run him over.

In the aftermath of that incident, Tennessee fled to a small hotel in Provincetown, where he spent the remainder of the night alone. He later said, "I knew then that it was all over between Pancho and me. The boy would soon depart."

In one of those strange coincidences known to readers of Charles Dickens, Tennessee was strolling down Lexington Avenue in Manhattan in late September of 1948.

He passed a delicatessen, thinking he would go inside and order a sandwich for dinner. In the deli, he spotted Frank with a friend of his, a straight (i.e., heterosexual) sailor. "Frankie, my god, I didn't know you were in town. Why didn't you look me up? I gave you my address!"

"I didn't want it to look like I was climbing on a bandwagon," Frank said, introducing him to his sea-going friend. "You've had such a big hit with *Streetcar.* I was afraid you'd think I was a star-fucker or something. I didn't want you to think I was exploiting our time together on the beach in P-town. Incidentally, I've seen *Streetcar.* Both the play and Brando were terrific."

With their food in hand, Tennessee invited Frank and the sailor back to his apartment in a building called Aquarius. After devouring roast beef and pastrami sandwiches, the sailor figured out what was going on. He excused himself to head back to New Jersey, leaving Frank to spend the night with

Tennessee.

Frank stayed over, the first of thousands of nights to come.

Almost from the beginning, Frank wanted to make their relationship permanent, but freedom-loving Tennessee wasn't so sure.

"Tennessee wasn't ready to settle down," Frank said. "He wanted to be with me three or four nights a week, the other nights he wanted to spend cruising for fresh meat. After all the hot sex, I thought we'd fallen in love, but Tenn wasn't there yet. That really hurt my feelings. In spite of my gruff exterior, I'm a very sensitive guy underneath."

Tennessee went to visit his stern, judgmental mother, Edwina Williams, in St. Louis. There, alone in his attic room, he came to realize that, "The young Sicilian was the guy for me."

When he returned to New York, he didn't know if Frank would be there or not. He'd given him a key to his apartment. "I found him sleeping in my bed. From that night on, he slept in my floating bed in rooms ranging from New York to Los Angeles. From London to Key West, with detours to Rome, Tangier, and Taormina, with side trips to New Orleans and Mexico."

[Tennessee was very depressed. After two big hits, Summer and Smoke *had opened in October of 1948 at the Music Box Theatre in Manhattan, in a production staged by Margo Jones. The play had a turn-of-the-early-20th-Century setting, the tale of a high-strung, unmarried minister's daughter, Alma Winemiller, who had a spiritual/sexual romance with a wild, undisciplined young doctor, John Buchanan, Jr. who had grown up and lived next door.*

Recipient of lackluster reviews, the play closed after 102 performances and represented a downturn in popularity for Tennessee.

Brooks Atkinson of The New York Times *blamed Margo Jones' direction for the failure of the play. But other critics were far from kind, one of them denouncing Tennessee's work as "a pretentious and amateurish bore." Yet another found it "a juvenile and sadly delinquent effort."*

In spite of its initial reception, the play would endure over the decades and eventually be defined as one of Tennessee's masterworks for the stage.

In 1961, Paramount purchased the property for a movie, assigning a gay director (Peter Glenville) and a gay star (Laurence Harvey) to help bring it to life. Geraldine Page starred as Alma. The film was nominated for four Academy Awards.

"Why Would Two Men Want to Share a Double Bed?" The Hotel Manager Asked.

Moving in with Tennessee, Frank began to make order out of the playwright's notoriously messy apartment. One of their first visitors, Christopher Isherwood, noted the change.

"Frank was very supportive of Tennessee," Isherwood later said. "He made everything work for him. He looked after Tennessee in a way that was uncanny. He was no goody-goody. He was just plain good. And he wasn't just some kind of faithful servitor. He was a lovable man with a strong will."

At night, Frank became acquainted with Tennessee's voracious sexual appetite. "Tenn just couldn't get enough. Sometimes, it was almost dawn before my cannon shot off its last round."

As Tennessee himself admitted, "my sexual feeling for the boy was inordinate."

In December of 1948, Frank and Tennessee set sail aboard the *Vulcania* from the Port of New York, heading for Gibraltar, where they would make their way to Tangier on the northern coast of Morocco. Tennessee had planned a reunion with his friends, Paul and Jane Bowles, who were married but turned to partners of their own sex for sleeping companions.

As Tennessee remembered the cruise across the Atlantic, "Several times during the night, I got up from my bunk and crossed over to Frankie's bunk in our stateroom."

In Tangier, Frank and Tennessee discovered the exotic life of the Medina and the peculiar sleeping arrangements in the household of the Bowleses. They also met the couple's Arab lovers—one a comely looking Arab boy no more than fourteen, for Paul, and Cherifa, a rather large Berber woman, for Jane. Cherifa was also the family's cook.

Tennessee's status as a jealous lover was reinforced when he accused Frank of having had sex with Paul. As it turned out, Frank was drawn to Paul, who supplied him with marijuana and other drugs, which were readily available in this international city of dubious expatriates from the far, and most debauched, corners of the world.

In Tangier, Tennessee solidified his friendship with Paul and Jane. Paul was a composer and author. In the upcoming year of 1949, he would write his first novel, *The Sheltering Sky,* which would make him world famous.

He had settled in Tangier in 1947, and the exotic city would remain his home for the remaining 52 years of his life.

Paul had composed the "incidental and optional" music for the stage versions of both *The Glass Menagerie* and *Summer and Smoke.* In time, he would also compose the music for Tennessee's *Sweet Bird of Youth* and *The Milk Train Doesn't Stop Here Anymore.*

Frank Merlo *(left)* and **Tennessee** in the 1950s equivalent of a same-sex wedding announcement, in a style suited to Key West.

Married to Paul since 1938, Jane was highly praised by Tennessee. She'd published her novel, *Two Serious Ladies,* in 1943. He claimed "she is the finest writer of fiction we have, even better than Carson McCullers, to whom she bears a physical resemblance. She was a charming girl so full of humor and affection and curious, touching little attacks of panic."

He was mildly alarmed to witness the beginning of her alcoholism, which would lead to her having a stroke in 1957, when she was forty. Her health continued to decline until her eventual death in 1973.

After saying goodbye to Jane and Paul, Frank and Tennessee "on a horrid ship with putrid food," sailed to Marseilles before heading east and then south to Rome, where they would spend a great deal of their time—sometimes five or six months a year—during their time together.

From Rome, Frank traveled to Sicily for a reunion with his family, while Tennessee remained in Rome writing a novel, *The Roman Spring of Mrs. Stone.* During the night, he patronized Rome's large community of hustlers, evoking the gigolos acquired by the protagonist of his novel. "Like the faded actress I am writing about, I, too, am 'drifting,'" he wrote to friends. The word "drifting" appears nearly two dozen times in the novel's opening pages.

Frank did not meet with approval, of course, from all of Tennessee's friends. Maria St. Just, a Russo-English actress *[She's described more fully at the end of this chapter]* was a close friend. She arrived in Rome in the wake of a series of "ugly, violent" fights the two men had had shortly after Frank's return to Rome from Sicily.

She found Frank "very detached, very run down. He is possessive and destructive of every relationship Tennessee has, which is bad for an artist like Tennessee, who needs some impetus—happiness or unhappiness—not just the nervous reactions of a 'Horse.'"

Throughout the 1950s, Frank and Tennessee would have a pattern of fighting and making up.

In a letter to Gore Vidal in 1951, Tennessee wrote that "Frank displays all the warmth and charm of a porcupine." At that point, Frank was telling Tennessee that they needed a vacation from each other.

He soon departed once again for his native Sicily, while Tennessee left for London, where a lot of handsome young British actors, dreaming of a role in one of his plays, sought out his company, especially during August of 1951.

But by September of that year, Frank joined Tennessee for a trip to Copenhagen, although both of them ended up wondering what they were doing there.

When they were together, Tennessee could show a surprising loyalty to Frank. Likewise, Frank could show extreme devotion to Tennessee when it came to protecting him from his enemies and detractors.

Tennessee was sensitive to slights to Frank when they traveled or were invited to parties.

Irene Mayer Selznick was still in Tennessee's life, in the wake of her having produced *A Streetcar Named Desire.* But when she invited him to one of her elegant dinners at the Hotel Pierre Apartments in Manhattan, she wrote a note.

"Oh, by the way, ask Frank to drop in after dinner, if he is so inclined."

"Tell her to go fuck herself," Frank told Tennessee.

Their sleeping arrangements at hotels often caused problems, especially when they checked in to find two twin beds after having requested a king-sized one. Most hotel managers quickly agreed to the large bed in view of Tennessee's increasing fame. However, at the Royal Orleans in New Orleans, the manager refused to let them share a room with only one bed.

In the lobby, Tennessee threw a hissy fit.

"We don't allow two men to share the same bed," the manager asserted. "Why would two men want to sleep in bed together?"

"So they can fuck!" Tennessee said. Then he stormed out of the lobby with Frank to check into a more accommodating hotel.

Back in Key West, in February of 1952, Tennessee wrote Oliver Evans, one of his closest friends. A poet and a teacher, Evans, under a different name, would be depicted in Tennessee's fiction as "a tireless gay cruiser."

Tennessee wrote that he was bored with Key West, "but Frank is out all night with the 'After the Lost Generation' crowd of guys and dolls who live on liquor and bennies, dancing on the fringe of lunacy. Frank dances with the dolls, possibly lays the guys."

Frank was also aware of Tennessee's promiscuity. As Tennessee confessed in a journal, he slipped off late one afternoon to a hotel with "these three queens." When he did return home, "a platter of meatloaf narrowly missed my head, followed by a bowl of succotash. Frank stormed out of the house and drove away. I picked up parts of the meatloaf off the Mexican tiles in the patio and ate it with much gusto. It was delicious."

The actress, Barbara Baxley, who starred in Tennessee's play, *Camino Real,* flew into Key West late in 1978 to film *The Last Resort,* based on Darwin Porter's novel, *Butterflies in Heat.* She told Porter, "From what I observed in 1953, Frank is absolutely essential to Tennessee. He would be lost without Frank. He anticipates his wish before Tennessee even expresses a desire. But he is quick to point out that he is no yes man. If Tennessee drifts into fantasy, Frank brings him back to reality. Both are lucky. Tennessee needs a practical person as a love object, and Frank gets to live with a great poet of the theater."

But the summer of 1953 found Frank and Tennessee separated again. Frank was in Rome, shacked up with a male prostitute named "Alvaro."

Tennessee was in Barcelona, patronizing hustlers along the beach, although he claimed he was despairing of them. "I'm tired of begging for crumbs," he wrote to a friend.

From the Hotel Colón in Barcelona, Tennessee wrote to Carson McCullers, telling her about Frank and himself, claiming, "relations with The Little Horse are strained."

By Christmas of 1953, Frank and Tennessee had reconciled and were entertaining their friends, such as architect Danny Stirrup, back in Key West for the holidays. In a letter to Oliver Evans, Tennessee wrote, "Frank is on his rare best behavior."

By that January of 1954, both Tennessee and Frank became aware that they were being spied upon, and not just by J. Edgar Hoover of the F.B.I., who by now already had an extensive file on Tennessee.

Naval Intelligence in Key West had begun to interrogate some twenty sailors who attended gay parties at Tennessee's home in Key West.

Confessions had been coerced out of at least twelve of them, who admitted to having had sex with either Frank or Tennessee. That had led to dishonorable discharges. Both Frank and Tennessee feared trouble from the government, but no harm came to them. Nor were they brought in for questioning.

By May of 1954, Tennessee did become alarmed at a number of gay murders in Key West. He wrote to friends in New York, "Some queens are getting their throats slit by demented sailors. A lot of them have gone underground here in Key West. Others have fled up the overseas highway to Miami."

[In January of 1979, Tennessee's home in Key West was burglarized on the 8th and again on the 14th, and Frank Fontis, Tennessee's gay gardener, was murdered.

Police searched Fontis' house for clues, finding more than a dozen original manuscripts of Tennessee's plays, which certainly would have value to a collector.

"Fontis was a very eccentric but harmless man, I thought, but it now appears he really wasn't my friend, and it took his murder to reveal that to me," Tennessee said.

Over the years, Fontis had stolen much memorabilia, including personal letters (some rather embarrassing), copies of the playwrights journals, and photographs, some taken of Frank in the mid-1950s that were "compromising," the police reported.

Near the end of his life, many rowdy young men knew Tennessee's address and would often drive by, tossing empty beer cans into his yard and yelling "FAGGOT." As Tennessee said, "These were not punks, but New York critics." On a few occasions, he was mugged in Key West after leaving the bars along Duval Street.]

By 1955, Frank's anxiety level seemed to reach a fever pitch. "Tennessee was also riddled with anxiety," he said. "Now my own nervous system was matching his." In addition to drinking heavily, Tennessee was smoking four packages of cigarettes daily. He also had developed an addiction to amphetamines.

Frank's non-sexual bonding with Danny Stirrup, known as "The Queen of the Conchs," grew stronger. Much time was spent at Stirrup's home where orgies were staged with sailors from the Key West Naval Base. When Tennessee was gone, the sailors were entertained at Tennessee's house.

When Tennessee was in residence in Key West, Stirrup was invited almost every night for dinner cooked by Frank. As such, Stirrup had a front-row seat to the deterioration of the relationship between Frank and Tennessee.

Stirrup remembered one quiet evening when Tennessee read a one-act play to both of them. He'd just written it. Usually, Frank was his biggest supporter and fan. But on this night, the scene turned ugly.

"Do you like it, Frankie?" Tennessee asked after his reading.

"I not only don't like it, I detest it," Frank angrily snapped.

"But why?" Tennessee asked. "Tell me what's wrong with it?"

"How in fuck do I know?" Frank asked, jumping up. "I'm not a playwright." Then he stormed out of the house and drove off into the night. Tennessee expected he'd return at dawn. But he'd

THE FLEET'S IN! When Tennessee was away, **Danny Stirrup** *(far left)* would sometimes bring as many as twenty sailors home for private parties. **Frank** *(seated on the far right)* would usually manage to seduce at least some of them. On this night, Danny and Frank entertain visiting Canadian "seafood.

driven to Miami Beach, where he picked up a beach hustler and spent a week with him at the Fontainebleau, hitting the bars at night. When he returned to Key West, he freely admitted those indiscretions to Tennessee.

"Not only the night of the play reading, but many nights during the months and even years to come, I witnessed such scenes," Stirrup said. "One night, I was invited to dinner, and Frankie had roasted a lamb. Before he could carve it, he and Tenn got into a fight, and Frank tossed the leg of lamb into Tenn's face. I had to drive him to the hospital. Frankie wouldn't go with us. He headed to Captain Tony's Saloon off Duval Street instead."

Tennessee: "The Night I Bedded Moby Dick's Ishmael" (Aka, Adolf Hitler)

Back in Rome in the mid-1950s, Tennessee wrote to friends that "Rome has never looked lovelier. We even have a chauffeur to drive us around. He's very handsome and well built. When he's not driving us, he's sleeping with Frank. The driver claims he bedded both Grace Kelly and Ava Gardner when they stopped off in Rome after the making of *Mogambo* with Clark Gable. Perhaps it's true, perhaps not. At least Clark *knew* both of these fine ladies. That's a Biblical reference. *Know* as in David *knew* Bathsheba."

While Frank was riding around with the hunky chauffeur, Tennessee sought other pastimes. Ever since he'd seen the versatile Italian actor, Vittorio Gassman, in the 1948 film, *Riso amaro (Bitter Rice),* he'd been mesmerized by the magnetic quality of this dashing and very cosmopolitan figure.

Tennessee was friends with the actress Shelley Winters, and was almost jealous of her during the two turbulent years (1952-1954) she was married to Gassman.

Tennessee had been mesmerized when he flew to Italy to watch Gassman star as Stanley Kowalski in *Um tram che si chiama desiderio (A Streetcar Named Desire).* "You're so different from Brando, yet so compelling," Tennessee had told him.

Although hailed as one of the greatest of all Italian actors, he had told Tennessee, "I'm not all that Italian. I was born in Genoa, but my father was German, Heinrich Gassmann. I dropped that extra N in the spelling of my name. My mother was a Pisan Jew."

[Whereas Tennessee could appreciate Gassman's performance as Stanley, he was horrified when he learned that Gassman's ex-wife, Shelley Winters, had been cast as Blanche DuBois in an unrelated English-language, 1955 production of A Streetcar Named Desire. *The play was presented "in the round" as an experimental production at the Circle Theatre in New York. Tennessee said that Richard Boone, the grizzly, craggy actor whose ambitions included a desire to direct, had cast Winters as Blanche "in a fit of madness."*

"Shelley was a tough broad from Brooklyn," Tennessee said. "To work on her voice, she told me she listened to southern accents on records as a means of getting rid of her New Yorkese. On stage, she never convinced me that she possessed the fragility of Blanche, but she tried very hard. Dennis Weaver was cast as Stanley. Shelley admitted to me that he didn't have the special sexual electricity that Brando generated. She was an expert on Brando's sexual electricity, having previously been 'electrocuted' by it."]

When Gassman learned that Tennessee was in Rome, he called his hotel and invited him for dinner.

"This was the first time I'd ever been alone with him," Tennessee said. "I found he had a sexual electricity all his own. He seemed very comfortable with me. Knowing I was homosexual, he treated me like he was dating a woman. Very gracious. Very well mannered. In a way, he seemed to be working overtime to overwhelm me with his macho charm, which he possessed in bushels."

Gassman was aware that Tennessee had rewritten his *Battle of Angels,* retitling it *Orpheus Descending.* At first, Tennessee thought he was "courting me so he could play Val Xavier."

Shelley Winters with
Vittorio Gassman

That, however, was not the case. He told Tennessee that when he and Shelley had lived in Hollywood, they had become close friends with Valentina Cortese, and her husband, the strikingly handsome actor, Richard Basehart, whom she'd married in 1951.

Gassman said that "both Dick and Valentina want to be cast in the leads for your Broadway production of *Orpheus Descending.*"

Privately, Tennessee had reservations about such casting, fearing Valentina was too young and beautiful for the role of "Lady." Basehart, however, in a snakeskin jacket might be enough of a sexual dynamo to be a convincing Val Xavier. Tennessee promised Gassman that he'd meet with both actors and discuss his revised play with them.

What took place after dinner between Gassman and Tennessee was revealed to author Donald Windham.

"Tenn told me that Gassman was rather matter-of-fact and most sophisticated about *après* dinner activities," Windham said. "He said the actor returned with him to his hotel room, where they had two more drinks."

"He just stood in front of me and removed all his clothing and then went and lay down in the middle of my bed," Tennessee said. "He then invited me to come over and enjoy him."

"You wrote such a good role for me as Stanley, so I figured you deserved to find out firsthand what turned on Shelley," Gassman said to Tennessee.

"Vittorio tasted as good as he looked," Tennessee told Windham. "A magnificent specimen of manhood. There was no foreplay. I was invited to go right for the target, and after about twenty minutes of intense activity on my part—after all, he'd had two bottles of wine—Mount Vesuvius erupted."

"After he got dressed, we ended the evening most formally," Tennessee said. "I expected at least a kiss on the cheek, but got a firm handshake instead. He congratulated me on being the world's greatest living playwright. I knew that already. What I wanted him to tell me was that I was the world's greatest cocksucker. If not that, at least better than Shelley."

After talking to Gassman, Basehart contacted Tennessee for a dinner rendezvous. Tennessee just assumed that he would show up with his wife, Valentina Cortese, but he came alone.

Tennessee had seen both stars when they ap-

Richard Basehart as Ishmael *(upper photo)* in *Moby Dick,* and as *Der Führer* in *Hitler (lower photo)*

peared together in *The House on Telegraph Hill* (1951). He'd been particularly impressed with Basehart's performance in the 1954 film *La Strada,* directed by Federico Fellini.

When Tennessee first met Basehart, he'd just finished playing Ishmael in Herman Melville's *Moby Dick,* released in 1956. Years later, in 1962, Tennessee would see him miscast, playing the *Führer* in the film, *Hitler.* "Who could possibly believe this handsome stud was Adolf?" Tennessee asked after sitting through the film.

Tennessee later bragged to Windham that he had also managed to seduce Basehart. "To the public, I always claim that I never go to bed with actors, especially those hoping to get a role. But that's just what I say in public. You know yourself I don't mean a word of that. Like any self-respecting homosexual, I seize upon every opportunity. What is a sex addict to do?"

"I think Gassman had cued Basehart on what to do," Tennessee said. "I'm sure he reported on our experience in my hotel room. With Basehart, it was a repeat of the same performance with Vittorio. He stripped off his clothing, including his boxer shorts, revealing Grade A government-inspected meat. The soft lighting in the room was perfect to display his body to me. He slowly walked around the room, giving me a chance to observe his body in motion. He was a beautiful man with his clothes on. Without his clothes, he was gorgeous. Gassman got away from me, but I insisted Basehart spend the night because I also wanted to make love to him in the rosy glow of dawn. He didn't protest. He slept beside me, snoring lightly. I was tempted to attack him in the middle of the night, the way I do with Frankie, but I contained my impulse until he woke up the next morning."

"Regrettably, after all that work," Tennessee said, "Basehart did not get to play Val, and his beautiful wife was not offered the role of Lady. Perhaps those two could have pulled it off. They certainly did make a lovely couple as long as their marriage lasted. They divorced in 1960."

Psychoanalyst Tells Tennessee:
"Abandon Homosexuality, Abandon Playwriting"

In the late 1950s, Tennessee often worked in his Manhattan apartment on East 58th Street while Frank remained at their home in Key West. As their relationship deteriorated, Tennessee wrote "A Separate Poem" to express his feeling about "the collapsing bridge across the river that separates Frankie and me."

Oh, yes, we've lost our island…
Our travels ranged wide of our island, but nowhere nearly so far
Of what cannot be spoken.

When we speak to each other
We speak of things that mean nothing of what we meant
To each other...a storm of things unspoken.

Windham said, "Tennessee was rich now, and didn't really need Frankie any more. He could afford servants. If he wanted sex, there were dozens of available wannabe actors or even major movie stars willing to drop trou for him. My god, even Elvis Presley wanted to play in movie adaptations by those 'queer writers, William Inge and Tennessee Williams.'"

"In the late 1950s, Tennessee was writing—how shall I put this delicately?—with a system filled with chemicals," Windham said. "That sounds so much better than 'drugs.'"

Plagued with constant anxiety, Tennessee indulged in substance abuse. He smoked two packages of cigarettes a day and drank at least a fifth of liquor, sometimes a lot more. He constantly downed pills. He spoke openly about his dependency on barbiturates, asserting "They unblocked my creative forces."

Many doctors disputed his claim about these mood-altering drugs, claiming that they had the opposite effect by "blunting his creative spark."

In 1957, after the commercial and critical failure of *Orpheus Descending,* and partly because of his collapsing relationship and ongoing crises with Frank, Tennessee became deeply depressed and underwent counseling, consulting a Freudian psychoanalyst, Dr. Lawrence Kubie, five times a week.

The doctor gave him some amazing advice, at least according to Tennessee. He claimed that he was urged to abandon Frank and covert to heterosexuality. Of course, that would necessitate a prolonged roster of dubious treatments and procedures.

Not only that, but the doctor, at least according to Tennessee, advised him to give up playwrighting. That latter claim seems especially dubious, but nevertheless, Tennessee insisted that it was true.

"For the first time in my life, I was so depressed that—at least for a while—I gave up sex entirely," Tennessee said. "Celibate as a priest. On the other hand, 'celibate as a priest' is not the right phrase, considering some of the priests I've known or heard about."

Eventually, Tennessee and Dr. Kubie ended their professional relationship. The doctor claimed that Tennessee was giving interviews in which he discussed his psychoanalysis. "As a result of those interviews, I'm losing some of my best patients," the doctor said.

Tennessee decided to ignore any further professional advice about abandoning his writing. Even though he was often devastated by the critical attacks on his reputation and his declining popularity, he continued to write almost every day. "I don't allow my decline to stop me, because I have the example of so many playwrights before me. I know the dreadful notices Henrik Ibsen got. So I keep writing. I am sometimes pleased with what I do—for me, that's enough."

Indeed, he continued to write one "critical stinker" after another, some of them closing after only a dozen or so performances.

At around this time, an American screenwriter, Meade Roberts, got to know and observe both Frank and Tennessee. Tennessee had gone to see a play by Roberts off-Broadway. It was called *A Palm Tree in a Rose Garden*. Inaugurated in November of 1957, it featured Barbara Baxley, one of Tennessee's favorite actresses, as the star.

Roberts was later hired to adapt Tennessee's *Orpheus Descending* to the screen, which he did under the revised title, *The Fugitive Kind,* starring Marlon Brando. Roberts also would adapt *Summer and Smoke* for the screen in 1961. He also wrote *The Stripper* (1963), starring Joanne Woodward, adapted from the William Inge play, *A Loss of Roses.*

Agent **Audrey Wood** is seen with her "two gold-plated money makers," **Tennessee Williams** *(left)* and **William Inge** *(center)*. In the 1950s, they had reigned as the leading playwrights of Broadway.

Roberts later said that Tennessee told him, "I am insanely jealous of Bill." Both had dramas opening on Broadway in 1957, Inge's *Dark at the Top of the Stairs* and Tennessee's *Orpheus Descending.* Whereas Inge's play was a big hit, Tennessee's play flopped.

"I could kick myself for introducing Bill to Audrey Wood, who later became his agent," Tennessee told Roberts. "I think Bill writes better regional dialogue than I do. Whereas he's Audrey's gentleman playwright, I'm her degenerate playwright."

Later, in Manhattan, when Frank was introduced to Roberts, he told him, "Tenn refuses to believe how much I love him. He goes around telling people that I will welcome his death so I can grab his millions."

Tennessee and Marlon Brando—
Farewells on the Road to Hell

Biographer Ronald Hayman wrote: "Tennessee felt certain he was unlovable, and his inability to believe the reality of Frank's love for him was even harder for Frank to accept than Tennessee's infidelities. Taking care of his lover had been not only Frank's main pleasure, but also his primary occupation. The more unneeded and redundant he felt, the more he neglected to take care of himself."

By January of 1960, Frank's health began to fail. He snapped at friends and was constantly fatigued. He cut off all sexual relations with Tennessee. Depressed and moody, he spent most of his days in bed. Every morning, he stepped on the scales, horrified at his increasing weight loss.

Frank did fly back to New York for a meeting with Tennessee in Audrey Wood's office to clarify his business arrangement with Tennessee. She told him that she would continue to send him ten percent of any royalties from productions of *The Rose Tattoo, Cat on a Hot Tin Roof,* and *Camino Real,* plus an allowance of $150 a week. Tennessee also turned over to him the deeds to two "conch houses in Key West." These were clapboard-sided fishermen's cottages which Frank rented out for extra income.

After the meeting with Wood, Tennessee told Frank goodbye, claiming he was going to pay a visit to Marlon Brando's apartment. He wanted to go alone, but Frank insisted on accompanying him.

Tennessee and Frank greeted Brando like old friends.

"Hon, the old faggot has come back into your life," Tennessee said to Brando, warmly embracing him.

"You never left," Brando said.

Over drinks—far too many for Tennessee—he told Brando that he feared he was going to become a library author instead of one whose plays are actually revived and performed.

Brando countered that he was going to become an actor written about in film schools instead of one seen on the screen. He told them that while making *The Fugitive Kind,* he'd taken a plane back to Los Angeles every weekend to edit and shorten the only film he had ever personally directed, the 1961 Western, *One-Eyed Jacks,* the way-over-budget film in which he also starred. "The God damn thing drove me into bankruptcy and ran up to eight hours."

He said that the other day, a college student had sent him his thesis. As part of an academic study, the student had maintained that *One-Eyed Jacks* was a homosexual movie. The thesis had claimed that Sam Gilman, Brando's best friend, who was also cast in the film, performed with "sexual innuendo" when playing opposite Brando's character of Rio. "In fact, the conclusion was that Sam Gilman and I, along with the rest of the cast, had made a homosexual movie."

"Welcome to the club," Tennessee said. "Everyone writes that about my plays."

Marlon told his guests that variations on the Horatio Alger story were the wrong reading material for America's youth. "Fame is a fraud and a gyp," Brando said. "The biggest disappointment of my life."

At the door, Tennessee and Frank kissed Brando on the lips. They did not know when they would see him again.

Tears welled in Tennessee's eyes when he told Brando that "on some glorious morning I'm going to create another Stanley Kowalski character for you to play."

"I'll be there for you," he answered.

Before heading down the hall, Tennessee looked back at Brando. "I'll race you to hell. Bet I'll get there before you do."

Brando would later claim that "he encountered Tenn deep into drugs and pills—but not quite as bad as Monty Clift. Tenn was clearly coming apart. Success is a deadly game, especially when you can't live up to your earlier successes. Just ask me."

[When his stage and screen performances had thrust him into the public arena in the 1950s, Brando had been part of an exclusive ten-member club whose films earned more than any other actors' in the entertainment industry. But by the 1960s, times had changed. The American public was growing tired of Brando's "poetic hooliganism." Despite Brando's brief comeback with the release of The Godfather *in 1972, the kids who had flocked to see* The Wild One *in the 1950s had grown up and sired rebellious children of their own. Now, they could scoff at the idol of their teenage years.*

To his new best friend of the 1990s, Michael Jackson (of all people), Brando confided, "My good-bye has been the longest good-bye in the history of show business. My tragedy was I didn't know enough to get off the stage when the play had ended."]

Bye Bye Blackbird, Bye Bye Frankie
[In Italian, "Merlo" translates as "Blackbird."]

In his play, *Suddenly Last Summer,* Tennessee's character of Sebastian was "famished for blondes," when he abandoned the Mediterranean and headed north to Scandinavia. In the summer of 1961, Tennessee left Frank behind in Key West as he sailed to the Greek island of Rhodes. There, he wrote to one of his best friends, Maria St. Just.

"I do not plan to return to Frankie. The Horse has done just about all in his power to shatter me and humiliate me, so I must find the courage to forget and put away a sick thing. But to be fair, it isn't easy to live thirteen years with a character walking a tight rope and a thin one over lunacy. But the time has come to 'cool it.'"

When Frank went to visit his family in New Jersey, Tennessee flew to Key West with a handsome young artist he'd met in New York. When it came time to write his memoirs, he could not remember the painter's name.

As the artist and Tennessee were making love on the living room sofa in Key West, Frank's friend, Danny Stirrup, emerged from the patio and saw them. Before midnight, he'd telephoned Frank in the north, where he was in the hospital for two days of extensive medical tests.

After leaving the hospital, Frank flew to Florida where he encountered both the painter and Tennessee. For the first hour, he didn't speak. Then he exploded. "Like a junglecat, Frankie sprang across the room and seized the painter by the throat," Tennessee wrote in his memoirs. He was forced to call the police to prevent strangulation.

The police delivered Frank to Stirrup's home for the night, and Tennessee, along with the painter, drove to Miami and checked into a motel.

Later, Tennessee confessed that the young man "wanted too much sex." So he paid the artist for a painting he'd left behind in Key West, the price of which was more than enough for him to buy a plane ticket back to his native San Francisco.

After that, Tennessee flew alone back to his new apartment at 134 East 65th Street in Manhattan. Within two months, he had launched an affair with a handsome young Frederick Nicklaus, an aspiring poet who had graduated from the University of Ohio.

Frederick was a cousin of the famous golfer, Jack Nicklaus. The poet would subsequently publish two volumes of poetry—*The Man Who Bit the Sun* (1964) and *Cut of Noon* (1971).

In 1962, while Tennessee was fretting over rewrites for *The Milk Train Doesn't Stop Here Anymore,* he decided to take Frederick to Tangier. Once there, they rented a 200-year-old house that had once been the harem of a sultan.

Almost from the beginning, Tennessee began to suffer through conflicts with the poet. He told Paul Bowles, "He's a decent companion but he can't do anything practical. Frank used to handle all these things for me. Freddie doesn't even know how to make a phone call. When we travel, it is nothing but chaos. Reservations are fucked up, Airplane flights are missed. He can't even put a key in the door and open it. As you know, the flushing of a toilet in Tangier is different from what it is in America. He can't even master the new way of flushing."

Leaving Morocco, Tennessee returned with Frederick to New York. He made arrangements to rent a small house on Nantucket, to which he also invited Sal Mineo and Rock Hudson, who had met and bonded with one another (and with Elizabeth Taylor and James Dean) in 1956 during the making of the movie *Giant*.

"Rock and Sal could give other men a case of penis envy," Tennessee later told Donald Windham. "They walked around our upper floor stark raving naked, with everything hanging out. We had to share a bathroom. Once, I caught them in a wild sixty-nine on our living room sofa. Both of these actors would have done great in porno. My only regret is that they did not invite me to join them."

After Nantucket, Freder-

The Merlo family, pictured in their New Jersey home in 1960. **Frank's mother** *(on the far left)* told her son, "I did not raise you to service some cocksucker."

ick and Tennessee flew to Key West, where they found Frank in residence.

For a while in January of 1963, Tennessee, Frank, and Frederick tried to live together in the same house. But it was hardly a convivial *ménage à trois*. Frank spent most days and nights alone and isolated in his bedroom. A black woman cook carried trays of food to him.

Jack Dunphy, the lover of Truman Capote, came to visit. He was very sympathetic to Frank.

Frank told Dunphy, "On seven different occasions, I've saved Tenn from suicide. But he's not grateful. Without me, there would be no Tennessee Williams."

I, too, lived in Truman's shadow," Dunphy said. "Unlike Frank, I'm also a writer, and I had to endure my work being compared unfavorably to his writing. I could see that Frank's spirit had been broken. I think that's what gave him cancer. He had been replaced by Frederick. Tennessee robbed Frank of his identity. He felt he had no recourse but to die."

Director John Huston arrived in Key West to discuss plans for the upcoming filming of *The Night of the Iguana* (1964) in Mexico. Tennessee decided to charter a boat to take him fishing. Part of the itinerary included some beach time on an uninhabited island that had been occupied during World War II by a naval lookout station.

As the vessel moored, Frederick jumped off the side of the chartered boat for a nude swim. Perhaps he spotted a shark or something. In panic, he screamed. He began flailing his arms and appeared close to drowning. He never explained exactly what happened, but it appeared to the crew that he could not swim at all. Responding with alarm, the captain's mate jumped in to save him, hauling his near lifeless body back on board.

In front of Huston, the captain and the crew, Tennessee gave Frederick "the kiss of life," a mouth-to-mouth contact that lasted for about five minutes.

After Huston left Key West, Frank—disgusted with the Tennessee and Frederick link— returned to New York.

By this time, Frank had decided to cut himself off completely from Tennessee. But one night, he experienced a sharp pain in his chest, and was rushed to the emergency ward of New York's Memorial Hospital.

Hearing that Frank was hospitalized, Truman Capote called on him and subsequently spread a horrible (and horribly exaggerated) story throughout the theatrical world that had the ultimate affect of discrediting Tennessee.

Truman had exaggerated, as was his way, asserting that he had found Frank in the hospital's charity ward. "It was like something from the Middle Ages," he reported, distorting the conditions at the hospital. "The patients, at least most of them, looked like corpses dug up in the graveyard. They were screaming in pain. Poor Frank is dying in conditions worse than what Olivia de Havilland experienced in that movie of the damned, *The Snake Pit.*"

Reacting in horror to the implications of the story, friends of Tennessee shamed him into flying to New York as a means of comforting Frank with financial aid. Arriving at Memorial Hospital, Tennessee had Frank moved, at his expense, to a private room.

Frank received cobalt treatments, which darkened and discolored the skin on his chest. After a few weeks, he was released into Tennessee's custody. He took him back to his apartment and installed him in his bedroom, establishing a bed for himself on a sofa.

"Each night, Frankie locked his bedroom door," Tennessee said. "The sound of that lock still haunts me and causes me pain. Did poor Frankie think I was coming in to ravish his skeletal body for my sexual pleasure? Perhaps it wasn't me, but death that he was locking out. All night lying there on the sofa, I heard Frankie coughing the cough of death."

As Frank's condition worsened, Tennessee had him recommitted to Memorial Hospital. This time when he checked in, he arrived in a wheelchair .

"I remember our last night together," Tennessee said. "I kept urging him to get some sleep. At one point, I asked him if he wanted me to leave so he could get some rest."

"No," he said. "I'm used to you."

Then Frank closed his eyes and drifted off. Those were his last words.

Since it was after official visiting hours, the night nurse asked Tennessee to leave. From the hospital, he went to a local pub and had a few drinks, returning at midnight to check on Frank's condition.

There, he learned from a doctor that Frank had died at 11PM.

The date was September 21, 1963. At the age of forty, Frank had succumbed to lung cancer after years of heavy smoking.

Tennessee went to the apartment of Elia Kazan. "I spent the afternoon sobbing in his bed. Frankie was dead, and the most dreadful years of my life were upon me. Something told me the worst was yet to come."

The next day, Tennessee resumed work on *The Milk Train Doesn't Stop Here Anymore.* He transferred many of his own feelings into the psyche of Flora Goforth, the agonized widow and retired actress he created as a character within the play. "Like her, I would go from room to room for no reason, and then go back from room to room for no reason, and then *out* for no reason. Like Flora, I was in mourning for having abandoned a loved one alone to face death by himself."

Two days after Frank's death, Tennessee wrote his friend, Maria St. Just:

"The Little Horse left us two nights ago. He died proudly and stoically. They say he just gasped and lay back on the pillow and was gone. I am just beginning now to feel the desolation of losing my dear Little Horse."

Gore Vidal was more cynical. "The Bird would mourn Frank ever after, quite forgetting that he had thrown him out several years earlier. A true romantic, the Bird associated love with death. And having lost to brain cancer what he always said was his first love, a dancer, the Bird was now mourning Frank."

Dotson Rader, the author, became friends with Tennessee in the 1960s. He claimed that the playwright often spoke nostalgically of Frank. "He created the atmosphere that enabled Tennessee to do the finest work of his career. In many ways, Frank was like a wife and mother to Tennessee. He nurtured him, loved him, worried about him, protected, praised, and comforted him, and kept him from harm."

In the wake of Frank's death, Tennessee was grief stricken, falling into a depression of drugs and despair that lasted for a decade. In 1969, he suffered a nervous breakdown. His brother, Dakin Williams, had him committed to a mental hospital in St. Louis, where Tennessee was held as a virtual prisoner for three months.

Dr. Feelgood Injects Tennessee and Truman with "Instant Euphoria"

From 1963 to 1969, Tennessee obtained most of his drugs from Dr. Max Jacobson, a German-born doctor in his 60s who administered amphetamines and other medications to such high profile clients as Marlene Dietrich, Cecil B. De-Mille, Eddie Fisher, Elvis Presley, John F. and Jackie Kennedy, Alan Jay Lerner, Mickey Mantle, and Anthony Quinn.

Jacobson was widely known as "Dr. Feelgood." During one of his profound depressions, Tennessee was taken to Jacobson by Robert McGregor, editor of *New Directions, [a literary review conceived by its founder in 1936 "as a place where experimentalists could test their inventions by publication."]*

Tennessee continued to drink large amounts of alcohol washed down with Nembutal, Seconal, Luminal, and Phenobarbital. He told his friends "I'm staying alive because of this witch doctor I'm going to."

The drugs helped him to deal with his low self-image. On his 54th birthday, he told a journalist, "I hate myself. I feel I bore people, I can't stand to look in the mirror because I feel I'm too physically repulsive."

His actress friend, Maureen Stapleton, tried to convince Tennessee that Jacobson was nothing but "an exploitive quack preying on celebrities."

By 1966, Tennessee had developed a drug dependence so powerful that it was manifested in toxic after-effects. He went with almost no sleep and at times seemed on the verge of hysteria. He became addicted to large dosages of a sedative, Doriden, which had been introduced in 1954.

In a conversational encounter with Truman Capote, Tennessee learned that he, too, was a "patient" of Dr. Feelgood's. Being Capote, the novelist filled Tennessee in on scandals associated with the quack.

"After getting a shot at the Carlyle, JFK pulled off all his clothes and danced around his hotel suite," Capote claimed. "He ran out into the hallway and started toward the fire escape until the Secret Service caught him and brought him back."

"Jacobson also told me that he gave his medical concoction to Nazi soldiers in 1934 and '35 and that Hitler couldn't get up in the morning without a shot," Capote claimed.

In 1936, because of his Jewish background, Jacobson decided his life was in danger. Consequently, he fled that year from Berlin.

Both Tennessee and Truman agreed that each of them experienced an "instant euphoria" after treatments from Jacobson.

Truman asserted that after receiving injections that he felt like Superman. "I feel I can fly when I come out of his office. Ideas for my work come at me with the speed of light. I can work for 72 hours straight with no sleep, not even a coffee break. If it's sex you're after, you can go all night on one of his injections."

Creep from Hell:
Max Jacobson
(Dr. Feelgood)

"Let me give you the names of some of his patients you might not have known—Sir Winston Churchill, Harry S Truman, Elizabeth Taylor, J. Edgar Hoover, Richard Nixon, Richard Burton, Judy Garland, Frank Sinatra, Ingrid Bergman, and Bette Davis. When Marilyn Monroe sang *Happy Birthday* to JFK at Madison Square Garden, she had come directly from one of Dr. Feelgood's cocktails."

[The Bureau of Narcotics and Dangerous Drugs seized Jacobson's supply; his medical license was revoked in 1975. Jacobson, also called "Miracle Man," ran out of miracles on December 1, 1979 and died.]

Tennessee's Five O'Clock Angel

After his death in 1983, many friends of Tennessee were shocked to learn that he had named Maria St. Just as his literary executor. "Who in the hell is Maria St. Just?" asked Elizabeth Taylor.

Born Maria Britneva, in Petrograd, Russia, Maria St. Just never revealed her age—by most accounts, she was born in 1921.

Her father, who had been court physician to the Romanovs, was murdered in one of the Soviet purges. In its aftermath, in 1922, her mother took Maria to live in London. As a girl, Maria studied ballet under the great Tamara Karsavina and later danced at Covent Garden.

As she grew into an adult, she befriended Sir John Gielgud, who got her work in the London theater. At one of his house parties, she met Tennessee Williams. Within minutes, he became her friend for life.

As time went by, he became her benevolent sugar daddy, and she fell in love with him, wanting to believe he was a lapsed heterosexual.

But when Frank Merlo evolved into a more or less permanent feature in Tennessee's life, she abandoned her pursuit of Tennessee. Instead she married the wealthy Britisher, Peter Grenfell, second Lord St. Just. From then on, she preferred to be addressed as Lady St. Just.

Maria and Tennessee seem to have shared what the French define as an *amitié amoureuse*. Although maintaining a friendly surface relationship with Frank, Maria resented him as both of them vied for influence over the playwright.

She also became jealous of the other women in Tennessee's life, including "that buck-toothed dyke," a reference to author Carson McCullers. Maria also was instrumental in turning Tennessee against his longtime literary agent, Audrey Wood.

Maria fancied herself an actress and wanted to star in Tennessee's plays. He denied her the role of Maggie in *Cat on a Hot Tin Roof,* although he admitted to using her personality as a role model in the development of some of his later characters. He used his influence to get her parts when he could, but in off-Broadway or in road show productions of his plays. She appeared as both Miss Alma in *Summer and Smoke* and as Blanche DuBois in *A Streetcar Named Desire.*

Maria flew in from London to witness Tallulah Bankhead perform in a Broadway (City Center) revival of *Streetcar.* Tennessee claimed that he had originally written the role of Blanche for Tallulah.

According to author Donald Windham, "Bankhead and Lady St. Just hated each other on sight, exchanging insults, much to the delight of Tenn, who was licking his lips at the prospect of a fight between them. He even thought there might be the seed of a play here based on two strong-willed actresses—perhaps Bette Davis and Miriam Hopkins, or Bette Davis and Joan Crawford. He did what he could to toss gas on the fire between Bankhead and Lady St. Just."

Gore Vidal also showed up to observe what was happening.

"Tennessee liked to surround himself with women who adored him but hated each other," Gore claimed. "He liked his drama both on and off the stage. Some writer called it a grotesque *gavotte* dancing around him. I don't know what Tennessee gets from these monster women—frankly, I couldn't tolerate them, including Maria St. Just, the so-called Lady St. Just, with whom I only pretended to be a friend. He had a large appetite for the grotesque in both his art and life. If these *monstres sacrés* provided him with the comforts of the damned, then that was all that mattered."

Of course, over the long duration of their friendship, Maria and Tennessee had arguments. He once flew to the Venice Film Festival just to achieve a reconciliation with "the raging Tartar, Maria, the Lady St. Just."

Perhaps sarcastically, he said he was accompanied by the "beautiful people"—Andy Warhol, Sylvia Miles, and Rex Reed. It was aboard the airplane headed to Italy that he developed a lifelong fixation on Joe Dallesandro, the Warhol star.

Director Elia Kazan said, "When Tennessee wanted a loyal, absolutely true reaction to his work, he turned to Maria St. Just. When he wrote his memoir, he sent it to her, then asked what she thought. She informed him that she put it where it belonged—in the wastepaper basket. He was hurt but didn't drop her. He suspected that in a very short time, he might hold that same opinion himself."

"To the end of his life, whatever distance separated them, he never lost touch with her," Kazan said. "He always counted on her when he was troubled or 'lost.' The truth saves. So does courage. He could count on her for both."

After his death in 1983, based on the terms of Tennessee's will, Maria and an attorney, John Eastman, were named co-trustees of the Rose Williams Trust, the legal entity, named in honor of his sister, which retained ownership, and controlled, the rights to all of Tennessee's literary work.

Almost immediately, Maria became known as a tyrant in her control of the revival of Tennessee's staples, and of productions of plays not previously produced. She even prevented publication of a biography of Tennessee by Lyle Leverich, even

Maria St. Just with **Tennessee**

though Tennessee had approved and agreed to it during the course of his lifetime.

In 1990, Lady St. Just published *Five O'Clock Angel,* a collection of letters addressed to her by Tennessee between 1948 and 1982.

In London, shortly after Maria's death on February 15, 1994, *The Independent* wrote: "Too rich to care about money, Maria St. Just was only concerned for the integrity of the performance in Tennessee Williams' plays which she was empowered to authorize."

Frank Merlo: Hobnobbing with the rarified cream of the Literati.
(Left to right) **Merlo, Windham, St. Just, Tennessee,** and **Sandy Campbell** in 1948

Chapter Seventeen

Truman and His Mother
Compete for the Sexual Affections of
John Garfield & Errol Flynn

Playing a Star-Studded Field

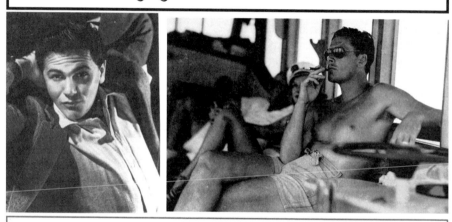

"**John Garfield** *(left)* was one of those thugs in a Bronx street gang that beat up faggots like me," Truman Capote said. "Almost for that very reason, I found him sexually alluring—a rugged, only half-ugly belligerent, and with a chip on his shoulder. He was also tough, cynical, and edgy, just what you want to pull into your bed on a dark night."

Before he became a victim of nymphets, booze, scandal, and premature aging, **Errol Flynn** *(right)* was the swashbuckling heir to Douglas Fairbanks, Sr., Before his zest faded, he was hailed as "fresh as the month of May," luring Truman Capote into his web, even though his mother, Nina, wanted him for herself.

Lillie Mae Faulk was only seventeen and

going to school when a traveling salesman, Archulus ("Arch") Persons, arrived in the sleepy little town of Monroeville, Alabama. She was hailed as the beauty of the county, but on the surface, he was no prize, with his bottle-thick eyeglasses and his thinning blonde hair. Yet he possessed a certain charm, and on frequent visits to Monroeville, he pursued her.

She found him sexually appealing, even though he was not handsome, but rather, short, round, and bespectacled. He had dark hair slicked back, and could have been a boxer, as he had a thick neck, powerful chest, and muscular arms.

The bookseller and literary archivist, Andreas Brown, later wrote that "Lillie Mae was a great Southern beauty, by the standards of her day. She stood five feet, with dark blonde hair." Brown considered her "a bubblehead—irresponsible, childlike, a case of arrested development."

She won a small beauty pageant sponsored by Lux. In later years, her son would exaggerate this contest, saying that, "My mother became Miss America," although that claim could quickly be disproven.

Marie Faulk Rudisill, Truman's aunt, later claimed that "Lillie Mae was so anxious to leave home that she married the first thing in pants that came along, jiggling a few coins in his pocket."

Lille Mae and Arch were married on August 23, 1923.

Almost from the beginning, the marriage was a disaster. It turned out that Arch had only enough money to provide for them for a week's honeymoon in a seedy boarding house near Gulfport, Mississippi, overlooking the Gulf of Mexico. After a miserable week, Lillie Mae was dumped back at the Faulk homestead in Monroeville as Arch set out on the road again as a salesman.

Lillie Mae wanted to get an annulment, but as weeks of indecision dragged by, she discovered she was pregnant. She wanted to abort her future son, but in Monroeville in 1924, pregnancies weren't easily terminated. "I was forced to have Arch's child," she later said. At no point did she ever call Truman "my child."

On an autumn morning deep in the heart of Dixie, Truman Streckfus Persons was born an unwanted child on September 30, 1924.

A Southern belle, whimsical and ambitious, **Lillie Mae Faulk,** later known as **Nina**, married Arch Persons for his money, only to find out on her wedding night that he didn't have any. Years later, she told her son, "I also found out he didn't have much else, either."

The upper photo was taken when she was "sweet eighteen," the lower one snapped at Mardi Gras in New Orleans, circa 1930.

Inherited Passions, Unbridled Lusts

246

Lillie didn't want him, but found the Faulk relatives willing to look after the child. The young boy was virtually adopted by his distant cousin, Nanny Rumbley Faulk, whom he called "Sook."

In his story, *A Christmas Memory* (1956), he described her: "Her face is remarkable—not unlike Lincoln's, craggy like that, and tinted by sun and wind."

As he grew up, his best pal was Harper Lee, a neighbor. In *To Kill a Mockingbird,* her megaseller of a novel, she provided a portrait of Truman as her character of "Dill Harris."

"*He wore blue linen shorts that buttoned to his shirt, his hair was snow white and stuck to his head like dandruff. As he told us an old tale, his blue eyes would lighten and darken; he habitually pulled at a cowlick in the center of his forehead. We came to know him as a pocket of Merlin, whose head teemed with eccentric plans, strange longings, and quaint fancies.*"

Tow-headed **Truman Capote** in Monroeville, Alabama. Virtually abandoned by his parents, he grew up in a bizarre house filled with aunts and distant cousins, amid nostalgia for a South that had "Gone With the Wind."

As Truman's aunt, Marie Rudisill, described Monroeville, "In the warmer months, the old men congregated on benches on the courthous grass, playing checkers, chewing tobacco, whittling sticks, or simply passing time, their liver-spotted hands crooked on their hickory sticks."

Truman reciprocated Harper Lee's creation of Dill Harris with the character of Idabel in *Other Voices, Other Rooms,* as inspired by Harper.

The young boy's days with his parents were numbered. They stashed him in hotel rooms when they went off separately pursuing other affairs. "Sometimes, I would scream until I finally fell asleep exhausted," Truman said. "I was constantly afraid of abandonment, which did come eventually."

"My marriage to Truman's father lasted in reality, not years, but as long as a plucked wildflower," Lillie Mae recalled. Later, in New York, she confided to friends that she had an estimated three dozen affairs during the course of her seven-year marriage. "It's always exciting when a man first drops his shorts," she said. "You never know what's in store for you: A small cucumber pickle or a huge carrot."

Her brother-in-law, John Persons, claimed that Lillie Mae specialized in "Greeks, Spiks, college sheiks wearing raccoon coats, and football players. She later preferred famous men, especially movie actors."

Her first famous big name conquest was one of the most celebrated men in America, the charismatic boxer, Jack Dempsey, a cultural icon of the 1920s who held the World Heavyweight Championship from 1919 to 1926. His aggressive style and exceptional punching power made him one of the most pop-

Young Truman had a slight resemblance to his real father, **Archulus Persons**. This snapshot was taken in Alabama in 1930. "Arch" was always upset that Truman took the name of his stepfather (Capote) instead of calling himself Truman Persons.

During the summer of 1923, Arch arrived in Monroeville in his chauffeur-driven black Packard, looking rakish in his Panama hat, white linen suit, and candy-striped silk shirt. Lillie Mae's first impression of him was, "He's got MONEY written all over him." But as time went by, Arch looked less and less like a movie star, and as it turned out, the Packard belonged to his grandmother.

ular sports figures in history.

Lillie Mae was sitting with her young son when Dempsey walked down the aisle of a train traveling between Memphis and St. Louis. He struck up a conversation with her and invited her for a drink in his compartment. She carried Truman with her. Once inside the compartment, Dempsey told his manager to take the young boy to the Observation Car for a Coca-Cola. For three hours, the manager acted as babysitter for Truman, until Dempsey finally came for them.

Before Dempsey parted with Lillie Mae, they made some sort of arrangement to keep in touch as a means of continuing their affair in some other city.

Somehow, Arch found out about this arrangement. Far from being angry, he interpreted his wife's friendship with Dempsey as a major commercial opportunity for him. He got her to persuade the boxer to appear as the featured VIP at Jack Dempsey Day in Columbus, Mississippi—a wrestling event Arch both organized and aggressively promoted. In the days leading up to the event some 12,000 tickets were reserved in the wake of a massive publicity furor. Extra wooden stands had to be constructed to hold the capacity crowds.

On the day of the event itself, only 3,000 spectators showed up because Columbus was hit that day with one of the worst storms in its history. Arch lost a lot of money and had to flee from his creditors.

One summer evening in 1925, Lillie Mae found herself in New Orleans, staying overnight at the Monteleone Hotel. That night, she met Joseph Garcia Capote, a former colonel in the Spanish

Later in life, **Truman** described the face of his distant relative, **Sook Faulk** *(left photo)*, as "Lincolnesque."

An American puritan, she was loving and protective of him when others mocked him. "She became the mother I never really had." She approved of almost everything he did, but warned him, "You can get into a lot of trouble wandering alone in the woods with a black boy--there have been stories of what happens to little blonde boys like you."

Army during the Spanish-American War. Beginning in 1894, he had been stationed in Cuba, defending the interests of the Kingdom of Spain. One of the most dramatic highlights of his military career had involved his unit's armed conflict against Theodore Roosevelt's Rough Riders during the Battle of San Juan Hill. *[This, the bloodiest and most decisive battle of the Spanish American War, occurred on July 1, 1898, a short distance south of Santiago, Cuba.]*

He spent the night in her bedroom, departing the next morning. They agreed to keep in touch by writing letters. Later, after migrating to New York, he obtained a good-paying job as the office manager of a respected textile-brokerage firm, Taylor, Clapp, & Beall. There, he met a beautiful secretary, fell in love with her, and married her. Despite that encumbrance, he continued writing letters to Lillie Mae, promising, "We'll get together again if you ever visit New York."

Back in Alabama, Lillie Mae got into trouble with the law. Arch had asked her to drive his car across the state line to the hotel where he was staying in Atlanta, Georgia. On the way back to Alabama, she was stopped for speeding by a patrolman. He became suspicious and forced her to open the trunk of her car, where he found a large stash of "bootleg hootch."

She protested that her husband had placed the moonshine there without her knowledge. She ended up spending two nights in jail—presumably cursing the day she ever met her husband—until she was rescued by the Faulk family, who managed to get the charges against her dropped.

After that, making her domestic matters worse, she learned that Arch had been arrested and jailed in Birmingham, Alabama, where he was facing charges of extortion and writing bad checks.

Lillie Mae fled from Alabama to Manhattan, where she found a job as a waitress in a restaurant on Lower Broadway. As what was defined at the time as a temporary, interim solution, she stashed young Truman at the Faulk homestead, which was owned by Jennie Faulk, her cousin, and populated by Jenn's two eccentric, middle-aged sisters and a

Lillie Mae, pictured here in the 1920s, was shocked, even horrified, when Truman confessed to her that he was different from other boys. He told her, "I will be brilliant, delicate, sissy, queer, homo—or shall I be formal, darling, and say 'homosexual?'"

The world famous boxer, **Jack Dempsey**, became Lillie Mae's first high-profile seduction, with many more to follow.

In his early days, the well-hung boxer posed for frontal nudes. After he became celebrated, his nude photograph became one of the hottest selling items in underground outlets for thousands of homosexual fans who viewed his nude frontals as valued collectors' items.

reclusive older brother. It was within this bizarre household that Truman passed part of his adolescence.

In time, he would define the Faulks as the inspiration for characters in his first novel, *Other Voices, Other Rooms.*

In New York, Lillie Mae, deciding that her name "too hillbilly," changed it to the more sophisticated "Nina." Even though he was married, and she was, too, she resumed her affair with Joseph Capote. During the next few years, she had at least three abortions, including one in Brooklyn that nearly killed her.

Her divorce from Arch was legally finalized on November 9, 1931. On March 24, 1932, after Joseph's own divorce was granted, he married Nina.

In the first week of September of that year, Nina sent for Truman to come and live with her new husband in their Brooklyn apartment. Unexpectedly, Truman bonded with his new stepfather. The tow-headed youngster had a high-pitched voice, "girlish manners, and an effeminate walk."

Nina complained constantly that "My son is a fairy," but Joseph assured her it would be all right. "In Cuba, we call such boys *mariposas,*" he said. "But I like the kid."

He liked Truman so much, he adopted him, changing his name to Truman García Capote. Arch was horrified to learn about his former wife's new husband, calling Joseph "a Dago New Yorker," and "A Cuban, the lowest form of a white person."

"The Slut of St. John's Military Academy"

In New York, beginning at the age of eleven, Truman began to write fiction. When other kids were doing their homework, he was spending three hours every afternoon writing.

In 1935, Truman attended the exclusive Trinity School in New York, a private preparatory school which had been founded in 1709. It was here that he had his first sexual experience. His English teacher had read his short stories and thought he was talented.

He began to walk him home from school. One day, he invited him to attend the Olympia Theatre on Upper Broadway to see a Clark Gable movie. The teacher led him to the back row. In the darkened theater, he began to fondle Truman and asked him to masturbate him. These secret rendezvous continued throughout the remainder of Truman's stay at Trinity. He later said, "I always had a marked homosexual preference, and I never had any guilt about it."

At Trinity, Truman joined the "Gay Blades," an ice-skating group on the city's West Side. He also appeared, cross-dressed, in a school theatrical, playing Evangeline St. Clare (the saintly and sometimes saccharine "Little Eva") in *Uncle Tom's Cabin.*

Nina was becoming increasingly alarmed that her son was "growing up to be a homosexual." In an attempt "to make a man out of him," she sent him to St. John's Military Academy at Ossining, New York.

"St. John's didn't make a man out of me, but I *made* half of its young men," Truman jokingly recalled later in life. "During the day, the boys made fun of my mannerisms. But at night, my services were in great demand. I was like a pretty young boy sent to prison. All of the boys wanted their chance at me, and they got it night after night. I was in Heaven. I practically seduced every boy in my dormitory and was very popular. Sometimes, they rewarded me with candy bars or some special gift. A few of them, such as the captain of the football team, actually developed a crush on me."

Back in Brooklyn, the Capotes (Joe and Nina) secretly began to court other lovers, as they seemed to have grown tired of each other. Joseph was gone for days at a time, pursuing women in Manhattan, and Nina developed a string of paramours. Hypocritically, she attacked Joseph for his philandering despite her many infidelities. Once, after confronting him for one of his affairs, she assaulted his testicles with her long fingernails until he bled. He was rushed to the hospital.

"When I came home, I was witness to several of her affairs," Truman claimed.

Nina remained slim, chic, stylish, and still beautiful, though, as the years went by, she spent more and more time maintaining her looks in the beauty parlor.

Songwriter Michael Brown remembered her. "There was something almost hysterical in her fluttering, in her incessant flow of words, in her coquettish behavior. There were two or three attempts at suicide as well, or so I heard."

Truman was eighteen when he posed for this photograph during his enrollment as a student at St. John's Military Academy.

"From Day One, I knew I would never become a soldier," he said. "But my life among Army wannabees had its advantages. It was at night in our dormitory that I learned about dicks, and I realized that they come in all shapes and sizes. These young men at the academy were at their sexual peak, and, for the most part, their only sexual relief came when I crawled between the sheets with them."

In 1939, Joseph moved his family to Greenwich, Connecticut, where Truman was enrolled in Greenwich (Public) High School. There, he wrote for the school journal, *The Green Witch*.

Phoebe Pierce Vreeland became Truman's best friend at high school. She later claimed that when Truman turned fifteen, he proposed marriage to her, claiming, "We can be buddies forever."

She was also introduced to Nina. "They were a strange pair and looked so much alike—the same coloring, the same high forehead, the same color eyes, the same mouth, the same body structure. Rather slim upper body, heavy hips and heavy legs."

"She was the first Southern woman I had ever met, and she scared me. Because she was not like a mother, at least not any mother I had met. She was a belle, extremely attractive and very attractive sexually. She was always beautifully dressed and had great style."

"When it came to Truman, she was always ricocheting—lovely at one point, terrible the next. In front of people, she warned him, '*You gonna wind up in the guttah.*'"

Mother and Son:
"Those Capotes, The Star F*#@ers"

After three boring years in Greenwich, Joseph and Nina moved to a large apartment on 1060 Park Avenue in Manhattan. Truman had not yet graduated from Greenwich High School. Consequently, he enrolled in the Franklin School, a private school on Manhattan's Upper West Side, from which he graduated in 1943. He never went to college.

It was during this period on Park Avenue, before her beauty faded, that Nina entered into her most high-profile romances.

Andreas Brown, the literary archivist, said, "Nina was very ambitious about being accepted into society. She wanted to be a member of café society, as it was called in those days. She pursued it with determination. She entertained, she spent money, and she lived well."

Her parties grew in prestige. Her invitations were eagerly sought by authors, playwrights, movie stars, and directors. "My mother became a social gadfly," Truman recalled. "Since Joseph was often gone pursuing whatever, she had a free range. Many famous actors were invited to stay over in her bedroom during Joseph's absence. She was 'auditioning' already established stars, including two or three female conquests."

Truman later told Carson McCullers, Tennessee, and others of his friends that Nina in the 1930s managed to seduce some of the leading male movie stars of that era, names not familiar to most movie-goers today, except those who watch Turner Movie Classics on television. For years, Truman bragged about Nina's seductive powers until people began to ask him, "And just who were those guys?"

Her conquests included Burgess Meredith, Warren William, Richard Barthelmess, and Lee Tracy, plus lesbian attachments to both Beatrice Lillie and Marlene Dietrich.

Designated as one of the most accomplished actors of the 20th Century, Burgess Meredith, originally from Cleveland, Ohio, was married to Margaret Perry when he became involved with Nina. Co-incidental to his affair with Nina, he was also sleeping with Tallulah Bankhead. By 1944, he would marry screen goddess Paulette Goddard, after the dissolution of her marriage to Charlie Chaplin.

In 1935, Nina was invited to a cast party after watching Meredith perform with Katharine ("Kit") Cornell in the Broadway revival of *The Barretts of Wim-*

Truman's Mommie Dearest;
Things They Talked About in Hollywood
(aka; Disadvantages of Living With a Precocious Child)

The film careers of Nina Capote's celebrity paramours spanned Hollywood's evolution from the Silents (as symbolized by **Richard Barthelmess**; *left)* to **Warren William** *(center)*, known for his pre-Code drawing room dramas; to **Burgess Meredith** *(right)*, shown as a *film noir* hero.

Truman evaluated each of his mother's lovers:

RICHARD BARTHELMESS: "In the silent era, Barthelmess represented what was considered the epitome of Victorian male beauty, something suspended between the glowing images of pre-Raphaelitism and the animation of moving pictures. Much of what he did on the screen was pure corn, but he invested every role with a combination of male strength and sensitivity."

WARREN WILLIAM: Warren William, in Truman's view, was an actor who "exemplified the 1930s. With the arrival of World War II, a different type of leading man was called for--Van Johnson, Alan Ladd—two fags, incidentally. In his heyday, no one could play a suave rotter like Warren. There was a deep, sophisticated tone to his voice. He was hardly a hero on the screen, playing roles such as a caddish womanizer or a misogynistic banker with a habit of bedding his secretaries. I saw him emerging from the shower one day. I never did a survey, but I think he was the best hung of Nina's lovers. if her screams were any indication. She told me, 'Going to bed with Warren is like taking it from a bull.'"

BURGESS MEREDITH: "Paulette Goddard, Tallulah Bankhead, and my dear Mom were welcome to Burgess Meredith," Truman claimed. "He did nothing for me. But I respected his talent and found him amusing. I encountered him decades later and asked him to tell me three or four experiences he had had that might come as a surprise to me. He willingly obliged."

"I once got a blow-job from Cole Porter," Meredith claimed. "In 1934, I bedded Amelia Earhart when she appeared with me on the 'Red Davis Radio Show.' When Charles Laughton and I did *The Man on the Eiffel Tower,* he asked me to shit for him so he could spread it on a sandwich. When I made *Rocky* with Sylvester Stallone, I found out he has a small dick. When I was married to Paulette Goddard, she complained to me that I was good for only one blast-off per night, whereas Charlie Chaplin could go for four or five times a night, and, once, she said, within a twenty-four hour period, he went nine rounds!"

pole Street.

Nina found Meredith amusing and sexy in a funny kind of way, but hardly the handsomest man she had ever seduced. She was in the audience on opening night of *The Barretts of Wimpole Street.*

"Just as I started my first speech, a woman in the second row had an epileptic seizure," Meredith told Nina. "Kit saved the day by vamping until the ushers got this catatonic lady out of the theater."

"Ingrid Bergman, Hedy Lamarr, and Marlene Dietrich lay in Burgess' future, but I got to him before those dames had their go at him," Nina later claimed.

"God knows I'm not a dashing swain," he told Nina. "But in a kind of mongrel way, I chased the foxes. Two of those foxes included Norma Shearer and Ginger Rogers."

"He was sexually liberated," Nina said. "He told me that once he was involved in a *ménage à trois* with a wealthy German lady and her lesbian lover."

"Burgess got uglier year by year, but when I was with him, he wasn't all that bad looking," Nina said. The critic, Wolcott Gibbs, said, "Meredith's extraordinary success on stage has practically nothing to do with what he looks like."

Truman was also privy to his mother's affair with Warren William, a film star who in the 1930s was nicknamed "The King of Pre-Code."

"I think she really wanted John Barrymore, but he eluded her," Truman said. "She settled for Warren instead. His distinctive mustache caused

"It was amazing that **Lee Tracy** *(photo above)* became a movie star," Truman recalled. "He didn't have all that much going for him. If he had any talent at all, it was for his rapid-fire banter and his saucy put-downs. He was a smartass on and off the screen."

"He did have a few exploits, like fucking Jean Harlow when they made *Bombshell.* He was a hellraiser and a heavy drinker. When he made *Dinner at Eight* with John Barrymore, the two went on a five-day-and-night binge, consuming so much alcohol that it nearly killed both of them."

"When I went to see Gore's disaster on Broadway, *The Best Man,* I went backstage to see this relic, born in 1898. The Georgia cracker told me, 'Gore Vidal is a better writer than you are.' I shot back, 'Nina told me you were the world's worst lover, a problem of erectile dysfunction.'"

him to have a certain physical resemblance to the Great Profile."

When Nina met Warren, he'd just filmed *Go West Young Man* with Mae West. "Nina took me to see *Satan Met a Lady* in 1936." Truman said. "Warren starred with Bette Davis. This plot later was called *The Maltese Falcon* when it starred Humphrey Bogart. Nina got Warren, but, years later, when we were shooting *Beat the Devil* in Italy, I got Bogie. So I had one up on her."

"Warren's heyday had ended when Nina first took up with him," Truman said, "although he worked steadily until his untimely death in 1948. He had a great personality both on and off the screen, and Nina told me that he was 'competent' in bed—that was her exact word. He was tall with a sharp nose. One of his biographers said, and I agree, that he was 'a wolf dressed as Granny with a smile.' He was from one of those frozen states—Minnesota, I think—and he was very debonair. He'd married in 1923, and was married until 'death do us part,' but he played the field."

"He was clever. He once showed me an early version of the Winnebago, a sort of apartment on wheels he could move around. He also invented a 'vacuum cleaner for lawns.' When I met him, he was doing research into the many uses of sawdust."

"As far as looks go, I always thought Warren looked like a combination of Basil Rathbone and Mischa Auer. I don't tell people that anymore, because they always say, 'Who in hell were those guys you speak of?'"

"Richard Barthelmess was Nina's third movie star conquest," Truman said. "For those not up on Hollywood history, he was nominated for the first Oscar for Best Actor back in 1928. He got into acting at the urging of that dyke, Alla Nazimova, a friend of the family. Nazimova was the godmother of Nancy Davis, who snared…what's his name? Ronald Reagan. Dick was a bit long in the tooth when Nina bedded him. Hell, he was born in 1895."

"Dick worked for D.W. Griffith, but he still had his looks when I met him. His heyday was in the 1920s when he was one of the highest paid actors in Hollywood. He was in this long-time marriage to Jessica Stewart Sargent when Nina met him, but like all actors, he liked a piece on the side."

"Dick used to appear with Lillian and Dorothy Gish, Griffith's famous sister act. He told me they were lesbian lovers. In *Broken Blossoms* (1919), Griffith cast him as a Chinaman opposite Lillian. He teamed with her again in *Way Down East* in 1920. Bette Davis gave him a blow-job when they made *Cabin in the Cotton* (1931)."

"Lillian told everyone that Dick Barthelmess was the most beautiful man she'd ever seen, but when I first met him, he had big circles under his eyes," Truman said. "He was

THERE IS NO DISPUTING TASTE

Truman never got to seduce his all-time fantasy, **Lloyd Nolan**, depicted above.

Nolan, a character actor from San Francisco, was never considered a male pin-up. He was twenty-two years older than Truman. "Nina took me to see Lloyd play 'the Polka Dot Bandit' in *The Texas Rangers* (1936), and I was hooked for life. I could spend an hour licking his armpits before I got around to the rest of him. He was a father figure for me, but a father I always wanted to commit incest with."

"With a few exceptions, he was definitely 'B' picture material, but I never missed one single film of his. I think he played Captain Queeg in *The Caine Mutiny* better than Bogie."

"On the screen, I lived out my sexual fantasies with him—the level-headed doctor with Lana Turner in *Peyton Place*. A murder victim killed by Anthony Quinn in *Portrait in Black*. I was glued to my TV set whenever he appeared in that TV series, *Julia*, which ran from 1968 to 1971."

"The great question I never answered was this: Would sex with Nolan have been as good as I imagined it?"

stoop-shouldered with a voice as high as that of John Gilbert, even though his career continued into the talkie era. He seemed rather smug to me, but that could have been because he was so fucking reticent. Nina told me she grew bored with his talk about social justice. She just wanted him to make love— and that was that."

"I'm grateful for Nina introducing me to Dick," Truman recalled. "I got one up on Gore and Tennessee. I bet they had never met any man who once fucked Theda Bara. Back in 1917, Dick made *Camille* with the original vamp."

Of all of Nina's movie star lovers, Georgia boy Lee Tracy was the least sexy of all of them," Truman said.

He became famous playing Hildy Johnson, the tough-talking reporter, in the original stage production of *The Front Page* (1928).

"He did well in films until he made *Viva Villa!* in 1933 with Wallace Beery. Desi Arnaz always claimed that Tracy stood nude on a balcony in Mexico and pissed on a military parade passing below. Desi was in the movie. He said that in Mexico from then on, if one watched the crowds, they would visibly disperse any time an American stepped out onto a balcony. MGM sacrificed Tracy in order to be allowed to continue filming in that country."

"You might say Lee Tracy 'pissed' away his stardom," Truman said. "The studio fired him and shot all his scenes with Stu Erwin instead."

"After that, in a sort of comeback role, Lee played Art Hockstader, a character loosely based on Harry Truman, in both the stage and film versions of *The Best Man* (1964). In case you don't know, that play was written by one Gore Vidal, Tarantula from Hell, a no-talent prick and asshole, the shithead faggot who can clear a room merely by walking into it, a thoroughly detestable creature who should have been removed from the planet years ago…by force, of course."

"Lee Tracy was not a party-goer," Truman said. He once said, 'I can count on one hand the number of parties I've been to.' Nina picked him up at the Plaza in Manhattan. He hated roots. At the time we met him, he'd never owned a home. He preferred hotels. He also found my presence annoying. 'If I ever get married, I will insist on no children,' he said. 'Who would want a snotty-nosed kid underfoot?' he asked."

"Lee was a wild card," Truman said. "When Nina met him, he got drunk a lot and did reckless things. He'd once been arrested in 1935. While intoxicated, he'd fired five shots through the floor of his kitchen into the occupied apartment below."

"Of Nina's many movie star beaux, the only one I could have had was Lee," Truman said. "I came home one day and found him lying nude and drunk in Nina's bed. I looked him over carefully and could easily have taken him. In his condition, he could not have put up much resistance. Had it been Clark Gable, Tyrone Power, or Robert Taylor, I would have jumped on and had some fun. But I just wasn't tempted."

"Actually, and I might as well tell you, my all time fantasy movie star, the one I dream about at least two times a week, is that character actor, Lloyd Nolan."

Nina Capote Pals Around with Bea Lillie and Marlene:
A Brush of Lesbianism

Sheridan Morley, in *The Oxford Dictionary of National Biography,* defined "Bea" Lillie, known in private life as "Lady Peel," with this description: *"Lillie's great talents were the arched eyebrow, the curled lip, the fluttering eyelid, the tilted chin, the ability to suggest, even in apparently innocent material, the possible double entendre."*

Many of her fans thought she was British born, but she entered the world in 1894 in Toronto. One of her most popular numbers was "There are Fairies at the Bottom of Our Garden." She gave the first ever performances of Noël Coward's witty ditty, "Mad Dogs and Englishmen."

Although an internationally known lesbian, she married Sir Robert Peel, 5th Baronet, in 1920.

She continued to seduce some of the towering figures in the theatrical world, including Judith Anderson, Tallulah Bankhead, Vivien Leigh, Katharine Cornell, Greta Garbo, torch singer Libby Holman, Gertrude Lawrence, and Eva Le Gallienne. But she helped engineer a few surprising male seductions, too, notably three towering figures from the era of silent films—Buster Keaton, John Gilbert, and Rudolf Valentino.

To that list of conquests can be added the name of Nina Capote. Tallulah brought Bea to one of Nina's fabulous parties, and the performer seemed enchanted with Nina, so much so that a "sleepover" was arranged. The next day, Tallulah called Nina to find out what had happened. "I just assumed you tasted the honeypot last night," Tallulah asked.

"Why tell you something you already know?" Nina replied.

Truman was not at all surprised that his mother indulged in an occasional lesbian fling. "All those grand old dames such as Kit Cornell were muff diving," he said. "Why not Nina?"

Tallulah and Bea were always in touch, Tallulah once defining her friend "as the funniest lady who ever stood in

Nina's lesbian affairs included some of the most visible and famous members of Hollywood's so-called "sewing circle," as typified by comedienne **Bea Lillie** *(left)* and **Marlene Dietrich** *(right)*.

257

shoe leather."

"Bea shared her wit and charm with us during two more parties, and then she was gone, never to return," Truman said. "But one morning, when I stumbled into the kitchen, I encountered Marlene Dietrich making what must be the world's greatest omelette. She'd been brought to one of Nina's parties by that social gadfly, Leo Lerman."

"I will never forget my first sight of Marlene," Truman recalled years later. "She wore a pair of rumpled pants and a shirt open at the neck. Her blue eyes stared straight at me as she saw right through me. Clean of makeup, the bone structure of her face was fantastic."

"Sit down," she told him. "It was an order and I obeyed," Truman said. "The omelette had the magic touch. I would get to know her much better during the Broadway production of *House of Flowers,* when she was always backstage, but that morning with Marlene remained one of the most memorable of my life. Nina was still in bed, and I was delighted. I wanted Marlene all to myself, and didn't want to compete with Nina for her attention."

After breakfast, Marlene shocked me," Truman said. "Even before our maid arrived, Marlene began washing glasses and dishes and straightening up the apartment after last night's party. What was she? Shanghai Lily? Or a *Hausfrau?"*

"Even back then, I craved gossip," Truman said. "I was dying to ask Marlene about her legendary love affairs, but didn't. Oh, how I wanted to hear stories of Maurice Chevalier, Colette, Gary Cooper (especially him), George Bernard Shaw, Barbara Stanwyck."

"At last night's party, I heard Marlene telling Burgess Meredith, 'In Europe, it doesn't matter if you're a man or a woman. We make love with anyone we find attractive.' How I wanted to be that sophisticated, although I had no desire to make love to a woman."

"Nina took me to see Marlene's movie, *Manpower* (1941), in which we heard she seduced both of her co-stars, George Raft and Edward G. Robinson. I was amazed that any woman would go to bed with Edward G., but Marlene must have had an iron-clad stomach to stomach him."

"Like Bea Lillie, Marlene soon disappeared from our lives, and it would be years before I got to know her during her Pearl Bailey/Yul Brynner period. We heard reports from the battlefields, as Marlene entertained the troops. Stories reached us that she was sleeping with Edward R. Murrow, General George Patton, Jr., General James Gavin, and even had a one-night stand with General Dwight D. Eisenhower. That Marlene! Hitler never got her, but others did, so many others."

In later years, Truman said, "God had a talent for creating exceptional women. Even in Heaven, *she* came up with one of her greatest accomplishments when she created Marlene Dietrich. Instead of my own life, I would much preferred to have been Marlene."

John Garfield:
The Postman Did Indeed Ring Twice

"He was one of the nicest people I've ever known. My mother saw him just once and tried to get him into bed with her."

—**Truman Capote**, on John Garfield

"Nina and I didn't agree on most things, but we were in complete agreement in our responses to the on-screen images of John Garfield and Errol Flynn," Truman said. "Both of us considered them the two hotties of the screen. Although Nina wanted both of them, she failed to get either one. Not me! I was the lucky one. I got both John and Errol in my bed, as unlikely as that seems. But you must remember that in the late 1940s, I was considered somewhat a pretty boy before age, booze, and Miss Time herself fucked me over."

"Had John stayed with those Bronx street gangs he grew up with, he might have become a full-time gangster, but he got involved with the Group Theater and became an actor," Truman said.

Garfield expressed it even better, saying, "If I hadn't become an actor, I might have become Public Enemy Number One."

At one point, Garfield told Truman that he went through a period of vagrancy, hitchhiking across the country, freight hopping, picking fruit in California for a dollar a day, logging in the Pacific Northwest. When he told writer/director Preston Sturges of these adventures, it catalyzed him into the creation of *Sullivan's Travels,* the 1942 movie that starred Joel McCrea and Veronica Lake.

Screenwriter Walter Bernstein said, "Garfield always had the face of a bar mitzvah boy gone just wrong enough to en-

Lana Turner and **John Garfield** flirt with sex and murder in their most famous movie, *The Postman Always Rings Twice,* a film adaptation of James M. Cain's 1934 novella about a drifter and a roadhouse owner's wife who rush into adultery and murder. The book was originally banned from the screen by the Joseph I. Breen office

When censorship eased, Lana and Garfield sizzled on the screen together, with Lana usually dressed all in white, from her turbans to her high-heeled pumps.

"Lana and I were told to tone it down a bit for the screen, but we made up for it later," Garfield claimed.

hance his appeal."

"By the time I got around to John, half the women in Hollywood had already had him, including Francis Farmer, Hedy Lamarr, Ida Lupino, Eleanor Parker, Ann Sheridan, singer Margaret Whiting, Shelley Winters, and a whole chorus line of showgirls, script girls, wannabe starlets, waitresses, and students of both sexes at the American Laboratory Theatre, where he trained in New York," Truman said.

"John was generous with his sex organ. He wasn't too particular where he put it. He was of the school that 'all cats are gray at night.' I was a beneficiary of his equal opportunity seductions."

"So was Lana Turner," Truman said "I fell in love with John when he made *The Postman Always Rings Twice* (1946) with her. She told me, 'John had a penchant for picking up girls, sometimes two at a time, and a reputation as a demon lover. That reputation was well deserved. He died young and in bed, which was understandable."

He was also sexually aggressive with his other co-stars. When he was introduced to Joan Crawford on the set of their joint venture, *Humoresque* (1946), she offered her hand for him to shake. He preferred to pinch her breasts instead. Taken aback for only a moment, she quickly recovered. "I think you and I are going to get on just fine on the screen and in the sack," she said.

The columnist, Sheilah Graham, former lover of F. Scott Fitzgerald, once spoke about Garfield with Truman at a party. "He makes love like a sexy puppy," she claimed. "In and out, huffing and puffing in quick gasps."

Tired of hearing about Garfield in bed instead of experiencing him firsthand, Truman made his big play for the drunken actor at a party at the lavish Manhattan apartment of celebrity collector, Leo Lerman.

"John was not a real homosexual—not at all," Truman claimed. "In bed, he treated me like he might respond to a young woman. He wanted only one thing, and you know what that was. As he made love to me, huffing and puffing, like Graham had told me, I thought not so much of him, but of the role he played with Lana in *The Postman Always Rings Twice*. He was such a turn-on for me. I saw that one picture eight times. One Saturday alone, I sat through it three times."

"In the post-coital glow, John sat on the living-room sofa, smoked a cigarette, had a drink, and

John Garfield posed *au naturel* at Warner Brothers for this publicity shot

talked to me about *Postman*. He said that the Joseph I. Breen office, the chief censor of movies, kept it off the screen for an entire decade, even though MGM had bought the rights for $25,000 in 1934."

Garfield claimed that two unauthorized versions of *Postman* had been made subsequent to the success of his original version, one in France in 1939 and another in Italy in 1942 by director Luchino Visconti.

Truman was shocked that Garfield didn't like his role in the movie. "We weren't allowed to let the sexual spark between Lana and me catch fire. There she was, all in virginal white, from her high-heel pumps to her turbans and platinum hair. I felt emasculated as Frank Chambers' playing against her interpretation of Cora, since she held all the power."

"I was told to tone down my character's complexities—a diversion from my usual acting style."

The next morning, as Truman later related, he came into his bathroom to find Garfield standing nude in front of the vanity mirror shaving himself.

"He had a semi-erection," Truman recalled. "I'd had John drunk. Now in the cold light of day, he was sober, and I wanted to try him out when he was in full control of his powers. I handed him a towel with a request. 'John,' I said to him. 'Would you rape me this morning, imagining I'm Lana Turner? And one more thing…Don't hold back. Don't be kind.'"

***

Truman was very distressed to hear over the radio that Garfield had died on May 21, 1952 at the age of thirty-nine. There was speculation that his long-term heart problems were aggravated by the stress of his blacklisting during the Red Scare, when he was accused of being a communist.

After he appeared on the Red Channels list, he was barred from future employment as an actor by Hollywood studio moguls for the remainder of his film career.

At his funeral in New York, Truman was among the estimated 12,000 fans who showed up. It was the largest funeral in the city since the untimely death of Rudolph Valentino back in 1926.

"John—or Julie, as his friends called him—came a long way in just a short time after having been born into a Russian Jewish immigrant family," Truman said. "His father was a clothes presser and part-time cantor. John knew early struggles and then, near life's end, had all these right-wing bigots like J. Edgar Hoover working to destroy him."

"Long before such Method actors as James Dean, Marlon Brando, and Monty Clift, there was John Garfield. At times, I think I'm one of the luckiest men alive: I got to make love to all four of those young men during their prime!"

Father and Son Swashbucklers, With Truman, On the Road to Hell

"Sean Flynn, son of Robin Hood, was so 1950s handsome, he could have been another Troy Donahue or Tab Hunter. Sadly, in spite of his superb physique, good looks, and his tallness—more than six feet—he lacked not only Errol's talent but his charisma. Errol Flynn was one of a kind. We may never see the likes of him in our generation."

—Gossip maven **Louella Parsons**

In public utterances, Truman was rather dismissive of his one-night stand with the swashbuckler Errol Flynn, "the Man in the Green Tights."

On the screen, Flynn had thrilled both Nina and Truman in such roles as *Captain Blood* (1931); *The Perfect Specimen* (1937); *The Adventures of Robin Hood* (1938), and *The Private Lives of Elizabeth and Essex* (1939).

At the time Truman met him at a Hollywood party, Errol had just completed the 1949 MGM film, *That Forsyte Woman,* which had teamed him with Greer Garson and Walter Pidgeon.

In the face he turned to the world, Truman was rather contemptuous of the drunken night he spent with Flynn. "If his name had not been Errol Flynn, I would not have even remembered our brief fling. We were both drunk, and I didn't have an orgasm."

"It also took him the longest time to have an orgasm himself, because he was so intoxicated." Truman claimed.

In contrast, privately to Donald Windham and a few selected friends, he gave a completely different and contradictory account.

Flynn's endowment was legendary. Iron Eyes Cody, the Native American actor who appeared in several films with Flynn, said, "Errol was so well hung that he was famous for it all over Hollywood. He often unzipped on the set in front of everybody, whipped it out for all to see...Just to set the record straight."

When Truman met Flynn, he had already enjoyed sex with the likes of Joan Bennett, tobacco heiress Doris Duke, aviator Howard Hughes, Woolworth heiress Barbara Hutton, Hedy Lamarr, Laurence Olivier, Argentine dictator Eva Perón, Tyrone Power, Lupe Velez, Gloria Vanderbilt, and director Edmund Goulding. Sometimes, Flynn entertained as many as four different starlets, simultaneously, in his dressing room. As he put it, "I just lie there reading the trade papers while they work on me."

His studio boss, Jack L. Warner, once said, "You know Flynn. He's got to be either fighting or fucking."

Before his life ended in 1959, Flynn himself estimated that he'd had sex with 12,000 to 14,000 different people. To him, the gender of his object of desire did not matter a great deal, as he took on all comers. In the last decades of his life, he seduced some of the sex symbols of the 1950s, ranging from Linda Christian to Rock Hudson.

On the night Flynn accompanied Truman back to his hotel, Truman learned one of the secrets of the lothario's sexual success: "Before entering his victim, he rubbed the tip of his penis with cocaine."

"Truman lied about not having an orgasm," Windham said. "He told me that he experienced orgasm the moment Flynn plunged in with that cocaine-coated head of his penis. It was true, apparently, that it took a long time for Flynn to achieve orgasm. Truman claimed that Flynn rode him for at least forty minutes before both of them erupted. 'It was the most glorious time I've ever spent in my life, knowing I was possessing Errol Flynn,' Truman told me."

There was more: Truman confided to Windham that Flynn passed out immediately after intercourse. "I took complete advantage. Until dawn broke across the Los Angeles skyline, I spent the early morning hours licking and sucking every single inch of his fabulous body, which was still in great shape in spite of his drinking, drugs, and dissipation."

"He was the tastiest man I ever had. I literally wanted to familiarize myself with every inch of that body. At one point, I turned him over and began with the nape of his neck, taking a long, long journey until I reached his little toe. I must have spent an hour on his rosebud alone."

An action-adventure roué, on screen and off, **Errol Flynn** thrilled millions of women and legions of gay men, including Truman Capote. He became legendary for his rapes (statutory and otherwise), public brawls, drinking binges, star seductions, and bisexuality. He was even accused by biographer Charles Higham of being a spy for the Nazis during World War II.

As regards his love of sailing, he claimed, "I always selected my crew very carefully. One of the captains I employed was a ruggedly handsome German, Manfred Lentner, who was wanted by Interpol. After he was caught spying on the Russians, he migrated to Berlin, where he went underground."

"There, he made his living as a pimp. When one of his girlfriends threatened to expose him as spy, he murdered her. Then he fled to Vienna, where he made a career of marrying women bigamously before robbing them of all their money. Boy, do I know how to pick 'em!"

"I found out much later that Errol, evocative of my own conflicts with Nina, had battles with his mother, Lily Marelle Young. She was a descendant of one of the mutineers on the *Bounty,* and she possessed the sword that had once belonged to Captain Bligh himself."

Errol as a youngster was a fearless rebel, often getting into trouble. She caught him once playing "doctor and nurses" with three girls from Sydney when he was only seven years old.

Marelle taught him that his penis was "something dirty" and that it should be concealed.

"I decided to make it a point to show her that my genitals were clean," Flynn said.

He would sunbathe in the nude on their terrace in Australia. He sometimes practically caused her to have a heart attack when he entered the family dining room not only nude but with a big erection.

"In his adult life, Errol was proud of his penis," Truman said. "At a party attended by Marilyn Monroe, he came out nude and played the piano by banging the keys with his erect penis."

"In spite of what I said, I really wanted to follow up on my night with Errol, and I called him several times, even wrote him a few letters. He didn't return my phone calls. Nor did he answer my letters."

"The night with him became one of the most unforgettable experiences of my life. For this quintessential hedonist, I was just another conquest to be made and quickly discarded. After all, he had 13,999 other sexual partners to get around to before he eventually killed himself, mired in alcoholism, his beauty long faded."

"In remembering Flynn, most of his lovers recall his penis and his incredible sexual technique," Truman said. "But there was so much more. He had the most engaging and charming smile, which he flashed often, showing his ivory white teeth. He had a flawless profile and a rugged square jaw. His hair was golden brown, and you wanted to run your fingers through it. The best for last: He had brilliant flecks of gold in his brown eyes. When he turned them on you, you melted and were willing to do his bidding, whatever his request."

"My heart was broken when I saw the last photo taken of Errol," Truman said. "His face had a thin layer of this spongy tissue that looked as if it has been inserted between skin and bone. Like his best friend, John Barrymore, he had destroyed perhaps one of the most perfect bodies that God ever invented."

To Windham, Truman whispered a secret that shocked him. His friend didn't know if Truman were telling the truth or not, although there were eyewitnesses in Havana asserting that the tale was indeed true.

In 1958, Sean Flynn, Errol's seventeen-year-old

Sean Flynn, "the son of Captain Blood and Robin Hood," followed in some respects the "wicked, wicked ways" of his father, Errol. Desperate for cash in Havana, he posed for frontal nudes for a gay photographer, and "peddled my ass" at one of the male bordellos that flourished at the time.

Errol gave his son some advice: "Like me, you are a 'perfect specimen' *[the name of his 1937 movie]*. You must work hard to develop a body that will thrill the girls and the homosexuals too. Don't overlook the homos. The boys are among my biggest fans."

son, found himself in Havana with no money. He had gambled away all his traveling money at the casinos. Twice he appealed to his mother, the French-born actress Lili Damita. Twice, she had acquiesced and sent bailout money, with dire warnings that it was the last time she'd rescue him in this way. After the third desperate incident, she turned him down. Short of funds himself, Errol could not bail out his son, as he had so many times in the past.

"A gringo doesn't want to be on the streets of Havana with no *dinero,*" Sean said. In desperation, he decided that all he had to sell was his own beautiful body. At that time, there were two dozen or so bordellos thriving in Havana, five or six of which were staffed by male prostitutes catering to a gay clientele.

Sean discerned, accurately, that many clients would want to have sex with the son of Errol Flynn. When Truman heard that Sean was prostituting himself in Havana, he flew there from where he was staying in Palm Beach.

"I got to enjoy a version of Errol that must have existed in the 1930s," Truman later told Windham. "The boy was a beauty and delightful, and he even reciprocated a bit when I made love to him. At least he let me kiss him and didn't lie there like a log, but was responsive. Errol and Sean Flynn, father and son…I'll never forget them."

Truman said that he cried when he read about Sean's disappearance and tormented death, probably as a prisoner of the Khmer Rouge.

[During the late 1960s, Sean developed a career as a freelance photo journalist, working under contract to Time magazine amid the bombs, bullets, and atrocities of war-ravaged Cambodia. On April 6, 1970, he and fellow journalist Dana Stone went missing on the road south of Phnom Penh. Despite the enormous sums of money his mother spent searching for her son, neither he nor his remains were ever found.]

Lillie Mae: After Many a Summer Dies the Swan

As a social gadfly, Truman, later in his life, collected a bevy of some of the most glamorous women on the planet, referring to them as his beautiful swans. [In some respects, Nina Capote, his own mother, had been the first of the beautiful swans in his life.]

Throughout the 1930s and 1940s, Nina had filled her life with beaux and fleeting one-night stands. It was a life devoted to the pursuit of hedonism. But by the 1950s, both Nina and Joseph Capote would face disaster, as their problems, long postponed, caught up with them. "There was a price to be paid for the lives we've led," his mother told Truman.

Truman was in Paris with his longtime lover, Jack Dunphy, when Joseph telephoned from Manhattan. It was a cold day in January of 1954. Joseph told him that Nina had swallowed a bottle of Seconals and was in the hospital in a coma.

Two days later, he called again. Nina was dead.

Truman booked the next flight to New York, where he ordered that her body be cremated. Perhaps it was his final act of revenge for her years of abandonment. All her life, she'd lived in fear of her body being cremated.

Not only did Joseph have to face the loss of his wife by suicide, but his own profligate spending had caught up with him. His Wall Street firm discovered that he'd embezzled $100,000 from the company. He was fired and ordered to pay back the money right away or else he would be officially charged.

The hedonistic life of **Joe Capote** and his wife **Nina** ended tragically.

This is the last known picture taken of them together before she committed suicide, and he was sent to prison for embazzlement.

He appealed to his adopted son, Truman, for money. Based on the success of plays he had recently written, Truman agreed to help, but he could not come up with all of the $100,000.

In 1955, Joseph pleaded guilty to embezzlement and was sentenced to fourteen months in New York State's Sing Sing Correctional Facility in Ossining, New York.

Even after his release from prison, Joseph remained a continuing problem in Truman's life. His adoptive father later remarried, but his precarious financial situation continued. At one point, Truman told a friend that "Joe's new wife has become an invalid living in a hospital at *my* expense."

Andreas Brown claimed that one reason Truman wanted to write his novel, *Answered Prayers,* was to expose the foibles and foolishness of Joseph and Nina Capote. Brown said that the "world of glamour and superficial values can easily dazzle and confuse and mislead impressionable, naïve younger people to want all of these things and to pursue them with a desperation almost like an addiction to a drug. It can end up very easily destroying people. And it does. And seems to have done just that in the case of Nina and Joe Capote."

Truman never really recovered from his mother's suicide. He later claimed, "She didn't kill herself because she was bored, or because she didn't like herself. She enjoyed her lifestyle. Someone killed my mother. Someone took her away. Who did that? Who did that to me?"

Chapter Eighteen

Scarlett O'Hara–She's Back!

Vivien Leigh's Identification with Blanche DuBois Sinks Her Into a State of Madness

Stanley Seduces Blanche Both On and Off the Screen

"Casting and then directing **Vivien Leigh** *(depicted in both photos, above)* on the London stage [in *A Streetcar Named Desire*] was my most painful undertaking," said her husband, Laurence Olivier. "I feared that because of it, I might even be stripped of my knighthood."

It had been his intimate friend, Hugh ("Binkie") Beaumont, who had convinced him to proceed with the project. Vivien's presentation of hundreds of stage performances of Tennessee's grueling role drove her to the brink of madness.

Laurence Oliver finally agreed to read the Tennessee Williams play, *A Streetcar Named Desire*. Putting it down, he told Vivien the drama was repulsive. "What are we dealing with here? Homosexuality? Nymphomania? Insanity? Incestuous rape? Have you ever heard of the Lord Chamberlain? Unlike on Broadway, stage morals are still censored in Britain. Have you forgotten that?"

Olivier was right. *Streetcar* would eventually be denounced in the House of

Commons as "low and repugnant." The Public Morality Council called it "lewd and salacious."

An official of the Royal Household, the Lord Chamberlain had licensed plays in England since 1737. Licensing actually meant censoring them. Such a policy was abolished in Britain in 1968.

The Lord Chamberlain later decreed that on stage Blanche could not reveal to the audience that she'd learned that her young husband had been the lover of an older gentleman.

"Dear boy, the great man of the British theater, I must override your objections to *Streetcar*," Vivien said to Olivier. "Bloody hell! This is the stage role of the

On the film set of *A Streetcar Named Desire* in Hollywood, **Vivien Leigh** told **Marlon Brando** that "Larry directed me as a bloody whore in the London production. To make it more authentic, I went nightly to Soho, the red-light district of the West End. I went to pubs, buying lager for the streetwalkers, talking to them and trying to understand them."

decade for an actress. You must not stand in my way. I've given you the limelight long enough. I never thought in my lifetime I would find a role to equal Scarlett O'Hara. At long last I have, and cannot allow your pettiness to block me. I will immortalize myself in this role, especially when I scheme my way to do it on the screen."

Her friend, Alan Dent, tried to persuade her to turn down the role. "It's not for you to play one of Tennessee Williams' walking and wandering casebooks, sluts, inconstant nymphs, the victims of men who could be sadistic and even cannibalistic."

A Streetcar Named Desire had opened on Broadway on December 3, 1947 to rave reviews. It had starred Jessica Tandy in the pivotal role of Blanche DuBois. The play had made an overnight sensation of its young male star, Marlon Brando, who was hailed on stage as "lightning on legs."

Vivien still exerted considerable emotional control over Olivier, and he agreed to direct her in *A Streetcar Named Desire*, opening at the Aldwych Theatre in London on October 11, 1949.

Although a bit leery of the subject matter within *Streetcar,* Hugh (Binkie) Beaumont had negotiated with its producer in New York, Irene Mayer Selznick,

"Deliberate cruelty is not forgivable. It is the one unforgivable thing in my opinion, and it is the one thing of which I have never, never been guilty."

—Blanche DuBois

former wife of David O. Selznick and the daughter of Louis B. Mayer. For Irene, her producing *Streetcar* was the biggest achievement of her career.

[A theater manager and producer, Binkie was known as the "eminence grise" of London's West End Theatre world. He often worked with Noël Coward and John Gielgud on productions, and may have done a lot more with both actors. Gielgud's friendship with Binkie survived even after he stole Gielgud's lover, John Perry, from him.

Binkie was one of the first in the British theater to promote Tennessee's work, and he was especially fond of performers, notably one named Richard Burton.]

Hugh ("Binkie") Beaumont was one of the most successful producers in the London's West End during the mid-20th Century. "When not staging productions, he must have seduced all the leading actors of the British stage," said Noël Coward. "He told me his favorite was not Larry Olivier, but Richard Burton."

"I am doing this play not because I want to but because Vivien demands that I do it," Olivier told Beaumont. "As you know, Blanche DuBois is led off to the madhouse at the end of the play. There is a strong possibility that Vivien as Blanche will be driven into total madness. I warned her of the risk of her scheme to play Blanche. At first I was going to say her 'mad scheme,' but I censored that tongue of mine at the last second."

As he signed on to direct *Streetcar*, Olivier became convinced that this was Vivien's last chance to erase the haunting ghost of Scarlett O'Hara. Whenever her role in *Gone With the Wind* was brought up, Vivien in the late 40s and early 50s had taken to saying, "Damn you, Scarlett O'Hara," Olivier said.

[Publisher's note: That phrase was so ingrained into the psyche of Vivien Leigh, and by extension, into the psyche of her husband, Laurence Olivier, that it was adopted as the title for Darwin Porter and Roy Moseley's award-winning 2010 biography of the famously troubled couple, Damn You, Scarlett O'Hara, The Private Lives of Laurence Olivier and Vivien Leigh © *2010, Blood Moon Productions.]*

"I thought," said Olivier, "that if her critics have one grain of fairness, they will give her credit now for being an actress and not go on forever letting their judgments be distorted by her beauty and Hollywood stardom as Scarlett O'Hara."

In May of 1949, Irene lured Tennessee from Rome to meet her in London to watch Vivien in two Old Vic performances, *The School for Scandal* and *Antigone*. "Let's see how David *[Selznick's]* beloved Scarlett O'Hara is holding up after all this passage of time," Irene said. "David told me she's quite mad, at least part of the time. Cecil Beaton informed me she's aged dreadfully."

"If Beaton is not being his queenly self, then the aging part would be perfect for Blanche DuBois," Tennessee said. "As you know, in my play, Blanche, too, has to deal with her fear of aging and has to confront her face in harsh light."

Tennessee liked Vivien's performance in *The School for Scandal* but thought she "is not really good in *Antigone*." Nevertheless, in a letter to his close friend, Donald Windham, he claimed that "she might make a good Blanche, more for her off-stage personality than for what she does in repertory."

Meeting her backstage after each performance, Tennessee found Vivien delightful. He noticed that she paid as much attention to his lover, Frank Merlo, as she did to him, which he thought was exceedingly kind and gracious on her part. She liked them so much she invited both of them to Notley Abbey, the 12th century manor house in Buckinghamshire, fifty miles northwest of London, which, at enormous expense, she, with Olivier, had renovated as a country retreat. There they would be joined by Olivier.

Tennessee's visit to Notley did not get off to a good start, as he and Frank arrived late. "Sir Laurence had gone to bed," Tennessee later said. *"Quelle insulte!"*

He also noted that the other visitor at Notley, Danny Kaye, Olivier's lover at the time, was "extremely quiet," which was uncharacteristic for the comedian. Unknown to Tennessee at the time, Vivien, Larry, and Kaye had become embroiled in a catfight before the playwright's arrival.

She had demanded that Olivier choose between Kaye and her. Insults were hurled for an hour or so, with no resolution. At breakfast the next morning, she seemed to have withdrawn her ultimatum and was charming and gracious to her guests, especially Frank. She was polite but cool to Kaye.

When Tennessee returned to New York, he told his agent, Audrey Wood, that he suspected Kaye and Olivier had become lovers. "Not on your life," Wood said. "Larry could have his pick of the most beautiful men in the British and American theater. Why would he choose Danny Kaye? I know for a fact that when Kaye wants sex with a young man, either in New York or Los Angeles, he pays for it."

Tennessee seemed adamant. "I know the ways of the human heart better than you, dear lady. Sir Laurence and Danny Kaye are lovers."

At dinner on their second night at Notley, Larry presided like a country squire, directing his conversation to Tennessee or Kaye, and virtually ignoring Frank and Vivien.

"Vivien was very nice," Frank recalled. "She included me in the conversation. After dinner, Kaye and Olivier excused themselves and went upstairs. Vivien looked disdainfully at their backs. Tenn retired to the library to write some letters, and Vivien invited me to go for a moonlit walk in her gardens."

"Outside in the night air, she told me that she sympathized with me for living with such a great artist."

"Tennessee must torment you at times the way Larry torments me," she told him. "Having a relationship with Tennessee or Sir Laurence must be something to endure. For causing us so much pain, we should get back at them. The bungalow is empty tonight. Do you like girls just a little bit?"

"I love women, but not in bed," he told her.

"Has the whole world turned gay?" she asked. "What are we poor girls to do?"

"Perhaps not hang out with men in the theater," he said. "Men who like to paint their faces and dress up in costumes every night are not the straightest arrows."

"That I have found to be true," she said. "At least Tennessee is open about his homosexuality. Larry likes to keep his secrets buried."

Her sudden sexual interest in Frank may have stemmed from the fact that before dinner Tennessee had confided in her that, in part, he'd based the character of Stanley Kowalski on Frank.

Later that night, he told Tennessee that Vivien had come on to him. "Don't flatter yourself," Tennessee responded. "She's just getting back at Sir Laurence who this very minute is probably in his bedroom plugging that red-haired comedian, whose art form has always escaped me."

When Tennessee came down for breakfast on the morning of his departure, he found that only Vivien and a house servant were up. Sir Laurence, Kaye, and Frank were still in bed.

A stately medieval manor house in Buckinghamshire, **Notley Abbey** *(photo above)* was the abode of **Vivien Leigh** *(upper right photo)* and **Laurence Olivier** *(lower left photo)*. Vivien did most of the decorating and supervised the daunting tasks associated with its restoration.

The Oliviers often invited house guests for the weekend, including, on one occasion, **Frank Merlo** *(upper left photo)* and his lover, Tennessee Williams.

To their surprise, they discovered that **Danny Kaye** *(lower right photo)* was also a house guest on the weekend of their arrival. "Tenn and I soon learned that Larry and Danny were lovers. The house was filled with tension between Danny and Viv. She got drunk the first night and after denouncing her husband, made a play for me while Danny was doing his thing upstairs with Larry."

"It was our first real discussion of the character of Blanche," Tennessee recalled. "I told her that Blanche was a demonic creature, the size of her feeling too great for her to continue to live without the escape to madness."

"I fear you have given me the blueprint to my own life," she told the playwright.

She appeared shocked when Tennessee told her, "You were not my first choice for Blanche. I actually took the script to Garbo and asked her to return to the screen as Blanche."

"I could never play such an involved and complicated person," Garbo had informed him. "I am too direct and masculine. I couldn't bear to tell lies and see things around corners like that girl."

"Garbo told you the truth," Vivien said. "If you want to bring the best Blanche DuBois on the planet to the screen, you're looking at her."

After a weekend at Notley, Tennessee returned to Key West where he told Truman Capote, "Larry Olivier is a great actor in that he preserves the myth of his long-faded romance with Vivien and brilliantly conceals his private unhappiness. Their romance died a long time ago, and only the ghosts of a love lost remains."

When a journalist once asked Tennessee his opinion of Vivien, he responded: "There may have been, in her time, as beautiful a lady, but if there was, I never encountered her. Her social behavior was a bit unpredictable owing to the nervous torment that I am afraid she always had to live with. She realized that I lived with the same nervous torment. When she was not tormented, she was capable of the most discreet and exquisite kindness."

Privately, Irene Mayer Selznick met with Olivier. She didn't want either Vivien or Tennessee to attend their meeting. "I have an idea I want you to incorporate into the British version of *Streetcar*. Gadge absolutely rejected it for Broadway." She was referring, of course, to Elia Kazan.

"I'm all ears," he said.

"To help goad Blanche into madness, I want Stanley Kowalski to rape her . . . by suggestion of course. After resisting him, I want her to begin to respond and dig her fingers into his back. He gets to her and she welcomes his lovemaking. But at a brutal moment, I want him to pull away from her and leave her gasping for breath and unsatisfied. I want him to stand up, with his cock put away, naturally, and laugh at her savagely, a final humiliation that will tip her over the top into pure madness."

He looked at her strangely, his face paralyzed with agony and dread. "Oh, dear, dear woman, I can't do that. It would destroy me and destroy Vivien. You see, once, in a rage, I did the very same thing to her. I can't live that moment again . . . ever!"

Although Irene had relinquished her rights to Binkie to move ahead with the London production of *Streetcar,* she continued to interfere as he prepared to open the play in the West End.

The big question involved who would be able to follow in the footsteps of Marlon Brando, who had been an international sensation, in the casting of Stanley Kowalski. "You must find an actor who is lustful and animal-like, yet needy," Irene lectured Olivier.

His choice surprised her. Seemingly from out of nowhere, Olivier plucked Bonar Colleano, who had been born in New York to a circus family traveling with Ringling Brothers. Near the end of World War II, Colleano had moved to England to become a resident.

When Vivien introduced Tennessee to Colleano, he whispered to her, "I could go for him. He's just my type."

"Too late, darling," she warned him. "I think my Larry has already engaged him for both onstage acting and off-screen diversion."

He was somewhat surprised of her open acceptance of homosexuality, but then, he reminded himself that she'd grown up in the British theater.

The American-born actor, working in Britain, **Bonar Colleano**, was exceedingly handsome, but lacked he emotional intensity of Marlon Brando. Nonetheless, Laurence Olivier cast him as Stanley Kowalski opposite Vivien Leigh in the London production of *A Streetcar Named Desire*.

Sitting in on the first rehearsal, Tennessee realized that Colleano had been woefully miscast as Stanley. He had begged Brando to come to England and repeat his role, but the actor had refused.

Even though Tennessee was not impressed with Colleano as an actor, he was saddened to learn of his accidental death on August 18, 1958. At the age of 34, he crashed his sports car in Birkenhead shortly after exiting from the Queensway Tunnel. He had just returned from Liverpool's New Shakespeare Theatre, where he'd starred in *Will Success Spoil Rock Hunter?* His close friend and fellow actor, Michael Balfour, was in the passenger seat. He required a hundred stitches, but ultimately pulled through.

In London, "A Pack of Apes Waiting to See Vivien Get Raped"

Back from a holiday in Switzerland, Vivien began to rehearse Tennessee's play. It had been announced in the newspapers that Laurence Olivier Productions would open *A Streetcar Named Desire* on October 11, 1949 at the Aldwych Theatre in London, with Vivien cast as Blanche DuBois, the tragic heroine of Tennessee Williams' drama. Bonar Colleano was cast as Stanley Kowalski. Renée Asherson starred as Stella, which Kim Hunter had played to such acclaim in New York.

Vivien had not seen Jessica Tandy's Blanche on Broadway, so she developed her own characterization. "I came to understand Blanche and ultimately love her," she said. "Blanche lives in her own dream world which is far preferable than the nightmare of reality."

Attending the first week of rehearsals, Irene Selznick did not like Vivien's interpretation of Blanche. Irene had perhaps been indoctrinated by the countless performances she'd watched of Jessica Tandy emoting as Blanche.

Olivier later told Ralph Richardson, "Directing *Streetcar* was humiliating for me. Irene Selznick is destroying my creativity. She is demanding that I present an exact replica of her Broadway hit. She reminded me, of course, that *Streetcar* ran on Broadway for years."

At one point, he confronted Irene, telling her that, "In Britain, Vivien and I are known as the King and Queen of the West End."

She shot back, "That's nothing. In Hollywood, my father, Louis B. Mayer, is an Emperor."

When Olivier was asked if playing Blanche every night was driving Vivien mad, he said, "Acting great parts devours you. It's a dangerous game."

"I wonder if Blanche's madness is contagious," Irene asked Olivier during rehearsals. "I hope Tennessee's play doesn't drive your girl over the cliff."

"It's a risk Vivien wants to take," he told her. "As you can see for yourself, she has the shaky emotional equilibrium of Blanche and she brings to life her delusionary colorations and deceits. The problem is, she can't turn off Blanche when she goes home. At times, she seems to become Blanche in real life. Playing Blanche seems to trigger bouts of hysteria and depression."

Years later, Olivier expressed regret about casting Vivien in *Streetcar*. "She was too much affected by the part she played. It had a great deal to do with playing Blanche DuBois and being ill in the same way."

The critics piled attack upon attack on Vivien for her performance in *Streetcar* and on Tennessee for writing it. All she would say was, "Of course, it's not a drawing room comedy." One reviewer, in town from Leeds, headlined his critique: *SCARLETT O'HARA DROWNS IN A CESSPOOL.*

A woman who arranged flower shows in Chelsea told the press, "It's sordid, a perfectly awful play that gets even more horrid every time I see it."

The London newspapers played up the "sex sensationalism" of *Streetcar*, and Vivien noted that on many a night, the audience flocking to see her as Blanche was "like a pack of apes waiting to see me get raped. I feel as if I've been bulldozed and can't believe I have to go through a gut-wrenching performance of Blanche every night."

After watching Vivien as Blanche onstage, critic Kenneth Tynan continued his life-long assault on her, claiming that Olivier's casting of her in the role had been a mistake. "Why not call it *A Vehicle for Vivien*. She plays Blanche like a bored nymphomaniac, a Hedda Gabler of the gin palaces."

Novelist and playwright J.B. Priestley on the BBC likened Vivien's performance to that of a bearded woman in a circus. He also said that Vivien's audiences were mostly men who on other nights might be catching a nudie girlie show at the Windmill.

Noël Coward, after seeing *Streetcar*, wrote: "Vivien magnificent; audiences sordid, theatre beastly."

After Dame Edith Evans saw the play, Vivien confided to her that it was hard "to shake off Blanche after playing her. I do not have the self-control and artistic discipline to bury Blanche once the curtain has gone down. Isn't playing Blanche like flirting with suicide?"

Dame Edith told her that "actors can shake off their roles faster than actresses."

In an interview with David Lewin, Vivien said, "I challenge any woman to be able to accept the scene when Blanche's face is held pitilessly under a naked light bulb and she is asked to contemplate what she will look like when her beauty has gone. Blanche is a woman with everything stripped away. She is a tragic figure and I understand her. But playing her has tipped me into madness."

John Gielgud delayed going to see her in *Streetcar*, because he'd heard the play was "loathsome." When he came backstage to congratulate her on a brilliant performance, he found her sobbing and shaking. Her lips trembled. "I fear she was near a nervous breakdown. I held her in my arms and let her have a good cry. Her demons were on parade that night. But were they really her demons? Perhaps they were straight from New Orleans and from the psyche of Blanche DuBois herself?"

During the time of Vivien's greatest emotional distress, she played Blanche night after night for eight grueling months, enduring attacks from critics who asked, "What is Scarlett O'Hara doing in this garbage?" Tennessee's play was also dismissed as "not fit for human consumption."

"The bitch queen of critics," as he was called, **Kenneth Tynan** privately admitted that he "had the hots" for Larry Olivier, but wrote horrible critiques of Vivien's stage performances.

Tynan claimed that "Vivien Leigh picks at a part with the daintiness of a debutante called upon to dismember a stag."

In the 1949 revival of *Richard III*, Tynan claimed "she quavered through the lines in a sort of rapt oriental chant."

As for her performance in *Streetcar*, Tynan wrote that, "The play should be retitled *A Vehicle Named Vivien*. Olivier is sacrificing his genius on the altar of his wife's paltry talent."

After the curtain came down on Blanche every night, Vivien's alcohol consumption reached new highs.

After 326 exhausting performances of *Streetcar* on the London stage, Vivien joined the producer, Alexander Korda, aboard his yacht for a sail along the Mediterranean.

It was during this trip that a rumor was spread the Vivien had gotten involved with a "sensitive" seventeen-year-old beach boy she'd met on the sands at Cannes. Korda privately told friends, "I think Vivien was just reenacting a scene from *Streetcar* in which Blanche flirts with such a young boy."

Vivien Cruises the Gay Bars with Tennessee

Three years after the 1947 release of *Streetcar's* opening on Broadway, and about a year after its 1949 opening in London, because of commitments in London to his Laurence Olivier Productions, Olivier remained behind as Vivien flew west, ultimately heading for Los Angeles. There, for $100,000, she had signed to appear as Blanche in the screen version of *A Streetcar Named Desire,* a film eventually released in 1951.

She was greeted with a Hollywood headline, *"SCARLETT O'HARA'S BACK IN TOWN"* as Vivien, after an absence of more than a decade, returned to the scene of her former glory. When facing overly deferential reporters, calling her Lady Olivier, she shocked journalists with the statement, "Her Ladyship is fucking bored with such formality and prefers to be known as Miss Vivien Leigh."

Charles Feldman had arranged for the Oliviers to inhabit the same Coldwater Canyon house, with its egg-shaped pool, where they'd stayed when they had filmed *That Hamilton Woman (aka Lady Hamilton)* during the autumn of 1940. Vivien set about making it more intimate and homelike for Olivier's return to Hollywood.

On the Warners' lot, she was given the former dressing room of Bette Davis, who had departed after the disastrous box office returns of *Beyond the Forest.* There was a certain irony here. Had William Wyler directed *Streetcar* as originally planned, he'd have preferred Davis as the actress to play Blanche. Consequently, Davis ended up losing both of the roles that brought Vivien Oscars, beginning with Scarlett O'Hara.

Tennessee arranged a reunion with Vivien in Hollywood, where he complained of censorship from the Breen office, which refused to allow the word "homosexual" to be even mentioned in relation to Blanche's dead husband or her promiscuity with military men. The Breen office also wanted to eliminate the suggestion that Blanche, prior to her arrival on the doorstep of Stanley and Stella in New Orleans, had been sexually involved with a seventeen-year-old boy.

A key reference within the Broadway stage version was the line, "I came into a room and found my young husband with an older man who had been his friend for years."

Broadway audiences clearly understood within that line the implication of ho-

Two English Roses (**Vivien Leigh** and **Laurence Olivier**) return (after her 1939 triumph in *Gone With the Wind*) to the glare of the unforgiving Southern California sunshine

mosexuality. But for the film version, the line was rewritten. Movie audiences heard, "He wasn't like other people."

Vivien's dear friend, Robert Helpmann, was also in Los Angeles at the time, and Tennessee sometimes joined them on their forays to the clubs of Hollywood. During this, the pre-Stonewall era, gay bars didn't exist as such, but there were many taverns where those seeking same-sex intimacies with a stranger could achieve that aim.

"We were looking for tricks," Tennessee said, "and Robert knew how to maneuver. If Vivien and I couldn't pick up something on our own, he could. Many of the men in this bar were bisexuals, and it wasn't difficult finding a handsome young man who'd want to fuck Scarlett O'Hara. The homosexual men in these bars loved Vivien and crowded around her. Larry might not desire her, but she soon learned that dozens of handsome young men wanted to be with her. Unlike her, Robert and I often had to pay."

"California has the most delicious men on the planet," Robert claimed. "These hunks come here to break into the movies, and the pick-ups are easy to come by."

Helpmann told Tennessee, "Vivien is certainly getting into her character of Blanche. She's picking up young guys like her character, a sort of Method acting approach."

Beautiful, unstable **Vivien Leigh**, playing the promiscuous, unstable Blanche DuBois.

Marlon Brando came to live with the Oliviers. He wrote his longtime lover, Wally Cox, in New York, "Her Ladyship has great tits and ass. After only three days, I wanted to fuck her so badly my teeth ached. I did. No more toothache. Sir Laurence likes to get serviced, too."

Although she had strangers in her bed, Los Angeles itself was a stranger to her. The city had changed, and in her opinion, for the worse. A horrible yellow blanket of smog lay over Greater Los Angeles, stinging her eyes and intensifying her coughing spasms.

Warner Brothers finally met Brando's demand of $75,000 to appear in the film version of *A Streetcar Named Desire*. Elia Kazan, who would direct the film, held out for the original Broadway cast. Consequently, Karl Malden and Kim Hunter were given the supporting roles that had made them famous on Broadway.

Jack Warner had preferred Burt Lancaster to Brando, but acquiesced to Kazan's vision. Warner, however, definitely didn't want Jessica Tandy. "She's known on Broadway, but except for a few rotten movies, no one knows who she is," the studio chief said. "Olivia de Havilland should do it, but the bitch is demanding $175,000. I've got Vivien Leigh for $100,000. Her husband is making a movie in Hollywood, and the nympho wants to be with the cocksucker."

Warner was referring, of course, to Laurence Olivier and his well-known homosexual proclivities.

"I can't stand the limey cunt!" Brando shouted at Elia Kazan after the first three days of shooting *A Streetcar Named Desire*. "Miss Vivien Leigh. Miss Scarlett O'Hara. Now Lady Olivier. 'Good morning, Mr. Brando.'" He imitated her accent perfectly. "'Good afternoon, Mr. Brando.' She'll suffocate me with her politeness. I can't wait for the rape scene!"

"If the censors will allow it," Kazan cautioned.

The first time Brando

The director, **Elia Kazan,** confronts **Vivien Leigh** *(left)* and **Kim Hunter** *(center)* during rehearsals for a scene between Blanche and Stella in *Streetcar*. Vivien protested that "Larry did not direct me this way in London."

Kazan responded, "You're not in Kansas any more, Dorothy. You're in Hollywood, and we'll do it my way."

sat down to talk to Vivien, he found a vulnerable character, not the "prissy English bitch" he'd envisioned. She reached out and gently touched his hand, as she spoke of the first time she'd read *A Streetcar Named Desire* in 1948. "I was touched by the haunting quality of Blanche," she said. "The play seemed to speak to a woman inside myself that lives within my own heart. Blanche DuBois is the *animus* of my own being. Talk about Method acting!"

That remark seemed to win Brando to her side. After that, and until the end of the eight-week shoot, he became almost inseparable from her.

He was full of questions about how she'd fared in the London stage production of *Streetcar,* which had been directed by her husband, Laurence Olivier. He was also anxious to learn of the feuds Olivier had catalyzed with Irene Selznick and Tennessee over cuts Olivier had made before the play opened in the West End of London.

One Saturday morning he drove her into the desert so she could breathe the fresh air. She'd had a struggle with tuberculosis and was having a hard time breathing in Los Angeles. "It's been ten years since Larry and I were here. Now there's this bloody smog. You're used to it. I'm not. It's like a yellow blanket that hangs over everything and doesn't go away. It stings my eyes and fills my lungs with poison."

He told her he knew of an inn thirty miles away that was outside the smog's radius. She could rest there for the weekend.

"When I first came to Los Angeles to play Scarlett," she said, "I remember oranges everywhere. Now those orange trees have vanished like my virginity."

"From what I was told, you and Larry had to live as secret lovers the last time you were in Holly- wood," he said. "Now you are the married Sir Laurence and Lady Olivier. The King and Queen of the London theater."

"It's a respectability I don't deserve, and a social responsibility from the throne I don't want. As you'll get to know me, and I hope you will, there is nothing respectable about me. In London I pick up taxi drivers and fuck them."

Startled, he looked at her. Had he heard right? Did she actually say that?

"Don't be surprised," she said. "I'm just as whorish as Blanche DuBois was, taking on all those soldiers at that army base."

On screen, **Vivien Leigh** throws a fit with **Marlon Brando** in *A Streetcar Named Desire.* The intensity and depth of feeling she brought to the role eventually brought her an Oscar.

Although the Blanche DuBois she was playing feuded passionately on screen with Brando's character of Stanley Kowalski, many of their nights were spent together making love.

She paused, lighting her own cigarette, as if remembering something he'd just said. "Forgive me, but you said Larry. Do you know my husband, Sir Laurence?"

"I met him a few years ago in New York when he came to see me in a play," he said. "I was very honored."

"I won't bother to ask you how well you knew Sir Laurence," she said, sucking the smoke deeply into her tainted lungs.

"It's just as well, because I won't tell you."

"Growing up in the theater, I am used to such things. I never quiz Larry about his private life. His first wife was a lesbian, you know. When he's with Richard Burton, Danny Kaye, Noël Coward, I ask no questions. Larry asks no questions of me either. I don't love him. We are only Sir Laurence and Lady Olivier in front of the press. When our pictures aren't being taken, we lead completely separate lives."

"If I ever get married, and I don't plan to, I will demand from my woman that I go on leading my separate life."

Driving through the desert with Vivien, Brando arrived at a wayside motel that seemed to evoke that dreary place she'd seen in *The Petrified Forest* with Bette Davis, Humphrey Bogart, and her friend and lover, Leslie Howard, her beloved Ashley Wilkes in *Gone With the Wind.*

They registered as "Petticoat Blossom" and "Durango Canyon." Inside the motel's best room, Vivien began to remove her clothing to take a shower. "Do you know," she said to him in the stifling heat of the desert bedroom, "I am part of the world's most beautiful, the world's most talented, the world's most admired, the world's most successful, and the world's most adored couple? If the world only knew the truth. Why don't you rape me like Stanley Kowalski raped Blanche DuBois?"

"An invitation I can't resist," he said, moving toward her.

After sex, he told her over a meal in a roadside diner that he hadn't liked her at first. "So fucking formal."

"Her Ladyship is fucking bored with formality," she said.

He broke into laughter before affectionately leaning over and kissing her on the nose. "I can't believe I've slept with Scarlett O'Hara. Rhett Butler's woman. You won't be the first woman that Clark Gable and I have shared."

"Trust me, Clark Gable never got into my pantaloons."

Oscar Night: Brando Loses to Bogie's African Queen But Vivien as Blanche K.O.'s Kate Hepburn

In His Memoirs, Tennessee Remains Silent About Vivien as Blanche

Details about Brando's relationship with Vivien would have gone unrecorded had he not confided in both Charles K. Feldman, the producer of *Streetcar*, and its director, Elia Kazan. The story of Brando and Vivien was just too hot for these two men to keep to themselves. When Tennessee arrived with his then-new lover, Frank Merlo, on the set of *Streetcar*, both Kazan and Feldman shared the news about Brando's sexual adventure with the two men, who were each anxious to hear (and eventually repeat) the latest gossip.

Meeting privately with Tennessee, Kazan told him, "I think that in casting Marlon with Vivien, Jack Warner has paired a gazelle with a wild boar. Even so, I told Vivien that we're going to make a great film and that both she and Marlon are going to walk off with Oscars—his first, her second. I also told her that it was time she set Hollywood on its ass again. After all, it's been a long time since she vowed never to go hungry again in *Gone With the Wind*."

During their time in Hollywood, both Tennessee and Frank visited the set of *Streetcar* every day. Tennessee told Frank that he was mesmerized by the chemistry on screen between Marlon and Vivien. "I always wanted that electricity between Jessica Tandy and Marlon, but didn't get it."

One day, after watching Vivien perform, Tennessee told Kazan. "She has brought everything to the role of Miss DuBois that I intended, and much more than I ever dared to dream."

One day, during lunch with Vivien, she told Tennessee, "It's all your fault. Your character of Blanche DuBois is tripping me into madness."

"I can understand that," he replied. "Blanche has already given me three heart attacks."

As Tennessee and Kazan continued to battle the censors, filming continued on *Streetcar* during one of the hottest summers in recorded Los Angeles' history.

Except for Brando, Jack Warner remained deeply dissatisfied with the cast. He still wished he had cast Olivia de Havilland in the role of Blanche, with her estranged sister, Joan Fontaine, playing Stella. When he couldn't get De Havilland, he asked Jane Wyman, recently divorced from Ronald Reagan, if she'd attempt the role. The answer was no.

Then, at the urging of David O. Selznick, Warner briefly considered David's wife, Jennifer Jones. The veto on Jones came from Irene Selznick herself, who was still bitter that David had dumped her for the younger and more beautiful star.

One week before shooting began, and even after Vivien had been signed, Kazan still held out for Jessica Tandy. He urged Warner to pay off Vivien, who by then had a signed contract, and hire Tandy to replace her.

"No way!" Warner shouted back at his director. "If I don't want to fuck Tandy, I have to assume that other men in the audience will feel the same way. Not one man wants a piece of Tandy's ass. She's got the sex appeal of Lionel Barrymore. Case closed!"

Even at the last minute, Warner pushed James Cagney for the role of Blanche's ambivalent boyfriend. But based on Karl Malden's success in the role on Broadway, Kazan held out for him instead.

Jack Warner and Kazan clashed bitterly over Kim Hunter, the studio honcho claiming that Hunter had a "negative screen personality." Warner preferred Anne Baxter, Ruth Roman, or Patricia Neal, who was at the time in the throes of an ill-fated affair with Gary Cooper. "Even Donna Reed would be better," Warner claimed.

"If you cast one of those actresses," Kazan threatened, "I'm walking off the picture. Kim Hunter will be brilliant playing a girl who likes to get fucked by Stanley—and fucked regularly. She's the one. I should know. I've already auditioned her in that department."

In only two weeks, Kazan managed to eradicate each of the stage directions Vivien had learned from Olivier during the staging of the play's production in London. A new and different Blanche DuBois was recorded on film. Not only that, but Brando told Tennessee that he was finding nuances in the role of Stanley Kowalski that he had never realized on Broadway.

"I made Vivien connect role with soul," Kazan later said. "She and Marlon are perfectly matched. Before my lens are two highly charged actors exploding off each other."

Privately, Brando said, "That delirium and despair you're capturing on the screen is Lady Olivier herself. She's writing a textbook of the madness that lurks within herself. I fear, though, that she's going over the deep edge with Blanche. She'll never come back."

Other cast members took note of Vivien's tottering on the brink of a nervous breakdown. Karl Malden, though deeply devoted to the skill and talent of Jessica Tandy, came to accept Vivien in the role of Blanche. "After all," he said, "she had star power. The film was riding on her. She was carrying all of us nobodies, including Marlon Brando himself. But she had a tenuous hold on reality."

In contrast to his ongoing struggles with Vivien, Kazan had no trouble directing Brando. He told Tennessee and Feldman, "There was nothing you could do with Brando that touched what he could do with himself!" Feldman was surprised by the fact that Brando had initially rejected the movie role of Stanley ("It'd be like marrying the same woman twice.") The producer was also surprised to learn that Kazan had originally refused the director's job, even when it was personally pitched to him by Jack Warner. ("I don't think I could get it up a second time for *Streetcar*.")

***

When the candidates for the Oscars were announced in 1952, Brando was nominated for an Academy Award for his portrayal of Stanley in *A Streetcar Named Desire*. His major competition came from the "sentimental favorite," Humphrey Bogart, for his starring role in *The African Queen*. Also nominated was Brando's former lover, Monty Clift, for his role in *A Place in the Sun*. The other contenders included Arthur Kennedy for *Bright Victory* and Fredric March for *Death of a Salesman*.

The same year, Vivien was nominated for best actress, her major competition being Katharine Hepburn for *The African Queen*. Brando's girlfriend, Shelley Winters, was nominated for *A Place in the Sun,* as were Eleanor Parker for *Detective Story* and Jane Wyman for *The Blue Veil*. Karl Malden and Kim Hunter were both nominated for supporting roles in their performances in *Streetcar*.

On Oscar night, three of the contenders associated with *Streetcar*—Vivien Leigh, Karl Malden, and Kim Hunter—walked away with Oscars. Brando lost to Bogie. Facing reporters, Kazan told the press, "Stick around, boys. Marlon's day will come."

In Hollywood, after seeing the final cut of *Streetcar*, Kazan had said, "After sitting through Vivien's performance as Blanche, I have my doubts. I should have gone with my first instincts and given the role to Geraldine Page or Julie Harris, either of whom could have played it better."

Later, however, after Vivien won the Academy Award for her interpretation of the role, Kazan claimed, "She deserved her Oscar. She would have crawled over broken glass if she thought it would help her performance."

Ironically, in his memoirs, Tennessee made no mention of Vivien as Blanche either on the London stage or in Hollywood's film version.

Chapter Nineteen

Tennessee and Gore in Pursuit of
Billy the Kid

"Paul Newman Is Going to Play Gore Vidal's Fag Cowboy"
—Jack Warner

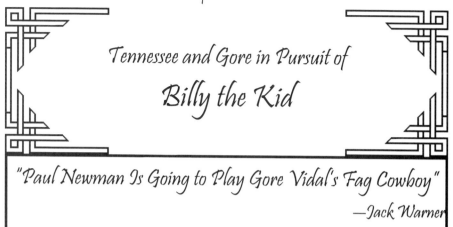

In the 1940s, I was not only one of New York's leading balletomanes, but I pursued 'dancers from the dance' after the curtain went down," said Gore Vidal. "It was a glorious time. I didn't dare fall in love with John Kriza and Harold Lang because the competition for them was too stiff."

In the *left and far right photos above*, **Kriza** is shown in separate scenes from his most popular ballet, *Billy the Kid*. In the center photo, **Harold Lang** (*left*, with **Gore** on the *right*) were photographed in Bermuda, where they serviced many members of the British navy.

The wildly promiscuous lifestyle of Tennessee Williams invariably led to his affair with Lincoln Kirstein, the scion of a rich Jewish Boston-based family. Kirstein had become a cultural icon, a sort of Renaissance man—writer, impresario, art connoisseur. As the English critic Clement Crisp wrote: "Kirstein was one of those rare talents who touch the entire artistic life of their time—ballet, film, literature, theater, painting, sculpture, photography—all occupied his attention."

He was instrumental in persuading George Balanchine and his ballet troupe to come to America. Together, the two men founded The Ballet Society, which was renamed as The New York City Ballet in 1948. Kirstein functioned as the company's general director from 1946 to 1989.

In 1941, Kirstein married Fidelma Cadmus, sister of the artist, Paul Cadmus. Discreetly, and on the side, Kirstein often checked into Manhattan's 63rd Street YMCA, where he seduced undergraduates from Harvard and Yale, sailors, marines, soldiers, and street boys, and indulged in casual sexual encounters in the showers. It was in the showers that he picked up Tennessee and became his sometimes lover.

Lincoln Kirstein was a towering figure on the American cultural scene. He also had an understanding wife who allowed him to bring home a studly array of temporary lovers.

Often, Kirstein took his boyfriends, including Tennessee, to live with Fidelma and himself in their house on Manhattan's East 19th Street.

Tennessee reported that Fidelma "was enormously gracious to this motley parade of young men who came and went from their guest bedroom. When I was there, Lincoln had in residence three studly young men in various colors."

During his sojourn with Kirstein and his wife, Tennessee spent time in Lincoln's library, where he discovered an inordinate amount of literature on Billy the Kid.

Based on that literature, and on dialogues with Kirstein, Tennessee learned that his host had commissioned a ballet in 1938, *Billy the Kid,* hiring Eugene Loring (another friend of Tennessee) as the choreographer. Aaron Copland was the composer. Its first performance in New York had occurred on May 24, 1939, and it had become wildly popular, famous for its incorporation of many cowboy tunes and American folk songs.

In Kirstein's library, Tennessee found and read a book devoted to the life of the infamous outlaw. The more he read about the life of William H. Bonney, the more he fantasized about this young man. Born in 1859, he'd been labeled "a murderous psychopath" by his enemies. Bonney's paradoxical image was that of both a folk hero and a notorious outlaw. He had killed his first victim at the age of fifteen.

Tennessee frequently mused over a legend that maintains that Billy the Kid somehow cheated death and ended up in Mexico with a bevy of beautiful *señoritas* available day and night to do his bidding. Tennessee eventually main-

Performing Billy the Kid in a "Sex Pouch"

tained that in any film treatment that emerged, he didn't want Billy to be slain.

He had seen the decorated American war hero, actor Audie Murphy, play the outlaw in a 1950s movie called *The Kid from Texas.* He didn't think Murphy captured the complexities of the outlaw and that he had merely "played the cardboard version."

In one of the coincidences of his life, Tennessee, as it turned out, was later ordered by producer Arthur Freed to write a scenario for a film about Billy the Kid for MGM. Back in 1941, MGM had cast heartthrob Robert Taylor, playing Bonner in a film entitled *Billy the Kid.* Of course, the most notorious film interpretation of the legendary renegade had been Howard Hughes's *The Outlaw,* the 1943 picture that starred the aviator's lover, Jack Buetel, as Billy. This was the controversial picture that introduced Jane Russell and her ample bosom to American audiences.

Tennessee seemed the least likely writer in America to be assigned the task of preparing a screenplay about Billy the Kid.

Louis B. Mayer ordered Freed to come up with a script about Billy the Kid. Under contract to MGM as a screenwriter, Tennessee at the time was struggling to adapt *Marriage Is a Private Affair* as a vehicle for Lana Turner.

On July 28, 1943, Tennessee wrote to his friend, Donald Windham. "I've been taken off the Lana Turner picture and reassigned. You won't believe this. Metro wants me to create a film scenario for a possible picture about Billy the Kid. Me, of all people. A Mississippi boy who's never ridden a horse. I have never viewed the Western genre as suitable for my particular talents. But this is Hollywood, and I need the paycheck."

Tennessee defined his latest job at that time "as good an assignment as I could hope for, but I am lazy about it, and have barely started."

He had written only eighteen pages of a scenario for Billy the Kid, before the project was dropped.

"In an ironic twist," Tennessee later said, "Gore Vidal would have a far greater love affair with Billy the Kid than I would."

Gore Vidal & Paul Newman
Collaborate in Launching
Billy the Kid as a Movie Legend

The jury's still out on **Billy the Kid (William H. Bonney)**, the subject of both photos above.

Was he a murderous psychopath or a folk hero? Gore Vidal pictured him as a repressed homosexual.

In Hollywood, Gore Vidal began working on a teleplay based on the life of Billy the Kid. Gore revealed that he'd become fascinated by the legend of the outlaw when his mother sent him to Los Alamos in New Mexico to attend a military school.

In the Southwest, Gore heard many tales, often contradictory, about the outlaw. "I read book after book about him, but I don't know why."

As revealed by Fred Kaplan in his biography of Gore, he "was fascinated by the American outlaw, identifying with him as someone permanently young, undyingly loyal to personal bonds, resolutely insistent on individual autonomy, and defiantly critical of injustice, especially state-sanctioned."

Somewhere along the way, Gore became convinced that William H. Bonney, born in 1859 as William Henry McCarty, Jr., and later known as Henry Antrim, was a repressed homosexual.

"We will make Billy's homosexuality so subtle that only the hip will get it," Gore told his friend, Paul Newman.

Harold Franklin was the chief of drama in the TV department of the William Morris Agency. He managed to interest Fred Coe, a producer at NBC, to produce Gore's *The Death of Billy the Kid.* Coe hired Robert Mulligan as the director, and the people at Philco gave it the green light.

Early in its production, Coe had agreed that only two actors could bring life to Billy the Kid, Marlon Brando or Paul Newman. After it became clear that Brando was unavailable, Coe offered the role to Paul Newman.

In the process of breaking up his first marriage at the time, Newman was having an affair with an actress from Georgia, Joanne Woodward. Gore already knew her—in fact, some newspaper reporters, unaware of the situation, wrote that Woodward and Gore were "engaged."

Tennessee privately commented on Gore's burgeoning friendship with Newman. "Gore was transferring his romantic fantasies onto Newman. I would also have romantic fantasies about this good-looking charmer, especially when he played Brick in my *Cat on a Hot Tin Roof."*

Gore told Newman that he wanted his teleplay to be "not so much about Billy himself, but about the people who created his myth." Newman seemed uncertain how

Producer Howard Hughes cast his discovery, **Jack Buetel** *(photo above)* as Billy the Kid in the controversial film *The Outlaw* (1943). Hughes told Howard Hawks, "Jack carries a gun on each side of hips and an even bigger one between his legs."

Tied up and ready for rape, **Jane Russell,** another Hughes discovery, became celebrated for her "two best assets," on ample display in *The Outlaw.*

286

to interpret that. Gore complimented Coe on his choice of Newman, though secretly. "Paul has both vulnerability and strength," Gore said.

On the set, both Gore and Newman felt that the teleplay could be "turned into a great movie," and that would eventually come to be.

But, first, it would be viewed by television audiences on July 24, 1955, when *The Death of Billy the Kid* was aired on *The Philco Television Playhouse.*

After seeing Newman perform as its protagonist, Gore claimed that it was his favorite of all his teleplays. But he added, "though by no means the most admired of all my TV shows."

During the months ahead, his friendship with Newman and Woodward deepened. Gore and Newman often met at the Château Marmont, plotting a project that would convince Warner Brothers to make a feature length film based on Gore's vision.

In his reworked script, Gore changed the title to *The Left Handed Gun.* That movie title evolved from the belief that the outlaw was left handed, although it is possible that that was a false conclusion drawn from a 19th century photograph that might have been reversed when printed.

The handsome actor with the world's most famous "baby blues," **Paul Newman** was a lot more alluring than the 19th century Billy the Kid who inspired his role.

Finally, Warner's gave the green light, even though its chief honcho, Jack L. Warner, had reservations. Gore viewed his revised script as a Greek tragedy with modern overtones. When Newman was cast, the joke on the lot was, "Paul is going to play Vidal's fag cowboy."

Arthur Penn, a young Turk from TV land, was selected to direct, and subsequently, was granted a modest budget of $700,000, with orders to shoot the film in only twenty-three days.

To trim costs, Penn used sets from the 1939 film, *Juarez.* A historical drama that had focused on the armed conflicts whirling around Maximilian I, a French-installed puppet monarch of Mexico, and Benito Juárez, the country's populist president, it had starred Bette Davis and Paul Muni. Exterior shots for *Left Handed Gun* were filmed near Santa Fe. During the shoot, Gore was working on another script, *The Catered Affair,* starring Bette Davis, and could not participate. Consequently, scriptwriter Leslie A. Stevens III re-

In *The Left-Handed Gun,* **Newman**, cast as Billy the Kid, was told to stand "as if you have a ten-inch cock."

configured the screenplay, following dictates from Warner, who wanted all suggestions of homosexuality removed. Not only that, but he demanded a happy ending.

Newman told Gore, "That's like filming a saga about the life of Abraham Lincoln that never mentions his experience at the Ford Theatre, and includes a divorce from Mary Todd Lincoln, and a ride off into the sunset in Kentucky with his true love, Joshua Fry Speed."

After reading the much-revised script, Newman also reported to Gore, "I feel disconnected from Stevens' script. Arthur Penn is shooting a very different script from yours."

Newman had no objection to playing gay. As a liberal, he'd always taken a stand for homosexual rights, asserting "Ever since I was a kid, I've never been able to understand attacks on the gay community."

Stevens refashioned the script, shifting the plot from repressed homosexual intrigue into more of a surrogate father-son drama, muting the Freudian subtext. Billy the Kid is depicted as "half boy, half man," who eventually interprets rancher Tunstall (as played by Colin Keith-Johnson) as a father figure. The half man part of Newman's character gets to deliver "the cojones" line of the movie: "I don't run. I don't hide. I go where I want. I do what I want."

Jokingly, Newman nicknamed Steven's script *The Left Handed Jockstrap.*

Penn later claimed that Newman "Method acted his way through the entire film." At one point, Newman curls up into a ball on the floor, a scene and an acting style that Penn interpreted as "pure James Dean."

"Through it all," Newman told Coe, "I feel Dean could have done a better job than me in this film. The thought is driving me crazy. Tonight, I'll have to have six extra beers."

Although Gore didn't like the revised script, he did compliment Penn for being an experimental director, creating a black-and-white movie that was cutting-edge, at one point employing slow motion and vision blur in a death scene.

In its bastardized, watered-down version, with bad editing, *The Left Handed Gun* opened in New York City on May 7, 1958, to disappointing box office.

Film critics were waiting with poison pens. The reviews were devastating, as New York writers didn't know what to make of "these television boys venturing into feature films." The reference was to Fred Coe and Arthur Penn. "Poor Mr. Newman," wrote Howard Thompson in *The New York Times*. "He seems to be auditioning alternately for the Moscow Arts Theater and Grand Old Opry, as he ambles about, grinning and mumbling endlessly."

One radio reviewer was particularly venomous. "For this type of role," he asserted over the air, "we need to resurrect James Dean from his grave. Maybe Marlon Brando could have pulled it off, certainly not little Paul Newman. A midget off screen, a midget on screen."

To the regret of both Gore and Newman, there was a critical backlash and a lot more unfavorable comparisons of the Newman interpretation to the acting of James Dean. As one critic wrote, "It's almost as if Newman is working at an excess of James Dean. That wouldn't be surprising, since the screenplay's Billy comes across as more misunderstood youth than cold-blooded killer."

Some reviewers regretted that the heroic soldier and World War II hero, Audie Murphy, didn't get to play Billy. "Visually, he would be perfect, and a better choice than Newman. Plus, surprisingly for Murphy's boyish appearance, he could do a killer-stare to make you believe he killed 100 Nazis in the war." *[Ironically, the critic who wrote that did not know that Murphy had already played Billy the Kid in the 1950 movie,* The Kid from Texas, *in which he gave a lackluster performance.]*

Not every critic attacked the film. Writing for *Time Out*, Tom Milne defined it as, "A key stage in the development of the Western." Also, based on favorable reviews and relatively robust box office in Paris, the French public appreciated the film more than their American counterparts.

In spite of its initial box office failure, Newman, in later years, spoke kindly about the film, calling it "way ahead of its time and still a classic in France." Gore himself continued to be disappointed at the way his script had been butchered and rewritten. He called it "a movie that only someone like the French could praise."

Even though he and Newman remained friends, Gore still expressed his resentment of the way the actor handled the film, as stated in his autobiography, *Palimpsest.* "Paul, no tower of strength in these matters, allowed the hijacking to take place." He was referring to Penn's ordering a rewrite of his script, as Newman stood by, not uttering a word of protest.

Ironically, in the dismal aftermath of Newman's second attempt to play Billy, Marlon Brando would star in *One-Eyed Jacks* in 1961, his character also based on the notorious Kid. *[Conceived and directed by Brando himself, it's a commercial and artistic failure, breathtakingly long and breathtakingly over budget.]*

"The Mark of Zorro is indeed on me," Newman said upon seeing *One-Eyed Jacks*. "I can't escape the curse of Brando. My wife even had to go make a film with him. Don't get me wrong, I love Brando dearly. When he calls me, I come running. Even after all this time, I still find him mesmerizing. But there are times on a bad hair day when I think I will always live in his shadow."

Arthur Penn once said, "Someday, film historians will have to judge *The Left Handed Gun* on its own merits."

That judgment came down in 2004, when film critic David Thomson wrote of Newman's portrait of Billy the Kid as "the intellectual's noble savage."

Otherwise, Thomson was devastatingly skeptical of New-

One-Eyed Jacks (1961), in which **Marlon Brando** played Billy the Kid, was his only directorial effort. He was also the film's star. Both aspects of his involvement were disastrous.

man's "blue-eyed likability. He seems to me an uneasy, self-regarding person-ality, as if handsomeness had left him guilty. As a result, he was more man-nered than Brando when young, while his smirking good humor always seemed more appropriate to glossy advertisements than to good movies."

The "Top Gun" Who Interpreted the Role of Billy the Kid

Sometime during the 1970s, John Calley became head of production at Warners. He'd been intrigued by the critical reappraisals of *The Left Handed Gun*, particularly Penn's own assessment that if his original version had not been edited so poorly, *The Left Handed Gun* would rank right up there with Gary Cooper's *High Noon* (1952).

Consequently, Calley called Penn and asked him to re-edit *The Left Handed Gun* into the original version he had wanted. But when a search was made in the archives at Warners, it was discovered that the unused footage had been junked.

Meanwhile, Hollywood's fascination for heroic *[or anti-heroic]* sagas about the American West continued. In 1989, Val Kilmer would star in an all-new in-terpretation entitled *Gore Vidal's Billy the Kid*. Of the fifty or so films made about the life of this psychotic gunslinger, Kilmer's was the most accurate in adher-ing to the actual events in The Kid's life—a greater, more artful, and more his-torically accurate depiction than either of Newman's previous interpretations on television and on the big screen.

Turner Home Entertainment financed a made-for-TV movie based on Gore's original concept of the outlaw.

There was much that was "authentic" in the script, including Val Kilmer's in-terpretation of Billy as "a dark version of the outlaw as a heroic innocent."

Gore had admired Kilmer's acting in *Top Gun* (1986) alongside Tom Cruise. Gore found Kilmer "the sexier of the two." Based on Kilmer's previous links to both Cher and Ellen Barkin, Gore assumed that he had a taste for older women.

Gore was pleased that this later version ad-hered more to his original concepts, enough for him to allow producer Frank von Zerneck to bill it as *Gore Vidal's Billy the Kid*. To everyone's regret, Americans did not flock in any numbers to see this dark, shadowy screen version, even though many critics hailed its premiere with fanfare. According to Gore: "I reworked the script, but I was pushing seventy years old. Perhaps I should have gone back to my original that I did in my twenties. In one early version I never submitted, I had a male-on-male love scene."

Val Kilmer as a "more artful" version of Billy the Kid

Gore's Pirouette Into the World of Ballet

There is a footnote to Gore and his fascination with Billy the Kid. It occurred in the late 1940s, a decade hailed as "The Golden Age" of ballet in America. Gore felt that ballet was significant enough in his life to devote an entire chapter to it, entitling it "Dancers: An Interval," in his memoirs.

After the War, and at the government's expense because of its designation as "rehabilitation," Gore attended ballet classes taught by George Chafee in New York. He never seriously entertained the prospect of becoming a ballet dancer, but he participated in the *barre* exercises as a means of healing his arthritic knee. Along the way, he became more interested in the dancers than the technique or the dance rituals themselves.

First came his ill-fated romance with Harold Lang.

Five years older than Gore, Lang, in 1944, had played one of the three sailors in Jerome Robbins' award-winning ballet *Fancy Free*. The other two sailors included Robbins himself and John Kriza. Two of these men would become Gore's lovers.

The inspiration for *Fancy Free* involved the shore leaves, during World War II, of three sailors "on the town" in Manhattan. The musical score was composed by Leonard Bernstein, with scenery designed by Oliver Smith.

Gore wrote that Bernstein's music "was a sort of marching song for all of us set free from the war."

All three "sailors" were to become icons in the world of dance. *Fancy Free* was adapted into a Broadway musical by Betty Comden and Adolph Green. It opened on Broadway in 1944 and featured such songs as "New York, New York." In 1949, MGM released its film adaptation, entitling it *On the Town,* starring Gene Kelly and Frank Sinatra.

In 1944, **Harold Lang** *(the central figure in both photos, above)* wowed Broadway in the musical *Fancy Free*. He also mesmerized Gore Vidal. When the musical was adapted into a film, *On the Town,* Lang lost the role to Frank Sinatra.

Gore met Lang one night when he was appearing on Broadway in *Look, Ma, I'm Dancin'!* (1948). Slightly shorter than Gore, the California-born actor actor/dancer had a trim, muscular body and looked much the same age as Gore, although he was five years older. "He had the palest blue eyes I've ever seen," Gore said, "his thighs were so strong they could lock you in a death grip. His smile was that of a roguish imp. He had an engaging personality that attracted both men and women to him like hound dogs at feeding time."

Gore wrote an unpublished short story about their first meeting "in a wood-walled bar in a beach town." Actually, it was East Hampton on Long Island.

That night, Lang invited Gore to his boarding house, but they didn't have sex until the dawn came. As Gore was dressing to leave, Lang said, "Let's have a roll in the hay." It would be the beginning of dozens of such seductions.

As the relationship deepened, Gore fancifully imagined that Lang was "like Jimmie come back to me." That was a reference to his former lover, Jimmie Trimble, who had died during the American invasion of Iwo Jima in World War II.

"In bed with Harold, and for the first time since Jimmie, I gave as much as I got," Gore recalled.

From the beginning of their relationship, Gore soon realized he'd have to share Lang with others, including his Broadway co-star, Nancy Walker, the actress and comedienne who had made her Broadway debut in the 1941 *Best Foot Forward.*

In the early autumn of 1948, after *Look Ma, I'm Dancin'!* closed on Broadway, Gore and Lang flew together to Bermuda, renting a cottage at low season rates. Their first days together were idyllic until one night, Lang informed Gore, "You don't satisfy me sexually."

After that pronouncement, Lang went out alone to the bars. According to Gore, "From what I gathered, he serviced half the British Navy. This hardly bothered me, since I was almost as promiscuous as he was."

Before the end of the trip, Lang told Gore that even though he would continue to sleep in the same bed with him, there would be no more sex.

"He told me I could lie beside him but couldn't have him," Gore admitted. "One night I was so desperate for sex, I raped him. That really pissed him off."

Even so, they lived together for one month, during October of 1948 at the Chelsea Hotel in Manhattan. Gore claimed that he was working on his fifth novel while pursuing four hours of ballet training a day.

At some point, they resumed their sexual relationship. Gore wrote that "Harold is just extraordinary when not running off to the dives of Harlem. He is really a sexual life force, giving it to both sexes. I've never seen anything like him and probably will never encounter the likes of him again."

Lang introduced Gore to his friend, Ethel Merman, the Broadway musical comedy star.

One night in her loud and stentorian voice, she confessed to him, "I fuck Judy Garland whenever I get a chance, and sometimes I shop for dresses for my best pal, J. Edgar Hoover. I can't wait to read *The City and the Pillar.* I don't read many books, but I love books about homos!"

Gore feared that Lang's addictive sex in public places would destroy his career, and urged him to arrange sessions with a therapist, Dr. Jules Nydes. Gore knew that during the day, Lang was having sex in the toilets of the New York City subway system. Lang began consulting with Nydes, but nothing seemed to help. Even when Lang was performing on Broadway in *Pal Joey* (1952), he was arrested three times by the police for sex in a public men's toilet. On at least two of those occasions, he was on his way to one of his performances, as the star, in a matinee.

At the urging of Anaïs Nin , Gore, too, had begun sessions with a therapist. But the psychologist ultimately dismissed Gore, telling him, "You think your shit doesn't stink."

Years later, when Leonard Bernstein visited Gore at his home in Ravello, the composer was turning sixty-nine and filled with memories. He recalled Jerome Robbins, John Kriza, and Harold Lang dancing together in a long-ago performance of *Fancy Free*. "I had all three of these sailors," Bernstein confessed to Gore. "Of them all, I would say that Harold's ass was one of the seven—or whatever number it is—wonders of our time."

Billy the Kid In a Jockstrap

During the remainder of the 1940s and into the early 50s, Gore continued to be one of the most devoted of Manhattan's balletomanes. He wrote to a friend: "I am submerged in the dance world."

At a bar patronized by dancers, Gore met John Kriza, who was famous for having performed in the Ballet Theater's production of Aaron Copland's *Billy the Kid* as choreographed by Eugene Loring.

Born in Illinois, the scion of blue collar Czech immigrants, Kriza was associated with the American Ballet Theater from 1940 to 1966. He originated roles in ballets choreographed by George Balanchine, Agnes de Mille, Léonide Massine, Jerome Robbins, and Eugene Loring. In time, he would dance for John F. Kennedy at the White House and for Nikita Khrushchev in the Kremlin.

After meeting Kriza at a bar, Gore told friends such as Anaïs Nin, "I now have a new lover."

"Johnny is about the sexiest thing that ever wore a pair of tights," Gore told Tennessee and other friends, including the designer and television ad executive, Stanley Mills Haggart.

Sometimes, Gore attended the ballet three times a week as he became more intensely involved with the ruggedly handsome Kriza, who had been one of the sailors in Jerome Robbins' *Fancy Free* in 1944.

Soon, Kriza and Gore were hanging out with some of the biggest names in the ballet world, including Antony Tudor, the English ballet choreographer, teacher, and dancer, who in 1938 had founded the London Ballet with, among others, his future lifetime lover, Hugh Laing. The legacy of Tudor's "psychological ballets" live on today. Mikhail Baryshnikov said, "We do Tudor's ballets because we must. Tudor's work is our conscience."

After seeing Tudor's ballet, *Pillar of Fire,* Gore defined him as "the missing link between Sergei Diaghilev and Martha Graham."

Kriza and Gore often dined with Jerome Robbins and were frequently seen with him when he was creating the dance sequences in Rodgers and Hammerstein's Broadway production of *The King and I* (1951). One night, Robbins showed up with his lover, Montgomery Clift. Sometimes Gore's friend, Ethel Merman, would join them. Robbins would work with Merman on *Call Me Madam* (1950) and on *Gypsy* (1959).

Gore's romance with Kriza did not develop into a grand passion, although they continued to have sex together for a number of years. Kriza's ballet company toured the United States. Bernstein said, "Johnny had at least three boyfriends in every major city, often young husbands. He had a beautiful body and was worshipped by dozens of men, and attracted equal numbers of women, too. A cult formed around him. He was known for 'great sex.'"

In his memoirs, Gore wrote: "Many men and women loved Johnny, who responded wholeheartedly in an absent-minded way. He had a large car that he called 'Florestan,' and together we drove down the east coast of Florida, receiving the homage of the balletomanes in the beachside houses. Eventually, he married another dancer and drank too much."

Kriza drowned in 1975 while swimming in the Gulf of Mexico near Naples, Florida.

After memories of John Kriza and Harold Lang had faded into the long ago, another famous, charismatic dancer came into Gore's life. He had fled as a political exile from Russia to the West.

Rudolf Nureyev.

John Kriza in the dance he performed before both John F. Kennedy and Nikita Khrushchev. Nikita hated it, but JFK said he liked it. Jackie's comment? "I adore John Kriza."

Entertaining American G.I.'s at a USO in 1945, and dressed as sailors, *left to right*, are dancers **John Kriza, Harold Lang,** and **Jerome Robbins.**

When the composer, Leonard Bernstein, visited Gore in Ravello, he bragged, "I slept with all three of them."

Chapter Twenty

Gore Vidal Seduces Jack Kerouac

Two Literary Icons Tangle in a Chelsea Sex Romp

"Semen Nurses, Castrators, Grave-Makers, & Crocodiles"
—*Kerouac's Evaluation of Women*

The unrelenting physical deterioration of **Jack Kerouac**, the literary icon of the 1950s Beat Generation, can be seen in this trio of photographs.

In 2003, Gore Vidal said, "A magazine reporter came to see me. After a lifetime of literary achievments, the first question asked was, 'What was it like fucking Kerouac?'"

In 1958, Gore encountered the Beat poet,

Allen Ginsberg. Since 1956, the native of Newark, New Jersey, had been both celebrated and denounced for his epic poem, *Howl,* which depicted heterosexual and homosexual sex at a time when sodomy laws made homosexual acts a crime in every state in the Union.

Howl became even more notorious when it became the subject of an obscenity trial, at the conclusion of which Judge Clayton W. Horn ruled that Ginsberg's epic was not obscene, adding, "Would there be any freedom of press or speech if one must reduce his vocabulary to vapid euphemisms?"

Gore admired Ginsberg for "his ballsy stands." Their discussion predictably turned to their mutual relationship with Jack Kerouac, whose 1957 publication of *On the Road* had also made him a celebrated figure hailed as "The King of the Beats." The novel was the postwar bible of the Beat Generation, its characters traveling across America, living their offbeat lives against a backdrop of heavy sex and heavy drugs interspersed with hot jazz and controversial poetry.

"When you first met Jack, he must have seemed like a dumb French-Canadian football jock to you," Ginsberg said to Gore.

Gore said that he had met Kerouac in 1949 when both of them were wearing formal dress in the Club Circle at the Metropolitan Opera House in Manhattan. As Gore remembered it, Kerouac was with a publisher, whom he was seducing, hoping to get his work into print. "I was with a

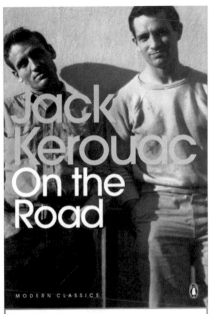

In September of 1957, Jack Kerouac's *On the Road* was finally published. In the edition whose cover is depicted above, **Neal Cassady** *(right)* along with **Jack Kerouac**, became cult figures. Initially, nearly every major publisher in New York turned it down.

friend of that same publisher. *[Although Gore refused to identify that person in his memoirs, he described the publisher like this: "He was a brilliant alcoholic writer with a fortune he was systemically losing. He told me that he'd paid for the sexual services of Kerouac, who was making a living hustling in New York in the late 1940s."]*

In his memoirs, Gore described his first encounter with Kerouac: "We are standing in the back of the opera box, which is so crowded that our faces are only a few inches apart. I feel the heat from his body. The eyes are bright and clear and blue; the body muscular, not yet bloated; a drop of water slides alongside his left ear and down his pale cheek, not sweat, but water that he must have just used to comb his thick black Indian-like hair. We were also coming on to each other like two pieces of trade—yes, I was attracted."

At the time Kerouac met Gore, he had already published *The City and the Pillar*. Kerouac's *The Town and the City* wouldn't be published until the following year.

Gore would not meet Kerouac again until the evening of August 23, 1953, when they came together at the San Remo Bar in Greenwich Village.

Kerouac was drinking with William Burroughs and Alene Lee, a beautiful black woman "with a tomboyish figure and mocha skin." She and Kerouac had become lovers, though he seemed embarrassed to be living with a black woman. He introduced her as a native of India, though no one was fooled by this deception.

Born to a wealthy family, the grandson of the inventor and founder of the Burroughs Corporation, the rather dour Burroughs was a close friend of both Ginsberg and Kerouac.

Burroughs had just found success with his first novel, *Junkie,* that year, although in time, he would become celebrated around the world for his third novel, *Naked Lunch* (1959), which would become highly visible. His greatest acclaim was yet to come when Gore met him.

In time, Norman Mailer would declare him "the only American writer who may be conceivably possessed by genius." The British author and critic J.G. Gallard called Burroughs "the most important writer to emerge since the Second World War," though Mailer actually thought he deserved that position.

Burroughs was already notorious when Gore met him. In 1951, he had shot his second wife, Joan Vollmer, during a drunken game of "William Tell" in Mexico City. He spend thirteen days in jail until he was rescued by his brother, who bribed Mexican lawyers and officials to release Burroughs on bail. Two witnesses were bribed to say that the gun had gone off accidentally while he was checking to see if it were loaded.

William Burroughs, as he appeared in a passport photograph. He and poet Allen Ginsberg briefly became lovers, although they were not sexually compatible. Ginsberg claimed that Burroughs was too emotionally demanding. "Not only that, but I don't want your ugly old cock."

Burroughs fled to the United States and was convicted, in absentia, of homicide and was given a two-year sentence, which was later suspended. At the time of Gore's meeting with him, he was working on his short novel, *Queer.*

Queer would not be published until November of 1985. Editors in the fifties considered the book's homosexual content obscene.

Gore remembered Burroughs as "looking like a traveling salesman who has traveled too far in a wrinkled gray suit."

Burroughs had previously expressed a sexual interest in Gore when he saw his picture on the book jacket of his novel, *Judgment of Paris* (1952). Writing to Kerouac, Burroughs said, "His novel is funny in places. The man is primarily a satirist and should avoid philosophizing and tragedy. Why will people insist on attempting what they are not fitted to do? Is Gore Vidal queer or not? Judging from the picture of him that adorns his latest opus, I would be interested to make his acquaintance. If a man of letters is young and pretty, and possibly available, my interest understandably increases."

Until their meeting in the San Remo bar, Gore had never seen Kerouac in casual dress. The last time he'd seen him at the opera, he'd worn a tuxedo. His present appearance in tight-fitting blue jeans and a muscle-revealing T-shirt evoked Marlon Brando in *A Streetcar Named Desire*. At the time, Gore was at the height of his good looks, and it was obvious that both Kerouac and Burroughs wanted him.

After only one drink, all four of them, including Alene Lee, left the bar and stood on the sidewalk. Lee asked Kerouac to return home with her.

"I've got to go with Gore," he told her. "Gore Vidal and Jack Kerouac—it's a historic occasion."

"You're drunk," she accused him.

Suddenly he crouched, repositioned himself, and then, athletically, stood on his head to convince her he was sober.

"It's either Vidal or me, goddamit," she shouted at him.

Then, when Kerouac did not rush to reassure her, she tersely proclaimed. "We're through," slapping his face before storming off into the night.

Then, for some reason, Kerouac suggested that Gore and Burroughs join him for a visit to Tony Pastor's, a lesbian bar flourishing at the time in Manhattan.

In a taxi en route to that bar, Burroughs was turned off by "the grotesque fawning of Jack over Gore. He even kissed his hand and called him 'dear,'" Burroughs said. "I had never known him to behave in such a manner."

After drinks with "some very tough women—not a lipstick lesbian in the bar—Burroughs, Jack, and I returned to the street," Gore recalled. "Jack began to perform some Tarzan-like antics on a lamppost, and Burroughs stormed away in disgust. I think he realized I was Jack's for the night and that I was not physically attracted to him."

Kerouac suggested that he and Gore rent a room together at the Chelsea Hotel for a "shack-up". On the way there, they stopped at yet another bar for a night cap.

"During our drinks, Jack tried to establish his heterosexual credentials," Gore said. "It didn't come as a surprise to hear that Anaïs Nin had been chasing after him. As a chicken hawk myself, I knew she was always chasing after some hot new artist, the way she'd done with me. Going after me didn't get her very far sexually."

"Anaïs told me that you're prejudiced against Negroes," Kerouac said.

"Even though you hang out with Allen Ginsberg, I hear you're anti-Semitic," Gore shot back.

"Perhaps it's my family background," Kerouac said. "My parents are from French Québec, where anti-Semitism flourishes. But Jew-hating is prevalent everywhere. The other day, I read a poll that showed that twenty percent of American soldiers stationed in West Germany believe that Hitler had done a lot of good exterminating the Jews. Let's hear one for the Holocaust!"

"Of course, being anti-Semitic puts you among some very distinguished members of the American literati." Gore said. "Some of our greatest artists were or are anti-Semitic, anti-black, and homophobic. Jew-haters are led by Ezra Pound—of course, he's crazy. Others include H. L. Mencken, T. S. Eliot, William Faulkner, Eugene O'Neill, E. E. Cummings, and Theodore Dreiser."

"My friend, Tennessee Williams, is anti-black," Gore said. "But he was born in Mississippi and never grew out of the youthful indoctrination implanted by his mother. Katherine Anne Porter doesn't like either blacks or gays, although she's had an affair with William Goyen."

"I met Goyen at a party at Anaïs's," Kerouac said. "She constantly praises his novel, *House of Breath,* claiming it's done in her style. I didn't know how Porter managed with Goyen. At Anaïs's party, he propositioned me."

"Then there is what I call homophobic homoerotics like J. Edgar Hoover and Graham Greene, our fellow author."

[Ironically, in the year to come, Gore would label Kerouac as a homophobic homoerotic.]

"Speaking of homophobic homoerotics, there is a belief that we're about to witness an onslaught of Jewish writers led by Norman Mailer," Kerouac said.

"Mailer calls James Baldwin—a friend of mine—a black faggot," Gore said. "He usually has nothing but snarls and sneers for me, as well. His latest victims are William Styron and James Jones."

"Styron told me that Mailer rages in frustration over his pent-up homosexuality, and actually wants to take it up the ass," Gore said.

"In his exact words, Styron said that 'James Jones is his cock-object, his secret desire. Mailer resents my close friendship with James. He's also jealous of James' talent. After all, which is the greater of the novels to emerge from World War II—Mailer's *The Naked and the Dead?* Or Jones's *From Here to Eternity?"*

With Kerouac, Gore decided to break his own rule about not having sex with anyone older than himself. At the time, he was twenty-eight years old; Kerouac thirty-one.

At the Chelsea Hotel, they checked in under their real names, Kerouac telling the night clerk that one day their signatures would be very valuable.

[Charles R. Jackson, author of The Lost Weekend, *the film version of which brought Ray Milland an Oscar, would commit suicide in a room here on September 21, 1968.]*

In their hotel room, if Gore's memory in the 1970s served him accurately, he recalled "no window shade—just a red neon light blinking outside, giving the room a rosy glow. Kerouac wanted to shower together, where I learned, to my surprise, that he was circumcised. For an instant, I saw not the dark, slackly muscled Jack Kerouac, but blonde Jimmie Trimble, my long lost blonde warrior lover of World War II."

Gore recalled that once in bed with Kerouac, he was the recipient of a blow-job. "That was right before I turned him over and sodomized him," Gore claimed. "He raised his head from the pillow to look at me over his left shoulder. His forehead was half covered with sweat, dark curls—then he sighed, as his head dropped back onto the pillow."

The next morning, Kerouac woke up with a hangover. He told Gore that he had no money and asked him for fifty cents to get home. Gore reached into his wallet and produced a dollar, admonishing Kerouac with, "You'll owe me a dollar."

Later, when Ginsberg heard this, he asked, "How cheap could Gore get? Didn't he think it was worth a dollar to fuck Jack Kerouac, considering he'd get literary mileage out of that seduction?"

As Kerouac later reported to the crowd at San Remo, "I gave Gore Vidal a blow job."

"He seemed rather proud of that," Ginsberg said. "That came as a complete surprise to everybody. If Jack ever admitted such a thing to anybody, he would be the blowee, not the blower."

Jack Kerouac never liked photographs of himself. He felt the photo on the left "makes me look like a serial killer," and that the one on the right "makes me look like I'm walking the streets willing to give a blow-job."

In later writings, Kerouac would devote a chapter to his seduction of Gore in his novel, *The Subterraneans.* He also dedicated a poem to Gore called "Mexico City Blues."

As Kerouac's biographer, Ellis Amburn, wrote, "His childhood and adolescence were lived in a pitch of romantic intensity and fulfillment rarely equaled in adulthood when he became tormented, and often paralyzed, by conflicting sexual passions. Kerouac saw his life as a sexual drama, as indeed it would prove to be, as he moved restlessly from homoerotic to bisexual and heterosexual liaisons."

Amburn commented on that transfer of cash between the two men. "Kerouac liked the designation because male prostitutes, often known as rough trade, can have sex with men and still think of themselves as straight. Vidal's delusions were of another order: He thought he was 'butch' enough to qualify as rough trade. Both, of course, were kidding themselves. They were two monstrous egos clashing in the night."

Gore later claimed that Kerouac "had employed his physical charms to advance his career as a writer. Sucking asses to get published."

Delta of Venus? or...An Overripe Persimmon?

Motivated by spite, Anaïs Nin telephoned Gore two weeks later. "I thought I'd tell you that Jack Kerouac spent the night at my apartment. He told me that you and he had sex, and that he did not enjoy it. He also said to me that he prefers my...shall we say, Delta of Venus."

"I suppose 'fruit' always tastes better when it's ripe, or, in the case of the persimmon, overripe." Then Gore put down the phone.

After the publication of *The Town and the City,* the Kerouac novel published in 1950, Anaïs joined other members of the literati eager to welcome the new novelist into their coveted circle. "The intellectual family of New York has spoken," said Norman Mailer. "After midnight and in voices like snakes and nettles and rats, hiss and titter, prick, and sip."

Before the decade ended, the success of Kerouac's *On the Road* aroused the jealousy of Anaïs as a writer. *[She was not acclaimed at the time.]*

Initially, she'd had praise for Kerouac, but when she met with him for a final time, she warned him that "*On the Road* contains pure lyrical passages, but its realism is too harsh for me. You ultimately don't want to write like Gore Vidal, now, do you?"

By then, their affair had long ago ended, or, as she put it, "Jack abandoned me when I could not keep up with his drinking at the Cedar Bar."

She failed to tell the truth: Based on her physicality as an aging *femme fatale,* Kerouac no longer found her alluring.

"Fucking Anaïs would be like plowing Edith Piaf on her last legs," he told his friend, Ginsberg.

Once, Gore Vidal's mentor, **Anaïs Nin** chided him about how Jack Kerouac much preferred her in bed to him. Gore responded by referring to her vagina as "an overripe persimmon."

In time, Kerouac got himself kicked out of the Cedar Bar for urinating in the bar sink and pouring his beer into the hat of artist Willem de Kooning.

Later, she had a chance encounter with Gore in Greenwich Village, when he was dining with Stanley Mills Haggart. For a while in the 1950s, Anaïs had dressed like a Beatnik herself, but she had quickly became disenchanted with the movement.

She told Stanley, "Jack's *On the Road* seemed like a gorilla when compared to Lawrence Durrell's novel, *Justine.* What a feast reading Durrell! A banquet! An orgy of words and colors, a riot for the senses—a male counterpart to my own novels, errative, elusive, penetrating, a sensuous jungle, a trapezist of images, a jungler, a master of a prestigitations."

Gore Is Raped by the Sex Symbol of the Beat Generation

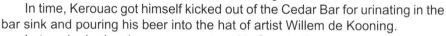

As an act of revenge for his rape by Gore, Kerouac sent his best friend and sometimes lover, Neal Cassady, to the San Remo Bar in Greenwich Village. His instruction was "to turn on your charm and sex appeal, pick up Vidal, and rape him in a room at the Chelsea Hotel before the rooster crows."

Neal was only too willing. He was known, in the words of Ginsberg, for "great sex and genitals stolen from a bull. Sometimes, I would just sit in the living room fondling Neal's genitals while we listened to jazz. That would really piss off Jack."

As early as the summer of 1949, Kerouac had written about Neal's bisexuality, one segment of which would be excised—for censorship reasons—from the original version of *On the Road.*

The censored section described a gay man who had traveled with them, stopping overnight with them in a motel room in Sacramento. Much to Kerouac's chagrin, he jealously witnessed Neal performing sex for pay. *[In* On the Road, *the character inspired by Neal was named "Cody."]*

Neal Cassady became the sex symbol of the Beat Generation after Kerouac immortalized him in *On the Road.* He was happy to have sex with anyone, male or female.

Ginsberg was ugly, but he and Cassady engaged in a torrid two-month affair. Collectively, they were referred to as "Beauty and the Beast."

[That night, the gangbelly broke loose between Cody and the skinny skeleton, sick. Cody thrashed him on rugs in the dark, monstrous, huge fuck, Olympian perversities, slambanging big sodomites that made me sick, subsided with him for money; the money never came. He'd treated the boy like a girl! You can't trust these people when you give them (exactly) what they want. I sat in the castrated toilet listening and peeking, at one point it appeared Cody had thrown over legs in the air like a dead hen...I was horrified."]

One of Kerouac's early works was entitled *Visions of Cody.*

Gore never wrote and presumably never talked about what happened that night he and Neal headed back to the Chelsea Hotel where he'd raped Kerouac.

Neal presented his version of the events of that night to Kerouac, Ginsberg, Burroughs, and others at the San Remo. "I raped Gore Vidal," he claimed. "Revenge is yours, Jack, and I enjoyed reducing this stuffy blue blood to a whimpering pulp. I expect to see him in here tomorrow like a puppy dog with his tongue hanging out begging for more."

According to Neal, "Vidal kicked and screamed, but I plowed him really good with my ass-splitting dick. Perhaps it was virgin ass, as he claimed, but I seriously doubt that. Even though he tried at first to fight me off, I ended up giving him two orgasms before I pulled out. I then forced him to lick me clean, real down and dirty sex. He became my slut for the night."

[Neal Cassidy is an American literary icon today, the subject of biographies, memoirs, inspiration for other writers, and a major figure in films. He stands as a towering image in the Beatnik movement of the 1950s and the psychedelic

movement of the sixties.

Born in Salt Lake City in 1926, Neal Leon Cassady was an exceedingly handsome boy who virtually lived on the streets in Denver after his mother died when he was ten. His alcoholic father was basically absentee, and Neal was wild, stealing cars and shoplifting. That landed him in prison, where he became top man to a lot of imprisoned gay men.

Released one month after World War II ended, he married a 15-year-old, LuAnne Henderson. They moved to New York, where he was befriended by Jack Kerouac and Allen Ginsberg, both of whom interpreted him as the fulfillment of their sexual fantasies.

In 1947, he had his marriage to the teenager annulled, and he married Carolyn Robinson. She called him "the archetype of the American man," although that was highly debatable. Her memories of him were recalled in her autobiography, Off the Road.

By 1950, he'd entered into a bigamous marriage to Diane Hansen, a beautiful model who became "Inez" in Kerouac's novel, On the Road. Although she was already married, Neal fell in love with her after meeting her at a party. Within five minutes, he was seducing her while she sat in a chair. After pulling up her dress, he buried his face in her crotch in spite of the presence of others in the room.

In 1958, Neal was sent to San Quentin on a charge of marijuana possession. By 1962, he met author Ken Kesey and became one of the author's "merry pranksters," a coven that formed around him, promoting the use of psychedelic drugs. Neal is believed to be the role model for the main character in Kesey's novel, One Flew Over the Cuckoo's Nest, which in 1975 was made into a hit movie starring Jack Nicholson.

Neal himself predicted "I will live forever in Jack's On the Road as the Dean Moriarty character."

Four days short of his forty-second birthday, Neal's body was discovered in San Miguel de Allende, in Mexico. The night before, he'd gone to a wedding party where he consumed a large dose of Seconal and a lot of pulque, a muddy alcoholic beverage concocted from the fermented sap of the maguey plant and hailed as a sacred drink by the Aztecs. Combined with the alcohol and Seconals he had ingested, it proved lethal.

After a night of heavy rain and strong winds, Neal's dead body, clad only in a T-shirt and a pair of jeans, was discovered beside some railroad tracks.

Kerouac, who was to die to following year, refused to believe that Neal had died. "He's just skipped out, probably to avoid the law. He's hiding

Carolyn Cassady, later immortalized in literature and on the screen because of her marriage to Neal Cassady, posed for this photograph in 1944.

The 1980 movie, *Heart Beat,* explored the unlucky, unhappy relationship among Neal, Kerouac, and herself.

out somewhere in Mexico. One day, he'll show up again, and I'll be there to welcome him back home, although home was a place he never found in life."]

"Queers Are Not Artists"

—Jack Kerouac

By the winter of 1953, Kerouac had soured on Gore. He began to attack him as part of a tirade against gay writers and homosexuals in general.

A group of Karouac's most devoted fans staged a dinner party in Greenwich Village that November. The author of *On the Road* agreed to speak to his faithful readers. Appearing drunk and drugged, he slid into a tirade attacking homosexual writers, notably Paul Bowles and Carson McCullers, but saving particular venom for Gore.

As Kerouac's biographer, Dennis McNally, wrote, "The writer was junked out on dolophines, his brain roiled with wine and goofballs. He delivered a befuddled post-banquet enconium."

McNally suggested that Kerouac had become jealous of Gore, viewing him as a symbol of mainstream literary success.

In another pronouncement, Kerouac claimed, "Queers are not artists. Truman Capote simpers, Gore Vidal stands legs akimbo in a baroque garden in Italy. Proust was the only fop who could write, but all the girls he wrote about were actually boys."

On November 23, 1953, Kerouac wrote a letter to Malcolm Cowley, an editor at Viking. "I see from the latest *New World Writing* where Gore Vidal is trying to tear you down to lift himself up to position of big new dean critic which is such a laff he's just such a pretentious little fag. Homosexuals are very powerful in American literature. Certain dull individuals who happen to be homosexual have grabbed off the limelight. Second rate anecdote repeaters like Paul Bowles, pretentious silly females with flairs for titles, like Carson McMullers (*sic*), clever dramturgists, grave self-revellers too naïve to see the shame of their position like Gore Vidal, really it's too much."

From Mexico City, Kerouac wrote Ginsberg about Gore's novel, *Judgment of Paris*. He called it "Ugily (*sic*) transparent in its method,

Photos of a young **Allen Ginsberg** for many viewers suggest a young Sal Mineo with a wider mouth. "In bed, I like straight men," he proclaimed. "They fuck me or else I blow them, maybe both. Then I fall in love with them."

the protagonist-hero who is unqueer but all camp (with his bloody tattoo on a thigh) and craptalk. The only good things are the satirical queer scenes. The critics expect us to be like Vidal, great god, regressing to sophomore imitations of Henry James."

While in Mexico, according to Ginsberg, Kerouac had a series of affairs with good-looking young Mexican boys. But that didn't prevent him from writing, in *Desolation Angels,* "I am nonqueer. But some 60 percent to 70 percent of our best writers (if not 90 percent) are queers."

Even though he was under attack by Kerouac, Gore privately envied the success of the best-selling *On the Road.* Marlon Brando had expressed interest in it, wanting to appear in a movie as "Kerouac's alter ego, the anti-hero of the novel."

Gore resented Kerouac for having picked up critical praise from such august literary lions as Lillian Hellman.

"My god, when Kerouac appeared in San Francisco, fans treated him like Elvis Presley, even ripping off his clothes," Gore said. "But in this age of total publicity, personality is all that matters."

Kerouac was candid in assessing his new found fame. "From all over America, both young men and women write me, and they are blunt—'I want to fuck you.'"

In January of 1956, Kerouac wrote Philip Whalen, a poet friend from Rocky Mount, North Carolina. "I can outwrite any sonofbitch in the world today, *and why now?* I'm the only one who's put in any time in it. You have your Gore Vidals who published 24 novels in 10 years. But the time he puts in is Hack-time."

In that same letter, he also attacked Ernest Hemingway, whom he always considered a closeted homosexual chasing after F. Scott Fitzgerald. Kerouac reserved special venom for Gertrude Stein. "She makes me puke with her dyke cuteness concealing all that venom."

If Kerouac disliked Gore, he positively loathed Truman Capote. It all began when Truman appeared with Norman Mailer and Dorothy Parker on a television show, *David Susskind's Open End,* which aired during the winter of 1959.

Whereas Mailer defended the Beat Generation, Truman attacked it. "None of them can write, not even Mr. Jack Kerouac. It isn't writing at all—it's typing."

For the rest of his life, thanks partly to Truman's pronouncement, Kerouac would be referred to by some critics as "the typist."

In its aftermath, Kerouac denounced Truman as "the most loathsome of faggots."

But Truman wanted the last word. He made a round of parties in New York and Los Angeles, with an additional biting assessment of his own. "I have it on absolute authority from a painter friend of mine who has gone to bed with Kerouac. He may be the darling of the Beat Generation if he doesn't take his clothes off. He's hung like a cigarette butt."

"I've Only Libeled Vidal"

— Kerouac

When Kerouac finished *The Subterraneans,* he sent a copy of the novel to his agent, Sterling Lord, in New York. Grove Press had agreed to schedule its publication of the 111-page semi-autobiographical novella in 1958. In it, Kerouac often wrote about friends and acquaintances, giving them fictional names.

In a note to Lord, Kerouac reassured him that the novel was "libel safe & fixed." However, he also issued a warning. "Perhaps the only libelous point is Ariel Lavalina, a recognizable portrait of Gore Vidal."

In the novel, Kerouac wrote about his encounter with a famous gay author. He goes with him to his hotel room, but passes out on the couch and does not have sex with him. There is no mention of him performing fellatio on Gore or being sodomized by him.

The novel also contains an account of his brief fling with Alene Lee, who was black. In the novel, he calls her "Mardou Fox" and writes of her carefree spirit and her contribution to the ambience of jazz clubs. Frank Carmody is clearly William Burroughs, and Adam Moorad is a recognizable Allen Ginsberg. Kerouac himself is Leo Percepied, who is depicted as a young novelist at the peak of his physical allure—"so beautiful that some found it impossible to look at him."

As Kerouac's alter ego, Percepied is sexually confused. At one point, he goes in for gay bashing, but later tells Mardou to go home alone. He then spends the evening with gay buddies, "later drooling over homosexual pornography" and listening to Marlene Dietrich records. He also goes cruising for sailors.

"Jack thinks he can partake of gay sex yet be part of society's straight tyranny," Ginsberg said to Gore.

"A wild delusion that will destroy him," Gore predicted.

One of the final MGM films produced by Arthur Freed, *The Subterraneans* went before the cameras in 1960. The African American character Mardou Fox, Kerouac's love interest, was seguéd into the character of a young French girl, as played by Leslie Caron. Comedian Arte Johnson was cast as the Gore Vidal character. In the aftermath of its distribution, the film lost $1.5 million.

George Peppard and **Leslie Caron** bring Jack Kerouac's *The Subterraneans* to the screen.

Seducing Gloria Grahame & Troy Donahue

Gore had his first real talk with Allen Ginsberg in 1958 (not in 1960, as Gore remembered in his memoirs). The two authors attended a party celebrating the publication of Kerouac's *The Dharma Bums.*

Ginsberg appraised Kerouac's latest novel as "an extraordinary mystic testament," although *The New York Times* headlined its review—*THE YABYUM KID: HOW THE CAMPFIRE BOYS DISCOVERED BUDDHISM.*

Henry Miller, Anaïs Nin's former lover, praised the book, but Kerouac modestly asserted that it was merely adequate as a means of keeping him supplied with cat food and brandy.

Reluctantly, Gore opted to attend the book party honoring Kerouac's latest achievement. "At least for the night we buried the hatchet," he said.

Gore embraced Kerouac when they came together again, later saying, "He was thick and sullen, about to lose his beauty for good. I told him that I recognized myself in the character of Arial Lavalina, but that he had not completely told the truth. 'Why did you, the tell-it-all-like-it-is writer, reveal everything about that evening with Burroughs and me and then go leave out what happened when we went to bed?' I asked him.

"I forgot," Kerouac claimed.

"I looked into his once clear blue eyes, but they were bloodshot, distant, really," Gore recalled.

Kerouac seemed eager to change the subject. "The world is taking notice of me...and how," he said. "Salvador Dalí and his wife, Gala, invited Ginsberg and me to Sunday brunch at the Russian Tea Room. After studying my face for a long time, Dalí told me that I was far more beautiful than Brando. Later, when I got up to take a leak, he followed me into the men's room, where he masturbated me, but only after I'd pissed."

Huddled together in a corner, Ginsberg and Gore talked about Kerouac. "I'm still in love with him, but he's become a hopeless alcoholic, and it's killing him," Ginsberg said. "Also, he's sounding more and more like his mother, denouncing Jews and faggots in that order."

His mother—"a prejudiced monster," in Ginsberg's view—was Gabrielle-Ange Lévesque of St-Hubert-de-Rivière-du-Loup in the province of Québec.

Critic Warren French tried to explain Kerouac's attacks on homosexuals. "He didn't have the guts to be gay and hated himself for it."

"Jack preferred oral sex to regular intercourse," Ginsberg told Gore. "That's why he'll

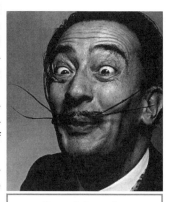

Surrealistic genius
or absurdist charlatan?
Salvador Dalí

never really forgive you for fucking him. He likes to eat both girls and beautiful boys. I blow him. He blows me, even though I'm not a beautiful boy. Neal Cassady was the love of Jack's life. He tells people he doesn't like to have sex with men, but continues to have one affair with a man after another. Of course, he practices cunnilingus a few times a year. He's a devotee of a woman's vagina."

[By the time Kerouac's book, Some of the Dharma, *his vast Buddhist Bible, was published in 1997, the writer had drastically changed his opinion about women. He'd begun working on the book in 1953, but it took almost half a century, long after his death, for it to go into print. It was a compendium of personal prejudices, meditations random notes, prayers, poems, and diaries setting forth his philosophy of life and his esthetic theories about "automatic writing."*

What astonished Gore was the misogynistic tone of the book, as Kerouac berated women. He wrote that "a woman's slit was a gaping wound that reminded me of homicide; Women make me sick."

Citing obscure, antiquated aspects of his own interpretations of Buddhist asceticism, he defined women as "semen nurses, castrators, grave-makers, and crocodiles. The true man eschews women, has no children, and seeks No-Return to the dreary wheel of life & death. He is constantly on his guard against lust and concupiscence & cupidity."]

At the 1958 book party, the surprise guests of the evening were Gloria Grahame and Troy Donahue—"two dubious celluloid idols" in Gore's estimation.

The year Gore met Donahue, that actor had appeared in three quickie films in a row—*Monster on the Campus; Live Fast, Die Young;* and *The Tarnished Angels.* Opposite Sandra Dee, beginning with *A Summer Place* the following year, he would become a major (but temporary) star and a teen idol. Gore found Donahue "blonde, blandly handsome, and a sort of pin-up boy."

Grahame was more intriguing. She had recently divorced the writer, Cy Howard, when Gore met her. She'd been in one of Gore's favorite movies about Hollywood, *The Bad and the Beautiful* (1952), for which she'd won an Oscar.

Her second husband had been the well-known film director, Nicholas Ray. Their marriage ended abruptly when Ray came home one day and found her in bed with his thirteen-year-old son, Anthony Ray. She later married her former stepson, in 1960, and produced two sons with him.

At the party, Gore was getting ready to leave when Kerouac cornered him. "Stick around. I know you have some of the voyeur in you. I've arranged with Gloria, Allen, and Troy for some entertainment."

"But your attacks..." Gore was astonished.

"Listen, Vidal, after a few drinks, I'm game for anything, as you'll soon see if you stay."

Gloria Grahame
...working with what she had.

308

At around 1:30am, Gore was invited to join Graham, Donahue, Ginsberg, and Kerouac in his bedroom for an orgy.

As Gore remembered it to Stanley Mills Haggart and others, "Kerouac's bed was filled with the smell of Indian incense, Candles were lit, and the place had an eerie glow. The only one I wanted to seduce was Donahue, but I felt he'd be up for grabs by all of them. Grahame was past her prime. The party got really raw...too raw, when everybody stripped down for action."

Kerouac announced to whomever was willing to take him on, "I am the fucker, not the fuckee, and, I must warn you, I believe in the long, slow fuck."

Grahame stripped off her clothes and lay down on the bed. She apologized "for the Tampax sticking out of my cunt" and, in lieu of vaginal intercourse, offered blow jobs to the men instead. She was mocking when she surveyed the penises up for grabs. "I've seen bigger cocks in kindergarden, but I'll make do with what I have to work with."

Seeing her condition, Ginsberg gave a lecture on the "glories of menstruation," explaining how in the animal kingdom, menstrual blood was an important component of lubrification.

Gore later claimed he believed that Kerouac wanted to demonstrate to him how devoted he was to sexual contacts with women. He removed Grahame's tampon and performed cunnilingus on her. He rose up only once to confront Gore. "Unlike you, I'm not put off by the scent of cunt blood."

During the orgy, in a far corner of the room, Donahue was sodomizing Ginsberg. Still clad in his underwear, Gore stood surveying the scene, not wanting to join either grouping.

Troy Donahue
...starring in an orgy

He later admitted, "Except for a slight interest as a voyeur to decadence, the scene did not intrigue me. It was Kerouac's show to reveal to me how straight he was. I was not impressed—in fact, rather disgusted by the whole scene. I put on my pants and quietly left."

Sea of Japan, travelling with Gary Snyder and Joanne Kyger after year-end half in India six weeks aboard on way home via Vancouver Poetry Conference, my Centre in Gary's hands early July 1963. We supped at temple nearby, Snyder snorkeled. Allen Ginsberg

Allen Ginsberg was never shy about appearing naked. His favorite expression of honesty was nakedness. "The poet stands naked before the world," he proclaimed.

Facing a heckler at a reading in Los Angeles, he stripped naked and demanded that the man do the same.

***

When Gore next encountered Ginsberg, the author of

Howl discussed some of the dynamics of that orgiastic evening. "Let's face it: Jack found himself in the bedroom with three faggots, and he had to show how macho he was. He had to reveal that he was a real cunt-man. After you left, everybody dipped into all sorts of combinations. As it ended up, Troy, not Gloria, was the belle of the ball."

After the death of Kerouac in 1969, in New York City, the poet said to Gore, "It was a tragic ending for Jack. He died on October 20. For breakfast, he'd opened a tin of tuna fish. He was sitting in his favorite armchair drinking Johnny Walker scotch. Believe it or not, he was making notes for a book about his father's print shop in Lowell. His wife, Stella Sampas, was in the kitchen. He yelled for her: 'I'm bleeding.' By the time he reached the hospital, it was too late. Blood was pouring from his mouth. His liver, after years of abuse, just exploded. Doctors operated on him to stop the bleeding, but he never regained consciousness. He was only forty-seven."

As Gore remembered his final encounter with Ginsberg, the poet was not in good shape. Gore described him as thin and beardless, with his right eyelid drooping. He complained of diabetes, high blood pressure, and an irregular heartbeat, and was surviving on macrobiotic food.

Ginsberg was heading off to Lawrence, Kansas to meet Burroughs for what would be his final visit. Burroughs was deeply self-involved and preoccupied with his heroin addiction.

"Were you two guys ever lovers?" Gore asked.

"He made many sexual advances to me," Ginsberg admitted. "I had no desire for him, but I gave in as an act of kindness."

In the words of Burrough's biographer, Ted Morgan, "Sexually, it was too bizarre to be satisfying to Ginsberg. For Burroughs, the act of sex underwent an amazing transformation. This reserved, sardonic, masculine man became a gushing, ecstatic, passionate woman in bed. The change was so extreme and startling that Ginsberg was alarmed."

Burroughs died in Lawrence on August 2, 1997, from complications from a heart attack he'd suffered the previous day.

Ginsberg was soon to follow. In New York, at the age of seventy, he died on April 5, 1997.

After being unsuccessfully treated for congestive heart failure, Ginsberg returned home. Knowing he was dying, he made phone calls to his friends for some final farewells.

His last call was to actor Johnny Depp, which he interrupted several times with wracking sobs.

Young **Johnny Depp**

Chapter Twenty-One

Lancaster "Tattoos" Magnani

Elmer Gantry Vs. the Roman She-Wolf

Tennessee Copes with La Lupa, Italy's Volcanic Earth Mother

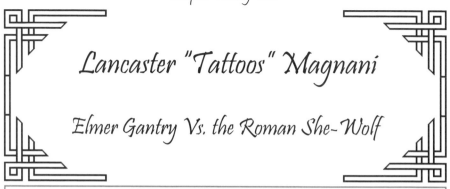

Anna Magnani, the pasionate, dark-haird *realismo* star of Robert Rossellini's *Open City* and Jean Renoir's *Golden Coach*, was selected as the female star of the film adaptation of Tennessee Williams' *The Rose Tattoo*. She was forty-six, but, in Tennessee's estimation, still thought of herself as a girl of twenty-eight.

Cast opposite her was Burt Lancaster, still at the peak of his celebrated male beauty.

"I tried to be the peacemaker," Tennessee said, "as these two enormous egos came together like two high-speed trains, heading toward each other on the same track."

After months of scheming, Burt Lancaster had been awarded with a star role in the film version of a drama by Tennessee Williams, *The Rose Tattoo* (1955) opposite Anna Magnani.

He had been cast as the buffoonish truck driver, Alvaro Mangiacavallo *[which translates from the Italian as "Eat a Horse"],* who woos a prickly widow, Serafina Delle Rose *[as played by Magnani]* back to life, romance, and love. The context was within a community of Sicilian immigrants uprooted and transplanted to the Mississippi shores of the Gulf of Mexico.

During the early stages of Burt's involvement with *Rose Tattoo*, Tennessee met with him for drinks at the Beverly Hills Hotel to talk over the upcoming film. But first, they had to clear the air about why Burt hadn't accepted the coveted role of Stanley Kowalski on Broadway in *A Streetcar Named Desire* in 1947.

"I realize now that the part was the greatest male role of the American postwar theater, and I'm still pissed off that I let it slip through my fingers," Burt said. "I wanted the part, but my business partner, Harold Hecht, nixed the idea, for which I will never forgive him."

Burt continued with a confession, "But frankly, I have to admit that Marlon did it better than I could have. As an actor, he's a genius, although genius is a goddamn dangerous thing to possess. Perhaps I'm lucky to be merely talented."

"Actually," Tennessee responded, "I

Tennessee Williams often didn't like the way an actress brought one of his characters to the screen, but he thought **Anna Magnani** was magnificent in the role of Serafina. On a personal note, he praised her ability "to live within society yet to remain so free of its conventions."

"In our later years, she picked up and discarded young men as fast as I did. It was what her heart desired, regardless of what others might think."

wrote a letter about you to Elia Kazan in 1947, telling him that I had met with you and that I was favorably impressed," Tennessee said. "I told Gadge that you had more force and quickness than I expected from the rather phlegmatic character you portrayed in *The Killers* with Ava Gardner. I also told him you seemed like a man who would work well under good direction."

"If I was phlegmatic in *The Killers,* it was because Ava drained me of all my testosterone throughout the course of the filming."

"I noticed that Mr. Hecht was guarding you like a trunk of gold from Fort Knox," Tennessee said. "That's understandable. You were his meal ticket."

"I'd teamed up with him," Burt said. "With his experience, who wouldn't? He was a former dancer with the Martha Graham troupe and the son of a Brooklyn iron contractor."

"Perfect qualifications to make it in the movies," Tennessee said. "For the film version, Jack Warner actually wanted you and Olivia de Havilland in the roles."

Tennessee Evaluates Lancaster's "Rose Tattoo"

"With that cast, it would have been altogether a different movie," Burt said. "I've learned that many of the roles I've played were originally offered to Marlon. Now for the big question. Did you offer the role of Alvaro in *Rose Tattoo* to Marlon before me?"

"I confess I did, but he turned it down," Tennessee said. "I've got to be honest with you, and this is not bullshit. I've thought it over and have decided that even though Marlon may have made a better Stanley, you'll make a better Alvaro.

Back to back, **Marlon Brando** *(left)* and shirtless **Burt Lancaster** were often rivals for the same screen roles. Burt had wanted to star in *A Streetcar Named Desire,* and Marlon had considered appearing as the alcoholic husband (a role Burt had made famous) in *Come Back, Little Sheba,* the 1952 film adaptation of a William Inge play.

Burt later said that the greatest disappointment of his career was when he lost the role of Don Vito Corleone to Marlon in *The Godfather.*

Of that, I'm sure. Actually, Marlon was afraid of the role. He told me that he feared Magnani would wipe him off the screen."

"I fear she'll do the same for me," Burt said.

"You and Marlon are two strange birds," Tennessee said. "It takes one to know one, so I've included myself in the flock. Certainly, God never created two more beautiful men than you two guys. Marlon makes it a point not to appear hostile to actors he competes with. They are a challenge to him. He told me he regularly seduces his male competitors as a means of understanding their weaknesses before surpassing them. Two of them come to mind: Monty Clift and James Dean."

"Add Burt Lancaster to that list," the actor said, ruefully.

"When *Streetcar* was being shot in Hollywood, my lover, Frankie Merlo, told me he had gone to Mushy Callahan's Gym on the Warner's Lot. He thought the place was empty at first. But then he heard noises coming from one of the shower stalls. He spied on you and Marlon showering together. You were soaping Marlon's back."

"Guilty as charged," Burt said. "With our clothes off, we're lovers. With our clothes on, we're bitter rivals. I once seriously considered having Marlon wiped out by some of my contacts in East Harlem where I grew up."

"As I'm sure you know, Marlon and I are both bi-," Burt contined. "We never compete for the same boys, although on occasion, we've gone for the same woman. Take that brassy blonde from Brooklyn, Shelley Winters for example, although what both of us saw in her I'll never know. Shelley and I had a back-street romance until Marlon came back into her life. After she met him, she ended our romance and told me to go back to my wife."

[Before the end of their rendezvous at the Beverly Hills Hotel, Burt told Tennessee that he expected to win the Oscar for his film appearance in The Rose Tattoo. *Actually, he would have to wait another five years when he carried home his Oscar for his appearance in the title role of* Elmer Gantry (1960).

In the future, Brando would continue to steal roles from Burt, most notably the part of Don Vito Corleone in The Godfather (1972).]*

As agreed, Tennessee accepted Burt's invitation to visit his suite at six o'clock the following evening for drinks and dinner.

Tennessee later recalled, "I was shown in by one of Burt's homosexual secretaries. He'd told me he always hired gay boys as his secretaries because 'they come in handy.' I think he carefully staged his entrance. After the secretary made a drink for me and then discreetly disappeared, Burt came out jay-bird naked from the shower. He stood before me in his living room toweling himself off, letting me appraise his body."

"You look fabulous in your clothes with that athletic body of yours," Tennessee told him. "And without clothing, you're a Greek God. You must spend at least three or four hours a day at a gym to exhibit a body like you're displaying in front of me."

"Forgive me…I'm an exhibitionist," Burt said.

"There is nothing to forgive," Tennessee said. "You're a ten-star road show attraction."

"Don't be disappointed by the look of my penis," he said. "I'm a grower, not a show-er."

"There is nothing disappointing to me at all. Quite the contrary."

As he sat down on the sofa, he told Tennessee, "I believe in the complicated life—that is, balancing kids, a wife, and a mistress or two, with occasional gay forays. I want to live life to the fullest. That's why I'm inviting you over here to sample the wares."

"It will surely rank as one of my more memorable invitations," Tennessee said, putting his drink down and heading for the reclining nude on the sofa.

The Rose Tattoo: Too Much Sex for Tennessee's Mother

In the wake of the success of *A Streetcar Named Desire,* Tennessee offered an option to produce his next play, *The Rose Tattoo,* to Irene Mayer Selznick, who had previously produced the theatrical version of *Streetcar.* After reading it in one night, she rejected it. "It's more suited to an opera than to a film," she said.

314

The next day, he presented the play to her rival producer, Cheryl Crawford, who telephoned five hours later to tell him, "I love it! It'll be a hit. Let's go into production!"

Tennessee later confirmed that whereas many of his plays had originally been conceived as acting vehicles for Tallulah Bankhead, *The Rose Tattoo* had been envisioned with Anna Magnani specifically in mind. As a result of that vision, Crawford called Magnani, and a meeting was organized for a locale in Paris, a city Magnani was visiting at the time, and not in her native Rome.

At their first dinner together, both Tennessee and Frank Merlo made it clear that they adored her and desperately wanted her to play the role of Seraphina on Broadway. Because of the language barrier, she bonded most amicably with Frank, often conversing with him in Italian, and not including Tennessee because "my no good English."

During that inaugural dinner, as she expressed herself in rapid, voluble Italian, Tennessee observed her closely. He agreed with the assessment of *Time* magazine, which had defined her as "the most explosive emotional actress of our generation."

In her native Rome, she was known as "La Lupa," which in her case translated as "a living symbol of the she-wolf." Tennessee had been stunned by the quality of her acting in the 1945 film directed by Roberto Rossellini, *Rome, Open City.*

In the press, Rossellini had called her "the greatest acting genius since Eleonora Duse." He'd also begun an affair with her, which had been widely reported in the press. The *Open City* film launched neorealism in Italian cinema, and *Life* magazine gave Magnani a rave, claiming, "She is one of the most impressive actresses since Garbo."

A month later, when Frank and Tennessee flew to Rome, Magnani had changed her mind about performing in the Broadway version of *The Rose Tattoo.* "The language is too hard for me. I'm not ready for the

Temperamental Divas at Work and Play: Anna Magnani and Tennessee Williams

In the upper photo, they are seen in Key West during the agonizing shoot of his play, *The Rose Tattoo.* Magnani was caught in a nail-biting rage of her co-star, Burt Lancaster.

In the lower photo, Magnani appears in a low-cut gown. Both of them brought their *"beau du jour"* to the formal affair.

315

live version of your play. But when the film is made, I'll be ready to speak in the right way. I'll practice my English every day. I will prepare myself for the role."

Disappointed, Tennessee returned to New York and helped Crawford re-cast the play, this time with Maureen Stapleton in the role of Serafina, and Eli Wallach as the truck driver, Alvaro.

Daniel Mann was the director. He'd later become the director of the film version as well.

Many critics objected to the heavy-handed symbolism of *Tattoo*. In a statement that might have been misunderstood (or not understood) by many theater-goers, Tennessee said, "*The Rose Tattoo* is the Dionysian element in human life, the lyric as well as the Bacchantic impulse. The transcendence of life over the instruments it uses. A celebration of the inebriate god."

Edwina Williams attended one of the performances, but found the play embarrassing—"all that talk of sex and lovemaking—how horrible."

In the play, Wallach—cast as the sexy truck driver—acquires a large tattoo, depicting a rose, on the center of his chest in commemoration of Serafina's late, lamented, and still mourned husband. The rest of the plot centers around Serafina's acceptance and acquiescence to the love which Alvaro unselfconsciously offers.

When the Tony Awards were passed out, *The Rose Tattoo* was honored as best play, and both Stapleton and Wallach also garnered awards as Best Actress and Best Actor.

After all that acclaim, the adaptation of the play into a film became inevitable.

"When You're Bored With Your Romans, Pass Them On to Me"

—*Tennessee to Magnani*

From Rome, Anna Magnani notified Tennessee that she felt her English was at last adequate for her involvement in a film adaptation of *The Rose Tattoo*. Consequently, he and Frank flew to Rome to retrieve her and bring her back to America, using the opportunity to coach her in the nuances of the script and her role within the screenplay.

When they rendezvoused in Rome, Magnani found Tennessee on the verge of a total mental collapse, with him entertaining thoughts of suicide. He was drinking around the clock, and he was also popping all sorts of pills throughout the day and evening, both sedatives and barbiturates.

In a letter to Cheryl Crawford, he wrote: "I am going through the worst nervous crisis of my life, and I don't know why."

Consequently, Magnani became his older sister and his Earth Mother. "I kept him from killing himself. Great artists have great pain. I should know."

He told her that he was kept alive by the inspiration of the words of D. H. Lawrence—"Face the facts and live beyond them."

It was during this visit that Tennessee formed what became his lifelong friendship with Magnani. He agreed with a writer's assessment of her: "She lacked the conventional beauty and glamour of a typical movie star. Slightly plump and rather short in stature, she had a face framed by unkempt raven hair and eyes encircled by deep, dark circles. She smouldered with seething earthiness and a volcanic temperament."

Roberto Rossellini defined her as "a forceful, secure, courageous man." *[Despite his assessment of her as a man, he'd launched a torrid affair with her before he succumbed to the (Nordic) charms of Ingrid Bergman.]*

In addition to Magnani, Tennessee easily made friends in Rome with personalities who included director Franco Zeffirelli. One night over dinner, Zeffirelli told him that, "I've known Magnani most of her life. When she started out in Rome, she sang in cabarets and was known as the 'Italian Edith Piaf.' She is called the most Italian of actresses, but she's not Italian at all. She was born in Alexandria to an Egyptian father and a Jewish mother."

***

Nearly every night during their stay in Rome, Frank and Tennessee dined with Magnani at a *trattoria* of her own choosing, most often in Trastevere. She told him she'd have preferred Luchino Visconti or Vittorio De Sica as the director of film version of *The Rose Tattoo*, but that she would settle for Daniel Mann.

In spite of her reluctance, he would helm her into the best performance of the year by an actress, garnering her an Oscar.

Mann was not without his credentials. In the same year (1955) as his direction of *The Rose Tattoo*, he'd also helm *I'll Cry Tomorrow,* one of Susan Hayward's best films, and he'd go on to direct Elizabeth Taylor in *BUtterfield 8*, for which she'd win an Oscar. A year later, he'd direct Marlon Brando in *Teahouse of the August Moon* (1956).

Tennessee noted that wherever she went in Rome, Magnani was treated like royalty. In restaurants, at the end of dinner, she would make the rounds of tables, gathering up bags of leftovers to feed to the stray cats of Rome, especially those that hung out in the Colosseum or at the Roman Forum. She also found a lot of cats living under Rome's bridges.

One of their evenings ended on the Via Veneto, where she fought off the paparazzi, denouncing them.

At her apartment house, Magnani and her *beau du jour* stood at the entrance to the elevator and bid Frank and Tennessee goodbye with lots of kisses and plenty of utterances of *Ciao, caro!"*

She lived on the top floor of the Palazzo Altier, close to the Pantheon. Tennessee always praised her taste in young men, who were "beautiful Italian stallions," although they rarely spoke English. "My nights are awful," she told

Tennessee. "I wake up in a state of nerves, and it takes hours to get back in touch with reality. The only way to do it for me is to be pounded endlessly by a young man such as the one standing here beside us looking bored. I have to select my studs carefully."

When Frank disappeared to hail a taxi for them, Tennessee whispered to Magnani, "I envy you your choice of young men. Will you be so kind as to give me your cast-offs, please?"

"Burt Lancaster, Big Tough Guy— What A Disappointment!"

—Anna Magnani

On September 2, 1954, Tennessee and Frank had flown to Rome in anticipation of hauling Anna Magnani to America for the debut of the filming of Tennessee's *Rose Tattoo*.

On the way back, after a stop in New York, they flew with her to Key West, which would become the setting for what the playwright had defined as a port in Mississippi along the Gulf coast.

During one of the flights, Magnani confided in Tennessee that she'd been having romantic fantasies about Burt Lancaster, her co-star. "He's my kind of man. I dumped my boyfriend in Rome, even though he wanted to come to the United States with me. I want to be free for Burt."

Tennessee didn't encourage Magnani in her dream, nor did he want to get involved. In his heart, he knew that the possibility of a romance between Magnani and Lancaster would be doomed from its debut.

Privately, he told Frank, "The bloom is off the rose. Anna is fifty-seven if she's a day."

On her first day on the set, Magnani was introduced to Burt. He immediately apologized for his haircut. "The makeup man snipped my hair since I had grown it long for *The Kentuckian* (1955). Maybe he'd had too many drinks. Look at it. I came out badly cropped and all fucked up. Now I'm stuck with it, unless I want to wear a wig. We're on such a tight schedule, I have to keep this crappy coiffure for the rest of the shoot. I've also got to show some flesh in this movie, so I've been working out night and day."

That evening over dinner, Magnani began to have misgivings over Burt. "Do all American actors spend most of their time worrying about their hairdos and their bodies? He didn't even compliment me on my looks."

"From what I've seen, American actors spend as much time getting camera ready as does Lana Turner," Tennessee said.

"Do you think Burt has a homosexual streak in him?" she asked.

"No, not Burt," Tennessee said, an obvious lie, since, from personal experience, he knew differently. "A very private survey conducted in secret in Hollywood found that 79% of Hollywood actors had had some sort of sexual experience with someone of the same gender, many of them when they were young. I discussed this with Dr. Alfred Kinsey, who knows more about the sexual habits of American males than anybody in the country. He speculated that if only actors had been included in the survey, 79% might be a low figure."

Tennessee wrote to some of his friends that "Anna's big scenes will be shot not in Key West but in a studio in Hollywood. For the moment, she's like a hungry tigress with a big hunk of juicy raw meat dangled outside her cage. She can't wait to dig into the meat."

He also revealed that Magnani had had her first fight with the director, Daniel Mann, after he suggested that she wear a *brassière* during the scenes she was filming. "What do you think I am?" she shouted at him. "A fucking animal? I'm not! I'm a woman who has tits. So why should I wear a cage?"

Day after day, Magnani flirted with Burt, making plays for him, but he wasn't responsive. One night, Frank and Tennessee were invited to a local movie hours on Duval Street, which had been rented by the film crew for viewings of the first rushes of film version of *The Rose Tattoo*. Both Burt and Magnani attended, along with most other members of the cast, administration, and film editors.

Based on his interpretation of the first film clips, Burt was skeptical, but Magnani was jubilant. After the screening, she climbed onto his back and rode him, piggy-back, up the aisle of the theater, kissing his neck passionately. That night, he agreed to drive her back to her motel.

The next morning, when Tennessee had coffee with her, she was very sad-faced. "I was terribly let down," she said. "A total disappointment. The end of my fantasy. I'm sure he's a homosexual." Then she held up her little finger in mock derision.

Later that day, Tennessee shared Magnani's anecdotes with Mann. "Obviously, I have a greater appreciation of the glories of Burt's penis than she does. If he wants me to sample it again, like I did in Hollywood, all he has to do is call, and I'll come running."

From that day on, Magnani and Burt clashed on the set, mainly because he accused her of trying to take over Mann's job and direct *Tattoo* herself, which was true.

"You're cutting the balls off Mann," Burt shouted at her in front of the cast and crew.

She shot back, "At least he has balls."

Increasingly alienated from Burt, Mann, and her co-workers, she began dining in her motel room on pasta that Frank cooked at home and brought to her. "She took out her frustration against Burt and Daniel at night," Frank said. "I always brought her two heaping platters of my pasta. One she'd eat and compliment me, telling me I made pasta like a true Sicilian. After dinner, she'd become enraged and toss the other platter of pasta against the wall of her motel room. When she checked out, the owner had to repaint the walls because they were streaked with spaghetti sauce."

One Sunday evening in Key West, Frank and Tennessee invited Magnani to their home for dinner. After the meal, she ranted and raged, suddenly breaking into Italian.

Tennessee thought she was emulating a bad actress in a silent film—"Think Gloria Swanson"—theatrically raising her hand to her forehead to convey an elaborate sense of anguish and despair.

After a few minutes of this, Tennessee turned to Frank. "What's the matter with Anna tonight?"

"Oh, she's just complaining that Burt's cock wasn't big enough for her."

Not surprisingly, Tennessee did not include that story in his memoirs. In fact, he didn't mention Burt at all.

Near the end of the shoot, Tennessee had to fly to New York to consult with Elia Kazan about casting for his new play, *Cat on a Hot Tin Roof.*

"I hope you can keep the peace between our two temperamental stars," he said to Mann. "After the picture is finished, you can put them in a boxing ring together and let them fight it out. Should one or the other murder each other, I'll fly back to Key West and rewrite the script as a murder thriller."

"Marilyn Monroe Is A Whore"

—Anna Magnani, shouting during the premiere of The Rose Tattoo

The premiere party for *The Rose Tattoo* was held at Manhattan's Astor Hotel on Deccember 2, 1955. Attending were Marilyn Monroe and Marlon Brando, who were having an affair at the time.

Tennessee escorted Magnani. They were greeted by the film's producer, Hal B. Wallis, who accurately predicted that Magnani would win the Oscar that year as Best Actress. Tennessee told Wallis that he had dedicated both the play and the film to Frank Merlo, and that he was going to donate ten percent of all future royalties to his lover for introducing him to the glories of Sicily.

Suddenly, Marilyn Monroe made a spectacular entrance into the crowded party. When the paparazzi spotted her, they pushed Magnani, the star of the picture, aside as they rushed to take pictures of the sexy blonde siren.

Magnani was furious at being treated "like a common streetwalker." As Marilyn paraded by her, Magnani screamed, *"PUTA! PUTA! PUTA!"* Then, perhaps realizing that the crowd didn't know what *PUTA* meant, she repeated, in translation, the allegation, yelling "WHORE! WHORE! WHORE!"

It required the diplomatic skills of both Tennessee and Frank, among others, to calm her down.

***

After seeing the final version of *The Rose Tattoo,* Tennessee said, "Anna's role as Serafina will surely be the apogee of her film career."

He later wrote: "She never exhibited any lack of self-assurance, any timidity in her relations with that society outside of those conventions she quite publicly exhibited. She looked absolutely straight into the eyes of whomever she confronted. During the golden time in which we were dear friends, I never heard a false word come from her mouth."

Although she'd previously rejected *Tattoo* as a star vehicle for herself on Broadway, Magnani agreed to perform the role on the stage of Dublin's Pike Theatre on May 12, 1957. Tennessee's original script called for a condom to fall out of the pocket of the male star. Director Alan Simpson feared that might be a problem for the conservative arbiters of the Irish stage. Therefore, he ordered the actor to mime the dropping of a condom.

Even so, Simpson was arrested by the police and charged with producing "lewd entertainment." His arrest drew protests from key members of Ireland's artistic elite, including Sean O'Casey, Brendan Behan, and Samuel Beckett. The police finally gave in to massive pressure and released him.

Marlon Brando escorted **Marilyn Monroe** to the premiere of *The Rose Tattoo,* a role that Tennessee Williams had asked him to play before he rejected it.

Anna Magnani bitterly resented the sexy blonde for showing up at her premiere, and for distracting all the photographers and reporters away from her.

In addition to other slurs, as regards Brando, Magnani shouted in Marilyn's direction, "I had him first, bitch!"

***

On September 26, 1973, ten years before his own death, Tennessee was at his home in Key West revising *The Milk Train Doesn't Stop Here Anymore,* thinking it might be a good vehicle for Michael York and Sylvia Miles. Actually, he was in imminent fear of his own death, as he suffered from high cholesterol, high blood pressure, and heart palpitations resulting from his acute anxiety.

A friend in Rome had just heard over the local radio that Anna Magnani, Italy's greatest actress, had died at the age of 65 in Rome from pancreatic cancer.

After sobbing for an hour, Tennessee wired two dozen red roses in honor of her long-ago appearance in *The Rose Tattoo.*

He later learned that during her funeral, large crowds of Romans had gathered in a final salute, the kind usually reserved for the death of a Pope. When her body was carried out from the church, there was massive applause greater than any she'd ever received after a performance.

With the roses, Tennessee had enclosed a brief message for the dead star:

"My Rose Tattoo, make room for me.
I'll soon be joining you in Eternity.
Love Forevermore, Tenn."

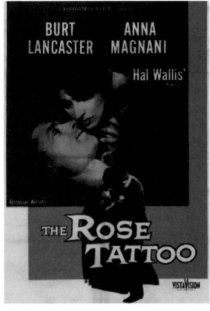

Chapter Twenty-Two

Tallulah Vs. Tennessee

Anima Vs. Animus–But Who Gets to Play the Dominant?

The Queen's Queen Bombs!!
(playing Tennessee's Blanche DuBois & Flora Goforth)

"In a fit of madness," **David Merrick** *(left)*, Broadway's reigning producer, brought Tennessee Williams' *The Milk Train Doesn't Stop Here Anymore*—which had failed in an earlier Broadway production—back to the Great White Way.

Perhaps as a publicity stunt, he delivered one of the campiest casting calls in theatrical history— the formidable **Tallulah Bankhead** *(center)* cast opposite the male screen heartthrob, **Tab Hunter** *(right)*.

With the hopes that she'd accept the role of the misguided matriarch, Amanda, director Irving Rapper sent Bette Davis the script for the film version of Tennessee Williams' *The Glass Menagerie,* to be filmed on the sound stages of Warner Brothers.

This was a surprise, because Davis was in disgrace with her longtime studio after the bitter blood over her last film appearance there. Horribly miscast and far too old, she'd played Rosa Moline in the 1949 box office disaster, *Beyond the Forest* with Joseph Cotten. The picture had been "condemned" by the Legion of Decency, and had ended Davis' career at Warner Brothers.

Yet although she was desperately in need of a good part, Davis rejected the role, writing to Rapper with, "I may have been too old to play Rosa Moline, but Mother Goddamn is far too young to take on mother roles, especially to a full grown girl."

"Don't touch me!" **Tallulah Bankhead** warns **Tennessee Williams**, who had put his hand on her mink-clad shoulder. "I can't stand to be touched, *dahling*, except by a lover, and then I find that some form of touching is necessary in most cases."

[Davis would also miss out on the two best female roles Tennessee ever wrote—that of Blanche DuBois in A Streetcar Named Desire *and that of Violet Venable in* Suddenly Last Summer.*]*

When Tallulah Bankhead heard that Davis had turned down the role based on an age issue, she said, "So, the Bitch Goddess has rejected the part, falsely claiming she's too young to play Amanda. Who does she think I am? Methuselah's mother?"

[Fortunately for Davis and her career, at around this same time, Claudette Colbert fell and seriously injured her back. Davis stepped in at the last minute to replace her in what became her most memorable role, that of Margo Channing in the classic All About Eve *(1950).]*

Still in need of an actress for the matriarchal lynchpin, Rapper called Tallulah and delicately asked if she'd agree to a screen test for Tennessee's Amanda.

"I don't faint at the idea," she said. "Perhaps you've heard I did a screen test to play a certain Miss Scarlett O'Hara. David O. Selznick, the shithead, thought I'd be better suited to play Belle Watkins, the whorehouse madam. Type casting, I'd call it. Of course, I'll submit to a screen test. Who in hell do you think I am? Katharine Hepburn? Bette Davis, God forbid? What a choice. Bette Davis or Hepburn. The choice is between a psychotic and a militant dyke."

Consequently, Rapper flew to Manhattan to conduct the screen test in the stifling heat of one of the city's hottest Augusts. He had dinner with Tallulah at

Tallulah Rides A Streetcar Named Desire for "The Queerest of the Queer Audiences"

her home, called Windows, in Connecticut. Over dinner, during which she drank only water, she said, "I love the idea of playing a Southern lady with pretensions of grandeur. I myself am an Alabama belle with actual grandeur. I don't have to pretend. Besides, I know how a Southern lady speaks more than Tennessee Williams. I could practically write Amanda's dialogue myself."

"That won't be necessary," Rapper told her, diplomatically. "Tennessee has done such an admirable job."

"Perhaps you're right," she said. "After all, Tennessee also fancies himself a Southern lady. I mean, let's face it: Tennessee *is* Blanche DuBois." Then she cackled at her own wit.

The screen test for *The Glass Menagerie* would span a period of four days, during which Tallulah told Rapper, "Her interpretation of Amanda brought that broken down drunken old hag, Laurette Taylor, acclaim on Broadway. My film role of Amanda will bring me that Oscar those idiots at the Academy denied me for my role in *Lifeboat.*"

During the first three days, Tallulah cooperated with Rapper, although she had had reservations about working with him at first. After all, he was known in Hollywood as Bette Davis's director, having helmed her in such classics as *Now, Voyager* (1942).

On her first day, Rapper came by her dressing room to check on her wardrobe for the test. He found her wearing only high heels and a turban. "How do you like my girlish figure, *dahling?*" she asked him.

Rapper admitted later, "As for her figure, the leaves of autumn had started to fall. Marilyn Monroe she isn't. Who is Marilyn Monroe, you ask? Wait a few months. Soon all of *tout* Hollywood will know who Marilyn is. I fucked her right before flying to New York."

In her stuffy New York dressing room, Tallulah looked at her tired face in the mirror. "I'm always playing the odds against tomorrow," she said. It was as if she were rehearsing the first line from her screen test in which Amanda begins to face the fact that that wicked old goddess, Time, was passing her by.

During the previous two weeks, Tallulah had diligently refrained from alcohol. After her first day of emoting for the camera, Rapper had pronounced her "letter perfect."

For three days, Tallulah continued filming, Rapper finding her consistently brilliant. He telephoned Jack Warner with the good news, although the studio mogul was very skeptical. It seemed as if he could picture only Olivia de Havilland in the role.

One scene almost brought a tear to Rapper's eyes. Tallulah, as Amanda, had to repair the hem of her daughter's dress, during which procedure she confronts the reality that her Laura is crippled with a withered leg. "The pathos on Tallulah's face was remarkable. She'd become Amanda, even better than the version Tennessee had put on paper."

Then came the fourth and ultimately defining day.

Rapper had scheduled a scene with Tallulah and Ralph Meeker, who had scored a major hit on Broadway when he'd starred in William Inge's *Picnic.*

"Meeker is up for the role of The Gentleman Caller," Rapper said. "This final test is really about him, not you. You have only four lines."

"I've seen Meeker in *Picnic*," Tallulah said. "My only fear is that I will not be able to restrain myself on camera and that I'll tear his clothes off and rape him. He's so goddamn sexy."

For reasons never fully explained, Tallulah on the day of her final test seemed to experience a momentary nervous breakdown, as if the anxieties of facing the reality of the camera had overwhelmed her. That morning, before she was scheduled for her appearance on the set, she'd downed one fifth of a gallon of Old Granddad.

When called, she swaggered onto the set on unsteady feet. "Rapper, you cocksucker," she shouted at him in front of the crew. "I'll direct this scene myself. Hell, I was making movies before you were born. No, come to think of it, you were around in 1918 to see me in my Silents, such as *When Men Betray, Thirty a Week,* and *Who Loved Him Best.* With me directing this big-dick stud here, Meeker will be better than Jack," *[She was making an obvious reference to John Barrymore, her former lover.]*

Tallulah Bankhead agreed to make a screen test with **Ralph Meeker,** hoping she might win the coveted role of Amanda in *The Glass Menagerie.*

At one point, she leered lecherously at Meeker, "Take it out, Good Looking. Let's see if you've got a two-hander."

The test, of course, was a disaster. Rapper claimed "Tallulah must have thought she was rehearsing for the role of that alcoholic singer, Lillian Roth, in *I'll Cry Tomorrow* (1955)."

After meeting Meeker, she told the director, Irving Rapper, "What are you going to do with a man like Meeker? Rip off his clothes and rape him--that's what!"

Although Rapper tried to conceal results of the final day's test from Jack Warner, a spy on the set reported the full details to the studio honcho, who was horrified.

He called Rapper, shouting, "Bankhead is out! We've already got our resident lush. His name is Errol Flynn. We don't need a female lush! My dream casting has fallen apart. I'm going with Gertrude Lawrence as Amanda and Reagan's former bitch, Jane Wyman, as Laura. Good luck with those two. Just don't let Wyman snip off your balls the way she did with Reagan. Speaking of him, I need to get rid of that joker like I did Dame Davis, your favorite actress. By the way, her tits have fallen."

Then he slammed down the phone.

How Tallulah Became Norma Desmond
(and Gay Miami's Favorite Icon)

Tallulah Bankhead always claimed that Tennessee created the role of Blanche DuBois in *A Streetcar Named Desire* with her in mind for the lead on Broadway. She also said that he had sent her the first draft of the play, and that she had rejected it because of its use of the word "nigger."

"As a Southern lady, I could not utter that word on the stage, and Tennessee refused to omit the line and write in something more appropriate."

This seemed too simplistic a justification for rejecting the role of Blanche. There were other problems, the most compelling of which she confided to novelist James Kirkwood (*A Chorus Line)* and to Darwin Porter one night at her townhouse. "Personally, I don't want to let this get out, but I've always detested the plays of Tennessee and his take on Southern degeneracy. I'm degenerate enough without depicting it on the stage."

"There's another reason," she continued. "Brando and I nearly came to blows—no, not those kind of blows, *dahling*—when we starred together in Jean Cocteau's *The Eagle Has Two Heads.* I think we would have assassinated each other if we'd starred together on Broadway. Did I tell you that at one point during the Cocteau play, during one of my big speeches, that Brando turned his back to the audience and urinated against the props?"

Even before Tallulah rejected the role of Blanche, Tennessee had second thoughts when he met with Irene Mayer Selznick, the producer. "I fear Tallulah

GREAT STARS HAVE GREAT PRIDE (AND GREAT PAIN)

Gloria Swanson, as Norma Desmond, being escorted to a mental asylum at the conclusion of *Sunset Blvd.* Most audiences were horrified.

Tallulah Bankhead, as Blanche DuBois, being escorted to a mental asylum at the conclusion of *A Streetcar Named Desire.*

The audience laughed and laughed.

327

would stamp too much of her own personality onto Blanche."

His words were prophetic.

When Tallulah heard about this, she defended herself. "Great stars have great personalities, and they stamp that personality on each role they play. Take John Barrymore and Sarah Bernhardt." Tallulah delivered her opinion in tones that eerily evoked Gloria Swanson playing Norma Desmond in *Sunset Blvd.* (1950).

Selznick agreed with her collaborative playwright. "The moth side of Blanche would be diminished by the tiger side of Tallulah."

Of course, the stage role of Blanche DuBois was eventually awarded to Jessica Tandy, and the film role to Vivien Leigh, whose interpretation of Blanche earned her a second Oscar.

After Tallulah had been dumbfounded by the success of Tandy and Leigh in their respective interpretations of Blanche, she was very receptive when Jean Dalrymple approached her to offer her the same role in a limited two-week run at New York's City Center in 1955. Since 1933, Dalrymple had consistently produced limited runs in repertory of successful plays starring Broadway names at popular prices.

"I never really liked the play," Tallulah told Dalrymple. "But I'm more sympathetic to Tennessee because of something I read in the paper the other day. He told a reporter, 'Tallulah is the strongest of all the hurt people I've ever known in my life.'"

When Dalrymple learned, to her amazement, that Tallulah had never seen the film version of *Streetcar,* she arranged a screening for her. "I detest Vivien Leigh ever since she stole the role of Scarlett from me."

Dalrymple later said that after sitting through a screening of *Streetcar,* Tallulah was impressed, "But she could not bring herself to give Vivien a compliment."

Later that night, Tallulah met with her best friend, Estelle Winwood. The aging actress told her, "Blanche DuBois will be the role of your career."

"Oh, *dah-ling*, every playwright from Lillian Hellman to Thornton Wilder has used the same line on me."

The following morning, Tallulah called Dalrymple and accepted the role, providing she could take home one-third of the box office receipts. Thinking Tallulah would be good box office, the producer gave in to this outrageous demand.

During the closing weeks of 1955, Dalrymple arranged for *Streetcar* to go into rehearsals at the Coconut Grove Playhouse near Miami. A young director, Herbert Machiz, was selected, with the understanding that this was the project that would catalyze his Broadway debut.

A week before rehearsals, Tallulah gave up drinking Old Granddad and tried to seriously tackle the complex role of Blanche. During her first meeting with Machiz, she was most gracious, but ominously added, "At times, I positively loathe Tennessee Williams and his fucking plays."

Machiz was intimidated by their first meeting. "She'd slashed herself with a coat of her Elizabeth Arden lipstick. Instead of tearing into me, she read to me letters from famous personalities in the theater, including Noël Coward, attesting to her talent as a stage actress. I read the play to her, and we discussed it at length. She seemed very open to suggestions. But that was merely the warmup. The first impact of her in the role of Blanche would later descend like a Florida hurricane."

"I do identify with Blanche," Tallulah told Machiz. "She is a Southern woman who drinks too much and is morbidly concerned with aging and rapidly losing her once fabled beauty, and an aristocratic lady who has fallen on bad days and has been a bit promiscuous in her past."

When Tennessee heard that Tallulah had arrived in Miami, he and his lover, Frank Merlo, drove up from their home in Key West to have dinner with the fading star.

They found her living in a mansion evocative of Norma Desmond's palatial home as it was portrayed in *Sunset Blvd.* Donald Windham's lover, Sandy Campbell, was staying in the building's guest cottage. "Oh, *dah-ling*," Tallulah said, greeting Tennessee, who introduced her to Frank. "You've given me a role, dear heart, that is harder to play than eighteen *King Lears* with a couple of *Hamlets* thrown in."

After dinner, when Frank went to fetch the car, Tallulah whispered to Tennessee, in reference to Frank, "You are so very nice to love such a hideous person."

That spectacularly callous statement, which caused Tennessee pain, was just the beginning of more hurt and sorrow to come for both of these strong, theatrical, ego-driven personalities.

"Frankly, Tallulah functioned better when Tennessee wasn't present," Machiz claimed. "Privately, he told me I was too weak to stand up against her. In his exact words, 'Tallulah is pissing on my Blanche. You've got to eliminate her playing Tallulah with her whiplash movements and her bronchial laugh. And that voice of hers. It's pure Tallulah, not the tremulous tone of Blanche. She'll get laughs where none were intended." *[As regards that final point, Tennessee was correct.]*

There was an immediate conflict over casting for the role of Stella. Tennessee preferring one of his closest friends, the Russian-born actress, Maria St. Just.

In advance of their first meeting, Tennessee told her that St. Just was not only a talented actress, but resembled Tallulah enough to be her sister.

Night after night, Tennessee's closest female friend (**Maria St. Just**, depicted here with **Tennessee**) "poisoned him" against Tallulah.

Tallulah detested St. Just on sight, denouncing Tennessee for bringing "this Cruikshankian cartoon into my presence. The nerve to say she looks like me! If she's not immediately removed from my presence, I'm storming out of here. I will not appear with her. You get rid of this little strumpet or I'll walk."

[St. Just later told Tennessee that she was surprised that Tallulah knew what Cruikshankian meant. At the time, he didn't know either. Sometime, during the period she had lived in London, she had learned that George Cruikshank (1792-1878) was a British caricaturist and illustrator of the works of Charles Dickens and other Victorian novelists.]

Later, Tennessee had dinner with Sandy Campbell, who was also his friend. "Tallulah's performance is disgraceful," he told the actor, who had been cast in *Streetcar* as the young man selling subscriptions to a newspaper. In the scene, Tallulah, as Blanche, flirts with him.

"You think you've got problems with Tallulah?" Campbell asked. "Last night, she took her role of Blanche flirting with me too far. She wanted me to fuck her. If faced with a gaping wound called a vagina, I would faint."

Privately, Campbell telephoned his older lover, Donald Windham, to complain. "I am caught between a rock and a hard place. Tennessee is smashed all the time, and Tallulah is in a stupor, downing sleeping pills in an attempt to calm her hysteria."

Windham advised "Get through it and it, too, will pass, and you'll be back in my loving arms once again."

[In New York and elsewhere, Tennessee and Frank had often bonded with Campbell and Windham as a gay couple to another gay couple.]

During rehearsals, Tennessee gave off mixed signals. After one of her try-outs, Tennessee climbed onto the stage and placed his head in Tallulah's lap. Soothingly, he told her, "You are playing Blanche as I wrote her."

Yet two hours later, he was threatening the producer, Jean Dalrymple, warning her that if Tallulah's performance didn't improve, he would shut down the play, not allowing it to open.

He had been goaded and encouraged by his iron-fisted friend, Maria St. Just, who had sat with him in the darkened theater. Tallulah, who hated her, would not have performed or emoted if she'd known that St. Just was in the audience. Throughout the course of Tallulah's trial run, St. Just kept whispering vicious attacks on her performance into Tennessee's ear.

Dakin Williams, Tennessee's brother, flew to Miami and observed firsthand the conflicts between Tennessee and Tallulah. "The battle between them was one of total exasperation. He thought she was being too grand. At one point, he warned her that as Blanche, 'You're being too flossy. This isn't Mayfair, you know.' On another occasion, he gave her a beautiful and expensive (black) Mark Cross handbag. She threw it back at him, saying, 'A lady always travels in brown. Never black. It's impossible for you to understand what a lady is.' They were often at each other's throats."

"And so they got through the trial run in Coconut Grove," Dakin said. "*A Streetcar Named Desire* was headed for New York. It was going to be one hell of a bumpy ride, to borrow a line from Bette Davis."

"Tennessee was drowning his sorrows in liquor and drugs. Tallulah was smoking marijuana—yes, this grand southern lady smoked pot before it became fashionable in the 60s. She also consumed a motley assortment of opiates. Before flying to New York, she told me she had to drink bourbon and branch water. 'Otherwise, Dakin, I feel when I'm sober that people, especially your brother, don't like me.'"

"Who could make this up?" Tennessee told Dakin before he departed. "And who is my Broadway baby? None other than the formidable Tallulah Bankhead. What in my life have I done to deserve such a fate?"

"Tallulah's Is The Worst Performance Ever of Blanche DuBois"

—Tennessee Williams, in an open letter to The New York Times

Tallulah's opening night, February 15, 1956, at New York's City Center evolved into both a disaster and a theatrical legend. "It was a gathering of the largest assemblage of gay men in the history of New York," crowed a reporter for the *New York Post.* "These men of all ages had come to see the actress they called 'The Queen's Queen.' Almost any line in the play that Tallulah uttered was interpreted as a sexually loaded *double entendre."*

In the aftermath of opening night, the press attacks on her were devastating, with the demographics of the opening night audience factoring heavily into the coverage.

"Opening night was campy hero worship," wrote critic Wolcott Gibbs. "There is, I suppose, no worship, no cure for this kind of vulgarity and stupidity in an audience, except possibly the employment of a machine-gun."

Tallulah was livid with anger when she read that. "What is Gibbs advocating? Genocide? A new Holocaust against homosexuals?"

She became even more furious when Tennessee was quoted as having denounced the opening night audience, referring to them as "so many goddamn faggots."

"Instead of America's most sensitive and lyrical playwright, he sounds like some ignorant redneck from my home state of Alabama. No, I forget. He was born in Mississippi. I should send Mr. Williams a note informing him that some people consider *him* a goddamn faggot. Takes one to know one."

One critic claimed that Blanche should not have been created "as a scapegoat for perverted gay humor," suggesting that Tennessee should have realized that certain lines in *Streetcar,* when uttered by Tallulah, could be widely misinterpreted, exaggerated, and satirized when filtered through a flamboyantly campy gay sensibility.

Writing in *The Daily Mirror,* Robert Coleman claimed that "Bankhead took the first act and kidded the pants off it, mocking Tennessee's words, satirizing them unmercifully."

At one point during her performance, Blanche looked up at her Gentleman Caller, Mitch, who was standing nearby. With her eyes directed theatrically toward the sky, she delivered the line, "I'm looking for the Pleiades, the Seven Sisters, but these girls are not out tonight. Oh, yes they are! There they are!" Then she pointed in the direction of the balcony, which was filled almost entirely with gay men. "God bless them, all in bunch, home from their little bridge party."

That line, and Tallulah's delivery, brought down the house, the laughter shaking the beams of the theater for a full five minutes.

The talented actress, Anne Meacham, the understudy for Stella in that production of the play, told Darwin Porter, "The gay men turned that moment on the stage into their private *Hallelujah Chorus*."

The ballerina, Tamara Geva, with her then-husband, actor John Emery, attended the opening night party. Emery had been Tallulah's first and only husband. Geva remembered passing by a bedroom, where, through the open door, she spotted Tallulah, alone, crying.

After the opening night hysteria, the reaction the following night was remarkably different. The audience was filled for the most part with conventional, middle-aged theater-goers who had been ardent Tallulah theater fans back in the 1930s and early 40s. There wasn't one unwanted laugh all evening.

Saul Colin, writing in London's *Plays and Players*, defined Tallulah's performance as "her best since Lillian Hellman's *The Little Foxes*. She was deep and tender, violent and sufficiently insane to appear normal, moving and coy, suffering yet concealing pain, a new dimension never encountered during the magnificent performances of Jessica Tandy, Uta Hagen, or Vivien Leigh."

Thomas R. Dash of *Women's Wear Daily* wrote that Tallulah gave "a performance that evokes all the subtle facets of Blanche's character, distilling the anguish, the heartbreak, and the pathos of a woman of tender sensibilities."

Walter Kerr of *The New York Herald Tribune* found Tallulah woefully miscast. "As a *persona* and a performer, Bankhead is notoriously indestructible. Blanche DuBois is a girl who deceives herself. There is no self-deceit anywhere in Miss Bankhead."

Dalrymple gave her own private assessment to Tennessee. "I have seen many actresses play your Blanche DuBois. They were sparrows. Tallulah is an eagle, but by play's end she was pinioned to the floor like a great bird brought down by her mocking fans."

On March 4, 1956, Tennessee joined the controversy by writing a letter (which they published) to *The New York Times*. In his letter, he revealed that in Coconut Grove, he and the director, Herbert Machiz, had called on Tallulah at her rented home.

"She asked me meekly if she had played Blanche better than anyone else had played her. I told her, 'No, your performance was the worst I have seen. The remarkable thing is that she looked at me and nodded in sad acquiescence."

He and the director gave her notes to improve her performance, and Tennessee said she worked valiantly to get rid of certain mannerisms.

He also commented on her notorious opening night performance as Blanche at City Center. "To me, she brought to mind the return of some great matador to the bullring in Madrid, for the first time after having been almost fatally gored, and facing the most dangerous bull with his finest valor. I am not ashamed to say that I shed tears almost all the way through and that when the play was finished, I rushed up to her backstage and fell to my knees at her feet."

Even though his letter to *The New York Times* was graciously, some say impeccably, phrased, Tallulah viewed it as condescending and went for years without speaking to him.

On a hot summer night in 1963, a call came in from Mexico. Tallulah's gay secretary, Ted Hook, *[who later operated famously as the manager of Manhattan's most celebrity-conscious bar, Backstage, in the theater district]* came to her bedroom, where she was watching TV. "It's Tennessee Williams. He's calling from Mexico and claims that it's urgent that he speak to you."

"What in hell does he want?" she asked. "Another revival of *Streetcar*? OK, I'll speak to him against my better judgment."

Throughout the short remainder of her life, she regretted having taken that call.

Why the Milk Train Never Even Got Started
"Tennessee Lured Me to Italy Under False Promises"
—Farley Granger

Tennessee's play, *The Milk Train Doesn't Stop Here Anymore,* may be unique in the annals of Broadway. It opened and closed and reopened and closed, all within a year. It opened in January of 1963 with a major star (British actress Hermione Baddeley), and ran for 69 performances at the Morosco Theater in Manhattan, then reopened in January of 1964 with Tallulah Bankhead and ran for five performances, closing after hostile reviews. In 1968, Elizabeth Taylor and Richard Burton would remount it as a film entitled *Boom!* It, too, was a dismal failure, some critics suggesting it should have been retitled as *Doom!*

The actual origins of *Milk Train* dated back to a summer a decade before in Italy. Frank Merlo and Tennessee had gone to their favorite country (Italy) for a months-long stay.

Tennessee and his lover, Frank, were introduced to the fabled Italian film director, Luchino Visconti, at a party in Rome. Visconti and Franco Zeffirelli approached the two Americans. Whereas Frank spoke Italian, and Zeffirelli spoke English, Visconti spoke virtually no English at all.

Therefore, in Italian, which had to be translated for Tennessee, Visconti said, "It is an honor for a famous homosexual Italian director to meet a famous homosexual American playwright. I'm Luchino Visconti, and this handsome darling man beside me is my beloved Franco Zeffirelli, who is destined to become one of the greatest of all Italian directors, like myself."

"I like a man of confidence," Tennessee said, enigmatically, with Frank translating.

Soon, all four of them agreed that the party was a bore, and Visconti and Zeffirelli took them on a tour of Rome's underground gay spots.

Before the night was over, Tennessee became mesmerized by the macho charm of Visconti, who had been born into an ancient aristocratic family in Milan, although he'd became a communist during World War II.

A young **Franco Zeffirelli** *(left)* meets **Tennessee Williams** *(center)* in the garden of the communist director, **Luchino Visconti** *(right)* in Italy in 1949. Tennessee later claimed, "They looked better in the nude than in suits."

All four of these men became friends. The next day over lunch, Visconti revealed a tantalizing secret to Tennessee and Frank. With Zeffirelli translating, he claimed that he wanted a movie script written for a film entitled *Senso.* He falsely claimed that he had already secured the participation of the male and female leads—Marlon

Despite many weeks of collaboration, and many failed promises and expectations, only a few lines of Tennessee's dialogue appeared in the final version of Visconti's historical romance, **Senso** *(photo below),* starring Farley Granger.

Brando and Ingrid Bergman. Bergman was living at the time in Rome after having been more or less banished from her film career in Hollywood based on her abandonment of her husband, Dr. Petter Lindstrom, and her subsequent marriage to the Italian film director, Roberto Rossellini.

"The concept must be fabulous, because Marlon even turns down some of my plays," Tennessee said.

On the basis of that all-star cast, Tennessee agreed to remain in Italy to work on an English-language filmscript. For lodgings and as a catalyst to his creativity, he rented a villa in the fishing village of Positano, along the Amalfi Drive, south of Naples.

But when he confronted the rough scenario and the historical background themes for *Senso,* Tennessee was less than inspired. It was not his kind of thing. Set in Italy around 1866, when the Italian/Austrian war of unification was coming to an end, it tells the story of an Austrian officer and his aristocratic Italian mistress within a lushly romantic setting.

Tennessee didn't feel any particular connection to the story. In his desperation, he called Paul Bowles in Tangier to work with him on creating dialogue for the script.

But instead of writing dialogue for *Senso,* which he produced very slowly, Tennessee spent more time on his short story, "Man Bring This Up Road," than he did on the script for *Senso.* He also spent a lot of time on the local beaches, cruising the handsome youths of Positano within the context of a depressed, impoverished, post-war economy. Many of them were sexually available, sometimes for only a meal.

After a few weeks, Visconti and Zeffirelli showed up for a weekend of script negotiations and sunbathing. "I gave them access to my terrace while I attempted to write dialogue, but my attentions were diverted to their nude bodies out there in the sun," Tennessee confessed to Maria St. Just. "From the look of things, it was obvious why those two were attracted to each other's manly charms."

Over dinner that night, Visconti delivered a bombshell. "Bergman has turned us down," he said. "Her Pope, her God, Rossellini, nixed it. I think he's jealous of me. Also, I met with my backers in Rome. Brando has agreed to do it, but those idiots in Rome think that Samuel Goldwyn's pretty boy, Farley Granger, is an even bigger star and would attract far more box office than Brando, who is not too popular in Italy at the moment."

Tennessee later said, "I felt I'd lost my hearing. These money people were rejecting Marlon in favor of this Farley boy. He had been acclaimed playing the gay murderer in *Rope* (1948), but I didn't think he was any good. He was also acclaimed for Hitchcock's *Strangers on a Train* (1951), but Robert Walker as the gay psychopath walked away with the picture."

"After the loss of Brando, I had even less enthusiasm for *Senso,*" Tennessee said. "Paul Bowles went back to Tangier after leaving a few pages of dialogue. Also, Visconti was offering me no remuneration for my work, so that took away what little incentive I had."

Tennessee did drive to the Rome airport to meet Farley at the end of his flight from New York. Visconti and Zeffirelli were there, too.

Farley remembered the event in his memoirs, *Include Me Out.* He had both fond and awful memories of this sprawling epic of two doomed lovers played out against the backdrop of the *Risorgimento [Italy's struggle for independence and unification, resulting in the establishment of the Kingdom of Italy in 1861].* In his memoir, Farley recalled the plush settings of La Fenice Opera House in Venice and the Villa Palladio in Vicenza, in the verdant north of Italy.

Farley was upset that Visconti spoke no English, but he was physically charmed by him, recalling in his autobiography that he "was a striking presence, darkly handsome, with a leonine head, chiseled features, and piercing dark eyes." He was introduced to the director's lover, Zeffirelli, who would be the assistant director on the picture.

Farley regretted having no meaningful dialogue with Tennessee at the time. "I went to my hotel to catch up on my jet lag. When I woke up, everybody had disappeared. I wouldn't see them again for a month."

In his memoir, he omitted many of the details about what happened to him in Italy. As one example, he rented a car in Rome and drove to Tennessee's villa in Positano. Frank Merlo was not in residence at the time, having left for a visit to his relatives in Sicily. Tennessee later told St. Just that he found Farley's ass "very fuckable, and he was a sweet, a dear, enchanting boy. But he is no Marlon."

Soon after, Tennessee bowed out of *Senso*. Visconti, plus five other writers, labored over the final script. However, when the film was released in America following its 1954 premiere in Italy, some of the dialogue by Tennessee and Paul Bowles was included in the English language version, which had been retitled as *The Wanton Countess* in anticipation of its American release.

Tennessee must have made some promise to Farley for a future role. Even though he did not find him suitable, he green-lighted his appearance as Tom (Tennessee's alter ego) in a 1965 revival of *The Glass Menagerie* on Broadway. Jo Van Fleet was cast as a rather tough Amanda, along with Hal Holbrook as The Gentleman Caller.

Samuel Goldwyn's own "golden boy," the American heartthrob, **Farley Granger,** flew in to star in the costume drama, *Senso*.

He later recalled his Italian experience: "You might say I got fucked by Tennessee Williams, Zeffirelli, and Visconti, quite a trio."

During the shooting of *Senso* in Italy, both Visconti and Zeffirelli became enamoured of Farley. The closely knit movie world of Rome buzzed with gossip that the two directors and the "beautiful *Americano* actor" were engrossed in a passionate *ménage à trois*.

"A British Battle Ax"
Rides The Milk Train To Broadway

Wherever he traveled, Tennessee sporadically began to write dialogue for his play, *The Milk Train Doesn't Stop Here Anymore.* He used his villa overlooking the sea along the *Costiera [i.e., Amalfi Drive]* as a setting for the play.

Nearly a decade would pass before the public would see *Milk Train* staged.

[The melodrama tells the story of the imperious Flora Goforth, who has retired to Italy after an extravagant life. Six-time-widowed, the American dowager is dictating her scandalous memoirs during her final days. She ingests a variety of alcoholic and chemical substances to help her sustain the illusion that death is not knocking on her door.

But it appears. The "Angel of Death" is a handsome poet and creator of mobiles named Christopher Flanders. He arrives at her villa either to freeload or to help Flora find salvation. Most of the play consists of convoluted dialogue between the star and Chris. Finally, Miss Goforth "goes forth" (i.e., she dies) after a long struggle with terminal illness.]

After years of struggle, Tennessee finally finished the first complete draft of *The Milk Train Doesn't Stop Here Anymore.* While he was in Rome, word came from the dashing Gian Carlo Menotti, the Italian-American composer and librettist, that he wanted to present the first-ever production of the play at his *Festival dei Due Mondi* in the hilltown of Spoleto, north of Rome.

Tennessee agreed to have dinner with him and his equally dashing lover, Thomas Schippers, who was one of the world's most famous conductors, highly regarded for his work in opera. Before moving in with Menotti, he'd shared the bed of Leonard Bernstein.

After the dinner, Tennessee agreed to allow his play to be previewed at Spoleto. "A great old British battle-ax was given the lead role of Flora Goforth," Tennessee said. He was referring to the character actress, Hermione Baddeley, who had once lived with actor Laurence Harvey. Baddeley told Ten-

Making beautiful music together, both on and off the stage, were composer **Gian Carlo Menotti** (left) and his handsome lover, the conductor and operatic maestro, **Tommy Schippers.** In tandem, they co-founded the stylish and by now world-famous *Festival dei Due Mondi* (i.e., the Spoleto festival).

It was they who arranged, for presentation at Spoleto, the world's first production of Tennessee's *Milk Train.*

nessee, "After my affair with the man we call 'Florence of Lithuania,' nothing in life is ever really too awful again."

In Spoleto, in July of 1962, on opening night, Baddeley gave a stunning performance as Flora Goforth. Even Anna Magnani drove up from Rome and pronounced her as *come magnifica!"*

Originally, Tennessee had planned to offer the part to Tallulah Bankhead for its eventual migration to Broadway. But he became so carried away that backstage, on opening night in Spoleto, he awarded the part, as it applied to its eventual run on Broadway more than a year later, to Baddeley. As he later said, "I still had some clout back then."

"You are my Broadway baby," he told Baddeley.

Tennessee spoke with disdain of the Spoleto Festival, calling it "mainly an ego-trip for the *maestro*, Gian Carlo Menotti, and his lover, Tommy Schippers. The climax was when Menotti and Schippers appear in white tie regalia and are charioted through the packed streets in a big new convertible, probably a caddy or a Rolls. Never mind. It was his kick, and I don't think I should knock another man's kick, nor his ego-trips, nor the fantasy world he lives in."

In previews in New Haven and Boston, critics praised Baddeley's performace, but attacked Tennessee's play. Nonetheless, it opened on Broadway during a city-wide newspaper strike in January of 1963 and ran for only 69 performances at the Morosco Theater. Even though the play was a failure, Baddeley was nominated for a Tony for Best Performance by an Actress that year.

Mildred Dunnock got raves as the sharp-tongued old Witch of Capri, "who floats in wearing gauzy brown, looking like a superannuated ballerina *prima assoluta.*" As the young poet, Paul Robeling was deemed "utterly unconvincing." Tennessee's script itself was interpreted as "the most disappointing" element of the production. Writing in *The New York Times,* Howard Taubman declared, "Mr. Williams' new play fails."

In spite of the failure of his play on Broadway, Tennessee did not give up. He kept rewriting the drama. In some ways, his creation of Flora Goforth reflected his own problems and personality. He'd lost confidence in his work, and feeling that "Broadway audiences have deserted me. I fear that in the future my plays will be presented at workshops starring wannabees with no talent."

Tennessee's most ardent fans made it a point to attend both of the (failed) Broadway versions of his *Milk Train.*

Most of them agreed that **Hermione Baddeley** (*photo above*) depicted the aged, jaded, and decadent Flora Goforth with far more bravura than Tallulah, who was the featured lead of the second version.

Tennessee was aging and morbidly concerned with his physical deterioration. At times, he predicted to friends, "Like Frankie Merlo, my death is imminent."

Flora Goforth to Tab Hunter:
"Us Swamp Bitches Don't Go in for Hand Kissing."

From Puerto Vallarta, in August of 1963, Tennessee spoke to Tallulah after many a chilly year. "Let's stop the border wars between Alabama and Mississippi," he said. "You always tell your cunties *[Tallulah's nickname for her servants]* to press on. I'm in Mexico right now shooting *The Night of the Iguana* with Richard Burton and Ava Gardner and belting down a few at night with Elizabeth Taylor. She's on the set during the day trying to protect her Welshman from the clutches of Ava Gardner."

Brushing aside past insults and injuries, he asked Tallulah to appear as the aging actress Flora Goforth in his rewritten version of *The Milk Train Doesn't Stop Here Anymore,* which had failed earlier that year.

Tallulah responded imperiously. "Although I swore I'd never appear in another play by one Tennessee Williams, have Audrey Wood send me the script tomorrow morning. I'll belt down some bourbon and branch water, brace myself, and read through it in one sitting."

She was true to her word. After reading it, she turned to her secretary, Ted Hook. He wants me to play "A promiscuous, pill-ravaged rip, born in a Georgia swamp. Tennessee obviously had me in mind when he conjured up that woman."

The following day, the director, Tony Richardson, called on her. The young English director was "one of the hottest on the planet," having scored a great success with the film *Tom Jones*. The bisexual actor was in a troubled marriage at the time to Vanessa Redgrave.

Amazingly, Richardson had never seen Tallulah perform when he met her. He also had not seen her most memorable film interpretation, her performance in *Lifeboat* (1944), directed by Alfred Hitchcock.

[When Lifeboat was screened for Richardson by David Merrick, the director told the producer, "I found her no livelier in that film than on the first night I met her."]

Richardson told Tallulah that the David Merrick Foundation was willing to give the play a sec-

Director **Tony Richardson** had hardly heard of Tallulah Bankhead when he was asked to direct her in *Milk Train*. When he met her in New York, he told David Merrick, "She's not up to performing the part."

After a week of rehearsals with her, Richardson said, "Her spectre is from the past, and she's the most unpleasant actress I've ever worked with. Let's blame it on her senility and decay."

ond try, blaming its initial failure on the newspaper strike. Richardson approved of Tennessee's rewrites, saying, "He's made his statement clearer now."

"At least clearer to you, *dah-ling*," Tallulah quipped. "This Flora Goforth sounds pretty muddled on drink and drugs, a condition I know only too well. I won't even have to act the part—I'll just be myself." Then she lit a cigarette and stared at him.

"It could be one of your defining roles on the stage," he said. "You don't want to be remembered just for Noël Coward's *Private Lives.*"

Her face flushed anger. She was aware that to this avant-garde New Wave director, she evoked the frivolous British Theatre of yesteryear.

"Who have you cast as my leading man?" she asked.

"Tab Hunter," he said, a bit too bluntly and defiantly for her tastes.

"Oh, *PLEASE*, *dah-ling*," she responded. "People are eating. You're not serious, are you?"

"Yes, I am," he said. "Tab has tremendous potential, which has been wasted as a teen idol in Hollywood. At thirty-two he's mature and is willing to work his butt off in this role."

"Or working his butt off in some other way."

Richardson seemed to resent Tallulah's implication that he wanted Hunter in the play so that he could seduce him. Richardson's enduring memory of his meeting with Tallulah involved being "wetted down by her white poodle, Dolores."

When Tennessee returned to New York, he called on Tallulah. She told him, "That Richardson prick doesn't give a fuck about Flora Goforth. All he's interested in is bedding Tab Hunter."

He was horrified at the sight of Tallulah. Since he'd last seen her, she had deteriorated badly. To make her condition worse, her hand was severely burned. A pack of matches had exploded when she was lighting a cigarette. Her doctor had told her not to bandage it because he diagnosed that access to the open air would make it heal more quickly.

"I don't know if David Merrick will be a lot of help either," Tennessee warned her, beginning to regret that he'd offered her the role. "That first-rate showman seems to be pouring all his energy into producing *Hello, Dolly!*"

"As for Richardson, don't blame him," Tennessee said. "Who wouldn't want to seduce Tab? Actually, Richardson first offered the role to Tony Perkins, Tab's lover. He would have been perfect. It was Tony who suggested that Tab play the part."

What Tennessee didn't tell Tallulah was that Richardson had not only wanted Perkins for the male lead, but that he had wanted to cast Katharine Hepburn as Flora Goforth. She had rejected the offer, invoking the excuse that, "Spence is ailing, and I must take care of him."

Her reference, of course, was to her platonic lover, Spencer Tracy.

When Tallulah finally met Hunter, she was most gracious. "How clean cut you look," she said. "Thank God I'm here, *dah-ling*, to corrupt you."

Later that afternoon, she complained to Richardson, "That Tab creature and I are going to get along like spitting cats."

When they weren't rehearsing, Hunter's presence, points of view, and conversation bored her. He'd recently filmed *The Golden Arrow (aka La Freccia d'Oro; 1962). [The story follows the tribulations of Hassan (Tab Hunter), a handsome adventurer who, viewers learn, is the lost heir to the throne of Damascus. When the sultan's daughter (as interpreted by Rossana Podesta) is abducted, Hassam vows to rescue her. He survives and triumphs over a wizard who turns men to stone, and a vengeful sorceress who rules an underground managerie of flaming monsters. Through it all he is aided by a trio of wise-guy genies, a flying carpet, a*

Tab Hunter, airborne on a flying carpet in *The Golden Arrow*, a performance and a film Tallulah mocked.

golden arrow, and a magic mirror.]

Under her breath, Tallulah asked her co-star, Ruth Ford, "Why doesn't he go take a flying fuck?"

At first, Ford—who had been cast as the "Witch of Capri"—and Tallulah bonded. Ford had been born in Mississippi, a state that neighbored Tallulah's native state of Alabama, and Ruth was married at the time to the bisexual actor, Zachory Scott, who had scored a big hit opposite Oscar-winning Joan Crawford in *Mildred Pierce* (1945). But as the days wore on, Tallulah realized what a scene-stealing role Ford had.

"Miss Ford was the only one in the cast who could light a fire under Tallulah," Hunter claimed. "The two women would stop at nothing to upstage each other, including kicking their chairs off their marks to subtly gain more audience attention."

At rehearsals, Tennessee grew increasingly dismayed by Tallulah's failure to grasp the role, especially the long, meandering speeches he placed into the mouth of Flora Goforth. "For the first time in her theatrical career, she couldn't remember her lines."

Hunter had his own reaction to Tallulah. In his memoirs, he wrote, "I saw this little old lady standing before me."

Sensing that Hunter would discuss her, critically, with his gay friends, she said, "Say anything you want about me, *dah-ling*, just so long as it's not fucking boring."

"What pissed me off was Tallulah's complete lack of professionalism, her inability to see beyond herself, beyond her reputation," Hunter said. "She was dissipating an incredible God-given talent, especially when she decided to turn anything—*anything*—into high camp."

The brilliant actress, Marian Seldes, had been cast as Tallulah's secretary. "During rehearsal, she had to cater to Tallulah's every whim, but she did it with grace and style, even when she had to run lines for Tallulah while she sat on the toilet," Hunter said.

"She *[Seldes]* tried hard to hold us all together, while Tallulah's insecurities threatened to blow us all apart," Hunter said.

Hunter resented some of the interviews Tallulah gave, within earshot, to reporters. At one point, she told a journalist from *The (New York) Daily News,* "Tab, gay? I don't really know, *dah-ling*. He's never gone down on me."

Once Hunter, in front of Richardson, was laboring through one of his longest and most difficult speeches. Nearby, to Seldes, Tallulah kept complaining loudly about her makeup.

Losing his patience, Hunter shouted at her. "Why the *fuck* don't you shut up?"

She looked indignant. "You are the rudest man I've met since Marlon Brando."

Before a fight could break out, Tennessee suddenly rushed down the aisle "flushed and disheveled," in Hunter's words, "cradling his Boston terrier and a silver flask from which he took copious swigs."

"President Kennedy's been shot! He's dying in Dallas!"

Tallulah dropped to the floor onstage, and uttered "an Alabama bawl," as Tennessee later recalled. "Ruth Ford, too, fell down on the stage and she cried even harder. Even in grief, Ford had to outdo Tallulah."

Hunter later claimed that on that date, November 22, 1963, the 1950s came to an end and that Bette Davis's "bumpy ride [Her memorable line from All About Eve] had truly begun."

When Tallulah recovered, she wrote a note to Jackie Kennedy. "Your husband's murder was one of the two most horrid moments of my life. The other was when my daddy in Alabama told me that Santa Claus did not exist."

When David Merrick finally got around to seeing a dress rehearsal, he appraised Milk Train as so bad that he threatened to shut down the show before its Broadway opening. "Tallulah just isn't up to it," he told a drunken Tennessee.

The playwright defended his star. "We've got to hang in there. Don't judge her by the rehearsals. I did the same thing with Laurette Taylor in The Glass Menagerie. She was awful during rehearsals, but pulled herself together and gave a performance that even today is part of theatrical legend. For all we know, Tallulah will surpass Laurette. Milk Train could become such a hit that Tallulah will be playing her until her dying day. She once told me that she wanted to die performing onstage."

"At the rate she's going, she will," Merrick snapped.

Previews in Baltimore were a disaster. A third of the audience walked out before the play concluded. Richardson flew off to London to deal with his troubled marriage to Redgrave and to cast an upcoming production of The Seagull. Tallulah vowed never to speak to him again.

With trepidation, Merrick bravely—or foolishly—forged ahead and opened Milk Train on New Year's Day, 1964, at the Brooks Atkinson Theatre in Manhattan.

On opening night, Tallulah's voice was weak. She was drugged from having ingested painkillers to stem the ache of her burned hand. Whenever she forgot a line, "she'd vamp until ready" in Tennessee's words.

At her final performance on Broadway, Tallulah once again attracted her gay camp followers. Marian Seldes told The New York Times, "Her cult shrieked with laughter at the most inappropriate moments."

John Chapman in The New York Daily News claimed that the opening night audience was one of the queerest since the early days of the Ballet Russe [He meant the Ballets Russes] in Monte Carlo.

"Most of the seats were filled with

Tab Hunter, with **Tallulah Bankhead** in *Milk Train*

342

screaming queens," Hunter said. "The play was nothing more than an excuse to wallow in their idol's patented *schtick*. We were props to her one-woman show."

One magazine asserted, "These gay lads had come to see a travesty and despite Miss Bankhead's sturdy refusal to commit one, they applauded, as though by their actions, they could call it into being."

Merrick closed the play after five performances.

Seldes said, "Tennessee was always so in and out of favor. You could almost chart his critical ups and downs, although it would break your heart if you did. But I wanted everything he did to be magic, and I was terribly disappointed that *Milk Train* didn't go over. It's an imperfect play, but it's beautifully imperfect."

After the closing, Tallulah put up a brave front. "I detest the theater, *dahlings*," she told reporters.

When Tennessee heard that, he differed. "Tallulah loves the theater with so much of her heart that, in order to protect her heart, she has to say that she hates it. But we know better when we see her on stage."

The failure of *Milk Train* had a lot to do with the lack of interest from audiences in the mid-1960s. They didn't want to line up at the box office to see a play with mystical overtones that asked them to contemplate an aging dowager's morbid obsession with her own impending death.

Milk Train has never died. In England, as late as 1994, actor Rupert Everett, in drag, played Flora Goforth.

Tallulah kept her promise and never spoke to Richardson again, even when he approached her one night at a party in Manhattan. She snubbed him brusquely.

The bisexual actor and director never repaired his marriage to Vanessa Redgrave, and she divorced him in 1967. In 1991, at the age of sixty-three, he died of AIDS in Los Angeles.

[In all, Tennessee had tried to get Tallulah to appear in at least six of his plays, beginning with his early version of Battle of Angels *and moving on through* The Glass Menagerie *and* A Streetcar Named Desire.

Unknown to most film and theater goers, he'd also tried to get her to star in two others of his dramas, not just The Milk Train Doesn't Stop Here Anymore. *Like her role as Flora Goforth, he wanted her to portray aging actresses.*

When she'd been performing as Blanche DuBois in Streetcar *at the City Center, he'd approached her, asking if she'd consider playing Mrs. Karen Stone, a retired actress, in the film version of his short novel,* The Roman Spring of Mrs. Stone.

Performances We Wish We'd Heard

Tallulah Bankhead *(right)* interprets a radio script with **Laurence Olivier** and **Vivien Leigh**

343

She had read the novella, but refused any involvement in any possible film adaptation. The 1961 role went instead to Vivien Leigh, cast opposite Warren Beatty, who played an Italian gigolo.

Tennessee had also offered Tallulah the role of Alexandra Del Lago in his memorable Sweet Bird of Youth. *Along with Paul Newman, Geraldine Page played that part in the 1962 movie version. Tennessee's interest in Tallulah's involvement in that play was mostly confined to the 1959 stage version of* Sweet Bird *on Broadway.*

She was tempted to embrace the play but rejected the offer because she was already committed to star in another play, Crazy October, *whose script had been written by James Leo Herlihy, her best friend. Estelle Winwood was in the play, as well as Joan Blondell. The producer, Walter Starcke, closed this campy play in San Francisco, not daring to send it to Broadway, where he had had much success with Christopher Isherwood's* I Am a Camera, *starring Julie Harris.]*

The last meeting between Tallulah and Tennessee came at a dinner party in Manhattan in 1965. "We had a wonderful time talking about those people we had either loved or hated," Tennessee said. "When it came time to say goodbye, we hugged and kissed. At that time, because of the excessive amount of libations consumed, both of us were feeling no pain. I hugged her longer than usual, perhaps realizing that it was for the last time."

In her final words, to him, she said, "Tennessee, you and I are the only consistently High Episcopalians I know."

That unlikely sentence marked the final words of her convoluted, tormented relationship with one of the most volatile personalities of the American Theater.

As he helped her into her limousine, he said, "If you or I have any lingering regrets, it's because neither of us got to bed Tab Hunter." She cackled as he shut the door on her.

To him, her limousine evoked a hearse. "It was the Black Maria that will soon be coming for me," he said.

Did She Become a Caricature of Her Own Sense of Camp?

Tallulah *(center)* performs in yet another disastrous play, *Crazy October*, with **Estelle Winwood** *(left)* and **Joan Blondell** (right)

344

Chapter Twenty-Three

Truman Beats the Devil, Gets Macho With Bogie, & Sleeps with Huston

A Screwball Cast Assembles in Ravello to Make a Screwball Picture

"Filming *Beat the Devil* was a hell of a lark," said its director, **John Huston**, who's in the sedan chair in the photo above. The creator of the film's nutty dialogue, **Truman Capote**, is hauling the director across a location somewhere in Ravello, a town later favored by Gore Vidal.

The stars of the picture included **Humphrey Bogart** and **Gina Lollobrigida** *(in upper left photo)*, and **Jennifer Jones** *(in lower left photo)*, during one of her brief reigns as a blonde.

In the film community's glory days of the early

1950s, Rome was known as "Hollywood on the Tiber." It seemed that every movie producer was in town either shooting a movie or selling one. At night, you could see Frank Sinatra, Elizabeth Taylor, *et al,* parading up and down the Via

Veneto to the delight of aggressive *paparazzi*.

In 1952, Carson McCullers and her husband, Reeves McCullers, were in town but not speaking to Truman Capote. He was there with his lover, Jack Dunphy. Once when the two couples encountered each other on the Via Veneto, each turned their head in the other direction.

Both had made scalding remarks about each other to their mutual friend Tennessee. "Capote exists in an extended state of faggotry, parroting my writing style," Carson charged.

Seriously Pissed-Off Southerners

Carson and **Reeves McCullers**. She'd just learned that Truman Capote had seduced her husband.

In retaliation, he defined her as "The eternal Muff-Diver, but then what is a poor, ugly, buck-toothed woman to do when married to a self-admitted homosexual?"

Carson had had many reasons for disliking Truman. They involved more than professional jealousy. She had discovered that he had had a secret affair with Reeves. And Truman had taken over a script-writing assignment that had initially been hers.

David O. Selznick was like a mother hen protecting the image of his wife, Jennifer Jones. He'd hired Carson to write the original script of *Stazione Termini* (1954), a film that would star Jones with Montgomery Clift, with whom Truman was having an affair.

[For its release in America, it was retitled Indiscretions of an American Housewife.*]*

After Selznick loudly and aggressively announced his dislike of Carson's script, he had hired Truman to replace her.

Around the same time, John Huston flew to Italy to direct *Beat the Devil* (1953), an offbeat movie that would star not only Jones, but Humphrey Bogart and Gina Lollobrigida, with the understanding that Carson would write the script. Huston may not have known that Selznick had fired Carson as scriptwriter for *Stazione Termini,* and that she'd failed miserably in her attempt to deliver anything resembling a film script.

Huston had acquired the rights to Claud Cockburn's novel, *Beat the Devil.* *[Cockburn had written it under the pseudonym "James Helvick." During the Red Scare launched by Senator Joseph McCarthy, he had been accused of being a Communist.]*

Bogie to Truman: "I told you not to swallow!"

346

Carson was determined not to fail in her second scriptwriting assignment. She wrote to Tennessee, "I'll show that little shit, Capote, which one of us is the real scriptwriter."

As scriptwriter for *Beat the Devil,* Carson had been Huston's third choice. He turned first to a New Yorker, Anthony Veiller, who would in time write 41 movie scripts from 1934 to 1964. He'd twice been nominated for Oscars for best screenplay, beginning in 1937 with *Stage Door,* starring Katharine Hepburn and Ginger Rogers, and in 1946, John Huston's *The Killers,* an adaptation of a short story by Ernest Hemingway. Veiller had just finished working with Huston on *Moulin Rouge* (1952), with José Ferrer and Zsa Zsa Gabor.

Perhaps not letting Veiller know, Huston also asked Peter Viertel to draft his own version of a scenario for *Beat the Devil.*

In Africa, Viertel had made *The African Queen* (1951) with Humphrey Bogart and Katharine Hepburn. In time, he would write a novel, *White Hunter, Black Heart,* a thinly disguised portrait of Huston while they were making the film.

[Viertel's looks and personality were the inspiration for Robert Redford's Waspish character, Hubbell Gardiner, in The Way We Were *(1974), with Barbra Streisand.]*

What's a Man to Do?

Bogie is caught between an inveterate liar (played by **Jennifer Jones,** *left)* and **Gina Lollobrigida** *(right).*

In the film, Lollobrigida's character is making overtures to Jennifer's husband, a dim-witted and bogus English peer.

When the completed scripts arrived at Huston's manse in Ireland, he could not finish reading either of them, as he later confessed to Bogie in Hollywood. "They stink," the actor said. "Get someone new, someone different, who can handle material like this."

That had led to Huston's unusual hiring of Carson McCullers, who accepted the job mainly because she needed the money. Privately, she admitted, "The material is as far from my own sphere of interest as Jupiter from Mars."

[Ironically, Huston would, more than a dozen years later, film Carson's third novel, Reflections in a Golden Eye *(1967), starring Elizabeth Taylor and Marlon Brando.]*

"The third script for *Beat the Devil* wasn't even a script," Huston said. He immediately fired Carson. One afternoon, he met with Selznick, who was visiting Rome to check up on his wife, whom he'd been told had fallen in love with the gay actor, Montgomery Clift.

Selznick reported to Huston the fine work Truman had done on *Stazione Termini* and suggested that the director hire him.

Actually, Huston had met Truman once before in New York at a party given

347

by Bennett Cerf, the publisher of Random House.

"He was the only man I'd ever seen attired in a velvet suit," Huston recalled. "It would have been a very easy thing to have laughed at him, if it had been anyone except Truman. I immediately fell for him—it didn't take me five minutes to be won over completely. He had a charm that was, to coin a phrase, 'ineffable.' He exerted that charm freely."

Before leaving Rome, Huston asked Truman for dinner. He showed up with his lover, Jack Dunphy. Huston was a well known homophobe, but Truman's effeminate mannerisms were of less importance to him than his wit and charm.

At dinner, Truman did an impersonation of Carson when Selznick had demanded to check on her work to that point on the script for *Stazione Termini*. Mimicking her Georgia accent with devastating accuracy, Truman mocked her. "Now just you hold onto your grasshopper a minute, David, while I go for a look-see. It's like finding a mouse in a barnful of newly mown hay. But I just know—as God is my witness—I just know that god damn script is somewhere heah. Doggone it, it must be under the bed. That's where Reeves hides out when I need to get fucked, which he never does. Too busy out cruising the boys in the streets of Rome at night. I swear on my left sugartit the script is hiding here. I'd better check the bathroom. I was reading it on the can. These pastas of Rome give me the runs."

When Selznick fired her, Carson complained to Tennessee, "That Selznick—what an ugly beast—came galloping into Rome and trampled me to death like a herd of stampeding buffalo."

Even so, she told him she'd made enough money to return to Paris. "Our housekeeper there, a direct descendant of Genghis Khan, has gone quite mad and is roaming the streets of Paris in a see-through *négligée.*"

After his fifth whiskey and three brandies with Huston, Truman agreed to take over Carson's scriptwriting job—"*Once again, my dear*"—and write *Beat the Devil,* which had already been scheduled for shooting in Ravello, south of Naples on the Amalfi Coast. Ironically, this town would become the future abode of Truman's nemesis, Gore Vidal.

Huston told Truman that he wanted the film to be a spoof of his early masterpiece, *The Maltese Falcon (released in 1941 as the first movie Huston directed),* which had also starred Bogie.

Truman already knew Jennifer, but he learned that other actresses had been considered for the role, including Jean Simmons and Audrey Hepburn. Bogie had recommended Lauren Bacall, but she'd signed to play one of the gold diggers in *How to Marry a Millionaire* (1953), co-starring Marilyn Monroe and Betty Grable.

Truman arrived in Ravello on a cold day in winter. He was wearing a red overcoat that came down to his ankles, accessorized with a ten-foot lavender-colored scarf. He was introduced to the supporting cast, which included the Italian bombshell, Gina Lollobrigida, Robert Morley, and Peter Lorre. Truman would record his impressions of the cast members in his journals.

Huston had told Truman that he'd wanted Sydney Greenstreet for the Morley role, but the character actor, who had retired in 1952, was desperately ill. He died in January of 1954.

Huston was somewhat reluctant to introduce Truman to Bogie. The actor defined anybody he disliked as "a fag." To Huston's surprise, Bogie bonded with Truman and soon was calling him "Caposy."

Bogie liked him so much, that Huston, in front of the crew, staged a mock fight. "He's mine, you bitch," Huston shouted at Bogie.

"You might have seen him first, but he swore on a stack of bibles that I'm better in bed than you are," Bogie shot back.

Bogie wrote to Bacall, "Capote is the kind of guy you want to put in your pocket and take home."

Huston liked Truman so much, he moved him into his private hotel suite, which caused the cast and crew to assume they were having an affair. Bogie spread the word that he was walking past their bedroom at night "I could hear Caposy screaming in ecstasy as John fucked him."

Truman complained to friends in Hollywood. "Bogie and John will be the death of me. They've nearly killed me with their dissipations. Half drunk all day and dead drunk at night. Once, believe it or not, I came around to wake up Bogie at six o'clock in the morning, as he had an early call. I found King Farouk of Egypt dancing the hula-hula in the middle of the floor."

He revealed that Jack Dunphy had fled to Naples, as he couldn't take it any more. "At least Jack will find diversions there. Naples has hordes of beautiful boys, all with olive skins and cocks the color of gold."

Although Truman was writing fresh pages of dialogue every day, he could also be a prankster. John Barry Ryan, who was assisting in the direction of the picture, said that Huston picked up a piano player in Rome, asking him if he spoke English. His answer was "yes." Consequently, Huston cast him as the purser. But soonafter, it was determined that the only English-language word the piano player knew was "yes."

After hearing this, Truman crafted the purser's spectacularly convoluted opening line: "Mr. Danruther, the captain of the *S. S. Niagara* presents his compliments and wants and wishes to inform you that owing to the failures of the oil pump, the sailing will be delayed."

Huston spent three days trying to extract those phrases from the lips of the piano player. "He never got it right," Ryan said.

The script centered around the piratical adventures of a motley crew of swindlers and ne'er-do-wells, each trying to lay claim to land rich in uranium deposits in Kenya. They are waiting for transport from a small port in southern Italy, where they plan to travel on an ill-fated steamer en route to Mombasa. The movie emerged as a parody of *film noir,* a style of movie-making that Huston himself had pioneered.

As the days proceeded, Truman became familiar with the major cast members. When he'd met Peter Lorre, the actor had grabbed Truman, locked him in a bear hug, and then stuck his tongue down Truman's throat. Huston told Truman, "That's just Peter's way of showing you that he has no prejudice against homosexuals."

Lorre had become familiar to American audiences after Fritz Lang had cast him as a child killer in the controversial 1931 movie *M.* When the Nazis came to power in Germany, Lorre, a Jew, had fled to Hollywood.

Today, he is best remembered for playing Ugarte opposite Bogie in *Casablanca* (1942).

Robert Morley was well aware of the eccentricities of both Huston and Bogie, having recently filmed *The African Queen* (1951) with them. According to Truman, "Morley was given an ungainly bulk, thick lips, a triple chin, bushy eyebrows, and he comes on like a pompous windbag. Yet with all these drawbacks, he's the best character actor to emerge from Britain. He and I engaged in a battle of wits, vying for the title of Queen of Repartée."

Like Truman, Morley had his own opinions about the other cast members. He told Truman, "Bogie is a nice man, but not much brain, really. As for Lorre, I always thought he was a rather unpleasant character, an unlovely man in every way. Have you seen him? He's hideous. He went to this homosexual hairdresser and got that excuse for a coiffure of his dyed blonde."

Beat the Devil was the first American film to star the Italian sex goddess, Gina Lollobrigida, who vied with Sophia Loren for roles. Before filming began, Loren told the press in Rome, "Gina's personality is limited. She is good playing a peasant, but is incapable of playing a lady."

In tribute to her physical assets, the French coined the term *"Lollobrigidienne"* to mean curvaceous.

Bogie told Truman he didn't like Gina very much, "but then, I was never a tits man. She makes Marilyn Monroe look like Shirley Temple."

"When I met Gina, she was married to this Slovenian doctor, Milko Skofic," Truman said. "I met him, but didn't understand why she'd married him. Perhaps his clothing concealed some hidden talent."

"I kept abreast of Gina as the years went by," he said. "I know she had an affair with Dr. Christiaan Barnard, that famous heart transplant surgeon from South Africa. He looked hot. She should have married him. John thought Gina looked like an apartment building with balconies—that John!"

In later years, Truman heard a rumor that Gina had seduced Fidel Castro

Gina Lollobrigida was cast as **Humphrey Bogart's** two-timing wife. Huston and Bogie called her "Lola Frigidaire."

when she became a photojournalist. She scooped other members of the press by obtaining an exclusive interview with him.

"Gina and Tennessee Williams are the only two people I know who managed to seduce Fidel," Truman told anyone who would listen.

"I never bonded with Jennifer Jones, although I wrote two of her scripts," Truman said. "She took her marching orders from David Selznick. Every day, at least five yellow pages of notes arrived from Selznick in Hollywood, instructing all of us what to do with Jennifer. When not before the camera, she spent most of her time running from this aggressive Neapolitan lesbian who looked like Anna Magnani on a bad hair day."

"In Rome, I did have a talk with David about his wife," Truman claimed. "Other than *Gone With the Wind,* his big epic was *Duel in the Sun* (1946), in which he'd cast Jennifer opposite Gregory Peck. He told me he'd patched together just the love scenes of Peck with Jennifer. He said that on some dark nights, he had them screened, 'during which time I jerk off,' he confessed to me."

During the course of the shoot, Truman invited the fashion maven, Carmel Snow, to visit the set. She was horrified at the dresses worn in their scenes by Jennifer and Gina. She immediately telephoned Paris and asked her new discovery, Hubert de Givenchy, to fly at once to Naples, where he was met by limousine and driven to Ravello, where he proceeded to redesign the costumes for the film's two female stars. *[Carmel Snow was the editor of the American edition of* Harper's Bazaar *from 1934 to 1958 and for many years, the chairperson of that magazine's editorial board.]*

The cast was surprised when "the fag hater," Huston, had moved Truman into his suite. His excuse was that he and Truman often worked throughout the night preparing dialogue for the scenes scheduled for filming the next morning.

"We hoped the company wouldn't know of our desperation," Huston said. "How close the dragon was breathing on our necks."

Truman later claimed that he was the sole author of the script. "John was often drinking and playing cards with Bogie. He was like Irving Berlin who had the little nigger boy in the trunk writing all his songs."

[Huston often entertained Truman with tales of his colorful life. In the course of his career, which stretched over half a century, he would receive fifteen Oscar nominations, winning two of them. Before coming to Hollywood, he had been an amateur boxer, a newspaper reporter, a portrait artist, in Paris, a cavalry rider in Mexico, and a documentary filmmaker during World War II. Author Ian Freer defined him as "cinema's Ernest Hemingway, a director who has never been afraid to tackle tough issues head on."]

Truman shared his opinion of Huston to anyone in the cast or on the crew willing to listen. "He's a classic seducer," Truman said. "His eyes are ungentle, as bored as a sunbathing lizard. He's a man of obsession rather than passion. He's a romantic cynic who believes that all endeavor, virtuous or evil, is simply plodding along, a check in the amount of zero."

"John was a mess," Truman confessed to friends. "In our suite, he always walked around in the nude, perhaps believing that the sight of his withered cock would drive me into wild passion. I've seen bigger and better. Often, he couldn't sleep and kept me up all night. The only way I could get him to sleep was to get him so drunk he passed out. He'd lie in the center of bed stark naked. 'Go to it, kid,' he'd instruct me. That was a laugh. He couldn't even get it up."

"We had an electric heater in our room. One night, he woke up at three o'clock and staggered toward the bathroom to take a horse piss. He tripped over the electric heater and started a fire. I shouted to him, 'Our room's on fire!' He shot back, 'Good, I've always liked the smell of smoke.' Thank God for Bogie. He came to our rescue."

One afternoon on the set, Truman did not show up with the anticipated pages of rewritten dialogue. One of the cast members told Huston "the little guy went down to Amalfi on the coast."

Huston went after him, finding him in a bar, getting drunk with a roster of A-list visitors. "I couldn't believe my eyes," Huston said. "There sat Capote entertaining Ingrid Bergman, Roberto Rossellini, Orson Welles, and George Sanders. Did I leave out a young filmmaker, Stephen Sondheim, who was in the area making a documentary?"

For the most part, Huston was enthralled with Truman's dialogue.

So was Bogie. "Line after line was pure Truman," he said.

Jennifer played a chronic liar in the film. Before one of her utterances, Truman had her say, "In point of fact..."

On another occasion, Morley, followed by his band of rapscallions, appears on deck, looking out at the ocean. "Take deep breaths," he tells his evil coven. "Every breath is a guinea *[a pound and a shilling]* in the bank of health."

The picture shut down when Truman had to rush back to Rome to face a perceived emergency in his apartment. He had a pet raven whom he'd named Lola. When he called his housekeeper, he asked her to put the receiver up to the bird so that the raven could hear his voice and talk back. No sounds emerged from the other end of the phone line. With alarm, Truman told Huston, "Lola is either sick or sulking. I've got to leave at once for Rome."

Once inside his apartment, he found out why Lola wasn't talking to him. Prior to his first "non-conversation" with the bird, the maid had left the window open, and the raven had flown away. "For me," said a sad-eyed Truman, "It was Bye Bye Blackbird."

Back in Ravello, mourning the loss of his pet, Truman returned to writing the script. But three nights later, when Huston came back to their suite, he found the writer's face swollen to twice its normal size. Truman was suffering from an impacted wisdom tooth. Huston called an ambulance to take him to a hospital in Naples. On the way out the door, Truman shouted back at Huston, "My shawl, my shawl! I can't go without my shawl!" Jennifer had presented him with a Balmain shawl, which he wore everywhere.

***

An arm-wrestling contest between Truman and Bogie became the fodder for an underground legend that still persists to this day. In an article in *Vanity Fair,* Lauren Bacall was asked about it.

As anticipated, she denied it, although she would have had no on-site knowledge. "Truman would have wished," she suggested.

One night, Truman attended one of the poker games with Huston, Bogie and two other crew members. When the men tired of poker, Truman challenged Bogie to an arm-wrestling contest. "I'll arm wrestle you in three different contests," Truman said. "If I win all three rounds, you'll have to submit to a blow-job."

"At first, Bogie thought I was joking until he looked into my face and realized I was deadly serious," Truman continued. "Huston and the two other guys urged Bogie to take the challenge. One of the drunks said, 'There's no way in hell this little fag will beat a tough guy like you, Bogie,'"

Bogie was drunk; otherwise, he might not have accepted the challenge. The First Round evolved into a major test of strength between the two men, but suddenly, Truman slammed Bogie's fist against the poker table. Round Two went much the same way, with Truman winning again. The poker players were astonished.

"This is it!" Huston warned Bogie. "If you don't win round three, you're a goner."

The director later recalled, "Truman sounded like a girl, walked like a girl, but when it came to arm wrestling, he was a little bull."

Truman once again won Round Three. Bogie was astonished, but looked as if he had no intention of carrying through with his part of the bargain. He staggered to his feet and headed for the door. Truman followed him and braced his foot behind Bogie before he punched him, sending him crashing to the floor. Truman then seated himself on Bogie's stomach. "A deal is a deal, Rick," Truman said, using the name of the bar owner in *Casablanca.*

Huston told Bogie, "As a man of honor, you must carry through on this commitment."

Finally, Bogie agreed he'd go through with it "if you'll get your ass off me." As he stood up, he looked Truman square in the eye. "I'm imposing one condition, however. Under no circumstances are you to swallow."

"It's not fair to change the deal at the last minute, but okay," Truman said. As he was leaving the room, he winked at Huston, indicating that he had no intention of honoring this last-minute agreement.

"By the time Bogie showed up late on the set the next morning, he had a cut on his lip," Huston said. "I ordered our makeup man to cover it up as best he could. Bogie was angry. He was denouncing Truman. 'That little devil didn't live up to our deal,' he told me."

"You mean, he swallowed?" Huston asked.

"Not only that, but he kept glued to it for another fifteen minutes when he'd drained the last god damn drop, that fucker."

Huston was vastly amused at Truman's physical assault on Bogie. "He put

Bogie on his ass and other unmentionable things," he told his crew.

After the film was wrapped, Huston told Bogie he was abandoning Truman and rushing back to Paris, "and my true love, Suzanne Flon."

But a few days later, Truman learned that instead, Huston had flown to England to "renew his old passion for Olivia de Havilland," who had stopped off in London before flying to the film festival at Cannes.

When most of the cast abandoned Ravello and migrated to London, Huston gave a dinner party for them. He appeared drunk before the meal began. Present were Bogie and Lauren Bacall. Huston attacked their left-wing politics. Gina was there, with her physician husband, Milko Skofic. Huston contemptuously called him, "a phony doctor." Then he attacked Gina, telling her that, "with all your beauty, you're probably a lousy lay."

He also announced at table that Truman was "the world's best cocksucker. But I think it is unforgivable to be a homosexual. I can say it! I'm not able to deal with homosexuals, except for Truman. But he's from another planet. Venus, I figure."

Later, when Bogie and Truman returned to Hollywood, he introduced him to his wife. Bacall defined the burgeoning friendship between Bogie and Truman as "the unlikeliest couple in the world. Truman was infectious because of his incredible brain and wit. This was before any of the bad stuff happened to him."

Beat the Devil failed at the box office. A lot of its audiences walked out. Many movie goers didn't understand it.

It fared better as time went by. Critic Roger Ebert claimed that *Beat the Devil* was the first camp movie.

A decade after its release, critic Pauline Kael wrote: "*Beat the Devil* is a mess, but it's probably the funniest mess—the screwball classic—of all time. It kidded itself, yet it succeeded in some original (and perhaps dangerously marginal) way of finding a style of its own."

Time magazine defined it as a screwball classic. As late as 1975, Charles Champlin, film critic at *The Los Angeles Times,* wrote: "However antic and loopy the circumstances of its making may be, *Beat the Devil* holds up as a fast and disciplined comedy, with a richness of invention which even now, after fifteen or twenty viewings, I find astonishing."

The copyright on *Beat the Devil* was not renewed, and it is today in the public domain.

Right before his death from cancer in 1957, Bogie issued his own critique: "Only phonies will like it."

In his future, Huston would become involved in creative projects with the other two members of "The Pink Triangle," playing Buck Loner in Gore Vidal's *Myra Breckinridge* and directing Ava Gardner and Richard Burton in Tennessee Williams' *The Night of the Iguana.*

Chapter Twenty-Four

Where Prostitutes Were Named After Flowers

Truman's All-Black Cast Mambos Its Way to Broadway

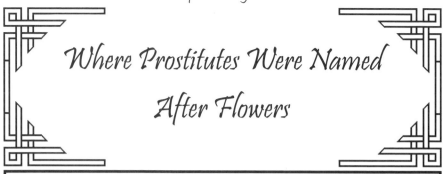

Black stars rule a Haitian world of prostitution and voodoo magic in the Broadway adaptation of Truman Capote's novella, *House of Flowers.* On the left, the talented dancer, **Geoffrey Holder**, portrays a witch doctor to **Diahann Carroll's** take as Ottilie, a symbol of Caribbean senuality, yet unsoiled in her innocence.

On the far right, **Pearl Bailey**—*"There's no one as good as me, honey"*—dominates the stage as Madame Fleur, who lost her virginity before she turned twelve.

It all began in 1948, when Truman organized a vacation in the Caribbean to celebrate his success as a novelist after the publication of *Other Voices, Other Rooms.*

Based on the increasing fame of Haiti among the avant-garde *[and the growing cognizance of its role as the cradle of Caribbean art]*, *Harper's Bazaar* commissioned some of the costs of Truman's trip to Port-au-Prince, Haiti's capital, where he worked on a travel article. That article later evolved into a short story, which he entitled "House of Flowers."

In the wake of his discovery that local nightlife didn't really exist in Haiti in any format he understood, he began to visit the local brothels, many of which were positioned amidst lush foliage on Bizonton Road.

Although he wasn't particularly interested in seducing any of the local prostitutes, he found them charming, *piquante,* coquettish, and fascinating, and he enjoyed their company. Most of them sat on rocking chairs waiting for customers to come along, an occasional black man but more often white foreign tourists, usually from either France or the United States.

Café society: In 1955, at the Blue Angel in New York City, a very gay **Truman Capote** entertains heiress **Gloria Vanderbilt** *(left)* and his star, **Pearl Bailey.**

He brought lots of cold beer for the girls to drink and learned that they had each been assigned French-language nicknames based on flowers or flowering shrubs such as Jasmine, Bougainvillea, Pansy, Tulip, Gladiola, and even Wisteria Lilac. The working girls would drink his beer and fan themselves with cardboard-backed illustrations of Jesus Christ.

His favorite of the impoverished city's many bordellos was called "The Paradise" (in English), run by a three-hundred-pound businesswoman, "Madame Fleur." She advertised her establishment as "a place that can satisfy any desire known to man."

Truman wasn't surprised that the *putas* were usually retired by Madame Fleur before they reached the age of twenty. "Most of my customers, especially those from the States, like them young," Madame Fleur told him. "*Très jeune, m'sieur.* In some cases, not even ten. I pick up a lot of kids at the border town, Dajabón."

[Dajabón, a blood-soaked market town on the northern end of Haiti's shared border with the Dominican Republic, with a population of about 10,000, is located on the Djabón River. That waterway is also known as the Fleuve du Masacre *because of its connection to the genocidal Parsley Massacre of an estimated 20 to 30 thousand Haitians ordered by the Dominican dictator, Rafael ("The Goat") Trujillo in 1937.]*

"There's a thriving market in Dajabón for both young boys and girls," she said. "It takes all kinds to make up God's world."

"Right now, I have only one young boy working for me," she said. "But when winter comes and business picks up, I might have three or four." She went into a back room and returned with a little boy who looked no older than ten.

In Haiti, Truman Encounters the Caribbean's Ultimate Stud

"He was slender, with large brown eyes, rather frightened," Truman said. "He seemed traumatized and, in spite of his profession, was very shy, afraid really. He wore a sleeveless undershirt, and there were bruises on his arms and back."

"His name was Juan, and he greedily devoured the candy I gave him," Truman said. "I made it clear to *Madame* that I was not a child molester. 'I much prefer Mandingos,' I told her."

"Well, I have plenty of those I can round up," she said. "Just give me the preferred height, weight, and the size of the whanger preferred—inches, not centimeters. I can round up what you want by midnight, even if I have to drag the stud from the bed of his wife."

"Not tonight, Joséphine," he answered.

"*M'sieur,* my name is not Josephine," she said. "If you must call me by my first name, it's Rosa. I was a working girl myself until I turned twenty and put on all this fat."

She looked down at Juan. "His mother died and he went to live with his grandmother, who didn't want him, She sold him to me for fifty U.S. dollars. For one of my girls for an hour, I charge tourists five dollars. Unless he's a Haitian man, and then I charge him only one dollar. Because Juan here is so special, I can ask as much as ten dollars."

In the course of one evening, Truman met the "prettiest girl among a lot of ugly ones in those rocking chairs."

"She was olive-skinned and an import from the old colonial city of Santo Domingo," he said. "She had three gold teeth and five silk dresses. Her name was Ottilie."

"Madame Fleur sold her every night as a virgin," he said. "How she managed to pull that one off I don't know. She said it was a special secret of hers, a secret she'd learned from her voodoo priest."

On another night, Madame Fleur was hysterical. She told Truman that Porfirio Rubirosa was flying in from Santo Domingo (Ciudad Trujillo) to talk with

Porfirio Rubirosa *(left)* married **Doris Duke**, the tobacco heiress and richest woman in the world, but preferred the whores of Haiti. On the right, the murderous dictator of Haiti, **François Duvalier ("Papa Doc")**, sets out with members of his dreaded private paramilitary, the *Tontons Macoutes,* to murder or castrate, or perhaps both, his enemies.

the *[terrifying, to Haitians]* Haitian dictator, François Duvalier.

"There is some shit about a border dispute," she said. "When Monsieur Rubirosa is in town, he always visits my Paradise."

Of course, gossipy Truman was well acquainted with the reputation of the legendary playboy, who had married Doris Duke, the tobacco heiress and the richest woman in the world. Nearly all of the conversation centered on his mammoth penis. His fame was so great that in many restaurants, when a guest wanted a giant peppermill, he told the waiter to bring a "Rubirosa." He was also nicknamed "Rubber Hosa."

He'd once been married to Flor de Oro Trujillo, *Generalissimo* Rafael Trujillo's whorish daughter.

In Hollywood, Rubi's list of sexual conquests had become part of his legend. They included Joan Crawford, Dolores del Rio, Ava Gardner, Susan Hayward, and Veronica Lake. He'd also seduced such prominent personages as Eva Perón, co-dictator of Argentina.

Rubi had once told a reporter, "I consider a day in which I make love only once as virtually wasted."

"I'd love to see that stud in action," Truman told Madame Fleur.

"You can, but it'll cost you twenty dollars," she said. She led him to a dark back room. There was a two-way mirror that opened onto her most elegant boudoir, a room with an elaborately carved four-poster bed.

"Rubi likes to keep the light on, so if you stand here, you'll be able to see everything."

Madame Fleur lived up to her promise. "She arranged for Rubi to seduce three of her youngest and prettiest gals," Truman said. "He put on quite a show—in fact, the best show of my life. The handsome gigolo lived up to his reputation. All the stories about him were true. Three years later, Doris Duke, at a party in the Hamptons, told me that Rubi's penis was the most magnificent she'd ever seen."

[Doris Duke (1912—1993) the America heiress, hedonist, art collector, and philanthropist, was the whimsical, imperious, and autocratic daughter of an almost unimaginably wealthy tobacco tycoon. In the lurid aftermath of her death, she left a fortune estimated at 1.3 billion and a carload of outrageous anecdotes and references.]

"I agree with you," Truman told her.

Duke looked at him. "And how in hell would you know?" Then she brushed aside her question. "Don't tell me. I don't want to know."

Although Truman didn't tell Duke, he announced to the world the size of Rubi's penis. He was quoted in print as saying, "It was six inches in circumference, an eleven-inch octoroon dick." He then whispered an aside. "A skilled fellator such as myself could even get it to stretch two or three more inches."

Truman's whisperings were based on the fact that he later introduced himself to Rubi at Madame Fleur's. Both of them shared a taxi back to the Hotel Oloffson—the best hotel in Port-au-Prince at the time, a seedy 19th-century gingerbread palace evoking something from a Charles Addams fantasy—where they were staying.

The next morning, a maid found Truman in Rubi's bed. Truman later said, "If it were late enough at night, Rubi didn't care what legs were open to him."

The Lavender Hill Mob Descends on Truman in Portofino

Early in 1954, the influential American-born Broadway producer, Albert Saint-Subber, wanted to mount a Broadway play based on Truman's short story, "House of Flowers." After a long confab, Truman agreed. Saint was most persuasive, and he was the "angel with the dough."

[Previously, Saint-Subber had traveled to Taormina (Sicily) to urge Truman to write a stage adaptation of his The Grass Harp, *which had been published in 1951, and eventually adapted into a vehicle for Broadway in 1952. It wasn't until 1995 that* The Grass Harp *appeared as a movie. The cast was more impressive than the drama: Walter Matthau, Jack Lemmon, Sissy Spacek; Charles Durning, Roddy McDowall, and Piper Laurie could not rescue it.]*

From the beginning of the stage adaptation of *House of Flowers*, Truman imposed a lot of demands. He wanted the distinguished English director, Peter Brook, to helm it; Virgil Thomson to write the incidental music, and Cecil Beaton to design the sets and costumes. Both "Saint" *[as Saint-Subber was nicknamed]* and Truman lobbied hard to convince those Silent Screen *duennas,* Dorothy and Lillian Gish, to appear in the lead roles of Dolly and Verena Talbo.

None of those original visions worked. Robert Lewis replaced Brook as director; the Gish sisters gave way to Mildred Natwick and Ruth Nelson. And even though Brooks Atkinson of *The New York Times* interpreted the final product as both "effortless and beautiful," *House of Flowers* never generated much business at the box office.

[Whereas Truman was completely inexperienced in creating a Broadway musical, Saint was very experienced, having previously won a Tony for Kiss Me, Kate, *a musical based on Shakespeare's* Taming of the Shrew. *It ran on Broadway from 1948 to 1951. Later, he'd produce seven Neil Simon plays, including* Barefoot in the Park, *and in 1973, he'd help launch the theatrical version of* Gigi *by Alan Jay Lerner and Frederick Lowe.]*

During the late spring of 1953, Truman and his lover, Jack Dunphy, planned to travel to Positano on the Italian Riviera where Dunphy would try to complete a novel and where it was understood that Truman would begin work on his stage adaptation of *House of Flowers.*

Prior to their departure for Positano, John Malcolm Brinnin, the poet and critic, attended a party that was conceived as both a celebration of Harold Arlen's birthday and a *bon voyage* party for Truman and Dunphy. Arlen, the creator of "Over the Rainbow" for Judy Garland, had agreed to write the musical score for *House of Flowers.*

"I remember Truman sitting on the floor, his head resting, using Arlen's knees as a cushion," Brinnin recalled. "In the corner was Marlene Dietrich encircled by the arms of Montgomery Clift. They were mutually transfixed and exchanged monosyllables now and then. But for the most part, they simply stood there, staring into one another's eyes. Dietrich wore a dress that was less like fabric, more like molten silver. Clift's suit was too big for him."

Once they reached the Italian Riviera, whereas Dunphy liked to be alone most of the time, Truman loved company. In Portofino, there were plenty of famous names with whom to associate, including the port's two most famous residents, Rex Harrison, and his wife, Lilli Palmer. Passing through town was a parade of stylish visitors, including John Gielgud and Truman's friend, Cecil Beaton. A coven of gay couples arrived, including Tennessee and Frank Merlo; Paul Bowles "with some Arab boy;" Noël Coward with Graham Payn; and Hugh (Binkie) Beaumont with John Perry (Gielgud's ex).

Poet and critic **John Malcolm Brinnin,** eventually a resident of Key West during its raunchy, pre-gentrification days, was a longtime confidant of Truman's. Truman even took Brinnan to hear Christine Jorgensen sing.

[*Jorgensen was the ex-G.I. who went to Denmark for a sex change operation that became an international cause célèbre. Brinnan remembered Jorgensen warbling "Getting to Know You" in "a half-croaking voice and moving through an upsy-daisy Patty-cakeman choreography on high heels that seemed about to collapse."*]

Truman labeled these homosexuals "The Lavender Hill Mob." With the exception of the snobby Gielgud—who was turned off by "that ghastly little voice, the world's longest fingernails, and dirty shorts,"—most of them gravitated to Truman.

In letters to friends in the States, Truman had comments about the resort's gaggle of other illustrious visitors. These included the Duke and Duchess of Windsor ("utter morons"); Henry and Clare Luce ("morons plus"), and Laurence Oliver and Vivien Leigh ("Apparently, Scarlett O'Hara has been released from the madhouse"). A surprise visitor was Greta Garbo, "who looked like Death with a suntan."

After Garbo's visit, Truman wrote to one of his best friends, Cecil Beaton, who had returned to New York. Truman fully understood how close Beaton was to Garbo. Nonetheless, he wrote: "Darling Cecil, I'm afraid Greta will never be a satisfactory person because she is so dissatisfied with herself, and dissatisfied people can never be emotionally serious. They simply don't believe in anything—except their own limitations." He later revealed that Garbo had spent most of their time together complaining about a pain in her neck.

[*Truman encountered Garbo again in February of 1955 in New York and wrote to Beaton: "She was looking extremely well—though her hair seemed a peculiar color: a sort of blondish lavender. I think she must have dyed it."*]

Back in Positano that summer of 1953, Truman complained that Noël Coward was trying to steal Jack Dunphy from him.

Eventually bored with Portofino, Truman announced to his friends there that he was leaving for Switzerland to visit Charlie Chaplin and his wife, Oona. She was one of his best friends.

During the Red Scare in America, Chaplin—who had remained a British citizen through the peak of his Hollywood fame—was charged with being a communist. Shortly after that, he flew from semi-retirement in French-speaking Switzerland to London for the premiere of his last American film, *Limelight* (1952). While there, the U.S. State Department told him he would not be allowed to return to the States.

After their visit with the Chaplins, Truman, with Dunphy, flew to Paris, where he found the city "dull and yellow" at that time of year.

In November of 1953, Truman wrote to his scholarly former lover, Newton Arvin, of John Gielgud's arrest, in October of that year, in London. An undercover police officer had apprehended Gielgud in a men's toilet in Chelsea, based on a charge of sexual solicitation of a male.

Truman called it "a dreadful rumpus over gents who interfere with gents. I'm terribly fond of John, and I talked with him on the phone last week. He seemed to be bearing up with a good deal of bravery and style. Still, it was a shocking thing to happen, malicious and stupid."

At his hotel, Truman was summoned to the phone. "It's Mr. Sister," Dunphy said. He and Truman always referred to Reeves McCullers as "Mr. Sister," because he had confessed to them that he was a homosexual.

On the phone, Reeves seemed on the verge of a nervous breakdown. He told Truman that his wife, Carson McCullers, had flown back to New York, leaving him with no money. Truman invited him for dinner, but he never showed up.

The next morning, he learned that Reeves had committed suicide by overdosing on liquor and barbiturates. Truman was among the handful of guests who attended his funeral in Paris, although he'd requested to be buried in Georgia.

Bad news came in pairs. Shortly after that, Truman received a call from New York, informing him that his mother, Nina Capote, had also committed suicide.

He decided to fly back for his mother's burial, leaving Dunphy and his dogs in Paris, where it was understood that they'd later catch a ship back to the Port of New York.

On the pier, as Truman told Dunphy goodbye, he lamented, "My youth is gone."

Truman Capote's friendship with **Greta Garbo** was not very widely publicized. At one point in 1949, he was going to travel to Paris with her for her comeback picture, its plot based on Balzac's 1834 novel, *La Duchesse de Langeais*. But the deal fell through.

***

After the failure of *House of Flowers* on Broadway,

Truman was not interested in continuing friendships with its cast and crew. However, he did maintain a relationship with its set designer, Oliver Messel. *[In the spring of 1960, Messel's nephew, Anthony Armstrong-Jones, became the Earl of Snowdon based on his marriage to Princess Margaret.]*

In London, Truman dined with Messel and his Danish companion, Vagn Riis-Hansen. In the aftermath, he wrote Cecil Beaton, fully aware that Beaton and Messel were bitter rivals.

"Darling Cecil, I dined with Oliver and his dear friend, a Dane. They were thrilled—absolutely thrilled—to be given 10,000 pounds to do Liz's clothes for *Cleopatra*."

[At the time, in 1963, Elizabeth Taylor and Richard Burton were in Rome, filming the horrifically expensive Cleopatra. *Later, in Rome, the epic film's director, Joseph Mankiewicz, fired Messel from any further association with* Cleopatra's *costumes and set designs.]*

When he later met with Beaton in New York, Truman claimed that because of Messel's new links, through his nephew, to Buckingham Palace, and because of Truman's friendship with him, "I expect the gates of Buckingham Palace will be open to me as well. So far, the queen—perhaps the poor dear has forgotten—hasn't invited me for tea. But it's only a matter of time. I'm sure she admires my work."

"Through Oliver, I was invited to this swanky party in Mayfair," Truman continued. "I met Prince Philip, who practically drooled over me. That man, I'm sure, has the hots for me. If he ever gets me alone, I know—*I just know*—that he'll rape me, and I will be forced to give in to his demands. The word around London is that Philip is extremely well hung. I can't wait to be deflowered, like one of my gals in *House of Flowers*."

Although Haitian whorehouses were not his *forte*. **Oliver Messel** *(photo above)*, England's most acclaimed theatrical designer, agreed to create the sets for Truman's *House of Flowers*.

His usual commissions involved designing and decorating houses for über-jaded and über-famous owners of homes in the U.K., Barbados, or the Caribbean Island of Mustique, where Princess Margaret maintained a vacation home.

In Messel, Truman found "a man after my own heart—we're two bitches in heat ready to set the world on fire."

Even the celebrated choreographer, **George Balanchine**, couldn't rescue *House of Flowers*, a play that never burst into bloom in spite of all the international talent that contributed to it.

"What is this thing called a mambo?" he asked.

Marlene Dietrich Lip-Locks with Pearl Bailey

In Manhattan, in 1954, *House of Flowers* was ready to go into production. Saint *[its producer]* and Truman huddled together to select its creative team and to cast it. Once again, Truman wanted Peter Brook, the English *Wünderkind,* to direct. *[Previously, he'd wanted him to direct* The Grass Harp, *but didn't get him.]*

As Saint and Truman were soon to discover, whereas Brook vividly understood how to direct virtually any play by Shakespeare, he was utterly lost in his attempts to direct a musical, especially one with an all-black cast. In England, he'd successfully directed such plays as *Romeo and Juliet* and *Love's Labour's Lost.* He had also directed productions at the Royal Opera House in Covent Garden, including the staging of Strauss's *Salome* with sets by Salvador Dalí. He'd also staged Puccini's *La Bohème* using sets created in 1899.

[In time, Brook would become famous for staging the controversial and very avant-garde work of the Franco-Greek playwright and laudanum addict, Antonin Artaud and his Theater of Cruelty. A prime example included the London premiere of Artaud's The Spurt of Blood.

Before coming to Broadway, Brook had directed John Gielgud in both The Winter's Tale *and* Measure for Measure. *None of this prepared him for what he'd encounter on Broadway, including Truman Capote, whose voice and effeminate mannerisms struck him as "peculiar."]*

Oliver Messel, the world's most acclaimed theatrical designer, agreed to design both the sets and costumes. Harold Arlen had already signed to write the play's musical score. As the crowning gem of *House of Flowers'* A-list associates, the great George Balanchine eventually signed on to choreograph the play's dance numbers.

Both Brook and Truman agreed that Pearl Bailey should play the lead, Madame Fleur, who ran the play's namesake bordello..

[Bailey had made her Broadway debut in 1946 in St. Louis Woman. *In 1968, Bailey would win a Tony Award for her starring role in an all-black production of* Hello, Dolly! *A staunch Republican, she would be appointed in 1970 as "America's Ambassador of Love" by President Richard Nixon.]*

Before casting even began, Truman was a bit taken back by Brook, who seemed apprehensive. "I am not familiar with people of the Negro race. Do they require any special handling?"

"I didn't know what to make of Truman Capote," **Pearl Bailey** said. "He prances into the theater wearing this large black hat more suitable to a witch and this huge black cape far too big for him. He looked like an old fashioned villain in some silent screen movie from the 20s. But he turned out to be a doll compared to our director, who threatened to send us back to Africa if we didn't get our numbers right."

363

Both Brook and Truman were surprised, even shocked, when Marlene Dietrich constantly showed up backstage, practically serving as Bailey's wardrobe mistress during the short run of the play.

As Marlene Dietrich's biographer, Steven Bach, wrote: "Marlene found time to make a few recordings of songs by Harold Arlen, on whom she doted and who doted back. She served as den mother and charlady for the cast of *House of Flowers* when it was in trouble out of town, advising Pearl Bailey to wear on stage jewelry of big rhinestones, not small diamonds. She rushed to Arlen's bedside when he was hospitalized in New York, persuading the police department that her missions of mercy to the man who wrote 'Stormy Weather' required an escort complete with screaming sirens."

Truman was at least mildly surprised when he walked into Bailey's dressing room and discovered Marlene and Bailey in a passionate lip-lock. He excused himself for intruding and departed. Later, he told Saint that "if Tallulah Bankhead can seduce Hattie McDaniel, then Marlene is entitled to Pearl."

Brook, Truman, and Saint rounded up the best black performers in New York, mainly dancers. These included Alvin Ailey; Carmen Da Lavallade and her husband, Geoffrey Holder; and Arthur Mitchell. Juanita Hall, who had leaped to fame as Bloody Mary in the Broadway version of *South Pacific,* was selected to play the pugnacious madam of a rival bordello. The beautiful Diahann Carroll was cast in the role of the play's love interest, Ottilie.

The Trinidad-born painter and dancer, Geoffrey Holder remembered meeting Truman at the time of the cast's first script reading. "He carried a large bouquet of red roses. Hopping, skipping, jumping around the theater, he gave each of us a rose. 'Pearl, a rose for you, *Dahhanne [Diahann Carroll]*, honey, a rose for you.' It was all so sweet—like a little elf."

Immediately, the show ran into trouble. Balanchine was not familiar with Caribbean dance traditions. "It took him hours until we finally figured out that he wanted us to do the

"During **Marlene Dietrich**'s affair with Pearl Bailey, she mothered both of us," Truman recalled. "After the show, she'd invite us back to her apartment, where she made the most divine omelettes for us. I'd leave at around one in the morning, letting Pearl and Marlene enjoy a sleepover.

"For a brief time, Pearl and Marlene were known along Broadway as the odd couple. But in show business, all sexual combinations are possible."

The performers in *House of Flowers,* especially Pearl Bailey, claimed that its director, **Peter Brook,** "treated us like slaves on the plantation. He knew Shakespeare, and he could direct Gielgud, but he was not the man to put us through our paces."

God damn mambo," Alvin said. "Why didn't he say so in the first place?"

Brook kept addressing the cast as "You People," which they resented. He constantly and loudly reaffirmed that, "I am not prejudiced against African Americans," which elicited a collective groan from the cast.

Herbert Ross replaced Balanchine when he bolted. Ross would go on to greater successes on Broadway, including involvements in both *Funny Lady* with Barbra Streisand, and in *Tovarich* with Vivien Leigh.

He would become more famous in 1988 when he married Lee Radziwill, sister of Jackie Kennedy. Radziwill, for a time, would become Truman's closest friend.

After *House of Flowers'* first tryout in Philadelphia *[November 24, 1954]*, Brook assembled the all-black cast for a meeting:

"Before leaving London, I was told that all you blacks were a lazy, shiftless lot, and that I'd have massive trouble working with you. After watching your performance last night, I think all of you should be sent back to Barbados or Africa, or wherever it is you came from."

In the immediate aftermath of the director's diatribe, Bailey stormed out of the theater, vowing never to speak to Brook again, and the rest of the cast was filled with seething hostility.

As the show limped toward Broadway, Truman told his friend, Brinnin, "*House of Flowers* has become an extended one-woman vaudeville act for Pearl Bailey."

But Arlen remained optimistic, telling Brinnin, "I just love Truman Capote. He's one of the most enchanting souls I've ever encountered."

The songs kept the show going, at least for a while. The audience heard such tunes as "A Sleepin' Bee," "Two Ladies in the Shade of de Banana Tree," "One Man Ain't Quite Enough," and "Don't Like Goodbyes."

On December 30, 1954, *House of Flowers* opened to lukewarm reviews on Broadway. Because of all the big names associated with it, and the music, it ran for 165 performances.

Dancer **Alvin Ailey** was broke throughout most of his life. When he was one of the co-stars in *House of Flowers,* it would be beyond his imagination that one day a street in New York would be named in his honor, and that a dance troupe would be established in his name.

Two talented dancers, **Carmen Da Lavallade** and **Geoffrey Holder,** fell in love and got married, one of the better things that spun out of *House of Flowers.*

Truman had assured them that their appearances in his play would make each of them an overnight sensation.

Nevertheless, it was still viewed as a failure. Messel's "wild and wonderful" sets came in for some of the highest praise. Critics also praised Arlen's music, but attacked Truman's script.

"It's one of those shows where everything seems to have gone wrong," wrote Walter Kerr in the *New York Herald Tribune.*

Truman was also attacked for being "a clumsy lyricist and an even worse librettist." Other critics found the show "as funny as an ingrown toenail." Yet another wrote, "There was too much gilding of the lily—too much manner for the matter."

Many found racist overtones in the show, which some people claimed depicted black people as stupid.

After reading the reviews, a drunken Truman called Saint at around three o'clock in the morning. "The fault is Pearl Bailey. We should replace her with somebody…help me name someone."

"Eartha Kitt, perhaps," Saint said. "She looks like she knows her way around a whorehouse."

"I think we should give it to a white Broadway musical star—take Mary Martin, for example. She could appear in blackface."

Despite Truman's drunken (and terrible) idea, Pearl Bailey retained her starring role until the end of the run.

Before departing for Europe, Truman assembled the cast and sang to them.

> *"My house is made of flowers,*
> *and fireflies climbed into my dome."*

House of Flowers, which would later be revived, is remembered today as one of Broadway's legendary failures, where great talents didn't manage to create the masterpiece that it could have been.

A 2003 review by critic John Kenrick stated, "It's high time that musical theater buffs stopped pretending that *House of Flowers* is a theatrical gem. After several disastrous productions, it is pretty clear that this musical stinks—and it always has."

Chapter Twenty-Five

Gore & Howard Austen

What Is This Thing Called Love?

Spying on Jackie Kennedy and FDR, Jr., and Pimping for Princess Margaret

"In my search for a lifetime mate, I found him in **Howard Austen** *(left photo above)*," Gore Vidal said. "It was at a gay bathhouse, the Everard in Manhattan. We made a commitment of friendship to each other--not sexual fidelity--and that commitment lasted for the rest of Howard's life."

"When I purchased **Edgewater** *(right photo, above)*, I planned to live there for the rest of my life. but that was a promise I didn't keep. It was in this house that I launched my political career, running for Congress. I hoped that one day it would lead to the White House. I was hoping to follow in the footsteps of my friend, JFK. He threw his weight behind my campaign, as did Eleanor Roosevelt. But I was in a Republican district, and they didn't like fags."

The most prolific sexual activity experienced by *Howard Austen and Gore Vidal occurred when they moved to Rome in the early 1960s. He was conducting research for his novel* Julian, *published in 1964, the first of what later developed into a series of historical novels.*

The choice spot in those days for picking up hustlers was the Pincio, one of the so-called "Seven Hills of Rome." Many of these handsome young hustlers posed their without their shirts. If they were questioned by the police, they claimed that they were auditioning for artists who daily selected a string of models to pose for the colonies of expatriate artists who had settled in the city, following in the traditions of (but without the talent of) Leonardo da Vinci and Michelangelo.

All that Gore and Austen needed to do was pull up in their Jaguar convertible [it had previously been owned by Robert Wagner], and the young men made themselves readily available, figuring that both Gore and Austen were rich, American, and willing to pay for their favors. Often, during Austen and Gore's seduction, they requested that the man pose, with an erection, for frontally nude photographs. Nearly all of them agreed to do that for an extra twenty dollars.

One summer evening, when the city was overflowing with tourists, many of them gay, Austen estimated that there were more than two hundred men for sale on the hill. "Making a choice was extremely difficult."

***

It was Labor Day, 1950, at the Everard Baths in Manhattan, and every cubicle was rented. Men of all descriptions and ages roamed the dimly lit corridors, with either a towel wrapped around their waist or else wearing a flimsy little cotton robe.

Howard Auster, a twenty-one year old Jewish man from the Bronx, spied a handsome Gore Vidal standing by himself near a blacked-out window. Gore was older, twenty-five. Auster approached him.

"I definitely came on to him, and he responded," Auster recalled years later. "He reached inside my robe and fondled my genitals before inviting me back to this seedy little cubicle."

"The sex wasn't all that good—in fact, it might be called a disaster—but we found we really dug each other," Auster said. "That night marked the beginning of a relationship that would stretch across the rest of the century."

"Gore likes to fuck, and he doesn't really like to be fucked, or to give blowjobs," Auster said. "On my first night with him, I would have ended up with blue balls if I hadn't masturbated."

Bronx-born Howard Auster worked at a Walgreen's Drugstore to pay his way through New York University, hoping for a career in advertising. After he graduated, in spite of top grades, no company would hire him.

Gore, his newly minted friend, told him that anti-Semitism was prevalent in advertising firms in those days. Gore suggested that he change his name, re-

---

"I Wanted to Buy Robert Wagner AND His Jaguar"

—Gore Vidal

moving the "R" at its end and substituting an "N." After he did that, "Howard Austen" was hired by an ad agency as an account assistant within the week.

Most weekends after that, from Manhattan, Austen would take the northbound train to the Rhinecliff Station, where Gore would be waiting in his car to pick him up and transport him to Edgewater, his elegant home on the Hudson.

On the Saturday night after his arrival on Friday, after dialogues with Gore, Austen would migrate down to Adolphs, a local tavern that drew patronage from both faculty and students at nearby Bard College. Nearly every weekend, Austen escorted back to Edgewater one or two of the students, or perhaps a professor if he were young and handsome enough.

Gore often invited VIPs to Edgewater, perhaps a member of the literati such as Saul Bellows or a foreign dignitary. Gore once introduced Austen to British MP Sir Henry (Chips) Channon. He told Gore, "I prefer men to women and royalty to either." Actually, Gore suspected that the MP was in love with the British playwright, Terrence Rattigan.

At first, Gore could not afford to pay Austen much money as his part-time secretary. He started him out on a salary of $20 a week, later raising it to $40. Gore was writing quickie pulp fiction, including a 1953 release of *Thieves Fall Out* under the *nom de plume* of Cameron Kay. He earned his usual fee of $3,000 per novel that eventually sold, retail, for twenty-five cents a copy.

In the early days of their friendship, Gore stayed with Austen when he visited Manhattan during sojourns away from his home at Edgewater. Austen's walk-up was near 57th Street. Later, Austen resigned his advertising job and went to live permanently with Gore. He also traveled with him, mainly to California and later to Italy. He began to manage Gore's affairs.

Two weeks into their relationship, Austen revealed his secret desire to be a pop singer. He began by singing "Night and Day" to Gore, and then proceeded to perform a medley of Cole Porter numbers.

He often sang for Gore's guests. One afternoon, Eleanor Roosevelt dropped in to discuss the possibility of Gore running for Congress one day on the Democratic ticket. "She was accompanied by what Gore described as 'two of Eleanor's Amazon Warriors'—in this case, two burly dykes who lived near her at Hyde Park," Austen said.

"After the first year of visiting almost every weekend, I eventually found my role in Gore's life," Austen confided to actress Claire Bloom. "I became not only his live-in companion, but his pimp, rounding up young working class boys, his favorite. I was also his secretary, his business manager, his playmate, his Greek chorus, and most of all, his Jewish mother putting him to bed when he'd had too much to drink and making sure he ate his vegetables."

"The next day, I got him up, made breakfast for him, and sat him down in front of his typewriter, into which I'd inserted a blank sheet of paper."

As more royalties came in, Gore moved Austen out of his small, third-floor walkup in Manhattan and into a larger apartment at the corner of 55th Street and First Avenue, the rent for which was $175 a month.

To make extra money at the time, Gore continued to write pulp novels such as *Death in the Fifth Position* under the pseudonym of Edgar Box. "He wrote that one in a week," Austen said, "for which he was paid his standard fee of $3,000."

Over the years, when Gore was asked the secret of their long-lasting marriage, he always replied, "No sex." However, close friends and acquaintances have challenged Gore's claim.

In Key West, Austen bonded with Frank Merlo, Tennessee's longtime lover. Both men discussed the perils of being the lover of a celebrated writer. Austen admitted to Merlo that he and Gore had had sex at the beginning of their relationship, but that they were always free to conduct affairs with other men. "We had many a three-way in the early days. I was always picking up a guy that I thought Gore would want to fuck around with."

He looked at Frank. "Do you pimp for Tennessee?"

"Not at all," Frank said. "He's his own talent scout. As America's hot playwright, he's got wannabee actors lined up at the door."

Letters that have surfaced from Austen to Gore during the early years of their relationship suggest that they were most definitely lovers.

Once, while Austen was still employed by the ad agency in Manhattan, Gore had to fly to California.

"Please hurry back," Austen wrote him. "My precious seed is going to waste in my dirty underwear before I send it to the laundry. I need relief. I need 'the man.' Love, Tinker"

[Tinker or Tinkerbell was Gore's affectionate nickname for Austen.]

In Los Angeles, Gore heard from Austen, with chastised him for not writing. "You must be getting a wonderful suntan out there. I can't wait for your return so I can check out every golden inch of your beautiful body. You are so handsome. I will check to see if you have a tan line or if you are bronze all over. I will pay special attention to your groin to determine if you wore that revealing bathing suit I bought you as a going away present, or *[if you]* went bareass."

At dinner parties, Austen did not have Gore's intellectual prowess, but he chose instead to amuse guests with indiscreet gossip.

He revealed incidents associated with their encounters with famous hosts. One night, he told actor Rod Steiger, "Gore and I were chatting with Johnny Carson before he went on *The Tonight Show* where Gore was to appear as a guest. We were drinking Scotch. Gore was called outside."

"I had to take a leak.," Austen continued. "I asked Johnny if I could use his dressing room. Just as I whipped it out, Johnny came into the room and stood beside me at the toilet bowl. 'Sorry, but I had to join you,' he said to me. As he took a piss, he told me that, 'You can look at it and salivate—no harm in that—but touching it or sucking it will have to be confined to your dreams.'"

In Manhattan, Gore and Austen attended parties and other events as a couple. At one party hosted by Garbo's former companion, Cecil Beaton, a dozen muscular, well-endowed men "served drinks in the nude and later were used as party favors," Austen said.

Noël Coward often invited them to dinners, parties, and special events when he was in New York. At one of them, Gore and Austen met Princess Margaret, who was Coward's guest of honor. "Gore spent most of the evening talking to her," Austen said. "They became great friends."

As the years went by, and as Gore's income increased, he and Austen moved to larger quarters, purchasing a brownstone in Manhattan at 416 East 58th Street. In their brownstone, Gore and Austen maintained a guest bedroom, which was frequently occupied by various guests. Gore wrote a note to red-haired Maureen O'Hara inviting her to stay with them. "You will be most welcome. Now you had better have a lot of gossip, and it should be more than your meager letter suggests." Gore confided to Austen that Maureen had walked into John Ford's office and caught him tongue-kissing Tyrone Power.

When another brownstone nearby (this one at 417 East 48th Street) became available, they bought it for $87,000 and restored the triplex on its top three floors and put it on the market for rent.

To their surprise, Franklin D. Roosevelt, Jr. was the first person to show up on their doorstep. They rented it to him, and he often invited Austen and Gore over for dinner.

[Franklin Delano Roosevelt, Jr. (1914 – 1988) was the fifth child of U.S. President Franklin D. Roosevelt and his wife, Eleanor. Although not associated with scandals as frequently as his elder brothers James and Elliott, Franklin Jr. was in frequent legal trouble, usually for traffic violations, He was married five times, once to a member of the du Pont family (Ethel du Pont), who committed suicide in 1965, sixteen years after their divorce in 1949. The family thought that FDR Jr. was the one most like his father in appearance and behavior.]

"Sometimes FDR, Jr.'s family went away, and Franklin remained in the triplex by himself," Austen said. "Well, not always by himself. Whenever he was living as a bachelor, we noticed Jackie Kennedy arriving to spend the night with him, discreetly leaving before dawn."

For a few months, Gore and Austen relocated to London, renting a flat there. Nina Vidal showed up for a visit, and Austen carried her baggage to their guest room. She hardly spoke to him, privately telling her son later that night, "I detest your friend."

During her stay, tensions mounted. Right before Gore kicked her out, she accused him of disgracing her among her social set. "Your being a homosexual is painful enough for me, but taking as your lover this horrible Jew boy who still speaks with a Bronx accent! It's too much for me."

He called a taxi and had her luggage delivered to the street outside their apartment house.

He would never speak to his mother again.

Franklin D. Roosevelt, Jr., pictured here with his celebrated mother, **Eleanor Roosevelt**, in 1962, the year of her death.

"Of all my boys, he was the most like Franklin, and that was both good and bad," she said.

When Gore was hired as a scriptwriter for MGM, he and Austen moved to Hollywood, where they lived temporarily at the Château Marmont, the retreat of celebrities who included Greta Garbo, off Sunset Boulevard. Austen picked up young hustlers on the boulevard and brought them back to service Gore and himself in their hotel room. From the garage, a client could escort a guest directly to his or her bedroom, without attracting attention by parading him or her through the lobby.

Before they were married, Paul Newman and Joanne Woodward lived together in a house in Malibu. They were such good friends with Gore that they invited Howard and him to move in with them.

In Malibu, Newman, Woodward, Austen, and Gore entertained many notables, including the diarist Anaïs Nin, the French author Romain Gary, and actress Claire Bloom, who delivered a devastating impersonation of Queen Elizabeth II. At the time, Bloom gave every indication of being madly in love with Richard Burton.

"It was obvious to me that Gore was madly in love with Paul," Austen confided to Elizabeth Taylor one night at a party.

"Who isn't, darling?" she asked. "He's so handsome. And those baby blue eyes. They are to die for."

Austen always opened and sorted Gore's mail before he read it himself. Years later, in 1965, Gore received a birthday card from Newman. It read: "I'm getting sentimental in my dotage, and long to crack a bottle with you as in olden days. It's been a long time since I've stared into your grateful eyes as you lovingly looked up at me with your knees on the floor of a urinal."

As far as Austen was concerned, that ended the debate over whether Gore had ever had sex with Newman.

Isherwood said that Gore confessed to him that he'd frequently had sex with Newman. "He apparently confessed to Tennessee as well. Gore also claimed that Newman had done it with guys on many an occasion. In Gore's words, "Paul Newman was a *bona fide* bisexual, but managed to keep it out of the press for the most part.'"

Christopher Isherwood and his young lover, Don Bachardy, often visited with Gore and Austen. "We related as one gay married couple to another young

Actress **Claire Bloom** was a close friend. Austen felt she might make an ideal wife for Gore.

Susan Sarandon, accompanied by Tim Robbins and her family, made several visits to visit Gore at his retreat in Ravello.

gay married couple," Isherwood said. "I liked to talk on almost any subject with Gore. The only part of the evening I dreaded was when Howard got up to sing for us. He was no Vic Damone."

One late afternoon, Isherwood walked with Gore along the beach. "He told me that after seeing Robert Wagner's brief appearance with Susan Hayward in *With a Song in My Heart* (1952), he'd fallen madly in love with the kid."

"He's my type," Gore said. "I like the clean cut, all American type. He's very masculine—a real beauty."

[In the 1940s, actor James Craig, a Clark Gable wannabe, had been Gore's type, too.]

In 1961, in Paris, Gore bought Robert Wagner's black 1961 Jaguar for $3,000. He later told Howard, "I'd love to have bought Robert Wagner instead."

From Paris, they drove south to Rome.

In Rome, Gore visited Ed Cheever's Gym every day and reported back to Austen on what was going on there. "One of the steam rooms should have been labeled the orgy room."

On occasion, he encountered Clint Eastwood taking a shower before a bevy of appreciative queens. Eastwood was in Italy making "Spaghetti Westerns" at the time. "Clint was on exhibit, but regrettably, he never showed it hard to the queens of Rome."

The rest of the day, Gore spent in a library, researching data on his historical novel, *Julian,* which would eventually be published in 1964.

In addition to the hustlers they brought to their apartment in Rome, Gore and Austen also hosted dinners for Sophia Loren, Audrey Hepburn, Marcello Mastroianni, and Federico Fellini.

Eventually, they moved to Ravello, along the Amalfi Drive, south of Naples, purchasing a villa there. Over the years, while living there, they often entertained many distinguished guests, none more notable than Hillary Clinton. Gore had written debating points for Bill Clinton when he faced off in a debate with then-sitting president George Herbert Walker Bush in 1992.

Perhaps Gore wanted to get even with Bush, Sr., for turning down his sexual advances when the future president was only

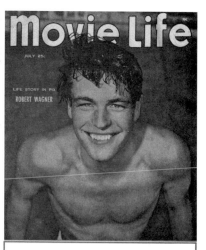

During the course of his Hollywood career **Robert Wagner** managed to survive the sinking of *The Titanic* in the 1953 film with that name, but did he survive the demands of its stars, the homosexual actor Clifton Webb and the bisexual actress, Barbara Stanwyck?

In *A Kiss Before Dying,* based on Ira Levin's first novel, Wagner murdered the wife of Paul Newman (Joanne Woodward), shoving her to her death from the top of a tall building.

"Natalie Wood and I had something in common," Gore Vidal said. "If he'd asked me, I would have walked twice with him down the aisle, just as she did."

seventeen years old and arrived at Exeter to pitch for the rival team from Phillips Academy.

To a friend, Gore wrote his impression of Hillary: "She is braced but edgy, uncommonly bright with a wry sense of humor, that, as a woman and a political figure, she dares not show the world."

While living in Ravello, Austen arranged orgies for Gore at their home. A parade of olive-skinned, muscular young men were often seen filing in on certain Saturday nights. One of them revealed to an Italian reporter that Austen paid them $20 each to participate in an orgy staged by him.

Their friend, actress Susan Sarandon, visited on occasion, remembering them as acting "like an old married couple" when she visited them in their home at Ravello, La Rondinaia, ["the Swallow's Nest"], accompanied by her companion, Tim Robbins.

Villagers in Ravello became aware of the parade of the rich and famous making their way across the square to Gore's home—on one occasion, Mick and Bianca Jagger. Woody Harrelson was a frequent visitor, telling Gore that he made $2 million a year in royalties from the hit TV sitcom, *Cheers.*

"When we were living in Ravello, Gore got a call from Princess Margaret, who wanted to spend two or three days with us," Austen said. "She asked Gore if it were all right for her to bring a companion. He said yes. The lover she brought over was Peter Sellers."

"At **La Rondinaia**, on the Amalfi Coast in the little village of Ravello, Gore and I settled happily for many years," Howard Austen claimed. "We had the best orgies along the coast, even better than those at Capri. But we cleaned up our act when visitors called, and those guests included everybody from Audrey Hepburn to Hillary Clinton."

"**Princess Margaret** *(above, right)* and I shared the same taste in men, and sometimes we switched partners," Gore Vidal claimed. "She visited me in our apartment in Rome and also at our beloved La Rondinaia."

"Margaret and I parted company, though, over **Peter Sellers** *(above, left)*. His masculine charm eluded me, and I wondered what she saw in him. In Ravello, I lent him a very snug bikini, hoping to discover some of his hidden charm, but I failed to find it."

"I was shocked at how far he went to ingratiate himself with Margaret," Austen said. "A real brown-nose. He told me that he'd had heart problems, but before mounting Her Royal Highness, he still used amyl nitrate as a sexual stimulant. That finally led to his fatal heart attack."

Theo Aronson, Margaret's biographer, wrote about her affair with Sellers, claiming that during her marriage to the Earl of Snowdon, Sellers purchased expensive camera equipment for her husband, knowing of his interest in photography. He even gave him a CIA bugging device.

In 1968, Sellers divorced Britt Ekland, and he informed Gore that Margaret's marriage to the Earl of Snowdon was collapsing. "I'm madly in love with her and expect to marry her," Sellers told Gore.

"Peter called her 'Ma'am, darling,' and he confided to me that her breasts were as large as Sophia Loren's—'the same cup exactly,'" Gore said.

Before she left Ravello, Princess Margaret whispered to Gore that "I have no intention of marrying Peter—call it a fling. You, of all people, know about flings."

"I wrote the book on the subject," Gore said.

Sometimes, Princess Margaret arrived in Ravello without an escort. Austen said Gore knew what she liked. "He once sent her off on a big boat with a good-looking guy sailor from Salerno who had the biggest cock on the Amalfi Drive. She came back with a happy gleam in her royal eye."

That night over dinner, Gore confided to Princess Margaret that Jackie Kennedy found Queen Elizabeth "pretty heavy going."

Margaret shot back, "But that's what she's there for!"

"Actually, Margaret had a dry wit," Austen said. "Over dinner, she told us that the Queen had uncommon talents. Gore asked her what they were."

"She can put on a very heavy diamond tiara while hurrying down a flight of stairs with no mirror," Margaret claimed.

Gore once wrote, "Princess Margaret is far too bright for her station in life, which she takes altogether too solemnly."

***

Over the years, Gore and Austen were frequent visitors to Hollywood, often discussing film projects that never materialized. By then, Gore had become an internationally celebrated man of letters and was often entertained by celebrities.

Barbra Streisand once fêted them at her home when she was having an affair with Don Johnson, who became famous for his TV series, *Miami Vice.*

Gore found the blonde-haired actor "very cute, just my type. I wonder if it's true that Sal Mineo has already had him."

At one point, Barbra revealed to Gore that she was urging Johnson to visit her doctor to have his foreskin clipped.

Later, he told Howard, "How dreadful. It shouldn't be cut off, but made love to."

375

"You never knew who Vidal and Austen were seen with," said Truman Capote. "I was a spy in the house of love. My contacts in Hollywood gave me up-to-date reports on their social contacts. One night, they were out with Robert Downey, Jr.; another night with Sidney Poitier and Joanna Shimkus. That dyke, Barbara Stanwyck, entertained them at her house. They were frequent visitors at the home of Elizabeth Taylor, although Gore got seriously pissed off at her, or so I heard. He told people, 'That bitch is getting fucked by Robert Wagner, and I haven't had him yet.'"

In the twilight of their years, Gore and Austen sold their villa in Ravello, returning to live in California.

Visitors became rare, and on many an occasion, Gore would claim, "I have no regrets."

Austen clarified that: "His life was filled with nothing but regrets. At night, he often talked about his great disappointment that he'd lost his bid for Congress. If he'd won, he planned in time to become Senator from New York and then run for president like his nemesis, Bobby Kennedy, did."

"Frankly, I think Gore would have made a great president if it were not for the heavy baggage of the gay thing," Austen claimed. "Of course, there was another problem. He was viewed as a pinko liberal."

As the years went by, Gore increased his consumption of Scotch. On many a night, he was drunk by eight o'clock. He liked to sit in front of the television set, watching the news. Austen said, "Gore became virtually glued to the TV during the impeachment proceedings against Bill Clinton, which he denounced as a Republican farce. He knew where all the bodies were buried, the most awful personal details about the senators. One night he pointed at this Republican jackass on TV and said, 'Look at that rat's asshole. Here he is, denouncing Clinton for a blow-job, and the shithead is the biggest cocksucker in Congress. He's sucked off so many pageboys, his mouth has locked into a permanent O. What a hypocrite!'"

Chapter Twenty-Six

The Amorous Pursuits of Gore Vidal

Gore Vidal's Claim: "I Seduced 1,003 Men, the Don Juan Legendary Total."

Movie Stars Rock Hudson, Dennis Hopper, Sal Mineo, & Tony Perkins Are Among His Conquests

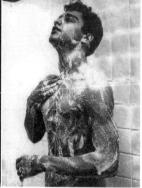

Gore Vidal didn't always get his man. He scored a bull's eye with **Rock Hudson** *(left photo above)*, and with **Sal Mineo** *(right)*. But Gore "struck out" after a baseball game in which a seventeen-year-old **George Herbert Walker Bush** *(center photo)* was the pitcher for the rival team. When he showered with the future president, all Gore got was "to cop a feel" before Barbara's future husband fled in terror.

Gore didn't exaggerate when he claimed that during his lifetime, he seduced 1,003 men, most of those conquests before he turned twenty-five. He and his companion, Howard Austen, when they were living in Rome, often had as many as fifteen young men in and out of their apartment in one week. The pair staged orgies where they could have had sexual contact with as many as eight men in one night.

During his early days in Hollywood, when he was a scriptwriter at MGM, Gore, like so many other young men in town, also seduced the occasional movie star before they became box office attractions.

He preferred hustlers to movie stars. Never a politician. Perhaps his sexual aversion to politicians stemmed from a aborted experience he had as a teenager.

During his prep school years at Phillips Exeter Academy, in Exeter, New Hampshire, Gore was assigned third base in a traditional baseball game with his school's longtime rival, Phillips Andover Academy, located across the state line in Andover, Massachusetts. *[The rivalry between these two elite schools, whose names are annoyingly similar, is the oldest in America. The fiercely competitive schools competed in their first ever baseball game in 1878, when Exeter defeated the boys from Andover 12-1.]*

The pitcher for Phillips Andover that day was George Herbert Walker Bush, the son of Senator Prescott Bush, a Republican

"I was only sixteen at the time, and several of my classmates at Exeter were homosexuals," Gore told a party one night at Tennessee Williams' house in Key West. "To put it bluntly, the pitcher from Andover was considered a hot piece of ass back then, a good looker, for those who liked the All-American type."

When **George H.W. Bush** was an aviator during World War II, many reporters wrote of how handsome he was, the *Austin American-Statesman* claiming, "He could very well be cast in a movie role of his true life story."

His most famous extramarital dalliance was with an Italian beauty named Rosemarie *(last name withheld)*, whom he met on a business trip to New York. He paid the rent on her apartment, and promised to divorce Barbara and marry her.

He broke off the affair in 1964, however. For a few months, Rosemarie considered, then rejected, suing for breach of promise.

"After we lost the game, I followed him into the showers to check out his body," Gore claimed. "I stood next to him as we both soaped up. I was particularly interested in his cock, which seemed generous enough, though flaccid. He had a long extended foreskin. I learned later that his teammates called him 'Skin,' a name that stuck to him even when he joined the Navy. He had a very lanky physique."

"I don't know if he ever got his dick clipped—you'll have to ask Barbara if she can remember," Gore said.

At Exeter, Gore Cruises 17-Year-Old George Bush, Sr. in the Shower Room After a Baseball Game

"I was very aggressive back then, chasing after the boys," he said. "All teenage boys are horny and will usually jump at the chance for any kind of sex. In the dorm, we called it the 'Princeton rub.'"

[Gore was referring to a form of sex known as frottage.]

"Georgie boy withdrew in horror from me when I reached out to fondle his soapy dick," Gore said. "He immediately fled from the shower, even though he was still soapy. He got dressed in a flash and was in his car heading back to Andover. At least I got to cop a feel from the cock that spewed the sperm that created the worst president in the history of the United States."

When Christopher Isherwood heard the story about Gore and the future president, he said, "I believe it. If Truman Capote had told me, I would have questioned it. But Gore was not a liar. I've cruised with him. He's a 'put your hand down there and grab the cock' type. Of course, that aggressive approach works better in Rome than it does in New York or Hollywood. Cock grabbing is how he made his intentions known."

***

In the mid 1950s, along with Howard Austen, Gore enjoyed life at the Château Marmont, an upscale hotel which was at the time one the best cruising grounds in Greater Los Angeles. His friend, Paul Newman, had turned him onto the place.

"In those days, Paul had the best of both worlds," Gore said. "He had a wife *[Jackie Witte]* stashed away somewhere, although I don't know if he still slept with her. He had Joanne Woodward in Hollywood, and he had, on occasion, Grace Kelly in one of the bungalows. What a life we had back in the good old days. Of course, the bisexuals were the lucky ones. Not being gender specific in their preferences, they doubled their chances of getting laid."

After a day of writing, Gore liked to hang out by the hotel pool, especially on weekends. Gore knew that the bisexual director, Nicholas Ray, occupied one of the bungalows, but he hadn't met him yet. He'd been greatly amused by Ray's campy Western, *Johnny Guitar* (1954), starring Joan Crawford battling Mercedes McCambridge. "Two dykes shooting it out," Gore told Austen.

One sunny Sunday afternoon, Gore came over and introduced himself to Ray, who had been described as a "silver-haired, chain-smoking *auteur* cursed with a romantic nature and a taste for vice."

Within thirty minutes, Ray and Gore got into an argument, Gore maintaining that the scriptwriter was more vital to a film than its director. Ray said, "If it's all in the script, why make the film?"

Despite their argument (or perhaps because of it), Ray invited Gore to a party he was hosting that night in his bungalow. He told Gore that he was putting together a film called *Rebel Without a Cause*. Released in 1955, it would star James Dean, Natalie Wood, and Sal Mineo.

"I've seen Dean before," Gore said, "at the Actors Studio in New York. He's always sucking up to Tennessee Williams, hoping he'll write another great part, the equal of...you know, Brando's part, the character of Stanley Kowalski in *A Streetcar Named Desire*."

In his yet-to-be-written memoir, *Palimpsest,* Gore gave a very limited overview of what happened at Ray's party that spring of 1955. "There were several bungalows around the pool," he wrote. "Nick Ray lived in one, preparing *Rebel Without a Cause,* and rather openly having an affair with the adolescent Sal Mineo, while the sallow Jimmy Dean sulked in and out, unrecognizable behind thick glasses that distorted myopic eyes."

On the set of *Rebel Without a Cause,* director **Nicholas Ray** was systematically seducing its young stars. Here Ray *(left)* is counseling **James Dean**.

Gore had gone to the party without Austen, who had wanted "to check out a wild new place" that had recently opened in West Hollywood. Gore later admitted that he had been tempted to put the make on Dean, only because he knew he'd been pumping it to Tennessee. But when Ray introduced him to Dean, Gore found him arrogant and insulting. "What a prick he was," Gore later said. "We hated each other on sight."

When Gore later chatted privately with Ray, the director told him that at first, he'd been reluctant to cast Mineo as Plato in *Rebel* because he felt he had no chemistry with Dean.

"Jimmy and Sal set out to prove me wrong," Ray confided. "Both of them came to my bungalow and stripped down and let me watch them make mad love to each other. They were explosive together. After that, I cast Mineo in the role which I had considered giving to this other young actor, Dennis Hopper. Later, I gave Dennis a smaller role in *Rebel.*"

Gay overtones in *Rebel Without a Cause* between **James Dean** *(left)* and a very young **Sal Mineo**. Nicholas Ray directed a scene of Dean deep-kissing Mineo, which ended up on the cutting-room floor.

Over their fourth drink, Ray and Gore discovered that they had something in common: Both were devotees of "boy ass."

"Since you and Dean didn't hit it off, you'll have to go for Sal, and I'll introduce you to Dennis. He's available, but only if you're important enough in the industry. Right now, you'll have to wait your chance."

"Dennis is entertaining his so-called sponsor, Vincent Price," Ray said, indicating an older and a younger man deeply involved in a private dialogue. "They're over in the corner. Take a look."

"Vince was obviously smitten," Gore later said. "When I talked to Price, he told me he was teaching young Dennis about art."

"And other things," Gore had snapped.

"Don't be a jealous bitch," Price said to Gore before walking away in a huff.

When Gore was alone with Mineo, he asked him out for dinner. "At first, Sal didn't seem too interested, until I told him I was Paul Newman's best friend. I also informed him that I was a script writer at MGM, and that I was working on a film script that had a juicy part for which he'd be ideal. Then our date was on."

The following night, because he wanted to be alone with Mineo, Gore asked Austen to disappear for the evening as a means of allowing him to pursue his private agenda, which in this case, involved Mineo. He'd heard some interesting recent gossip about the young Bronx-born actor.

"Ray told me that Sal was madly in love with Dean, and he was going to depict that love on the screen," Gore said. "As director, he planned to include a scene where Dean and Sal would kiss passionately on film."

[*Ray carried through on his vision. During the filming, he shot a scene of Dean as Jim and Mineo as Plato sharing a prolonged and very deep kiss. The two actors got carried away and Ray had to yell "CUT! CUT! CUT!"*

The head office heard rumors of this kiss and immediately shot off a memo to Ray: "It is, of course, vital that there be no inference of a questionable or homosexual relationship between Plato and Jim."

Ray later told Gore, "I had to kill the kiss scene, saving the clip for some future restorer to insert into an unexpurgated version of Rebel Without a Cause. *But I fucked the studio and got away with something, at least. I retained a scene of Sal with those adorable brown eyes of his gazing up with love at Jimmy. At least the gay guys in the audience will get it."*]

Then Ray filled Gore in on some additional background about Mineo, claiming he'd been broken in while still a kid on Broadway. "When they starred together in *The King and I* on Broadway in 1951, Yul Brynner fucked him almost every night before they went onstage."

"My God," Gore said. "Mineo must have been only twelve or thirteen years old. Aren't there laws in New York against child molestation?"

The dinner and the sex between Gore and Mineo apparently got rave reviews. Both of them, the actor and the writer, claimed to be bisexual, "Everyone's supposed to be bi," Mineo told Gore. "What's wrong with being bi?"

"Kid, you're preaching to the choir."

Gore later told Austen and others, "Sal has an uncut cock that expands to nine inches. Before that,

Yul Brynner as King of Siam. The costumes were historically correct, but the camp factor was there, too

I used to make the pronouncement that a man with nine inches is impossible to find. But as the years went by, I encountered many of those nine inch cocks, even a twelve inch cock. If you find one of those, get married right away."

***

Gore was only beginning his sexual conquests around the hotel pool. More young actors were to come, so to speak.

Two weeks after Nicholas Ray's party, he placed an urgent call to Gore in his hotel room at the Château Marmont. "I've got a conflict in my schedule, too much of a good thing," he told Gore. "You've got to help me. I'd made a date with Dennis Hopper tonight. But at the last minute, Natalie Wood called, and she's free after all. I'd invited her before I called Dennis, and she'd said she was busy, but her plans fell through. I'd rather fuck Natalie than Dennis, but I can't reach Dennis on the phone."

"Where do I come in?" Gore asked. "My advice is to have a three-way."

"Natalie's too young for that," Ray said. "Please do me a favor. I'll make it up to you. The next hot actor who shows up on my casting couch, I'll toss to you. I've agreed to meet Dennis in the bar. I want you to stand in for me and invite him to dinner. I'll leave fifty dollars for you in an envelope at the front desk. If you guys hit it off tonight, so much the better."

"I find Dennis more appealing than your buddy, Dean," Gore said.

"Since you're an ass man, it'll work out just fine, since you told me you don't like to suck dick all that much. Dennis doesn't have much up front."

"You've got yourself a deal," Gore said. "I think the kid is good looking. Vincent Price sure thinks so."

"He's free of Vince tonight," Ray said. "Dennis is all yours."

Gore later told his long-time friend, Stanley Mills Haggart, "Dennis looks like a clean cut kid, which, as you know, I prefer. He's the type of guy voted Student Council President." Of course, Gore made that appraisal long before Dennis entered his drugged-out weirdo phase.

Over dinner that night, Hopper seemed more interested in talking about his burgeoning film career than in Gore's script writing. Ray had cast him as a gang member named "Goon" in

In Cecil B. DeMille's *The Ten Commandments*, **Vincent Price** *(left)* played a wicked (but rather campy) slave driver who is eventually murdered by Anne Baxter. Young **Dennis Hopper** *(right)* was being taught about "art" by Price...and about other things, too.

Rebel Without a Cause.

Like Sal Mineo, Ray himself, and so many others, including Natalie Wood, Hopper seemed to have developed what Gore called "James Dean fever."

From what he gathered from Hopper, he was having affairs not only with Dean, but with his best pal, Nick Adams, an aspiring actor, as well. He was also pursuing starlets on the side.

Despite a debauched life, Hopper looked fresh and innocently wide-eyed, even dewey.

He'd driven Gore to his favorite pizza joint in his new red Austin convertible purchased with money he'd earned from his recently signed movie contract.

After pizza, he took Gore to Googie's, known as a "zippy, populuxe-style coffee shop where the stars gathered on Sunset Strip." Paul Newman frequented the place, accompanied by Tony Perkins at the beginning of their torrid affair. They often came in with Vampira, a Goth and very campy TV hostess who drove around Hollywood in a long black hearse she'd nicknamed "Black Death."

Hopper told Gore that the other night, he had been here with Dean. "Frank Sinatra walked in to check out the joint. He was with the actress, Marilyn Maxwell. Spotting Dean, he ordered the waiter to bring Dean a glass of milk. Sinatra also gave the waiter his comb to deliver to Dean."

As Gore looked up, he noticed Anthony Perkins entering the café, accompanied by Vampira. The pair headed for their table. "It must be Tony's night off from Tab Hunter," Gore whispered to Hopper.

As Perkins and Vampira sat down to join them, Hopper didn't speak to him. Gore learned later that Hopper viewed Perkins as his chief rival for quirky, neurotic parts.

Gore enjoyed seeing Perkins again. By the pool, back at the hotel, he'd found him not only handsome, but charming and intelligent. At least he had something in common with Perkins: Both of them considered Newman one of their best friends.

[Years later, Gore said, "In 1960, Alfred

In Los Angeles, The Finland-born "horror hostess" **Vampira** (aka **Maila Nurmi**), was known as the original fag hag, hanging out with James Dean and Tony Perkins, becoming their mother confessor.

She also, for the benefit of 1950s late-night TV audiences, dressed in "Goth black," screamed, fainted, lay in a coffin, and seductively loitered within a mock cemetery.

Rail thin, shy, and handsome, **Tony Perkins** immediately caught Gore Vidal's roving eye. If a director needed a stuttering, quivering wacko, he called on Perkins.

Hitchcock, in Psycho, *made the ideal choice in selecting Tony, an all-American boy next door, to play a mama's boy harboring secret demons of shocking violence and perversity."]*

After Googie's, Gore's next stop was Hopper's apartment. Even at that stage of his career, he was into drugs. He'd told Gore that it had all begun when he learned to sniff gas fumes from his grandfather's truck, which he said made him high, often leading to hallucinations. He also admitted that he and Dean consumed "grass and peyote." In addition, he consumed a combination of heroin and cocaine, which would later be known as "speedballs."

Ray had been correct about Hopper's lack of endowment. He stripped down and lay on his stomach, waiting for Gore to penetrate him.

In the afterglow of sex, Hopper seemed embarrassed and wanted to reassert his heterosexual credentials. "I like drugs and liquor, but what I'm really addicted to is sex. I can have virtually any starlet in Hollywood, just for the asking. In a period of forty-eight hours, I'm likely to bed eight women. I look at sex like drinking beer—a can of beer, a woman, a can of beer, a woman."

"Sounds monotonous to me," Gore said as he put his clothes back on. He couldn't resist a putdown before departing: "Frankly, I think you should always be the fuckee, not the fucker."

***

Anthony ("Tony") Perkins telephoned a few days later. Gore knew that he was the son of the famous stage and screen actor, Osgood Perkins. Tony was in town to film *Friendly Persuasion* (1956), in which he played a gentle pacifist farm lad, the Quaker son of Gary Cooper and Dorothy McGuire. Gore had gone to see Tony when he'd played a gay student during part of the run of the long-running Broadway production of *Tea and Sympathy* (1953). He'd wanted to go backstage to congratulate him, but didn't.

Having seen him beside the swimming pool of the Château Marmont several times, Gore was surprised to learn that he didn't occupy a room at the hotel.

"I will when I get my next paycheck," Tony said. "In the meantime, I'm living in this janitor's room across the street. Right now, the building has no janitor, and the owner is renting the room to me. Why don't you come with me and see where I live?"

"I don't mind love in the afternoon," Gore said.

On the way across the street, Gore said, "There's an item in the morning paper. Louella or Hedda, I can't remember which bitch. It said that you are the new Brando. Is that true?"

"That's for me to know and you to find out," Tony said.

"I intend to," Gore said, "even if I have to move a janitor's mop and pail to do so."

Later, during Gore's report to Stanley Haggart, he said, "Tony is great sex, a beautiful boy with a beautiful cock and body. But he's a little weird in bed. No wonder his best female friend is Vampira. Tony spends a lot of time sinking his teeth into your neck, I think he really wants to go for blood, but holds back."

"Come on, Gore," Haggart said. "A lot of lovers, gay and straight, attack the neck. It's supposed to turn people on."

Later, after sex that day, Tony and Gore headed once again to Googie's.

Over coffee, Gore found Tony brimming with ambition. "He was riding a roller-coaster to fame."

"I'm going to all the right parties, meeting all the right VIPs," Tony said. "I want to be a movie star and enjoy all the trappings. I want to drink champagne with the big boys—Zanuck, Dore Schary, Jack Warner...whomever."

Provocatively, Gore inquired about the status of Tony's relationship with Tab Hunter.

"It's a real problem," he said. "To protect our careers and keep our private lives secret, we have to sneak around. We can never be seen together except on a double date. Of course, we drop the ladies at their doorsteps with a fleeting kiss on the cheek. If we're going to an event, we arrive in separate cars and leave separately."

"Sounds like a high degree of paranoia," Gore said.

"About the only place we dare go together is the Vista Theater, a movie revival house in Silverdale. It's very remote, and nearly all the audience is gay."

"Sorry to hear you guys have to sneak around so much," Gore said.

"Tab feels there are serious issues damaging our personalities," Tony continued. "His point is that one has to adopt a *persona* in this town. After a while, at least according to Tab, you become that *persona*."

"I'd say that half of Hollywood—perhaps a hell of a lot more—is living a *faux persona*," Tony claimed. "You know, Joan Crawford as a doting mother; Cary Grant as a ladies' man who—in private—chases boys; or Bogie, the tough guy who'd be the first to run from a fight."

"There's more," Tony said. "I also lead a secret life from Tab. I'd like to slip around and see you, too."

"I think that's wonderful," Gore said. "You're hot!"

"Speaking of hot, there's still more," he said. "In a few minutes, Robert Francis will walk through that door. He's that gorgeous young actor who appeared in *The Caine Mutiny* with Bogart."

"I saw him," Gore said. "The ensign, a real dish."

"Hollywood doesn't know it, but he's Howard Hughes' boy. Our aviator friend supports him." Then Tony looked up. "He's com-

Saddled with one of those phony 1950s names, **Tab Hunter** represented the decade's ideal of male beauty: Blonde, handsome, boyish, likable, self-effacing. He was the heartthrob of gay Hollywood.

ing here now."

Tony introduced Gore to Robert Francis.

"I'm honored to meet *Screen World's* most popular personality of 1954," Gore said.

"And I you, Mr. Vidal," Robert responded.

Seated together, facing Gore, Robert and Tony each looked like manifes-

tations of Adonis to him. He'd later tell Haggart, "No wonder Hughes is apeshit over Robert—a swimmer's build, a clean-cut look, and that faddish brush-cut from his barber."

Gore and Robert must have signaled their attraction for each other, but Tony didn't seem to mind at all. He confessed that he never liked to be seen out with only one male. "I like at least three at my table."

"The third person is called a beard," Gore said.

Robert said he wanted to learn to fly and that Hughes was teaching him. He was aware that Gore's father had been America's aviation czar during the 1930s, and he asked Gore many questions. At times, Tony felt left out of the conversation.

After about an hour of this, Gore invited them back to the Château Marmont, where he was having a few people in for cocktails, including not only Haggart, but Christopher Isherwood and his young artist lover, Don Bachardy.

Bachardy later remembered the event. "Tony Perkins never talked queer, or in any way acknowledged his queerness to us. I suppose it was much more usual then to be secretive. Of course, he was carrying on with Tab Hunter, we were told on good authority. Be that as it may, Perkins was always by himself at these get-togethers, or so I heard from Gore."

Before leaving Gore's party, Haggart invited the other guests for cocktails late the following afternoon at his beautiful home in Laurel Canyon. As an interior designer, it was a showplace built around a pool with a lovely little guest cottage in the back. Both Robert and Gore accepted, although Tony had another commitment.

The toy boy and paid companion of the billionaire mogul Howard Hughes, **Robert Francis** *(both photos above),* played the field whenever the bisexual aviator was away seducing one of his female stars.

Francis made a fatal choice in his attempt to become, like Hughes, an airplane pilot.

Haggart also invited Austen, who was not at Gore's cocktail party. "He's still in New York on business, but he sends his love," Gore said.

***

[Christopher Isherwood and Don Bachary would not encounter Tony Perkins again until the late 1970s, when super-agent Sue Mengers threw a party for Gore at her home.

In addition to the May-December couple (Isherwood and Bacardy), she'd also invited actor Jack Nicholson, who had become a good friend of Gore's. He showed up with Angelica Huston. Other guests included Paul Newman and Joanne Woodward, along with producer Ray Stark and fashion maven Diana Vreeland.

Bacardy spoke to Perkins' biographer, Charles Winecoff, telling him that he and Isherwood next saw Perkins in the late 1970s. He'd married Berry Berenson in 1973, and the couple had had two children, Osgood and Elvis.

Before his marriage, according to Winecoff, Tony had had affairs with Rudolf Nureyev, composer Stephen Sondheim, and dancer-choreographer Grover Dale.

Having turned down Jane Fonda and Brigitte Bardot, he'd had his first heterosexual experience at the age of 39 with Victoria Principal, when working on the 1972 film, The Life and Times of Judge Roy Bean.

At the Mengers household, Isherwood and Bachardy approached Tony. "He suddenly looked panic-stricken," Bachardy said. "He looked around for his wife and children, and kind of bid them to him before he would even say a word to us. 'My life is different,' he whispered to us. He was treating us like we were the Popes of Queerdom, and seemed to fear we'd talk some sort of dirty fag talk to him. Did he honestly think that his marriage could make him straight?"

[Perkins died on September 12, 1992, at his home in the Hollywood Hills, suffering from AIDS-related pneumonia.

Nine years after that tragic day, on September 11, 2001, in Boston, Beren-son boarded the doomed American Airlines Flight 11, presumably heading for Los Angeles. Seized by terrorists in midair, it crashed into the North Tower of Manhattan's World Trade Center, killing 87 passengers and crew members, five terrorists, and approximately 1,600 other people within or near the building itself.]

***

Late the following afternoon, Gore showed up at Stanley Hag-

Dark, brooding, and pensive. **Tony Perkins** was the ideal choice to fatally stab Janet Leigh during the shower scene of *Psycho*.

Some of his sex partners claimed he had a "taste for blood" off the screen as well.

gart's party with Robert Francis. Ominously, Haggart whispered to Gore, "Aren't you afraid of getting wiped out by Hughes? I was told that Robert is his boy."

"I'll take my chances," Gore said.

"In attendance at Haggart's party was Gore's former friend, Anaïs Nin. It was obvious, as Haggart watched, that the relationship between the two had dimmed, but at least they were still on speaking terms.

Haggart always had Golden Age stars at his parties. At this one, one of the guests was the petite redhead, Nancy Carroll, one of moviedom's leading ladies from the dawn of the Talkies, and a former mistress of Joseph P. Kennedy. Joan Blondell was another guest, as was Alexis Smith.

Gore was stunned when Haggart introduced him to the novelist Ayn Rand, with whom Gore later got into a political argument. After she left the party that night, Haggart told Gore, "I used to live near Ayn. One night, when I invited her to dinner, she brought this huge manuscript called *The Fountainhead*. I managed to read only eighteen pages of it."

"The bitch is a crypto-Nazi," Gore responded.

[It was the use of that term that in 1968, at the Democratic National Convention in Chicago, would involve Gore in a multi-million-dollar libel suit with right-wing commentator, William F. Buckley, Jr.

Buckley had shot back, "Now listen, you queer! Stop calling me a crypto-Nazi, or I'll sock you in your goddamn face and you'll stay plastered."]

Both Gore and Robert were delighted to meet Haggart's long-time friend "from the old days," Jon Hall. Side by side with Dorothy Lamour, who wore a sarong, he had once thrilled movie-goers in pulpy, tropical sagas that included *The Hurricane* (1937) and *Aloma of the South Seas* (1941). The virile star photographed so well in Technicolor with Maria Montez, that no one seemed to notice that he couldn't act. "All I had to do was wear as little clothing as possible," he told Gore.

"And that's why we salivated so over you," Gore told him.

"Any time they needed a swashbuckler, a stud in a fairy tale, and a seminude South Sea adventurer, I got a call," Hall said. "But the

Dorothy Lamour and **Jon Hall** in the pulpy 1937 romance, *The Hurricane,* made the sarong a fashion statement around the world.

phone hasn't been ringing too much these days."

"I think you still look great," Robert said.

[Haggart was one of the last friends to see Hall. Suffering from cancer, he fatally shot himself on December 13, 1979.]

The guests departed at seven. Haggart asked Robert and Gore to stay for a supper he'd cooked himself. Later that night, all three men took off their clothing and went for a nude swim in his pool.

Since it was getting late, Haggart invited Robert and Gore to spend the night in his guest cottage. Both of them accepted.

They were stunned by the décor. An interior designer, Haggart had introduced the then-shocking colors of chartreuse and royal purple to the American consumer through layouts in magazines which had included *Family Circle.*

Gore said, "I've never slept on chartreuse sheets before. At Nina's house, only starched white was used."

Robert smiled at him and said, "You won't get all that much sleep tonight."

The next day, before Robert had risen for breakfast, Gore joined Haggart and Jon Hall on the terrace. The fading movie idol had spent the night with Haggart in the main house.

When Gore realized that he was in safe company, he said, "Robert Francis is a gift from the Gods. We had a wonderful night together."

Gore seemed to fall in love with Haggart's guest cottage and used it not only during his stay at the Château Marmont, but when he and Austen moved into their Malibu residence with Paul Newman and Joanne Woodward."

"Using the cottage, with its private entrance, gave him the privacy he craved. "I don't want to be seen hauling my tricks through the living room." Gore said.

After Gore was installed in the cottage. Robert became a frequent visitor. Tragically, the stardom predicted for Robert Francis never happened. On July 31, 1955, Robert and his co-pilot died when their small, one-engine plane crashed after take-off from Los Angeles.

Tony Perkins finally accepted an invitation and showed up on several nights to come, as did Sal Mineo.

As long as he stayed in Hollywood, Gore continued with his movie star seductions. The biggest star of all lay in his immediate future.

***

When Jackie told her husband, Senator John F. Kennedy, that Gore was working for MGM as a scriptwriter in Hollywood, he called his brother-in-law, Peter Lawford, who had married Kennedy's sister, Patricia. "Peter, invite Gore to go out with you. Let him attend your parties in Santa Monica. Make him feel welcome, the way you do with me. Except if you fix him up, make sure it's a boy, not one of those glory holes you hook me up with."

Lawford promised that he would. Consequently, he called Gore at MGM and invited him to visit Patricia and him at a Saturday night party at their home in Santa Monica, a beach-fronting house that had once been owned by Louis B. Mayer.

At the party, Gore was introduced to Patricia Kennedy Lawford, who told him, "Gore Vidal, you're practically a member of our family...or something like that."

Both of them shared memories of Jackie, Gore telling of when they had the same stepfather—a reference to Hugh Auchincloss.

As an avid movie-goer, Gore had long been fascinated by the screen charm of Peter Lawford. He found the British-born actor very good looking and sexually appealing.

He'd heard that his mother, Lady May Lawford, was privately known as "Mother Bitch."

[Six months into her pregnancy, after informing her devoted husband that he was not the father, he had committed suicide in front of her. Peter was born three months later.]

Most of what Gore had learned about Lawford came from reading the Hollywood gossip columns. He had seduced some of the most widely publicized movie goddesses of the 1940s, including Ava Gardner, June Allyson, Lucille Ball, Rita Hayworth, and, in a much publicized mini-drama, Lana Turner. As a bisexual, he'd once enjoyed the sexual favors of a married couple, Tony Curtis and Janet Leigh, but on separate occasions. Ironically, he had affairs with both of Ronald Reagan's wives, Jane Wyman (after her divorce from Reagan) and Nancy Davis (before her marriage to him).

Director George Cukor had told Gore of Lawford's homosexual life, having seduced the young actor himself. Cukor revealed details about Lawford's long affair with Robert Walker, who had had an extended affair with Nancy Davis himself.

Lawford also had a years-long affair with Van Johnson, and sexual dalliances with men as diverse as Clifton Webb and Noël Coward too.

As a sexual athlete, Lawford had pursued beach bunnies while surfing, as well as prostitutes of both genders. At MGM, he'd specialized in young male extras and studio messengers.

When Gore was introduced to the formidable Lady May, she immediately launched into an attack on the Kennedy family, knowing that Gore knew both Jackie and JFK. She called them "a bunch of barefoot Irish peasants. By marrying my son Peter, that Patricia bitch hopes to link herself with British aristocracy. My God, the next thing I hear, old Joe Kennedy will be buying a title for her. There have been a lot of those for sale since the war ended."

"I told Peter he should have married Elizabeth Taylor," she continued. "She's always been in love with him. Besides, Elizabeth is going to make a lot of money one day, and then Peter could support me in the style to which I am accustomed."

At that point, Lady May asked Gore to bring her another gin and tonic. "The Queen Mother and I share the same taste in drink."

Gore and Lawford had met at the height of their sexual allure, and each of them seemed attracted to the other. Away from the other guests, out on Lawford's terrace overlooking the Pacific, they agreed to slip away on a date that coming Wednesday night. To maintain privacy, Gore suggested they use the guest house of Stanley Haggart, because Gore had access to it, and because it had a private entrance.

Lawford warned him, "As a member of the Kennedy family, I have to be more discreet than I was in those good old days at MGM. Did you know that Jack wants to run for president, perhaps become vice president before that?"

"With Papa Joe's money, he has a chance," Gore said.

That Wednesday, Lawford did arrive at the secluded guest cottage. But as Gore told Haggart the next day, "Peter and I will be friends in the future, but not lovers." He admitted, "We're not sexually compatible. He's a great cocksucker—in fact, oral sex is his thing with both men and women. But he wouldn't let me fuck him, which is what I wanted to do, and I've never been good at giving blow jobs, which is what he wanted."

Gore shared some of Lawford's sexual secrets with Haggart, asserting that Lawford's interest in oral sex began when his governess fellated him when he was only ten years old. Lawford claimed that he'd climaxed. He also told Gore that his first experience with male sex also came when he was ten. A famous American correspondent in London encountered him in a hotel corridor, forced him into his bedroom, and raped him.

"Surely, it wasn't Edward R. Murrow?" Gore wanted to know. "During one of his visits to London?"

Lawford chose not to reveal the name of the journalist, adding, tantalizingly, "I'm sure you were a daily reader of his column."

"Cukor had already told me what a lousy lay Peter was," Gore told Haggart, "and Truman Capote goes around spreading the word about what a lousy lay I am. So there were no great combustions between Peter and myself."

In the future, Gore and Lawford would be nodding acquaintances at parties, but hardly inti-

Dashing, romantic, and wholesome, **Peter Lawford** gets familiar with **June Allyson** in *Good News* (1947).

At the time, she was having an affair with a congressman, John F. Kennedy.

John F. Kennedy *(left)* holds the first child (**Christopher**, born 1955) of his brother-in-law, **Peter Lawford** *(center)*, and his sister, **Patricia Kennedy Lawford** *(right)*.

At the time, JFK was a Senator from Massachusetts.

391

mate friends. "Sal Mineo, in time, told me that he and Peter became hot-to-trot lovers," Gore said. He remembered Lawford in his memoirs, not writing of their sexual link, but referring to him as "Jack's plenipotentiary to the girls of Hollywood. Jack asked both Peter and me on separate occasions endless questions about the availability of this or that star. He was particularly interested to know if Shirley MacLaine had a red pussy."

***

Before she flew to Texas to film scenes for *Giant* (released in 1956), Elizabeth Taylor threw a party at her home, inviting some of her co-workers from her past at MGM. She also included some of the cast members of her upcoming film based on the massive Edna Ferber saga. Her party's guest of honor was the film's director, George Stevens. Cast members from *Giant* included her co-stars, Rock Hudson and James Dean, who would be living in the same house in Mafra, Texas.

Gore had known Elizabeth at MGM, and he was invited. Later in his involvement in Hollywood, he would write the screenplay for one of her most famous movies, *Suddenly Last Summer* (1959), based on a Tennessee Williams play.

Gore was very anxious to meet Hudson, who at that time was the most talked-about actor in gay Hollywood. Almost every day, there was a story about him in the press, often speculating about the type of girl who he would one day marry. Only the other day, Gore had read an entire magazine article speculating about whether Hudson slept in the nude.

Everybody seemingly gossiped about Hudson behind his back. John Wayne had said, "What a waste of a face on a queer. You know what I could have done with that face?"

Much of the gossip about Hudson intrigued Gore. Unlike most young Hollywood males, Hudson had been known to extend "mercy fucks" to such Golden Age icons as Joan Crawford and Tallulah Bankhead or Errol Flynn and Tyrone Power. During the making of *Giant,* he'd have affairs with Sal Mineo, with Elizabeth herself, and with James Dean before those two highly competitive male co-stars launched a famous feud.

Of all the available men at the party, Hudson approached pint-sized Mickey Rooney, who had long been identified with his hostess, Elizabeth, since the days when they were both child stars at MGM.

Rooney later told people at the party, "Rock sent a male friend over to invite me to his house, because he was having some gay guys over. I turned

392

down the invitation. I thought Rock knew I liked girls."

From across the expanse of Elizabeth's living room, Gore took in the sight of Hudson surrounded by three young men. He'd have to wait his turn for an introduction, as he wanted to get to know this tall, handsome, muscular actor noted for his easy going charm and sexual allure.

Gore had heard that Jane Wyman had fallen madly in love with him during their recent filming of *Magnificent Obsession* (1954). "I bet he showed her a hotter time than Ronald Reagan," Gore told Elizabeth.

"Oh, Ronnie's not so bad," she answered. "He's a forty-minute man, unlike Senator Kennedy, who's a two-minute man."

That Hudson was one of the best-endowed actors in Hollywood was common gossip. The blonde-haired actress, Mamie van Doren, a Marilyn Monroe clone, had said, "The boulder his agent *[Henry Willson]* named him after must have been a big one. Rock is very well-endowed."

When Gore finally got to talk to Hudson, he found he was without airs and pretensions, and he spoke with an honesty and candor about his life in Hollywood. After Elizabeth's party, he invited Gore to his home for a midnight swim. The invitation rejected by Rooney was accepted by Gore.

Hudson admitted that, "I'm living with this hot guy who right now is visiting his parents in San Diego. It's always good to have prime beef at home, but even more exciting is to capture something outside on the hoof."

Hudson excused himself "to work the room," as he called it, but agreed to leave at midnight. Gore was instructed to follow in his own car.

Before deserting Gore at the party, Hudson introduced him to Roddy McDowall, a longtime friend of Elizabeth's.

"I never made it with Roddy," Gore later confessed to Haggart. "But every male star at MGM had, or so I heard.

As Gore soon learned, Roddy knew more about the secrets of Hollywood stars than any other actor around—the cover-ups, the blackmail, the abortions, the furtive affairs, especially among married stars, the closeted homosexuals, the back alley deals, even the penis size of every popular male star, gay or straight. Although Hudson surfaced near the top on the penile chart, Clark Gable was near the bottom.

Roddy showed no sexual interest in Gore, but introduced him to Tom Drake, a handsome young actor he'd known from his days at MGM. Before meeting Drake, Roddy warned Gore, "He's still carrying a torch for Peter Lawford, but he's available."

Drake was scheduled to play Elizabeth's brother in another upcoming film, *Raintree County* (1957). He'd also be cast almost decade later in her film, *The Sandpiper* (1965).

Gore told Roddy, "I think I fell in love with Tom when he appeared as "the boy next door" with Judy Garland in *Meet Me in St. Louis* (1944).

Gore liked Drake right away. Even though about eight years older, the Brooklyn-born actor still retained his good looks and quiet charm. Haggart was throwing a late Saturday night bash for his Hollywood friends, and Gore invited

Drake to drive over to Laurel Canyon to attend. Drake said he'd be delighted.

"Don't bring an escort," Gore cautioned. "I'll be your escort."

"I was hoping you'd say that," Drake answered.

***

After midnight, at Hudson's pool party, Gore counted at least thirty-five young men in various states of dress or undress. Some wore the skimpiest of swimwear, including flimsy *caches-sexes,* as they were known on the French Riviera. Others were completely nude.

Exercising his muscular body, actor **George Nader** *(depicted above)* was Rock Hudson's best friend.

Below, **Rock Hudson**, fresh from the shower, is arranging another date with a man. Once, Gore was invited to take a boat ride with these two handsome men to Catalina Island. "Those guys pulled off their swimming trunks," Gore said. "For the first time, I believed God created man in his own image."

For the occasion, Hudson himself appeared in conventional bathing trunks, the kind he'd wear in an upcoming picture with Doris Day. He introduced Gore to actor George Nader, who seemed as well-built as Hudson.

Gore also met the talent scout and theatrical agent, Henry Willson, who was sloppy, fat, and known for auditioning the hottest hunks in Hollywood, including Guy Madison and Rory Calhoun. Gore looked for either of them at the party, but they weren't there.

"Mr. Willson," Gore said. "Your reputation has preceded you."

"Don't believe those rumors that I'm a lecherous, dirty old queen," Willson said. "I take a bath every day—never alone, of course, so you can strike 'dirty' from my list of credits."

Gore cast a skeptical eye at Willson, with his hawkish nose that evoked a bird of prey sniffing out his next meal, plus a protruding lower lip that implied a deep capacity for petulance. He noted that he was a chinless wonder, with feminine hips and sloping shoulders, along with legs shorter than those of Elizabeth Taylor.

Sensing that Gore was evaluating him critically, Willson said, "I don't need male beauty to seduce a boy, gay or

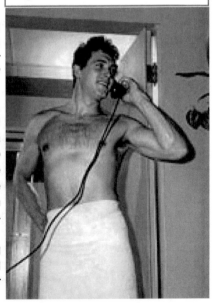

straight. In Hollywood, all you need is power. If you've got that, you can have virtually any actor, even if straight. You'd be surprised at how many straight boys drop their pants for me and show it hard if I can get them a role in a movie."

Before meeting Willson that night, Roddy had warned Gore that "Willson is like slime that oozes from under a rock you don't want to turn over. Henry operates the busiest gay casting couch in the history of Hollywood."

The highlight of the evening came when someone began broadcasting a recording of Rosemary Clooney singing a duet with Marlene Dietrich. From the pool house emerged Hudson and George Nader, each wearing only a pink bow tie with cherry-red polka dots.

"My God," Gore later recalled. "I couldn't believe those two. There was meat there for the poor."

At two o'clock that morning, Gore was invited up to Hudson's bedroom.

"I didn't know if we'd make it or not," Gore later reported to Haggart. "But I knew one thing. He wasn't going to put that club in me. If he had, I'd surely have to be rushed to the hospital. Holy shit! As it turned out, he liked to get fucked. He shot off while I was in the driver's seat. We had a great old time, and set up future dates with each other."

Months later, Gore claimed that his times with Hudson fell into two different periods: "pre-*Giant* and *après-Giant.*"

"We made it together several times before his trip to Texas, but it never happened after his return, although I made repeated calls to him," Gore said. "We never argued. He just drifted off, as he was faced with incredible temptation. One night at another party at Elizabeth's home, I ran into Rock again. This time he seemed locked into an affair with Troy Donahue, the hot new blonde-haired sensation."

Later that night, both Rock and I shared the toilet bowl in Elizabeth's bathroom. We had to take a leak. He whipped it out for me, the last I ever saw of such splendid equipment. He also confided a secret to me."

"Troy Donahue is one of Hollywood's great cocksuckers. But there's not much down there between his legs."

***

Former child star, **Roddy McDowall**, was Elizabeth Taylor's best friend. He knew all the dark secrets of Hollywood, but refused to write a memoir.

Henry Willson *(left)* told truck driver Roy Fitzgerald (later renamed **Rock Hudson;** *right)*, "I can turn you into a big Hollywood star, but you've got to put out...and I'm insatiable."

That Saturday night, Tom Drake showed up at Haggart's home in Laurel Canyon. As was his custom, Haggart had assembled his usual coven of current and faded stars, some from RKO, where he'd worked as an extra in the 1930s.

On this occasion, there were no women present, only men, all of whom were actors, most of them has-beens. Guests included Alan Ladd, Ramon Novarro, Jon Hall, William Haines, Francis Lederer, and Eric Linden.

At this point, Drake's movie career was in decline. As he said himself, "It's been a long time since I've seen *The White Cliffs of Dover,*" a reference to a movie he'd made in 1944.

He was, however, finding acting jobs in television series, notably NBC's *Cimarron City* and CBS's *Perry Mason.*

Drake had told Gore and Haggart, "The membership in my fan clubs from the 1940s has dwindled down to just three loyal members. My bobbysoxers have all moved to the suburbs and are married with children."

That night, after the actors retreated from Haggart's party, Gore and Drake remained. Before retiring to the main house with Jon Hall, Haggart delivered a chilled bottle of champagne to his guest cottage.

Haggart didn't see Gore and Drake again until one o'clock the following afternoon. He assumed that their mating had been successful.

But after breakfast, Drake pulled off his swimming trunks and went for a nude swim. Haggart was eager to know what had happened the previous night.

"We're very compatible," Gore told him. "Tom's a great bottom, just like I prefer 'em.'"

"My cottage is always open to you guys," Haggart promised.

"You're going to have to change those chartreuse sheets a lot for us," Gore said. "That one's ass, as you can see for yourself, is in need of pounding. No wonder Peter Lawford dumped him. He's more into passive sodomy than he is into active fellatio, Peter's favorite pastime."

MEET ME IN ST. LOUIS

Tom Drake *(featured in both photos, above)* won the hearts of both the American public and **Judy Garland** when he appeared as "the boy next door" in her blockbusting 1944 musical, *Meet Me in St. Louis,* a frothy celebration of small-town nostalgia filmed during the darkest years of World War II.

In the 1940s and 50s, the handsome young actor was "passed around" from one bed to another, seduced by the likes of such men as Peter Lawford, Merv Griffin, and Gore Vidal.

In the years ahead, both Gore and Haggart were saddened to see Drake's film and TV work dry up.

He ended up selling used cars. The last time he ran into Haggart, he told him, "I'm heading for oblivion."

Drake died of lung cancer in 1982.

***

In May of 1955, Gore previewed a television play called *Visit to a Small Planet,* which he later reworked for the Broadway stage. It made its debut on the Great White Way in February of 1957 and ran for 388 performances. It starred Cyril Ritchard, who also directed. Eddie Mayehoff was his co-star, and both actors were nominated for a Tony Award for their performances.

In a nutshell, Gore had written a satire on post war paranoia in the United States, as spearheaded (disastrously) by the notorious senator from Wisconsin, Joseph McCarthy.

The play is the story of Kreton (Ritchard), a time traveler who has arrived on earth from a distant planet with the intention of witnessing the American Civil War of the 1860s. En route, he made a miscalculation and lands on Earth a century later than he wanted.

In 1960, to Gore's dismay, Paramount adapted his play into a movie starring Jerry Lewis as Kreton, the alien from outer space. *The New York Times* wryly observed, "Having run short of stratospheric monsters, the movie people have recruited Jerry Lewis as the latest arrival from Outer Space."

The review was an attack, defining Lewis as "a jazzy intruder from above who flabbergasts and heckles a rather dim-witted Southern family, performs some pratfalls and magic tricks warmed over from *The Invisible Man,* and finally streaks away in his space ship. Naturally, Lewis is hanging on by his fingernails and yelling his head off."

When the play had originally been adapted for television, a young actor, Indiana-born Dick York, had showed up for an audition. Gore had already seen him perform with his friend, Joanne Woodward, in live television broadcasts. He'd also appeared in such Broadway hits as *Tea and Sympathy* and in William Inge's *Bus Stop,* which had been seen by Gore.

He liked York and immediately bonded with him. As he later told Woodward, "Dick and I sent the right signals to each other, and not from Outer Space."

Even though York had married Joan Alt in 1951, a relationship that would last until his death in 1992, Gore knew that York was a homosexual.

After dinner on their first night together, Dick and Gore ended up in the writer's apartment. "He was very submissive," Gore later told Haggart, who had returned to New York to occupy his Greenwich Village townhouse. "Unlike the hustlers I rent, I didn't have to pay Dick. He's very willing and very passive in all the right ways. It's not much of an affair, but the kid appeals to me in some way." *[Although he called York a kid, he was only three years younger than*

Gore.]

The on-again, off-again affair lasted until 1958, when York suffered a back injury that would prove permanently disabling. He was filming a movie with Tab Hunter, Gary Cooper, and Rita Hayworth entitled *They Came to Cordura*. A stunt backfired, and York suffered a back injury that would cause him pain for the rest of his life.

Even so, although in great pain, York starred with Elizabeth Montgomery and Agnes Moorehead in the hit TV sitcom, *Bewitched,* in the 1960s.

At one point in the series, York became so ill, he could no longer perform. From that point until the series ended in 1972, Dick Sargent played the role of Darrin Stephens. Ironically, Sargent had originally been offered the part in 1964, but turned it down for another sitcom that failed.

Largely bedridden, York battled pain for the rest of his life, becoming at one point addicted to pain killers.

Gore Vidal was but a distant memory when he died on February 20, 1992.

***

"Gore's screwing around with movie stars definitely lasted through the 1950s," said Haggart. "Often, these liaisons took place in my guest cottage in Hollywood, or in my townhouse on Leroy Street in Manhattan. After that, they became very rare."

"With a notable exception here and there, Gore's sexual involvements were mostly with hustlers until the end of his life. Rock Hudson, Sal Mineo, Tom Drake, and Robert Francis belonged to his glorious youth. He still preferred handsome, well-built men, but they were hardly movie stars, and not likely to become such in their futures. Also, except for Nureyev, Gore's sideline as a balletomane also dimmed."

Dick York became most famous for his portrayal of the self-inflicted sufferings of a fussy, Cold-War era suburbanite, Darrin Stephens, in the long-running TV sitcom, *Bewitched.*

In the upper photo, he's positioned uncomfortably between his wife (**Elizabeth Montgomery**) and his witch of a mother-in-law, Endora, as played by **Agnes Moorehead**.

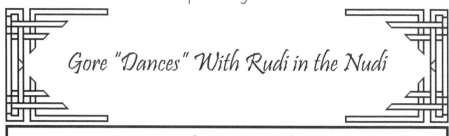

Chapter Twenty-Seven

Gore "Dances" With Rudi in the Nudi

From Russia With Love—Tales of Tatar Tail

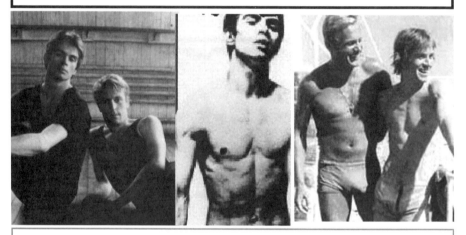

When he was younger, Gore Vidal shared **Rudolf Nureyev** *(who appears in each of the three photos above)* with many other lovers, especialy ballet dancer **Eric Bruhn** *(left photo)* and with **Tab Hunter** *(right)*. "I'm too good a lover not to share my body with others," Nureyev said.

"I don't care what the magazines say, I am *the sexiest man alive!" So proclaimed Rudolf Nureyev: "Just ask Lee Radziwill. Just ask Tab Hunter. Just ask Jackie Kennedy. Nobody in the world can resist me. Everyone who has ever gone to bed with me has fallen madly in love with me!"*

Ever since the late 1940s, Gore Vidal had been a balletomane, seeking out dancers such as John Kriza and Harold Lang and seducing them. He'd also studied ballet himself, though he was not particularly good at it.

In 1961, Gore was mildly intrigued when he read in the newspapers that the premier Russian ballet dancer, Rudolf Nureyev, had defected to the West, turning himself over to police officers in Paris and asking for asylum.

Gore read that Nureyev had been born in 1938 on a Trans-Siberian train racing across the Soviet Union to meet his father, a Red army political commissar.

The papers claimed that Nureyev was known for "his rebellious character and non-conformist attitude." Suspecting he might defect, KGB agents in France, using a ruse, tried to lure him back to Moscow. But quick-witted Nureyev knew he was being lied to and suspected that if he returned to Russia, he's be imprisoned.

Rudolf Nureyev

As Gore remembered it, he was in Paris when he read an article by Oliver Merlin in *Le Monde*, describing Nureyev, who was being increasingly referred to as "Rudi" in the press:

"I will never forget his arriving running across the back of the stage, and his catlike way of holding himself opposite the ramp. He wore a white sash over an ultramarine costume, had large wild eyes and hollow cheeks under a turban topped with a spray of feathers, bulging thighs, immaculate tights. This was already Nijinsky in Firebird."

As Gore proclaimed to Howard Austen, "I've got to possess this ballet god."

Rudi, within a week of his defection, signed up with the Grand Ballet du Marquis de Cuevas, and Gore attended a performance of Rudi's *The Sleeping Beauty* with Nina Vyroubova.

Gore went backstage and was introduced to Rudi by the theater manager, who told him that Gore was a famous American writer and "the brother of Jackie Kennedy."

It was suggested that Gore's connection to the recently elected American president, John F. Kennedy, might lead to Rudi becoming an American citizen.

Rudi desperately wanted to meet this author with such close ties to Kennedy's White House. He accepted Gore's invitation, and the ballet dancer and Gore returned to the author's hotel suite in Paris. Austen was no problem, as he'd been booked into a separate room on another floor.

Over champagne, Rudi told Gore that, "My creativity as a ballet dancer is very much akin to my sex drive."

Gore found this stimulating. He was even more aroused when Rudi pulled off all his clothes and performed a scene from *Le Sacre du Printemps (The Rite of Spring)* that Vaslav Nijinski had performed at the Théâtre des Champs-Élysées in Paris in 1913.

Rudi re-created the role of a nymph and, like Nijinski in the original, he danced an act of masturbation. But whereas Nijinski (on stage, at least) had only mimed masturbation, in front of Gore, Rudi actually masturbated.

"Before his dance had ended, I had already planned its *climax,*" Gore later told Howard Austen and others.

The Reincarnation of Nijinski, Spewing Sperm in The Rite of Spring

That evening marked the beginning of other nights that would be played out around the world, mainly in New York, London, and the Amalfi Coast of Italy.

"We were on-again, off-again lovers," Gore said. "I knew better to want more from him, and I also knew that I would never possess him, as he'd known many lovers, perhaps even some female ones, in his future."

The designer, Stanley Mills Haggart, was in Paris at the time, writing a guidebook to that city for the Frommer Guides. When Haggart visited with Gore, his friend revealed that he and Rudi were having an affair.

"On our second night together, Rudi went into the bathroom and came out naked," Gore said. "He lay down on his stomach on the thick carpet. 'Take me,' he commanded."

After it was over, Gore claimed that Rudi had wanted to have sex with him like that "just to show off my back *[his words]*. It is very beautiful, *non*?"

"Yes, you have an incredibly beautiful back," Gore told him. "But with an ass like that, who in hell looks at your back?"

Gore also told Haggart that "Rudi considers taking of his ballet tights as the beginning of foreplay. He likes to be taken when he's all hot and sweaty. He also thinks the aroma of smegma from his uncut penis stimulates lust in his partner—that, of course, is a matter of *taste.*"

Within weeks, Rudi had fallen in love—not with Gore, but with Erik Bruhn, the Danish soloist ballet dancer at the Royal Danish Ballet in Copenhagen. Gore soon learned that Bruhn and Rudi had become lovers.

Even though he was in Verbier, Switzerland, at the time, Truman was among the first to learn of the Vidal/Nureyev affair. "Gore had the hots for Rudi," Truman claimed. "Word spread through the ballet world. Even though Rudi had taken Bruhn as his permanent lover, Gore showed up at his performances with his tongue hanging out."

Truman wrote Cecil Beaton. "I don't understand Nureyev. What sort of sex life does he have? Is he in love with Erik Bruhn? Myself, I think Nureyev is repulsive. But then Gore and I have never agreed on this subject of what constitutes attractiveness."

Truman later said, "As for Rudi, Gore can have him. Besides, I understand he fucks like a jack rabbit."

Truman may not have been completely honest in dismissing Rudi to Beaton. Later, he claimed, "Everybody, man or woman, wanted to fuck with Rudi, and most of them did, even the Kennedys. Whether he was dancing *Swan Lake* or *Romeo and Juliet,* all eyes were glued to Rudi's ample crotch. I sampled it myself. All nine and a half inches of thick Slavic meat."

Back in New York, Haggart also entertained Gore and Rudi at his large townhouse on Leroy Street in Greenwich Village. For a party in honor of Rudi, Haggart invited dancer/choreographer friends of his who wanted to meet Rudi. The guest list included Martha Graham, Alvin Ailey, Joyce Trisler, and James Mitchell, who brought his lover, Farley Granger.

The former actress and ballerina, Tamara Geva, was also invited. She had been married to George Balanchine and also to Tallulah Bankhead's only husband, actor John Emery. She was Russian herself and could help Rudi convey his thoughts to the other guests, since his English was very poor.

"After dinner and over drinks in the parlor, Rudi at one point disappeared into the bathroom," Haggart said. "He came out completely naked and took his seat on the sofa between Martha and Joyce. These were all very sophisticated people, and so everybody just continued talking as if there was nothing out of the ordinary. Of course, dancers are used to backstage nudity."

"After midnight, all the guests departed," Haggart said. "Gore asked if he and Rudi could stay over in one of my guest bedrooms. I told them, 'Move in if you like.'"

On a very different occasion, Gore called Haggart and invited him to the apartment of actress Monique van Vooren. She was out of town, and she had given Rudi the use of her apartment while she was away.

"I'm an interior designer myself," Stanley said. "and I was highly amused when I walked into the apartment. The décor was something that Liberace and Mae West combined might have created. A huge candelabra rested on a white grand piano, a touch of Liberace."

When I investigated more thoroughly, I found that liquor bottles had been placed inside the piano. It was a bar, not a piano. Everything was in white—the carpet, the furnishings. Affixed to the ceiling, directly over the bed, there was a very large mirror, just like the one in Mae West's apartment in Los Angeles."

"Even though the day was bright and sunny, Rudi had pulled the draperies. He told me he was terrified."

Across the street from the apartment was the Russian Consulate, under heavy guard by KGB agents.

"They have orders to kidnap me and bring me back to Moscow," Rudi told Haggart and Gore.

This was not paranoia on Rudi's part. His life was in far more jeopardy than he feared at the time. In the 1990s, it was revealed that Nikita Khrushchev had signed an order demanding that Soviet agents assassinate Rudi.

***

Monique van Vooren wrote in her 1981 book, *Night Sanctuary,* "Rudi was tortured and tormented by his sexuality. He was ashamed of being a homosexual."

In Diane Solway's *Nureyev: His Life*, published in 1998, she wrote that he preferred "rough trade, pickups, sailors, lorry drivers, and the like."

"Rudi went in for rent boys and hustlers, but he seduced an amazing number of celebrities, and I include myself on that list," Gore said. "Some of his choices surprised me—take Tab Hunter, for instance."

The strikingly handsome, blonde-haired matinee idol of the 1950s even admitted in his autobiography to having an affair with Rudi, writing about his "bone-white body with blue veins clad only in a silver *lamé* swimsuit."

What especially intrigued Gore were Rudi's rumored Kennedy seductions, including both Jackie and her sister, Lee Radziwill. Even more astounding was an affair with Bobby Kennedy, whom Gore had long suspected of being a deeply closeted homosexual. He later speculated about this in his memoirs.

In *Palimpsest,* Gore claimed that Rudi confessed that he and Bobby "did share a young soldier, American soldier," in Rudi's words.

Julie Kavanagh, who wrote the definitive biography of Rudi, added another RFK/Nureyev link.

Alexander Grant of the Royal Ballet claimed that he and Rudi were having an intimate talk at Arthurs *[the leading nightclub in Manhattan in the 60s]* when Bobby Kennedy approached them.

Abruptly, Bobby asked, "Hey, what's going on between you two? Break this up!"

It seemed that RFK wanted to take possession of Rudi, and he pulled him away and disappeared with him into the night.

Rudolf Nureyev Dancing "to the Last Drop" in Paris

In Paris, Rudi invited Gore to see his 1977 film, *Valentino,* in which he impersonated that great lover of the Silent Screen, "The Sheik." British director Ken Russell guided Rudi through a difficult role with many costume changes. His wardroom ranged from gangster-style pin stripes, flowing Moorish *djellabas,* and Argentinian-style gaucho pants, as well as scenes where he appeared without clothes at all.

Long after the last dying embers of passion's fire had turned to ashes, Rudi and Gore still remained friends, especially when Rudi purchased a little rocky island off the coast of Positano, along the Amalfi Coast, south of Naples. The islet had previously been owned by Léonide Massine, the great Russian choreographer, who had built a villa there. Gore, of course, lived in the nearby hilltop town of Ravello.

In his memoirs, Gore relates, "I would come down from Ravello to visit him. Then, with seigneurial courtesy, he would come to see me by the sea, where he would let his AIDS-wasted body collapse beside the pool."

"I spent the night with Rudi and was awakened the next morning at nine o'clock," Gore said. "A boat filled with tourists was circling the island, and a woman's voice on a loudspeaker was extolling the glories of Rudi's achievements in ballet."

"After breakfast, we went into a room below, which was covered with ceramic tiles from floor to ceiling," Gore said. "It was crowned with a dome. Rudi told me he wanted to be buried in the center of the room under that dome—this was, in fact, his mausoleum."

"For lunch and dinner, the cook served only potatoes cooked in myriad ways—no meat or vegetables," Gore said. "The cook was fat, Rudi, of course was not."

"I knew Rudi practiced unsafe sex, but he seemed to think he was immune from AIDS," Gore said. "In 1984, he told me that he'd tested positive for HIV, but he didn't change his sexual habits. He kept insisting that, 'There is nothing wrong with me. My Tatar blood is pure as a mountain stream in Siberia.' But by the summer of 1991, I noticed a remarkable decline in his health. When I saw him in Paris in the spring of 1992, I knew he was dying."

Deep in December, **Gore** *(left)* in Ravello with **Nureyev** on his last legs.

Gore attended Rudi's final ballet performance in *La Bayadère* at the Palais Garnier in Paris. During the ten-minute ovation that followed, Rudi needed help to walk across the stage.

Later that night, he told Gore, "The main thing for me is my dancing. Before it withers away from my body, I will keep dancing until the last moment, the last drop."

In his memoirs, Gore recalled Rudi's final visit to Ravello. It was in the August before he died.

Gore remembered that Rudi looked thin and exhausted. "He sat on my sofa, drinking white wine. He could go on for hours without talking. He did come alive for ballet gossip."

As Gore reported it, Rudi said, "Peter Martins—he kill wife, no? No. Sad. Saw him when he was sixteen. In class. Big cock hangs here. I make move. Erik Bruhn say, 'No, too young. Go to jail.'"

[Peter Martins, the very talented and hard-driving Danish classical dancer and choreographer and one of the luminaries of the ballet world, served for many years as the artistic director of the New York City Ballet.]

Gore claimed that Rudi's face was ravaged but still beautiful. "He was still very much the Tatar king. The upper body had begun to waste away, but the lower was still unaffected—legs powerful, and the feet, for a dancer, not too misshapen, no hammertoes."

The last time Gore met with Rudi, the dancer told him, "I will soon be joining Erik somewhere, someplace. He and I will dance a *pas de deux* into eternity."

Rudi died on January 6, 1993 at the age of 54. He was buried at the Russian cemetery in Sainte-Geneviève-des-Bois near Paris, a pilgrimage site even today for his still-loyal fans.

On his last visit to Paris, Gore placed yellow roses on his grave and included a note:

THANKS FOR THE MEMORIES

—G. V.

Chapter Twenty-Eight

Gore Confronts "Mother Goddamn," the Very Difficult
Bette Davis

Gore Gets Down and Dirty with Guy Madison
"The Leading Male Sex Symbol of the Postwar Era"

Gary Merrill *(left)* not only made love to **Bette Davis** as Margo Channing in *All About Eve*, but he married her. Gore Vidal later said he found the Joseph L. Mankiewicz script "the most devastatingly venomous, witty, and literate script of 1950—I wish I'd written it."

Instead, he was assigned to another Davis script, *The Catered Affair* (1956), co-starring a young **Debbie Reynolds**, showcased with a frumpy-looking Bette in the right-hand photo. "Hollywood has forgotten me," Davis told Gore. "I hope your script and my acting will reignite my career." They didn't.

In 1945, at war's end, as Gore was ending his tour of duty

in the U.S. Army, he was a frequent visitor to Hollywood. He usually found his mother, Nina Vidal, drunk, and he didn't want to stay with her.

Her best friend was Doris Stein, and she invited Gore, during his visits, to stay with her family. She was married to the powerful Jules Stein, an entrepreneur and Hollywood player who had taken $1,000 in capital and had eventually built a billion dollar force in the world of mass entertainment. He was one of the founders of MCA, Inc. Starting out as an eye surgeon, he later became the world's largest producer of film entertainment.

He found Gore brilliant and talented, predicting he'd go far if he decided to devote his life to screenwriting instead of novels.

When Gore met him, Jules was the agent to such stars as Bette Davis, Betty Grable, Joan Crawford, Greta Garbo (although she was retired), Ingrid Bergman, Frank Sinatra, and Jack Benny, among dozens of others.

One night, Jules drove Gore to the Hollywood Canteen, which had been

Bette Davis, the belle of the Hollywood Canteen. As one sailor told The Hollywood Reporter, "You could always count on Miss Davis if you wanted to get laid."

That comment did not appear in print.

founded during World War II by Bette Davis and John Garfield to provide entertainment for servicemen, many of whom were going off to battle the Japanese in the Pacific, and perhaps to their imminent deaths.

Jules was head of the Hollywood Canteen's finance committee, charged with fund raising. At the Canteen, major stars such as Barbara Stanwyck and Betty Grable, danced with servicemen. Jules immediately introduced Gore to Bette Davis, the Queen of the Canteen.

"It was obvious to me that Jules was in love with Bette," Gore later said. "When I first met Bette, I had no idea that in a decade or so, I'd been writing a screenplay in which she'd star."

"I had heard that she was nothing but majestic arrogance," Gore said. "Not on this night. She was a petite little thing, no Lana Turner, but not ugly either. She kissed Jules and me, but was enveloped by a bevy of gay servicemen who adored her. She was very, very popular."

During the course of its existence, some two million servicemen were entertained at the canteen, dancing to the sound of Kay Kyser's band. "Hormones raged and romances soared," one reporter wrote. "Young, untested, and unknown servicemen danced with Betty Hutton, Ida Lupino, and Hedy Lamarr, among others. Bing Crosby often showed up to warble."

"Before I left Hollywood for duties in the Aleutian Islands, Jules drove me

---

"If you cast her as a Bronx housewife, Bette Davis will play her as Queen Elizabeth the First"

—Dore Schary, Director of Production (later, president) of MGM

---

back to the canteen for one final visit." Gore said. "After all, I was a serviceman in need of entertainment. Bette wasn't there that night, but Jules introduced me to Marlene Dietrich, who showed up in a costume of gold body paint, hard to describe. She asked me to dance."

"As she danced real close to me, she made her intentions rather obvious," Gore said. "Apparently, she found me attractive, but there was no way I was going home with a powerhouse of a woman like that."

"Before the night was over, I danced with Jane Wyman, who was married to Ronald Reagan at the time. She just seemed to be doing her duty, no sparks between us. However, when I went to the men's room, I was cruised by Za-chory Scott. I'd just seen him with Joan Crawford in *Mildred Pierce.*"

"I wanted to leave with this devilish hunk, but didn't want to embarrass Jules," Gore said. "At the time, he didn't know I was gay."

"I never got to seduce any male stars at the canteen. Later, I heard that Tru-man Capote, the lucky little fart, on very different occasions, got the pants off both Errol Flynn and John Garfield. How he managed to do that, I'll never know."

Although Gore more or less failed as a novelist, he did not abandon that form of writing forever. Soonafter, he began to achieve monetary success with teleplays, some of them adapted from successful works presented in books or even other films.

He was aided by the support of an administrative pow-erhouse, Martin Manulis, a Brooklyn-born CBS director best known for creating the television series *Playhouse 90.* The show came to epitomize what is known as "Tele-vision's Golden Age of Live Drama." Insofar as his rela-tionship to Gore, Manulis said, "I was his mother, wet-nurse, and psychiatrist."

Zachory Scott...
cruising Gore

[Manulis became known for commissioning teleplays based on the works of such established writ-ers as William Faulkner, Clifford Odets, Ernest Hemingway, and F. Scott Fitzgerald. Fre-quently working against the grain of commonly accepted belief patterns, he would eventually cast Robert Redford as a Nazi or "monster" Boris Karloff as a dignified man deeply in love. In time, he also produced movies, his most heralded being Days of Wine and Roses *(1962).]*

Manulis assigned Gore to adapt Faulkner's short story, *Smoke.* Manulus at first thought Gore was so handsome, trim, and fit that he might become a leading man, instruct-ing his underlings to "Bring him in front of the

Ronald Reagan with **Jane Wyman**
....When Love Was Young.

407

camera instead of having him write scenes for it." But Gore preferred writing.

Smoke was so successful that Gore was then commissioned to adapt Faulkner's "Barn Burning."

["Barn Burning" which first appeared in Harper's Magazine in 1939, is a short story dealing with social inequities and vengeance as viewed through the perspective of a young, impressionable child.]

Suddenly, Gore was turning out teleplay after teleplay—Henry James' *The Turn of the Screw;* Stephen Crane's *The Blue Hotel,* and "A Sense of Justice" for Philco Playhouse, with a stellar performance by E.G. Marshall.

Not all of Gore's ideas went over, however, especially when he suggested a TV series that would cast the extremely handsome Louis Jourdan as The Devil. In another script, he wanted to send a young physicist back to the year 1865, where he would prevent the assassination of Abraham Lincoln. For each thirty-minute teleplay, Gore was paid $1,500, good money back in the mid-1950s.

Gore joined the coveted list of major teleplay writers, including Rod Sterling and Paddy Chayefsky. "I am the King of Television," he announced to his mother, Nina, who had predicted utter failure for him.

Sometimes friendships, even an occasional romance, rose from one of these productions, since the principals worked together so closely together, often into the dawn hours.

In March of 1955, he had been asked to adapt the George Kaufman/Edna Ferber Broadway hit *Stage Door* for the TV series, *The Best of Broadway,* to star Rhonda Fleming and Diana Lynn. Katharine Hepburn and Ginger Rogers had already co-starred together in a highly successful film adaptation of that Broadway play. Released in 1937, it was also entitled *Stage Door.*

During the business associated with its TV remake, Gore met the very beautiful Rhonda Fleming, who was hailed as "The Queen of Technicolor" because her fair complexion and flaming red hair photographed so well in color.

He found Fleming striking, although his sexual interests lay elsewhere. He did write a womanizer friend of his, "Tonight, I dine with Rhonda Fleming. Tell me how much you envy me."

He did, however, find Diana Lynn so appealing that he became involved in a series of platonic dates with her that stretched over five years.

Gore was often invited to Hollywood parties, and he needed to show up with a woman. "Only Tennessee dared attend these parties with Frank Merlo on his arm," Gore said.

He would invite Lynn, who was between marriages at the time. She was a pianist, a child prodigy, who turned to film roles, having scored her biggest success in Preston Sturges' *The Miracle of Morgan's Creek. (1944)*. She'd even appeared with Cary Grant in *Every Girl Should Be Married* (1949), and with

Diana Lynn
...a roll on the carpet

Ronald Reagan in *Bedtime for Bonzo* (1951).

Gore remembered Lynn as "having this elegant sort of kittenlike manner with very sharp eyes, a pert nose, and an attractively angled face. Her look radiated with good humor and intelligence."

Dominick Dunne, a writer and investigative journalist, was a friend of Lynn's. He later said, "If Gore Vidal could ever have loved a woman, it would have been Diana. Gore was mad about her. Let's call it a special friendship."

Lynn wasn't as straight-laced as Gore had originally perceived. At a Hollywood party for couples only, Gore and Lynn were the only unmarried couple there. As she walked through the room greeting everybody, she gave each of the men a kiss on the cheek. On the terrace, Lynn confessed to him, "You know something? I've had every single husband in this room."

DID YOU SAY "UNPRESIDENTIAL?"
A Role that a Future World Leader
Would Regret

Diana Lynn (Gore Vidal's "beard") with **"that naughty chimp"** and an ill-advised **Ronald Reagan** in *Bedtime for Bonzo* (1951)

Jules Stein found Lynn "cute and tiny, dreaming of becoming the next Grace Kelly. I once asked Gore if they'd ever rolled in the hay together. He told me they hadn't, but that once, they had rolled around on his carpet."

"It was sad what happened to the girl," Stein said. "She died of a stroke in 1971 at the age of forty-five."

"At the same time that Gore was going out with Lynn, he was also seen with Joanne Woodward, who, unknown to us for a time, sneaked around with Paul Newman," Stein said. "Hollywood columnists wrote about Gore's romances with Woodward and Lynn. Those gals, Hedda Hopper and Louella Parsons, pretended to be awful dumb in those days of deceiving the public."

"Gore wasn't screwing either Lynn or Woodward, but I suspected he was sucking off Newman on the side and plowing Hedda Hopper's son, William Hopper, every other Saturday night," Stein said. "Newspapers, except for *Confidential* magazine, never printed shit like that back in the good old days."

As Gore later wrote in his memoirs, "I kept loving company with Diana for several years, with no thought on either side of marriage, the central God in the American pantheon during the Age of Eisenhower."

In May of 1955, Manulis got Gore the assignment of adapting Ernest Hemingway's *A Farewell to Arms,* into a 60-minute teleplay, part of the TV drama series, *Climax.*

Director Allen Reisner cast the blonde heartthrob Guy Madison in the lead, opposite Diana Lynn, who had fallen in love with Madison the moment she'd seen his brief appearance as a sailor in *Since You Went Away* (1944).

To Gore, Madison represented the epitome of the post World War II male sex symbol. He was one of the star attractions from talent agent Henry Willson's coven of pretty boys, which included Rock Hudson, Rory Calhoun, Troy Donahue, Tab Hunter, Robert Wagner, and dozens of others collectively forming "The Beefcake Brigade."

Lynn arranged the first run-through of the made-for TV drama at Gore's apartment. Madison showed up in tight-fitting blue jeans and a white T-shirt, revealing the outline of his pecs. For Gore, it was love at first sight.

"I'm Guy Madison," the icon said, flashing his famous smile.

Before the night ended, Gore realized "the hunk could be had." After kissing Lynn goodbye on the street, Madison was invited to stay over.

As Gore later told Tennessee and others, "He spent the weekend. I didn't want to let him go. I would have liked to have held on to him, but the competition for that guy was just too severe."

"Guy told me that Willson operated the hottest and busiest casting couch in the history of Hollywood," Gore said. "He calls himself a flesh peddler. He always takes a pound of that flesh before he peddles one of his guys on the open market. In Hollywood, there are many takers."

"As an actor, Guy was a bit wooden in *Farewell to Arms,*" Gore said. "I fear our attempt at Hemingway bombed, but Guy certainly was a fringe benefit to me for my adaptation. He was three years older than me, but looked ten years younger and had a great body—and he sure knew how to use it. Lots of practice, I'm sure. Also, Guy—whose original, pre-Hollywood name was Robert Moseley—was the only person I ever met from Pumpkin Center, California.":

"My fling with Guy didn't work out, so I went back to taking Diana out at night," Gore said. "After giving her a fleeting kiss and a promise to call in the morning, I headed for Santa Monica Boulevard to locate my hustler for the night."

[Later, in 1957, another member of Willson's stable of good-looking men, Rock Hudson, would make A Farewell to Arms *into a full-length movie, playing opposite Jennifer Jones. Previously, Gary Cooper and Helen Hayes had co-starred together in a previous film adaptation, released in 1932, of the same Hemingway novel.]*

Heartthrob **Guy Madison**, the subject of both photos above, became every gay man's fantasy in Hollywood. "For me, the dream came true," Gore claimed.

Bette Davis' "Little Ronald Reagan" Gets Cast as a Homosexual

In July of 1955, Dore Schary, chief of MGM (he'd replaced the tyrannical Louis B. Mayer) chose Gore to write a big screen adaptation of Paddy Chayefsky's teleplay, *The Catered Affair.* MGM had purchased the movie rights and had selected the very talented Richard Brooks, as director. *[Not to be confused with Peter Brook, the English director disastrously associated with Truman Capote's* House of Flowers, *Philadelphia-born Richard Brooks was also a screenwriter, a novelist, and occasional film producer.]*

Brooks had a lot of clout at the time, as he had just directed the hugely successful *Blackboard Jungle* (1955). Two big hits lay in his immediate future, including Tennessee Williams' *Cat on a Hot Tin Roof* (1958) and Sinclair Lewis' *Elmer Gantry* (1960).

Gore signed on as a scriptwriter for $2,000 a week, and immediately met for luncheons in the MGM commissary with fellow scriptwriters. Leonard Spieglegass, who spoke with a voice evocative of Noël Coward's, was the king of MGM scriptwriters at the time. At the writers' table in MGM's commissary, he warned Gore not to show up his fellow writers by producing more than three pages of dialogue a day.

Schary was pleased with the choice of Ernest Borgnine as the male lead, cast as a Bronx taxi driver and the scruffy husband of the dowdy Aggie Murley, a character famously portrayed in Chayefsky's TV teleplay by character actress Thelma Ritter.

[Ironically Ritter had portrayed Davis' maid in All About Eve *(1950), and now Bette Davis had "surpassed" Davis once again, having been chosen by Brooks to replace Ritter in the role of the Bronx housewife on screen. "I am really pissed off," Ritter told Brooks in an angry phone call.]*

Schary, however, didn't want Davis, whose career was in great decline, at the time. "Davis will turn the role into grand opera. She'll play it like Queen Elizabeth I."

Brooks, however, won out, and Schary caved in.

Schary also objected to Brooks' casting of Debbie Reynolds in the film as the beautiful, well-adjusted bride-to-be.

"She's a musical comedy star wrapped up with that closeted fag, Eddie Fisher," Schary said. "There are a hundred young stars in Hollywood who would be more convincing." Again, Brooks prevailed, and Reynolds got the part.

Borgnine had just won an Oscar for playing the lead role in *Marty* (1955), cast as a warmhearted

Thelma Ritter
perfecting the art of dry-witted, stinging Brooklynese.

but ugly man, a lonely, self-deprecating Bronx butcher who tenderly woos a shy schoolteacher.

Bette was hoping that her portrayal of Aggie Hurley, an offbeat role for her, would also earn her another Oscar.

Gore was convinced that Bette's biggest challenge would involve her ability to gracefully transition herself from glamour roles—one of the best examples was that of Margo Channing in *All About Eve*—into character parts.

Gore hadn't seen Davis since her days back at the Hollywood Canteen. He noted that while living in Maine, she had put on several pounds. "Wardrobe will not have to pad her dresses, and makeup can let her keep those thickened jowls," Gore told Brooks. "While I'm working on the screenplay, Bette is practicing her Bronx accent."

Filming began on *The Catered Affair* in January of 1956, even though the producer, Sam Zimbalist, didn't like Gore's script. He complained to Brooks, "Vidal at several points abandons the naturalistic dialogue of a Bronx housewife. He has Bette dip into her role of Margo Channing. And tell the bitch to get rid of those Bette Davis mannerisms, for God's sake."

Bette invited Gore to lunch in the MGM commissary. "I saw little Ronald Reagan last night at a party. He was with his new wife…that starlet, I can't remember her name."

[Ever since she'd starred with Ronald Reagan and George Brent in Dark Victory *in 1939, Bette had referred to the future president as "Little Ronald Reagan."]*

"I was paid $35,000, little Ronnie $1,258."

Gore was astonished that after all these years, Bette still remembered the exact figure Reagan had earned on that film. "The joke was on him," she continued. "Ronnie went through the entire movie not knowing he had been cast as a homosexual."

"Well, Bette, did you realize you were playing a lesbian?" Gore provocatively asked.

"What in hell do you mean?" she retorted. "I married George Brent in that movie."

"Please, I watched *Dark Victory* the other night," Gore said. "It's obvious that Geraldine Fitzgerald is in love with you. How could you not have noticed the lesbian subtext? Just listen to Tallulah Bankhead sound off on the subject. When she did *Dark Victory* on Broadway in '34, she told me she definitely was aware she was playing a lesbian."

Bette Davis with **Ronald Reagan.** As an inebriated gay blade, the character played by Reagan was not macho enough to earn the love of a woman like Judith Treherne in the movie version of *Dark Victory.*

"Bankhead should know all about playing a lesbian. As for Reagan, he is a BAD ACTOR. Jack Warner wanted him to play opposite me in *This Our Life* (1942). I nixed him in favor of George Brent, who was also my lover off screen as well."

***

On the night of April 20, 1956, *The Catered Affair* was previewed at the Fox Beverly Theater in Beverly Hills, garnering mostly positive reviews. Many critics, however, thought Bette was far too regal a character to be convincing as a Bronx housewife.

Bette thought *The Catered Affair* would become one of her more remarkable achievements, a showcase for her versatility on the screen."Her heart was broken when the film didn't duplicate Borgnine's success with *Marty,* and she didn't walk off with another Oscar," Gore said.

[When Reagan functioned as governor of California (1967-1975), he told certain friends, "I don't care for the Lady (i.e.,Bette Davis) personally, professionally, or politically."

Margo vs. Eve:
WHEN DIVAS CLASH

Margo Channing, as played by **Bette**, addresses Eve Harrington, as played by **Anne Baxter,** in a key scene from *All About Eve*

"I took time out from fucking Bette Davis to appear in this scene with her," **Gary Merrill** claimed, unchivalrously.

His friend, actor-dancer George Murphy, repeated his comments. But over the years, both Reagan and Davis softened their positions on each other...somewhat.

In 1987, when Bette was honored in Washington, D.C. at the Kennedy Center for her lifetime achievements, Reagan paid her an ambiguous tribute. "Bette Davis, if I'd gotten roles as good as yours and been able to do them as good as you, I might never have left Hollywood."

In spite of that, in 1989, Davis rejected Reagan as a presenter at the Film Society of Lincoln Center in New York City. The event had been staged in her honor.

However, after he left his office as U.S. president in 1989, she said, "Reagan was not a very talented actor, but he gave a very good job as president, and he made us all very patriotic. I miss him."]

Gore Confronts Bette's Drunk, Abusive, (and Nude) Husband,

And Bette Gets Sado-Masochistic with Gary Merrill

One night, Bette invited Gore to her home for dinner. At the time, she was still married to Gary Merrill. He'd played her lover in *All About Eve*. Celeste Holm, one of the film's co-stars, claimed that "Gary and Bette spent more time banging off screen than emoting on screen."

When Gore arrived at Bette's home, Merrill was not there. Neither was her daughter, Barbara Davis Sherry, who apparently was visiting a girlfriend's home. *[In 1985, Davis's daughter, using her married name (B.D. Hyman), published a highly critical and highly controversial memoir of her mother,* My Mother's Keeper, *which chronicled Davis as an overbearing and emotionally destructive alcoholic, and detailed a wrenchingly difficult mother-daughter relationship.]*

"It was a night to remember," Gore later said. "It was obvious that the Merrill/Davis marriage was coming apart, and I heard plenty about it from a raging Bette."

"He's drunk all the time," she charged. "Not only that, but he doesn't satisfy me in bed. I demand satisfaction from a man—or else out the door he goes."

"When Gary is bored and wants to stir things up, and for no apparent reason, he will physically assault me or my daughter, B.D. Once time, Gary came home and found B.D. visiting with her girlfriend from school. He beat up both of them, and I had to pay off the family with my own money. Before they took the money, they insisted on having their daughter examined by a doctor to determine that she had not been sexually assaulted by Gary. Not only that, but when he comes into the house, he heads for the bedroom and pulls off all his clothes. He walks around the house nude, not only in front of B.D., but also in front of visitors."

After Gore and Bette were served dessert, Merrill stormed into the house. He was dead drunk.

"Gary, this is Mr. Gore Vidal, a distinguished novelist who's writing the screenplay for *The Catered Affair,*" Bette said.

"I've heard of you," Merrill said, not bothering to shake Gore's hand. "You're in that Christopher Isherwood, Tennessee Williams set, aren't you?"

Upper photo: A daughter's brutal (and bestselling) portrait of her famous mother.

Lower photo: **Bette** (age 78) was not amused.

"Guilty as charged," Gore responded.

Merrill went over to the liquor cabinet and poured himself a stiff drink before disappearing into the downstairs bathroom.

Bette and Gore adjourned to her living room, where a maid served coffee.

In a few minutes, Merrill emerged from the bathroom, "stark, raving jaybird naked," as Gore later expressed it. "He wasn't the first man I'd seen in the nude, so I didn't faint on sight. I think he'd been playing with himself to look more impressive."

"Gary, I suggest you wear a towel in front of our guest," Bette enunciated in her most "socially proper" voice.

"I don't think this faggot wants me to wear a towel, now, do you, Mr. Distinguished Writer?" Merrill asked.

"It's your home and you can suit yourself," Gore said.

"In that case, I have a request for you, Mr. Distinguished Writer." Then Merrill's face turned bitter. "Mr. Faggot, why don't you suck my dick?" Then he shook his penis near Gore's face. Gore studied it rather clinically. "Give me a raincheck," he said, rising from his chair and heading for the hallway. He called back to Bette, thanking her for the dinner.

Before he could leave, Bette and Merrill were engaged in a knockout fight. He did not come to her rescue, because he believed that this physical violence was merely a form of foreplay.

As Bette's biographer, Barbara Leaming, wrote, "Bette often sought to provoke Gary to the physical violence she appeared to confuse with ardor. She goaded him with reminders that he failed to earn as much money as she did at acting, and with merciless mockery of his inability to satisfy her in bed. She would shove and push at Merrill until he knocked her to the floor with his fist. Whereupon Bette would let loose blood-curdling shrieks of pain, shouting 'DON'T HIT ME!'"

Bette Davis Makes Alec Guinness "The Scapegoat" —
and Gore Launches a Feud with Novelist Daphne du Maurier

In 1959, at MGM, Gore was asked to adapt a literary work into a movie script. In this case, it involved a reworking of *The Scapegoat,* a crime thriller originally written (and published in 1957) by the English author, Daphne du Maurier. MGM's intention involved using it as a vehicle co-starring Bette Davis in a supporting role opposite the supremely talented English actor, London-born Alec Guinness.

[In time, Guinness would be best known for his six collaborations with director/producer David Lean, including The Bridge on the River Kwai, Lawrence of Arabia, *and* Dr. Zhivago. *At the time of her collaboration with him, Bette had seen only one of Guinness's movies, the 1949 black comedy,* Kind Hearts and Coronets, *in which Guinness had interpreted the roles of eight different char-*

acters. That film's director had been Robert Hamer.]

The Scapegoat's plot involved a French nobleman who encounters his exact lookalike (a French-speaking Brit) and, through a trick, trades places with him. The unwitting British lookalike eventually learns that the Frenchman has murdered his wife and wants his British "twin" to be blamed and convicted for the crime.

Davis had reluctantly agreed to play a supporting role because she needed the money. She was cast as the nobleman's formidable, overbearing, and dope-ridden mother, *La comtesse de Gué*, and her scenes would depict her in bed.

After Bette was introduced to Guinness, she reported to Gore, "I find him overbearing, egotistical, snotty, and a dreadful actor." As for The Scapegoat's director, Robert Hamer, she said, "The son of a bitch was drunk when I met him."

Bette also complained to Gore that when she agreed to her involvement in the picture, she had been promised Cary Grant as the male lead, but he'd turned the role down.

Based on a screenplay by Gore Vidal, **Bette Davis** in *The Scapegoat* played the drug-addicted dowager, Countess de Gue, the mother of **Alec Guinness**, an actor she loathed. She told Gore, "Gay actors like Guinness can be so temperamental."

He had no comment. Pictured separately in the upper row, as well as together in the lower photo, **Bette Davis** *(left)* and **Alec Guinness** *(right)*.

After having drunkenly ventilated her complaints to Gore, Davis was horrified when she ran into him the following day. She'd just learned that Guinness was also the co-executive producer of the film, and that as such, he'd have enormous control over the final scenes and the editing. She'd later accuse Guinness of "maliciously leaving out my best scenes, which ended up on the cutting room floor."

When Guinness heard rundowns of Davis' many grievances, he (at first) was gracious. He told Gore, "Not only did Bette not trust Hamer, but she was suspicious of me right from the beginning. She seemed to think I was going to steal scenes from her. I had no intention of doing that, and was falsely accused.

Miss Davis did not like any of the British crew, especially Hamer and me."

When Bette's vicious and oft-repeated attacks later reached the press, Guinness responded, "Bette Davis entirely missed the character of the old countess, and she wanted to be extravagantly overdressed and surrounded, quite ridiculously, by flowers. She spat out her lines in her familiar way, like she was attacking Miriam Hopkins in one of her old movies. She is a strong and aggressive personality. She held me responsible for the failure of her performance, which she might more accurately have attributed to herself."

Guinness also battled with Gore over his script, defining it as "fussy."

When Du Maurier was shown the rushes, she also attacked Gore, claiming that "He has saddened me by making a disaster out of my novel."

Guinness later contributed to the growing feud, intoning, "It was a film that should never have been done with that lamentable script of Vidal's."

Wanting someone to blame, Du Maurier continued her public criticisms of Gore prior to the film's release.

Gore counter-attacked, asserting: "Her novel, *The Scapegoat,* is dreadful. I also don't appreciate the bitch going around calling me 'the hack from Hollywood.' I've tried to exercise tact and patience with this supreme best-selling author, and Guinness treats her like a potential werewolf at dusk."

Despite his contentions with Guinness and Du Maurier, Gore bonded with the alcoholic director, Robert Hamer. "We maliciously read Du Maurier's prose out loud," he said, "savoring the rich tautologies, the gleaming oxymorons, and the surreal syntax."

Hamer introduced Gore to his so-called girlfriend, Joan Greenwood, an English actress known for her slow, precise elocution and her husky voice. Gore had seen her as Gwendolen in the 1952 film version *The Importance of Being Earnest*.

"Hamer privately told me that Joan claimed she was 'too small to be entered," so their lovemaking was limited," Gore said. "Actually, Hamer was mainly homosexual. One drunken night he came on to me."

Plagiarist? **Daphne du Maurier** and the cover of the first edition of her crime thriller.

Below, a poster for the movie that both du Maurier and Davis hated.

417

Du Maurier's biographer, Margaret Forster, claimed that "Du Maurier's denial of her bisexuality unveiled a homophobic fear of her true nature."

When the author attacked Gore on his homosexuality, he fired back. He'd learned from Noël Coward that Du Maurier had had affairs with actress Gertrude Lawrence and with Ellen Doubleday, the wife of her American publisher. Vengefully, in response, Du Maurier told a reporter, "I find it impossible to get through any book Vidal ever wrote."

Gore vollied back with: "At least my work isn't plagiarized."

[As a literary scholar, Gore made it a point to investigate frequently aired charges of plagiarism in Du Maurier's work, and he found that these accusations had merit. Gore discovered embarrassing similarities between Du Maurier's Rebecca *and a novel,* The Successor, *written by a Brazilian, Carolina Nabuco. In addition, Du Maurier's famous short story,* The Birds *(1952), later adapted into Alfred Hitchcock's 1963 film, was very similar to Frank Baker's novel,* The Birds *(1936). Finally, her 1959 short story, "Ganymede," contained many similarities to Thomas Mann's semi-autobiographical 1912 novella,* Death in Venice.]*

Months later, when Bette met Gore in Hollywood, she said, "Making *The Scapegoat* was one of the most unpleasant experiences I've ever had on any set. Guinness is an egomaniac."

"At least you were spared the lesbian advances of Daphne Du Maurier," Gore told her.

Years later, Gore was approached by two middle-aged filmmakers planning to film a TV documentary on the life and career of Bette Davis. He granted a filmed interview with them. Later, to his surprise, he learned that the project had been abruptly cancelled.

Months had gone by when Gore, by happenstance, encountered one of the filmmakers at Chasen's in Los Angeles, Gore asked what had happened to their documentary.

In response, Gore was told that "The young powers that be at our studio, the ones with the money, had never heard of Bette Davis."

Chapter Twenty-Nine

Tennessee's Cat on a Hot Tin Roof Generates Sound, Rage, & Fury

Elvis Presley Vs. Paul Newman: Who's the Man?

Ben Gazzara and **Barbara Bel Geddes** *(left photo)* stunned Broadway audiences with their daring performances of Tennessee Williams' *Cat on a Hot Tin Roof.* Gazzara was bitterly disappointed when his role for the play's adaptation into a movie was assigned to his fellow Actors Studio disciple, Paul Newman. In the aftermath of that, throughout the 1980s and 90s, Gazzara ended up playing tough guys, pornographers, and degenerates.

The husband of **Elizabeth Taylor** *(depicted in the right-hand photo, with* **Paul Newman***),* Mike Todd, urged her not to appear as Maggie the Cat. To reinforce his argument, he took her to see Kim Stanley performing the role in London. Backstage, he urged Stanley "Help me convince Elizabeth not to attempt this role. No one's gonna believe that any man wouldn't want to go to bed with my wife."

Elizabeth defied him and made the film with Paul Newman. Todd died in a plane crash during the shoot.

Maggie the Cat (later retitled *Cat on a Hot Tin Roof*) got off to a rocky start. Deep in his drug-induced paranoia, Tennessee charged that his loyal and longtime agent, Audrey Wood, "detested my play. She even wrote me asking if I had 'flipped out.' She claimed she didn't understand it."

To Tennessee, under fire, Wood denied these accusations. "I received a large, rather bulky and disorganized man-uscript," she said. "Most of it had been typed on hotel stationery from various parts of the world—Key West, Los Ange-les, Mexico, Rome. Some pages were even handwritten."

"I stayed up until four in the morning, reading every word of this disjointed ma-terial, which had enough dialogue for three or four plays. If presented in its en-tirety, the play would have opened at four o'clock in the afternoon, with the curtain rung down by midnight or later. But from the beginning, I realized its great potential, and, of course, I understood it, including the theme of latent homosexuality. My God, half of my clients, including Bill Inge, were gay."

"I wrote Tennessee that when a shorter draft emerged, *Maggie the Cat* would be his best play since *A Streetcar Named Desire*. Not only that, but I told him that with the proper script—one that would appease the Production Code in Holly-wood—I could get the best movie deal ever for him, at least half a million dollars, enough for him to retire—with Frankie Merlo."

With his revised play, by now officially retitled *Cat on a Hot Tin Roof*, Tennessee and Audrey went first to Cheryl Crawford, who had previously functioned as producer (1950-1951) of the theatrical ver-sion of *The Rose Tattoo*. Tennessee was greatly disappointed when she re-jected his latest play, claiming "There is not one character the audience can root for."

In January of 1955, Wood won the approval of Playwrights' Company to produce the play on Broadway, knowing that—based on its theme of impotence and repressed homosexuality—that it would be controversial.

The play focused on the interactions of characters rarely assembled to-

During the first week of rehearsals, Paul Newman became so exasperated with Elizabeth's performance as Maggie that he complained to director Richard Brooks. "She's giving me nothing to work with," he protested.

"Just wait until the camera is turned on her," Brooks responded. "Then she'll be-come the feline temptress, Maggie the Cat."

"All in a day's work."

Paul Newman discussing Grace Kelly, Vivien Leigh, and Elizabeth Taylor

420

gether on Broadway, centering around members of a rich family, owners of an important plantation in the Deep South. Featured were Brick, a former athlete and now an alcoholic, and his sexually frustrated wife, Maggie the Cat.

Brick is in mourning in the wake of the suicide of his friend, Skipper. It was obvious to hip and sophisticated playgoers in 1955 at the Morosco Theatre in New York City that Brick was really in love with Skipper, but had rejected him. Skipper had slept with Maggie to prove that he was not homosexual, but during their interlude together, he was impotent. This was supposedly a key element that contributed to his suicide.

Brick's parents, Big Daddy and Big Mama, were some of the strongest roles ever written for Broadway. The play opens as Big Daddy returns from the hospital. He thinks he was given a clear bill of health, but his greedy family, including Sister Woman, Brother Man, and their "no neck monster children," are fully aware that he is dying of cancer.

In New York, in January of 1955, Tennessee met with the play's director, Elia Kazan, who had previously helmed *A Streetcar Named Desire*. He was shocked at the massive rewrites Kazan demanded. "I fear my original intention has gone the way of my virginity!" he told Kazan. Nonetheless, he agreed to follow Kazan's advice on the rewrites. He told Frank Merlo, "I'm desperate for a success."

While working on revisions, Tennessee left New York for Tulane University in New Orleans, where Maureen Stapleton, one of his favorite actresses, was starring in his one-act play, *27 Wagons Full of Cotton*. She played Flora, a somewhat stupid farm wife whose husband, Jake, destroys a neighbor's cotton gin.

In the year that followed, the play would be adapted into the film, *Baby Doll.*

Before the end of February, Tennessee found himself back in New York to approve the casting of the play. Several major stars wanted the role of Brick, but ultimately, it went to Ben Gazzara, with Barbara Bel Geddes cast as his wife, Maggie the Cat. In the past, many producers, including Howard Hughes at RKO, didn't think Bel Geddes was sexy enough.

Gazzara asked Tennessee where he got the title for his play.

"It came from my father, Cornelius," Tennessee said. "He used to tell my mother, Edwina, 'You're making me as nervous as a cat on a hot tin roof.'"

Tennessee became quite fond of the New York-born Gazzara, whom he found had a rugged sex appeal. Like Frank Merlo, he was of Sicilian origin. "I have a thing for Sicilian men," Tennessee confided to Kazan.

The actor told Tennessee that his drifting into acting rescued him from a life of street crime.

Rough, virile, and unconventionally handsome, Gazzara later admitted, "I was a babe magnet, also attracting a lot of interest among the gays."

At around the time Tennessee met Gazzara, he was engaged in affairs with both Eva Gabor and Marlene Dietrich. Audrey Hepburn would later fall in love with him.

At his favorite Manhattan hangout, Harold's Show Spot, Gazzara told Tennessee, "Eva sure likes my Italian salami."

Tennessee responded, "And who among us can resist it?"

Gazzara confided to Tennessee, "At the Actors Studio, Marlon Brando and James Dean both chased after me."

Tennessee was skeptical of all this name dropping. Drunk at the time, he challenged the actor. "I must see this mighty weapon of yours."

"Okay," Gazzara said. "Drop by my dressing room one night. I'll flash for you, but won't promise to do anything else, since I'm a man for the ladies."

Tennessee sighed. "So many actors have falsely used that line on me."

Tennessee approved of Gazzara, "an actor with sexy legs," for his portrayals of Brick, but he felt that Bel Geddes "was not much of a cat, not complex enough. She's also too wholesome for my text. A Broadway

Life magazine valued the acting talents of **Barbara Bel Geddes** more than Hollywood did. Although she'd scored a big success on Broadway in *Cat on a Hot Tin Roof*, she was not asked to repeat her role in the movie version.

whore would have been better in the part. Someone more obviously neurotic."

At a rehearsal, Tennessee protested to Kazan, "Bel Geddes is fuckin' with my cadence."

The actress overheard his assessment, and ran from the stage in tears.

During rehearsals for *Cat*, Kazan began to lose his patience with Tennessee. One afternoon, the playwright wandered in drunk from lunch, and plopped down in the middle of the orchestra seats. He didn't like Bel Geddes in the part, and he let it be known. He called out to her, "More melody in your voice, Barbara. Southern girls have melody in their..."

At that point, Kazan cut him off. He wanted his choice of actress to know that he'd protect her from onslaughts from Tennessee. Kazan walked over and slipped into a seat beside Tennessee, warning him that with another outburst like that, he'd walk off the play. Properly chastised, Tennessee quietly left the theater.

Tennessee also objected to the casting of Burl Ives as Big Daddy. "But he's a singer," Tennessee protested.

"Ives stays in the play," Kazan shot back. "Right away, I had to let Tennessee know I was the guy with the big balls."

"Ives was perfect for Big Daddy," Kazan said. "I'd seen him drunk one night, macho and rampant, aroused to the point where he was looking for a fight, anywhere and with anybody. He was Big Daddy to his toenails. But also, the Lion Roaring in Winter."

Tennessee heartily approved of the rest of the supporting cast—Mildred Dunnock as Big Mama, Pat Hingle as Brother Man, and Madeleine Sherwood as Sister Woman.

When they premiered in Philadelphia, Tennessee invited Gazzara to dine. His fellow guests included Carson McCullers, John Steinbeck, and William Faulkner.

Faulkner was in love with Jean Stein, a member of *Cat's* production staff. "I felt a terrible torment in the man," Tennessee wrote in his memoirs: "He always kept his eyes down. Finally, he lifted his eyes once in response to a direct question from me, and the look in his eyes was so terrible, so sad, that I began to cry."

Even before the play opened on Broadway, rumors surged through Hollywood that *Cat on a Hot Tin Roof* would eventually reach the screen. Even before any movie star saw the play, many actresses wanted to get their claws in the role of Maggie. Interested parties included Marilyn Monroe.

On opening night, March 24, 1955, Marilyn showed up with Lee Strasberg of the Actors Studio.

After the curtain went down that night to the sound of wild applause and standing ovations, Marilyn arrived backstage, where Gazzara saw her talking to Tennessee for at least fifteen minutes.

Finally, she walked over to congratulate Gazzara. Wearing dangerously elevated high heels, she said to him, "I hear you may play Brick in the movie opposite me," using the purring voice of a cat.

Gazzara wondered if Tennessee had promised her the film role.

Before giving Gazzara a wet-lipped kiss, she slipped him her phone number, informing him that she had to go to a party. "Call me and then drop by my suite after ten o'clock. I'm busy until then. Let's see what our off-screen chemistry is like." Then, she seemed to appraise his body. "From the looks of things, I expect an explosion. Tennessee and I like Italian men."

[Ironically, during rehearsals, Tennessee had come backstage to instruct Gazzara, "Distance yourself from Maggie," he said. "Whether the audience knows it or not, you are playing a homosexual."]

Cat on a Hot Tin Roof ran for 20 months and earned Tennessee a Pulitzer Prize.

A 1974 revival by the American Shakespeare Theatre in Stratford (Connecticut) featured Elizabeth Ashley as Maggie the Cat, with Keir Dullea playing Brick. Tennessee restored much of the text which had been removed, under instructions from Elia Kazan, from the original.

On Broadway a revival in 1990 starred Kathleen Turner, who was eventually nominated for a Tony Award based on her performance as Maggie.

In 2003, another revival starring Ashley Judd received only lukewarm reviews.

In 2008, an African-American production opened on Broadway.

The latest revival was in 2013, with Scarlett Johansson playing Maggie the Cat.

Grace Kelly, as a Candidate for Maggie the Cat, Goes Slumming with Paul Newman

Tennessee was in Barcelona in July of 1955 when Audrey Wood notified him of the half-million dollar movie sale of *Cat.* He wrote Frank Merlo, "That means we don't have to worry about the hard stuff for another ten years, I guess. We'll be old girls by then, and can get our social security when it runs out, and by such little economies as saving old teabags and turning collars and cuffs, we can eke out a comfortable elderly existence in some quaint little cold-water walk-up in the West Nineties in New York."

Paul Newman's appearance as Brick on the screen opposite Elizabeth Taylor in the 1958 release of *Cat on a Hot Tin Roof* was preceded by a bizarre sequence of casting sagas which included not only Tennessee, but Grace Kelly, Vivien Leigh, and Elvis Presley.

The dramas began in 1954 when Tennessee was still working on the Broadway play. Three days before opening night at the Morosco Theater, he was still working on it. Months before its premiere, there had been much speculation in the press about *Cat. The Los Angeles Times,* in an embarrassing piece of misinformation, labeled it as a comedy.

Newman's involvement in the play began with a phone message that came in to a publicist at Warner Brothers. The message was from "G.K." The publicity department was savvy enough to know it originated with Grace Kelly. When word of this got back to Tennessee, and when he called her back, she arranged a meeting with him.

If casting had gone differently, Paul Newman would have played the role of Brick on Broadway alongside Grace Kelly. But the deal fell through because of events which eventually concluded, in April of 1956, with Kelly's widely publicized marriage to Prince Rainier of Monaco.

During his early years in Hollywood, Newman had had a brief fling with Kelly at the fabled Château Marmont, after having met her previously at a party in her Manhattan apartment. Both of the nascent stars had quickly moved on to other conquests.

Now, in anticipation of a role in Ten-

The cool, serene beauty, **Grace Kelly**, won the 1954 Oscar for her role in *The Country Girl.* She played the bitter, aging wife of a slipping actor, hiding her beauty behind big horn-rimmed glasses and a shapeless sweater.

nessee's play, after some phone dialogues with Kelly, Newman agreed to meet her at a secluded restaurant in San Fernando Valley, where he was ushered into a back room where Kelly was waiting for him with a strange man in shadows. To his surprise, Newman quickly realized that the man was Tennessee.

[Director Elia Kazan and Tennessee had first seen Newman perform in the 1953 Broadway production of William Inge's Picnic. Ralph Meeker had played the lead, and director Joshua Logan had cast Newman as the rich boy, Alan, who loses his girl (Janice Rule) to the seductive drifter.]

After that performance, both the director and the playwright had congratulated Newman.

"You were just beautiful," Tennessee exclaimed, embracing Newman. "But spectacularly beautiful. Up to now, I thought Marlon was the most beautiful man I'd ever seen on stage. Now you come along, making my fickle heart waver. With you on the stage with Ralph Meeker, all homosexuals will have a difficult choice. Do they want to see sexual menace or do they want to worship at the altar of male beauty?"

Newman was embarrassed by Tennessee's adulation, but he returned the compliment. "It's an honor to get a seal of approval from America's greatest playwright."

"With a compliment like that," Tennessee said, "all you have to do is blow in my ear and I'll follow you anywhere. One of these days, I'm going to write a role for you, one so great you'll always be remembered for it."

"A promise I'll hold you to, Mr. Williams," Newman responded.

Encountering Tennessee again after so much time made Newman think that perhaps that promise, hastily concluded backstage at *Picnic,* might soon be fulfilled.

Kelly rose from the table with the grace of a swan to kiss Newman on the mouth. Tennessee also stood up for him, kissing him on both cheeks, and recalling their previous meeting on Broadway.

After very routine chatter and congratulations on the recent accomplishments of each of these artists, Kelly assumed a rather business-like aura. "Tennessee has the most divine proposal. He's at work on a Broadway play. It's called *Maggie the Cat.* He's proposing that I open the play on Broadway, run with it for 85 nights, then turn it over to—say, Kim Stanley. During that time, I'll sign a contract to appear in the movie. I'm crazy for the idea of the movie, but appearing on Broadway terrifies me."

"Grace Kelly in a new Tennessee

Impish, and as enigmatic as a cat, **Tennessee Williams'** *Cat on a Hot Tin Roof* originated as a short fiction piece entitled "Three Players of a Summer Game." Its theme dealt with spiritual anguish and emotional impotence.

Williams play?" Newman said. "What a dynamite idea. How do I fit in? Will I be the guy who gets Maggie purring?"

"Like a true Hun, you get right to the point," Tennessee said. "You'd be cast in the male lead, and you don't get the frustrated Maggie purring at all. You'd be playing her closeted homosexual husband."

"I've got balls enough to do that if I don't have to wear pink," Newman said.

"Actually, your role—that of Brick—is very masculine, even sexy," Kelly said. "Like me, you'd agree to appear in the stage version, followed by the movie."

"In the play, Maggie has a foul mouth and is very earthy," Tennessee said. "In other words, Grace would be playing against type. I like that kind of casting."

"And me?" Newman asked.

"You'd be in silk pajamas throughout most of the play," Tennessee said. "Often showing that sculpted Davidesque chest of yours, arguably the most beautiful in Hollywood. God created your chest for silken tongues to lap."

Then he turned back to Kelly. "How I envy Grace here for having sampled the world's tastiest specimen. As for me, an aging queen can only dream of what a delight that must be."

Showing a slight embarrassment, Kelly laughed to mask her feelings. "It seems that you've gone through your fixation with Brando and turned to more modern stars. Paul is the embodiment of the new breed taking over Hollywood."

"You're known for appearing with older stars," Newman said. "Gary Cooper, Clark Gable, Ray Milland, James Stewart. It might be fun for you to work with someone closer to your own age."

"It'd be more than fun," she said. "We'd burn up the screen, but only after setting Broadway on fire."

"There's also a great role for a character actor," Tennessee said. "Big Daddy. I have Orson Welles in mind."

"He's certainly big enough," Newman said. "If a deal can be made, I'll go for it. I don't have to read the play. Knowing that Tennessee wrote it is good enough for me. I'm sure it'll be a masterpiece."

At the end of dinner, a rather handsome young man with a slight growth of beard appeared in the rear of the restaurant to escort a drunken Tennessee back to his car.

The playwright didn't bother to introduce his hustler/driver. "I was writing all my roles for Brando," Tennessee said, rising on wobbly legs. "But he's getting too beefy to play a Tennessee Williams leading man. Today I'm cre-

Paul Newman was never one to object when the director called for him to disrobe.

426

ating characters like Brick who are lean, mean, and astonishingly beautiful. Men who inspire sexual fantasies, regardless of the viewer's persuasion."

He looked his driver over skeptically. "Right now I'm studying the world of hustlers. Someday I'll cast you as the lead in one of my plays where you'll play a hustler. I envision Tallulah Bankhead playing an aging, has-been actress opposite you." Then he gently kissed Paul on the lips before heading off into the night with his paid companion.

Without Newman knowing it, that was his first preview of the hustler role of Chance Wayne *[Sweet Bird of Youth]* that he'd eventually play both on Broadway and on the screen.

Months later, Newman told Audrey Wood that, "I left Grace and Paul in a sleazy joint to work things out for themselves. That cockroach palace was pretty poor digs for a glamorous future princess. But back then, Grace in Hollywood liked to take off those white gloves. Or, as Gary Cooper told me, 'Grace looks like a cold dish with a man until you get her pants down. Then she explodes.'"

Scarlett O'Hara (Vivien Leigh)
Lobbies for the Role of "Yet Another Southern Woman"

After purchasing the film rights for *Cat on a Hot Tin Roof,* Metro-Goldwyn-Mayer considered George Cukor as its possible director. But from the beginning, MGM knew there would be problems with the script, especially as regards the homosexual issues.

Broadway audiences had been enthralled with its homoerotic subtext. Nonetheless, the studio felt it had to "launder" this Pulitzer Prize-winning drama before it "went out to be viewed by every little homophobic town in America."

The film's producer, Lawrence Weingarten, felt that Cukor might know how to adapt the script into something acceptable to mass audiences, in spite of (or perhaps because of) the director's own homosexuality.

Tennessee knew Cukor and thought he'd be ideal to direct the film version of *Cat.* But he became alarmed when Cukor wanted Vivien Leigh to play the role of Maggie the Cat on the screen. "Whereas she was just the right age to play Blanche DuBois," Tennessee said, "Scarlett O'Hara is getting a bit long in the tooth to play Maggie the Cat. Nearly two decades have come and gone since Rhett Butler carried her up those antebellum stairs for the fuck of her life."

"Since Cukor was fired as the director of *Gone With the Wind* back in 1939, perhaps he wants to use *Cat* as his final chance to direct Vivien Leigh," Weingarten said.

When Tennessee flew into Hollywood, Cukor invited him to his house for a reunion with Vivien, who had performed so brilliantly in *Streetcar.*

Cukor stated that he had asked Montgomery Clift to play Brick, but that Clift had rejected the role because "the character of a closeted homosexual, I guess, was too close to home."

427

When Tennessee came face to face with Vivien again, he was shocked by her appearance. She had aged badly, and she even appeared a bit matronly, hardly his image of Maggie the Cat.

She kissed him on the lips. "Thank God, dear heart, you came over to visit with George and me. My enemies claim I'm washed up in Hollywood. Not at all. I've been waiting for the right script to lure me back. I've always thought of myself as a stage actress, but I've done all right in films."

"All right?" Tennessee exclaimed. "Two Oscars and countless great roles?...That's a lot more than just 'okay!'"

"You're such a darling," she said. "By the way, Larry *[Laurence Olivier]* sends his love."

As the director, the playwright, and the actress settled in for a rather drunken evening, Tennessee noticed that Vivien was visibly shaking. She kept reaching for Cukor's hand for reassurance. "Oh, dear heart," she said to Tennessee. "I'm terrified of taking on such a

Vivien Leigh called George Cukor, who at the time, and before he was replaced, was operating as *Cat on a Hot Tin Roof*'s director.

"Darling, I'm ready to play Maggie the Cat. As Scarlett O'Hara proved, I can play a Southern belle."

challenging role in front of that see-all movie camera. I get exhausted so easily these days. There are spells of depression that descend. I call them 'ghosties.' I must warn you gents that when I'm tired and depressed, I'm a mess. As you know, playing Blanche DuBois nearly drove me over the brink. But having been married to Larry all these years, I can certainly play a sexually frustrated wife like Maggie the Cat."

Tennessee regarded both Cukor and Vivien as old friends. But after four hours of drinking and talking with them, he feared that their ideas of a screen version of *Cat* differed remarkably from his own. Nonetheless, he left Cukor's home realizing that MGM would never let Vivien play Maggie. He also suspected that Cukor's mission to defy the Production Code, and to insert homosexuality directly into the context of the movie, would doom him as the director of choice.

Discreetly, Tennessee chose not to mention his fears or reservations that evening.

***

In the weeks that followed, producer Pandro S. Berman was brought into the debate over the film script of *Cat*.

Previously, during his long-ago tenure as chief at RKO, he'd overseen Cukor's cross-gendered allegory, *Sylvia Scarlett*, starring Cary Grant and

Katharine Hepburn. It had been a box office disaster, so Berman immediately took a dim view of having Cukor direct the film version of Tennessee Williams' controversial play.

Berman told Lawrence Weingarten that if he weren't careful, Cukor would turn *Cat* into "a fag piece." Berman had become exasperated when Cukor, against his wishes and instructions, had announced to the press that the movie, like the play, would have to deal up front with the issue of homosexuality.

"Who in hell does this queer think he is?" Berman asked Weingarten. "We're not allowed to even mention the word 'homosexual' in a movie. What does Cukor want? A flashback, showing Brick sucking off Skipper in their football heyday. Fire Cukor!"

The battle intensified between Cukor and MGM. Finally, the director withdrew. He told Louella Parsons, still the industry's reigning gossip maven, that he could not maintain the integrity of Williams' play because of the censorship being imposed on its film adaptation. "I am not sure the public will like this play or understand it," Cukor said. "But I just couldn't do an emasculated version, and I don't see how the movie itself could be properly presented."

Originally commissioned to direct *Cat on a Hot Tin Roof*, gay director **George Cukor** wanted to make Brick's repressed homosexuality a focal point of the production.

MGM emphatically disagreed.

With Cukor off the picture, so went the casting of Vivien. Weeks later, after it was announced in the papers that Elizabeth Taylor would be starring as Maggie the Cat, Vivien placed a call to Tennessee. "Elizabeth replaced me in *Elephant Walk*, so why not *Cat on a Hot Tin Roof*?" she said, bitterly.

"No one could ever replace you," Tennessee responded, gallantly. "You're an original."

Vivien also revealed to him that Paul Newman, who would have been a potential co-star for her if she had been awarded the female lead in *Cat,* had visited her at Cukor's home and spent the night. "He was such a nice gentleman," Vivien claimed. "The next day, he sent flowers. So many men I pick up—gardeners, garage mechanics, whomever—just give me a pat on the ass the next morning and say, 'Thanks for the memory, Scarlett.'"

Newman later discussed the role of Brick with Tennessee, comparing it to his own life: "As a kid, I was split into two different personalities. Dad wanted me to be a tomboy, a great athlete, then a commercial gent. My mother appealed to my sensitive side—the artist, the poet. The character of Brick is perfect for me. All my life, one side of me wanted to live life with a guy like Skipper in *Cat;* the other side was tempted to fuck the living shit out of Maggie the Cat and be the heterosexual my fans wanted me to be."

"My Boy Elvis Will Not Appear in this Perverted Crap!"

—Col. Parker

With both Vivien Leigh and George Cukor out of the picture, Richard Brooks, the film's director, and Lawrence Weingarten, its producer, came up with new ideas for casting.

Brooks called Lana Turner, telling her, "It's almost certain that MGM is going to ask you to play Maggie the Cat in the movie version of the Tennessee Williams play, *Cat on a Hot Tin Roof.* We want you to come in for a reading with Paul Newman. He's one of the stars who's up for the role of the male lead."

"I'd be thrilled to play Maggie the Cat," Turner said. "I saw it on Broadway. I can be a hell of a lot more feline that Barbara Bel Geddes, darling. I'd adore playing opposite Paul. Who is his competition? Don't tell me…Ben Gazzara!"

"You're not going to believe this," Brooks said, "but yesterday, I got a call from none other than Elvis Presley. I told him about you. He'd love to play Brick to your Maggie."

"You've got to be kidding!" said Lana. "Lana Turner and Elvis Presley starring together in a raunchy Tennessee Williams drama of the Old South!"

"A distinct possibility," Brooks told her. "But you've got the billing out of order. It would be listed as 'Presley and Turner.'"

When Tennessee landed in Hollywood, he learned that Elvis was in town, having flown in from Las Vegas. He'd heard from the cast of *Cat* on Broadway that Elvis had attended a performance, but that he had not come backstage to greet the cast. At the time, Gazzara was fully aware that Elvis was in the audience, but at no time did it occur to him that Elvis wanted to play Brick, a repressed homosexual.

When Elvis called with an invitation, Tennessee eagerly accepted. But in advance of his meeting with Elvis, he called Weingarten. Tennessee had learned that Elvis wanted to make a serious movie and Tennessee thought he'd be ideal as Brick.

"The brass is considering casting Elvis as Brick, with Lana Turner as Maggie," Weingarten said. "Their eyeballs are registering dollar signs at the box office."

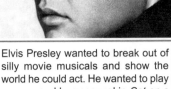

Elvis Presley wanted to break out of silly movie musicals and show the world he could act. He wanted to play a repressed homosexual in *Cat on a Hot Tin Roof.*

Horace Logan, the affable long-term host of *Louisiana Hayride,* said, "That son of a bitch, **Col. Tom Parker** *(photo above)* ought to be hung up by his balls. He practically destroyed one of the greatest talents that ever lived. Elvis could have walked off with an Oscar for *Cat.*"

"Elvis with Lana!" Tennessee said. "That's Hollywood!"

A paid companion drove Tennessee to Elvis' rented home and stayed in the car throughout the course of Tennessee's visit. A member of Elvis' Memphis Mafia let Tennessee in and offered him a drink, telling him that "The Boss" would be down in fifteen minutes when he got off the phone.

A short while later, Elvis bounced down the stairs. Back then, he was still in good physical shape, and Tennessee was impressed with his startling good looks, even better in person than on the screen. He radiated vitality.

"Mr. Playwright," Elvis said to Tennessee. "Welcome. I want you to let me be your Teddy Bear—specifically I want to play Brick in *Cat.*"

"Well," Tennessee said. "That's a startling casting idea. At least you won't have to fake a Southern accent."

Col. Tom Parker *(left)* said, "My boy Elvis *(right)* can shake that fuckable ass of his and pull in millions."

He was neither a colonel nor a Parker. He fled from his native Holland after murdering a woman in a fit of rage and was an illegal immigrant in America.

"No one can play a Southern boy like Elvis," the singer said. "The part has my name written on it. I want a meaty role. I'm tired of all this shit Colonel Parker tosses my way. I can't go through the rest of my life shaking my butt and swinging my hillbilly pecker—covered in pants, of course—in front of a lot of screaming teenage gals."

["Colonel" Tom Parker, a former circus roustabout with a shady background, became Elvis' rapacious business manager. He consistently demanded (and got) a fifty percent agent's fee, and a hell of a lot more. In essence, he functioned as Elvis' crooked Svengali.]

"I, for one, would be delighted to see you on the screen as Brick," Tennessee said. "But from what I hear of this colonel of yours, he won't let you do it."

"Fuck Colonel Parker," Elvis said, flashing anger. "I'm seriously pissed off at him. There are just so many movies I can do like *Loving You.*"

"I'm all for you," Tennessee said. "I find you very charismatic, but I must say I fear the deal can't be worked out."

"You leave that to me," Elvis said. "I've got clout in this town." He settled back with his drink on a large sofa.

"I hear that cute little Jew boy, Paul Newman, is also up for the role," Elvis said. "But he ain't Southern. Newman's got Yankee written all over him. It takes a guy like me to stand up to both Maggie the Cat and Big Daddy."

"Paul has been talked about," Tennessee said.

"I think he's too old," Elvis said. He's ten years older than me…at least."

"I don't make casting decisions in films…regrettably," Tennessee said.

"I hear Newman's a nice guy, and I think he and I can settle this competition the way we do it in Memphis," Elvis said.

"You mean, duke it out?" Tennessee asked.

"Note quite," Elvis said. "I thought of a little contest between me and Newman. Of course, we both could invite Marilyn Monroe over, and each of us could plug her. Then she could award the prize to the best man for a roll in the hay."

"I'm sure Marilyn would find that most intriguing," Tennessee said.

"Actually, I had another contest in mind," Elvis said. "Both Newman and I are world class beer drinkers. What I'm suggesting is that I have him over, and that we both fill up on brew. Then when we want to get rid of some of the suds, we go out into my moonlit garden. Let my boys be the judge. We stage a pissing contest like we do in Memphis. Whoever can piss the farthest gets to play Brick."

"I won't say this is a first for Hollywood," Tennessee said, "and I can't say it's not been done before, but this is a most intriguing contest. I'm a bit of a voyeur, if you'd like me to judge the contest."

"I don't think me or Paul could trust you when we whip out our dicks," Elvis said. "We've heard stories."

"You're probably right. I wish you luck in throwing the largest arc of golden showers."

Tennessee remembered that sometime during the remainder of the evening, he and Elvis each passed out from drink and drugs. Two members of the Memphis Mafia eventually placed Tennessee in the back seat of his car for the ride back to his hotel.

A few nights later, Newman called: "Good news. I won the pissing contest that Elvis came up with. I'm your Brick."

Weingarten called the following day with a different slant on casting. "Tenn, I've got to be upfront with you. Years ago, Elvis wanted to star in Inge's *Picnic,* but Col. Parker nixed that idea, too. Now, he's forbidden Elvis to appear on the screen as Brick. He claims you're the biggest queer in Hollywood, and that you've crafted the role as a 'fucking piece of shit about a repressed homosexual.' Those are his exact words, of course, not mine. He claimed that if Elvis appears in *Cat,* it'll destroy his fan base. He had more to say on the subject, too, giving me a lecture about sex."

"What exactly are the Colonel's view of sexual relations?" Tennessee asked.

"Okay, if you must know!" Weingarten said. "The Colonel told me, in his words, that 'God made a man and a woman. He gave a man a dick and a bitch a hole. God's intention was to have a man stick his thing in a cunt and make babies. It was not God's intent for a man to stick his thing up another man's ass. Assholes are made for shitting, not fucking.' Then he went on to say, 'As long as I'm able to smoke a cigar, my boy, Elvis is not appearing in this perverted piece of crap.'"

"Sounds like a New York drama critic to me," Tennessee said.

At around midnight, Tennessee had fallen asleep in front of his TV set.

Then a call came in from Richard Brooks in his capacity as the director of *Cat.*

"Forget Grace Kelly," Brooks said. "Forget Vivien Leigh. Forget Lana Turner. MGM has its Maggie the Cat to play opposite Paul Newman. I've just returned from a late night meeting with the brass. A contract has been signed. Miss Elizabeth Taylor Todd is your Maggie. No doubt, she'll soon be meowing after you."

"Not as long as Mike Todd is still alive," was Tennessee's immediate response. "I know Elizabeth. She'll make a great Maggie, although I think I might have preferred Marilyn Monroe."

"Dream on," Brooks said. "Marilyn is the Queen of Fox. We want the role to go to MGM's Queen. With this role, Elizabeth is a sure-fire Oscar winner."

A Male Beauty with Glacial Blue Eyes
Meets a Female Beauty Whose Eyes are Violet

Elizabeth Taylor faced life-threatening pains while she was pregnant during late September of 1957. An abortion was suggested, but she eventually submitted to a dangerously premature caesarean, which led to the birth of Frances (Liza) Todd, weighing four pounds, fourteen ounces.

During her time in the hospital, her husband, showman Mike Todd, entertained her with plans to film *Don Quixote,* with the understanding that Elizabeth would play the scruffy, shrewish Dulcinea.

Her friend, Truman Capote, came to visit her. They had become friends through their mutual interest in Montgomery Clift, and Truman had called on Elizabeth on occasion, begging her to help rescue Monty Clift from his latest physical and emotional breakdown.

Truman said he was drawn to Elizabeth because of what he defined as her "hectic allure," apparently referring to a lively intelligence and a raucous, often raunchy, sense of humor.

"She was very bright and even gave me unknown books by rather famous writers to read—P.G. Wodehouse, for example."

After Elizabeth survived that dangerous pregnancy, and with the infant out of danger, Truman went to visit her in Westport, Connecticut, where she and Todd had rented a 23-room mansion. "I found her in the front yard buried under a dozen Golden Retriever puppies."

Almost immediately, she asked about Clift. "He's starting to pick up rough trade," Truman said. "These guys sometimes beat the shit out of him. Monty seems to enjoy it. And he's still crazy for those pills."

Almost in passing, Truman told Elizabeth that he was leaving a script that had been entrusted to him by Tennessee. "He wrote you a note. The package is in your study."

In the whirlwind that encircled the Todds, she didn't open the package containing the script, and its note, until months later.

One day in her study, when recovering from a severe back pain, she noticed the script from Tennessee and opened it, settling in to read it. The play was *Cat on a Hot Tin Roof*. In his note, he had scribbled, "The role of Maggie the Cat is waiting for you. Sharpen those claws of yours."

The Broadway play came and went, and Elizabeth attended one of its performances with Todd. Later, the couple had dinner with Tennessee at Sardi's. Elizabeth told Tennessee, "I'd give my right nipple to play your Maggie the Cat."

Todd responded to the room at large, "Elizabeth Taylor could seduce any man, even your Brick fag."

When MGM finally cast her in the film opposite Paul Newman, she was elated. "When the man with the glacial blue eyes meets the girl with the eyes of spring violet, the great movie romance of the century will surely unfold," one columnist wrote. "How can two such sex symbols resist the magnetism of each other?" That columnist had obviously not read the "fine print" about how the character of Brick most definitely resists Maggie.

Ben Gazzara was bitterly disappointed when he didn't get the role of Brick in the movie version. "It went to Newman," he told his friends. "Tennessee has a crush on him, in spite of the fact he has skinny legs and I have the legs of a Roman centurion."

Shooting on *Cat* began on March 12, 1958. When Elizabeth met Newman on the set, she said, "You're more beautiful in person than on the screen, if such a thing is possible," she said.

"You took the words out of my mouth," he answered. "Surely, you are the most beautiful woman in the world, maybe in the universe, for all I know."

Tennessee arrived during the first week to greet Elizabeth and Newman. He had lunch at the MGM commissary with the film's director, Richard Brooks. Over sandwiches, Tennessee was informed that MGM had rejected the first draft of the script in which Brick confesses to Maggie both his homosexuality and his undying love for his best friend, Skipper, who had committed suicide.

"You've got to understand my dilemma," Brooks pleaded with an irate Tennessee."The Production Code doesn't even allow us to mention the word 'homosexual' on the screen."

James Poe, who had worked on the script of Todd's *Around the World in 80 Days* (1956), showed up to meet Tennessee. The lunch crashed downhill from there after Poe informed the playwright he'd been assigned "to clean up the script."

Tennessee stormed out of the luncheon, but both Newman and Elizabeth kept him abreast of the revised script, which was relentlessly being watered down.

Near the end of the film's final version, Maggie lies to Big Daddy, asserting falsely that she is pregnant, and Brick backs her up in her lie. In movie's final scene, he tosses a pillow into position beside Maggie on their bed. The movie ends with the couple's "horizontal reconciliation," with the implication that Brick will penetrate Maggie and make her pregnant. As part of the film's happy ending, previous wrongdoings and misunderstandings blissfully fade away.

***

Throughout the filming of his play, Tennessee received calls from both Taylor and Newman, each complaining about the other. Newman charged that "Elizabeth is totally lifeless working with me. We have no chemistry at all. She's holding back."

During any of several calls that Elizabeth placed to Tennessee, she charged that during rehearsals, "He's doing everything he can to steal every scene from me, even indulging in male burlesque. He's been stripping down to his underwear and running around, anything to distract from my best dialogue."

But when the actual filming began, Newman called Tennessee to say that he'd changed his mind. "When the camera is turned on her, she becomes radiant, a much better actress than I ever imagined."

He also told Tennessee, "Although a great deal of my motivation has been removed by the censors, I'm struggling to make Brick a creditable character."

Then Brooks telephoned Tennessee with bad news. "Elizabeth, the one with the 'Oh! So delicate health,' has taken sick. Her doctors told me it's developing into pneumonia. I'm going to try to shoot around her until she recovers. MGM is furious because her contract expires on June 1. After that, they'll have to more than double her salary, which right now is $125,000. Warner Brothers is charging only $25,000 for Newman's services. To be on the safe side, we're negotiating with Carroll Baker to replace Elizabeth if we have to."

While Elizabeth was sick in bed, Todd boarded *The Lucky Liz* in bad weather for a flight to New York, in anticipation of being fêted at an upcoming Friars Club dinner at the Waldorf Astoria. What happened next generated headlines around the world.

On March 22, 1958, caught in a violent storm over New Mexico, the plane went down over the Zuni Mountains, killing everyone aboard.

As soon as the first radio reports came in, Brooks called Tennessee. Elizabeth had already been notified. "I just heard from her house," Brooks told Tennessee. "She's hysterical."

Later, Tennessee learned that Elizabeth, consumed with grief, had run out into the street. "I was Tennessee Williams' *Baby Doll,* you know, with the little panties?" she said. "I fell onto my knees in the street, shouting, '*No, not Mike, Not Mike, dear God, please not Mike.*' I was almost run over by a car."

Tennessee later said, "I came to visit Elizabeth only once, and I found her deranged. In the wake of Todd's death, she was reaching out for love. Paul came over to comfort her, and she insisted he spend the night. He was seduced. Then, for a while, she felt she was in love with Mike Todd, Jr., Then she developed this fixation on Eddie Fisher, her husband's best friend. I knew she had never liked Eddie. One night at a dinner, she referred to him as 'the bus boy.'"

"I was there to greet Elizabeth when she returned to work in April of 1958," Tennessee said. "She was visibly shaken, but a real trouper, determined to finish the movie. We were proud of her, and Paul was wonderful to her."

When the picture was wrapped, Tennessee was invited for a look at the final cut. He cringed throughout the screening, and Newman, sitting beside him, shifted nervously in his seat. When the lights came on after that tossed pillow scene, Tennessee rose to his feet.

He looked first at Newman. "You were fabulous. One tasty morsel. And Elizabeth, you look so sexy no gay man could ever turn you down."

Then he turned to Brooks. "You emasculated my play. You bastard!" Then he stormed out of the studio.

***

On September 20, 1958, when *Cat on a Hot Tin Roof* opened in theaters across the country, Elizabeth was denounced as "the other woman." She was accused of breaking up the marriage of America's so-called sweethearts, Debbie Reynolds and Eddie Fisher.

But instead of segueing "Notorious Liz," as she was labeled, into box office poison, publicity generated by the illicit romance had movie-goers lining up to gaze upon "this Jezebel."

When *Cat* opened at theaters in New York City, Tennessee went to the movie house where people were lined up to buy tickets. He shouted at them, "Go home! This movie will set Hollywood back fifty years." *[At the time, Tennessee was tanked up on amphetamines, liquor, and barbiturates.]*

Cat was eventually nominated for Best Picture, Best Adapted Screenplay (in spite of Tennessee's ongoing assaults), Best Director (Brooks), Best Actor (Newman), and Best Actress (Elizabeth).

Both Elizabeth and Newman lost, respectively, to Susan Hayward (in *I Want to Live*), and David Niven (in *Separate Tables*).

Cat on a Hot Tin Roof was MGM's biggest hit of the year, and polls in the autumn named Elizabeth as the number one star in Hollywood. In a call to Tennessee, she said, "Notoriety worked in my favor. Apparently, the public wants to go into a darkened movie house and gaze upon a scarlet woman. Baby, I'm not scarlet...I'm purple."

In years to come, *Cat on a Hot Tin Roof* would go before the cameras again, as it did in 1976 in a television version that received mixed reviews. A husband and wife team, Natalie Wood and Robert Wagner, starred with Laurence Olivier (of all people) playing Big Daddy, and with Maureen Stapleton as Big Mama. It received many negative reviews.

Again, in 1984, another TV version was produced by American Playhouse, starring Jessica Lange and Tommy Lee Jones in the lead roles, supported by such talent as Kim Stanley and Rip Torn. The sexual undercurrent that had been muted in the 1958 MGM film was restored in a more permissive era. In the aftermath, Stanley walked off with an Emmy for her interpretation of Big Mama.

Chapter Thirty

Gore's Ménage à Quatre?
(Perhaps Not, but Perhaps....)

Gore & Howard Move in With (Then Unmarried) Paul Newman and Joanne Woodward

It was the beginning of a beautiful friendship, as **Gore Vidal** *(left)* confronts **Paul Newman** *(right)*, "pretending" to be challenging him for conjugal rights to **Joanne Woodward** *(center)*, a mistress he'd taken during the closing months of his deteriorating marriage to his first wife, actress Jacqueline Witte.

He later told Gore, "My marriage to Jackie is increasingly empty, yet I can't stand the thought of leaving my family." But he did.

Gore first met Joanne Woodward at a party in

Manhattan in 1952. She was introduced to him by William Gray, who had been her friend at Louisiana State University. Later, she introduced Gore to her "beau," a handsome young television and theater actor. He was making his first film, *The Silver Chalice, [released in 1954]* with Virginia Mayo. His name was Paul Newman.

For a brief time, Gore and his platonic long-time companion, Howard Austen, lived together at the Château Marmont in Hollywood. So did their newly minted friends, the "married-to-Jackie-Witte-at-the-time" Paul Newman and his mistress, the very talented actress, Joanne Woodward.

The château-inspired hotel, located off the Sunset Strip, was ideal for those who led shady lives in the Eisenhower 1950s.

As *The Los Angeles Times* phrased it, "No wonder people come here to have affairs—it's got that air of history, where you know a lot of people did things they weren't supposed to do." Indeed, if details about the shack-up of Woodward and Newman had been known to the general public at the time, it could have seriously damaged their promising careers.

Newman remembered overhearing Harry Cohn, founder of Columbia Pictures, telling Glenn Ford and William Holden, "If you're going to get into trouble, do it at the Château Marmont." Although that advice had not been directly aimed at him, Newman took it seriously.

Although **Joanne Woodward** and **Paul Newman** look serenely happy in this photo, their relationship got off to a rough start. Knowing that Newman was still tied to his wife, Jackie, Woodward tried to make him jealous by getting engaged to other men, such as playwright James Costigan. She also flirted with Gore, suggesting that their platonic relationship might not necessarily remain platonic.

The film director, Nicholas Ray, had told Newman, "If you're a novelist or actor from New York, you'll feel at home in this dark, rambling old French castle. It's not part of the state of California. If you want to pick up a garage mechanic with dirty fingernails, you can hustle him up on the elevator directly from the garage to your hotel room. Chances are, no one will see your comings and goings. After he's spurted, slip him a twenty and send him on his way. On the way up in the elevator, you can unzip him and cop a feel to make sure he's worth the twenty before you actually get him up to the room and undress him."

It was around the pool at the Marmont that Woodward began to read Gore's

---

Gore Makes a Bid for President of the United States, With the Understanding that He'd Marry Joanne Woodward and Make Her His First Lady

---

novels, including *The City and the Pillar.*

"I'd like to live to see the day when Hollywood has advanced to the point that it will make a movie based on *The City and the Pillar,*" Newman told Gore.

"I doubt if that day will ever come," Austen said. "Not in my lifetime."

When Woodward read *Judgment of Paris* she sent Gore a telegram, as he was out of town. It read, "AT YOUR FEET ARTISTWISE SUCH A BEAUTIFUL MIND BETWEEN THOSE FLAPPING EARS."

[Gore's Judgment of Paris, *a witty odyssey of self-discovery, published in 1952, prompted John Aldridge at* The New York Times *to describe Gore as "easily the most precocious, versatile and prolific member of the newest generation of novelists now under 30."]*

It was at the Château Marmont that Newman and Gore plotted to convince Warner Brothers to film a movie version of *Billy the Kid*, the role Paul had originally played on TV. It was there that Gore agreed to turn his teleplay into a full script ready for the cameras.

Based to some degree on the quartet's *[Woodward, Newman, and Gore, with Austen]*, frequent dialogues beside the Château's swimming pool, they became known as Hollywood's most notorious *ménage à quatre.* But this was not necessarily the case.

Sometimes, when Newman was at the studio, Woodward and Gore got involved in intense discussions about Gore's vision of one day running for President of the United States.

"Of course," Gore cautioned, "the specter of homosexuality might rear its ugly head during the campaign." Presumably, it was Woodward herself who volunteered to consider marrying him as a means of providing "cover."

"I wouldn't mind playing the role of First Lady," she said. "It would be a hell of a lot better than this stinking part I've got in *A Kiss Before Dying [released in 1956].* And it also might be a hell of a lot more inter-

Joanne Woodward and **Paul Newman** as they appeared in 1958 in *The Long Hot Summer,* one of the best movies they ever made. Supposedly, it was based on two short stories by William Faulkner, but its real inspiration was Tennessee Williams' *Cat on a Hot Tin Roof,* which was already an acclaimed Broadway hit. The executives at 20th Century Fox wanted to show MGM that they, too, could spin a tale of twisted Southern passion.

They even cast a big "Big Daddy" in the form of Orson Welles, who on and off the screeen was a "dissipated, bloated mess."

Welles held Newman in contempt. "He's a little guy physically, but he has a certain pizzazz. He frowns and rolls his eyes, and I guess a lot of women find that sexy."

esting than sitting around this pool waiting for Paul to make up his mind to divorce Jackie and marry me."

[The reference was to Newman's first wife, Jacqueline Witte.]

There remained another questions. What to do about Howard Austen?

"Perhaps we could let Howard permanently occupy the Lincoln bedroom, rent free?" Gore said facetiously.

Fred Kaplan, in his biography of Gore, quotes Woodward as saying, "I think if we had gotten to that point and Gore had said, 'Let's get married,' I might very well have done so. Because I was very fond of him. Many people have had that sort of marriage. I can't imagine how long it would have lasted. I would have driven Gore crazy, or he would have driven me crazy."

Both Newman and Woodward configured themselves as Gore's celebrity supporters, as did Eleanor Roosevelt, when he unsuccessfully ran for Congress in a Republican district in New York State in 1960.

How the Gore Vidal / Paul Newman Liaison Inspired Jealousy in Other Writers

One day, Monty Clift arrived beside the pool at the Château Marmont when Newman and Woodward were away. He confided to Gore that he'd originally been offered the Robert Wagner role opposite Woodward in *A Kiss Before Dying.* "I turned it down," Clift said. "Cheap melodrama. Actually, I recommended that Paul should lobby for the role. 'Play a murderer,' I told him. I thought it would help him get over his squeaky clean image. In love, he knows

a lot about betrayal and deceit, lies even. As smart as she is, I bet Woodward doesn't know much about the secret life of Newman. Do you?"

"I'm discovering him day by day," Gore said. "But I do know that he's devious enough to take a mistress and that he plays around."

"Have you had him yet?" Clift asked.

"No, but it's only a matter of time," Gore said. "He's my number one priority, but I'll have to strike like a cobra at the right moment."

Eventually, Newman, Woodward, Gore, and Austen found a new landlady, actress Shirley MacLaine, who collectively rented them her cottage in Malibu. Subsequently, they abandoned the Château Marmont.

Once a sailor, **Paul Newman** was the best-looking man to ever come out of Shaker Heights, Ohio.

Newman's marriage to Jackie Witte had all but expired at this point. He was waiting for divorce papers to be filed.

Meanwhile, at the Actors Studio in Manhattan, Lee Strasberg told Tennessee, "Joanne Woodward will never really have Paul. He likes to share himself with other admirers, both male and female."

Christopher Isherwood, who had recently dined with Tennessee, claimed that the playwright "was bubbling over with jealousy over Gore's decision to live with Newman."

"I am certain that when Joanne is away, Gore is pawing those golden inches and sucking him dry," Tennessee told Isherwood. "Do you think Gore cold resist Paul walking around that beach house in a pair of tight-fitting jockey shorts? Paul drinks a lot, especially beer. It's inevitable that seduction is going to take place one night when the moon goes behind a cloud. Ask any gay man: The difference between a straight sailor and a gay sailor is a six-pack."

The unorthodox *ménage* maintained by Newman, Woodward, Vidal, and Austen became the hottest news racing along the Hollywood grapevine, but escaped serious scrutiny in the press. Once again, there was much speculation about the various sexual combinations the household might pursue. Even an ongoing four-way orgy was suggested, with Newman as the main object of communal desire.

In his memoir, *Palimpsest,* Gore addressed the rumor of a sexual tryst between Newman and himself. "I should note here that over the years, I have read and heard about the love affair between me and Paul Newman. Unlike Marlon Brando, whom I hardly know, Paul has been a friend for close to half a century, proof, in my psychology, that nothing could ever have happened."

The logic (or lack thereof) of such a statement could be loudly challenged. The world has long been peopled with fifty-year friendships that began as youthful love affairs.

During Newman's lifetime, Gore protected the actor's image. But after his death, Gore informed close friends that "I did Paul on rare occasions. It was hardly a romance. Sometimes, when we were alone in the house, he would appear at my bedroom door in the nude. He just wanted to be done, perhaps to relieve sexual tension. He thought I would enjoy it to a point. But I wanted so much more, even though I knew he didn't feel it was right, or didn't want to give more than what I got. He was a beauty, and I did enjoy him. After all, he knew I wasn't getting anything from Howard."

"Paul Newman Is Trapped in a Fake Celluloid World"

—*Anaïs Nin*

Reunited with her younger second husband, Rupert Poole, in Los Angeles, Anaïs Nin, the diarist, drove to Malibu for lunch at the Vidal/Newman/Woodward/Austen household.

At their home, she warmly embraced Gore and Austen, who introduced her to their housemates, Woodward and Newman. Later, Anaïs would dismiss both of them as "starlets."

Later, Anaïs spoke to her friend, the novelist, James Leo Herlihy [author of Midnight Cowboy], who was trying to convince Newman to star in the 1962 movie adaptation of his 1960 novel, All Fall Down.

[The role Herlihy was proposing for Newman— that of a good-looking, hedonistic drifter—bore many similarities to the one he eventually played in Hud (1963). The role that Herlihy was proposing in All Fall Down eventually went to Warren Beatty.]

"Newman is just as much of a narcissist as Gore is," Anaïs later told Herlihy. "But he disguises it completely, and, like the most skilled of actors, puts up a mask to confuse the world. I suspect he will go far in an industry that is all about illusion."

"There is no self-awareness in this handsome young man at all," she claimed. "He is an obvious homosexual, but does not dare admit that to himself. He's a selfish rogue while pretending to be benevolent, supporting all the right causes. He has a facile charm but no depth. In spite of the hot sun out here, he already knows that California is a cold, harsh land. He does not want it to hurt him. So what will he do? What must he do? He will inflict emotional pain on others, therefore avoiding the pain of having the blows strike him first."

"I predict he'll have a miserable life in Holly-

Gore introduced Paul Newman to the diarist, **Anaïs Nin**. Later, she gave a devastating psychological appraisal of this "cardboard starlet."

Gore claimed, "I think Anaïs had the hots for Newman and secretly masked her desire for him behind all this psychological blabber she picked up from sleeping with her psychoanalyst, Dr. Otto Rank, whose mentor had been Sigmund Freud."

wood," she said. "Beneath all of his swagger, I suspect there is a sensitive man lurking somewhere there. He can't be frank with himself. It's obvious that he can't have a dialogue between his own flesh and his true spirit. He has no soul, or, if he does, it is hidden behind the package of surface beauty that he presents. I advised him to write down his dreams and try to analyze them, or get help from an analyst. I even volunteered to help him myself, but he rejected me. Amazingly, he told me, 'I don't dream.' What is a man without dreams?"

"His whole life is a deceit, a cover-up, and I join him in that," she said. "I, too, as you well know, am torn between two lovers. This balancing act has made me a mistress of deceit myself. Liars need to keep track of what they say. I have a secret Book of Lies that I write in daily. That way, I can remember what I told one lover and what I told another."

"I feel sorry for Newman because he will never be what he wants to be," Anaïs said. "If he wants to be a movie star, then he has to be as fake and artificial as Marilyn Monroe. He has to become a sort of dream figure for the women of America. American women are shallow. They always go for the superficial. They make gods and goddesses out of cardboard caricatures. I predict Newman will turn into a cardboard figure. There will be no reality to him. He can't be real."

"He's moving into a world foreign to him," she said. "He'll be an alien in Hollywood, as if he's landed from another planet. We'll never know who Paul Newman is, because he doesn't know himself. Perhaps one harsh, brutal morning, when the world tumbles in around him, he'll look into the mirror and see himself for the first time. But it will frighten him. He'll immediately reach for that mask to put on again, the one that conceals him from himself."

"While pretending to be one thing, which he isn't, he'll live a secret life in the shadows," she said. "He'll grab pleasure where he can find it and then flee from it back into this fake celluloid world. A tragedy, really. But, this is, after all, Lotusland."

Gore Pursues Paul Aboard a Yacht on the Aegean Sea

In 1958, Paul Newman finally married Joanne Woodward. "And then all of us, including Howard, lived happily ever after," Gore wrote.

Of course, he was exaggerating, but Newman and Woodward did spend part of their honeymoon in London with Gore and Austen, who had rented a flat on Chesham Place. Woodward remembered it as "very dark and very cold."

Woodward arrived pregnant at their apartment, and during her honeymoon, she miscarried. "Had it been known that she was pregnant on the honeymoon, her career might have ended—hard to believe today," Gore said.

In his memoirs, Gore wrote: "The Newmans made a calculated choice to present themselves as a folksy, lower-middle-class, all-American couple when, in actual fact, he came from a wealthy family in Ohio that had sent him to Yale, while Joanne was the daughter of a vice president of the publisher, Scribner's."

The by-now-famous quartet reunited again for an extended period in 1961. Gore had just completed his second most controversial novel after *The City and the Pillar*. It was entitled *Myra Breckinridge*.

As a celebration of their shared decade of friendship, they chartered a yacht together for a sail through the Greek islands with a final destination at Rhodes. Collectively, they departed from Piraeus with a captain and a small crew. The seas were stormy, and all of them were sick at times from the turbulent sea. The cruise was badly conceived and badly organized, and the year was not good for exploring Greece, a country that was midway through a series of military coups and plagued with chronic civil unrest.

Gore later recalled, "Our idiot captain brought us too close to an island where 10,000 political prisoners were jailed. We were fired upon by the Greek navy. Officers boarded our boat. Two of them recognized Paul as an American movie star. Not wanting to generate headlines by creating an international incident, they retreated. We were saved from arrest as potential Pimpernels."

By this time, Woodward had had enough. "Get me off this fucking boat!" she shouted at Newman. When the opportunity arose for her to board a ferry back to Piraeus, she jumped ship and sailed away, heading for London to watch plays in the West End.

Throughout the cruise, regardless of the island or port on which they landed, Newman's arrival was greeted with hysteria, with youthful voices shouting "POLE NOO-MUN!"

In his second book of memoirs, *Point to Point Navigation,* Gore wrote about an encounter they had on the island of Mykonos. Here, a tall, Giacometti-style woman vaulted aboard their yacht, claiming she was a Hohenzollern princess of Prussia. Newman ordered Gore to get rid of her, but he and Austen found that her limbs were "made of fettuccine. This self-styled heiress to Frederick the Great slithered herself free of us and rushed into Paul's stateroom, where she relieved herself of what seemed to be a gallon of *[vomited]* ouzo on his bunk."

Later, when Gore relayed anecdotes about his trip to Tennessee in New York, *[and perhaps as a means of inflaming his jealousy],* he confessed to having enjoyed intimate relations with Newman after his wife abandoned the ship. "Paul never looked sexier and more macho than he did in the Greek islands," Gore claimed. "We both grew beards. He walked naked around his stateroom, a sight for my sore eyes. I viewed that as a green light."

"Joanne was in England, and I took advantage of her horny husband. When I came to his bed at night, I did the dirty deed. He always managed to explode, so I assumed he enjoyed it. We were never close like a romantic couple, and it was very mechanical. But I enjoyed it."

From all appearances, Newman was attracted to Gore's mind, perhaps not his body. "He exposed me to literature and was very familiar with the ancient world. He told me stories of the ancient Greeks that were mesmerizing. He constantly set off a buzz in my head. I think I came to realize what a great chance I had to get educated when I met Gore."

As the years went by, Gore saw Newman and Woodward only periodically.

In Washington, in 1994, having been invited to address the National Press Club, he received a call from Newman, who wanted to hear his speech. Newman proposed that on the evening of the day of Gore's speech, that they have dinner with Bill and Hillary Clinton at the White House only four days before the midterm elections.

"Since no one else in Washington was talking to the Clintons, I agreed to go," Gore said.

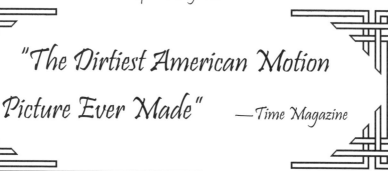

Chapter Thirty-One

"The Dirtiest American Motion Picture Ever Made" —Time Magazine

"I Want to Be Your Thumb-Sucking Baby Doll" —Marilyn Monroe to Tennessee

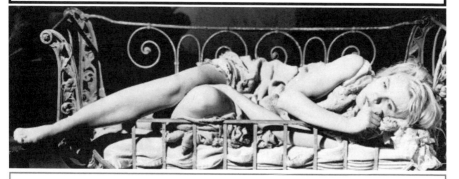

Jack Garfein, the husband of **Carroll Baker**, who's pictured above in *Baby Doll,* grossly misinformed her that Marilyn Monroe had been Tennessee's first choice for the film's female lead. That had not been the case. He had been misinformed.

Baker later claimed that "Tennessee's script was a sheer delight, full of humor and poetry--in fact, the dialogue was just scrumptious. Was I playing a dumb blonde role like Marilyn?"

Although there were many poignant aspects to her character, the answer was "yes." The script called for Baby Doll to inform her husband, as a means of proving how enlightened she is, that she's a magazine reader.

In the summer of 1955, Tennessee was living in Rome

with Frank Merlo, working on the script for *Baby Doll* and also writing dialogue for a new play, *Sweet Bird of Youth.* He was also downing an inordinate amount of Seconal and guzzling gin martinis.

Elia Kazan had already expressed an interest in making a film version of *Baby Doll* for Warner Brothers. But, as before, both of them had different ideas about the script. Originally, Tennessee had wanted the play to be more of a comedy, and he perceived, with alarm, that Kazan seemed more intrigued with the idea of turning it into heavy drama.

In a letter to Kazan, Tennessee wrote: "*Baby Doll* is not a part for Grace Kelly or Deborah Kerr. It's a role for a sexy little *comedienne*. Baby Doll is about as genteel as Paddy's Pig. She is touchingly comic, a grotesquely witless creature, about as deep as kitty-cat's pee. Who the fuck gives a shit if she is, was, or ever will be fulfilled as a woman? Woman's fulfillment is your game, not mine."

Originally, Tennessee had conceived of *Baby Doll* as an overweight bundle of horror, with fat arms, bulging calves, and thick ankles, a latter-day, three-hundred pound version of Anna Nicole Smith

Always restless, Tennessee later migrated to Madrid, even though he claimed, "That's one city in Europe I truly hate."

He was in the Plaza Mayor, having a martini and contemplating *Baby Doll,* when critic Kenneth Tynan accidentally encountered Tennessee, sitting alone nursing a martini of his own.

Tynan recorded his impression of Tennessee at the time: "He had that sleazy fat-cat smile and raffish saunter, with hair like a nest of small, wet serpents. He fits into every country he visits, including Spain, where he becomes a Spaniard; or Italy, where he becomes an Italian; or Greece, where he becomes a Greek fisherman. Only in London and New York does he seem out of place, looking like a retired bandit."

***

First written in the summer of 1936, 27

Carroll Baker *(upper photo)* stares with not-so-innocent eyes between the spokes of Baby Doll's crib, where she spends most of the day sucking her thumb.

In the *lower photo*, her husband, a role interpreted by Karl Malden, goes for her neck, indicating that when he finally gets his virginal wife to bed, he's likely to behave like a vampire.

"I Could Have Killed Marilyn Monroe."

—Carroll Baker

Wagons Full of Cotton was published in *Manuscript* magazine. In this version, the Southern plantation owner is busy ginning 27 wagons of cotton, while his fat wife fans herself on the veranda and flirts with the plantation overseer, who is a rather small man. The man constantly flicks his riding crop in her direction, ostensibly fending of flies, although there is a hint of sadomasochism in his gestures.

Eventually, she invites him upstairs to her bedroom--that is, if he promises not to hurt her.

As source material for a movie, director Elia Kazan found the one-act play too weak. He struck upon the idea of combining it with another of Tennessee's one-act plays, *The Unsatisfactory Supper.* Consequently Tennessee delivered a reading that summer of this other play to the summer residents of Nantucket, the audience including the notable playwright, Thornton Wilder.

The Unsatisfactory Supper was originally entitled *The Long Stay Cut Short.* It was based on an incident in the playwrights' own life. his maternal grandmother, Rosina Dakin, had come to live with his parents, Cornelius and Edwina Williams. She became the cook, but Cornelius objected to her fare, especially all those collard greens cooked in greasy fatback.

The one-act play was published in 1945, but it was never produced on stage until 1971, in London, where it was severely criticized.

During the process of combining the plays, both Tennessee and Kazan had slimmed down Baby Doll until she was a sexy "child woman," still living in a baby crib and sucking her thumb.

Her father gave her away in marriage to an older, lecherous man, Archie Lee Meighan, the owner of the local cotton gin. There were conditions attached—her husband had to provide for her and could not consummate the marriage until Baby Doll's 20th birthday.

At the time the film begins, Baby Doll is only nineteen, and Archie Lee can hardly wait "to plow her." In the meantime, he drills peepholes through her bedroom wall, hoping to spy on her nudity.

The plot thickens when a foreigner, Silva Vacarro, moves to the nearby countryside with a more modern and efficient cotton gin, stealing Archie Lee's old customers. No longer a small and wizened man, Silva has morphed into a handsome, sexy Sicilian.

With his furniture confiscated and facing bankruptcy, it becomes clear that Archie Lee cannot meet his obligation of providing for Baby Doll.

Consequently, he burns down Vicarro's cotton gin, and Vacarro, seeking revenge, tries to snatch Baby Doll from him.

Based on his previous success with *A Streetcar*

Marilyn Monroe's lover, jaunty **Frank Sinatra,** ridiculed her efforts to interpret the dramatic roles of Tennessee Williams' heroines. "Perhaps you and I could co-star together in the musical version of *Streetcar,*" he mockingly told her.

Named Desire, producer Charles Feldman, an on-again, off-again lover of Marilyn Monroe, had been constantly calling Tennessee and Kazan, asking them, "When are we going to make another great movie together? You guys are hot!"

As news of this Tennessee/Kazan collaboration heated up, Feldman flew to New York to meet with them, suggesting that Warners was willing to pay handsomely for the film Rights to *Baby Doll*. Williams and Kazan were still working on the screenplay.

At the Actors Studio in Manhattan, Kazan tried out an early version of *Baby Doll,* casting Karl Malden as the frustrated husband, and Carroll Baker as Baby Doll Meighan *[i.e., the Flora character of 27 Wagons.]*

For the film version, Eli Wallach would be cast as Silva Vaccaro, with Mildred Dunnock playing Rose Comfort, *The Unsatifactory Supper's* cook.

In its first stage production, *27 Wagons Full of Cotton* was performed at the Playhouse Theater in Manhattan in 1955. It starred Felice Orlandi (who Tennessee defined as "my type"), Maureen Stapleton, and Myron McCormick.

Tennessee Auditions James Dean

Beginning with the 1950s, Marilyn Monroe had entertained dreams of starring in a play by Tennessee Williams.

One night in 1952, at Peter Lawford's house in Santa Monica, a drunken Marilyn was sharing her dream with Sammy Davis, Jr., Dean Martin, Frank Sinatra, and Lawford himself. She claimed that she was considering touring America with Marlon Brando in a road show version of his Broadway success, Tennessee's play, *A Streetcar Named Desire.*

"Marlon would get a chance to be Stanley Kowalski again, and I, of course, would play the doomed heroine, Blanche DuBois. I'm sure Tennessee would love the casting."

"SHUT UP, MARILYN!" Frank Sinatra shouted at her. "You don't know what in the fuck you're talking about. As Blanche DuBois, you'd be laughed off the stage. Stick to those dumb blonde roles."

In tears, she ran from the living room and locked herself into one of the guest bedrooms. Sinatra stormed out of the house, but the temperamental star later apologized when he wanted her body.

That fantasy dream faded, of course, but three years later, another possibility arose.

In 1955, Marilyn Monroe was in Manhattan, attending the Actors Studio, when she first heard of Tennessee's latest play, *Cat on a Hot Tin Roof.* Her informant was James Dean, who was arranging a rendezvous with her, but not "until I take care of some unfinished business."

"Tennessee told me he's writing this play about a repressed homosexual married to this hot-to-trot wife named Maggie the Cat," Dean told Marilyn. "He thinks the part of the young husband would be ideal for me, although I'm not very repressed. I think his audition will consist of an expert blow-job."

"Sounds like fun," she said. "If the part's right, maybe I could play Maggie the Cat."

"Tennessee said that both roles are sexy." Dean looked at Marilyn and winked "Can you act sexy, doll?"

"Try me!" she shot back.

"It's a deal, but give me a raincheck for right now. Of course, I'd rather get a blow job from Marilyn Monroe than from Tennessee Williams."

"Those are about the most romantic words I've ever heard spoken to me," she said, kissing him goodbye and wishing him luck. Before he left, she said, "I guess men sometimes have to lie on the casting couch, just like us girls."

Marilyn had briefly met both Tennessee and Truman Capote when they were in Hollywood writing screenplays. Even though Tennessee knew her only slightly, he opted to invite her to a tea he was hosting for his mother, Edwina Williams, at the St. Regis Hotel in Manhattan. He definitely knew that Edwina would be impressed if he invited Marilyn. When she arrived, she did not disappoint.

At the St. Regis, all the guests had already arrived except Marilyn, who was invariably late. She made a spectacular entrance, as described by writer Lois Banner:

"Everyone stopped what they were doing, freeze-framed with their drinks, hors d'oeuvres, or cigarettes halfway to their mouths. A path was cleared, and Marilyn walked through. She wore a simple black silk slip dress with thin shoulder straps and nothing on underneath. Her skin was a luminous alabaster, with pearly blue and rose tints. Marilyn was more beautiful in the flesh than on film."

Marilyn, eager to be cast as "a Baby Doll virgin."

Her relationship with Tennessee merited a few friendly words and a kiss on the cheek. She'd been intimately involved with director Elia Kazan. Although he was not present at the tea, he was set to direct *Cat on a Hot Tin Roof* on Broadway.

In addition to her affair with producer Charles Feldman, Marilyn and Kazan had been lovers for years. Their love affair had been turbulent, much of it conducted within the privacy of the Feldman home. Kazan confessed to that once-secret relationship in his memoirs, *A Life:*

"In the morning light, I'd listen to her stories. Sometimes, she wept. I gave her comfort. Ignite her and she'd explode. On many a dawn, I would put on one of Charlie's white terrycloth robes and drive Marilyn home. She often wore white. I'd put down the top of the convertible, and we'd drive through the empty

Elvis, longing to appear "in a drama by either of those two fags," a reference to Tennessee Williams and William Inge.

streets and boulevards of Los Angeles, two 'mad monks,' singing and laughing."

Kazan remembered one evening when Marilyn attended a post-Academy Awards celebration at Feldman's house following the Oscar sweep of *A Streetcar Named Desire*. Kazan had rented a suite at the Beverly Hills Hotel for the night, and he asked Marilyn to leave the party with him. She told him that she couldn't because she had to meet her new lover, Joe DiMaggio, at ten that night. "He's asked me to marry him, and I'm afraid you and I are going to have to break it off."

"I don't care how late it is, I think you owe me a farewell fuck," Kazan told her. "I'll leave the door to my suite unlocked, and you're to come in, regardless of the hour."

As Kazan remembered it, it was 3:30am when Marilyn arrived. He woke up just as she was pulling off her clothes. "Incidentally, even though married to DiMaggio, Marilyn never cut off my conjugal rights," Kazan claimed.

Elvis With Marilyn—Co-Starring Together?

Months later, Marilyn, on a date with Marlon Brando, complained to him that, "All the great women's roles are being written by gay guys these days." She was referring to the play *Bus Stop,* which had been written by William Inge, a former lover of Tennessee's. On Broadway, it starred Kim Stanley. Later, the role of the sexy saloon singer pursued by a horny cowboy would be hers in the play's 1956 incarnation as a film.

She told Brando that she was flying to New York to attend the Broadway premier of Tennessee's *Cat on a Hot Tin Roof,* scheduled for its debut on March 24, 1955.

For the big opening night, Marilyn flew into New York and asked columnist Walter Winchell to escort her to Broadway to see Barbara Bel Geddes perform in the role of Maggie the Cat opposite Ben Gazzara.

As Winchell later noted, "Marilyn sat through the play mesmerized. It was obvious she was dying to play Maggie the Cat in the film version."

The first person Marilyn met backstage was Tennessee himself. "I know you created the role of Maggie the Cat just so I could play it in the movies," she said to him.

At first, he looked stunned. Then he said, "Something like that. If you'll excuse me, I've got to head to the men's room to barf. I do that when I fear the opening of one of my plays will lead to failure."

Backstage, Marilyn hugged and kissed Ben Gazzara, the star of the play, but avoided confronting Bel Geddes. She looked around for Tennessee, but he had mysteriously disappeared.

Winchell and Marilyn were invited to the cast party, an event scheduled at Gracie Mansion, the official residence of the mayor of New York. She found that an odd venue, and wondered how Kazan had ever managed to arrange such a high profile setting.

Wearing a skin-tight gold mesh gown, Marilyn made a grand entrance at Gracie Mansion, her hair a shining platinum. She managed to steal the thunder from the then-married couple, Debbie Reynolds and singer Eddie Fisher, who were famously hailed at the time as "America's Sweethearts."

In a corner of Gracie Mansion sat a sulking Tennessee, who had slipped into the party virtually unnoticed. He was all by himself.

A waiter had served him an entire bottle of white wine. Marilyn went over to him and congratulated him on his "stunningly brilliant play with a great movie role for a blonde bombshell."

Pretending at least for a minute to be a Southern gentleman, he told her how glad he was to see her again. "You've caught me between barfs."

"After tonight, I know you're the greatest playwright on Broadway," she said. "*Your Cat on a Hot Tin Roof* is mesmerizing. For an actress, the role of Maggie the Cat is a dream part. With such a success under your belt, why do you look so sad?"

"It's going to be a disaster—the critics will rip the flesh from my bones. I caught my agent, Audrey Wood, leaving the theater fifteen minutes before the curtain fell. She was like a rat fleeing a sinking ship."

"Don't worry," she said. "The reviews will be terrific. I just know it."

One of the mayor's aides came to fetch him for something, and he excused himself.

She reached out to him before he left. "Could we have dinner some night? I want to talk to you about the role of Maggie the Cat."

"Of course," he said.

"I'm staying at the Waldorf Towers," she said. "I'd love to hear from you."

"Consider it done," he said before walking away. She suspected he was drunk. Even though she'd slipped him her phone number, he seemed so intoxicated, he might not remember.

Two weeks later, a call from him and an invitation to dinner came into her suite. In the lobby, she met Tennessee and his Sicilian lover, Frank Merlo. He was young and dynamic. Tennessee told Marilyn that Frank was "the role model I used for Stanley in *A Streetcar Named Desire*."

On the way to an Italian restaurant in Greenwich Village, she sat between them for the bumpy ride south.

Frank knew the owner of the restaurant, and he personally retreated to the kitchen to order the house specialties. Soon he came back, finding his lover and Marilyn talking about who might play key roles in the movie version of *Cat*.

"Would you believe that Elvis Presley wants to play Brick?" Tennessee asked. "I can just imagine what Colonel Tom Parker would say about his boy playing a repressed homosexual still in love with a dead football hero."

"And for the Maggie role?" she asked.

"Would you believe they're talking about Lana Turner? I once was hired to write a screenplay for her. I never got beyond the brassière."

"At least they're not considering Bel Geddes," she said. "She's all wrong for the role. Just ask Howard Hughes. He told me that she doesn't have it at all."

"I fought with Gadge *[Elia Kazan]* over casting her. She's not the kind of actress I appreciate. But—and I know you know him well—when he makes up his mind, it's hard to budge him. He has this theory. Barbara was once fat. Of course, she slimmed down. Gadge thinks that women like that still doubt their sex appeal. That's why they try extra hard to convey a strong sexual appetite."

"That sounds silly," she said, looking over at Frank, who seemed to be hanging onto her every word. "Maggie should be real sexy on screen. In fact, dare I say it myself, some people consider me real sexy."

"I think you invented sex," Frank chimed in, gallantly.

"You might be terrific in the part," Tennessee said. "Barbara is a cool, somewhat cold-looking blonde. But I conceived of Maggie as a sizzler on stage."

"Well, if Marilyn can do anything, she can sizzle," Frank said.

"I'll try to lobby for you," Tennessee promised. "As for the man, I was considering Marlon Brando, but he told someone that he will never appear again on Broadway in a Tennessee Williams play. Why, I don't know. Maybe he'll do it on the screen, but I hear he's going to turn it down. I also hear Paul Newman wants to do it, but I think he looks too pretty-boy Jewish to portray the son of a plantation aristocrat in the Deep South."

"Ben Gazzara might want to repeat his stage role in front of the camera," she said. "That reminds me. I'll call him up and audition him at the Waldorf Towers to see if he and I have any chemistry. Regardless of who plays Brick, the one thing I know is that I am Maggie the Cat. Can't you just hear me saying, '*SKIPPER IS DEAD. I'M ALIVE. MAGGIE THE CAT IS ALIVE!*'"

"You'd be electric in the role," Tennessee said.

"Don't give it to Elizabeth Taylor. She can't act."

"I'm considering playing Big Daddy myself," Tennessee said.

"You'd be wonderful."

***

After sitting impatiently through the screen version of *Cat on a Hot Tin Roof,* Marilyn wrote a note to Tennessee at his home in Key West. "I could have played Maggie so much better," she said. "I hate to say this, but Elizabeth just doesn't have the sex appeal the role calls for, and I'm sure you'll agree."

Months later, Marilyn lamented to Brando. "I thought Tennessee adored me. So what happens? The role of Maggie the Cat goes to that damn Elizabeth Taylor. You and I should have done it."

"I hear she's also going to film Tennessee's *Suddenly Last Summer* with Monty," he said.

"Just my luck. I get the dumb blonde comedies, and Taylor gets the meaty dramas. *Hollywood!*"

"Marilyn is Too Old—And Not Enough of a Virgin"

—Tennessee

Based on what she'd heard, Marilyn felt that the star role in Tennessee's *Baby Doll*—scheduled to be shot in the state of Mississippi—would be ideal for her. But its playwright *[Tennessee]* and its director *[Kazan]* had other ideas.

First, Marilyn called Marlon Brando, her sometimes lover, and arranged a date. She'd heard that Warner Brothers had already signed him for the film's male lead of Silva Vaccaro.

At his home, she found Brando rather vague about any commitment. "Let's talk movies tomorrow," he told her. "In the meantime, how about a good old fashioned fuck from my noble tool?"

[Brando turned down the role, the movie part eventually going to Eli Wallach, with Karl Malden cast in the second male lead, with support from character actress Mildred Dunnock playing Aunt Rose Comfort.]

Dunnock had originated the role of Big Mama in *Cat on a Hot Tin Roof,* losing the movie part to Judith Anderson. Dunnock's most famous scene has remained her role as the wheelchair victim in *Kiss of Death* (1947). The film's psychotic villain, Tommy Udo (played by Richard Widmark), pushed the woman in her wheelchair down a flight of stairs to her death.

Not getting anywhere with Brando, Marilyn, the next day, read that Kazan, Tennessee, and Tennessee's agent, Audrey Wood, had checked into the Bel Air Hotel. She immediately called Kazan to arrange a late-night rendezvous.

When she confronted him, she found he had more on his mind than the production woes associated with *Baby Doll*. He had been summoned to testify in front of the House Committee on Un-American Activities (HUAC), which had revealed his youthful affiliations with the Communist Party. To save his career, he had been forced to name names of former colleagues who also had been communists. To the horror of his left wing friends, including Brando, he named such associates as Clifford Odets and Paula Strasberg.

Many in Hollywood turned against him, except Tennessee, who did not approve of what he did, but was at least empathetic. He said, "It's a sad commentary on our times. Human venality is something we must not only expect, but forgive."

Marilyn later claimed to her best friend, Jeanne Carmen, "Elia was one depressed man, but at least before the night ended, he rose to the occasion. He didn't offer me the role of Baby Doll,

Tennessee asked a question few men have had to answer: "What is a man to do when faced with a choice between Marilyn Monroe and Elizabeth Taylor?"

For very different reasons, a small and select group of other men (Eddie Fisher, Paul Newman, Nicky Hilton, and John F. Kennedy) have faced the same dilemma.

but neither did he turn me down. I think it's mine."

In a call to Tennessee, Kazan told him of Marilyn's obsessive desire to play Baby Doll. "She's nearly thirty, and Baby Doll, as you've written her, is a teenage virgin. Marilyn's a good *comedienne*, but not much more. And she comes with baggage. Not only is she completely neurotic, but she's got Paula Strasberg tagging along to direct the picture for her."

As expected, a call from Marilyn rang in Tennessee's hotel suite that afternoon.

"What could be better box office than a movie starring Marilyn Monroe and Marlon Brando, directed by Elia Kazan and written by the great Tennessee Williams?" she asked.

"I don't like the billing," he said.

"*Baby Doll* can transform my career and send me off in a new direction," she told him. "Maybe I'll be taken seriously as an actress."

He explained to her that he did not have the right to cast the movie, but would give her bid serious consideration.

In several biographies, the claim is made that Marilyn was Tennessee's first choice for the role of Baby Doll, and that she lost the role because of Kazan's objections. One night at his home in Key West, Tennessee told Darwin Porter that he, too, thought Marilyn was not only too old, but inappropriate for the role of the thumb-sucking nymphet. "Not one movie-goer would believe that the on-screen Marilyn had not been fucked," Tennessee said. "She was not that good an actress and certainly no virgin. I heard she'd lost that to Howard Keel when she was thirteen."

Bypassing Marilyn, Kazan was fascinated by the icy blond sex symbol, Carroll Baker, having watched her in the rushes of *Giant* (1956), starring James Dean, Rock Hudson, and Elizabeth Taylor. Kazan envisioned her as perfect for the role of the child-like wife (in name only) of the character played by Karl Malden.

Kazan invited Tennessee to the Actors Studio in Manhattan to witness a scene between Malden and Baker. Lee Strasberg tipped Marilyn off about this audition, and unexpectedly, she showed up to witness the scene as it unfolded with her young rival for the role.

Before her audition for Kazan and Tennessee, Baker had experienced what she described as a terrifying nightmare, in which Tennessee became "a gigantic, white, round balloon with a pig's head. His face was stark white and bloated with two round rouged spots on his puffed-out cheeks. He tells Kazan, 'We'll have to fatten her up. Her breasts will have to be globular.'"

In Carroll's nightmare, Kazan had protested, "But you've already created a bizarre character, and I want to use a normal girl to bring her to life."

In response, Tennessee said, "But this girl is dull, dreary, and titless. I want a sexy 'piglette.'"

Before her tryout scene at the Actors Studio, Baker learned that Marilyn, who was conspicuously in the audience, was a contender for the part. "I wish my breasts were as big as hers," Carroll lamented.

454

Baker's husband, director Jack Garfein, had more or less been left with the impression that if Baker did well in the tryout, the part would be hers, unless Kazan decided to go for the box office draw of Marilyn herself. Even so. it was a surprise when Marilyn walked into the Actors Studio as a prominent member of the audience.

Baker remembered the blonde goddess wearing a patterned scarf, a pink angora sweater, and oversized sunglasses. "Her thin cotton pants might have been grafted to her flesh," Baker later said.

All eyes focused on Marilyn, as she pursed her lips and lisped, "Hello, Jack," to Baker's new husband.

"I was so jealous, I could have killed her," Baker wrote in her memoirs. "She made the word "Jack" sound positively obscene."

Baker remembered Marilyn's approach toward her: "She was like a perpetual-motion gel. If her hips weren't gyrating, she was winching her shoulders, or swinging her pink fuzzy tits, or making that sucking fish-pucker mouth. Everything about her stated: 'I'm yours. Take me. Use me.' I thought I smelled the fruity aroma of sex."

After watching Baker and Malden emote onstage, Tennessee jumped to his feet. "That's it! Carroll, you are it!" He rushed up onto the stage and embraced her. "Baby, you're our *Baby Doll*," he sang out.

Seated in the third row of the audience, Marilyn, too, jumped up from her seat. In tears, she made her way to the exit.

***

Barbara Leaming, one of Marilyn's many biographers, speculated about what would have happened if Marilyn had starred in *Baby Doll*:

"Had she been directed by Kazan at that stage in her career, she probably would not have become as dependent on the Strasbergs. What need would there have been for Lee Strasberg if it had been Kazan who enabled Marilyn to do her first important dramatic role? What need would there have been for Paula Strasberg, her acting coach? Had Marilyn done well in a film written by Tennessee Williams, quite possibly she would have been treated differently by the public, and even by the industry. And who could say what would have happened to Marilyn's relationship with Arthur Miller had she gone to Mississippi in November of 1955 with Kazan?"

The Catholic Hierarchy Tries to Suppress Baby Doll

Baby Doll was released throughout the United States on December 18, 1956 to immediate controversy. The Roman Catholic Legion of Decency, guardian of movie-goers' morality, condemned it.

Variety noted that this was the first time in years that Legion censors condemned a major American film that had already received the approval of the

Motion Picture Production Code.

Time magazine defined *Baby Doll* as "just possibly the dirtiest American-made motion picture that has ever been legally exhibited."

Hellfire and dragon flames came with particular force from Cardinal Francis Spellman, who functioned as the sixth Catholic Archbishop of New York City from 1939 to 1967, and who was described by journalist Michelangelo Signorile as "one of the most notorious, powerful and sexually voracious homosexuals in the American Catholic Church's history." He had not seen the movie, but denounced its "immoral and corrupting influence."

"In the Vatican," Kazan privately claimed, "they call him Cardinal Nellie Spellman because they know he's as gay as a Christmas goose. He and his fellow cross-dresser, J. Edgar Hoover, should put on their gowns and their pumps and actually see the picture. I'd call Nellie the Sammy Glick of the Catholic church."

In public, Kazan defended the movie, claiming, "I like it better than *A Streetcar Named Desire*. *Baby Doll* is more ambivalent. It combines comedy and social significance, passion, and farce."

Tennessee issued a statement to the press. "I can't believe that an ancient and august branch of the Christian faith is not larger in heart and mind than those who set themselves up as censors."

In defiance, Warners plastered Times Square with a block-long billboard depicting Baker sucking her thumb. She had eighty-foot legs and ten-foot eyebrows.

The Catholic Church forbade Catholics from seeing *Baby Doll*, which evoked howls of protest from the American Civil Liberties Union as a violation of the First Amendment.

James A. Pike of New York City's Episcopal Cathedral of St. John the Divine countered Spellman's assault, asserting that there was more sensuality in *The Ten Commandments, [the 1956 religious and historical epic produced and directed by Cecil B. DeMille]* than in *Baby Doll*.

As stated by Pike, "It is not the church's duty to prevent adults from having the experience of this picture, but to give them a wholesome basis for interpretation and serious answers to questions that were asked with seriousness."

At Oscar time, Carroll Baker vied for Best Actress, losing to Ingrid Bergman for *Anastasia*. Mildred Dunnock, up for Best Supporting Actress, lost to Dorothy Malone for *Written on the Wind*. Tennessee was nominated for Best Adapted Screenplay, although he should have shared that recognition with Kazan.

In later years, Eli Wallach, the film's co-star, defined *Baby Doll* as "one of the most exciting, daring movies ever made. People see it today and ask, 'What the hell was all the fuss about suppressing it?'"

Chapter Thirty-Two

A Hatchet Attack on Hollywood's Bad Boy in His Domain

Truman Interviews Marlon Brando

In the most bizarre role assignment of the decade, **Marlon Brando** was cast as a Japanese in the 1956 melodrama, *Teahouse of the August Moon*. He is depicted in both the *left and right photos*, above, with **Truman Capote** in the middle.

Brando certainly wished Truman "Sayonara" *[goodbye, the title of his 1957 movie]* after the journalistic hatchet job Truman crafted, based on their interview in a Tokyo hotel room.

That was not all that Truman did to Brando that night in his hotel suite...

Truman Capote invited Marilyn Monroe to see

Marlon Brando and Glenn Ford starring together in the 1956 release of *The Teahouse of the August Moon*. Both the author and the blonde goddess were amazed to see Marlon accessorized with "Jap makeup" *[Truman's words]*.

On their way to the movie house in Los Angeles, Marilyn confessed, "As you know, I've repeatedly had Marlon, but I've also had a one-night stand with Glenn Ford."

During Ford's involvement in the shooting of that film in Japan, he had be-

come one of Marlon's premier enemies, as their two powerful egos
clashed.

"I've had Marlon, too," Truman
bragged, "but I don't expect I'll ever get
Ford, so you have to give me a blow-
by-blow description after we see the
movie."

Truman had read all the details associated with the Glenn Ford vs.
Brando feud. It had begun when Marlon publicly attacked the actor's performance in *Human Desire,* a 1954
movie based on Emile Zola's *La Bête
Humaine.* Zola's novel had originally
been filmed in France by Jean Renoir
in 1938.

After seeing *Human Desire,* Marlon told the press. "Ford is hopelessly

In *Teahouse of the August Moon,* **Marlon
Brando** (center) played Sakini as secretly gay.
Here he depicts a Nipponese matchmaker, try-
ing to unite **Michiko Kyö** *(left)* with **Glenn
Ford.**

boring on the screen. He just stands there on camera, waiting for accidents to
occur. He is totally wooden."

Two years later, after director Daniel Mann cast both of these temperamental stars—sarcastically referring to them as "the male versions of Joan
Crawford and Bette Davis"—in *The Teahouse of the August Moon,* it was inevitable that they'd continue to clash.

In an artistic decision that surprised (and dismayed) almost everybody,
Marlon was cast as a Japanese national named Sakini. Before heading off to
Japan, he told friends, "I'm going to paly Sakini as gay, and naïve America will
never know the difference."

On the set of *Teahouse,* beginning with the first day of shooting, Marlon
denounced Glenn Ford, calling him, "a second-rate William Holden, but without Holden's 'hard-on" on camera. "Ford stumbles and stammers, and his performance means nothing, says nothing, goes nowhere."

In retaliation, Ford claimed that Marlon was nothing "but a vain showoff."

Months later, after the movie was released, one reviewer asserted that
casting Marlon and Ford in the same picture was like having a love scene between Marjorie Main and Tab Hunter."

Teahouse stands as one of the three worst pictures Marlon ever made.
"That's why Truman was shocked when he heard that Marlon's next film, *Sayonara* (1957) would necessitate his return to Japan. "At least Marlon won't be
playing a Jap this time," Truman said.

The film was based on that sprawling mess of a novel by James A. Michener. A romantic tragedy, *Sayonara* told the tale of an American (Marlon) falling
in love during the Korean War with a Japanese entertainer.

Joshua Logan was signed on as the director.

Marlon had rejected the role three times and was chronically unhappy with the script. He'd later tell Truman, among others, "I could piss a better script in the snow than this shit!" However, he needed the $300,000 fee his contract provided, and he also believed that *Sayonara* would represent a plea for racial tolerance. At the time, American occupation forces legally opposed marriages between its servicemen *[many of whom were based in Japan, or had been sent from the front in Korea for medical treatments or for R&R in Japan]* and Japanese women.

When Marlon met Logan, the director shared a secret with him. "Tennessee Williams offered me the directorship of *Streetcar* before Elia Kazan read it. I should have accepted. Under my direction, you would have been an even greater Stanley Kowalski."

Marlon would later share his impression of Logan with Truman. "At last, I've met a man more high strung and quixotic than I am. He's driven by demons, maybe bigger ones than those that sometimes overcome me. Fits of depression descend on Logan like summer rain. Sometimes the rain turns into hurricane gales."

Even before his departure to Japan in anticipation of his interview with Marlon, Truman began dredging up gossipy secrets. They included the fact that Audrey Hepburn had rejected the role of the film's female lead. "If I play an Oriental, I'll be laughed off the screen," Hepburn had informed Logan.

The role was eventually awarded to Miiko Taka, a second-generation Nisei-American working for sixty dollars a week at a travel agency in Los Angeles.

Marlon made no attempt to seduce Taka, but confessed to Truman, "I must have fucked every Japanese girl involved with *Sayonara.*"

The moment he arrived in Tokyo, even before interviewing Marlon, Truman began picking up "tidbits of information." Logan told him that one night Marlon took a "deep-throated kisser" home with him. "She bit Marlon's tongue so badly it caused it to swell. Mumbles was really Mumbles for a day or so."

When Truman, a Southerner himself, saw rushes of Marlon in *Sayonara,* he was surprised at his Southern accent, deriding it as a "cornpone and chittlin'" type of speech pattern.

During the actual interview, Marlon would be far too candid in his mocking of Logan to Truman. Marlon told Truman, "In one scene, I did everything wrong I could think of. I rolled my eyes, grimaced in the wrong place, and used irrelevant gestures. When I was finished, Logan smiled and said, 'It's wonderful, Marlon. Print it!'"

Marlon also admitted to Truman, "I'm just walking through the part—nobody knows the difference anyway."

[In spite of Marlon's assessments of his performance in Sayonara, *as expressed to Truman, his performance was nominated for an Oscar as Best Actor of the year.]*

"It Was Nothing More than a Blow-Job"

In a disastrous move that he'd regret for the rest of his life, Marlon agreed to meet with Truman in January of 1957 at the Miyako Hotel in Kyoto. Capote had been assigned to write a piece on Marlon for *The New Yorker*. Marlon hadn't seen the writer since he'd performed in *A Streetcar Named* Desire more than a decade before, on Broadway. At that time, Marlon had shared an erotic moment with Truman and his friend, Cecil Beaton.

Marlon learned that Beaton was also in Kyoto with Truman, but he pointedly invited only Truman to dinner at his hotel—not Beaton, even though he'd posed nude for him several years before.

Before the meeting, Truman had reassured Marlon that the first part of the tape-recorded interview would be on the record, followed by the candid remarks later "of two old friends getting together to share a memory or two." It sounded innocent enough.

Joshua Logan, however, didn't fall for Truman's reassurances and had, in fact, barred him from the set of the picture. Horrified to learn that Marlon had granted the interview, Logan telephoned Marlon's suite to warn him, "He's a vicious queen and he'll destroy you."

"Don't worry your sweet noggin one bit 'bout this little tadpole," Marlon said, using the exaggerated Southern accent he'd adapted for his character in *Sayonara*. "I can't go into details, but Truman worships me. The piece he'll probably write on me will sound like that silly fodder printed in *Photoplay* magazine."

"I'm not so sure," Logan said. "I've heard this guy gossip at parties. He's not that kind to you. He tells everybody that he and Cecil Beaton seduced you. He even claims that you posed nude for Beaton. I've even heard him describe your dick to enraptured audiences. Personally, I think he's got it in for you. He knows you're one of the most powerful icons in America. Capote loves to shatter icons. To expose them for having clay feet. He'll do the same to you."

"Before the night is over, I'll have Capote sucking on my noble tool," Marlon predicted.

"So you think," Logan told Marlon. "I just read the little fucker's *The Muses Are Heard*. He treats human beings like bugs to be squashed underfoot."

[The Muses Are Heard was Capote's non-fictional lampoon of the Porgy and Bess *troupe traveling in Russia.]*

"I know Capote," Marlon assured Logan. "I can handle the little Southern faggot just fine. I will speak only the usual crap to him. Stuff fit to print. He will not get a look into my soul. My soul is a very private place."

Carlo Fiore, Marlon's best friend, remained in Marlon's suite during the first hour of what became an infamous encounter between the author and the actor. Arriving with a bottle of vodka under his short arm, the diminutive Truman— "slim and trim as a boy"—minced into Marlon's cluttered suite.

With his high-pitched, nasal voice, he greeted Marlon with a kiss on the lips and a handshake for Fiore. Although not a teetotaler, Marlon rarely drank much alcohol.

But in front of the suspicious Fiore, Truman started pouring the liquor for

Marlon, preferring a "courtesy sip" for himself. Fiore later recalled that Truman used "his eccentric charm and sly manipulation to get Marlon to drink that vodka."

The interview began at 7:15pm, with Fiore departing an hour later. Privately, out of earshot from Capote, Fiore told Marlon that he'd call him "every hour with an emergency. This will allow you an excuse to escape from the pansy's clutches." Marlon agreed to that. Fiore kept his promise, but Marlon ignored the so-called emergency calls and kept talking nonstop to Truman until 12:30am the following morning.

Sitting with pages of a script scattered around him, Marlon opened up to Truman as he'd done to no other journalist. He revealed very personal moments about his mother, Dodie; about his private views on friendship, love, and marriage; about what a lousy director Logan was—and on and on, one personal revelation piling up on top of another.

During this long ordeal, Truman took no notes, as he was known for his "unfailing memory."

Truman later claimed that Marlon, throughout his long ramblings, "sounded like an educated Negro using big words only recently learned."

Later Truman revealed the secret behind the success of his interviewing techniques: "You make the victim think he's interviewing you. I told Marlon some of my most personal secrets, even about my mother. Naturally, we shared homosexual secrets with each other. Slowly, ever so slowly, I began to spin my web. By opening myself up to Marlon, I got him to open up like a flower petal facing the dawn. He began to reveal himself as he never had before. The more he talked, the more confessional he became. After the first hour, I knew I was on to a big story. My victim was trapped. I came for an interview but went away with insights that no other writer had ever gotten."

As his opening gambit, Truman described his recent rendezvous with Yukio Mishima, the successful Japanese novelist and playwright who would commit *hari-kiri*, publicly, on November 25, 1970, as a samurai-inspired act of defiance against the modernization and corruption of the Japanese psyche.

"As a lover, Yukio found me inadequate," Truman claimed. "But in exchange for his own hospitality in Japan, he told me that when he comes to New York he wants me to arrange for him to suck a big white cock."

Having seduced each other before, Truman and Marlon were frank in discussing their homosexual affairs. Marlon told Truman of his involvement with Clifford Odets, Tennessee Williams, Laurence Olivier, and Leonard Bernstein. Truman finally left a drunken Marlon in his suite.

The next morning, Marlon told Fiore that his hours with Truman had been better than any session he'd ever had with his analyst. "And it didn't cost me a fucking cent."

Despite having had no sleep all night, a gleeful Truman telephoned Logan, who'd arrived early on the set of *Sayonara*. "Oh, you were so wrong about Brando," an ecstatic Truman informed the director. "Last night your star talked my head off. I got my man." He paused for dramatic effect. "In more ways than one!" Then Truman hung up the phone on a bewildered Logan.

On the *Sayonara* set, later in the day, when a hung-over Marlon showed up for work, Logan confronted his star. Logan wasn't at all concerned with the morality involved in Truman's seduction, but about any bad publicity that might be generated for *Sayonara*.

"Did you go to bed with Capote?" Logan demanded to know.

"If you call 'going to bed' getting a mere blowjob from the little monster with the succulent mouth," Marlon said, "then OK, I went to bed with him."

Yukio Mishima
Was Truman lying?

***

In the weeks ahead, Marlon began to fear that he'd be embarrassed by Truman based on what would appear in *The New Yorker*. In May, Marlon sat down and wrote him a three-and-a-half page, single-spaced, handwritten letter. Marlon's letter, later released to the press by Truman, was filled with an bizarre choice of words, misspellings, and unusual grammatical constructions.

"It is, indeed, discomforting to have the network of one's innards guywired and festooned with harlequin streamers for public musing, but, perhaps it will entertain. I am sorry, in a way, that you didn't complete your plans for the full travesty you had planned to do because it has come full upon me, that there are few who are as well equipped as yourself to write, indeed, the comedy of manners."

This letter was written before Marlon actually read the interview. But the gossipy Truman had told "everybody I know about it" even before publication. Word had traveled back to Marlon, who was aghast.

Entitled "The Duke in His Domain," Capote's profile of Marlon appeared in *The New Yorker* in its edition of November 9, 1957. In the article Marlon was depicted as an overweight, self-indulgent, self-delusional movie star pretending to be on a diet while stuffing himself with French fries, spaghetti, and apple pie. And that was just for openers.

"The interview could have been so much worse in print if I had wanted to reveal all I knew about Brando," Truman later recalled. "If I'd written about the homosexual liaisons of Marlon's, I could have destroyed his career. As it was, I was kind to him. Of course, my profile was not just a journalistic revelation. More of a celebrity *exposé*. But actors should be exposed for what they are: mental dwarfs."

The New York gossip columnist, Dorothy Kilgallen, defined Truman's article as "a real vivisection."

Her rival columnist, Walter Winchell, wrote that the article was "the type of confession usually confined to an analyst's couch."

Marlon's sister, Jocelyn, called the article "a well-written, bitchy hatchet job!"

Enraged, Marlon called Logan to apologize for having been so critical of him in the article. "That little bastard spent half the night telling me his problems," Marlon said. "I felt the least I could do was tell him a few of my own. If I ever run into the pissy queen, I'll kill him!"

Logan chided Marlon that, "You should have done that before you let him into your room."

Truman never responded to Marlon's heartfelt plea to suppress the profile. But the author did have a post-publication comment, which he expressed to a reporter.

"Brando apparently felt that my profile of him was an unsympathetic, even treacherous, intrusion upon the secret terrain of a suffering and awesome sensibility. I thought it was a sympathetic account of a wounded young man who is a genius at acting but not markedly intelligent."

Seething with anger, but also painfully humiliated, Marlon called on George Glass and Walter Seltzer to press a lawsuit against Truman, seeking the advice of these two savvy Hollywood insiders. Glass had first met Marlon when he'd been working as a publicist for Stanley Kramer. A one-time publicist himself, Seltzer had turned producer.

When the men got Marlon to confess that he actually did make the revelations as reported by Truman, they advised him to drop the lawsuit.

Feeling dejected and powerless to fight back, Marlon sighed before getting up to leave their office. At the door, he paused and looked back at the men.

"I was sandbagged!"

Gore Beds Marlon

Gore Vidal was a self-admitted sexual predator, claiming that he'd had sex with more than a thousand people, mostly men. "My near contemporaries," he wrote in his memoirs, "were Jack Kennedy, Marlon Brando, and Tennessee Williams. They were all keeping up with me."

It was inevitable that Gore would encounter Marlon one night. The occasion occurred in 1965 at the London apartment of the British critic, Kenneth Tynan, and his wife, Elaine Dudley. The left-wing couple were known for the flexible boundaries of their open marriage.

Gore's friendship with Kenneth and Elaine had originated in the 1950s, when both of them had visited him at Edgewater, his circa 1825 mansion on the Hudson River in New York State.

In Elaine's own memoir, she wrote: "Once, and once only, Gore and I went to bed together. Next, let us say that we chose to bathe in the pure, refreshing streams of friendship rather than shoot the perilous rapids of physical love. Which is not to say I wasn't in love with Gore, because I was. If platonic love is not based on passionate feelings, how can it sublimate itself and ascend to the heights?"

Gore had already seduced her husband on numerous occasions. Tynan had always fascinated Gore with his command of the English language and his devastating critiques. In London by the 1960s, he'd become a poster boy of the radical chic, derisively defined as a "champion of champagne socialism."

Gore was even fascinated by the way Kenneth smoked his cigarettes.

"Bette Davis he was not. Kenneth gingerly held a 'fag' *[English slang for a cigarette]* between his ring and little fingers. Alec Guinness caricatured him brilliantly in his 1951 British comedy, *The Lavender Hill Mob.*"

Politically, Gore and Kenneth were aligned. Their sexual tastes, however, were dissimilar. Kenneth's leaned aggressively toward sadomasochism. "I get my greatest satisfaction by caning a young bird or boy on their bare bums. I also like to hurt and humiliate women."

In a late night program for the BBC, he became the first Brit to use the word "fuck" on air. The immediate response was outrage, which fumed its way all the way to the House of Commons, where Kenneth was censored. In the aftermath of that reprimand, he wrote a letter to Queen Elizabeth, suggesting that a fit punishment for a reprimand would be for her "to spank my bottom."

Her Majesty did not respond.

Gore was also fascinated by Kenneth's close friend, Marlene Dietrich. Accompanied by Kenneth, he once attended one of Dietrich's concerts. Later, he read Kenneth's critique of a performance that had included her rendition of "Where Have All the Flowers Gone?":

"On stage, Dietrich stands as if astonished to be there, like a statue unveiled every night to its own inexhaustible amazement. She shows herself to the audience. She knows where all the flowers went—buried in the mud of Passchendaele, blasted to ash at Hiroshima, and napalmed to a crisp in Vietnam—and she carried the knowledge in her voice."

Gore was invited to a party in London hosted by Kenneth and attended by Marlon, who was filming *The Countess from Hong Kong [released in 1967]* at the time. In that movie, Marlon co-starred with Sophia Loren under the direction of Charlie Chaplin, a man Marlon came to detest.

Among the distinguished guests at the party were Richard Harris, who was drunk, and director Michelangelo Antonioni. Harris and Marlon were not speaking to each other, based on a feud that began during their joint filming of *Mutiny on the Bounty* (1962).

"I idolized Marlon until we made that movie together," Harris claimed. "Then it was Shitsville. The man is crazy and some days he didn't even bother to show up, keeping cast and crew waiting as millions were wasted."

In one scene, Marlon, cast as Fletcher Christian, was supposed to strike Harris.

As Harris' biographer, Robert Sellers, wrote: "Brando was absorbed with the Method and mumbling away, so his blow, when it finally came, was the dampest of squibs. Harris responded with a mock curtsy and waggled a limp wrist in the air. Brando didn't get the joke. Take two, and again, the blow was almost non-existent. Everybody wanted to see how Harris would react. They weren't disappointed. Thrusting his chin forward, he propositioned, 'Come on, big boy, why don't you fucking kiss me and be done with it?' Brando glared back, white with rage. Harris then kissed Brando and hugged him, 'Shall we dance?' Angry and embarrassed, Brando stormed off and afterwards, the two men each refused to appear on the set together."

The hellraiser at Kenneth's party was clearly Harris. He had the habit of wet-lipping everybody, man or woman—that is, everybody except Marlon, whom he pointedly ignored.

In front of this party's highly permissive roster of guests, in lieu of a kiss from Harris, Marlon dared his host, Kenneth, to escort him into the bathroom "for a full-on-the-mouth kiss as proof of our friendship." Kenneth accepted the dare, and Gore noticed that they remained, secluded alone and in the loo together, for fifteen minutes or more.

That provided Gore with the opportunity to move in on Harris. "I suspected he was far too intoxicated to take note of which sex I belonged to," Gore later told Kenneth.

Gore openly propositioned Harris, who politely rejected his offer. "I'm such a horny bastard I might have gone off with you if it were a normal night. But tonight, I promised to fuck Soraya."

[He was referring to Soraya Esfandiary Pahlavi, an actress and the second wife of Iran's Shah Mohammed Reza Pahlavi. She had been Harris' co-star in the film, Three Faces of a Woman *(1964).]*

"I need a woman to haunt me, to tear my insides out," Harris confessed to Gore. "As for a love affair, if it doesn't end tragically, I will be horribly disappointed. My ideal woman is a beautiful, mute nymphomaniac who runs the local boozer."

After Kenneth emerged with Marlon from the loo, he told amusing stories about himself to his guests. Later, during an evaluation of his host, Gore said, "As a raconteur, I found Kenneth more amusing than Noël Coward, whose stories were too clean for me."

Then Kenneth launched into a discussion about the "glories of masturbation," claiming that once, at Oxford, he'd delivered a speech that both promoted masturbation and called for a repeal of British laws associated with homosexuality and abortion. Gore agreed with the critic's opinions.

Then Harris chimed in, "When I was a teenager, I masturbated every night to this photo of Merle Oberon. After I fucked the real thing in Hollywood, I decided I preferred masturbating to her picture instead of actually mounting her."

"People don't know what to make of me now," Kenneth said. "But when I was a young man, I created a sensation wherever I went. In Oxford, someone once described me as 'a tall, beautiful, epicene youth with pale yellow locks, Beardsley cheekbones, a fashionable stammer, plum-colored suit, lavender tie, and a ruby signet ring.'"

"When I was called up for National Service, I was outrageously camp. I showed up in a floppy hat, a red velvet coat that Oscar Wilde might have worn, scarlet painted fingernails, bright red lipstick, lots of green eyeshadow, and enough Yardley scent to sink the Bismarck. I was rejected as 'medically unfit.'"

As the night wore on, Gore was also fascinated by the Italian director, Michelangelo Antonioni, who produced enigmatic mood pieces in the form of such films as *L'Avventura* (1960); *La Notte* (1961); and *Eclipse* (1962). He defined these works as his "trilogy on modernity and its disconnects."

Gore and the director agreed that they both loathed the word "morality." Antonioni claimed that "stereotyped morality is sustained by people out of cowardice and sheer laziness."

Harris was one of the first to leave the party for his date with the "discarded Empress of Persia," as he called Soraya.

He stopped off to give Gore a lip-lock. "I'm sorry I couldn't grant your request tonight," he said. Then he took Gore's hand, placed it on his crotch, and said with enigmatic black humor, "Perhaps as a future date. But you've got to promise not to fall in love with me, and drink weed killer."

Before the end of the evening, Gore would find himself included on the long list of Marlon's alleged lovers. In his memoirs, written by Gore when Marlon was still alive, he tried to lay those rumors to rest. For public consumption, Gore denied having had sex with Marlon. Privately, however, to Kenneth and others, he admitted, "We did the dirty deed."

Once, when asked by a reporter about Marlon's sexuality, Gore was dismissive. "Anyone with a great deal of sexual energy and animal charm is going to try anything."

Kenneth would later tell friends that Gore and Marlon spent the night together in a double bed in his guest room.

Gore told Tennessee, Kenneth, and Howard Austen that "I didn't actually have an affair with Marlon. We went to bed and we had sex, but that was hardly an affair. Actually, it was nothing memorable. Neither of us wanted to repeat the act or advertise the fact of our mutual conquests. Marlon and I disagreed on too many subjects to want to maintain a longtime relationship. Besides, both of us had too great an ego."

Over breakfast, after Marlon left Kenneth's apartment for an early appearance at the film studio, Gore told Kenneth, "One of my real reasons for wanting to sleep with Marlon was a one-upmanship I play with Tennessee and that creature who calls himself Truman Capote. I knew both of them had already had sex with Marlon—especially Tennessee."

"Frankly, Marlon is not Stanley Kowalski," Gore said. "Not at all. He was only acting the part, rather convincingly, I might add. Kowalski was a straight, macho, fucker. Marlon is far too kinky for that."

"He did tell me that you're the best butt paddler in London," Gore said to Kenneth, "where the competition is keen for that title. In fact, as a nation, Britain has made butt paddling a fine art."

Chapter Thirty-Three

The Queering of Ben-Hur

How Gore Camouflaged The Homoeroticism of Ancient Rome

In one of the most controversial scenes in *Ben-Hur*, **Stephen Boyd** *(left)* and **Charlton Heston** *(to the right of Boyd, and also in the right-hand photo)* share a communal bond in memory of their boyhood, when they were inseparable friends.

"Chuck is trying to look macho throughout our bonding," Boyd later said, "but I was playing Messala like Gore Vidal intended. We had been boyhood lovers, according to Gore, and I'm looking at Chuck with lust in my eyes. Any fool can see that. But Chuck missed the point of the scene."

In 1958, while Gore was still working as a

scriptwriter at the financially troubled Metro-Goldwyn-Mayer, producer Sam Zimbalist called him in for his new assignment. With the studio on the verge of bankruptcy, the brass at MGM decided that it needed a blockbuster to lure potential movie-goers away from their TV screens and back into the movie houses.

"The studio was in such bad shape that its executives were like dinosaurs facing a dramatic change in the weather," Gore said.

Gore had a lot of respect for Zimbalist, based on having worked with him before. Zimbalist had begun his career at MGM at the age of sixteen as a film cutter, and had moved on to direct *King Solomon's Mines* (1950) and *Quo Vadis* (1951), both of which had received Oscar nominations as Best Picture.

Producer Sam Spiegel had told Zimbalist, "Vidal is not half as good as he thinks he is, but he's twice as good as the others."

As Gore walked into Zimbalist's office that day, he remembered him "as a tall man with a wen *[a protruding cyst]* on the side of his neck. He was smoking a cigar from Havana before the importation of Cuban cigars became illegal. An assistant came in with a large mug of coffee only half filled. Sam took a cup of heavy cream and poured all of it into his coffee."

In its 1925 silent version, *Ben-Hur*, with its S&M implications, was the role of a lifetime for gay actor **Ramon Novarro** *(right)*, and the cinematic comeback for horse-hung **Francis X. Bushman** *(left)*.

Here, they glare at each other—or is it foreplay?

Zimbalist got right to the point. "MGM has decided to remake *Ben-Hur*. We want you to come up with a new script."

"My heart sank," Gore recalled. "One year before, I had turned down the job of writing a new script for *Ben-Hur,* and I was placed on temporary suspension."

Ben-Hur had originally been announced as an MGM candidate for a remake in December of 1952, starring Robert Taylor and Stewart Granger, but plans for it had been shelved.

"MGM wants you to go to a screening with me this afternoon to see the silent screen version with Ramon Novarro, the fag actor, and Francis X. Bushman," Zimbalist said.

Needing the money, Gore agreed to work on the script. But he wanted to make a deal. He would accompany the film crew, which included the film's director, William Wyler, to Rome for an agreed-upon period of three months, after which he wanted to be released to pursue other interests. Those included trying to find a producer to bring his play, *Fire to the Sea,* to Broadway.

That endeavor ended in failure when a medley of producers told him, "No one wants to see a play about the (United States') Civil War."

"If I recall," Gore shot back, "that's what many money people told David O. Selznick when he went to them with *Gone With the Wind.*"

Gore also wanted to write a novel entitled *Julian*, about a 4th Century, C.E.,

Gore is Summoned to Save MGM from Bankruptcy

468

Roman emperor.

After sitting through a screening of the 1925 silent version of *Ben-Hur.* Gore told Zimbalist, "It holds up pretty well. That chariot race between Ben-Hur and Messala was amazing—as dramatic as ever."

Over dinner that night, Gore was introduced to William Wyler, who had reluctantly signed to direct *Ben-Hur,* with the understanding that it would be shot in Rome. Ironically, Wyler had been a production assistant on the first version of *Ben-Hur* some thirty-five years before.

When Wyler met Gore, he told him, "Be assured that it takes a Jew like me to make a good film about Jesus Christ."

Wyler was a formidable choice as director, having previously helmed such pictures as *Mrs. Miniver* (1942) and *The Best Years of Our Lives* (1946), both of which had won Oscars for Best Director.

Invariably, their dialogue turned to casting *Ben-Hur.* "We're considering asking your buddy, Paul Newman, to play Ben-Hur. He and Liz Taylor are already shooting *Cat on a Hot Tin Roof* on the lot, as you know," Wyler said.

"Paul won't do it," Gore predicted. "But I'll call him and make sure. After starring in *The Silver Chalice* (1954), he assured me he'll never appear again onscreen in a cocktail dress showing off his skinny legs."

Gore was right. When he telephoned Newman later that night, he rejected the role, even though it was one of the most sought-after star roles in Hollywood that year.

Within two days, a contract—revised to Gore's specifications—was delivered to Gore's office. It had been rewritten to expire after his completion of his agreed-upon three months of work on script issues associated with *Ben-Hur.*

"The messenger boy was a real good-looking kid," Gore said. "He was hot, and smart as paint as they say. I felt he could be had. I made several suggestive remarks to him. I felt he was picking up on my vibes but pretending to be naïve. He didn't fool me. This mother fucker looked like he'd been having sex ever since his tenth birthday."

"Why don't you tell me your name in case I need your services again?" Gore asked.

"I'm Jack Nicholson," the boy responded. "I want to be an actor."

"That's an original idea around here," Gore said. He later recalled, "As the future bigtime star left my office, I checked out his ass. I decided it was a great ass, but that he was a fucker, not the fuckee."

Three days later, at a luncheon in the MGM commissary, Gore was invited to have a meal with Wyler and Zimbalist as a means of bringing him up-to-date on their casting ideas for the film. Because shooting was scheduled to begin within a few weeks, there was an urgency to sign up actors, especially since Newman had turned the role down.

"We offered the role to Rock Hudson," Wyler said. "He's a fag, but disguises it. He's got the physique. When we called his people over at Universal, they told us they already have their prize stud booked up. He's just not available."

"I called Marlon Brando," Zimbalist chimed in. "He told me he hated himself on the screen in that 1953 version of *Julius Caesar,* and he's not anxious to return to Rome for another of those 'sword and sandals' epics."

"I thought Burt Lancaster would be ideal," Wyler said "After I called him, he said he'd love to play Ben-Hur, but he had already committed himself to another film next week."

With a sense of wry amusement, Gore noted that each of the actors mentioned during that casting pow-wow was either homosexual or bisexual.

"Guess who we finally came up with?" Zimbalist said. "Charlton Heston. He's agreed to do it."

Gore reacted skeptically. "He has the charm of a wooden Indian."

Casting the key role of Messala, the Roman officer, was also convoluted. The idea choice was Victor Mature, who had scored a big hit in the 1949 release of *Samson and Delilah* for Cecil B. DeMille. But he was not available. Neither was Steve Cochran, the second choice. Finally, the handsome Irish actor, Stephen Boyd, agreed to play Messala. Again, to Gore's private amusement, he knew that Mature and Cochran were bisexuals and Boyd a homosexual.

"Don't Let Heston Know He's Playing a Gay Ben-Hur"

In 1958, aboard a plane with Wyler and Zimbalist, Gore flew to Rome, a city he hadn't visited in a decade. It was still suffering economic devastation in the wake of World War II.

For his first day on the job, Gore arrived by taxi at the 150-acre Cinecittà Studios with its nine sound stages. MGM had rented the entire compound, and Gore heard the sound of hammers from the construction crews. Ancient Rome and First Century Jerusalem were being re-created on the back lot, centering around a sprawling rendition of a Roman hippodrome, a historically accurate replica of the ancient world's venue for chariot races.

For this, the film's 1959 version, its frantically scripted plot would revolve around the feud between figures interpreted by Boyd and Heston, instead of the 1925 version's feud between characters played by Ramon Novarro and Francis X. Bushman.

The film was budgeted at $15 million, modest by today's standards, but in the late 1950s, the most expensive ever allocated for a film.

Gore made it a point that day to introduce himself to the Italian director, Federico Fellini, who was also working at Cinecettà, on pre-production for his next film, *La Dolce Vita.*

Gore invited Fellini for a tour of the mammoth sets of *Ben-Hur.* As a scholar of ancient history, Gore instantly noted problems on the developing sets. In a facsimile of the kitchen of Ben-Hur's mother, the set designer had placed a basketful of tomatoes. Gore told him that the tomato did not exist in the land of

Ben-Hur at that time. He also criticized the re-creation of ancient Jerusalem with domes, pointing out that this form of architecture would not exist in Jerusalem for another five centuries, with the arrival of the Muslims.

Back in his office, on his desk, Gore found a badly organized script the size of a New York City telephone directory. "If that script had been shot, it would take up twenty hours of screen time. What I held in my hand was a silent movie, with miles and miles of dialogue, some of it written in a sort of poetic style, much of it stilted and too formal for the screen. Where was Cecil B. DeMille now that we needed him?"

Throughout most of the 1950s, MGM had hired a dozen screen writers to try to re-create *Ben-Hur* as a talking picture. The script Gore was given represented the combined efforts of two popular writers, Maxwell Anderson and S.N. Behrman.

"This photograph shows that he has no intention of ever joining a monastery."

Ramon Novarro in a publicity still for MGM's 1925 film, *Ben-Hur*. Even his pubic hair is showing.

Gore had not seen either of Behrman's two most frequently produced plays, *Biography* (1932), and *End of Summer* (1936). He'd read *Biography,* which lamented a political landscape divided between left- and right-wing extremists, leaving little space for a tolerant and humane middle ground.

Gore had seen both of Anderson's "Tudor plays," but only when they reached the screen—*Mary of Scotland* (1936) with Katharine Hepburn; and *The Private Lives of Elizabeth and Essex* (1939), starring Bette Davis and Errol Flynn.

Gore immediately discovered a loop in the plot: Ben-Hur and Messala had been intimate boyhood friends. Years later, they meet as strong-willed, testosterone-permeated adults, whose personalities and politics differ widely, even dangerously.

Initially, as adults, Heston is a land-owning, fervently patriotic Zionist Jew; Messala an aristocratic Roman officer and a ruthless and foreign conqueror. Although their reunion is affectionate, they soon after quarrel bitterly over sovereignty and politics. A mutual

In contrast to Novarro, **Charlton Heston**, in the 1959 remake of *Ben-Hur*, decided that the silent screen star looked "too faggy," so he butched it up.

loathing follows, and a rivalry that leads to Messala's death during that infamous and heart-racing chariot race.

Gore protested to both Wyler and Zimbalist that there "is no motivation for all this fury." Consequently, he came up with a strong motivation.

He suggested that Ben-Hur and Messala had been boyhood lovers. Meeting again as adults, the more decadent and more permissive of the two, Messala, was still in love with Ben-Hur and wants to resume their sexual relationship.

Ben-Hur, however, as a virtuous, Old Testament-thumping Zionist, righteously rebuffs Messala's advances. As for Messala, hell hath no fury like a horny Roman soldier rejected in love—and from a Jew, no less.

At first, Wyler and Zimbalist were aghast at this plot enhancement, since at that time the word homosexuality could not even be mentioned on the screen.

Charlton Heston *(left)*, when he saw the rushes for Ben-Hur, said, "I practically did a male burlesque show. But I launched my career as a nude model, so I was accustomed to revealing a lot."

In his recollections, Gore said, "Without being aware of it at first, I was recycling the plot from my *The City and the Pillar* novel. Fortunately, neither Sam nor Willy had read it. For a while, they sat in stony silence, looking at me like I was some crazed pervert."

Finally, Wyler said, "How do you propose going about depicting this...what shall I call it? A gay romp between Ben-Hur and Messala? Keep in mind, this is *Ben-Hur, a Tale of Christ*. Not 'Boy's Night Out at the Baths.'"

Gore assured the producer and director that the romantic love between Messala and Ben-Hur would be depicted indirectly, almost subliminally—nothing overt.

"I won't even mention it in a single line of dialogue," Gore promised. "The actors can use their eyes to suggest it. The average movie-goer will not get it, but gay men will. When Ben-Hur rejects Messala's overtures—which are only suggested—and refuses to support the Roman occupation of Israel and Judea, Messala's face can reflect not only a rejection of his political beliefs, but thwarted love as well."

"If it's played correctly, the love that will not dare screech its name can be subtly indicated," Gore said. "We can show the proud, arrogant Messala abasing himself before his former love, a lowly Jew boy."

Wyler rose to his feet. "God damn it, we'll try it. At this point, I'll try any scene short of actual cocksucking. We're desperate to get some strong motivation going here!"

Wyler, Zimbalist, and Gore decided to bring the sexually sophisticated Boyd, a homosexual himself, into the loop. Wyler insisted, however, that he preferred to direct Heston's scenes as Ben-Hur without "the Big Cornpone *[his nickname for Heston]* ever realizing what in the fuck was going on. Under no circumstances is Heston to know that the scenes he'll be acting have a homoerotic undercurrent, subliminal or not."

Zimbalist wondered if Wyler and Gore could pull this off. "Surely the Big Cornpone isn't that dumb."

But apparently, he was. In his memoirs, Gore noted that "Heston was imitating Francis X. Bushman's style and mannerisms as they'd appeared in the film's 1925 silent screen version, tossing his head, chin held high, oblivious to what was going on from the other actors nearby. Boyd at one point winked at me. He was in character."

Wyler thought their game was up, when Heston gained access to the rushes. "But even during his face-to-face encounters with a lovesick Boyd, Heston didn't get it that they were playing a gay love scene."

Based on what he said during an interview years later, in 1977, Heston appeared to have finally understood the subliminal messages a bit more clearly, appearing better informed by the gay undercurrent in *Ben-Hur*. "The story behind *Ben-Hur* isn't really about Christ," Heston said. "It's certainly not a story about Ben-Hur and Esther, either. It's a love story between Ben-Hur and Messala, and the destruction of that love and the world they had known."

"In the wake of that destruction," Heston continued, "there remained only hatred and revenge—it's a vendetta story."

Gore & Stephen Boyd—A Romance that Survived Only Until the Filming of Ben-Hur Was Finished

Although Gore was introduced to each of the film's supporting players, his eyes and attention were focused on the very handsome Stephen Boyd. The two men bonded. After his second night in Rome, Boyd moved into Gore's hotel suite.

One of the actresses in *Ben-Hur*, Missouri-born Martha Scott, had dinner at a *trattoria* in Trastevere with Gore and Boyd. "If they weren't in love, they were definitely lovers," she later told Wyler. "It was very obvious, based on the looks they exchanged between them, and the many personal jokes and innuendos they shared."

Gore and Boyd also dined with the English actor, Jack Hawkins, who had been assigned one of the film's lead roles. Gore remembered that he smoked three packages of cigarettes a day, which later led to cobalt treatments and his eventual death from throat cancer. He, too, agreed that Boyd and Gore were lovers.

Years later in a pub in Dublin, near the end of Boyd's short life, he told one of the authors of this book, "Gore and I were mature. We both knew that our affair would last just for the duration of the picture. When *Ben-Hur* was over, so were we."

Before the end of his three-month contract, from Rome, Gore wrote to Paul Bowles in Tangier, "I am doing a fast rewrite of this mammoth epic called *Ben-Hur*. I started at the beginning, while my co-author, Chistopher Fry, a nice little man who looks like the way Shakespeare must have looked, started at the end and works toward me. It is predicted that, as writers, we shall meet at the char-

473

iot race."

The writing credits for the movie are still protested today. Gore maintained that he wrote half the script, but the Screen Writers Guild did not agree. Nor did they credit Fry. In a final judgment, they ruled that Karl Tunberg crafted most of the script.

"Sam would have protected my interests," Gore later said. "But he died of a stroke before the picture's release."

MGM's gamble with *Ben-Hur* paid off. It was a box office bonanza, playing to capacity audiences around the world. It was nominated for a dozen Oscars, taking home eleven of them, including Best Picture, Best Director (William Wyler), Best Actor (Charlton Heston), and Best Actor in a Supporting Role (Hugh Griffith).

"Heston hated me by the end of the picture," Gore said. "At his acceptance speech before the Academy, he thanked Fry as the writer and left out any mention of Tunberg or me."

[Throughout most of his life, Heston managed to convey a squeaky clean image, even though he began his career as a nude model.]

***

In 2008, in the aftermath of Heston's death, details about his private life faced exposure in the tabloids. He was "Outed" as a bisexual, his early affair with a very young Sal Mineo exposed.

During his lifetime, he came under heavy "fire" as president of the NRA (National Rifle Organization). Barbara Stanwyck mocked his performance as Moses in *The Ten Commandments* (1956). "Chuck has a bad memory. He still thinks he's parting the Red Sea."

In Mark Windurn's Web blog, a site known for some of history's most notorious recitations of Hollywood gossip, this short defining entry about the actor was worded like this:

"CHARLTON HESTON— Right-wing gun kook. Reportedly likes young girls—and, if rumors are to be believed, young boys, too. Abuser of women, Alcoholic."

When Gore read that, he said, "I couldn't agree more."

At an NRA convention, it was clear that **Charlton Heston** was already showing symptoms of dementia.

Chapter Thirty-Four

Breakfast at Tiffany's

The Saga of a Hillbilly Child Bride from Texas Who Runs Away and Becomes a Hooker

But Will It Be Filmed With Marilyn or With Audrey Hepburn?

Photos above: **Marlene Dietrich** *(left)*; **Marilyn Monroe** dancing with **Truman Capote** at El Morocco *(center)*; and **Marilyn** *(right)* impersonating….well, Marilyn Monroe."

SHOW-BIZ AMBITIONS AND CASTING DREAMS GONE AWRY

Truman's best friend, Cecil Beaton, turned him on to Marilyn after he photographed her. He told Truman, "She's a hidden bisexual, narcissistic, unkempt with hygiene problems, a hypnotized nymphomaniac, as spectacular as the silvery shower of a Vesuvius fountain, an undulating basilisk. Her performance is pure charade, a little girl's caricature of Mae West. She is quintessentially America, conjuring up two straws in a single soda, juke boxes, running nylons, and drive-in movies for necking. She is a composite of Alice in Wonderland, Trilby, and a Minsky burlesque artist."

"I'm fascinated," Truman exclaimed.

Soonafter, Truman announced his intention of rewriting *The Blue Angel* (the movie that had made Marlene Dietrich famous) as a vehicle for Marilyn. But Dietrich had other plans, and became a saboteur.

Truman Capote liked to ingratiate himself

with iconic women, including the likes of Jacqueline Kennedy and Elizabeth Taylor. In the 1950s, Marilyn Monroe was the hottest property in Hollywood, and he wanted to become more intimately involved with her.

He'd heard that 20th Century Fox was considering remaking Marlene Dietrich's *The Blue Angel (Der Blaue Engel;* released in 1930*),* which had made the German actress an international star. Truman informed Fox that he'd like to write the screenplay. On that pretense, he called Marilyn in New York and invited her out to dinner.

Dietrich had a lot of spies, and someone tipped her off that Truman was negotiating with Fox to rewrite *The Blue Angel* as a screen vehicle for Marilyn. Dietrich was horrified, perhaps fearing that Marilyn might interpret the role of Lola Lola better than she had in the late 1920s.

As Dietrich told her friend, critic Leo Lerman, "I decided to sabotage the project before Miss Monroe and Miss Capote got their hands on a property that belonged to me and my legend."

Shortly before Marilyn was scheduled for her dinner with Truman, Dietrich sought her out, knowing that whatever happened between them would be directly transmitted to the gossipy author.

On January 5, 1955, Marilyn announced she had organized a press conference to launch her newly formed Marilyn Monroe Productions, with herself as president. At the time, "Marilyn's Svengali," photographer Milton Greene, was micro-managing her career. He was luring her into classic film properties, perhaps Dostoevsky's *The Brothers Karamazov,* where she'd be cast as Grushenka.

Greene was also a friend of Dietrich's, and consequently, it was he who arranged a meeting between the *femme fatale* of the 30s and early 40s with the *femme fatale* of the 1950s. "The world's most glamorous grandmother" allowed herself to be caught on camera standing next to the protruding breasts of the more youthful

Marlene Dietrich in *The Blue Angel*, the controversially *risqué* film that made her an international star after its release in 1930.

She's pictured here with **Emil Jannings** (an actor who was more famous at the time than she was) as a stuffy professor who is charmed by her cabaret savvy and sensous charms.

Truman and Marilyn Flirt With "The Blue Angel"

and more immediately desirable Marilyn.

At the last minute, Truman slipped into the press conference, claiming that he was covering the event for *The New York Times,* which he was not. Surrounded by reporters, he remained inconspicuously in the back of the room as a means of not being spotted by either Dietrich or Marilyn.

La Dietrich and Truman had never been friends, but they'd become involved in each others' lives during the Broadway run of *House of Flowers,* when Dietrich was having an affair with the star of his musical, Pearl Bailey.

Dietrich had already informed Greene, "I'd like to take a bite out of Marilyn."

Dietrich, of course, was part of an expanding group of Hollywood lesbians and bisexuals widely identified by insiders as members of "the Sewing Circle." They included Greta Garbo and her close friend Salka Viertel, Barbara Stanwyck, Janet Gaynor, Mary Martin, Kay Francis, Jean Arthur, Agnes Moorehead, and Katharine Hepburn. Author John Baxter once "outed" these women in an article that included a surprising name among the group's members: the silent screen vamp Gloria Swanson, a very closeted bisexual.

At the time, Truman was clearly aware of Marilyn's own bisexuality, although such a revelation would have deeply shocked movie-goers during the repressed 1950s. Since then, however, dozens of Marilyn biographies have described her bisexual impulses and involvement, including a sexual tryst with Hollywood's most notorious bisexual, Joan Crawford.

Marilyn, with photographer Milton Greene, dreaming dreams not meant to be.

Marilyn had told Truman that she had long been fascinated with Dietrich's lore, legend, and image. She'd been particularly impressed with photographer Eve Arnold's photographs of Dietrich that had run in *Esquire.*

The Berliner had been positioned against a bare soundstage, without her usual outrageous frills and with very little makeup. Based on that example, Marilyn convinced Arnold to photograph her in the same way she'd shot Dietrich.

Consequently, in the autumn of 1955, Arnold photographed Marilyn in ways markedly different from those which had previously catered to her image as a "dumb blonde." One photograph showed her simply dressed, in a park reading James Joyce's fa-

Milton Greene *(right)* promised to photograph Marilyn in a style that would evoke Garbo. He introduced her to **Marlene** (center) instead.

mously opaque novel, *Ulysses,* even though she didn't understand it. One of Arnold's photos depicted Marilyn as Eve "at the dawn of time," slithering through tall marsh grass.

Marilyn immediately rushed prints of Arnold's photos to Truman, as she trusted his "bitchy judgment." He told her, "It's about time you showed the world there's more to you than that Lorelei Lee character you portrayed in *Gentlemen Prefer Blondes.*

[In 1958, Richard Avedon would photograph Marilyn impersonating the great sirens of Hollywood, including Clara Bow, Theda Bara, Lillian Russell, and Marilyn's favorite, Marlene Dietrich.]

After Marilyn's press conference, Dietrich invited her back to her apartment. When they were alone, Dietrich got immediately to the point:

"I hear the stupid swine boys at Fox are preparing to film *The Blue Angel* again, the movie that made me a star. I must talk to you about this."

Marilyn seemed somewhat embarrassed that Dietrich was aware of Fox's vision for a modern adaptation of *The Blue Angel.* Originally released 1930, Dietrich's iconic version had been directed by von Sternberg and starred Emil Jannings, who was an immensely popular star in Germany at the time. Dietrich had famously interpreted the role of Lola Lola, a petty bourgeois Berlin tart with dazzling legs and a come-hither manner. One German critic wrote that she played the role with a "callous egotism and cool insolence."

Although nervous about being alone with Dietrich—she'd heard tales— Marilyn was eager to be in the company of one of her early role models. She'd already seen most of her American movies from the 1930s.

In a memoir, *My Story,* published more than a decade after Marilyn's death, Marilyn is alleged to have written: "I was young, blonde, and curvaceous, and I had learned to talk huskily like Marlene Dietrich and to walk a little wantonly and to bring emotion into my eyes when I wanted to. And though these achievements landed me no job, they brought a lot of wolves whistling at my heels."

Marilyn's evening with Dietrich would later be penned as the first entry she would make in the leather-bound diary Greene had given her as a Christmas present. En route with Dietrich to her apartment, they discussed not *The Blue Angel,* but author Truman Capote.

"Milton told me you're having dinner with Capote tomorrow night," Dietrich said to Marilyn. "Keep your guard up. He pretends to be your friend, and then spreads the most vicious gossip about you. His latest claim was that when he was visiting me, he witnessed Eleanor Roosevelt emerging nude from my bedroom. He claimed that Eleanor had long had a crush on me. That may be true, of course, and, if so, I don't blame her. *BUT CAPOTE, OF COURSE, DID*

Philanthropist, visionary, and liberal spokeswoman for many causes benefitting humanity, the then-maligned, now-revered former First Lady, **Eleanor Roosevelt.**

Truman claimed that Marlene Dietrich had an affair with her.

478

NOT SEE ELEANOR EMERGE NAKED FROM MY BEDROOM!"

Later, inside Dietrich's apartment, as the women sat drinking champagne on a champagne-colored sofa, Marilyn decided to bring up *The Blue Angel*: "I want you to know I'm thrilled at the idea of playing Lola Lola. Of course, I could never create the performance that you did."

"Of course not, darling, and I understand that," Dietrich said. "Zanuck is out of his mind to think of redoing *The Blue Angel*. Every actress in Germany wanted to play Lola Lola, even Leni Riefenstahl, Hitler's filmmaker and mistress. The search for an actress to play Lola Lola was not equaled until David O. Selznick began his search for Scarlett O'Hara."

"Do you have any advice on how I should play the part?" Marilyn asked, appearing more innocent than she was, as she later confessed to her diary.

"Von Sternberg said the part called for an actress to represent a new incarnation of sex. At first, he didn't want me. He said my bottom was all right, but that Lola Lola must have a face."

"What an odd thing to say," Marilyn said. "You have one of the most fabulous faces ever seen on the silver screen."

"That's true," Dietrich agreed, "but Josef and I had to invent that face the way you invented your Marilyn Monroe character. Lola Lola must be an irresistible presence, singing on a barrel and showing off her *derrière*. She must have electricity and charm, her songs crackling with sex. She must be corrupt, decadent—actually vile—and evil."

"I don't know if I could be all that," Marilyn said. "That's a pretty tall order."

"I understand," Dietrich said. "Even when you're playing a slut on screen, you project a virginal innocence. The actress Lola Lola, in contrast, must be an alley cat screaming for a tomcat, especially in that song, 'Tonight, Kids, I'm Gonna Get a Man.' Lola is jaded, lustful, naked in her emotions. A harlot who can destroy a man, especially the professor in the film. It calls for a voice singing out, late at night, in a crude German *Bierstube*, cutting through the smoke of a cabaret catering to perverts."

Dietrich continued with her daunting pronouncements, as Marilyn's insecurities reached a feverish pitch. "Critics have written that the screen character of Lola Lola must never be repeated, that I have immortalized it. If any actress dares, she will be weak lemonade on the screen. It could destroy an actress's career. Audiences might get up and walk out on the wrong Lola Lola. Whereas your sensuality is wholesome and real, Lola Lola is an artificial creation of the night. She is the wrong image for you. Edith Piaf would understand that. So would Greta Garbo. When men flock to see one of your movies, they want to see the Marilyn Monroe they love—not some prostitute in a Berlin cabaret. Men want someone who will make love to their prick—not castrate them."

Marilyn burst into tears, as Dietrich moved closer to her, taking her in her arms and comforting her. "I can't play Lola Lola," Marilyn sobbed. "It's not for me."

"A wise decision, my dear. You need to go on to greater parts, like you said in your news conference, not be a low-rent German trollop, a devouring female predator."

Over a harmoniously flavored *coq au vin*, Dietrich intoned, "Your attempt to play Lola Lola would be as foolhardy as an attempt to star as Scarlett in a remake of *Gone With the Wind*. You'd be laughed off the screen: Don't do it! You are an all-American girl, not Lola Lola. European characters, especially those who worked the cabarets of 1920s Berlin, are not for you. Don't allow yourself to be ridiculed and mocked."

Marilyn later recalled that she fell asleep in Dietrich's arms and in her bed, as the chanteuse sang softly in her ear.

Ich bin die fesche Lola,
Der Liebling der Saison.

***

The next evening, at a dinner with Truman, Marilyn thrilled him by reporting all the details of her night with Marlene. "Lesbian sex with me is only an occasional thing," Marilyn confided to Truman, who spread the word privately along his grapevine: "Marlene is very oral and very skilled. She did her own thing down there, but I didn't reciprocate."

"It was worth staying over for the career advice and to taste her scrambled eggs the next morning, for which she is so famous. She's a good cook and would have made a wonderful wife for Josef Goebbels. Isn't he the one who liked her movies so much?"

"In the late 30s, Goebbels, then in charge of propaganda films at UFA, beseeched her to leave America and to return to movie making in Berlin, but Marlene refused," Truman said. "Hitler was a fan of Marlene's and considered her the epitome of a German wife. But she wasn't *Der Führer's* favorite blonde goddess."

"And who might that have been?" Marilyn asked.

"It was Alice Faye," Truman answered. "He had all of Faye's movies smuggled into Germany. It's said that he watched *Alexander's Ragtime Band* (1938) a total of thirty-eight times."

[Eventually, in 1959, Fox followed through on their plans to release a reincarnated film version of The Blue Angel. *But instead of Marilyn Monroe, it starred May Britt in the Dietrich role, with Curt Jürgens as the lovesick professor. Directed by Edward Dmytryk, it was a commercial disaster. Marlene was delighted, claiming, "I told those idiots at Fox not to remake it."*

Truman never wrote one word of the script, and, of course, Marilyn was only discussed abstractly as a potential contender for the character of Lola. Instead, also released in 1959 and directed by Billy Wilder, she made Some Like It Hot, *in which her co-stars, Tony Curtis and Jack Lemmon, played most of their scenes in drag.]*

Marilyn's Sexual Fixation on Abraham Lincoln

"In Hollywood, I'm just another movie star," Marilyn told her mentor and manager, Milton Greene. "But in New York, I'm treated like an exotic creature descended from the planet Venus. Everybody is extending invitations."

"To my party tonight," he told her, "I've invited Truman Capote. He wants to know you better. He said he danced with you one night at El Morocco."

[An iconic photograph was taken of Truman dancing with Marilyn at the famous night club. At five feet eight inches in height, she towered over him, as he was five inches shorter. So as not to accentuate the differences in their height, she had kicked off her high heels and danced with him barefoot.

Capote's close friend, John Malcolm Brinnin, became infuriated when he saw the photo after it appeared in Time *magazine. He disapproved of the increasing frequency and intensity of Truman's involvements with glamorous jet-setters of Broadway and Hollywood. He wrote to Truman with a reprimand: "Was this the portrait of Artist as a Young Man? Joyce's motto was, 'Silence, exile, and cunning.' What's yours?"]*

"Truman is very flamboyant," Marilyn said to Milton Greene. "The press calls him an *enfant terrible*, whatever in the hell that means. When he comes, send him back here *[to a back bedroom of Milton Greene's house, where Marilyn was living at the time]* while I get dressed. I've never read anything he wrote, but he seems like a more interesting character than anything he can create on a page."

"Truman told me he found you fascinating at dinner the other night," Greene said. "He knows more indiscreet gossip than anyone in New York. As an example, he privately tells friends that he knows the dick size of every major star in Hollywood, and what they like to do in bed. He writes it all down in some diary, which may be published one day when the world has grown more sophisticated."

"Who did he tell you had the biggest one in Hollywood?" she asked. "I'd cast my vote for Milton Berle."

"Would you believe John Ireland?" he answered, "at least according to the Truman Capote Bible. Ireland fucked Monty Clift when they made *Red River*, that picture with John Wayne. Joan Crawford also awards Ireland top prize, and she should know. She's fucked every big star except Lassie."

"Thanks for the tip," she said. "I'll have to work Ireland into my schedule."

"I asked Capote to show up early so the two of you can gossip over a pre-party drink. When the party is in full blast, he becomes the center of attention, with a crowd clustered around him as he tells one outrageous story after another. Much of what he says is actually true, but he does embroider things a bit. He says all good Southerners never let truth get in the way of a good story."

"Send in my amusement for the night," she said.

When Truman did arrive for the party, two hours early, Greene directed him to Marilyn's quarters. He knocked on her door. She called for him to come in.

Not finding her in the bedroom, he heard her voice summoning him to the bathroom, where she was taking a bubble bath.

"Hi," he said, "Truman Capote, first in your boudoir and now in your *toilette*." He spoke in a high-pitched voice, and had grown up shunned by other children because of his "sissyish traits." In the way he walked and talked, he was different from most men, with that babylike, slightly artificial voice. She would remember him as a writer "trapped forever in boyhood, as if refusing to mature."

As Truman himself later said, "The way I spoke in the fourth grade is the way I talk now. When I was growing up, everyone told my mother I should have been born a girl. She even took me to psychiatrists hoping to find a drug or therapy that would turn me into a boy. In spite of my odd behavior, I always had to be myself."

And that is what he presented to Marilyn, who seemed mesmerized by him. He immediately established his credentials as a gossip. Gazing at her in the claw-footed tub, he said, "The last time I saw a movie star in a bubble bath, it was Errol Flynn. After I bathed him and dried him off, I discovered what 'in like Flynn' means."

She giggled. "You're my kind of guy, Truman. What a name. It sounds so presidential. Why don't you wash my back for me so we can get better acquainted? I hope you won't get too turned on."

"You can rest assured that I won't," he said, taking off his jacket and moving toward her. "Half the men in America would want to be in my shoes right now, and I'm not even tempted."

As he reached for the soap, he said, "You must tell me everything about Joe DiMaggio. I want all the details. Cock size. Duration in the saddle. Cut or uncut? I suspect uncut. The exact taste of his semen. What does he prefer? Fellatio? Analingus? Around the world? The missionary position?"

"My, you're an inquisitive little demon. But I like you for some perverse reason. Joe's biggest bat is not the one he uses on the field. If that's all it took, we'd still be married."

"Lucky girl!" he said. "How I envy you." He began an expert soaping of her luscious back.

As she emerged from the bath, he helped dry her off. She put on a robe. In her bedroom, he sat on a chair beside her dressing table, sipping a glass of champagne that Greene's cook had delivered. The cook thanked Marilyn.

After the cook left, Truman asked Marilyn, "Why is she thanking you?"

"This afternoon, I peeled potatoes for her and snapped beans for dinner tonight."

One of Marilyn's biographers, Fred Lawrence Guiles, in his book, *Legend*, wrote: "*[Marilyn]* was never very serious with Capote. They spoke a secret language liberally sprinkled with sex and gossip."

Marilyn heard Greene's party guests arriving, but she wanted to extend her private time with Truman. He noticed that she was reading a book about Napoléon Bonaparte and Josephine. "I didn't know you were interested in history," he said.

I'm not, but when I visited Marlon Brando on the set of *Désirée* (1954), where he played Napoléon, I became interested in playing Josephine in a movie focused on her. Perhaps you'll write the script for me."

"Perhaps," he said. "But unlike Josephine, I wouldn't have gone to bed with Napoléon. His cock was too small. I've seen it."

She looked astonished. "How in hell could you have seen Napoléon's cock? I didn't know you were that old."

"Before he was buried, someone cut off the emperor's little penis, and preserved it in alcohol. Today, it's owned by this old queen in Connecticut. He exhibits it on occasion. It looks pretty withered these days. Perhaps it was an inch or two longer in the days of the French Empire."

"That is such a ghoulish story. It's delectable,"

"Speaking of small cocks, can Senator Kennedy satisfy you?"

"We manage," she said. "Don't tell me you've been to bed with him too."

"Not at all," he said. "What I don't understand is why everybody thinks the Kennedys are so sexy. I know a lot about cocks—I've seen an awful lot of them—and if you put all the Kennedys together, you wouldn't have a good one. I used to see Jack when I was staying with Loel and Gloria Guinness in Palm Beach. I had a little guest cottage with its own private beach, and he would come down so he could swim in the nude. He had absolutely nuthin'."

"Unlike you, I haven't seen all the cocks I want to see," she said. "But I'm not on the East Coast to chase after them—at least that's not my first goal. As you know, I want to be a serious actress."

"If you mean that, I've got the right acting coach for you, since you seem to have left Natasha Lytess back in California," he said. "She's a British actress, rather old at this point: Constance Collier."

"I've heard of her," she said.

"Constance is the best acting teacher in New York. If you'd like to meet her, I can take you to a luncheon this week. I've been invited to her apartment. Greta Garbo and Katharine Hepburn will be there."

"Garbo?" she asked in astonishment. "And Hepburn? Are they still taking acting lessons?"

"No, they're admirers. Will you accept?"

"Are you kidding? I'd be honored. But I don't know what to wear."

"A single string of pearls and Chanel's little black dress."

"Can't wait," she said. "But I fear I'll be speechless."

"I wouldn't worry about it," he said. "All three of them are dykes, and each of them will be salivating when you walk into the room. You don't have any skin blemishes, do you?"

"No, but why do you ask?"

"Hepburn won't go to bed with any gal with blemishes on her skin," he said. "But Garbo doesn't mind all that much, considering that she slept with Marie Dressler."

There was a sudden knock on the door, and Milton Greene's voice announcing, "Marilyn, the guests are here, and you're the guest of honor. Shake your ass, girl. Norman Mailer's here. So is Gene Kelly. He's with a real cute trick. I bet if you work it right, you can take the hunk from Gene."

Truman rose to his feet. "I don't care who they are. Kelly always manages to get them first before anyone else in Hollywood, even beating out Joan Crawford."

Marilyn called that she'd be right out after putting on her high heels. "I'm anxious to meet this Adonis," she whispered to Truman, "With Amy hanging on to Milton all the time, I haven't been getting much."

"In that case, after Constance's luncheon, I can arrange a date for you with Porfirio Rubirosa. After all, the two richest women in the world, Doris Duke and Barbara Hutton, spent millions on that eleven-inch octoroon dick. But I can get it for you for free."

"Is that why in a restaurant when some men request a peppermill, they ask for a Rubirosa?"

"You learn quick, gal. Now it's showtime. There are a lot of important people out there tonight. It's time for you to become Marilyn Monroe."

On the way out the door, he took her by the arm. "By the way, I forgot to ask. Why in hell do you have a picture of Abraham Lincoln by your bedside? That's weird."

"I've always had this fantasy about going to bed with Honest Abe," she said. "I know it's crazy, but that's how I feel. Since he's cold and in his grave, I'll settle for someone who reminds me of him. Call it second best, since I can't have the real thing. He's coming to the party tonight, if he's not already here."

"You have stumped me on that one," he said. "Who might this august personage be?"

"My next husband," she said. "Arthur Miller."

"Marilyn, Meet Katharine Hepburn and Greta Garbo"

—Truman Capote

Truman escorted a nervous Marilyn Monroe along West 57th Street, not her favorite part of Manhattan. He'd instructed her to dress, act, and talk like Grace Kelly. He also told her not to be too apprehensive. "Garbo will be intoxicated by your innocence. I mean, your innocent look, and Katie will adore you because you have no skin blemishes."

Arriving at the apartment door of Constance Collier, the "secretary" to the actress and drama coach, Phyllis Wilbourne, showed them in to the dark, dank apartment where the furnishings had been young in 1901.

Although she had scheduled and defined the event as a luncheon date, Collier was attired in a mauve-laced evening gown. Looking like a character from an Oscar Wilde play, Collier sat on a battered sofa upholstered in fading red velvet. She extended a frail hand to Marilyn, as Truman made the introductions.

"My dear," Collier said, "I'm nearly blind, but the luminosity of your face and golden hair illuminates this old room."

"I'm honored to meet you," your Highness," Marilyn said, curtsying.

"Oh, Marilyn, Constance is not the Queen of England," Truman said.

"That is true, Truman," Constance said, "but I should have been. I'm regal enough."

As they settled in and Constance was smoking her second cigarette, Truman explained that Marilyn wanted to take acting lessons from her. "In essence, she wants to reinvent herself as an actress."

"I want to so much," Marilyn said. "All the men, all the glamour, all the jewelry and gowns are not important. After all, I'm not using Elizabeth Taylor as my role model."

Collier complained that she was losing feeling in both her hands and feet. Then she said, "I suppose I could teach you something about acting. At any rate, I need the money to supplement my meager income. My little darling, I could start you out by teaching you how to interpret the role of Ophelia. Once you master that, you can succeed in any part. The one thing I can't teach you is how to play sexy."

"I already know how to do that," Marilyn said.

"I'm sure you do," Collier said.

"You're so elegant," Marilyn said. "I wish I knew how to be elegant."

"Darling, I've had decades to become who I am. Of course, I inherited exotic features."

Then, like all actresses on their last legs, she wanted to relive past glories. "I inherited some of my features from my Portuguese grandmother. Believe it or not, I was considered one of the great beauties of the early 20th century stage."

"Queen Victoria must have adored you," Truman said.

"Truman, you're such a nasty little demon," Collier responded, "but I always

| Constance Collier | Katharine Hepburn | Greta Garbo |

like to have you around to sharpen my sense of bitchery."

She spoke in a fading voice that still retained a husky, contralto quality. "My mother was an actress. She wrapped me in a blanket and left me backstage, nursing me between acts. At the age of three, I toddled out onto the stage, cast as Fairy Peaseblossom in *A Midsummer Night's Dream*."

As Collier wandered down memory lane, Marilyn evaluated the room, its walls covered with decaying, saffron-colored wallpaper highlighted with antique racing horse prints. On the sofa with Collier lay a little black fox terrier, which Collier stroked with one hand, holding a golden cigarette holder in the other hand. Marilyn also spotted the largest brandy inhaler glasses she'd ever seen.

With her weak eyesight, Collier followed Marilyn's gaze, quickly adding, "Those glasses haven't been used in years. I'm diabetic."

A large portrait hung on the wall. Marilyn asked, "Was he your husband?"

"Constance is not the marrying kind," Truman quipped.

"Truman, sometimes you smart-ass bitches think you know it all, but get it wrong. Marilyn is right. I was once married to an Irish actor, Julian L'Estrange. It was a perfect arrangement. He traveled most of the time with a young pianist, Albert Morris Bagby, who took care of my wifely duties. Julian was a homosexual and beautiful husband and a marvelous companion if I ever needed to be escorted to a gala. He died in this apartment, in Albert's arms, in 1918, while I sat in the corner having a brandy and smoking a cigarette."

Fortunately, the ringing of the doorbell broke Collier's reminiscences.

With a forceful, confident stride, Katharine Hepburn came into the room wearing rose-colored slacks and a battleship gray jacket. She'd applied only a slash of lipstick, no other makeup, and her hair was pulled back into a tight bun. "This divine creature must be Marilyn Monroe, America's reincarnation of Helen of Troy."

"Miss Hepburn, I'm honored. Ever since I was a little girl, I've gone to see your movies. You were great as Mary of Scotland."

"Oh, you sweet girl, never tell an aging actress you enjoyed her movies when you were but a toddler. It will only add another line to my face."

"Your face will be eternal," Truman assured her. "You're one of the very few actresses from the Golden Age who will be appearing on the screen when you're ninety."

"Oh, Capote, you always say such flattering bullshit to old actresses. Later on, you tell your friends what you really think of all of us battle axes."

Seated on the sofa with Marilyn and Collier, Hepburn learned that Marilyn was going to study acting with the aging duenna. "What a

Constance Collier
in her heyday, as Cleopatra

486

fabulous idea. Constance taught me every stage secret I know."

"And a lot more," Truman said with a smirk.

"Marilyn, why didn't you lobby to get me that Jane Russell role in *Gentlemen Prefer Blondes*?" Hepburn asked. "I would have been terrific."

Marilyn seemed taken aback. "I don't know…I'm sure…"

Truman came to the rescue. "There is a role you could play, Katharine. I've read an early draft. It's from Tennessee Williams' *The Garden District*. You'd be ideal as Violet Venable, a cold bitch and tyrannical mother. Marilyn could play the beautiful twenty-five-year-old who ran away with your poet son, Sebastian, to write his annual poem. In the plot of the play, you're trying to get a young doctor to lobotomise the girl and erase the unpleasant memory of how your son was killed."

"Tennessee himself has told me about this play," Hepburn said. "I'd be cast as a faded beauty who is now an old harpy. When I was younger and more beautiful, I was used as bait to attract the young men my son sexually desired. It's a play about perversion. From what Tennessee told me, it includes both incest and cannibalism."

"Oh, Miss Hepburn, you're too much of a lady to undertake such a role," Marilyn said.

"I wish you could convince Capote and Tennessee of that. The last I heard from him—he's down in Key West—he told me he's working on another Broadway play. He wants it to co-star both Bette Davis and me."

"I've worked with Bette," Marilyn said. "You know, on *All About Eve*. She's not the actress you are—and not nice at all."

"Truer words were never said," Hepburn said.

"Oh Kate," Truman said. "You survived Hollywood in the 1930s, going from John Barrymore to Marlene Dietrich to Howard Hughes. You've seen it all. If there's something you missed, I'm sure Spencer Tracy will fill you in."

"Truman, dear heart, you remind me of a naughty little chihuahua who has never been house broken."

Hepburn turned to Marilyn again. "Constance is a wise choice as a drama coach—the very best, in fact. She has a real zest for all that is good and wonderful in life. You will blossom under her, find dimensions in yourself as an actress you never knew existed. I should know. She did wonders for me."

The ringing of the doorbell signaled the arrival of the remaining guest, mystery and all.

Greta Garbo entered the room, an Hermès scarf covering most of her head and dark sunglasses concealing a good part of a fabled face that had not been seen on a movie screen since 1941.

Throughout the luncheon, Hepburn ate heartily as Garbo nibbled. She rarely took her eyes off Marilyn and seemed enchanted by her. Marilyn also seemed transfixed by Garbo, even more so than by Hepburn.

Collier retreated a bit, giving way to her age and a consumption of far too much alcohol.

Tanked up on pre-luncheon vodka and wine that had been set out on the table, Truman became even more provocative. "Katie, I've often wondered about something: Other than Bette Davis, female impersonators such as T.C. Jones like to imitate you. But I've never seen one of these drag queens do Greta."

Collier suddenly seemed to revive. "Let me answer that. I know why. Among all the great film stars, Garbo cannot be impersonated. Her appearance and femininity are unique. She has the cold quality of an Arctic mermaid. She really is hermaphroditic on screen."

Truman remained silent, but wanting to tell Collier that she'd stolen that impression from a magazine interview with Tennessee.

Garbo didn't seem insulted to be hermaphroditic, and actually seemed proud of it. Hepburn seemed to suddenly become even more articulate. "Greta is to be congratulated for representing the aspiration of both sexes, uniting the two sides of her nature, the feminine and masculine, in every role she's ever played. Her freedom from being trapped in either gender allows her to create a cryptic amorality in each part she plays."

"I allow a film-goer to create his or her own fantasy," Garbo said. "I do not let them look inside me— only inside their own dark desires."

"The miracle is that such a face as Greta's can even exist," Hepburn said before turning to face the star. "I know at times you must feel regret, even view it as tragic, that you were given the responsibility of owning such a face. Your look represents the apogee of the progression of the human female face."

"Oh, please," Garbo said, as if dismissive of all this praise. "Let me finish my salmon, and quit speaking of me as if giving a eulogy at the funeral. I am still alive, still enjoying the comforts of the damned, such as they are."

Collier's secretary served her favorite dessert. Before tasting it, Marilyn wanted to know what it was.

"It's junket, my dear," Collier said. "I first discovered it in my nursery."

"What is junket?" Marilyn asked. "I thought that was a trip you took with some man."

"It's a British dessert," Collier said. "It's made with sweetened flavored milk with rennet. Rennet, of course, is the lining membrane of a calf's stomach used for curdling milk."

"I'd better skip it today," Marilyn said. "I'm watching my figure."

"So is everybody else at this table," Truman added, his remark meeting with stony silence. Recognizing his gaffe, he quickly changed the subject.

He turned to Garbo. "When I was a twelve-year-old boy, I got very mad at you during one long, hot summer in the South. I'd had this awful mishap when a pack of ebony-colored boys, perhaps eight in all, brutally raped me. I was incapacitated for the rest of the summer. During all that time in bed, I wrote a play called The Most Beautiful Woman in the World. I sent it to you with a fan letter, asking if you'd star in it on Broadway. You never answered me, and I nursed this grudge against you until I was nineteen. I later burned the play."

"I'm so sorry I ignored you," Garbo said. "Too bad I'm too old to play in it now, since I'm no longer beautiful."

"But you *are* beautiful," Marilyn said. "Amazingly so. People say I'm beautiful, but I don't think so. I'm sexy-looking, but only after I've applied a lot of whorish makeup. Otherwise, I think I look like a milk maiden from Norway."

"In my home country of Sweden, the young men always journeyed in summer to Norway to seduce its beautiful young women," Garbo said.

"Miss Garbo, do you think you'll ever return to pictures?" Marilyn asked.

"Thank God Marilyn didn't use that awful word, 'comeback,'" Hepburn said.

"That proves that she saw *Sunset Blvd.*," Truman chimed in. "Gloria Swanson as Norma Desmond objected to the word 'comeback' too."

"Over the years, I've considered it," Garbo said. "I've always wanted to play Dorian Gray, based on the Oscar Wilde play. If I do, I'd like you, Miss Monroe, to play one of the girls that Dorian seduces and destroys."

"Garbo and Monroe," Collier said, "What box office! I could see a Best Oscar for Greta, but would she be nominated as Best Actor or Best Actress?"

"I'd be terrified to appear opposite you on the screen," Marilyn said. "But since you'd be cast as a man, I guess I might pull it off if Miss Collier coached me. There's no way I'd appear on the screen in a woman-to-woman role with you. I'd be mocked."

"I, too, wanted to do a film with Greta," Hepburn said. "*Mourning Becomes Electra*, with George Cukor directing. The year was 1947. I failed to convince Louis B. Mayer."

After the luncheon, Garbo excused herself to visit the bathroom. Marilyn was next. After emerging from the toilet, Garbo slipped Marilyn her private phone number. "Call me," she whispered. After thanking Collier and hugging Hepburn and Truman, she departed.

Likewise, Hepburn departed fifteen minute later, but not before inviting Marilyn to visit her at her home in Connecticut. Marilyn said she'd be honored.

Out on the street again, Truman warned Marilyn, "If you accept invitations from those two regal dykes, you might have to sing for your supper."

"What in hell do you think I've been doing all these years?" Marilyn said. "Call me the canary."

"I must congratulate you. You've come a long way from the days when you were the teenage bride of that sailor boy—I don't care to remember his name. Now, you're dating from the A-list: John F. Kennedy, Katharine Hepburn, and Greta Garbo. Speaking of big name legends, who does that leave out? Let me see—Charlie Chaplin and Albert Einstein?"

"Been there, done that."

Truman came to an abrupt stop in the middle of the sidewalk. "Like me, you're known for telling some tall tales. A whoremonger like Chaplin, I can believe. But you must admit that Einstein is a bit of a stretch."

"Silly boy, didn't you read in the papers that Einstein told an interviewer that I was his favorite movie star? After that, what could I do but get in touch with him? I wanted him to explain to me his theory of relativity. I simply cannot understand it."

In the weeks leading up to the acting coach's death, Marilyn visited Collier's apartment two or three times a week for acting lessons. The two women became close. Marilyn later said, "She opened up doors within me that I had kept locked all my life," without explaining to Truman exactly what she meant.

In April of 1955, Truman called to tell her of Collier's death. Marilyn was deeply saddened.

As a keepsake, Collier had given Marilyn a playbill from her 1906 performance as Cleopatra, in which she appeared on stage crowned in silver and carrying a golden scepter ornamented with a replica of the sacred golden calf.

Truman asked Marilyn if he could be her escort at the funeral, and she gratefully accepted.

Arriving dressed all in black, with Truman on her arm, Marilyn sat through the service "gnawing an already chewed-to-the-nub thumbnail," in Truman's words, "periodically removing her spectacles to scoop up tears bubbling from her blue-gray eyes."

After the service, she told Capote, "I hate funerals. I don't want a funeral—just my ashes cast on the waves by one of my kids, if I ever have any."

Collier's "secretary," Phyllis Wilbourn, whom Marilyn had come to know, was at the funeral, too. Marilyn offered her her deepest sympathy and was happy to learn that Hepburn was going to take her in. She would remain as Hepburn's "secretary" for the next forty years—there was talk.

Long after Collier's death, Truman published what the actress had articulated about Marilyn's talent or lack thereof:

"Oh yes, there is something there—a beautiful child, really—I don't think she's an actress at all—certainly not in a traditional sense. What she has is this presence, a certain luminosity, a flickering intelligence. These marvelous traits could not be captured on stage because they are too subtle, too fragile. Her wonder can only be caused by the camera. It's like a hummingbird in flight. Only a camera can freeze the poetry of it. But anyone who thinks this girl is simply another Harlow or harlot or whatever, is mad. I hope, I really pray, that she survives long enough to free the strange lovely talent that's wandering through her like a jailed spirit."

"Skip the Canned Dog Food and Have Breakfast at Tiffany's With Truman."

—Tennessee's Career Advice to MM

Marilyn did not always get along with Truman. When he learned of her secret trysts with playwright Arthur Miller, he spread the word.

One afternoon, during one of his visits with Marilyn in her new Manhattan apartment, she warned him, "I've got connections with Murder, Inc. I could have you bumped off if you don't stop gossiping about Arthur Miller and me. We're not ready to go public with our relationship yet. One call to Sam Giancana, and your wispy little voice will be heard no more."

"Marilyn, how can you threaten me with such a thing? I'm completely loyal to you. Not a word of your affair with Arthur has escaped from my succulent mouth, which is being put to finer uses these days."

"I bet!" she snapped, sarcastically.

Months later, in a letter to Cecil Beaton, Truman wrote: "By the time you get this, Marilyn Monroe will have married Arthur Miller. Saw them the other night, both looking suffused with a sexual glow. I can't help feeling this little episode will be called Death of a Playwright."

The saga of the Miller/Monroe romance became tabloid fodder, one headline citing them as THE INTELLECTUAL AND THE NAKED VENUS. Robert Levin, a magazine writer, claimed, "The upcoming marriage of the pin-up girl of the age and the nation's foremost intellectual playwright seems preposterous." *The New York Post* referred to the coupling as, "America's number one representatives of the Body & the Mind."

Marilyn told Truman, "We're going to have the greatest kids in America. With my beauty and his brain, how can we go wrong?"

***

Although many scripts were presented to her, Marilyn did not work during the entire course of 1959. The role that interested her was that of Holly Golightly in Truman Capote's *Breakfast at Tiffany's*, based on his best-selling novella, published that same year (1959).

"When I created the character of Holly, I had Marilyn in mind for the role,"

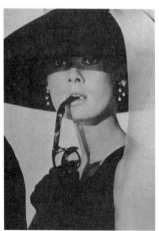

Holly Golightly is a slut.
(Two Views of **Audrey Hepburn** in *Breakfast at Tiffany's*)

491

Truman asserted.

To his friends, Truman referred to Marilyn as "unschooled, but enormously brilliant."

At one point, he claimed that Marilyn had deliberately intended to "sabotage" Arthur Miller's *The Misfits* through her aggressive lobbying for the role of Holly Golightly, which was eventually released as a movie in 1961. As her biographer, Barbara Leaming, put it, "She seemed eager to subvert Arthur's plans. If he was willing to put up with anything to get his picture made, then she, apparently, was ready to do anything to stop it."

"Meeting with Tennessee Williams and his lover, Frank Merlo, Marilyn presented her dilemma to him. "Which picture should I make? Arthur Miller's *The Misfits* or Truman Capote's *Breakfast at Tiffany's?*"

"It's no contest," Tennessee advised her. "Go for Capote's Holly Golightly. Miller's play is about rounding up mustangs for the slaughter house, where the meat will be canned as dog food. Is he out of his mind? Who would want to see a play about that?"

"Don't condemn it too much," Frank cautioned him. "After all, you wrote a play about beach hustlers cannibalizing a homosexual in Italy. I'd rather eat horse flesh that human flesh."

"Of course, Holly is another slut role for me, but you've made up my mind for me," she said.

"Slut roles can be fabulous," Tennessee said. "I hear Elizabeth Taylor's going to play a slut in *BUtterfield 8.*"

"Call that type casting," Marilyn said.

Truman went on to work with Marilyn during his creation of two of the scenes from *Breakfast at Tiffany's*, excerpts which she performed in front of the highly critical Actors Studio.

Later, Susan Strasberg recalled Marilyn's performances of the scenes at the Actors Studio, but only after she'd seen the completed movie version. "It was a great moment for Marilyn and should have been captured on film. Audrey Hepburn, who eventually got the role, was wonderful, if you could believe such a delicate little creature could be a working whore. I don't mean that Marilyn was sluttish, but she looked like she was familiar with the profession. Actually, she would have brought a dimension to *Breakfast at Tiffany's* that Audrey didn't. But Marilyn had earned such a bad press for all the delays on *Some Like It Hot* that Blake Edwards, the director, didn't want to use her, fearing she'd break the bank."

"Paramount Double-Crossed Me" —*Truman Capote*

"Moon River Stays in the Picture" —*Audrey Hepburn*

"I'd rather have cancer than a dishonest heart."

—Holly Golightly in Breakfast at Tiffany's

The winds of autumn were blowing against the face of Truman Capote as he strolled Fifth Avenue in New York City. It was 1958, and his novella, *Breakfast at Tiffany's,* had been published. He was window shopping the bookstores, all of which displayed his novella in their front windows.

His main character, a prostitute in spite of his denial, was on her way to becoming an iconic figure in American literature. Truman would later claim that of all the characters he'd created, Holly Golightly remained his favorite because of her free spirit.

Over the years, many women would be listed as the inspiration for the character of Holly, notably Marilyn Monroe. But other candidates included the heiress Gloria Vanderbilt, Doris Lilly, Phoebe Pierce, Carol Marcus, and Oona Chaplin, wife of Charlie and the daughter of Eugene O'Neill. Many friends of Truman's also felt he drew heavily upon the character of a young Nina Capote, his mother.

One woman unrelated to any aspect of Truman's novella, Bonnie Golightly, was so angered by the use of her name that she sued for nearly a million dollars. Of course, the case was ridiculous and was thrown out of court. "I heard that the woman was fat and middle-aged," Truman said. "That's like Joan Crawford claiming that she was the basis for Lolita."

Most of the novella's reviews were favorable, and Truman felt he had a best-seller. The attacks, however, would be what he remembered. He was especially infuriated by novelist William Goyen, who reviewed *Breakfast* for *The New York Times Book Review* in an article that appeared on November 2, 1958.

Goyen disparaged Truman, defining his novel as "perhaps the last of the old-fashioned Valentine makers. He dwells in a doily-story-world entirely of his own making."

In a letter to the poet, John Malcolm Brinnin, Truman wrote: "How is that for a piece of sour grapes bitchy? What a psychopath!"

The attack on *Breakfast* that appeared in *The New York Times* was followed by a brief unsigned dismissal published in *The New Yorker,* for which Truman had once worked and contributed. *Breakfast* was denounced as "empty nostalgia."

George Peppard and **Audrey Hepburn** as they appeared in *Breakfast at Tiffany's*. Initially, both were attacked as "unsuitable for the roles."

Truman wrote them a letter of protest, attacking their review as "condescending, with an unserious, unjust, and meaningless wisecrack."

As anticipated, Gore Vidal stood by his stubborn position of maintaining that "Holly Golightly is a mere redrawing of Sally Bowles from Christopher Isherwood's *Berlin Stories.*" Gore to some degree was accurate, but he failed to note that Holly's character was far more complicated, with far more nuances, than that of Bowles' in pre-war Berlin.

Unexpected praise for Truman came from Norman Mailer: "He is tart as a grand aunt, but in his way, he is a ballsy little guy, and he is the most perfect writer of my generation. He writes the best sentences word for word, rhythm upon rhythm. I would not have changed two words in *Breakfast at Tiffany's,* which will become a small classic."

Many actors, including several at the Actors Studio, wanted to play the male lead, a writer who hustles a rich woman for a living. When Marilyn heard that George Peppard was a leading contender, she went to the Actors Studio, with Truman, to watch him perform in a nude scene in bed with a woman.

"A lot of actors would have kept on their boxer shorts, but not George," Truman said. "He was obviously proud of his equipment—and with good reason—and he flashed for his fellow actors in the studio, including Lee Strasberg. Marilyn and I were mesmerized by his beauty."

Eventually, Peppard married actress Elizabeth Ashley, who became his second wife in 1966. Truman agreed with Ashley's description of her new husband. "George Peppard looked like some kind of Nordic God—six feet tall, with beautiful blonde hair, blue eyes, and a body out of every high school cheerleader's teenage lust fantasy."

Ever the voyeur, Truman was privy to the secret friendship that Peppard had developed with a fellow hunk, Paul Newman. It had begun when they were cast together in the TV drama, *Bang the Drum Slowly,* which had first aired on *The United States Steel Hour* in 1956.

"I knew both Paul and George, and often saw them huddled together as if oblivious to the rest of the world," Truman said. "I wouldn't exactly call it a love affair. But I bet they had great sex together. They would often wander off together, including a secret weekend together in New England. I wished they'd invited me along as chaperone. At least they could have let me watch."

"Looking at the two of them would give a queen an orgasm," Truman said. "If some studio ever remakes *Gone With the Wind,* the director should cast George as Rhett Butler and Paul as Ashley Wilkes. I couldn't quite pull off the role of Scarlett, but in blackface, I could do the Butterfly McQueen role perfectly. I already have her voice."

Months later, when Peppard was cast in *Breakfast at Tiffany's* with Audrey Hepburn, Marilyn complained to Truman, "Audrey Hepburn got George, the man intended for me."

Unlike Truman, Blake Edwards, the director of *Breakfast at Tiffany's,* was unhappy about the casting of Peppard. He'd never viewed one of his movies until Edwards went to see *Home From the Hill* (1960), in which Peppard played the neglected son of land baron Robert Mitchum.

"After seeing George on the screen, I got down on my knees and begged Martin Jurow and Richard Shepherd, the producers of *Breakfast at Tiffany's*, not to make the film with Peppard. 'He is a piss poor actor,' I told them, an ex-Marine and all that shit. I wanted Robert Redford, but ended up with Peppard. Paul Newman could have done it, too."

Truman's greatest disappointment involved the casting of Audrey Hepburn as Holly Golightly. "I adore her, but she was wrong for the role. It was tailor made for Marilyn. She would have been absolutely marvelous. She wanted to play Holly, too, to the extent that she worked up two whole scenes all by herself and did them for me. She was terribly good, but Paramount double crossed me by hiring Audrey."

In a surprising reaction, Audrey agreed with Truman, even though Holly, in time, would evolve into her most iconic film statement. "I feared I lacked the comic sense the part called for. Holly was an extrovert. I'm an introvert. I was pressured into doing the movie. But it made me a nervous wreck. I lost sleep. I lost weight."

Truman was also displeased with the enormous liberties that Hollywood was taking with his plot. "In my book, Holly is really rather bitter, and Holly Golightly was *real*—a tough character, not an Audrey Hepburn type at all. Holly had something touching about her, a portrait unfinished. Marilyn had that quality. Audrey did not. I also objected to turning my serio-comic tale of a lonely, wandering girl in Manhattan into a mawkish Valentine to New York City."

In a nutshell, Truman had once described the role as "the story of a child bride from Tulip, Texas, who runs away from home to marry the richest man in the world, but ends up joining the ranks of the world's oldest profession."

Audrey brought in her friend, the fashion designer Hubert de Givenchy, to create her wardrobe, which included "the Little Black Dress" she wore at the beginning of the film. It became one of the most iconic items of clothing in the history of the 20th Century. In 2011, it sold for nearly a million dollars.

Tiffany's (the jeweler) wanted to hire Audrey to hawk its products in their print advertisements, but she rejected their lucrative offer. "I don't want to become known as Miss Diamonds," she said.

Despite Audrey's objections and appraisals, millions of fans worldwide found her irresistible as Holly. At Oscar time, she received her fourth nomination as Best Actress, losing to Sophia Loren for her role in *Two Women.*

One horribly false note was sounded by casting Mickey Rooney as Holly's grotesque Japanese neighbor, "Mr. Yunioshi." Truman accused Rooney of "ludicrously overplaying the role."

For her role in the movie as "The Other Woman," Patricia Neal received her first movie offer in years. She jumped at the chance to play a society matron who supports the struggling young writer portrayed by Peppard. She worked well with Audrey, Blake Edwards, and "Gorgeous George," as she called him.

"George's character was written with a battered vulnerability that was totally appealing," Neal remembered. "But it did not correspond to George's image of himself as a leading man. He seemed to want to be an old time movie hunk. At one point, Blake wanted him to sit on my lap. George and Blake almost came to blows over that scene. In the end, George played the role as he wanted to, and I always felt that Blake should have stood his ground. The film would have been stronger—and so would George Peppard."

When the final version of *Breakfast* was screened for the brass at Paramount, Martin Rankin, the head of production, objected to the song "Moon River," demanding that it be cut from the film.

A defiant Audrey Hepburn rose to her feet, shaking her fist at him. "OVER MY DEAD BODY!" she screamed.

Breakfast at Tiffany's was a box office hit, although it drew a fair amount of criticism. One reviewer wrote that "Audrey Hepburn carries the picture, but her fragile grace doesn't really fit the hillbilly-turned-Manhattan pub crawler Capote imagined. She is, however, a hundred times more engaging than the wooden Peppard."

The New York Times defined the movie as "completely unbelievable but wholly captivating."

In 1966, Broadway producer David Merrick attempted to adapt *Breakfast at Tiffany's* into a musical, starring Mary Tyler Moore and Richard Chamberlain. Merrick opted to scrap the project's original script, as conceived by the theatrical veteran Abe Burrows. Its replacement derived from an unlikely scriptwriting candidate—Edward Albee. "At least Edward adhered more closely to my original concept of Holly," Truman said.

During its inaugural previews at Broadway's Majestic Theater, beginning on December 12, 1966, the musical adaptation of *Breakfast at Tiffany's* ran for nearly four hours. Despite its heavy advance ticket sales, Merrick pulled the plug after only four previews. Then he placed an infamous infomercial in *The New York Times,* asserting that he shut down the show "rather than subject the drama critics and the public to an excruciatingly boring evening."

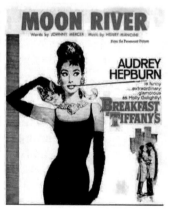

"Moon River," the song that almost didn't make it into the film version's final cut, went on to win an Oscar for Best Song, and became one of the proudest achievements of Henry Mancini and lyricist Johnny Mercer, especially when it was sung by Andy Williams.

Chapter Thirty-Five

Fidel Castro
Radical, Revolutionary, & Media Star

How Tennessee's Sexual Fantasy Became MM's Conquest

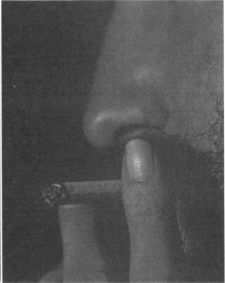

Icons of the 20th Century
Ernest Hemingway *(left)* and cigar-smoking **Fidel Castro** *(right)*

"I was intimidated by Hemingway the first time I met him in Havana," Tennessee recalled. "He was not my kind of a man, living with bullfighters, boxing world champions, hunting big game. Of course, I liked bullfighters and boxers, but for different reasons. The 'big game' I pursued was different from his."

In contrast, Fidel Castro was Tennessee's "dream man. I wanted to be kidnapped by him and be his love slave,"

Promising funds and assistance for whatever Hollywood studio would endorse the project, the Cuban dictator sought Tennessee's help in the production of a movie that would have starred Marlon Brando interpreting Castro, and Marilyn Monroe in the role of his revolutionary mistress.

Tennessee Confronts "Mr. Macho," Ernest Hemingway

During their early struggles in Hollywood, Marilyn

Monroe and Shelley Winters roomed together to cut down on expenses. After they moved out and into better quarters, they remained friends and saw each other when no lover was on the immediate horizon.

One bored, rainy afternoon in Hollywood, Shelley visited Marilyn, finding her washing her hair and painting her toenails scarlet red.

The two men-chasers often shared revelations about their wide-ranging love affairs, present and past, sometimes plotting strategies for future conquests.

Marilyn claimed that early in 1955, she'd had an affair with James Dean, whom she'd met at the Actors Studio in New York.

"Who hasn't?" Shelley asked.

"Jimmy and I used to play games in which we'd reveal our darkest secrets," Marilyn said. "In one game, we both had to name very unlikely people we'd slept with. He named Barbara Hutton, Howard Hughes, Tallulah Bankhead, and J. Edgar Hoover."

"Not surprising," Shelley said. "Jimmy would go down on a doorknob. And who did you name, my dear?"

You can guess one of them: Charlie Chaplin," Marilyn said.

"I know all about how you fucked Charlie," Shelley said, "because I was screwing his son, Sydney. Now for the other three—and this had better be good, not a twice-told tale."

"Jimmy Hoffa, Fidel Castro, and Albert Einstein."

"Are you bullshitting me, or just fantasizing?" Shelley asked. "I'm sort of inclined to believe you, because you've had some strange bedfellows. Ever since you shacked up with Senator Kennedy, Hoffa's been on your tail. He thinks Kennedy will become President in 1960, and he wants to have blackmail evidence on him."

"As for that ugly little mutt—who's sorta cute—that Maestro of the Theory of Relativity, he told a reporter that you're his alltime fantasy," Shelley said.

"As for your screwing

James Dean told Marilyn that the only reason he attended the Actors Studio in Manhattan was to meet potential lovers.

"I didn't like the way your guru grilled me. I think he's just using you to bring money and fame to his god damn studio."

Although **Marilyn** sharply disagreed with Dean about Strasberg, they made plans to become "the screen team of the 1950s.

"Forget Katharine Hepburn and Spencer Tracy. They can play grandparents. You and I are what the public wants to see today."

498

around with Fidel, I don't know unless you made a quick trip to Cuba from Florida, or perhaps from Mexico, where you're always hanging out. *Variety,* or some such rag, reported that the rebel leader fell in love with your Lorelei Lee image in *Gentlemen Prefer Blondes* and that he has seen it more than a dozen times."

Cruising Sailors in Key West,

And Being Entertained by "Superman" in Havana

In 1941, still licking his wounds from the theatric failure of *Battle of Angels,* Tennessee moved to Key West for the winter. "Swimming was an important part of my life, and I felt this was the only place along the Eastern Seaboard where the water would be warm enough to go swimming, year-round. It was only sixty miles off the coast of Cuba."

He checked into a little boarding house, the Tradewinds, which stood on Duval, the town's main street. There, he formed a bond with the daughter, Marion Vaccaro, of its owner. Vaccaro, became one of his most cherished *confidantes*—his "Partner in Crime," as he liked to call her.

Even though she was married to Regis Vaccaro, one of the heirs to the Standard Fruit Company, Marion and Tennessee cruised the sailors along Duval at night, often hauling "our blushing trade" back to the inn.

Tennessee claimed that Regis was "the worst alcoholic I have ever known in my life. When he wasn't soaked in alcohol, he was high on ether. When Regis got mad at you, he'd remove his glass eye and toss it at you. The eye often landed in your soup."

Leaving Regis drunk in one of the back rooms at the Tradewinds, Tennessee and Marion often flew to Havana for what he called "riotous weekends."

"She was an alcoholic nymphomaniac, and we often patronized bordellos that hired handsome, well-hung young men who catered to both genders."

At night, they attended one or another of the fourteen "Superman shows" that featured studly men with fourteen-inch penises having various forms of sex on stage.

"When Marion sobered up, she often called her friend, Billie Burke, who had played the Good Witch in *Wizard of Oz,*" Tennessee said. "They had remained lifelong friends ever since Marion had been the tutor to her children during her stormy marriage to showman Flo Ziegfeld."

"One night at the Tradewinds, I was the meat in the sandwich between two nude, drunken sailors," Tennessee recalled. "Marion suddenly handed the phone to me because Miss Burke wanted to speak to me. There I was chatting with this sweet old thing, who told me her life's desire was to appear in a play by Tennessee Williams. The talk didn't go as I expected. Miss Burke, as it turns out, is not what she appears on the screen. In her heyday, Marion told, she and Flo Ziegfeld used to fight over who was going to sleep with which of his showgirls that night."

"Papa Hemingway Was a Closeted Homosexual

With a Transgendered Son Called Gigi (later, Gloria)"

—Tennessee Williams

After Fidel Castro seized power in Cuba, Tennessee and Marion continued to take the 90-mile flight from Key West to Havana, at least until the dictator closed all the bordellos and shut down the live sex shows, denouncing them as a product of decadent imperialism. "The role of the new government in Cuba is not to exploit our young men and women as a means of providing sexual relief for frustrated, rich Americans."

In 1959, Tennessee and Marion flew to Havana for another of their "raucous weekends," where they came face-to-face with the "two most macho men of the Caribbean," expatriate Ernest Hemingway and Fidel Castro.

Shortly after they'd checked into a suite at the Hotel Nacional, Tennessee received a call from Kenneth Tynan, the British critic and friend of Gore Vidal.

"Would you like to meet Hemingway?" Tynan asked. "Before you replaced him, he used to be the most famous writer living in Key West."

"I'm not so eager, Tennessee said. "I understand he can be very unpleasant to people of my particular temperament."

"Don't worry about that," Tynan said. "I'll be there to protect you. I think you ought to meet Papa. After all, he is one of the great writers of your time or mine."

Tennessee was very nervous about meeting Hemingway, and Marion had to mix him three martinis before he could face the ordeal. Finally, he donned a yachting jacket with gold buttons and a yachting cap before walking along Old Havana's waterfront to the Floradita *[Old Havana's most iconic bar and café]*, where Hemingway was already getting tanked up on *mojitos.*

Tynan was seated with Hemingway at an outdoor table. He introduced the two writers.

"That bitchy queen, Tynan, later wrote a completely inaccurate account of this historic meeting that was more amusing than truthful," Tennessee later asserted. "I admit, though, that Hemingway and I were not plugged into the same electrical circuit, and that I was rather awkward in the beginning."

"In Key West, I often dance to the music of this all-black band at Sloppy Joe's along Duval Street," Tennessee told Hemingway. "I understand it was your favorite hangout, and that your signature is still carved onto one of its bar stools."

"I left more behind than my carving," Hemingway said. "Don't tell anyone, especially a book collector: I also left some discarded manuscripts behind the bar."

Then Tennessee tried to flatter Hemingway: "What I admire about your writing is that you care about honor among men."

500

"What kind of men are you referring to?" Hemingway asked. "Men who have honor never talk about it."

There arose a strained silence at the table, and Tennessee made another stab at conversation. "I realize that no sane person would ever confuse the writing of Tennessee Williams with that of Ernest Hemingway. But a recent piece in *Time* magazine at least put us in the same club together. According to the esteemed editors at *Time*, you and I belong to the 'Cult of Dirt.'"

"What in hell are you talking about?" Hemingway asked.

"In October of 1956, *Time* ran this piece that included an appraisal of us by Robert Elliot Fitch," Tennessee said. "He was the Dean of the Pacific School of Religion at Berkeley. He called us part of a cabal of 'the Cult of Dirt,' whose fellow members include Eugene O'Neill, Norman Mailer, and James Jones. We were referred to as the 'Merde Mystics.' His exact words, and I remember them well, were, 'Each writer is trying to replace Christian values with a debased secular morality.' Fitch called me the High Priest of this cult, accusing me of epitomizing the mystique of obscenity, especially in my play, *Cat on a Hot Tin Roof.*"

"I wrote *Time*," Tennessee continued, telling them I was flattered to be the High Priest of something, even something called *merde.* I went on to say I would not have exercised the subterfuge of using a foreign word for it."

Hemingway seemed to ponder this anecdote for a moment. "I guess what this Fitch faggot is suggesting is that we're Shit—that's the word. I could care less what some crazed Christian fanatic says about me." Then he ordered another *mojito.* "When I wrote my novel, *Across the River and Into the Trees, Time*—or some such piece of shit like that—said that I had become a caricature of myself as a writer."

"I have this friend, Miss Tallulah Bankhead, who once told me that at the end of our lives, all of us become caricatures of ourselves."

"Perhaps your Miss Tallulah was right," Hemingway said. "By the way, I think I fucked her once—or was it Marlene Dietrich? We'll all be dead soon anyway, and what does it matter what someone thinks of us?"

"At least no one ever accused us of writing like each other," Tennessee said.

"I regret to say, I've seen only one of your plays, *A Streetcar Named Desire,*" Hemingway said.

"Dare I ask?" Tennessee said. "What did you think of it?"

"It was saturated with death," Hemingway responded. "After my experience with Gertrude Stein and F. Scott Fitzgerald, I don't normally seek out the company of fellow writers. I prefer the company of bullfighters, garage mechanics, street cleaners, bartenders, and bordello madams."

"Once, I was crammed into this bar in Paris, and seated next to me was Ford Madox Ford, who passed wind all evening—read that 'farted bigtime,'" Hemingway said. "Do you have many writer friends?"

"A few but, I must confess, I'm jealous of their achievements," Tennessee said. "Carson McCullers is a friend."

"I know of her but I can't bear to read her," Hemingway said. "Some critics rank her *The Heart is a Lonely Hunter* as a better piece of literature than my *The Sun Also Rises*. I can't bring myself to pick up a novel by a lesbian writer like McCullers. I have a theory that a woman can't write a novel unless she receives a deep penetration from the male animal on a regular basis."

"Carson thinks like a man, I can assure you," Tennessee said. "In 1946, I was dying in Nantucket, or at least I thought I was. She arrived in a baseball cap with that radiant crooked toothed grin of hers. She rescued me from the throes of death, and I started to polish my *Streetcar* play the very next morning."

"Speaking of lesbian women writers, I once chatted with Miss Katherine Anne Porter," Hemingway said. "She told me that your plays give off 'lurid flames.'"

"She must have been talking about *Summer and Smoke,*" Tennessee said.

"You mentioned you felt you were dying," Hemingway said. "Each morning as I rise to face my typewriter, I experience a minor death. It's like a bullfighter facing that moment of truth in the ring."

Perhaps as a means of flaunting his credentials as a critic of the arts, Tynan suddenly joined in the sparring between the two writers.

"The Spanish have a word for it. *Duenda.* Perhaps the word is familiar to you, Ernest. There is no English equivalent. It denotes the quality without which no flamenco singer or bullfighter can conquer the summit of his art. *Duenda* is the talent to transmit a profoundly felt emotion to an audience of strangers with the minimum of fuss and the maximum of restraint. There are examples, of course—Laurence Olivier has it, Maurice Evans does not; Billie Holiday has it, but Ella Fitzgerald never reached it. It is the quality that distinguishes Ernest Hemingway from John O'Hara; Tennessee Williams from William Inge."

Neither writer had any comment after that. Tennessee changed the subject. "In Key West, I knew your second wife, Pauline."

[Hemingway was married to Pauline Pfeiffer from 1940 to 1945.]

"I know she died in 1951," Tennessee continued. "Did she die in great pain?"

Hemingway looked toward the sea and paused for a long time before he replied in very Hemingway-like prose: "She died like everybody dies, and after that, she was dead."

"Forgive the indelicacy of my rude question," Tennessee said. "I've had a run of bad luck lately coming up with new ideas for plays. My critics claim I'm repeating myself. And my psychiatrist tells me I should pursue more heterosexual themes."

"In Key West, there's so much talk about you and your legacy that I came up with an idea for a play about a struggling writer living in Paris with his first wife," Tennessee said. "Of course, I won't call her Hadley."

[The reference was to Elizabeth Hadley Richardson, married to Hemingway from 1921 to 1927.]

"In my play, the young writer and his wife would become friends with a very stately, rather macho, lesbian writer, and her lover, who is known for her recipes. Of course, I'm referring to Gertrude Stein and Alice B. Toklas. The first act will be set in Paris. I see it as a sort of "Lost Generation First Act" of the expatriate community living in Paris in the 1920s."

"The hero of my play outgrows his first wife," Tennessee continued. "Of course, as Pauline's friend, I know her much better. I know she came from a wealthy Catholic family. In my play, she persuades the young writer to convert to her religion. They have two sons, one of whom, Gregory has a problem with his gender assignment."

"In my play, I will change the name of Pauline to Paula," Tennessee said. "When her son turns nineteen, he is arrested as a male trying to enter a women's toilet, not as a voyeur, but because he thought of himself as a woman born into a man's body. The writer calls his wife and informs him of the arrest of their son, whom they've nicknamed 'Gigi' throughout most of his life. The shock of the news, along with her failing health, leads to her having a fatal stroke."

"Much of my play will deal with father-and-son issues," Tennessee continued, "Part of it will be about a son growing up in the shadow of a very macho father. For a while, he becomes a celebrated athlete in school and later finds release killing elephants in Africa. But he never gets over the fact that a real woman is hiding in his body, struggling to get out. He will ultimately become transgendered."

[Ernest Hemingway's son, Gregory Hemingway, also known as Gloria Hemingway, underwent a sex change operation in 1995. As Gloria, he was arrested on a beach in Miami as he was wandering about in the nude. Perceived to be a woman, he was charged with indecent exposure and committed to the Miami-Dade Women's Detention Center, where she died of a stroke on October 1, 2001.]

"My son has the biggest dark

Papa Hemingway (left) with his tormented son, **Gregory**, were estranged for many years. Gregory sent his father a note in 1954 to congratulate him for being awarded the Nobel Prize for Literature. Ernesto sent him $5,000 in return.

Gregory wrote a memoir of their strained relationship entitled *Papa: A Personal Memoir* that had a thin cutting edge of malice.

Living in the shadow of his father's fame, Gregory once claimed, "What I really wanted to be was a Hemingway hero." But as the years went by, his dreams changed. What he wanted to be—and ultimately did become—was a woman named Gloria Hemingway.

In 2001, at the time of his death in a woman's jail in Miami, he had never completed the long process of transformation from male to female.

Throughout his tortured life, Gregory, a medical doctor, battled bipolar disorder, alcoholism, drug abuse, and what he defined as "gender dysphoria."

side in the family except for me," Hemingway said, heatedly. "That story is far too complicated for a mere play—in fact, I will not allow you to dramatize such a personal invasion of my private life. I suggest that instead, you write a play about the troubled marriage of F. Scott and Zelda Fitzgerald. You would find it far more rewarding to invade their heads than mine, and you would understand both of them better. As for you, it is impossible for the homosexual mind to understand what motivates me."

The Great Spanish Matador, Antonio Ordóñez

— "His Success Involved a Blend of Scars & Cojones"

In Havana, at the Floradita, still at table with Hemingway, Tennessee decided to switch to the more neutral topic of bullfighting.

"In Madrid, I got to know your friend, Antonio Ordóñez," Tennessee said.

"That young Andalusian is the first undisputed *torero de epica* since the death of Manolete in 1947," Hemingway said. "Manolete spent his last moments alive on the right horn of a Miura bull."

"I have seen all the great bullfighters of my day, and, to me, Antonio is *Numero Uno,*" Hemingway continued. "He knows that bullfighting is not a tragic conflict. Rather, it is a lyrical dance, a partnership between the bull, who must inevitably die, and the man, who may die."

"One afternoon, Ordóñez took me for a drive in his Rolls Royce from Madrid to Segovia," Tennessee said. "Instead of chasing a bull in the ring, he pursued cars on the road. He was a speed demon, passing every vehicle in sight, sometimes at 100 miles per hour. Once, he almost collided into a large oncoming truck. We just missed it by two seconds."

"He seems to want to defy death every day of his life," Hemingway said.

"One afternoon, before one of his appearances in Madrid, he invited me to watch him dress," Tennessee said. "He even showed me what he called his *cogidas,* as you know, scars on his thighs."

"Do you think he would talk to you and show us his *cogidas?*" Hemingway asked.

Tennessee didn't understand the wording of such a curious question. "Oh, I'm certain he would. He's a most accessible boy. Not only did I see his *cogidas,* but his *cojones* were on ample view, too. Now I know

The celebrated bullfighter, **Antonio Ordóñez** *(left)* with the bullfighting aficionado, **Ernest Hemingway**, who wrote the definitive English-language book on the art, *Death in the Afternoon.*

Here, they are seen together in Málaga, Spain, in 1959, taking in the Andalusian sun.

why he's so popular with the ladies. The evidence was before me."

"Don't let Antonio mislead you," Hemingway said. "Most bullfighters pad their crotches. Let's face it: Mother Nature didn't make all men equal. Sometimes, the male penis is as different as my penis is from that of F. Scott Fitzgerald."

Surrounded by adoring fans, **Ordóñez** receives their applause in his form-fitting "suit of light," showing off his prodigious endowment.

Tennessee Williams, who had seen him get dressed, later said, "Seeing was believing—it practically came down to his knee."

Antonio seemed very concerned with money," Tennessee said. "He refers to U.S. dollars as '*Washingtones.*' He said he has a lot of people to support."

"Yes, he's a family man with mistresses and their children to support," Hemingway said. "In 1953, I urged him not to get married. I warned him that wives inhibit a bullfighter and imbue him with their fears. They want to keep their husband's *cojones* intact. Wives also don't want their husbands ending up with a femoral artery slashed or a punctured lung. Antonio told me that he's stabbed 150 bulls to their death in a moment of truth in the ring. But he never knows if the next bull horn he encounters has his name on it."

"Will you be returning to Madrid any time soon?" Tennessee asked.

"Alas, I'm growing bored with bullfighting. I find that the young hustlers in the ring today adhere to a self-castrating style that merely passes for bullfighting," Hemingway said. He never explained what "self-castrating" meant. Then he turned to Tennessee. "What is your opinion of bullfighting?"

"Perhaps my reaction is strange, but I think bullfighting today is the only place where you can see the sword being used for the purpose for which it was invented."

"I'll Never Open a Play on Broadway Again"
—Tennessee Williams

"*F. Scott and Zelda Fitzgerald embody concerns of my own, the tortures of the creative artist in a materialist society. They were so close to the edge. I understood their schizophrenia and their thwarted ambition.*"
—Tennessee Williams commenting on *Clothes for a Summer Hotel*

As ironic as it seems, Tennessee, in 1976, took Hemingway's long-ago advice. He began working on a play revolving around the troubled lives of F. Scott and Zelda Fitzgerald, entitling it *Clothes for a Summer Hotel.* It would be the last of his plays to debut on Broadway during his lifetime.

The play revolved around a one-day visit Scott pays to Zelda at the Highland Mental Hospital in Asheville, North Carolina. It included a series of flashbacks highlighting scenes from their turbulent marriage in the 1920s.

For inspiration, the play drew upon Tennessee's frequent visits to his mentally incapacitated sister, Rose, who had also been committed to a mental hospital.

Starring Geraldine Page as Zelda, and directed by José Quintero, *Clothes for a Summer Hotel* opened at the Court Theater in Manhattan on March 26, 1980. Stricken by a critical assault from the press, the play closed after fourteen performances. At the debut of its short run, New Yorkers faced a paralyzing blizzard and a transit strike.

En Famille: **The Fitzgeralds** left to right: **F. Scott**, their daughter, **Scottie**, and the mentally disturbed **Zelda**.

Throughout the course of their stormy marriage, she taunted her husband that he didn't "measure up" to her other male lovers. She also accused him of being a homosexual, lusting after Ernest Hemingway.

"I'll never open a play on Broadway again," Tennessee vowed. "I can't get a good press from *The New York Times,* and critics Harold Clurman, Brendan Gill, and Jack Kroll hate me. I put too much of my heart into my plays to have them demolished by some querulous old aisle sitters."

***

In his memoirs, Tennessee described his meeting with Hemingway: "He could not have been more charming. He was exactly the opposite of what I'd expected. I had expected a very manly, super-macho sort of guy, very bullying, and coarse spoken. On the contrary, Hemingway struck me as a gentleman who seemed to have a very touchingly shy quality about him."

Maria St. Just, one of Tennessee's closest female friends, claimed that he maintained quite a different point of view in private. "All his life, Tenn felt that Hemingway was a closeted queer and that the love of his life was F. Scott Fitzgerald. When Gertrude Stein forced Hemingway to face that reality, he never spoke to her again. He was extremely jealous of Fitzgerald, but also extremely passionate. It was unrequited love."

"Tennessee once told me, 'Papa (Hemingway) has an unnatural concern about queens,'" St. Just said. "'Not only that,' Tennessee said, 'but he writes uninterestingly about women.'"

"If that is true," St. Just responded (to Tennessee), "then you are normal, as you can write only interestingly about women."

***

Tennessee's friendly relationship with critic Kenneth Tynan did not last through 1959, based to a large degree on that meeting in Havana with Ernest Hemingway.

Their relationship collapsed after Tennessee read what Tynan had written about his latest play, *Sweet Bird of Youth,* in *The New Yorker:*

"The writing is operatic and hysterical, as if it had long been out of touch with reality. A dust bowl, one feels, is being savagely, obsessively plowed, in defiance of known facts about soil depletion and the need for irrigation. I recognized nothing but a special, rarefied situation that had been carried to extremes of cruelty with a total disregard for probability, human relevance, and the laws of dramatic structure."

Hemingway fared better from Tynan's pen than did Tennessee. "Hemingway has his own ideal of manhood, which he projects onto the American mind—a noble savage, idly smoking, silhouetted against a background of dead illusions."

Fidel to Tennessee: "Only From the Waist Down"

In Havana, at the Floradita, after bidding Hemingway goodbye, Tynan informed Tennessee that he had a two o'clock appointment with Fidel Castro at his headquarters. The rebel leader had granted Tynan an interview. He later said, "Tennessee begged me to take him along. He confessed that 'Fidel is my dream man. If I can't have him, Che Guevara will do just fine.'"

Consequently, Tynan invited Tennessee to tag along. "His revelation didn't surprise me at all," Tynan said, "because I was aware that Tennessee was not attracted to the typical pretty boy actors of Hollywood as much as he was to rugged macho types like Castro."

When Tynan, with Tennessee, reached Cuba's government headquarters, they were told that Castro was in a cabinet meeting and that he'd make himself available when it was over.

[During this early stage of Castro's administration of Cuba, the U.S. had not yet declared a state of emergency or hostility with the flashy young revolutionary leader. Castro had been a guest in Dwight and Mamie Eisenhower's White House, and the U.S. was pursuing a course of watching, waiting, and evaluating their strategies that affected Cuba and the U.S. presence and investments there. All of that would radically change with the debut of the Cuban missile crisis under JFK's administration in 1961.]

Tennessee later recalled, "We sat around until five o'clock before we were ushered in, but it was worth it. When I was introduced to Castro, he called me 'The Cat Man.' I was flattered that he'd heard of my play, *Cat on a Hot Tin Roof.*"

With a trusted aide at hand, Castro granted Tynan his interview, in which he discussed the goals and intentions of the United States in its relationship with Revolutionary Cuba. Tynan was then dismissed, but Tennessee was asked to remain for a private meeting with Castro.

"At long last, I was alone with my idol, *[except for an interpreter, although Tennessee suspected that Castro spoke and understood English]* though I felt he didn't plan to rape me,"

Castro told him that before he became a revolutionary solder, he'd wanted to be an actor. "I once appeared uncredited in a film shot in Mexico," Castro revealed. "I had only one line of dialogue. I think I should buy up all the copies."

After this preliminary chat, Castro got to the point of their secret huddle. "What do you know about the film that producer, Jerry Wald, intends to make about my early life, and the events leading up to the overthrow of the government?"

"I do know something," Tennessee said. "A screenwriter friend of mine, Meade Roberts, has been hired to write the screenplay. He also has expressed interest in adapting two of my plays for the screen."

[Tennessee was referring to the upcoming movies, The Fugitive Kind (1960), which would star Marlon Brando, and Summer and Smoke (1961), in which Geraldine Page and Laurence Harvey took the lead roles.]

"I understand that your friend, Marlon Brando, has been offered the chance to play me on the screen," Castro said. "I think Brando would be ideal. I saw him play your character in that Desire Streetcar movie."

"I didn't know the role of 'Revolutionary Castro' had been offered to Marlon," Tennessee said. "But I think he'd be ideal. Marlon is a revolutionary, too, in his own way."

"I want you to do me a big favor," Castro said. "Be a sort of eyes and ears for me in Hollywood. Please call Roberts and Brando when you get back and report to me about what's going on with the film. Now for the big surprise. I also want you to contact Marilyn Monroe. I'm sure she's a friend of yours. Several people have told me that she's spoken out in favor of me and my revolution. Not only that—from what I hear she's got this big fat infatuation with me."

"Who hasn't?" Tennessee asked, signaling his interest, which Castro did not acknowledge.

"Since it's a Hollywood film, I know some ro-

In the early 1950s, **Fidel Castro** dreamed of becoming a Spanish speaking movie star, and he appeared in a movie shot in Mexico.

He was also a devotee of American cinema, with Marilyn Monroe being his dreamgirl.

The **Revolutionary Castro** was photographed in the Cuban Sierra in 1958 before his descent on Havana. He survived countless assassination attempts by the CIA and the Mafia. He is today both a myth and an icon. To the very end, he stuck to his original slogan— "Socialism or Death."

mantic interest will be interjected," Castro said. "I want Roberts to write a strong role for a character based on my mistress in the mountains, to be played by Marilyn. She can be depicted as a guerilla fighter like me."

"I want it to be known that I will provide everything a producer will need to shoot this movie in Cuba," Castro said. "Errol Flynn loved Cuba and was going to launch a film industry here. Maybe Wald's film will be the beginning of many films to be shot in Cuba. It will certainly help our economy."

The moment I return to the States, I will contact Meade, Marlon, and Marilyn to convey your desires," Tennessee promised.

A fiery orator, **Castro** ultimately became a brutal dictator, sending screaming victims to his torture chambers. His links to the Soviet Union during the Cuban missile crisis almost brought on World War III.

"If you'll do all this for me, and keep me informed, I guess you're entitled to something as a reward. I've always suspected from what you've said to several people—I have my spies—that you, like Marilyn, consider me what you Americans call 'a dreamboat.' Is that true?"

"It's useless for me to hide it," Tennessee said. "You are my ideal man."

"I am not a homosexual, but we might work something out," Castro said. "I'm headed for my private steambath right now, and I'm inviting you to come along. But I must warn you: It's mainly to give you the voyeur's pleasure of taking a good look. If anything happens—and I don't know that it will—it can only be from the waist down. Anything above my waist is strictly off limits."

"*Anything* would be the fulfillment of a dream to me," Tennessee responded.

Then, Tennessee disappeared with Castro into his private quarters for the next two hours. It's known that both of them entered the steambath nude and that later, each received massages from two young Cuban women. Whatever else happened is not known.

Tennessee refused to tell Tynan, or even Marion Vaccaro. To her, he said, "I don't want to be rounded up and castrated, which I'm told is the punishment for homosexuals in Cuba."

However, after his return to Florida, New York, and then Hollywood, he set about fulfilling Castro's requests.

NO EXIT: Tennessee's Interactions with Jean-Paul Sartre & Simone de Beauvoir

Later that evening, after time spent with Castro, Kenneth Tynan arranged for Tennessee to meet Jean-Paul Sartre and his mistress, Simone de Beauvoir, at a café in Havana. Previously, after encountering these French existential writers in Paris, he had invited them to a party. Neither of them had showed up.

Before meeting them, Tennessee fully understood that both of them were spectacularly distinguished figures in the world of French letters. Yet he had never read any of their works. Consequently, Tynan delivered a brief overview of their status and literary/theatrical accomplishments.

[One of the leading figures in post-World War II French philosophy and Marxism, and a key player in the philosophy of existentialism and phenomenology, Jean-Paul Sartre (1905-1980) was a French philosopher, playwright, literary critic, novelist, screenwriter, and political activist.

Although he was awarded the Nobel Prize for Literature in 1964, he refused it, saying that he always declined official honors and that "a writer should not allow himself to be turned into an institution." Eventually, he rejected the concept of Literature itself, having concluded that it functioned ultimately as a bourgeois substitute for genuine commitment in the world.

His work influenced post-colonial political theory, radical politics, sociology, and concepts of the absurd. When French President Charles de Gaulle was asked by his security forces whether Sartre should be arrested because of his involvement in the anarchist/student riots of 1968, De Gaulle answered, "One should not attempt to arrest Voltaire."

For years, Sartre was closely associated with the prominent feminist theorist Simone de Beauvoir (1908-1986), with whom he shares a grave in Paris' Montparnasse Cemetery.

Among other seminal works, De Beauvoir was known for her treatise The Second Sex. *Originally published in French, in Paris, in 1949, and later translated and distributed worldwide, it's interpreted as a seminal tract of contemporary feminism.]*

"My God, these two sound like someone Gore Vidal should meet," Tennessee said. "I can't talk about any subjects that might interest them. I'll have to look for little windows in our con-

French writers and intellectuals **Jean-Paul Sartre** and **Simone de Beauvoir** were lovers. Before meeting with them in Havana, Tennessee feared, "I'm too low brow to carry on a conversation with them."

Although at first they were supporters of Castro and his revolution, the pair ultimately turned on him because of his atrocities. In the late 1960s, they charged in the French daily, *Le Monde*, that Castro was imposing the same repressive system on Cuba that Stalin had forced on the socialist countries.

versation, where I can interject a thought or two without appearing like a bare-foot boy from Mississippi."

Later, Tennessee recalled that De Beauvoir was "the icy lady," although Sartre was far more gracious. "I understand, Mr. Williams, that you write plays."

"I attempt it," Tennessee said. "I'm also told that you, too, write plays."

"The play of mine that might interest you most is called *Les Mains sales (Dirty Hands;* 1948). In it, I explore the problems associated with being a polit-ically engaged intellectual."

"I think that Mr. Williams would find your play, *Huis clos (No Exit)* closer to his own personal dilemma," De Beauvoir said, enigmatically.

"Among those of your plays produced in Paris, which might interest me the most?" Sartre asked.

"You've already missed out," Tennessee said. "Jean Cocteau organized and produced a very French, very 'Cocteau' version of *A Streetcar Named De-sire.* I think he somehow managed to interject Marie Antoinette into this back-street drama in New Orleans. Cocteau wanted to direct the play, at least originally, as a vehicle for his lover, Jean Marais."

"I remember my first meeting with Cocteau," De Beauvoir said. "I was with Jean Genet. Cocteau's torrential flow of conversation made me dizzy. He spoke with acrobatic dexterity. With his hands, he traced hypnotic arabesques in mid-air. He has a narcissistic streak, but that does not restrict his vision."

"Unlike me, Cocteau believes the poet should hold himself aloof from the follies of war and politics," Sartre said.

"He told me that Hitler's sheer celebrity mitigated his crime. In his words, 'Folly is the prerogative of a Lord, and a Lord is he who lords.'"

"I also met your friend, Mr. Genet," Tennessee said. "He reminded me of Mickey Rooney. Speaking of Hitler, I'll always remember a story Genet told us. He said that something good came out of the Nazi invasion of Paris. He claimed that the city was filled with beautiful, blonde-haired, blue-eyed young men who turned to Genet and his gay friends for love on the darkest night. The soldiers of the Third Reich might be raping the French people, but Genet considered each of his rapes from a Nazi soldier as an absolute delight."

"Perhaps it's better that a Nazi soldier turn to one for love-making instead of some more hideous assault," Tynan said in one of the few comments he contributed that evening.

"I came to Cuba to meet Castro and to speak with Che Guevara," Sartre said."Che is not only an intellectual, but also the most complete human being of our Age. He is the most perfect man of the 20th Century."

"I, too, have a crush on Che," Tennessee said. "And I've never met him. What about Castro?"

"For the most part, I am in sympathy with his goals," Sartre said. "However, I told him that I am violently against the persecution of homosexuals by his regime. To his face, I compared such horrendous activity as comparable to the Nazi persecution of the Jews. Homosexuals are the Jews of Cuba."

"I, too, have identified and felt sympathy for the plight of the homosexual,"

De Beauvoir said. "Like the homosexual, women historically have been considered deviant, abnormal. Men have been held up as the ideal toward which women should aspire. Such an ideal limits a woman's success, as it does for the homosexual. For feminists, and homosexuals, to assume their rightful place in society, these old assumptions about emulating 'normality' must be set aside forever. And that's because both groups have always believed in transcendence, a lofty plâteau where one, a woman or a homosexual, needs to take responsibility for oneself in a world where one chooses one's freedom."

After acknowledging De Beauvoir's artfully passionate speech, Tennessee rose from the table, reaching for Tynan's hand. "It's getting late and I must meet my lady friend, a wonderful poet named Marion Vaccaro. She and I plan to spend the rest of the evening in our favorite Havana bordello, the aptly named Garden of Delights. They have such lovely boys there. One thing that can be said of a Cuban boy (and not of an American or French boy): No Cuban boy ever lets you leave his bed unsatisfied."

Then he turned to Sartre. "Are you here to patronize the bordellos?"

"I do not need to patronize bordellos like Genet," Sartre said. "Simone and I are perfectly content with each other. However, when she senses I am growing bored and need more stimulation, she will introduce me to one of her young female lovers."

"I am so very gratified that both of you stand up for us lesser mortals when faced with tyranny," Tennessee said. Then he kissed both Sartre and De Beauvoir on both of their respective cheeks and parted from Tynan in anticipation of meeting Marion for a night in the bordellos. Later, at the bordello, they would occupy adjoining rooms with paper-thin walls.

Tennessee recalled, "That way I could use peepholes to check up on the action next door to me, and Marion could do the same. On some nights, each of us liked what was on the other side more than what we'd already bought and paid for, and we'd quickly change partners and proceed with our erotic dance."

Marilyn Monroe: "Revelations from a Tarnished Heart"

In New York, Marlon Brando was the first person Tennessee called. The actor said he'd like "to appear as Fidel on the screen, but it all depends on the script. If it's written by John Foster Dulles *[then the hawkish U.S. Secretary of State]*, NO WAY!"

"But if Castro is played as a true revolutionary, a friend to the downtrodden," Marlon continued, "then I'll green light it. As for Marilyn, my sweet babe, I've always wanted to star in a movie with her. I think on screen together, we'd be dynamite."

Producer Jerry Wald seemed elated with Castro's invitation to turn over Cuba's facilities and perhaps financial aid to a film crew arriving on his shores.

Tennessee had always interpreted Wald as an intriguing character, as he

512

was said to have been the model for Budd Schulberg's novel, *What Makes Sammy Run?*.

After talking to him, Tennessee told his literary agent, Audrey Wood, "Jerry is a vulgarian in the David O. Selznick mold, but he has a brutal instinct for what will play on the screen. We might consider him as the producer of one of my plays. If he can conquer Hemingway and D.H. Lawrence, why not Tennessee Williams? Although right now, I hear that in addition to the Castro project, he's buried deep in a film adaptation of Joyce's *Ulysses*."

After his dialogue with Wald, Tennessee sent a message to Castro that he would be presented in a favorable light on the screen, regardless of the reservations of the Eisenhower administration.

Tennessee also placed a call to Meade Roberts, who told him he was halfway through writing a script. When Meade heard that Marilyn might get involved, he promised to rewrite the woman's role, making it as strong as that of the male lead.

Roberts was the first to reveal to the world at large that Tennessee had a crush on Castro. Even before he met Castro, Tennessee once told Roberts that he'd dreamed of being kidnapped by Castro and Che Guevara and being reconfigured as their love slave.

"He wanted me to go to Cuba with him, way back when Castro and his guerillas were still hiding out in the mountains. I told him, 'If you go and get kidnapped, MCA will ransom you. After all, you're Tennessee Williams. No one will ransom me. I'm only Meade Roberts.'"

Brando had told Tennessee that he felt Marilyn Monroe would be most receptive to portraying Castro's mistress in any film shot in Cuba. Tennessee found politics boring, and until he talked to Brando, he didn't realize that Marilyn, in the wake of her marriage to a left-wing playwright, Arthur Miller, had become increasingly political. "She's even to the left of her husband," Brando claimed.

Marilyn had joined SANE (Committee for a Sane Nuclear Policy). She signed up with fellow stars who included Brando, Shirley MacLaine, Peter Lawford, and Gene Kelly.

In the late 1950s, Marilyn had begun to seek out men who sharpened her awareness of international politics. She'd become a friend of Lester Markel, the Sunday Editor of *The New York Times.* At one point, he took her on a tour of that newspaper's offices.

From Hollywood, she wrote to Markel, stating her view that American newspapers were biased against "Fidel C.," her obvious nickname for Castro. After she was elected alternate delegate to the Connecticut Democratic caucus, she began to announce her views on the men she wanted to run for the highest two offices in 1960.

Her choice for president was William O. Douglas, the Supreme Court Justice. She feared that his divorce might be a strike against him, especially among Catholic voters. "To balance that factor," Marilyn claimed, "why not run a charismatic young politician as the vice presidential candidate. John F. Kennedy."

Then she muffled a giggle. "I found Jack very presidential."

When JFK was nominated for president, Marilyn actively campaigned for him, attending rallies at the home of her former lover, Peter Lawford, who was married at the time to Patricia Kennedy. Tennessee accompanied Marilyn to one of these fund-raising rallies and contributed $1,000 to JFK's political campaign.

Marilyn once stated her own policy toward Cuba, a set of ideas which she shared with Tennessee: "I think Fidel C. is awfully cute and very, very sexy."

"I saw him first, Queenie," Tennessee said jokingly.

"The Batista regime was bleeding Cuba dry," Marilyn said. "I heard the brutal dictator stashed away billions in Swiss banks. I think Fidel C. is a true man of the people. He is the savior of his country, regardless of what Eisenhower and Dulles think."

Tennessee transmitted Castro's invitation for Marilyn to visit him in Havana and to star as his mistress in a movie about his revolutionary days. "I will be his mistress both on and off the screen," she told Tennessee, who reported it and all the other developments associated with events in Cuba to his lover, Frank Merlo.

Around the same time, in a real life drama that seemed like something out of a Hollywood movie itself, Marilyn increased her sexual involvement with JFK, an affair that had actually begun in the 1950s. To complicate matters even more, she also launched an affair with Robert F. Kennedy, then the Attorney General of the United States.

Presumably, over "pillow talk," RFK indiscreetly told her about the government's plans to murder Castro.

Rumors circulated about JFK and Marilyn, at least among the press corps, but her affair with RFK was not well known. Arthur Schlesinger, a Kennedy loyalist and RFK biographer, later said, "Bobby was human. He liked to drink and he liked young women. He indulged that liking when he traveled, and he had to travel a great deal, especially to California."

Marilyn had long been involved with Johnny Roselli, mob boss Sam Giancana's West Coast henchman. For a time, Giancana became secretly involved with the CIA in a plan to assassinate Castro. When Roselli became embroiled, he came up with his own scheme, one involving Marilyn.

Roselli had learned that she was Castro's favorite movie star. He also knew that the Cuban leader would extend an invitation to her to visit him in Havana if she asked.

At the time that Roselli was plotting such a trip for Marilyn, he seemed unaware that Tennessee had already involved her in another, entirely separate, invitation to visit Cuba to make a film.

"With Marilyn in Havana, Castro would surely want to pop her," Roselli told his associates. "We could arrange for Marilyn to poison him, using some kind of

Gangster **Johnny Roselli** wanted to lure Marilyn Monroe into a plot to poison Castro in Havana. Later, he was part of the cabal sent to murder Marilyn herself.

chemical that didn't take effect right away, giving her time to get her shapely ass out of the country."

A renegade cabal found the plot bizarre, citing how risky it was. But Roselli moved ahead with his plan anyway.

Giancana ordered Roselli to visit Marilyn in New York to see if she'd participate in such an grisly and outlandish scheme. "Even with the blackmail we have on Marilyn, including all those incriminating photographs we have, we can't force her into a stunt like this," Giancana said. "She might even think we're insane. And we're not at all sure she'd want to take such a risk. Just because she's fucking our new President doesn't make her a super patriot."

When she met with Roselli, Marilyn pretended to acquiesce with his scheme to kill Castro. But her real objective involved double-crossing both Roselli and Giancana. She wanted to get as much information about the plot as she could, and then fly to Havana to warn Castro about what was going on.

At least that is what she reported to Tennessee.

During the months ahead, the worlds spinning around Marilyn grew even more complicated. She told Tennessee that over "pillow talk" with RFK, she'd learned that he, too, was spearheading yet another plot to kill Castro.

"Apparently, Marilyn had many arguments, even fights, with our esteemed Attorney General over his plan to eliminate Castro," Tennessee said. "She argued against it, and in retaliation, Bobby accused her of being soft on Communism."

To an increasing degree, Marilyn was being influenced by a former lover, Frederick Vanderbilt Field, who was at the time living in Mexico City. The wealthy scion of the Vanderbilts had been charged with communist activities and had served a jail term. After he was released from prison, he began an expatriate life in Mexico City. He influenced Marilyn' s political beliefs. Vanderbilt himself was a strong supporter of Castro and his revolution.

Marilyn's involvement with both Roselli and with her communist and/or socialist friends did not escape the attention of J. Edgar Hoover at the FBI. At one point, agents were feverishly compiling dossiers on both Tennessee and Marilyn. She was viewed as a potential threat to the security of the United States. Tennessee, however, was ultimately dismissed as "a harmless faggot."

An agent concluded that the playwright was more interested in visiting the all-male bordellos of Havana than he was in any political activities. "After Castro shut down the whorehouses, Mr. Williams lost interest in visiting Cuba," an agent concluded.

After the disastrous fiasco associated with the Invasion of the Bay of Pigs [April, 1961], increased complications—including the threat of a nuclear war— prompted producer Jerry Wald to shelve the plans for a film about Castro.

Meade Roberts was told "It's too hot, too controversial. I've got to pull the plug. Marlon has bowed out, and I've told Marilyn it's off."

***

515

Both Marilyn and Tennessee were heavily drugged during the 1960s, and not always the most coherent of people. *[Wald and Marilyn would each die in 1962.]*

Robert Slatzer, Marilyn's former lover and longtime friend, was allowed to read pages in her Red Diary, in which she wrote about the plot to kill Castro.

José Bolanõs, Marilyn's last lover, an actor wannabe, later claimed that Marilyn did visit Castro. "She left Mexico City in disguise and flew to Havana. I warned her that she was playing a dangerous game, but she didn't listen to me. She told me she was going to inform Castro of what was going on with Bobby Kennedy. Because the Kennedys were cutting her off, she remained loyal to Castro.

"I met Marilyn at the airport when she flew back to Mexico City, but she refused to tell me what had happened during her time with Castro. I just assumed they'd had an affair," Bolaños claimed.

"She was consuming large amount of alcohol and drugs, and seemed confused about what she was actually doing," Bolaños said. "It was a terrible time, I feared Marilyn was self-destructing."

Tennessee left several messages for Marilyn to call him, but he later reported, "She never did. The last time I talked to her, she seemed completely unglued. But so was I at the time."

After Marilyn's death during August of 1962, Tennessee, for several weeks, attempted to write a play he'd entitled *Revelations from a Tarnished Heart*. The plot would follow somewhat that of *The Milk Train Doesn't Stop Here Anymore*. In both plays, an aging actress would be depicted dictating her memoirs.

In *Revelations,* the blonde goddess, a facsimile of Marilyn, would be having an affair with a handsome, dashing American president, as well as a charismatic young dictator of some Latin American country. These two men are arch enemies, threatening to destroy each other, and the goddess runs back and forth between each of their ideologies and each of their beds.

The dictator, depicted as a "sex god," was not modeled on Castro, but on Tennessee's fantasy version of Porfirio Rubirosa, the Dominican playboy.

Most of *Revelations* would take place as the goddess fretfully lay in bed, dictating her memoirs. There would be flashbacks to the bedrooms of both the U.S. President and that of the Latino dictator.

Eventually, Tennessee abandoned the project, as he had abandoned so many other plays in his past. At his home in Key West, he told author James Leo Herlihy and Stanley Mills Haggart that, "I decided I really didn't know enough about political intrigue to pull this one off. Besides, I think if I had gone forward, I would have been murdered. They got Marilyn. Maybe I would have been next. I definitely felt my life would be in jeopardy should I have continued. The play contained too many dangerous secrets, and sometimes you can know too much for your own good."

Chapter Thirty-Six

"I Want To Be Mrs. Tennessee Williams"

—Diana Barrymore

The Curse of the Barrymores

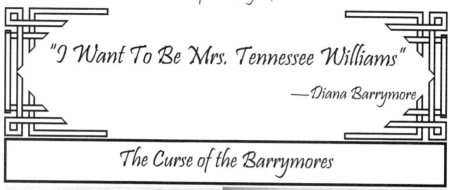

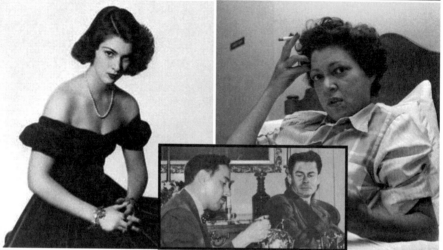

Once hailed as a great beauty, **Diana Barrymore** *(left)* disintegrated into suicidal depression and alcoholism *(far right)*. She told Tennessee, "I've lost my way. I was John Barrymore's daughter, and I never lived up to my promise. Neither did he. But I'm going to try to find my way back."

That never happened. She never found the road back, and was possibly murdered.

For a time, she lived with Tennessee. "She could outdrink me," he said. "Bloody Marys to start the day. Martinis all afternoon. Straight gin to fortify her until dinner--a quart of it. Three stingers before the meal arrives. A double brandy with soda throughout the meal. After dinner, she orders a demitasse. (She) pours out half the coffee and replaces it with brandy. Then eight more stingers before she rises and staggers to her feet."

Photo insert: **Tennessee** chats with poet **Gilbert Maxwell** in 1945.

In the final year (1960) of Dinah Barrymore's life, both Tennessee Williams and one of his best friends, the poet Gilbert Maxwell, would become intimately involved in her turbulent murk. Maxwell would fall in love with her, and she would fall in love with Tennessee.

Tennessee's brother, Dakin Williams, summed up his sibling's romantic entanglements at the time: "If Tennessee had put such a scene in a play, no one would have believed it or accepted it: A poet *[Gilbert Maxwell]* is in love with a beautiful and talented but flawed actress *[Diana Barrymore]* who is (or says she is) in love with a famous playwright *[Tennessee Williams]*, who in turn is in love, spiritually, with his sister *[Rose Williams]*, who had become a kind of lovely china doll, and he is living in sin with a former pharmacist's mate in the Navy *[Frank Merlo]*."

The American film and stage actress, Diana Barrymore (1921-1960), was the daughter of "The Great Profile," John Barrymore, and the second of his four wives, Blanche Oelrichs, a poet, playwright, and theater actress known by her pseudonym, "Michael Strange." *[John Barrymore's stormy marriage to Oelrichs lasted from 1920 to 1925.]*

John Barrymore, *(depicted above)* squandered one of the great talents of the American theater, as he descended into acute alcoholism. When this picture was taken at the end of his life in 1942, stage memories of his Hamlet, Richard III, and Mercutio had faded. He was making "B" pictures, a grotesque parady of himself.

Introduced to John by one of his leading ladies, Cathleen Nesbitt, Blanche had been defined as "the most beautiful woman in America" by the French portrait artist Paul Helleu.

As she was growing up, Diana had little contact with her estranged father. During a perfunctory reunion with his daughter after an absence of many years, the famous star of the stage and silent screen said, "you are my little girl three wives back, are you not?"

She later remarked, "Father wasn't really certain just who I was."

A casual remark made by her father wounded her deeply. "Diana is a horse's arse, quite a pretty one, but still a horse's arse."

Before she even left school, she had evolved into a flamboyant alcoholic. Even so, she decided to pursue a career as a movie star, mainly because of her beauty and her famous association with the Barrymore name.

Diana and her mother also became estranged, especially beginning in the summer of 1942, when Blanche became romantically involved with her lifetime companion, Margaret Wise Brown, the author of many children's books.

That summer, Diana signed a contract with Universal, which launched a

"Diana was murdered. She did not commit suicide."

—Tennessee Williams

major publicity campaign, billing her as "The Year's Most Sensational New Screen Personality." She became bogged down in booze and drugs, and she was soon disparaged as "The Barrymore Brat" around Universal. Studio chiefs felt she was following in her father's self-destructive footsteps. He'd died in 1942, broke and drunk after a long run of forgettable "B" pictures.

Diana would emulate her father's behavior with a series of drug-related disasters punctuated with severe depressions, extended stays in sanitariums, and suicide threats.

Diana also had a sex addiction. Arthur Lubin directed her first picture *Eagle Squadron* (1942) in which she co-starred with Jon Hall. Lubin said, "She was oversexed—that girl couldn't get enough. If I needed her to film a scene, she could always be found in one of the men's dressing rooms, usually that of Jon Hall. She wore him out so much he didn't have much left to give to his screen role."

As the world braced for its most disastrous war, **Diana Barrymore** posed as a bathing beauty for the July 31, 1939 edition of *Life* magazine. With her stellar pedigree, she was set to pursue a career as an actress. The prediction was that she would have a fabulous screen career.

After Hall, Diana set out to seduce some of the leading male actors of her day. The list is long—Eddie Albert, George Brent, Rory Calhoun, Brian Donlevy, Henry Fonda, Van Heflin, Leif Erickson, cowboy icon Lash LaRue, Victor Mature, Don Porter, and James Stewart. Somehow, she managed also to seduce the famous novelist, Sinclair Lewis.

When Blanche died in 1950, Diana was left with only $300, all that remained of a once-vast family fortune.

In 1949, Diana was offered her own television talk show, but she failed to show up for its premiere broadcast. If she had, she would have been the host of the first TV talk show in history.

During part of the 1950s, Diana entered into the lowest point of her life, becoming a virtual derelict, shoplifting and stealing vegetables from a supermarket. A doctor warned her, "You're on a dreadful merry-go-round: Alcohol, barbiturates, stimulants. If you don't get off quickly, you will die."

In 1957, Diana published her autobiography, as relayed to Gerold Frank. Entitled *Too Much, Too Soon,* a Cinderella story told in reverse order, it became a bestseller. Tennessee read it avidly, believing that he understood this troubled actress, who had been born to a heritage of beauty, breeding, and wealth, but who had stumbled tragically through a blighted life.

He was touched by her uninhibited published account of her notorious life. After having suffered through the depths of degradation, she finally summoned the courage to pull herself up and valiantly start again, trying her chance on the stage. She played Maggie the Cat in 1958 in a road show version of *Cat on a Hot Tin Roof,* and received respectable reviews.

In Philadelphia, she appeared in another of Tennessee's plays, this time interpreting the key role of Blanche DuBois in *A Streetcar Named Desire.* By this time, Diana had met the poet, Gilbert Maxwell, who had become besotted with her. She urged him to prevail upon Tennessee to drive to Philadelphia to watch her perform as Blanche.

Two weeks before the Philadelphia premiere, she'd suffered a tragic accident. One night, she'd taken two sleeping pills, but awoke at midnight. Famished, she went to the kitchen and, in her drowsy condition, put an entire stick of butter into an iron skillet in which she planned to scramble some eggs.

Before she could scramble the eggs, she fainted, falling against the skillet. As she collapsed onto the floor, the hot butter in the skillet scalded her right thigh, seriously damaging it. She managed to call for an ambulance and was rushed to the hospital.

The first doctor who examined her gave her some alarming news: "Miss Barrymore, your leg might have to be amputated." Somehow, her fighting spirit was aroused, and she summoned other specialists, who were able to save her leg. When she returned to rehearsals in anticipation of her Philadelphia premiere, she was still in severe pain, with an obviously bandaged leg.

Gilbert and Tennessee arrived in Philadelphia to watch Diana perform as Blanche during the late spring of 1959.

Tennessee sensed the physical pain she endured during her appearance as Blanche. "I suspected she was on the bottle again," he told Gilbert. "At one point, when she sat down, she looked as if she had throbbing hemorrhoids. But through it all, she displayed a certain gallantry, and the powerful Barrymore madness got her through her last three scenes brilliantly."

Maxwell, still enamored with her at the time, was the first to reach her backstage. "In the harsh glare of a backstage exposed light, I saw that the bones of her neck and spine, revealed in a low-cut black dress, were much too evident. She was a sort of urchin-girl-woman, too thin, too high strung, supersensitive, and somehow touching."

When Tennessee encountered Diana backstage, he said, "Her dress was soaked with perspiration, as if she had been standing under a shower. When I embraced her, I was frightened because her breast was heaving with such a dangerous intensity. I whispered to her manager, 'Don't you think we'd better call a doctor?'"

Tennessee's Coven of Lost Women

Another close friend of Tennessee's, Paul Bigelow, noticed that "Diana Barrymore soon joined Tenn's coven of lost ladies, who included Maria St. Just and Marion Vaccaro. Diana saw in him a savior for both herself and her career. Like the other ladies, she imposed on him. She was invited to do so because he saw her as a defeated soul in every way, much like himself, and so, he took her on as a project. This, of course, turned out very badly, very savagely, with a good deal of mutual abuse."

The director of the Philadelphia production of *Streetcar,* George Keathley *[founding director of the Studio M Playhouse, a theater in Coral Gables, Florida]*, observed both Tennessee and Diana during that summer of 1959. "Both of them were drinking heavily and taking far too many drugs," he asserted. "Diana also procured young men for Tennessee, the way the Elizabeth Taylor character did for the fictional Sebastian in *Suddenly Last Summer.* She also helped him dress in drag for private parties, something I'd never heard that he'd done before. In spite of all this, she believed that Tennessee might not permanently be a homosexual. She became passionately dedicated to turning him straight."

Diana soon became a fixture in his life. They were seen everywhere together, from New York to Key West, from Havana to Rome. Newspaper columnists, feigning to appear more innocent than they really were, predicted that wedding bells would soon be ringing.

Even Audrey Wood, who should have known better, told Tennessee, "I don't think it will be long before I'm a flower girl at your wedding."

From Rome, Diana wrote to Dakin Williams: "Our trip to Italy has been idyllic, although Tennessee also took along Marion Vaccaro. I have never been so happy. Just to sit at your brother's feet and to light his cigarettes is pure joy."

Back in New York, Diana bought a new blue mink coat, and wore it as Tennessee accompanied her to the theater and to dinner at Sardi's. Once, he took her to a performance of his one-act play, *I Rise in Flame, Cried the Phoenix,* starring Alfred Ryder in Tennessee's overview of one of his idols, D.H. Lawrence. Viveca Lindfors played Lawrence's wife, Frieda.

[Many critics claim that D.H. Lawrence was Tennessee's major literary inspiration, although Tennessee himself claimed that it was Anton Chekhov first, then Lawrence. Donald Windham and Tennessee had based their joint play, You Touched Me!, *on a short story by Lawrence. Frieda, his widow, had granted the rights.*

In addition to that, Tennessee wanted to write his own play about D.H. and Frieda—hence, the Phoenix *drama. He wrote, "Lawrence felt the mystery and power of sex as the primal life urge, and was the life-long adversary of those who wanted to*

"**D.H. Lawrence** (*left*) was a highly *simpatico* figure in my literary upbringing," said Tennessee. "The collaborative play I wrote with Donald Windham, *You Touched Me!,* was based on a Lawrence short story. I visited his widow, **Frieda** (*right*), when her husband died. She wrote a beautiful, unsentimental memoir. As he lay dying, he said, 'I think it's time for the morphine.'"

keep the subject locked away in the cellars of prudery. Much of his work is chaotic and distorted by tangent obsessions, such as his insistence upon woman's subservience to the male, but all in all, his work is probably the greatest modern monument to the dark roots of creation."]

Diana took Tennessee to see the film adaptation (*Too Much, Too Soon*; 1958) of her infamous autobiography. Dorothy Malone starred in it as Diana, and a debauched-looking Errol Flynn played John Barrymore, who had been one of Flynn's best friends and drinking partners.

Tennessee and Diana shared many intimate secrets together. One night, when she made it clear that she wanted him to be her fourth husband, he asked her about the first three. She'd been married to the actor and tennis player Bramwell Fletcher (from 1942-1946); John Howard (for a brief period in 1947); and finally another actor, Robert Wilcox (from 1950-1955). "Of them all, Wilcox was the love of my life, although he once nearly beat me to death during one of his violent assaults on me."

She seemed to hold no grudge against Wilcox: "Noël Coward told me that a woman should be struck regularly, like a gong. He's right. Women are no damn good." She went on to tell Tennessee that the only writers she ever read were Ellery Queen and Tennessee himself.

Most of these revelations took place in her Manhattan apartment, its walls covered with framed photographs of John Barrymore. She always made herself up to look especially lovely for Tennessee. He remembered one night when she came to the door wearing a scarlet silk blouse, tapered black slacks, and ballet slippers that she claimed were once owned by Pavlova.

"I felt she was a woman trying to save her own life from the depths she'd known," he said. "She seemed to be desperately reaching out for that affection that had been denied to her by her parents. She seemed so eager to please me that she was almost living in a perpetual state of panic."

In 1957, Diana Barrymore published her best-selling memoir, *Too Much, Too Soon*, a "Cinderella in reverse" story.

She desperately wanted to recover and to inform all those columnists (especially Walter Winchell and Hedda Hopper), that she was on top once again, no longer the girl whose "bloated face and drunken grin" had been sprawled across the front page of so many tabloids. That day never came.

In a scene from the movie adaptation of her memoir, **Errol Flynn**, cast as Diana's father (John Barrymore), confronts **Dorothy Malone**, playing Diana.

Diana projected a glorious future for herself *[as an actress]*, and for Tennessee *[as a playwright]* on Broadway. "You'll write great roles for a woman, and I'll star in them. You and I will become the hottest ticket on Broadway."

Their "romance" often encountered hurdles, many of them from Frank Merlo, who was already sifting through the embers of the fire that had once burned so passionately between Tennessee and himself. One night, Tennessee invited Diana, Anna Magnani, and Marion Vaccaro to his Manhattan apartment for drinks and a light supper.

Early in the evening, Audrey Wood telephoned and said that she needed the final draft of *Period of Adjustment,* Tennessee's most recent play at the time, before her meeting with backers the following morning. Frank was dispatched to deliver the script to her home.

When Frank returned, he found Magnani chatting in the living room with Vaccaro. He barged into the bedroom to find Tennessee in a huddle with Diana. He dragged her out of the bedroom and pushed her across the living room and out the door. He was normally friendly with Magnani, but that night he viewed her as "one of the co-conspirators," so a few minutes later, after screaming denunciations, he tossed the Italian diva out of the apartment, as well as Vaccaro.

All of their respective relationships survived that violent night, but bigger problems for Tennessee and Diana loomed on the horizon.

The Sweet Bird of Youth
Doesn't Fly Over the House Anymore

Shortly after Tennessee let Diana Barrymore read the first draft of his *Sweet Bird of Youth [which eventually opened on Broadway in 1959],* she rushed to see him at once. "You have written the perfect role for me, the part that will put me over the top. I'm destined to play the Princess Kosmonopolis or, as you also call her, Alexandra del Lago. *I AM THAT PERSON.* I understand her to my toenails."

He was hesitant, as he was engaged in private negotiations with Geraldine Page, discussing the possibility of her in the role opposite Paul Newman, whose interest in appearing in the play had already been expressed.

Under heavy pressure, Tennessee arranged a reading for Diana in front of Elia Kazan. Neither Tennessee nor Kazan were impressed with her delivery.

"She held no surprises in the role," Tennessee said. "She failed to grasp the nuance of the character of the princess. She so identified with the character that she was simply reading her lines instead of getting into the part."

At the end of her reading, Tennessee said, "I had to live through one of the most painful moments of my life. I had to tell her, 'Diana, this is simply not your role.'"

Later that afternoon, Diana threw herself into Gilbert Maxwell's arms. "My hatred of Kazan burns black," she said. "If he had not wanted to play Svengali to Miss Page, I would have been cast in the Broadway production. That woman is *me*—I, too, was *FINISHED* at the age of thirty-six—I AM Alexandra del Lago."

She later relayed to Gilbert a story about how, one afternoon, she slipped into the theater and watched Page and Newman in a complete dress rehearsal of *Sweet Bird of Youth*. "I was chain smoking and biting my fingernails," she said. "I was like a hungry dinosaur devouring flesh. Page was playing my role."

Diana was equally outraged by Paul Newman. As she later told Gilbert: "I have no respect for this boy whore. He's an actor who has prostituted himself before playwrights and directors in his younger days. Do I have to name them? Tennessee himself, William Inge, Joshua Logan. Newman used that pretty face and great body, plus a minimum of talent, to advance himself as an actor. I have never found myself spread-eagled on anyone's casting couch, and I never will. I was never as morally callous as Newman is."

Gilbert said that at no time did Diana ever attack Tennessee. "Her love for him, however, turned out to be just short of traumatic."

She did vow that day to "move heaven and earth" to play Alexandra del Lago in its London production. But that was not to be, either.

Later, Diana told Tennessee, "I know I've lost the role on Broadway, but I want to play the Princess in the London production. Standing before you, in the flesh, is the REAL Alexandra del Lago."

Tennessee, however, was still unconvinced. Consequently, he offered a consolation prize.

Diana Barrymore—Live Fast, Die Young

Tennessee arranged with director Herbert Machiz to schedule a reading for Diana during the casting of the pivotal role of Catherine Holly *[the role famously interpreted by Elizabeth Taylor in the film version]* for the Chicago stage production of *Suddenly Last Summer*. "It was a magnificent reading, and she performed brilliantly," Tennessee said. Consequently, he agreed to fly to Chicago for the premiere of this road show.

He later wrote that, "My foredoomed friend, Diana Barrymore, made a great personal success in Chicago, with Cathleen Nesbitt, John Barrymore's former friend, cast as Violet Venable."

After Chicago, he flew to Key West to work on future projects.

It was here, on January 25, 1960, that he received word from Gilbert: "Diana was found dead this morning."

The official report was that she had died from an overdose of liquor and sleeping capsules.

Suffering both guilt and grief, Tennessee flew north to attend the funeral. At the gravesite, he chatted with Violla Rubber, Diana's former manager.

"She told me that when they discovered the body, Diana's bedroom was in absolute shambles," Tennessee said. "It appeared that an act of violence had occurred in spite of the official explanation of her death. She was found naked, face down, with blood streaming out of her mouth. There was a very heavy marble ashtray shattered against the wall, and other evidence of a violent struggle. I think someone murdered her, accidentally perhaps, but she was definitely killed by some other hand. She had succumbed to the curse of the Barrymores."

Diana was known for picking up strange men in bars, usually while intoxicated. Because of her famous name, many hustlers assumed she kept a large stash of money in her apartment. There was speculation that she brought home a hustler who went on a search for money that wasn't there. Perhaps in an altercation, she was killed. Her death was believed to be a random incident, perhaps accidental—not one that was premeditated.

Diana Barrymore
1921-1960; Rest in Peace

Gilbert later wrote that Diana had been "lonely, disturbed, scared, brave, violent, snobbish, resentful, loving, compassionate, and wildly generous. Tennessee and I knew her for little more than about a year before she died—and a woman must be extraordinary to leave behind her, in the minds of two such hardened veterans of emotion, the conviction that neither of our lives has been the same since that bleak winter of her passing."

Sweet Bird Segués into The Roman Spring of Vivien Leigh

In London, a telephone call came in for Vivien Leigh, informing her that the financing for a play about Eva Perón, the former First Lady of Argentina, had collapsed.

Vivien was on the verge of a mental collapse, as she was in the throes of divorcing Laurence Olivier, who wanted to marry a younger actress. Vivien was forty-eight at the time. Olivier had informed her that Joan Plowright, as a condition of their marriage, was insisting that he break off his long-term homosexual relationship with the American comedian, Danny Kaye.

Two weeks later, she met with Tennessee, who was in London at the time. He told her that he wanted her to star as the lead in *The Roman Spring of Mrs. Stone*, and he presented her with a copy of his novella.

It was the story of a fading actress whose husband had had a fatal heart attack on a plane en route to Rome. As a result, she decided to live in Rome, where her loneliness leads her to a dashingly handsome gigolo.

Tennessee told Vivien that Warren Beatty had been cast as the Italian gigolo. She was unfamiliar with his work. She was shown photographs of Beatty. Later, Vivien told her companion and lover, Jack Merivale, "I think there have been some casting couch sessions between Mr. Beatty and Tennessee, but I can't be sure, of course. We'll fly to Rome to make the movie. I hear there's a strong role for Lotte Lenya playing a pimp countess."

The German actress and chanteuse, Lotte Lenya, befriended Vivien during the shooting and became her confidante. "At first, she disliked Beatty intensely, really didn't care for him at all, but he exerted a powerful charm and ended up seducing her."

It has also been reported that Vivien was involved sexually with her handsome, dashing chauffeur, Bernard Gilman.

Richard Burton, who knew Vivien intimately, later said, "She and Beatty were at it in broom closets, across billiard tables, and in telephone kiosks. There also were all these stories that he fucked Tennessee, too."

Later, Tennessee reflected on the short, unhappy life of Vivien.

"Vivien Leigh was the most profoundly lovely actress and woman I ever knew," said Tennessee. "And, she was a warm, generous person. She had no idea she was so ill the last time we met, but I could tell she hadn't long. I glad she went fast. Her film role as Blanche was all her own and quite genuine. But I liked her work in *The Roman Spring of Mrs. Stone*, which is the only film version of anything I wrote that I truly admire. It just worked."

After Donald Windham, Tennessee's longtime friend and fellow author, went to see *Roman Spring*, he said, "This is Tenn's first fictionalized self-portrait after his success, and it displays a hair-raising degree of self-knowledge. For the rest of his life, Tenn, like Mrs. Stone in the film, will be paying a succession of beautiful young boys for the rent of their bodies for the night."

Karen Stone (**Vivien Leigh**) tangles with **Warren Beatty**, cast as an Italian gigolo in *The Roman Spring of Mrs. Stone*.

Chapter Thirty-Seven

Sweet Bird of Youth:
The Actor as Hustler

"Paul Newman Uses Love Like Most Men Use Money"

During its adaptation into a film, director Richard Brooks was assigned the unenviable task of removing the homosexual overtones from Tennessee's play, *Cat on a Hot Tin Roof.* Now, he was faced with what the studio called "censurable material" during the film adaptation of *Sweet Bird of Youth.* It starred **Paul Newman** *(in both photos, above)* as the hustler and **Geraldine Page** *(right)* as the aging actress who pays for his services.

The studio demanded that the ending of the film version be changed. Instead of being castrated at the finale, as Tennessee had written into his play, the hustler (Chance Wayne) would merely get beaten up. And he could not be depicted as having transmitted a venereal disease to his girlfriend, Heavenly Finley. Instead, the plot was revised to show Chance knocking her up, instead.

On the verge of buying out his contract with Warner Brothers, Paul Newman agreed to make one final film for the studio that had held him in bondage for such a long time. He later said, "I had to make *The Young Philadelphians.* They had me trapped, but I knew from the start the picture would be a disaster."

What he really wanted to do, early in 1959, was appear in a drama on

Broadway playing Chance Wayne, the hustler in Tennessee Williams' *Sweet Bird of Youth*. Even as Newman was shooting *The Young Philadelphians*, he was secretly meeting with Tennessee to discuss his involvement in the play and possible actresses who might co-star with him.

Tennessee convinced Newman that he should sign a contract to star in *Sweet Bird of Youth* on Broadway. Asked to comment on his return to the New York stage, Newman said, "You wake up in the middle of the night and find yourself drenched in sweat. You have this terrible fear that your fraud will be discovered, and you'll be back in the dog kennel business. That's why it's good to work on Broadway as well as in Hollywood. You know you'll get the hell kicked out of you once in a while, but if you don't you'll fall back on a lot of tried-and-true tricks an actor always has stashed away in his pocket."

In *Sweet Bird of Youth,* **Paul Newman** and **Geraldine Page** were perfectly cast as the hustler and the has-been über-star.

But when Tennessee had first presented her with the script, Page told him, "I'm not that thrilled at playing a has-been. There are too many Alexandra Del Lagos around as it is. I'm also afraid I'll overact the part, the way Swanson did in *Sunset Blvd.*

Unknown to Newman at the time, Tennessee had first shown the play to Marlon Brando. After reading the script about the doomed hustler—a gigolo servicing the physical and emotional needs of a faded movie star—Brando flew to Key West to discuss his possible involvement. He later dropped out after being told that producer Cheryl Crawford and director Elia Kazan really wanted "pretty boy Newman" in the role.

Brando later regretted that he didn't pursue the role of Chance Wayne more

How the Fading Star of Sunset Blvd.
Inspired the Über-Diva of Sweet Bird of Youth

—

Male Prostitution, Alcoholism, Drug Addiction, Venereal Disease, Racism, and Castration—Each of These Is an Element in Tennessee's Latest Play.

aggressively. "I know more about hustling than Newman," he said. He also regretted not having appeared in the film version of *Cat on a Hot Tin Roof* opposite Elizabeth Taylor. "I know more about being a homosexual than Newman," he said. "It's very clear to me that Tennessee modeled Alexandra del Lago after Tallulah. I surely know how to appear opposite Tallulah better than Newman does. Besides, I hear my prick is bigger than his."

For the role of Alexandra Del Lago (aka Princess Kosmonopolis), Tennessee first offered the part to his dear friend, Anna Magnani, whom he'd visited in Rome. Producer Cheryl Crawford later said, "Tenn must have been on something at the time. Magnani is all wrong for the part. The role calls for an American star, and the Hollywood Hills is full of women who can play has-been actresses: Lana Turner, Ava Gardner, Rita Hayworth, Lauren Bacall—the list is long, indeed."

Magnani had never viewed a Newman film, and she demanded to see an image of him. Frank Merlo, Tennessee's longtime companion, found a publicity shot of Newman and presented it to the Italian diva. She studied it seriously for a moment and then ripped it to shreds. "No! No! No!" she shouted at Tennessee. "I can't play with this man. There is no poetry in his face."

After Magnani wisely turned down the role, Tennessee presented it to Tallulah. After all, he'd written the part with her in mind. She read the script and told Tennessee that she'd seriously consider it. Immediately she wanted to know what actor would be cast as the gigolo opposite her. "Not Marlon Brando!" she yelled at Tennessee, puffing furiously on a cigarette. "I will never work with that bastard again."

"No, it's not Marlon. I want that divine creature, Paul Newman, to play Chance opposite you. His golden velvet body was designed by God herself to grace pink satin sheets."

"I must meet this Apollo," she said. "I've only seen one of his movies, *Cat on a Hot Tin Roof*. After seeing him shirtless, I decided I must have him. After all, I went to Hollywood with only one purpose in mind—not to make those stupid movies I did, but to fuck that divine Gary Cooper. Why don't you arrange for me to meet God's new wonder? Have you had him yet, *dah-ling*?"

"Not yet, Princess," he said, "but Bill Inge has. If Inge can get Newman, so can I. I'll place a hundred dollar bet with you that before *Sweet Bird* ends its run, I will have had him."

"You're on, *dah-ling*" she said. "I like bets. My whole life is a bet. Right now I'm betting against the clock. What perfect type casting *Sweet Bird* will be for me. A fading has-been of an actress. Look at me, *dah-ling*. I used to be Tallulah Bankhead."

To his friends at Actors Studio, Newman recalled his first meeting with Tallulah in her apartment. After being introduced to him by Tennessee, she went

> *"Relentless caper for all those who step*
> *The legend of their youth into the noon."*
>
> —Hart Crane

right to the point. "How big is your cock, *dah-ling*?"

"That's for you to find out later tonight," Newman said.

"A promise I will hold you to," she said. "Come in, dear one. I'm already seven drinks ahead of you pansies."

"I'm not a pansy," Newman protested. "I'm a happily married man."

"Oh, please, *dah-ling*, people are eating," she said. "Sit down and tell me all about your divine self. I'm especially interested as to why you haven't put out yet for my devoted friend here. After all, he wrote your greatest part in that *Cat* movie, and I think you'd owe him one."

Trying to be as sophisticated as this worldly pair, Newman looked over at Tennessee. "I do owe you one," he said. "But you can only have me from the neck down—and not tonight." He glanced toward Tallulah. "It appears that I'm going to be booked up this evening."

For three hours, Tallulah amused Newman and Tennessee with her quick wit and drunken charm.

"Oh, God, *dah-ling*," she said. "I've had everybody from Hattie McDaniel to John Barrymore. I struck out with Ethel Barrymore, however. When I propositioned her, she slapped my face."

As she went on and the drinking continued, she said, "I've tried several varieties of sex. The conventional position makes me claustrophobic, and all the other positions give me either a stiff neck or lockjaw."

By one o'clock in the morning, both Tennessee and Newman were ready to leave. As they rose to bid her good night, Tallulah urged Tennessee "go run along into the night, *dah-ling*. I know you're meeting up with this new kid on the block—Warren Beatty, I think that's his name. He's going to appear in Bill Inge's *A Loss of Roses*. He also wants to audition for you. Good luck tonight. This Warren Beatty sounds divine."

Newman started to leave with Tennessee but Tallulah possessively grabbed his arm. "Not you, *dah-ling*. Tonight you're going to experience first-hand what brought such enchantment to Sir Winston Churchill."

***

Tallulah later claimed she'd turned down the role and the chance to star opposite Newman in *Sweet Bird of Youth* because she'd already committed to an involvement in *Crazy October*, a play written by her friend James Leo Herlihy. Her co-stars would be Estelle Winwood and Joan Blondell. Even though Herlihy graciously offered to tear up her contract, she said she felt that "would not be right. If anything, *dah-ling*, Tallulah is loyal to her friends," she said.

The pivotal role eventually went to Geraldine Page, Newman's close friend from the Actors Studio.

Years later, Herlihy told Darwin Porter, "I think Tallulah was afraid to go on the stage as Alexandra Del Lago. Tennessee had modeled the character on her, and she would have been better in the part. Let's face it: Tallulah is a debauched, drug-addicted ex-film queen, and Geraldine is not."

530

"With Paul Newman and Tallulah Bankhead starring in the same play, those two would have had theater-goers lined up for blocks," Herlihy predicted.

One afternoon at the Actors Studio, Newman told Rod Steiger and Lee Strasberg, "In Tennessee's play, I'm a male whore. Guess who is giving me tips on how to play the character? Steve McQueen. In his teenage years, he had a lot of experience selling his meat to guys."

For the play, Kazan had assembled what was perhaps the most talented cast on Broadway during its 1959 season. Although she'd been considered too young for the part, Geraldine settled beautifully into the role of Alexandra Del Lago.

Even during rehearsals, she electrified the cast with her interpretation of this boozing, washed-up actress. Vain, insecure, and desperate, she played it with raw emotion, and she would well deserve the award she eventually won for her interpretation—a Golden Globe for Best Actress in a Drama.

Diana Hyland played Heavenly Finely, Chance's former girlfriend. In the play, Chance takes Alexandra Del Lago back to his hometown in Florida to hook up with Heavenly again. But before leaving town, he'd infected her with a venereal disease, forcing her to have a hysterectomy.

Heavenly is the daughter of Boss Finley, a brutal figure who rules the town. The role was played on the stage by veteran actor Sidney Blackmer. Rip Torn, who would later take over the role of Chance, was cast as Boss Finley's son and Chance's avowed enemy.

Torn and Geraldine would marry in 1963, a union that lasted until her death in 1987.

Madeleine Sherwood was brilliantly cast as Boss Finley's discarded mistress. Bruce Dern, who became a great drinking buddy of Newman's, was cast in a small role.

Making some excuse to Kazan and presumably to his family, Newman flew to San Juan for a long weekend with Tennessee. Both the actor and playwright were world-class drinkers, and they shared a suite together at El Convento Hotel. One old-time retainer there remembered them checking in.

When asked about it during an interview, Tennessee, as predicted, denied their weekend together. "I have never auditioned actors that way," the playwright claimed, although his statement wasn't true. "Besides, Paul Newman is too big a star to lie on a casting couch."

Frank Merlo revealed to Tennessee's friend, Stanley Haggart, that during "pillow talk," Tennessee had confessed that he had indeed serviced Newman one weekend. "I knew it would be my one and only chance to have him, and I took advantage of it, just as I did with Marlon way back in those early days in Provincetown."

Although Frank and Tennessee were lovers, they had an open relationship and talked about their lovers with each other. Newman sometimes spoke to his *confidants*, but he never mentioned that San Juan weekend with his friends, so far as it is known.

"Let's just call it *The Lost Weekend*," he told Kazan upon his return. Newman was referring to a film Ray Milland made in 1945, where he'd won an Oscar for playing an alcoholic.

Tennessee also told Frank that after their weekend together, Newman had quipped: "Now, God damn it, the next time you have a great part, you come to me, not Marlon Brando. Who's the man, baby?"

Privately, Elia Kazan told Tennessee that "Newman was too much of a pretty boy for the part. I'm going to dye his hair red to make him look more sleazy, and I'm also going to order him to get his hairline shaved. I want audiences to see him with a receding hairline. That will make him look over the hill. After all, he's playing a gigolo past his prime."

Initially, Kazan feared that Newman was not adequately portraying the vulnerability of Chance. Then Kazan came up with a plan, although he knew it would be brutal on the actor. He never gave Newman one compliment for his work, although he praised almost everything Geraldine did.

Years later, Kazan confessed to Tennessee that he'd deliberately "cold-shouldered" Newman throughout the rehearsals.

"Chance Wayne is terribly insecure, uncertain of his manhood, possibly gay, and afraid of tomorrow. By destroying his self-worth, I'll make Newman a more believable Chance Wayne on opening night," Kazan said.

In spite of his brutal treatment during rehearsals, Newman had only kind words to say about Kazan, who had so intimidated him. "Kazan has broad shoulders, and his invention, patience, and imagination are extraordinary," he later said. "Not once did the man who'd directed Brando compare me to him, and for that I was God damn grateful."

Before opening night, Newman tried to hide his private intimacies with Tennessee from Kazan, but he did make one confession. During one drunken night, he'd gone to bed with Geraldine Page. "I was always planning to do it, but we finally committed the horrible sin. We're both Method actors. We felt it would make our characters more believable if we knew each other as David knew Bathsheba."

Kazan congratulated him on his good judgment. Unknown to Newman, the director was not the best person to keep a secret. After Kazan's appearance before the House Committee on Un-American Activities, where he "outed" fellow Communists, Brando had nicknamed him "The Squealer." Kazan liked to discuss the private sex lives of stars he'd directed, including not only Brando but James Dean as well.

On March 10, 1959, *Sweet Bird of Youth* opened on Broadway at the Martin Beck Theater. The play had a shattering climax when Boss Finley's goons come to seek their revenge on Chance for deflowering Heavenly. Led by Rip Torn, the bully boys of the Old South descend to castrate Chance, presumably so that he'll never again ruin the life of another young woman.

Even though Newman played a heel, there were tears in the eyes of some first-nighters when he delivered his climatic line. "I don't ask for your pity, but just for your understanding—not even that—no, just for your recognition of me in you, and the enemy, Time, in all of us."

At one point, critic Kenneth Tynan asserted that Page played Alexandra del Lago with "a knockout flamboyance and dragout authority. She brought the entire audience to its feet, screaming and clapping. She and Newman staged a *coup de théâtre.*"

Later that night, Tennessee told Audrey Wood, "I was Alexandra del Lago from start to finish, drinking too much, taking drugs, and purchasing male flesh by the inch. I've probably made every speech she made. And I meant them twice as much."

Newman received his best reviews to date in Tennessee's play about lost youth. So far, not one review has surfaced in which his acting was compared to that of Marlon Brando. Had he become his own man as an actor at last?

As the play became more deeply entrenched within its run, Newman received many visitors backstage, many of them world-famous stars.

One of Newman's strangest visitors was an aging former hustler who sent him a note backstage inviting him to have a beer with him after the show. "I was the guy Tennessee based the character of Chance Wayne on," the note read.

Newman was intrigued enough to instruct the stage manager to show the man backstage. When he opened the door to his dressing room, he encountered a no-longer young man who looked unkempt, a kind of over-the-hill Tab Hunter. Somehow the years of heavy drinking and a wasted life had taken a toll, but, even so, Newman saw the remains of the hustler's former beauty.

He shook Newman's hand. "I'm Mitch Parker," he said. Once, when Frankie and Tenn broke up, I filled in. Back in those days I could get a hundred a night."

Newman invited him across the street for a beer, and the two men talked until the bar closed down. He believed Mitch's story, and the former hustler showed Newman several snapshots documenting his association with Tennessee.

"I was actually castrated," he said. "That's where Tenn got the idea. It wasn't on the orders of a political boss. Back then, I let men do me for money, but I screwed gals on the side. I once got caught. That was in a town down on the Panhandle. The husband and some of his friends kidnapped me and took me to an abandoned cornfield where they cut my balls off. I had broken up with Tenn at that time. I wrote him begging for some money, but he never answered. I read in the paper about the play. It sounded familiar. I knew I was Chance Wayne. I never shacked up with a movie star, but I told Tenn about the year I lived with this rich woman in Boca Raton. She had once been a great beauty, but time had passed her by. I just know you're playing me."

"And well I might be," Newman said. It was getting late. He slipped him a one hundred dollar bill and watched him disappear down a rainy street in the Broadway district.

As he watched him go, he speculated on the fate of Chance Wayne at the end of the play. To him, the Chance Waynes of the world just seemed to disappear in the vastness of the American wasteland, perhaps escaping into an early death.

"The World's Most Beautiful Male" Seduces "The World's Most Beautiful Female"

It was Tennessee who brought Ava Gardner to see the play. Perhaps imitating Ernest Hemingway, the playwright had always wanted to see Ava cast in one of his plays. Although somewhat pleased with Geraldine Page's performance, he felt Ava would bring a "tragic loveliness" to the character of Alexandra Del Lago. He'd not been too happy that Geraldine was playing the role with a harpy's screech and looked rather blousy. He felt that the film version should present his character as a greater beauty, albeit faded.

At the end of the performance, Ava told Tennessee that the role of Alexandra del Lago "hits me in the belt. Did you base this character on me? I'm called a man-hungry movie star. I'm virtually retired now and certainly a has-been. That pill-popping and heavy drinking comes close to having been inspired by the life of Ava Gardner. The whole world knows that I ripped off Rita Hayworth's life in *The Barefoot Contessa*. Now it's time I got roasted."

Ava Gardner
Still lovely, but no longer
an ingenue.

Even so, she wanted to meet Paul Newman. "He's like so many men I've loved temporarily, then had to discard and move on to the next one."

Meeting Newman, she found him enchanting. "When you took off your shirt, I swooned. I always wished Frankie had a better chest. All of his growth went into his cock."

He'd already been warned that Ava had a "potty mouth," so he wasn't at all surprised to hear that line coming from what he viewed as one of the most beautiful creatures on Earth. In some ways, he found her beauty more arresting than that of Elizabeth Taylor herself, or so he would claim later to his friends.

Tennessee invited Ava and Newman to join him at a hidden tavern in the Broadway district. Actors often gathered there after curtains fell.

"So what did you think of our little drama tonight?" Newman asked Ava.

She was not a woman to mince words: "I'm from North Carolina, honey, a real Tarheel. We call a spade a spade. There's some pretty strong stuff here— a male whore, drug addiction, alcoholism, racism, venereal disease, and castration. That castration thing was a bit over the top. I shuddered to think that America's reigning male sex symbol might be losing the source of his power."

"It gives me nightmares just to think about it," Newman responded. "I find myself touching the family jewels every night just to convince myself that they're still there."

"You need a beautiful woman to fondle them and to reassure you that you're indeed still intact."

Tennessee later claimed he was rather insulted by Ava's critique.

She very accurately predicted that the writing would have to be cleaned up for the screen. "Yet, the day will come when Hollywood can present realistic drama. I want to be the first actress to use the word 'fuck' in a major motion picture, but Elizabeth Taylor will probably beat me to it, since every third word that comes out of her usually begins with F."

Tennessee, who knew Hemingway only briefly, quizzed her about working on the film adaptation (1957) of his novel *The Sun Also Rises*.

Ava spoke eloquently of the "last days" of Errol Flynn and Tyrone Power, who had each co-starred with her in that movie. Shortly after their involvement in its filming ended, both stars would meet early deaths, Power in 1958, Flynn in 1959.

Ava told Paul and Tennessee that she'd dated both Power and Flynn back in the Forties. "When they showed up on the set of *The Sun Also Rises*, both of them looked like old men. They had prematurely aged. You know, of course, they used to be lovers."

"I didn't know that," Newman said.

"They must have made a lovely couple," Tennessee said. "I think they were the most beautiful men I've ever seen on the screen." Then he flashed his famous grin at Paul. "That is, until this divine creature came along."

"Flattery has already gotten you everywhere," Newman quipped.

Quick to pick up on the innuendo, Ava said, "Oh, I see. You two fellows already know each other."

"Don't worry," Tennessee said. "The passage will not appear in my memoirs."

"Half of my lovers, including Howard Hughes and Peter Lawford, were secret cocksuckers," she said.

Tennessee laughed, but Newman did not. In some way, as he'd later confess, Ava was one of the most outspoken women he'd ever known.

"Flynn especially was a spectacular wreck, not a magnificent wreck," Ava said. "He was far too gone to be magnificent at anything. I should know. We tried it again one night for old time's sake. Forget it."

535

"You'd be perfect for the role of a lost exile from Hollywood," Newman said, abruptly changing the subject.

"Oh, darling," she said, "I fear I am indeed Alexandra del Lago, and don't really need to prove it by playing her in a movie."

"Perhaps some time with me would convince you," Newman responded.

At that point, Tennessee jumped up from the table. "I'll pay the tab and leave you two love birds alone. He's good, Ava. Enjoy." He kissed both Newman and Ava on the lips before wandering into the night like some lost feathered bird.

No one knows for sure what transpired that night, because Newman and Ava, at least in this case, didn't indulge in Monday morning quarterbacking after Saturday's game. Tennessee, however, always maintained that they connected, at least for a one-night stand. "It must have been a lovely coupling," Tennessee said, "the world's most beautiful woman, a bit past her prime, coming together with the world's most beautiful man."

In spite of their night together, Newman never managed to convince Ava to accept the role of Del Lago. He did tell Elia Kazan that Ava Gardner "is one of the world's most fascinating creatures. She is Venus." He might have been referring to her 1948 film, *One Touch of Venus*.

"You're Going to Be My Next Husband"

—*Lana Turner to Paul Newman*

Lana Turner made another entrance into Tennessee's life when she became one of the many actresses flying into New York to evaluate his new play. There weren't that many great parts for aging actresses, and Lana wanted to see if she felt comfortable with the role before making a play for it back in Hollywood. "After all," she told Tennessee, "MGM owes me a few favors. I practically saved them from bankruptcy in the 40s."

Over a drink at Sardi's before the curtain went up on *Sweet Bird of Youth* that night, Tennessee and Lana laughed about his former days at MGM when he'd been assigned to work on the screenplay of *Marriage Is a Private Affair* in which she had starred. *[Although Tennessee had fretted for days over the project, he ultimately could not relate to the plot, joking to friends that he was working on a "celluloid brassiere for Miss Turner," as described in an earlier chapter of this book.]*

"What happened to you at MGM?" Lana asked Tennessee.

"The studio heads finally decided that I would never be able to produce a screenplay for you," Tennessee told her. "So they reassigned me to write a scenario about Billy the Kid. That was more Gore Vidal's fantasy than mine. Then they asked me if I wanted to write a scenario starring Margaret O'Brien. I told them where they could shove Little Miss Margaret. Finally, MGM and I parted ways."

"Finally, MGM and I parted ways, too," Lana said. "But I may come back if I get cast in your *Sweet Bird*."

Throughout the performance of *Sweet Bird of Youth*, Tennessee noted that Lana studied Geraldine's every movement and expression "like a hawk."

Lana told Tennessee she'd loved the play but, like her best friend, Ava Gardner, she feared it would have to be "cleaned up" for film audiences.

She was all charm and grace when Tennessee escorted her backstage for a reunion with Newman, whom she'd once known intimately back in Hollywood. Right in front of Tennessee, she kissed him. It was a long and lingering open-mouthed kiss that forced her to repair her makeup in front of his dressing room mirror.

Looking exotic, **Lana Turner** wanted both Paul Newman and the role of Alexandra Del Lago.

"I'm in New York all alone," she told Newman.

He wasn't sure where her other lovers—or could there be a husband?—were. He'd lost track of her many entanglements. "I need someone by my side at all times," she said. "I'm so dependent on a man. But aren't most women like me?"

"I can definitely assure you that most women aren't like Lana Turner," Newman said.

"I've always been alone," Tennessee said, not revealing his many companions over the years. "I have always depended on the kindness of strangers I meet along the way."

It was agreed that Tennessee would take both Lana and Newman to dinner at Sardi's before retiring for the night. Lana wanted to go dancing later, and Newman agreed to be her escort.

At Sardi's, all heads turned as Lana walked in, escorted with Newman on one side and Tennessee on her other.

After dinner, Lana, with Newman, in a limousine, migrated to a night club uptown. As the stunningly beautiful couple entered, a hush fell over the patrons. She looked gorgeous, sheathed in a clinging white evening gown that was slit high up the side and low down the front. Her blonde hair was cropped short.

Dancing in Newman's arms, she told him, "Everybody is looking at us. We'd make a fabulous pair on the screen."

"Everybody is looking at you," he corrected her. "To attract attention, I think I'll have to take off my jacket, shirt, and undershirt."

"Later, darling," she whispered into his ear.

Newman did not share details of his subsequent visit to Lana's hotel suite.

537

He'd seduced her before, finding her clinging and desperate.

Even though he didn't give a blow-by-blow description of what happened that night with Lana, he did share an intimacy two nights later over drinks with Tennessee.

"As I was leaving her suite the following morning, she held me close and delivered a shocker. 'You may not know it now,' she said to me, 'or even tomorrow. But one day in the not-so-distant future you are going to become my next husband. Note that I said next and not last husband.' With that tantalizing remark, she shut the door in my face."

"I Want To Play a Male Whore"

—Elvis Presley to Paul Newman

Newman was stunned when he received a note from the stage door security guard. He was used to beautiful movie stars arriving backstage to greet him, often on the pretense of wanting to appear as Alexandra del Lago in play's movie version. He told Frank Sinatra when he came to visit one night that he felt that many of these glamorous stars "are just coming backstage to hook up with me so that they can fuck me."

Sinatra had laughed at the remark, telling him that an entire lineup of screen queens, ranging from Joan Crawford to Ingrid Bergman, had arrived at the stage door to greet the new sensation of Broadway, Marlon Brando, when he had appeared in *A Streetcar Named Desire*.

"Fuck those broads who appeal to you and tell the rest of them to go home and use a dildo," was Sinatra's advice.

One note that arrived was the most startling of all. Not from a women, it was from Elvis Presley.

Was he still bitter over not being allowed to appear as Brick in *Cat on a Hot Tin Roof*? Intrigued, Newman told the guard that he'd meet Elvis when the curtain went down. In a return reply, Elvis told him that he'd be waiting outside in a white limousine, its windows darkened so that fans could not peer inside to discover him.

After the show, outside on the street, one of Elvis' "boys" opened the back door of the limousine and ushered Newman inside. There, Elvis was waiting, swigging blackberry brandy directly from the bottle. "Haul your ass in here, kid," Elvis said. "I'll take you for a ride."

"Another pissing contest?" Newman asked. "Don't tell me you want to play Chance Wayne in the movie."

Once again, **Elvis Presley** wanted to be cast in "that hustler role written by one of those queers."

538

"No more pissing," Elvis said. "You won that round."

[*Elvis was referring to a drunken night in Hollywood when he challenged Newman to a pissing contest in his garden to determine who could urinate a golden shower over the longest distance. The winner would get to play Brick in* Cat on a Hot Tin Roof.]

"We've got some serious business to talk over tonight," Elvis told Newman. "And, yes, MGM has offered me the role of Chance Wayne. Fuck what Colonel Parker says. I'm gonna play that male whore. No one ever takes me seriously, as a film star, considering the shit I do." He swigged more from the brandy bottle. "But that day is gonna change."

"Actually I think you might be great as a hot-headed redneck male prostitute," Newman said.

"Thanks for the compliment," Elvis said. "Hal Wallis wanted me to appear in *The Rainmaker* (1957) with Katharine Hepburn and Burt Lancaster. I was set to do it, but the deal fell through. All the serious roles I've been offered I never got to do. That scumbag Parker saw to that. He sabotaged every deal."

In the suite of the king of rock and roll, Newman confronted a much more mature and rather bitter Elvis, not the man he'd encountered before. He continued swigging the blackberry brandy, but he was also popping pills. Newman suspected the drug was Seconal, a now-controlled substance that was evaluated as relatively harmless in the late 50s.

Years before, Elvis had been considered quite the Southern gentleman, but the star tonight was snapping orders at his staff. He was rude and flashing a bad temper, but not at Newman, whom he continued to treat with respect.

"Col. Parker is a bloodsucker," Elvis claimed, "and he's virtually ruined my film career with junk movies. This time, thanks to Chance Wayne, I'm gonna defy the fucker."

"I've got to ask you," Newman said. "Why am I here? I have no control over casting. If you want the part, you've got it. You're the hottest thing in town. I think that you playing opposite Ava Gardner would be the biggest grosser of the year."

"Ava Gardner," he said. "I've never fucked her. Frank Sinatra told me he'd cut off my dick if I plunged into that succulent pussy."

"This time, no pissing," Newman said. "If you want the role, it's yours. I'd love to play Chance Wayne on the screen, but it's yours for the asking."

"That would make me a heel," Elvis said, before turning to one of his boys from Memphis. "It's time my best friend here and I did some serious drinking. Get us a pitcher, asshole. We're ready to start chug-a-lugging screwdrivers."

When Elvis turned his attention back onto Newman again, his voice became softer. "I'd be a fucking son of a bitch if I took something you wanted," Elvis said, standing up and starting to pull off his clothes. "That's why I'm here to make a deal with you. I just learned that MGM is willing to pay you $350,000 for starring as Chance Wayne. Elvis is going to offer you $350,000 for NOT being Chance Wayne. You can find an even better script that will also pay you $350,000. That means you can double your money. Sounds God damn fair to me."

He continued to strip down to his jockey shorts. "I'm not trying to turn you on, although I know you go for the boys. My masseur has arrived. I'm taking youth treatments. Would you believe I'm starting to sag a little bit here and there? After all, I was born in 1935."

"Want to hear an even sadder story?" Newman asked. "I was born ten years before that."

Two of Elvis' boys wheeled in a hospital bed with a curtain around it. They were followed by a masseur who looked a bit effeminate. "I know Fido here doesn't look like much of a man, but he's got the most skilled hands of any masseur in America. He's from Haiti. A High Yaller."

The mulatto smiled at Newman and motioned for Elvis to go behind the curtain. Pulling down his jockey shorts, Elvis stepped inside and apparently got up onto the rolling bed. From behind the curtain, Elvis continued to talk to Newman, who sat on the sofa enjoying the best screwdriver he'd ever tasted in his life.

After fifteen minutes of conversation, Newman heard Elvis shout, "You god damn cocksucking faggot." Then he stormed outside the curtains, knocking the masseur in the face. The masseur fell to the floor as a nude Elvis, boasting a semi hard-on, started kicking the young man in his ribs.

Two of Elvis' boys suddenly appeared and restrained him. "Get that faggot out of here! He was trying to jerk me off." A third member of Elvis' boys emerged with a red silk robe which he slipped on. "Better give him $10,000 to buy him off so the queer won't sue me."

And then the screen goes black.

***

A few hours before his next performance of *Sweet Bird of Youth*, Newman was relating the story about his encounter with Elvis to Geraldine and Kazan.

But their dialogue was interrupted, and consequently, Newman never finished his story of what had had happened earlier that evening with Elvis.

In panic, Tennessee Williams suddenly came rushing down the aisle of the theater. "I'm dying!" he shouted. "I've just come from my doctor. He says I have inoperable cancer. I'm dying! This is the last play I'll ever write."

This was the beginning of fifty such outbursts from the playwright, each announcing his imminent death, until the inevitable moment when the day of doom actually arrived.

Princess Rita (Hayworth) Considers the Role of Tennessee's Princess Kosmonopolis

Sweet Bird of Youth ran on Broadway for 375 performances.

Newman recalled his last performance as Chance Wayne at Manhattan's Martin Beck Theater. "I remember my last night going to the theater. I swallowed two jiggers of honey for energy and for my throat. I felt completely exhausted. I must have been in the hot shower for thirty minutes. I broke down and started crying like a baby. Then it came to me: I'd never say Tennessee's words again. I'll never have that kind of quiet near the end of the third act. Never that specific kind of quiet, as a hush came over the theater."

***

After the run of the play had ended, during the long gestation period it took to adapt Tennessee's play, *Sweet Bird of Youth*, to the screen, Newman received a call from Orson Welles. It surprised him because the talented director/actor had made his distaste for Newman known during the filming of *The Long, Hot Summer* (1958).

Yet during his phone conversation with Newman, Welles was at his most charming. It soon became apparent that he was shopping for the proper vehicle in which to star his former wife, Rita Hayworth. "She'd make the perfect Alexandra Del Lago," Welles predicted. "The screen requires a softer, gentler del Lago, not that brash harridan Geraldine Page played on the stage."

In some ways, Newman agreed with him. When Welles invited Newman and Richard Brooks, the upcoming director of *Sweet Bird*, for a joint meeting at Rita's house, Newman eagerly accepted, although Welles explained that he would not be present at the gathering.

Newman had always wanted to meet Rita, as she'd long been on the A-list of stars he planned to seduce. During his stint in the Navy, he'd had a pin-up of her pasted to the inside of his locker door. In some ways, he found Rita far more enticing than Ava Gardner, a comparable beauty.

When Rita graciously received Brooks and Newman into her home, he was struck by how different she was from her screen image as showcased in her 1946 classic, Gilda. She was dressed simply in slacks and a blouse, and wore little makeup.

Time had been a bit cruel to the Love Goddess of the 1940s, a vivacious, sexy, and desirable woman known for her sunny smile and the come-hither glint in her eye. In many ways, this newest incarnation of Rita would be perfect as a fading movie star. She was a fading movie star.

During their time with Rita, Newman and Brooks met a realistic, straight talking woman without the glamorous

Rita Hayworth told Paul Newman, "It is no longer 1942, but I'm still a love goddess."

moves of Lana Turner, who could never stop playing Lana Turner even when the cameras were turned off for the night.

In spite of her bizarre marriages—among them to Orson Welles himself, and to Prince Aly Khan as well—there was something very wholesome about Rita, Newman had read that after her divorce from the Argentine singer, Dick Haymes *[their marriage had lasted from 1953 to 1954]*, she'd married producer James Hill. But Hill was nowhere in sight.

Newman complimented her on her recent performance in *Pal Joey* (1957). "Do you know that Mae West was originally offered the part?" she said. "Mae probably could have done it better."

"I doubt that," Brooks said.

Brooks and Newman discussed the possibility of Rita appearing in *Sweet Bird of Youth*. But later, when the two men talked about it together privately, they expressed their belief that she didn't really want to appear as the fading actress, and that she'd been cajoled into meeting with them because of Welles. Still in love with Rita, he was trying to jump-start her dying career.

Her reddish auburn hair looked as lustrous as ever, but she was smaller than she appeared onscreen. Her maid kept supplying her with highballs, and Newman matched her drink for drink. Brooks held back.

"As Alexandra del Lago, I could be what I am, a fading star," she said. "I might as well let it all hang out. Somehow people think I'm as old as Joan Crawford and Bette Davis. I started so young—that's why they think that."

"*You Were Never Lovelier*," Newman told her, evoking the title of her 1942 movie.

"Thank you, dear," she said. "I've had a lifetime of compliments, but now they fall on suspicious ears. I know what I look like. I know what time it is. Like Alexandra del Lago, I, too, am battling that old enemy, time."

"Would you be our Alexandra?" Brooks asked her.

"Let me think about it." She turned to Newman and took his hand, holding it up to her cheek. "This beautiful man here and I could light up the screen, like Glenn and I did in *Gilda*." *[She was referring, of course, to her frequent co-star, Glenn Ford.]*

The maid came back into her living room with three more highballs, but when she started to hand a drink to Brooks, Rita motioned for her not to. "If you have to go, I understand," Rita said. Brooks did not have to leave so soon. "I'd like Paul to remain behind. We can sit in my garden and talk about appearing on the screen together. It'll give us a chance to discover each other. I think in this role I can show the world I have some depth. All my life, Rita Hayworth has had only a few good moments, everything else was about image."

At the door, she kissed Brooks on the cheek. "Thank you for coming, dear one," she said. "We'll see if this offer leads to anything." He noticed that she was holding Newman's hand at that point.

"Well, you two take care," he said.

Brooks was the source of information about the meeting between Newman and Rita, and the director knew nothing of what happened after he left. Newman never confided in him.

Brooks' last memory of Rita was her standing with Newman at the doorway and looking into his eyes. Her gaze was penetrating, yet somehow suspicious. Her final statement was somewhat enigmatic. He would remember it for years.

"Before the night is over, I must convince Paul I'm not Gilda."

A few weeks later, Metro-Goldwyn-Mayer rejected the idea of casting Rita.

"They Castrated My Play"
—Tennessee, After Seeing the Movie Adaptation of Sweet Bird of Youth

Sweet Bird of Youth, in a "castrated" version, wouldn't reach the screen until 1962. As the gigolo and the fading actress he serviced, it starred the actors who had originally made it famous on Broadway, Paul Newman and Geraldine Page.

Repeating their Broadway roles were Rip Torn and Madeleine Sherwood. Ed Begley was contracted to play Boss Finley in the film version, as was Shirley Knight to appear as Heavenly, the girlfriend. The very talented character actress, Mildred Dunnock, was assigned to the role of Heavenly's Aunt Nonny, who is sympathetic to Chance.

The contract that legally committed him to an appearance as Chance Wayne in the film represented Newman's most lucrative financial deal to date, ensuring him a fee of $350,000 for his performance, plus a percentage of the take. He'd finally arrived on the A-list of movie stars, where he would remain for a very long time.

Because of studio pressure, Richard Brooks was forced to water down the original script, just as he'd been ordered to do in *Cat on a Hot Tin Roof*. Instead of a castration, Chance suffered a beating at the hands of Boss Finley's goons.

And instead of being infected with a venereal disease, Heavenly undergoes an abortion. The biggest change, and one that infuriated Tennessee, was the happy ending Brooks added to the film. Heavenly and Chance run away, presumably toward a happy future, although that hardly seems likely after what has come down before.

Sweet Bird of Youth, advertised with slogans that included *HE USED LOVE LIKE MOST MEN USE MONEY*, premiered on March 21, 1962. Unlike the play, the vanilla film version of Tennessee's drama bombed, as audiences stayed away in droves. For the most part, film critics panned the movie. But when it came time for Academy Award nominations, *Sweet Bird*, in spite of its flaws, was not ignored.

The film brought Academy Award nominations for some of its actors, including Geraldine Page as Best Actress in a Leading Role. She would lose that year to Anne Bancroft, who had appeared in *The Miracle Worker.* Shirley Knight was nominated as Best Actress in a Supporting Role. But it was Ed Begley, nominated as Best Actor in a Supporting Role, who walked off with an actual Oscar.

It took another quarter of a century for *Sweet Bird of Youth* to open in a theater in London's West End. It premiered on July 8, 1985, at London's Haymarket Theatre. Lauren Bacall, formerly known as "Bogie's Baby," played the role of Alexandra del Lago. She was certainly typecast as a faded film actress.

In a foolish decision, Elizabeth Taylor in 1989 agreed to star as Alexandra del Lago in a remake of the film. She captured none of the nuances of Geraldine Page and gave one of the flattest on-screen characterizations of her career.

Casting actor Mark Harmon as Chance made the few viewers who watched the 1989 version of *Sweet Bird* realize just how good Newman and Geraldine had been in the original, both on stage and on the screen.

Troy Donahue Tries to Kill Tennessee Williams

Troy Donahue, more of a male pin-up than an actor, burst onto the screen in the late 1950s. He was blonde, blue-eyed, blandly handsome and often confused with Tab Hunter, his rival. He and another blonde, Sandra Dee, had their fifteen minutes of fame in such saccharine movies as *A Summer Place* (1959). That same year, Donahue and Dee had also packaged themselves into that Lana Turner soaper, *Imitation of Life.*

Donahue was smart enough to know that his place in the Hollywood Sun would soon turn to Twilight, as the pretty boys of the 1950s faded into the reality of the 1960s with the emergence of such newer "anti-heroes" as Dustin Hoffman.

Long before Tab Hunter tried to reverse the downward spiral of his career through appearances on Broadway with Tallulah Bankhead in *The Milk Train Doesn't Stop Here Anymore,* Troy made an aggressive assault on Tennessee. He felt that if he snared the role of the good-looking hustler in the film version of *Sweet Bird of Youth,* he would reach an entirely new audience, and demonstrate to studios that he could tackle a really tough dramatic role.

Donahue's career had been launched by the King of the Casting Couch, Henry Willson, who changed the name of a lowly truck driver (Roy Fitzgerald) and put him on the road to stardom as Rock Hudson. During his reign from 1957 to 1967, Rock became the most popular movie star in the world. Willson, the controversial gay starmaker of the 1950s, also played a major role in the film careers of Rory Calhoun, Tab Hunter, Alain Delon, Robert Wagner, and Guy Madison.

Willson changed Donahue's name from Merle Johnson to Troy Donahue, and he became what Inside Hollywood called "the latest slab of beef on Willson's Meat Rack."

Willson got Troy a role in Rock Hudson's *The Tarnished Angels* (1957). The other men in Willson's stable asked Hudson about their clan's newest blonde stallion: "Great cocksucker, tiny dick," Hudson responded.

Tennessee had attended some of Willson's all-male parties, and subsequently, he telephoned the playwright and asked him to arrange a private dinner with Donahue. "He's the new James Dean," Willson assured Tennessee.

Over dinner, Tennessee was most gracious to Donahue, who was making himself plainly available, as he'd been instructed to do. What Donahue, or even Willson, didn't know was that Tennessee preferred dark-complexioned, Mediterranean-derived young men, to the All-American blonde look, as represented at the time by Donahue.

At one point in the evening, Tennessee told Troy, "I understand that you invade the fantasies of pubescent girls. My Chance Wayne is different. He's a hardened hustler who is running out of time. You look like you have several years to go before the bloom fades from the rose."

"I can play a different type," Donahue

After making love to **Troy Donahue** *(both photos, above)* Rock Hudson was cruel, telling him, "You need to work on that willowy chest of yours and add another three inches to your dick."

Lower photo, Troy is seen in the melodramatic *A Summer Place* (1959) with co-star Sandra Dee, two confectionary screen concoctions that didn't survive the Eisenhower 1950s.

said. "I wish you'd seen me in *Imitation of Life.* I was cast as this sullen thug who beats up his mulatto girl friend, played by Susan Kohner. I was a racist brute."

"My night with Troy did not end up in bed," Tennessee recalled in the aftermath of their dinner together. "I did not go for his facile charm, or even for his looks. He seemed quite shocked when I rejected his invitation for a roll in the hay. I don't think anybody had ever turned him down before."

"However, I was still a bad boy. I promised I'd recommend him for the role of Chance Wayne, although I knew that some bigger names, perhaps Paul Newman, would eventually be signed for the role instead. Even Elvis was eager to play the role, even though I doubted whether Colonel Tom Parker would let him do it."

"Not really wanting to deal with Troy, I quit accepting his phone calls," Tennessee said. "This seriously pissed him off."

Through Willson, Tennessee began to hear reports that Donahue had begun drinking early in the day. "He tells me he's got to have a drink or two before facing the cameras."

Three weeks later, Willson complained again to Tennessee. "Troy is mixing codeine with his vodka."

Unlike Tennessee, his friend and rival playwright, William Inge, had more than a few sexual interludes with Donahue, who hustled him for the male leads in *Bus Stop* with Marilyn Monroe and also for a role in *Picnic* with Kim Novak. *[The male lead in* Bus Stop *eventually went to Don Murray, with the starring male lead in* Picnic *going to William Holden.]*

Even after the failure of those inaugural attempts to extract commitments from Inge for a starring role in one of his plays, Donahue made additional attempts to seduce Inge during his campaign to snag the male lead in Inge's screenplay for *Splendor in the Grass* (1961), opposite Natalie Wood. That film's director, Elia Kazan, eventually awarded the coveted role to Warren Beatty.

Donahue made one final attempt at stardom, "moving heaven and hell" to play John F. Kennedy in *PT 109,* but losing out to Cliff Robertson—after Beatty rejected the role.

In the wake of all these lost opportunities, Troy sank so deeply into despair that his house at 1234 Wetherly Drive in Los Angeles became known for its midday drug orgies. Guy Madison once visited it, discovering that Donahue was "completely zonked. He didn't know what planet he was on. The house was filled with degenerates just hanging on and hanging out. Everybody was drugged."

At one point, Donahue became involved with Lili Kardell, who became his fiancée in 1961. A minor actress, she had appeared in a Nazi-themed spy comedy entitled *Looking for Danger,* but was even better known for going out on two or three dates with James Dean. Kardell eventually filed an assault-and-battery suit against Donahue, seeking damages of exactly $60,450.

An out-of-court settlement was reached as a means of avoiding public exposure of Donahue's violence and drug addiction.

Tanked up on alcohol and fueled by LSD, a belligerent Donahue arrived at a Hollywood party attended by Tennessee. LSD had set off adverse psychiatric reactions in Donahue, filling him with anxiety, paranoia, and delusions.

He had developed a hatred toward scriptwriters and directors, especially gay ones. He retained particularly intense hatreds for Kazan, Tennessee, and Inge. In his paranoia, Donahue held Tennessee responsible for the failure of his career, and for not coming through with the role of Chance Wayne in *Sweet*

Bird of Youth. [Actually, as defined by the terms of his contract, Tennessee did-n't have the power to cast the role even if he'd wanted to give the part to Don-ahue.]

Donahue had told Willson that, "Tennessee just used me and discarded me." Perhaps in his delusion, he'd substituted Tennessee for William Inge, who had to a greater extent trivialized and taken advantage of his career-related hopes, ambitions, and dreams.

When Tennessee encountered Donahue at that party, he found the failed actor "itching for a fight."

"I quickly moved on, almost fearing his belligerence," Tennessee recalled.

Also present at the party was celebrity psychic John Cohan, who for years had been a friend and confidant of such stars as Elizabeth Taylor. His relations with a host of stars were revealed in his candid memoir, *Catch a Falling Star: The Untold Story of Celebrity Secrets,* published in 2008, with revelations about Natalie Wood, Merv Griffin, River Phoenix, John F. Kennedy, Jr., Elvis Presley, Mick Jagger, and Rudolf Nureyev.

Cohan was also a close friend of Nicole Brown Simpson, the murdered wife of O.J. Simpson.

Cohan freely admitted that "the love of my life" was Sandra Dee, who at one time was married to Bobby Darin. Ironically, Donahue had been her most fa-mous co-star.

[Cohan's revelations have been frequently reported by Cindy Adams, the
popular columnist for The New York Post. *She was the first to report on the story of Eliz-abeth Taylor bearing a love child in the early 1950s. As widely publicized by Adams, Eliz-abeth had confessed to Cohan that she'd given birth to a baby girl named Norah, who was eventually adopted by a family in Ireland.*

Taylor also delivered another shocker to Cohan, asserting that her former husband, Richard Burton, had died from some AIDS-related disease.]

At the party, Donahue seemed enraged at Tennessee, falsely accusing him of work-ing to destroy his film career, which was not true at all, although Tennessee had done nothing in particular to promote it either.

"I don't write roles for Troy Donahue," Tennessee told Audrey Wood.

"The only role that I ever wrote that he could conceivably play was that of the inse-cure, closeted gay husband in *Period of Ad-justment,* a part that went in the film version to Jim Hutton, who starred opposite Jane

Celebrity Seer **John Cohan** came between a drugged-out Troy Donahue and Tennessee Williams

Fonda.

At the party, overcome with a sudden rage, Donahue, according to Cohan, darted toward Tennessee, grabbed him around the throat, and began to choke him. The playwright was so startled that he made no attempt to fight him off.

Fearing he would choke Tennessee to death, Cohan rescued him from the assault. He pulled Donahue off from Tennessee, who fell on the floor coughing and sputtering.

Shortly thereafter, Donahue was removed from the building.

"All those future plays, although not as good as the ones from the 40s and 50s, would never have been written if I hadn't moved quickly," Cohan said. "Troy was so deranged that he clearly had an intent to kill, that awful night."

Gloria Swanson Plots "Yet Another" Comeback

At a private screening in Hollywood, Tennessee had seen Gloria Swanson emote in *Sunset Blvd.* (1950), playing the deranged silent screen vamp Norma Desmond, lost in a vanished world of her own delusions. He would later tell scriptwriter Meade Roberts that, "I was shattered by the film. It is wonderfully awful. Amazingly, the part called for a bad actress, which made it ideal for Swanson, who was never an actress at all, but a creation of her own imagination."

When Tennessee went to work on the theatrical version of *Sweet Bird of Youth,* the play's early readers noted the parallels of his new script with *Sunset Blvd.* Tennessee had met and had lunch with Swanson during the mid-1950s, but in his letters to friends, all he reported was that mere fact, and not the essence of what transpired between them.

However, he told Frank Merlo and others that he used the occasion to probe Swanson for any background details on *Sunset Blvd.*, one of his most mesmerizing films he had ever seen.

She did reveal that until right before filming began, she had expected to appear opposite Montgomery Clift as her kept man. At the last minute, however, Monty had bowed out, and the role had gone to the more traditionally masculine William Holden. Holden's involvement virtually assured him of major stardom playing the role of the sullen but attractive gigolo, Joe Gillis.

Holden had once told Tennessee at a Hollywood party that in the 1940s, he had been known "for throwing mercy fucks to antique pussies." Tennessee was too much of a Mississippi gentleman to ask Swanson if she had ever managed to seduce her handsome co-star.

He was surprised when she revealed to him that originally, the film's director and screenwriter, Billy Wilder, had offered her role to Mae West, during the early period when *Sunset Blvd.* was still conceived as a black comedy rather than the drama it became. In the first script, Norma Desmond was to have been a has-been burlesque queen. West had flamboyantly rejected the role, claiming that "None of my fans will ever believe me as a has-been."

In a complete reversal of types, Wilder then offered the role to Mary Pickford, America's Silent Screen sweetheart from the 1920s, who also rejected it. Swanson had been a last-minute choice, although Pola Negri, her 1920s rival, had also been briefly considered.

Tennessee wanted to know which of the silent screen stars inspired the iconic role of Norma Desmond.

Swanson responded that she had been informed by Wilder and his fellow scriptwriter, Charles Brackett, that it was Mae Murray, the star of Eric von Stroheim's silent screen hit, *The Merry Widow,* with John Gilbert.

Murray herself went to see *Sunset Blvd.* and later remarked, "None of us floozies was that nuts!"

[Mae Murray, the wistfully pretty dancer and ingénue who had tangoed with Rudolph Valentino during her early days in New York, just faded away, slipping into delusion and poverty. In 1964, a year before she died at the age of seventy-five, she was found wandering the streets of St. Louis, not knowing where she was or even who she was.]

Mae Murray, extravagantly beaded and coiffed, as a 1920s star during the film industry's Silent Era. She was said to have been the inspiration for the character of Norma Desmond.

In 1958, Swanson toured the Southern states in her Rolls Royce and paid a sentimental journey to Key West, where—known at the time as an "Army brat,"— she'd lived in 1908 with her father. It was here that she'd made her singing debut at the Odd Fellows Hall.

Immediately settling into Key West, she went on a futile search for staples of what had become her health-conscious diet, fertilized eggs and chemical-free meat. *[Although she found neither of those items, the Spanish limes she discovered at an open-air market brought back long-forgotten childhood memories.]*

Swanson had a compelling reason for being in Key West other than as a vacation. She had read the script for Tennessee's newest play, *Sweet Bird of Youth,* and she considered its female protagonist, Alexandra del Lago, as "the perfect role for me."

Consequently, she telephoned Tennessee *[also in Key West at the time]* who invited her to his home for dinner. His lover, Frank Merlo, cooked three of his specialties that night, but when Swanson, resembling a fashion plate

Uber-Diva and Survivor:
Gloria Swanson

549

from 1928, arrived, she handed him a piece of boiled chicken breast. "Make that my dinner," she commanded, "with a glass of white wine."

She and Tennessee spent the early part of the evening talking about her fabulous past. She discussed her former lover, Joseph P. Kennedy, and her off-screen romances with suitors who had included Valentino and Aristotle Onassis.

"I've been married so many times, but my first marriage *[to Wallace Beery]* should have sworn me off marriage for life. I lost my virginity to him on my wedding night, which I thought would be my ticket to heaven. It turned out to be a fast ride to hell. In pitch blackness, he brutalized me. As he whispered filth into my ear, he ripped my insides apart before falling asleep and deeply snoring. I spent the rest of the night huddled on the bathroom floor, swathed in towels to soak up the bleeding and ease the pain."

"After a few weeks, I told him I was experiencing stomach cramps. He gave me some medicine to swallow to ease the cramps. I woke up in a hospital where the doctor told me I had suffered a miscarriage. I learned the medicine he'd given me was actually poison."

She and Tennessee finally settled in for some serious discussion about her candidacy for the role of Alexandra del Lago. She said that she knew he must have been inspired by *Sunset Blvd.,* which he did not admit.

"Ever since I played Norma Desmond, I've been handed nothing but rip-off scripts from that movie," she told him. "In every case, I turned them down. I did not want to go through the rest of my life endlessly playing Norma Desmond."

"But in your *Sweet Bird,* I found an almost poetic interpretation of the role of an aging actress. Not only that, but I liked the idea of your having Alexandra make a comeback. Everybody said *Sunset Blvd.* would be my comeback picture. I want *Sweet Bird* to be my second comeback. It's almost assured that if I get rave reviews on the road, I'll be offered the screen role. After all, even though millions of fans from my silent films have died off, *Sunset Blvd.* generated millions of new ones. I want to be your Alexandra del Lago, relentlessly battling the enemy of us all, time itself."

In response to all this, Tennessee was exceedingly polite and, at the end of the evening, he assured her that he'd do everything he could to get her the role.

But after she'd left, he told Frank, "It will never happen. Even though she might play the role to packed houses, her mere presence would distort the integrity of my play. Everybody in the audience, especially our gay brethren, will be buying tickets to see Norma Desmond in *Sunset Blvd.,* not Alexandra del Lago in *Sweet Bird of Youth.* Her personal legend is too overpowering. She'd be Gloria Swanson up there on the stage, and not immerse herself into her new incarnation. I'm going to cast my vote against her."

"You know, Tenn, that it will break her heart," Frank said.

"I regret that," Tennessee said. "Poor Gloria has had her heart broken a thousand times. But I'm sure she's used to it by now."

Chapter Thirty-Eight

The Night of the Iguana *(the play)*

Tennessee's Last Great Work for the Theater
Before his Fall from Grace and Popularity

"The Cry of the Caged Iguana, The Lament of the Sacred Misfits, the Demons of Frantic Sex"

Bette Davis *(left photo)* made a spectacular entrance as the beachboy-chasing Maxine Faulk in Tennessee Williams' last big hit on Broadway, *The Night of the Iguana*. Her co-stars were **Margaret Leighton** and **Patrick O'Neal**, pictured with **Tennessee** *(center)* on the right.

When O'Neal spurned Bette's sexual advance and he rejected her, "World War III was declared." Bette lost the film role to Ava Gardner.

"Tennessee Williams' theme in *The Night of the Iguana*

is perhaps the most pervasive in American literature, where people lose greatly in the very shadow of the mountain from whose peak they have had a clear view of God. It is the romance of the lost yet sacred misfits, who exist in order to remind us of our trampled instincts, our forsaken tenderness, the holiness of the spirit of man."

—Arthur Miller

Bette Davis had lost out on the chance to play Amanda Wingfield in *The Glass Menagerie,* Blanche DuBois in *A Streetcar Named Desire,* and Violet Venable in *Suddenly Last Summer.* However, wearing a Hallowe'en-colored orange wig in Tennessee's 1962 Broadway play, *The Night of the Iguana,* She had her chance to star in a role by the playwright whose work had so far eluded her.

Tennessee was thrilled when she'd agreed to star in the play. Along with Tallulah Bankhead, he'd long had a fascination with the temperamental star. Even if his play had flaws—and he suspected that it did—he knew that legions of Davis' fans, especially gay ones, would flock to see her perform in it on Broadway.

Tennessee based the setting of *Iguana* on time he'd spent in 1940 at a Pacific coast Mexican backwater, at a small, seedy hotel. "That summer, much of Mexico was overrun with Nazi Germans," he wrote. "A party of them arrived at my hotel, jubilant over the fire-bombing of London. There was an attractive girl in the party, and I said 'hello' to her. She glared at me and growled, 'Sorry, I don't speak Yiddish.' Apparently, she assumed that all Yankees were Jewish."

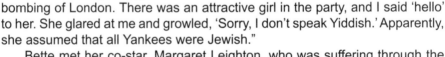

Bette Davis hated her co-stars and announced she was leaving the show. Tennessee urged her to stay, claiming it would shut down the play itself. "Bette, at this point in our troubled careers, both of us desperately need a hit. Don't walk out."

He later told her replacement, Shelley Winters, "I did not admire Bette's performance. Only the tickets she sold. What a bitch!"

Bette met her co-star, Margaret Leighton, who was suffering through the final months of her turbulent marriage to the English actor, Laurence Harvey. The director, Frank Corsaro, introduced Bette to Leighton. "We don't have to be friends, do we?" Bette asked. "When I made *All About Eve* with Celeste Holm, I never spoke to her except on camera."

Ever the lady, Leighton chose not to be drawn into an early catfight with the volatile Hollywood movie star.

Up to then, Bette had been shown only pages of her own dialogue, given to her directly by Tennessee, who was frantically rewriting them every day. However, when she saw Leighton run through her scenes, she realized that the more experienced stage actress was the production's star, the one with a role calling for depth and sensitivity. Leighton was cast as Hannah Jelkes, a

An Enraged "Mother Goddamn" Denounces Margaret Leighton and Tries to De-Pants Patrick O'Neal.

Nantucket spinster and portrait artist who traveled around with her aging grandfather, Nonnon *[played in the production by Alan Webb]*, "the world's oldest living and practicing poet." Jelkes *[as played by Leighton]* earned a meager living painting portraits of tourists in the local town square, while Nonno recites poetry.

Fanatically jealous of Leighton, Bette became her provocative self: "I understand you're still married to that cocksucker, Laurence Harvey," she said to Leighton one afternoon. "I noticed he hasn't come backstage to visit you during rehearsal. Where is he? Busy cruising the men's toilets in the subway?"

Leighton chose not to answer.

Bette began to have arguments with Tennessee, urging him to cut much of Leighton's dialogue and enlarge her own part in the play. "The public will be coming to see me, not Margaret Leighton. The role should have gone to Katharine Hepburn, not this relative unknown. Davis and Hepburn—a sure fire Broadway hit."

"Actually, I did offer the role of Hannah to Hepburn, but she turned it down," Tennessee said.

From the beginning, Bette had conflicts with her director, Frank Corsaro. "He's not a director. I hear he's a libretto writer for operas. Also, he's from that moronic Actors Studio in New York, which gave us Mumbles *[a disparaging reference to Marlon Brando]*. I can't stand Method acting."

Her most volatile relationship would be with the male star of *Iguana,* Patrick O'Neal. The reason it quickly turned sour began with a very flirtatious Bette.

O'Neal, too, had studied at the Actors Studio. Born in Florida, he had directed training films for the U.S. Army during World War II. Beginning in the 1950s, he was seen mostly as a guest star on television programs. *Iguana* would be his first big role on Broadway.

At first, Bette pursued O'Neal, as she had done previously with a host of other co-stars who had included George Brent, Henry Fonda, and Franchot Tone; and directors such as Anatole Litvak, Vincent Sherman, and William Wyler. Every afternoon, she invited O'Neal for drinks in her dressing room, where she made romantic overtures to him. Disinclined to such a liaison, he somehow managed to flee from her clutches.

She confided to Tennessee, "I am seriously thinking of making Patrick my next husband in lieu of my failed marriage to Gary Merrill."

Twenty years Bette's junior, O'Neal was eventually invited to her townhouse on Manhattan's East 78th Street. Finally, he made it clear that whereas he respected her as an actress, his feelings for her were not romantically inclined. She immediately denounced him as a homosexual.

The next day during rehearsals, she turned on him, accusing him of trying to be a "dimestore Marlon Brando, mumbling incoherently like a babbling fool."

Her abuse continued on a daily basis, although O'Neal at the time was on the verge of a nervous breakdown, as was Tennessee.

Both of them were making almost daily visits to the office of Dr. Max Jacobson, where they were being injected with a murky blend of vitamins, hormones, glandular secretions, and amphetamines.

Sometimes, Jacobson was not available because of his frequent excursions to Washington, D.C., where he was injecting his "miracle" drugs into then-President John F. Kennedy and, unknown to the president, into Jackie. Celebrated by dozens of prominent clients from the world of media, show-biz, and politics, with very little supervision of medical practices later defined as both destructive and addictive, Jacobson was dubbed "Miracle Man" or "Dr. Feelgood."

One day, O'Neal and Tennessee encountered Truman Capote in Jacobson's waiting room. The gossipy author said, "Guess who was in here last week? Marlene Dietrich with Eddie Fisher. Mickey Mantle was here the week before. And need I identify a certain rock 'n roll star? Max flew to Memphis to shoot him up. He's also visited the home of Nelson Rockefeller."

O'Neal constantly complained to Tennessee about Bette, accusing her of being "a psychotic bitch. She's crazy. She accuses Maggie and me of sabotaging her performance, whatever that means. She rants at us and curses us. Listen, I'm not too steady on my feet, and at times, I don't think I can take it."

As he had (accurately) predicted, O'Neal eventually "Lost it." One afternoon, he lunged toward Bette to choke her. Corsaro restrained him. O'Neal later confessed to Tennessee. "As you know, Max *[Jacobson]* is out of town, and I need a shot."

"So do I," Tennessee responded.

After O'Neal's aborted assault, Bette fled to the home of a friend in Westport, Connecticut. There, she remained in seclusion in a tiny bedroom upstairs, refusing to accept Corsaro's calls.

Charles Bowden, the producer of *Iguana,* did not like Corsaro and blamed him for not getting along with Bette. "She is a highly complex woman, a major actress who even managed to stand up to Warners during that studio's heyday. She earned her position by fighting like a tigress for good roles. She's like a cackling mother protecting her chicks. In the theater, you must learn to work with tem-

Bette Davis denounced **Patrick O'Neal** to Tennessee. "This god damn Method actor piece of shit gives a different performance every night. It is his attempt to sabotage my performance and embarrass me in front of my devoted fans. I'm on to that bastard!"

Before her final performance, Bette told **Margaret Leighton**, her rival, "I'm so happy to have worked with such a congenial actress. I'm soooo glad everyone, especially O'Neal, found you so charming and brilliant. I'm sorry I irritated you with my professionalism. You obviously like doing it your way much better. Well, now you can, my dear."

peramental actresses. You should know that from your opera background, dealing with divas."

Tennessee and Corsaro drove together to Westport to plead with Bette to come downstairs to the living room to meet with them. Finally, she agreed to a confrontation, during which she made a series of demands, including that both Leighton and O'Neal should be replaced. Once again, she demanded that Tennessee enlarge her part and cut down certain scenes focusing around Leighton.

Those scenes just happened to be vital to the structure of the play, and also Leighton's best dialogue. Tennessee agreed to work on that, although he had no intention of acquiescing to Davis' demands. Corsaro explained that O'Neal and Leighton had contracts that could not be broken.

Finally, and very reluctantly, Bette agreed to open the play in a tryout in Rochester. "No one has ever heard of Rochester, and it is far, far away from the critics of New York City," Bette said. "If we bomb there, you can get Bowden to shut down the play and not bring it to Broadway."

Before Corsaro and Tennessee left that house in Westport that day, Bette reminded them that the theater party bookings, which were heavy, were based entirely on one name—"That of Bette Davis."

"After my last three failures on Broadway, I concede that, indeed, you have a point." Tennessee responded.

"Satan" Mauls Tennessee,
& Bette Exiles Her Director from Chicago

After her boycott, in Manhattan for *Iguana's* final rehearsals, O'Neal said Bette seemed to have undergone a personality change. "Instead of that bitch, Mildred, in *Of Human Bondage,* she became Margo Channing pursuing Gary Merrill in *All About Eve.* When I came to her dressing room for a drink, she locked the door. Then she really came on to me. Once again, I had to decline. I seriously feared I wouldn't be able to get it up for her."

"The next day, the Bitch Goddess was back in all her fury," O'Neal said. "It was even worse for me, because now I had rejected her for the second and final time."

Tennessee flew to Rochester for his play's opening night. He was shocked, after the curtain rose, that the raucous audience was treating *Iguana* like a black comedy instead of as a serious play. Bette brought wild laughter to many of the wrong moments, evoking for Tennessee the gruesome memory of Tallulah Bankhead, as Blanche DuBois, inadvertently but inevitably sabotaging a production of *A Streetcar Named Desire.*

At the end of the opening night performance, however, it was Leighton who received the loudest applause. Unlike Bette's, her role was taken seriously.

Backstage, Tennessee observed that Bette's face was filled with fury. When she came out on stage, she was greeted with polite applause, "something that the Queen of England might deliver after a command performance," Tennessee said.

That night, Bette managed to trip and fall backstage, and was rushed to a hospital in an ambulance. When Corsaro and Tennessee went to see her the next day, they found her in a wheelchair. She informed them that she could not complete the bill in Rochester and that her understudy would have to perform in her place.

When Bowden heard the news, he was immediately tempted to close *Iguana* in Rochester. Corsaro suggested that Bette be replaced with Shelley Winters. *[Ironically, it was Shelley who would take over the Maxine Faulk role on Broadway after Bette's three-month involvement.]*

Two days later, Tennessee visited Bette, and—in a reversal of her earlier position—she assured him that she'd be recovered in time to appear on stage in Detroit, their next stopover.

The Night of the Iguana, as presented in "Motown," evolved into an intensely personal disaster for Tennessee, with long-lasting implications for his relationship with his companion, Frank Merlo.

Satan, a gift from Anna Magnani, was a black Belgian shepherd dog that had far greater affection for Frank than for Tennessee. They had opted to bring Satan with them during this stress-permeated trip.

Beset with production problems, and uncomfortably installed in a hotel suite on their first night in Detroit, Tennessee stepped over Satan to get into bed with Frank. The dog suddenly lunged at Tennessee, biting both of his ankles to the bone and going for Tennessee's throat until Frank pulled him off. Then Frank locked Satan in the bathroom. The following day, he took him to a vet to be put to sleep.

In the meantime, Tennessee had to be rushed to the hospital. Overnight, "my ankles had swollen up to the size of elephant legs," he said.

When Corsaro came to visit him, he found that Tennessee on antibiotics and pain-killers was completely irrational. When Frank left the room, Tennessee told Corsaro that Frank had commanded Satan to attack him. "He wants me dead so he can steal my money. He didn't dare kill me himself, so he had Satan attempt to do it. Before I passed out, all I remember was Satan with those large fangs going for my throat."

[Darwin Porter, who as a favor to Tennessee and Frankie, used to exercise Satan through walks along Duncan Street in Key West, remembers the dog as slobbery and amicable, and wonders whether the dislocation of life on the road during the road show of Iguana, *coupled with Tennessee's erratic behavior, didn't set the dog off.]*

Recovered somewhat, Tennessee, with his bandaged feet shuffling along the Detroit sidewalks in large bedroom slippers, took the train with Frank and the cast to Chicago, where more turmoil awaited them.

Very late one night, from a corridor of the hotel in Chicago where she'd

556

been installed in a suite, Bette observed O'Neal leaving Margaret Leighton's accommodation. Although the actor had rejected her, he had—to Davis' fury—begun an affair with her rival. At that point, her pent-up rage against both Leighton and O'Neal virtually exploded.

She decided to take it out on Corsaro, who had previously been supportive of her grievances. She confronted Bowden, threatening to fly out of Chicago unless he removed Corsaro from the theater—"never to return." Later, she upped that demand, insisting that she would not perform unless Corsaro was banished from Chicago altogether. "I can't even stand to be in the same city with this Actors Studio Method stooge."

Subsequently, Corsaro was hastily banished from the production, provided with enough incentives to quickly, but with enormous bitterness, get out of town.

By default, Tennessee became the production's director. Unlike Corsaro, he stood up to Bette, reminding her that she was no longer the Queen of Hollywood, but an aging actress in the twilight of a distinguished film career, not a stage career.

"I will not do the rewrites you want before the opening on Broadway," he informed her. "I will not ruin my play to appease your monstrous ego." Then he stormed out of the theater, leaving her reduced to tears.

She ranted. She raged. She called him "a goddamn, cocksucking faggot son of a bitch."

Throughout the remainder of the run in Chicago, she started to miss performances, evoking a scene from *All About Eve*. Once, when it was announced that Miss Bette Davis would not be appearing, nearly three-quarters of the audience rose from their seats and headed to the box office to demand a refund.

Tennessee, no temple of mental health himself, also had to nurse Leighton through a suicide attempt. He later wrote to his friend, Maria St. Just: "I believe that I am the only one who knows that Maggie is quite starkers!"

The waiters in a Chicago restaurant witnessed a demonstration of how unstable O'Neal was. He dined with Audrey Wood, Charles Bowden, and Tennessee.

After Tennessee left the restaurant, heading back to his hotel, O'Neal got into a fight with Bowden, who refused to fire Bette. "Patrick was drunk and without his shots from Max Jacobson," Wood said. "He rose to his feet and turned over a table laden with cocktails, coffee, and *canapés* into our laps. Waiters came charging toward our table, shouting, 'Catch him! Stop that lunatic!'"

O'Neal fled through the restaurant's front door, nearly knocking down Tennessee, who was standing on the curb in front, waiting for a taxi. The waiters chased after O'Neal, but he eluded them.

Corsaro later said, "By the time the cast from hell left Chicago, Bette had virtually wrecked Patrick's performance. Even when I was forced out of the theater by Bette, I knew that Patrick had become a mere shadow of himself, thanks to Miss Davis."

O'Neal later admitted, "I was terrified to open on Broadway with Davis, not knowing what she would do. At this point, both Tennessee and I were plunged into some dark night. At least in New York we could find rejuvenation from those injections from Dr. Feelgood."

Bette Receives Broadway's Most Thunderous Ovation

It was the evening of December 28, 1961. In her dressing room, Bette Davis, with the assistance of a gay hairdresser, placed a "catsup-colored wig" over her own hair and checked her makeup in the mirror, as she prepared to face a Broadway audience for her New York debut of *The Night of the Iguana.*

Much of the theatrical world, along with stellar lights from Hollywood, had flown in to see the play. "They're not coming all this way to see a new degenerate play by Tennessee, but to watch me in this goddamn fright wig make a horse's ass out of myself."

She checked her appearance in a full-length mirror. Dressed as a slatternly widow, Maxine Faulk, she was determined to play the role as a "female Stanley Kowalski." She wore a pair of hip-hugging jeans "with my middle-aged flesh hanging out over my belly."

According to the script, Maxine's first appearance follows in the immediate wake of having been seduced by one of her well-hung Mexican beach boys.

One of the actors, Christopher Jones *[who later married Susan Strasberg]* impressed Bette: "From what I saw in those tight pants of his, he had meat for the poor."

The curtain opened, depicting a decaying ramshackle set, suggesting the Costa Verde Hotel in a Mexican backwater. "I was cast as the nympho bitch who runs the joint," Bette said.

When Bette walked onto the stage that night, she received what some reported to be the most thunderous ovation in the history of Broadway, the applause lasting for at least ten minutes.

Patrick O'Neal had to wait impatiently in the wings before she called out, "Shannon!," signaling that he was to come on stage and that the play could begin.

Tennessee was impatiently pacing back and forth in the theater's lobby, but he rushed in to see what all the thunder was about. Bette later claimed, "This was even better than going on stage to receive an Oscar."

As Bette's biographer, Barbara Leaming, wrote: "This short, scrawny, self-proclaimed Yankee dame, with legs spread, wide arms akimbo, her head held high," was enjoying one of the most glorious moments of her turbulent life.

It was clear to all the critics that although Bette's role was the more flamboyant, Leighton had delivered the award-winning performance. When admirers rushed backstage to greet Bette, O'Neal stood ten feet away, analyzing the scenario with skepticism. Bette was surrounded with everybody from Lillian Gish to Eleanor Roosevelt, from Judy Garland to Helen Hayes.

Carson McCullers tried to comfort Tennessee, who told her he feared a massive assault from the critics. He angered her, however, when he gave her some good advice, which she did not heed: "Whatever you do, do not publish your latest novel, *Clock Without Hands.* I read the manuscript. It is considerably flawed and it will damage your literary reputation."

Many months of bitter silence would pass before she agreed to speak to him again.

***

When it came time for awards, Bette was deeply disappointed when Leighton walked off with a Tony for Best Actress in a Drama. Tennessee was honored for writing the Best Play of the Year, an award that would forever elude him in the future. He also received the New York Drama Critics Circle Award for Best Play.

On April 4, 1962, Bette dropped out, informing Bowden, "I can't stand the horror of working with this cast, especially Leighton and O'Neal, who offer me no support whatsoever. It has been plain murder for me having to go onto that stage every night with those two bastard assholes."

As disgusted as she was with *Iguana,* Bette was disappointed when she lost the role of Maxine Faulk in the play's 1964 film adaptation, the part going to Ava Gardner. Davis had told Hedda Hopper, "I'm praying that I get the role. Everything Tennessee Williams writes is better on screen than on stage."

It was Shelley Winters who signed on to replace Bette onstage in *Iguana.* "Miss Davis brought in the cash, and Miss Winters, appearing every night tanked on Jack Daniels Tennessee sour mash whiskey, managed to fill the balcony with her fans," Tennessee said.

In Hollywood, Bette told Olivia de Havilland, "I made the worst mistake of my life appearing in Tennessee's *Iguana* crap. It was my all time worst performance. But I've signed to do another picture. I just know I'm going to win another Oscar. I play a former child star opposite Joan Crawford in a film called *What Ever Happened to Baby Jane?"*

***

In 1976, *The Night of the Iguana,* as directed by Joseph Hardy, was revived at the Circle in the Square Theatre in Lower Manhattan. The stars included gay actor Richard Chamberlain as the Rev. Shannon, with veteran actress Dorothy McGuire as Hannah and Sylvia Miles as Maxine.

For the many actresses who have interpreted the role of Maxine Faulk, from Bette Davis to Ava Gardner, critics have noted that, "It is a coveted role for middle-aged stars who want to wriggle out of the girdle of Hollywood glamour and liberate their inner slobs."

There have been subsequent revivals as well, including a critically acclaimed London production at the Lyric Theatre, starring Woody Harrelson as the Rev. Shannon, in all his broad sonorousness and whiskey-rotted virility.

559

Bette Davis to Tennessee:

"The marquee shouldn't read '*The Night of the Iguana* with Bette Davis.' It should read 'Bette Davis in *The Night of the Iguana*.' I'm playing second fiddle to a goddamn IGUANA! Nobody knows what an iguana is, but everybody's heard of Bette Davis."

Chapter Thirty-Nine

THE DEBATE STILL RAGES

Did Tennessee Perform Fellatio on Senator John F. Kennedy?

"Tennessee Williams had a wild crush on Jack Kennedy. I told Jack, and he thought it was a horse laugh—he was greatly amused."

—Gore Vidal

There are a number of books out there similar to *Who's Had Who*, a title published in 1990 by three authors: Simon Bell, Richard Curtis, and Helen Fielding. The best of the lot is Mart Martin's *Did He or Didn't He?*, published in 2000, revealing details about the intimate sex lives of 201 famous men.

Martin, along with many other writers, includes on John F. Kennedy's list of conquests everyone from Hedy Lamarr to LeMoyne (Lem) Billings. In his book, Martin wrote, "Kennedy was the frequent recipient of nonreciprocal fellatio from Billings. Meeting in prep school *[Choate]* in 1933, the two became lifelong friends and even toured Europe together."

As has been frequently reported, Kennedy enjoyed many temporary *ménages à trois* with his brother-in-law, Peter Lawford. A bisexual secretly in love with the President, Lawford was forced to procure many a starlet *du jour* for encounters with Kennedy, some of them three-ways, a few with Lawford as a participant.

On some of the compilations (including Mart Martin's) of names of Kennedy's lovers, Tennessee Williams' name appears. Additionally, a description of JFK's sexual

In 1958, even with a bad eye, **Tennessee Williams** proved that he was a better marksman than **John F. Kennedy** *(left)*, who's standing next to **Gore Vidal**, at the Kennedy compound in Palm Beach.

encounter with Tennessee has appeared in a number of other books as well, and Gore Vidal *[who introduced JFK to Tennessee, and because the assertion is so prevalent]* has even mentioned it in his writings.

Gore more or less dismissed the possibility of an intimate encounter as an urban myth, but those closer in friendship to Tennessee than Gore repeat it as "gospel truth," having frequently heard it from the mouth of the playwright himself.

Over the years, an assertion of a sexual link between JFK and Tennessee has been promulgated by some of his closest female friends, including Maria St. Just, Marion Vaccaro, and Margaret Foresman.

Look at the ass on Senator Kennedy!" —*Tennessee Williams*

"Bird, you can't cruise the future President of the United States!" —*Gore Vidal*

How Did It All Begin?

In 1958, before going to Hollywood to write the screen version of Tennessee's play, *Suddenly Last Summer,* Gore flew to Key West to confer with the playwright.

Before the end of his sojourn there, Gore suggested that Tennessee should travel with him to Palm Beach for an afternoon with the future president of the United States, John F. Kennedy. At the time, he was still serving as a Senator from Massachusetts.

[It was Jackie was wanted to meet Tennessee more than JFK did. Of course, their 1958 meeting in Palm Beach with Tennessee occurred before she occupied the White House, but in 1961, she told Gore, "One of the glories of living in the White House is that you can meet almost anybody you want to." As a demonstration of that, one of the first celebrities she invited to dinner was Greta Garbo. At that dinner, JFK embarrassed Jackie by asking Garbo, "Did my father seduce you?"

Garbo's sphinx-like face remained an enigma. She neither denied nor admitted it.]

Tennessee was apolitical. To Gore's astonishment, he had never heard of Senator Kennedy. "Well," Gore responded. "You will hear of him, because he's going to run for President of the United States—sooner than later. Then the whole world will hear of him."

Northbound traffic from Key West was heavy that day, and in Palm Beach, Jackie was getting restless, wondering if Gore would actually show up at all, with or without Tennessee. Fortunately, the cook had prepared a lunch featuring cold lobster, so that any delay in serving it would not complicate her role as a hostess.

Arriving an hour late, Gore was filled with apologies.

Ever the courtly Southern gentleman, Tennessee was introduced to Jackie. "You're far too pretty to be a First Lady," he told her. "Perhaps a movie star. I'm sure you could play roles suitable for the near departed, Grace Kelly, or the still-with-us, Audrey Hepburn."

Jackie was flattered, and confided to Tennessee that she had once entertained the possibility of becoming an actress instead of the wife of a Boston politician.

"Jack's office used to be right across from Richard Nixon's," Jackie told Tennessee. "One afternoon, when Jack was away making one of his endless speeches, Nixon made a pass at me."

"Jackie just blurted this out," Tennessee recalled. "I think this was my signal that the luncheon would be filled with indiscreet gossip. Later, as time went by, I discovered that Jackie and I shared some things in common. Both of us had powerful crushes on Marlon Brando."

Jackie led Gore and Tennessee out onto the lawn, where JFK was target shooting. From the looks of things, he was a poor shot, having missed every bull's eye at which he'd aimed.

When Tennessee was introduced to JFK, the playwright was startled. JFK complimented him on what a brilliant play *Summer and Smoke* was. Tennessee was used to receiving compliments for *A Streetcar Named Desire,* and was pleasantly surprised the JFK had cited his enjoyment of one of his lesser works.

Even though one of his eyes was severely nearsighted, Tennessee shouldered JFK's gun and scored a bull's eye with his first shot. The future U.S. President was impressed and put his arm around Tennessee in a congratulatory, very macho hug.

Jackie had already told Gore that Jack, when introduced socially to a homosexual, always asserted his male virility to that person in an intimate way: "He flirts with them and, I think, basks in their adoration of his manhood."

"Better that than burning them at the stake!" Gore responded.

Then Jackie headed back inside the house to check whether the long-delayed lunch was ready, and JFK walked ahead to wash up, since he was sweaty. Tennessee remained on the lawn with Gore, checking out the future President's retreat. "Look at that ass!" Tennessee said to Gore.

Gore scolded him. "You can't cruise our next President."

"Let's stop all this talk about him being President," Tennessee said. "With that voice of his, those good looks of his, and his hip nature, he will never go over with the public. He'd be a rage in Hollywood. He's more of a leading man than president. He'd look great on screen making love to Arlene Dahl or Lana Turner."

"I'm sure he's already been there and done that," Gore responded.

Over lunch, Jackie told Tennessee, "I'm jealous of Tommy Auchincloss, my halfbrother. It's a family legend that you took Tommy to Coney Island in 1951."

"I have no recollection of

Jack Kennedy and **Jackie** looked fabulous in formal wear, the most glamorous couple ever to inhabit the White House. However, they could dress informally, as when vacationing in Palm Beach.

Most of the films of them at play, including Jack on the golf course, were shot in black and white. However, some color footage remains. Jack had an addiction for wearing pink pants, which were considered very daring in 1961. Jackie told Gore, "He even likes my panties to be pink."

that event," Tennessee said. "I don't know how old Tommy would have been in 1951, but it never happened. Besides, New York has laws against child molestation."

JFK joined in the laughter. Much of the other gossip centered on Elizabeth Taylor, who was contracted to appear in the upcoming film version of *Suddenly Last Summer*. JFK didn't appear to even be vaguely interested in her co-star, Katharine Hepburn, but—much to Jackie's annoyance—he pumped both Tennessee and Gore for gossip about Elizabeth.

"I saw *Cat on a Hot Tin Roof* three times," JFK told them.

"I saw it, but objected to how Richard Brooks was forced to obscure Brick's *[the character played by Paul Newman]* homosexuality," Jackie said. "I think there should be more openness on the screen. When Jack becomes President, I want him to fight to get rid of all vestiges of that old-fashioned Production Code. It's stifling in its conformity, and I want it to die with the Eisenhower years."

"Oh, my God," JFK said. "The future First Lady is a rebel in the making! Wait until Dad hears about this."

What happened next remains a matter of conjecture, even to this day. Jackie asked Gore to drive her to Worth Avenue for a shopping expedition, as she needed to buy some summer dresses.

As she headed out with him, JFK warned her, "Don't spend too much money. I'm not as rich as people think."

Left alone with JFK, Tennessee later claimed, "He pumped me for gossip about stars, including Marlon Brando, of which I knew intimate details, but also about Joan Collins, of which my information was very limited."

"After we rested a bit after lunch, he suggested we go for a swim," Tennessee said. "I told him that a daily swim was almost mandatory for me. He invited me into the changing room."

"He stripped naked before me, telling me that he always swam in the nude, something he'd learned from his mother, Rose Kennedy, who he claimed still swims jaybird naked at her age."

"After we swam for a few laps in his pool, we returned to the changing room to dry off," Tennessee said. "I couldn't help myself, but my eyes fastened on his crotch. I told him that swimming was just

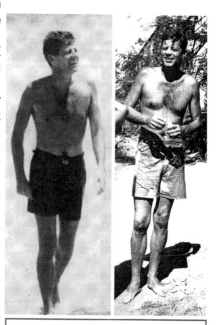

Jack Kennedy was very thin and often looked frail. But he was never ashamed of showing off his body—in fact, he strippped down more frequently for the camera than did any other president. His nearest rival was Ronald Reagan, who posed for beefcake photos during his years in Hollywood.

one of my favorite pastimes. I guess I made my dark desires rather obvious."

"He went over to the sink for a minute and seemed to fluff himself a bit before turning around to display an erection. What else could I do? If Gore were right, he would soon become President and could command me, as his loyal subject, to do his bidding."

"I must confess, it was not one of my most memorable blow-jobs. In fact, I think it was over in about two minutes of intense suction on my part. He was a fast shooter. His cock was only average, perhaps a little less than average, but then, I've never been known as a size queen."

As Tennessee later relayed to Margaret Foresman *[his notoriously raunchy drinking buddy and long-time Managing Editor of* The Key West Citizen*]*, "The President-to-be did give me a compliment. 'You're good!,' he told me."

"Then we put on our clothes and went back into the house, where he invited me for sundowners. I changed my mind about him. I now decided he had the makings of a President. It was obvious that he was used to being serviced instead of doing the serving himself. Call it 'Imperial Privilege.'"

"I did lose out in one respect, however," Tennessee recalled to Foresman. "JFK became famous for saying, 'I'm not finished with a woman until I've had her three ways. With me, he could have had at least two ways. But he never invaded my second portal."

Months after JFK was elected president in 1960, Tennessee parroted a line from his inaugural address to the American people: "I didn't ask what my President could do for me. Instead I asked what I could do for my President."

***

[Although Jackie admired Tennessee, they never became friends. In 1976, she was seen dining with Andy Warhol and Tennessee in a Manhattan restaurant.

"Jackie seemed a bit nervous about being with Tennessee, and he seemed a bit nervous about hanging out with Jackie," Warhol later recorded in his diary. "All Jackie kept talking about was household business, beautifying the home, where to buy this and that, and so forth. She sounded like a glorified housewife, although, of course, she wasn't."

"What I really wanted to ask Tennessee was, 'Did you really go down on Jack Kennedy?' And what I really wanted to ask Jackie was, 'Did you know that Tennessee once went down on your husband?' But discretion prevented me from going where angels fear to tread."

Chapter Forty

The Night of the Iguana

(The Movie)

Burton & Taylor & Tennessee
Chase Iguanas and Sex Partners in Mexico

Left photo: **"Liz and Dick,"** or "Dickie," as she called him, created a media frenzy every time they appeared in public during the filming of Tennessee Williams' play, *The Night of the Iguana.* Whether smiling, scowling, or cursing, the pair stirred up frontpage news both in Mexico and the U.S. Much of what Elizabeth said could not be printed: "My best feature is my gray hairs, both on my head and covering my vagina. Each hair is named Burton."

Right photo: The motley stars of *Iguana* assembled for a group photograph. *Standing, left to right,* **Sue ("Lolita") Lyon**; prim and proper **Deborah Kerr**, and whorish **Ava Gardner**. *Seated,* brilliant and dissipated, and as jaded as the defrocked priest he was portraying, is **Richard Burton.**

The arrival of the "scandalous" Elizabeth Taylor and Richard Burton in Mexico City occurred on September 22, 1963. As mobs descended on the airport, it became an international media event. Although she hadn't been cast in the movie, Elizabeth was accompanying Burton to Mexico, where he'd be filming Tennessee Williams' *The Night of the Iguana.*

Losing her purse, part of her wardrobe, and even her shoes, Elizabeth made it through the crowd with the help of strong-armed security guards. "Fuck this!" she shouted at Burton. "They think we're the Beatles!"

Even before they left the airport, "The Liz & Dick" show entertained the masses by staging a big fight over a missing case of jewelry, each blaming the other for its disappearance. The box later turned up in a packed suitcase.

A press conference had been scheduled, but Burton refused to attend. However, he did issue a statement. "This is my first visit to Mexico. I hope it will be my last."

In a short time he would change his mind and buy a vacation home there.

Elizabeth had a different opinion. She told the press, "I have always wanted to come back to fucking Mexico. I like fucking Mexico." The Mexican reporters printed her remarks but left out the two adjectives.

Initially, there was a lot of misunderstanding in the press, headlines claiming that Elizabeth, not Ava Gardner, would be the female star of the movie.

John Huston, the project's director, had wanted Marlon Brando to play the defrocked priest, but Ray Stark, the producer, favored either Richard Harris or William Holden. Finally, they settled on Burton. Ava Gardner had been their first choice as the notorious innkeeper, but Melina Mercouri was also held out as a replacement.

Under the scorching Mexican sun, *Iguana's* director **John Huston** *(left)* tells **Tennessee** that he had originally wanted Marlon Brando instead of Richard Burton to star as the defrocked priest. However, the film's producer, Ray Stark, Huston informed him, had preferred Richard Harris or William Holden.

"I flew to Switzerland and lied to Burton, telling him, 'You were my one and only choice,'" Huston said.

For the role of Deborah Kerr's grandfather, Nonno, Tennessee wanted Carl Sandburg, America's most famous playwright, but he was in failing health. The role instead went to Cyril Delevanti.

According to Elizabeth's secretary, Dick Hanley, who accompanied the famous pair, Elizabeth arrived "pissed off" at director John Huston. In fact, by the second day, she was already lambasting him as "an ugly, old, mean, withering fart," charging that he had mentally abused her friend Monty Clift during the filming of both *The Misfits* (1961) and *Freud* (1962).

In retribution, the director rather ungallantly chose to bring up the subject of how Elizabeth was "shameless" in stealing Mike Todd from Huston's former

Marilyn Monroe's Latest Lover Crawls Into Bed First With Elizabeth, and Then With Tennessee

wife, Evelyn Keyes.

Zoe Sallis showed up in Puerto Vallarta. It was common knowledge that she was Huston's mistress.

In 1963, Puerto Vallarta was a seedy little fishing village lying three hundred miles north of Acapulco. Tacky and not very well known, it became instantly famous when Elizabeth and Burton arrived and put it on the international tourist map. Tennessee would soon arrive to join in the chaos.

The actual shooting of *Iguana* took place on the

Merrily We Roll Along

As a horrified extra *(right)* looks on during their bus tour through Mexico, **Grayson Hall** *(center)*, cast as a tour guide and chaperone for nymphet Lolita **Sue Lyon** *(left)*, really wants to take her to bed. But since that wasn't possible, she vowed to "move all the mountains in Mexico" to keep Burton's paws off her.

isolated peninsula of Mismaloya, which had no road access to the mainland and could be reached only by boat. The only inhabitants on Mismaloya were Indians who lived in thatched huts and survived on fishing.

Elizabeth and Burton and all their massive amounts of luggage were taken to Puerto Vallarta and delivered to "Gringo Gulch," an upmarket neighborhood where Americans had purchased a number of vacation homes. Locals had another name for it, referring to it as *La Casa de Zoplotes* (the House of the Buzzards) because it lay near a garbage dump.

Whereas Burton had an actual part in the filming, Elizabeth was on site to see that he didn't go astray in the arms of any of his female co-stars. They included man-eating Ava Gardner, Deborah Kerr, and Sue ("*Lolita*") Lyon.

Elizabeth also had to keep her eye out for at least fifty whores, some of them diseased, who had arrived from Mexico City to service the film crew. At least half of that number of male hustlers had also come to Puerto Vallarta to service homosexual members of the crew. "I'm sure Tennessee will be royally entertained," Burton said.

Arriving at the port, Elizabeth feared she'd be assigned to some shack, but was delighted by Casa Kimberley, the villa provided for her. In fact, she liked it so much that she eventually bought it for $40,000.

Burton liked the ramshackle port, too, and in time, he built a villa across the street from Casa Kimberley, connecting the two properties with a footbridge that linked the two buildings from points within their respective second floors. Its design was inspired by the Bridge of Sighs in Venice. "I can run across the bridge and escape from Liz when she becomes a raging harridan," Burton told his assistant, Michael Wilding, who—as her former husband— was all too familiar with her rages.

It would take almost a novel to untangle the past and present romantic entanglements that whirled around the cast and crew of *Iguana*. Before it was over, Kerr told the press, "I'm the only one here not shacked up with somebody."

She left out the fact that she was accompanied by her husband, Peter Viertel, the scriptwriter who had previously worked with Huston on *The African Queen* (1951) with Humphrey Bogart and Katharine Hepburn. Viertel had also been the former lover of Ava Gardner.

There were other sexual embarrassments unfolding. Huston had a reunion with Gardner, with whom he'd once had a torrid affair. Huston had also once pursued Kerr.

Elizabeth knew that Kerr had had a sexual tryst years before with Stewart Granger, but she was not certain if Burton had had an affair with her in Britain.

Relationships between Burton and Wilding were still friendly, and Elizabeth had no animosity toward him. It had not been a bitter divorce. They were both involved in the rearing of their two sons, and both of them loved their boys very much, even though neither of them would ever win any awards for parenting.

Wilding was no longer lusting for Elizabeth. He showed up with a beautiful Swedish actress, Karen von Unge. She recalled, "Michael was a dear, sensitive man who should have been a great painter. Here he was, carrying suitcases of chili for Elizabeth from Chasen's in Los Angeles because she asked for them. She simply asked, and men did—it was that simple."

Huston looked upon Wilding as "a pathetic figure. He was once a big star in England, but he gave it up for Elizabeth. What did it get him? Now he serves her drinks and picks up dog poop for her. He's like the Erich von Stroheim character in *Sunset Blvd.*. Formerly married to Gloria Swanson in the movie, he becomes her butler."

Anticipating feuds or muggings, Huston passed out derringers to key members of his cast. These were the kind of small pistols that late 19th-century card sharps were known for concealing within their sleeves. With the pistols, he gave each person a silver bullet with a name etched onto it. Even though she was not a member of the cast, the derringer he gave Elizabeth was gold-plated.

Unlike the others, Elizabeth received five bullets, each with a name on it—Richard Burton, Sue Lyon, Ava Gardner, and Deborah Kerr. The director also included one with the name of John Huston.

On seeing Elizabeth again over drinks, Gardner said, "Dear heart, you and Richard are the Frank (Sinatra) and Ava (Gardner) of the 1960s."

Evelyn Keyes, though not in Mexico, was present—at least in the group's collective memory. Elizabeth had stolen Mike Todd from her following Keyes' divorce from John Huston. Keyes was now married to Artie Shaw, who had been Gardner's former husband.

The plot thickened when Budd Schulberg, author of the Hollywood novel, *What Makes Sammy Run?* and the screenplay for *On the Waterfront*, arrived to seduce Gardner. Viertel had once been married to Schulberg's former wife,

Virginia Ray.

In a conversation one day at the beach with Elizabeth and Dick Hanley, Viertel confessed that he had abandoned his pregnant wife to run away with Bettina, arguably the most famous French fashion model of the 1950s. "She later dumped me for Aly Khan."

"I know Bettina," Elizabeth said. "I know Aly Khan, too. Oh do I know Aly Khan!"

"Huston tried to console me when I lost Bettina," Viertel said. "He told me 'Aly Khan is one swell guy.' Then, when Aly Khan fucked Huston's wife, Evelyn Keyes, I told him, 'It's okay, John, Aly is one swell guy.' He punched me in the mouth. I love John, though. He's fucked everybody from Marilyn Monroe on the set of *The Asphalt Jungle* to Truman Capote on the set of *Beat the Devil* when they shared a double bed. He even screwed a neo-Nazi woman in London who gave him syphilis—something he later referred to as 'the Hitler clap.'"

When she wasn't due on the set for a day or so, North Carolina-born **Ava Gardner** could outdrink any man in Mexico, even **Richard Burton.**

According to John Huston, "She could go on all night and on through the following night and through the next day and the next night and the next. Although a beautiful woman, she had a big pair of *cojones* on her— Those Tarheel women!"

When Viertel left to return to the set, he, as a man of the world, kissed both Elizabeth and Hanley on the lips before departing.

Tennessee arrived in Puerto Vallarta with Frederick Nicklaus, a young recent graduate of Ohio State University. Tennessee told Huston, "Frederick is the world's greatest living poet, though not discovered as of yet."

"You've already introduced Freddie boy to me in Key West," Huston reminded the drugged playwright.

"I've dealt with Bogie, so I know how to handle difficult, temperamental personalities," Huston later said. "Williams is an odd bird, always in flight. He can also 'fly' off the handle at just a perceived insult. Not only that, but he is eccentric, a sex addict, a pill pusher, an alcoholic, and, perhaps, a genius. A genius is always difficult to handle. I already had Ava Gardner, Richard Burton, and Elizabeth fucking around. Now, Tennessee with his fat wallet would soon be buying every good looking Mexican lad at the port."

Tom Shaw, Huston's assistant director, detested Tennessee and his volatile personality. In his bulldog manner, he said, "I hated the mean son of a bitch. I was having a drink at the bar, and he was berating the shit out of this poor Mexican bartender. At the time, I didn't recognize who he was. I said to myself, 'Who is this asshole?' He was a vicious kind of faggot."

One night over drinks, the key players were asked by Herb Caen, the San Francisco columnist, what they most wanted in life. Huston said, "Interest."

Gardner wished for "Health." Burton opted for "Adventure," Viertel for "Success," and Deborah Kerr "Happiness." Elizabeth chose "Wealth."

Tennessee requested, "Better sex."

James Bacon, the veteran Hollywood reporter who'd once seduced Marilyn Monroe, arrived on the scene. "I'm from Hollywood, and I knew both John Barrymore and Errol Flynn, but I'd never seen such heavy drinking. One night in a tavern, Burton downed twenty-five straight shots of tequila, using Carta Blanca beer as a chaser."

Tennessee and Huston could almost keep up with him.

"I was in no condition myself, but I often had to put Burton to bed at his villa long after Elizabeth had retired," Tennessee said. "He begged me to help him get undressed, so I took advantage. He didn't specifically ask me to, but I also removed the Welshman's jockey shorts. I figured I wouldn't get a chance like this very often—to see what appealed to the stately homos of the British theater like Olivier and Gielgud in the 1940s, and to so many fine ladies."

The cast and crew were constantly besieged by reporters, Elizabeth claiming, "There are more press guys and *paparazzi* here than fucking iguanas."

Whereas reporters from California relished writing about the heavy drinking and the behind-the-scenes romances, the Mexican newspaper *Siempre* denounced the entire cast and crew of *The Night of the Iguana*. It attacked the "sex, drinking, drugs, vice, and carnal bestiality of this gringo garbage that has descended on our country." *Siempre* also cited "gangsters, nymphomaniacs, heroin-taking blondes, and the degenerate American playwright, Tennessee Williams."

One night, while drinking with Elizabeth, it became clear that her body was a sea of insect bites. "Welcome to Puerto Vallarta," she said, "with its tropical heat, cheating lovers, poisonous snakes, deadly scorpions, hot pussies, and giant land crabs. Of them all, the most devouring are the goddamn chiggers, which dig in real deep and can only be removed with scalpels."

The local Catholic priest attacked Elizabeth as a "wanton Jezebel" and called on the President of Mexico to deport her as an undesirable alien. When Tennessee's arrival was publicized in the press, the priest also called for his removal from Mexico as well. "We do not need another notorious homosexual coming to Mexico to corrupt the morals of our young men."

A drunken Elizabeth was asked one night how she'd describe the three women in the cast. She obliged: "Gardner is lushly ripe for a middle-aged woman; Kerr is refined and ladylike until you get her in bed, or so I'm told; and Lyon is...well, let's just say nubile. No wonder James Mason had the hots for her. When making *Lolita*, he temporarily gave up his interest in boys."

When Tennessee, in a Puerto Vallarta tavern known as the Casablanca Bar, was asked for his opinion of the Taylor/Burton romance, he said, "They are artists on a special pedestal and therefore the rules of bourgeois morality do not apply to them."

Burton was sitting with Tennessee when he made that pronouncement. When Burton himself was asked for a comment, he said, "I am bewitched by the cunt of Elizabeth Taylor and her cunning ways. Cunt and cunning—that's what the attraction is."

Graham Jenkins, Burton's brother, was also in Puerto Vallarta, and he had a more sensitive view of the Taylor/Burton affair. "Richard discovered how much he really needed Elizabeth, and his surrender to her was total. Of course, they still fought like cats and dogs. Each of them was mercurial. But they truly loved each other, and that was so evident. That did not mean that each of them could no longer see with their roving eye. Rich especially would always have that."

For the most part, Burton was pleased with his role, telling Tennessee, "After this film is released, those boys in the press will stop calling me Mr. Cleopatra."

The one thing Elizabeth liked about Tennessee's play was the dialogue. "It contained some of the most bitch wit ever recorded."

Over a private drink she had with Huston and Tennessee, she told them, "Believe me, no one adores Ava Gardner more than I do. Such a fine actress, if the role isn't too challenging. I think you'll make a good picture. Regrettably, if you'd chosen me for the role of Maxine, it would have been a great picture, and I would win another Oscar to give the one I have company."

"I'm sure you're right, my dear," Huston said. "Right on target. Forgive my mistake in casting."

***

Before his departure from Mexico in October of 1963 for New York, Tennessee hosted a party at his rented villa near Elizabeth and Burton in Gringo Gulch. He'd invited both of them to attend, but only Elizabeth had shown up.

There, she met Jose Bolaños, a Mexican screen writer who was enjoying a certain vogue. After the murder of Marilyn Monroe on August 4, 1962, he was getting a lot of press attention and being widely hailed as her last and final boyfriend.

Bolaños told Tennessee that he and Monroe had mutually committed themselves to get married, although some of her friends said that Monroe had promised to remarry Joe DiMaggio.

Bolaños was working on a TV commercial twenty-five miles to the south, but had come to Puerto Vallarta with the hope of meeting and ingratiating himself with Elizabeth as he had with Monroe.

Tennessee had been charmed by the charismatic young Mexican and had set up the meeting for him with Elizabeth, presumably without Burton.

Tennessee defined him as a Latin lover archetype, evocative of both Fernando Lamas and Ricardo Montalban. Bolaños was dark and handsome, with a magnetic personality. The night of their meeting, Bolaños told Elizabeth and Tennessee that his dream involved coming to Hollywood and putting both Lamas and Montalban "out of business." Secretly, he hoped that by attaching himself to Elizabeth, she could use her influence to help him break into the American film industry.

573

Elizabeth might have paid scant attention to Bolaños except for two reasons: He was the only man she'd met in Puerto Vallarta who qualified for that "revenge fuck" she'd planned as a means of getting even with Burton for seducing Gardner. Also, she was tempted by the idea of learning intimate secrets about Monroe's last lover, especially if the fallen star had considered Bolaños as marriage material.

The Mexican screenwriter, **Jose Bolaños** *(appearing in both photos above)*, announced that he was going to marry **Marilyn Monroe**. "I will be her new husband and the last lover she will ever need," he boasted to a newspaper in Mexico City.

But before the wedding, Marilyn was murdered. That forced Bolaños to look for a new gig. Subsequently, he showed up in Puerto Vallarta with the intention of stealing Elizabeth Taylor "from Old Man Burton."

At Tennessee's party, Bolaños exuded masculinity, and as Elizabeth would tell Dick Hanley, "He stood so close to me he was practically rubbing that big package up against me."

On his own turf within Mexico's film community, Bolaños was known as a "star fucker," having previously seduced such aging screen divas as Merle Oberon and Dolores Del Rio.

On the patio of Tennessee's rented villa, lit by colored lights, Bolaños danced both the rumba and the samba with Elizabeth. Tennessee had hired a six-member band, each of the members appearing in tight white pants and shirtless, as per the playwright's request.

According to his reputation, Bolaños specialized in making a woman feel like she was the only female on earth.

The screenwriter mesmerized Elizabeth with his tales of working in the film industry in Mexico. He had been an intimate friend of the late, great modernist painter, Diego Rivera, and was also close to the Spain-born director Luís Buñuel, a towering figure in experimental cinema.

Bolaños also invited Elizabeth to see the Mexican historical epic, *La Cucaracha (aka The Soldiers of Pancho Villa;* 1959), whose screenplay he had written.

She pumped Bolaños for any details he could supply about Monroe's final weeks alive. Hanley came over to join them. "Bolaños was very clever," he said. "He did not speak unkindly of Marilyn, but he placed Elizabeth on a higher pedestal. About three times, he told her that 'you are, of course, a far greater star than Marilyn, who possessed neither your talent nor your beauty.'"

"Your beauty is a natural beauty," Bolaños told Elizabeth in front of Hanley. "Marilyn had to become Marilyn Monroe by acting the part, dressing up, and painting her face. With no make-up on, I'm sure you'd look stunning. Surely no one on the planet has eyes as beautiful as yours."

Hanley drove Elizabeth and Bolaños to his apartment, where they disappeared upstairs. He waited downstairs in his car for two hours. When Elizabeth finally came down the steps, he drove her home. She told him that Bolaños had asked to remain in Hanley's apartment for the night, not wanting to drive after dark on the impossibly treacherous roads.

Back in his own apartment, he found a nude Bolaños asleep on his bed. Very gently, Hanley draped a sheet over him. "Lucky Marilyn, lucky Elizabeth," he later told Roddy McDowall.

"The next morning, I made breakfast for him," Hanley said. "He also let me make love to him, but only in exchange for a big favor."

"I know you're her secretary," Bolaños said, "and you can arrange for me to have a rendezvous with her in Hollywood. I want to be in her life. She'll tire of Burton. He's an old man of failing powers, I heard. I want to be nearby when she replaces Burton."

"You've got yourself a deal, but I'll expect my pound of flesh."

Bolaños sighed. "All of you *mariposas* want that. So if you deliver Elizabeth Taylor to me, you can have me on occasion. After all, I'm the most sought after male in all of Mexico."

Bolaños was already aware of the important roles Tennessee had written for men, including the character of Stanley Kowalski in *A Streetcar Named Desire,* and the role of Brick in *Cat on a Hot Tin Roof.*

Consequently, Bolaños asked Hanley to call Tennessee immediately to ask if he could spend the day with him, and possibly the night.

Tennessee was only too eager to invite Bolaños over, telling Hanley, "If Marilyn and Elizabeth can go for him, why not me?"

In the aftermath of that call, Tennessee spent a day and a night with Bolaños before he headed out of Puerto Vallarta the following morning.

Tennessee was so taken with Bolaños that he promised to write a role for him based on the archetype of a dashing young Mexican. "The part will be ideal for you."

Of course that was an empty promise. Tennessee never came through for Bolaños.

***

On most mornings, Tennessee met Elizabeth at her villa. Together, they headed out, wading through chickens, naked children, and mange-encrusted mongrel dogs. He and Hanley carried the makings of a picnic with them, to be shared with Burton later when they reached the remote peninsula where filming was occurring.

Huston liked to launch his day with five Bloody Marys, and Elizabeth and

Tennessee joined him.

One day, Elizabeth was feeling ill and Tennessee went alone, telling Huston that he stood ready to write additional dialogue.

Huston told him, "I don't think we're going to get much shooting done today. The heat is crushing, and Burton disappeared into Ava's dressing room at ten o'clock. They may be in there for the day."

As author Nancy Schoenberger wrote: "Ava seemed to come alive in Burton's presence. The press were not just covering a congregation of some of the world's greatest talents and personalities in a remote Mexican village, they were waiting—hoping?—that Burton and Taylor's vaunted love affair might founder on Ava Gardner's dangerous shoulders."

The coming together of the drunken, poetry-spouting, lust-filled Welsh actor and the Tarheel *femme fatale* and sex symbol had sparked "meaningful eye contact," as Huston described it to Tennessee.

Portraits of the *Iguana* cast, including **Sue Lyon** *(upper left)* and **Richard Burton**, with an anguished **Ava Gardner** pictured below. "Every eligible red-blooded Mexican man in that part of the country was after Ava, and many of them got lucky," Huston said.

The director didn't like the way Tennessee handled Ava's character. He accused the playwright of turning her into a female spider. "You've got it in for women. You don't want to see a man and a woman in a love relationship."

One day before noon, both Gardner and Burton got drunk on a local moonshine known as *raicilla.* It was made from the agave plant. Gardner called it "cactus piss."

Huston defined it to Tennessee as "a cactus brandy stronger than tequila." Burton told him that the way to drink *raicilla* was straight down. That way you can feel it going into each individual intestine." When Elizabeth tried it, she said, "I hear it's made from cactus. Tell the fuckers who brewed it that they left the god damn needles in it."

One evening when Elizabeth was suffering from "*turista,*" Hanley drove Tennessee and Burton to the Casablanca Bar. To Hanley's surprise, a sultry Gardner was waiting there for him. Burton turned to Dick, "I can always count on you for being discreet around Her Ladyship."

Actually, Burton was wrong about the degree to which Hanley would remain discreet.

"After Ava and Richard consumed enough alcohol to resink the *Titanic*, they retired to one of the hot-bed shanties out back, where they disappeared," Hanley said. "I wondered if Richard would be able to get it up in his condition. I sat in the bar with this beach boy hustler waiting for their return."

"Tennessee hired this other hustler and seduced him in our car. Ava and Richard were gone for about three hours. When both of them finally emerged, they were barely able to stand up."

"I literally had to toss them into the back of our car, where they cuddled up with Tennessee for the ride back home," Hanley said.

The next day Elizabeth suspected that something had happened between Ava and Burton. She also suspected that something might be going on between Burton and Sue Lyon, who played the rigidly chaperoned blonde nymphet in *Iguana*.

In some ways, Lyon's casting in that role had been influenced by her involvement, in 1962, of Stanley Kubrick's *Lolita*, an adaptation of the novel by Vladimir Nabokov (*Lolita*) about a middle-aged man's sexual obsession with an adolescent girl.

Burton, incidentally, had seen Lyon's film interpretation of Lolita three times, exhibiting a keen interest in both the film's concept and in its protagonist, of which Elizabeth was emphatically aware.

Elizabeth wasn't the only person struggling to keep Burton away from Lyon. At the debut of filming, she had arrived in Puerto Vallarta with her boyfriend, Hampton Fancher III. Huston's biographer, Lawrence Grobel, described the boy as "a tall, pale youth ravaged by love." Soon after his arrival, Fancher warned Burton, "I tend to be murderously inclined."

The circumstances which led to Burton finally being left alone with Lyon involved the fact that her boyfriend, as it turned out, was married. His young wife arrived unexpectedly on the set one day. Fancher would marry Lyon before the year ended, after his divorce became final.

As Lyon remembered it, "Richard drank so much at night that the alcohol literally oozed out of his pores the next day. It gave off a terrible odor."

One night, Tennessee served as a "beard" to protect Burton during one of the actor's secret flings with Lyon. He'd told Elizabeth that he was going drinking with Tennessee to discuss future roles for them.

Instead, he left Tennessee in the Casablanca Bar, talking with yet another hustler, while he and Lyon disappeared upstairs into a private room.

***

Tennessee could not wait around for the shooting to end. He had to fly back to New York to face other commitments. He was in a Broadway theater when he heard the news about Kennedy's assassination. He later heard that both Elizabeth and Ava Gardner took the news rather badly. Both of them had had flings with the assassinated president.

"So did I," Tennessee said enigmatically, with no explanation.

In the future, Tennessee would deal with Elizabeth and Burton again when they filmed *Boom!* in Sardinia, based on his play, *The Milk Train Doesn't Stop Here Anymore.*

But Truman was also a friend to the Burtons, and would have several encounters with them.

So would Gore Vidal, when he urged Elizabeth to interpret the role of a transsexual in his controversial film, *Myra Breckinridge*, starring Mae West.

Truman Writes a "For Real" Sex Scene Featuring Elizabeth Taylor and Eddie Fisher in BUtterfield 8

Elizabeth Taylor and Truman Capote had known each other for years, their relationship mostly stemming from their mutual friendship with the doomed Montgomery Clift. Truman encountered her on frequent occasions, and he shared some of the most dramatic moments of her life with her.

During the shooting of her Oscar-winning role playing a prostitute in *BUtterfield 8* (1960) *[Elizabeth was starring opposite Laurence Harvey and her then-husband, the singer Eddie Fisher]*, the scriptwriters of Hollywood went on strike.

Despite the *[supremely inconvenient]* strike in force at the time, she wanted her dialogue sharpened and extra scenes added. She especially wanted changes in the script to include love scenes between Fisher and herself. Prior to her involvement in script changes, the onscreen relationship between her character and Fisher's character had been strictly platonic.

Consequently, she approached both of her friends, Tennessee Williams and Capote, to tweak the script for her. Whereas Tennessee was reluctant to get involved but agreed to rewrite some of it, Truman was delighted with the unpaid assignment.

When he came to discuss its details with Elizabeth, he found her distraught, almost on the verge of tears. She told him, "I have to work. I have no money. Eddie has no money. Debbie Reynolds took it all when they divorced…every last cent."

Soon, she and Truman jointly conceived of a torrid love scene "under the sheets" between Fisher and herself. Truman devised a scenario that director Daniel Mann claimed was perhaps too hot to film. Eventually, however, Mann's curiosity became voyeuristically intrigued, and he arranged for the scene to be shot, albeit with a sense of caution.

On the set, on the day of the actual filming, both Fisher and Elizabeth *[who were married to each other at the time]* stripped completely nude and crawled together under the sheets.

As Fisher later claimed, "Having the camera on Elizabeth and me and with that faggot, Capote, drooling at the mouth, turned me on. I had sex with Elizabeth. We really went at it. She liked it rough, and I delivered."

Later, in his memoirs, he denied that he had a climax, but Elizabeth, in dialogues with Truman, insisted that he did.

"It was evident that Fisher was blasting off inside Elizabeth," Truman said. "From the look on her face, she was also experiencing an orgasm. She was not good enough an actress to fake it."

Later, their scene was judged as too hot for the screen, and it ended up on the cutting room floor.

Elizabeth Taylor later confided to Truman Capote: "**Eddie Fisher** *(depicted with Taylor, above)* fucked me better on camera than he did at home. Could it be that he needed an audience?"

Richard Burton & Truman Capote Share A Drunken, Three-Day Collaboration at The Plaza?

Kay Meehan, who was married to Joseph Meehan, the former head of the New York Stock Exchange, was one of Truman's "swans." In the wake of the publication in *Esquire* of early chapters from his controversial novel, *Answered Prayers,* all of his other swans had deserted him because of their scandalous and thinly veiled portraits of themselves.

The other swans weren't returning his calls, but when he phoned Meehan asking if she'd join him for lunch at Manhattan's Plaza Hotel, she accepted. She arrived to find Truman on one of the banquettes, engrossed in a head-to-head huddle with Richard Burton.

Because of that day's heavy rainfalls, she entered the Oak Room like "a drowned rat" *[her words].* There, she found Truman and Burton going over his lines for his upcoming Broadway appearance in *Equus* (1976), in which he would interpret the role of a psychiatrist.

"A tape recorder was on, and he and Truman were rehearsing dialogue line by line," she said. "It was obvious that he was picking Truman's brain. The contrast in their voices was amazing, with his squeaky high-pitched tones and Burton's husky baritone."

"I had a fabulous time, and I think Truman was testing me but also rewarding me. After all, all his other swans had flown away, and he was seeing if I were still loyal. He hadn't told me that Burton would be there. If he had, I would surely have accepted his invitation. He wanted to see if I'd appear at a rendezvous where he'd be the only other person there."

Later, there was speculation among the swans and others that Burton would somehow reward Truman for helping him rehearse his lines in *Equus.* Babe Paley—no longer committed to any sense of discretion about Truman's private life—openly exposed the idea at parties.

It was later learned that Truman and Burton spent three nights together in a suite at the Plaza, ostensibly to work on the actor's stage presence and delivery. Gore Vidal later sarcastically remarked, "I'm sure the little midget was rewarded for his services. I'm certain that he wanted to learn firsthand what turned Elizabeth Taylor on. The Devil's most devious angel just had to know the secrets of everybody who was a media event."

"Eddie [Fisher] Claims That You Made a Pass at Him"

—Elizabeth Taylor to Truman

In February of 1961, Joseph Mankiewicz, the director, was working almost around the clock to complete the script of *Cleopatra,* to star Elizabeth Taylor. She and her then-husband, Eddie Fisher, flew to London, where filming was to begin.

On March 4, just as the cameras began to roll, illness struck as Elizabeth became incapacitated with a severe case of Asian flu.

Fisher demanded the best care for her, and summoned Lord Evans, the personal physician of Queen Elizabeth. He ordered an oxygen tent for her and a portable toilet, the same one used by Her Majesty when she traveled to remote corners of the Commonwealth.

Fisher also ordered around-the-clock nurses for her. In the early morning hours, a night nurse noticed that Elizabeth's face was turning blue, and she was gasping for breath. She called the desk and shouted for them to get a doctor quick.

In a touch of irony, some doctors were having a late-night reception at The Dorchester. Among them was Dr. J. Middleton Price, one of the best anesthesiologists in the British Isles. He was rushed to Elizabeth's hospital suite. "She had turned blue as the sea," he said, "and was unconscious. I estimated that if I had not gotten there, she would have died in fifteen minutes."

The doctor picked her up by the heels and tried to make her lose some of the congestion in her chest. That did not succeed. Next, he stuck his finger down her throat, hoping to make her gag and breathe again. Still, nothing happened. He then pounded her chest,

"So the doctor started gouging at my eyes," Elizabeth related in her memoirs. "He gouged like mad and I opened my eyes…I took a deep breath, which kept me alive."

Dr. Price determined that only a tracheotomy would save her life. But the operation had to be performed in a hospital, although it was very risky to move the patient. He decided, however, that it was worth the chance, and an ambulance was summoned to The Dorchester.

With dome lights flashing and sirens wailing, she was rushed to the private London Clinic where Dr. Terence Cawthorne awaited her. He performed the life-saving tracheotomy by drawing a scalpel across the soft part of her throat right above her breastbone. Here, he made an incision allowing him to insert a breathing tube connected to a respirator.

His diagnosis was acute staphylococcus pneumonia, which is most often fatal. She would retain a small scar at her throat for the rest of her life, although she would in most instances cover it with a piece of jewelry.

Still desperately ill, she was put in an iron lung as a means of controlling the rate of her respiration and linking it to just the right amount of oxygen.

Seven doctors, including Lord Evans, were at her bedside. Dr. Evans even gave Queen Elizabeth a daily bulletin on his famous patient. It was Dr. Evans who also discovered that she was suffering from anemia, and he ordered blood transfusions, intravenous feedings, and doses of antibiotics. He also prescribed a rare drug, staphylococcal bacteriophage lystate, which Milton Blackstone, Fisher's agent, personally carried with him aboard a hastily scheduled flight to London.

During her stint in the hospital in London, Elizabeth had been fed intravenously through her ankle.

While Elizabeth Taylor was confined to a hospital bed, she asked Truman Capote to take her husband, **Eddie Fisher** *(photo above)*, out to dinner in London. Perhaps too eagerly, he agreed.

The next day, Fisher told his wife, "Never again! The little devil reached under the table and groped me. He told me, 'Some reports have you heavy hung; others claim it's a small sausage.' He said he wanted to find out the truth for himself!"

Regrettably, that caused an infection in her lower leg. As she admitted in her memoirs, "I almost lost my leg…I just let the disease take me. I had been hoping to be happy," she said. "I was just pretending to be happy. But I was consumed by self-pity."

Early on the morning of March 6, a radio station in Pensacola, Florida, broadcast the news: "Elizabeth Taylor is dead. Doctors in London fought to save her, but it was hopeless. The little girl who won our hearts in *National Velvet* died a living legend."

The news was picked up and broadcast on other stations before a bulletin was issued from London: "Elizabeth Taylor is not dead. She is the hospital in a fight for her life, but is still very much with us."

London tabloids began preparing "Second Coming" headlines.

A few newspapers published her obituary, and Elizabeth got to read a summation of her life. She later commented, "These were the best reviews I ever received, but I had to die to get these tributes."

On March 10, the first optimistic bulletin was released, claiming she had made "a very rare recovery."

Later, she defined the experience as "absolutely horrifying. When I would regain consciousness, I wanted to ask my doctors if I was going to die. But I couldn't make myself heard. Inside my head, I heard myself screaming to God for help. I was frightened. I was angry. I was fierce. I didn't want to die. I stopped breathing four times. I died four times. It was like falling into this horrible black pit. Dr. Evans later told me I lived because I fought so hard to live."

Also residing at The Dorchester, Truman Capote was one of the first guests allowed to visit her after her operation. He recalled it as a "media event, with the streets clogged with fans and the idle curious." At her request, he slipped in a magnum of Dom Pérignon and some books to read, mostly his own.

"I visited her in London in the hospital when she had that tracheotomy. She had what looked like a silver dollar in her throat. I couldn't figure out what held it in place, and it surprised me she wasn't bleeding or oozing. A few nights later, I went out with Eddie Fisher. The next afternoon, Elizabeth told me that Eddie thought I was trying to make a pass at him. At that moment, she played a trick on me and yanked at the plug in her throat, spurting out champagne—I'd brought her a magnum of Dom Pérignon—all over the hospital room. I thought I was going to pass out."

Fans on every continent mourned her, even though she was still clinging to life, but just barely. Mobs of people descended on the London Clinic for around-the-clock vigils.

Each day, her condition improved until it was finally judged safe for her to leave the hospital, though in a vastly weakened condition.

On March 27, Elizabeth, in a wheelchair, made one of the most spectacular exits from a hospital in the history of England. Wrapped in sable, with a white scarf covering her neck, and in preparation for her flight to New York, she was handled with the care of a porcelain doll as London bobbies held back threatening hordes and a mob of paparazzi. Airport security nestled her into a kind of canvas sling, and lifted her into the waiting plane.

With *Cleopatra* delayed once again, Elizabeth was coming home. She predicted to Fisher that "Cleopatra will never sail down the Nile on that barge of hers."

Spyros Skouras, President at Fox, sued Lloyds of London for three million dollars, but settled for two million, as compensation for the production delays on their attempt to film *Cleopatra* at Pinewood.

In a huddle, Wanger and Skouras decided that England was no place to film an exotic epic like *Cleopatra*. They agreed to scrap $600,000 worth of sets at Pinewood and to relaunch the filming in Rome in September of 1961, allowing Elizabeth time to recuperate.

Chapter Forty-One

A Trio of Illustrious Drunks

(Tennessee, Elizabeth Taylor, & Richard Burton)

Going "Boom!"

Welcome to the Stoned Age: Drug Addiction, Alcoholism, Depression, & Self-Destruction

In one of the cinema's worst cases of miscasting, **Elizabeth Taylor** agreed to portray an aging, ravished, has-been actress, opposite **Richard Burton**, who was far too ravished himself (*left photo above*) to be convincing as an alluring young poet in his early 20s.

To the right, **Elizabeth** in her elaborate Kabuki headdress invites "The Witch of Capri" (played by the British wit, playwright, and man-about-London **Noël Coward**) for a black fish dinner. The script suggested that in their respective pasts, both the homosexual Coward and "Sissy Goforth" (as played by Elizabeth) had competed for the affections of the same young men.

"I cannot live alone," Tennessee protested to Audrey Wood. "I need to feel the beating of a human heart on the pillow next to mine, even if I have to pay for it."

Thus, with Frank Merlo long dead, Tennessee began to hire a series of paid male companions. "Love has nothing to do with it," he said. This lifestyle pattern would continue until his death.

Unless he was incapacitated or ill, a series of young men, hired for their youth and looks, entered his life, some of them for no longer than a month or two. For the most part, he paid them between $200 and $300 a week.

"They were attracted to my fame and money," he later said, "and I'm sure in most cases it was a grin-and-bear it situation when I made love to them."

He never lacked companions. Once, at the Dorchester Hotel in London, he told Noël Coward, "It seems that wherever I go, when I check into a hotel, the entire male staff, from bartenders to room service waiters, make themselves available to me, for a price, of course."

"Welcome to the club, dear heart," Coward responded. "That's the fate of bloody old rich sods like us."

Tennessee Williams *(left)* poses in 1968 with his paid companion, **Bill Glavin**, whom Tennessee accused of having an affair with Elizabeth Taylor.

"Life with the illustrious playwright was like standing at the Gate to Hell," Glavin reportedly once said.

Tall, handsome, articulate William (Bill) Glavin entered Tennessee's life in 1964. Mike Steen, the director and a friend of Tennessee's, introduced this young man from Arlington, New Jersey, to Tennessee. Glavin reminded Tennessee that he'd met him very casually after a party several months before. "You complimented me on what a nice ass I have," Glavin told the playwright.

"I don't remember the occasion," Tennessee said, "but it sounds like me."

Glavin found Tennessee "very lonely, like something was wrong." He was not employed at the time, and Tennessee asked him to fly with him to California. The invitation was accepted. Glavin is today widely recognized as Tennessee longest live-in companion since Frank Merlo.

Tennessee later told Maureen Stapleton that "Bill is my Chance Wayne," a reference, of course, to the gigolo character in *Sweet Bird of Youth,* who rents out his services to the aging actress, Alexandra del Lago.

Tennessee later said that Glavin was the best looking of all his companions and had the best ability to organize his life.

From the beginning, Glavin became aware of Tennessee's drug addiction. He noted that Tennessee moved on unsteady feet, his speech often slurred.

He became more and more reluctant to attend public gatherings or private parties. He still loved getting awards, however, and usually tried to pull himself

Tennessee's Final Romance—What's Love Got to Do With It?

together to fly somewhere to accept an honor.

Sometimes, when Tennessee and Glavin would enter a restaurant together, the playwright would collapse and fall down en route to a table.

Maureen Stapleton remained one of his loyal friends, although others had deserted him. "Most people who saw Tenn on wobbly legs assumed he was drunk," she said. "But it was more than pills, especially the injections of speed he was receiving from the notorious Dr. Max Jacobson *["Dr. Feelgood"]*. I urged him to go into rehab and cut off this quack. Tenn listened politely, but showed up at Feelgood's creepy office the next day for shots."

Outside Manhattan, Tennessee had set up a network of doctors in such cities as Key West, Miami, San Francisco, Rome, Los Angeles, New Orleans, and Madrid.

Glavin defined Jacobson as "a witch doctor, a frightening man."

Nonetheless, Dr. Feelgood remained Tennessee's physician of choice. "I have incredible vitality when I get one of his injections," Tennessee told Glavin. "I get way ahead of myself as a playwright, you know. I move into another dimension. Never in my life have I enjoyed writing so much."

Glavin noted that even in his drugged state, Tennessee rose from bed each morning to write on his portable typewriter for three to four hours. "Sometimes, he would toss his writing of the morning into the wastepaper basket, claiming, 'I'm just no good anymore.'" Often, he focused his attention on scripts that had not only already been performed on the stage, but had been made into films." One morning, Glavin discovered that he was "revisiting" *Summer and Smoke*.

Glavin was quickly drawn into what Tennessee called "my gypsy life." He seemed never to want to stay anywhere for more than two weeks. He paced the floor like a caged lion, eager to run away—perhaps to Taormina in Sicily, where he'd gone with Frank Merlo, perhaps to London, but most often back to his modest home in Key West.

Shortly after meeting him, Glavin moved in with Tennessee, first occupying the thirty-third floor of an apartment on West 73rd Street in Manhattan.

When an old woman friend of Tennessee's came to visit—Glavin defined her as "a human wreck"—she warned Tennessee (after Glavin had left the room) about his companion: "How do you have the nerve to live on the thirty-third floor with a small concrete balcony, with somebody who has eyes like those of Glavin?'"

The following day, Tennessee moved out of the apartment, eventually occupying a suite at the St. Moritz Hotel on Central Park South.

[Glavin had to be a very understanding and tolerant soul to live with Tennessee. The playwright grew increasingly paranoid, frequently asserting that "people are plotting my death." He also began to tell friends, "I'm dying from an inoperable brain tumor." There were fears that he would commit suicide, because he talked about it often.

For no apparent reason, and without justification, he accused Glavin of being disloyal. He even accused him of being a thief, although he could not itemize or name any items stolen.

A Long Day's Journey to a Mental Asylum

By the late 1960s, Tennessee was out of control, even calling the Los Angeles police to report that he'd been kidnapped. He ordered Glavin in and out of his life, and seemed to thrive on the turmoil he created. He came to believe that his frantic lifestyle was an important catalyst for his writing. He once told Glavin, "If I got rid of my demons, I'd lose my angels," which was his way of saying that his demons were his muse.

As his condition grew worse, Tennessee often wandered into the living room of wherever he was staying and asked, "What town is this? New York or Key West?" When his entire body started to shake, he'd stagger about, looking for more pills. His hands shook so badly, he was unable to type. He'd often babble incoherently.

Sometimes, he'd shout and order people around him, including Key West friends Danny Stirrup *[an interior designer who was creating a modern kitchen for Tennessee]* and Margaret Foresman *[managing editor of the local newspaper, The Key West Citizen]*, even Glavin, out of his house. Then he'd burst into tears and call each of them, begging them to come back. He'd tell Foresman, "Go and find Glavin. He's probably at Captain Tony's Saloon, cruising."

Tennessee told friends that his relationship with Glavin was not sexual, consisting of sex only four or five times in five years. He also said that Glavin was bisexual. Later he accused Glavin of having sex with Elizabeth Taylor on the set of *Boom!* in Sardinia.

As the 1960s dragged on, his consumption of controlled or illegal substances increased. After having taken so many drugs, he seemed to build up a resistance, which required stronger and stronger doses.

In September of 1969, when he returned to Key West, he told Glavin that his house was surrounded by enemies with machine guns. "They are going to break in and kill me," he claimed.

He sent Glavin away for a week or so, asking his friend and drinking buddy, Foresman, to occasionally check on him during Glavin's absence.

During that period, Tennessee rose early, with the intention of writing. According to Foresman, he fainted while making coffee for himself, and fell onto the hot coils of the stovetop, severely burning himself. Rushed to the hospital, he was treated for burns, but later released into Foresman's custody.

In the immediate aftermath of that incident, she realized what a dangerous condition he was in. She felt inadequate to care for him because of the responsibilities of her own newspaper duties.

Consequently, she telephoned Dakin Wiliams in St. Louis, and he flew to Key West. He found that Tennessee's vision was blurred, his walk unsteady, and that at times, he would retreat, sleeping, as in a coma, for twenty-four hours at a time.

"My brother was popping pills like they were jellybeans," Dakin said. He prevailed on Tennessee to fly back with him to St. Louis, where he would receive first-class treatment at the Barnes Hospital.

There, three doctors separately examined Tennessee, ultimately declaring, "He has a violent, destructive personality and exhibits suicidal tendencies." He was confined to the Renard Psychiatric Division of the hospital, where he was denied both visitors and access to a telephone. Dakin was told that his brother was going "cold turkey" into rehab and would, no doubt, experience horrible withdrawal symptoms.

"The withdrawal almost killed Tennessee," Dakin claimed. "He had seizures and suffered two heart attacks. He almost died."

"I refused to ascribe to paranoia my conviction that the resident physician intended to commit legalized murder upon my person, and very nearly succeeded," Tennessee later claimed. "I crouched like a defenseless animal in a corner while the awful pageantry of those days and the nights went on, a continual performance of horror shows, inside and outside my skull. I intended to survive."

When Tennessee was allowed phone calls and visitors, including his aging, increasingly senile mother (Edwina Williams) and Dakin, he created a scenario of horror. He told Foresman that not since Olivia de Havilland descended into *The Snake Pit [a reference to her Oscar-winning performance in the 1948 movie]* had anyone suffered as much. "The conditions eerily evoked the way mental patients were treated in medieval times." Of course, these were gross exaggerations, as he'd received expert care.

Upon his release, he said, "Now I know how Marilyn Monroe felt when she was locked away in a mental ward."

Back in Key West , he told friends, "I feel like Blanche DuBois when she was hauled off to the insane asylum. Unlike poor Blanche, I escaped. I also have greater sympathy than ever for my sister Rose and her confinement."

Darwin Porter, then a young bureau chief for *The Miami Herald* in Key West and a journalistic colleague of Foresman, was one of the first to entertain Tennessee and welcome him back to Key West after his confinement in the mental ward. Foresman drove him to Porter's house for dinner.

"Tennessee looked better than he had in years, in spite of the horrendous ordeal he'd

Portrait of a Troubled Family from St. Louis

Left to right, **Dakin Williams,** the family matriarch, **Edwina,** and **Tennessee** himself.

Tennessee never forgave his brother for committing him to a mental asylum.

587

been through," Porter claimed. "After dinner, he wanted to be driven with Margaret to Captain Tony's Saloon, where people he knew welcomed him. Margaret consumed five drinks, but Tennessee had only one glass of bourbon. He told us he was taking only two pills a day. Unfortunately, this was only a lull before the storm. Many of his habits with drugs and alcohol would return, but he never reached that point of desperation that he did in 1969."

For Dakin's contribution in saving Tennessee's life, he met with his attorney and had his brother removed from his will. He also refused to speak to his brother for the rest of his life.

By 1970, Tennessee was spending his final months with Glavin. He told Porter that he suspected his companion had had an affair with Margaret Foresman during the time he had been confined to the mental ward. Porter knew that this was not true, but Tennessee was not convinced.

"Then, for no reason at all, he accused Glavin of sabotaging his work," Porter said.

"Bill knows I live for my work," Tennessee said.

"If anything, Glavin encouraged him to work and tried to make conditions possible for him to do so," Porter said. "Tennessee was unfair and unreasonable to someone who had stood by him through some of the worst years of his life. But he wouldn't listen to reason. His relationship with Glavin crashed to a bitter end."

"Tennessee also turned on Foresman, who had been his drunken friend," Porter said. "He accused her of being a woman of 'profligate ways,' which was more or less true. Her sex partners had included Richard Nixon's friend, Bebe Rebozo; Burl Ives; and the baseball player, Ted Williams, but there was no evidence that she and Bill Glavin ever had an affair. Tennessee remained convinced, however, that they did."

"He told me never to show up on his doorstep with Margaret in tow ever again," Porter said. "His exact words were, 'Margaret Foresman and Bill Glavin are *persona non grata.*'"

"I drove him to the airport to catch a flight to New York, with connections through Miami," Porter said. "From then on, I was introduced to a series of paid companions who changed as rapidly as the sunsets over Key West's Mallory Docks. Victor. Another Bill. Jeff. Ramon. Dean. Johnny. Mel. The young men became a blur, even to Tennessee himself."

"And then there were the plays," Porter said. "One failure after another, and I attended every one of them, always finding some merit, some poetry, in all of them. The critics were harsh, even cruel. Tennessee thought they were deliberately cruel, and that was the one thing Blanche DuBois could not forgive."

Maria Callas, Katharine Hepburn, Simone Signoret, & Ingrid Bergman

Each Say "HELL NO!"

But Elizabeth Taylor Is Recklessly Ready to "Goforth"

"People don't like sustained success."

—Elizabeth Taylor

Audrey Wood, still Tennessee's agent, pulled off a remarkable deal. She sold the movie rights of *The Milk Train Doesn't Stop Here Anymore* for $50,000, and even got an additional $100,000 for Tennessee to write the screenplay. Producer David Merrick was stunned, since previously, he'd already produced the play on Broadway on two separate occasions, the first with Hermione Baddeley and later with Tallulah Bankhead. Both productions had flopped.

Tennessee learned that Joseph Losey would be the director, and subsequently, he and Bill Glavin, during the closing months of their relationship, flew to London to meet with him. In America, Losey was a controversial figure, having been blacklisted during the communist witch hunt scare, as spearheaded by Joseph McCarthy, during the early 1950s.

Losey had studied in Germany with Bertold Brecht and had accumulated a string of impressive credits, notably the film, *The Servant* (1963), by Harold Pinter. A superb study of brooding decadence, it had co-starred James Fox and Dirk Bogarde. It was the story of how a corrupt manservant had become the master of his employer.

In England, after his meeting with Tennessee and Glavin, Losey was concerned with their physicalities and the perceived states of their health. Glavin said he'd have to undergo surgery for some gastrointestinal problem, and Tennessee confessed that he was suffering from "terminal hemorrhoids and the bloody mess of my rosebud."

Privately, Glavin told Losey that Tennessee had become heavily dependent on drugs, especially Doriden *[a sedative normally used for the treatment of sleep disorders]* and that the drug seemed to be driving him deeper and deeper into paranoia.

Losey was disturbed by this admission, and wondered if Tennessee would be able to complete the scriptwriting project.

Tennessee liked what Losey held out as a promise. "I want to make a visually lyrical film in a beautiful island setting about both the welcome and the terror of an aging actress facing death."

Losey didn't like the title of *Milk Train,* and consequently, Tennessee agreed to change it to *Goforth,* in honor of the play's leading character, Flora Goforth, who is "going forth" into death.

In London, Tennessee wanted to know if Losey missed—because of the Blacklist—not working in America. "I'm in sympathy with you. I'm surprised that J. Edgar Hoover didn't put me in a dungeon as a communist homosexual."

"I'm not really that bitter anymore," Losey said. "If I had not been expelled, blacklisted, I would probably own three Cadillacs, two swimming pools, and millions of dollars—and I'd be dead. It is terrifying. It is disgusting. But you can get into the money trap. A good shaking up never did anyone any harm. I'm still here, and I'm still working, I'm still creative."

There remained the problem of casting. For some reason, Tennessee wanted Sean Connery to play the male lead, that of the "Angel of Death," a young poet, Chris Flanders. *[Tab Hunter had starred in the role with Bankhead on Broadway.]* At the time, Connery was about thirty-seven years old, and the role demanded a young man in his early 20s.

For the female lead, both Losey and Tennessee came up with a surprise *[but probably brilliant]* choice, Maria Callas. But both the opera diva and Connery turned down the roles. Losey then pursued James Fox and Simone Signoret, again to no avail.

Losey was also having trouble casting the "Witch of Capri," Flora Goforth's gossipy island neighbor, a role which had previously been portrayed on Broadway by Mildred Dunnock.

Losey approached Dirk Bogarde to accept the role, but was turned down. "It's too high camp for me, and would spoil my macho image," the gay actor said.

Compelled to flee from the U.S. during the communist witch hunts in the 1950s, **Joseph Losey** sought work abroad. Along came an offer to direct Elizabeth Taylor and Richard Burton in *Boom!*.

"With Tennessee added to the mix, it was like running an insane asylum."

Losey reminded him that he'd played a gay character in the 1959 film, *Libel,* and again in the 1961 film, *Victim,* but Bogarde still refused. "I was gay in those films, but not a queen."

Losey then approached Katharine Hepburn. After reading the script, she was furious, telephoning Losey to denounce him. At first, she told him how offended she was to have been offered such a small role. "Not only that, but the character is perverse. As you know, I appeared on the screen as Violet Venable in *Suddenly Last Summer.* That is the last time I want to play one of Tennessee Williams' perverse characters. I am a very normal woman. I do not understand perversity—never have, never will."

Finally, Losey, in another surprise casting call, decided he wanted Noël Coward to interpret the role of "The Witch of Capri." At first he expected to be turned down, but Coward said he'd be delighted to play "This queen of High Camp. It would be a lark for me." Subsequently, Coward agreed to sign a contract.

Losey still hadn't signed the leads. He thought Ingrid Bergman and James M. Fox might be ideal. But when Bergman read the script, she raised violent objections. "The role is vulgar, and I've never been known to play vulgar women. I can't even say the word 'bugger' without blushing."

Tennessee was in Key West with Glavin when Losey called him. "You won't believe this. "Elizabeth Taylor and Richard Burton are signing to do the movie. Burton doesn't really want to do it, but Elizabeth does. Burton said he'll do it because they need the money to meet their extravagant living expenses."

"I love Elizabeth," Tennessee told Losey, "and I have great admiration for Burton as an actor. But Flora, or 'Sissy Goforth' as I call her, is an actress whose face has been ravished by time. Tallulah was the right age, but was in such desperation she couldn't wrap herself around the dialogue. Tab Hunter looked right for the part, but couldn't pull it off."

"I'll be really blunt with you," Losey said. "With Burton and Taylor cast as the leads, we can raise the rest of the money we need to make the film. In spite of their recent financial failures on the screen, the couple is still bankable."

Then, before ringing off, he told Tennessee, "Incidentally, the title of Goforth has been nixed. We've retitled it as *Boom!*"

En route to the film's location in Sardinia, Tennessee and Glavin stopped in Portofino, where Elizabeth and Burton had anchored their yacht. There, accompanied by various members of their family, they were visiting Rex Harrison and his alcoholic wife, the Welsh actress, Rachel Roberts.

Tennessee warmly embraced Elizabeth, who kissed him directly on the mouth. Burton followed suit, even giving him a flicker of his tongue. "I did god damn all right playing Maggie the Cat and that poor girl in *Suddenly Last Summer,*" Elizabeth told Tennessee. "And Richard did just fine as that defrocked pervert in *Iguana*. I think we can pull the rabbit out of the hat one more time."

Tennessee was delighted to hear that. But what disturbed him, as he later claimed, was the instant physical attraction between Glavin and Elizabeth. Perhaps Burton noticed it, too. "From the moment I introduced Elizabeth to Bill, she looked like she wanted him to fuck her. It didn't help matters that whenever she sat down, that miniskirt she was wearing, the shortest I'd ever seen, clearly revealed her crotch. Bill, it seemed, couldn't take his eyes off that 'bush of fire' that had already enflamed so many suitors in the past, including President Kennedy."

The Burtons and the Harrisons, along with Tennessee and Glavin, gathered for pre-dinner drinks at La Gritta Bar along Portofino's waterfront. It was clear that Roberts was already drunk.

Tennessee announced to everyone at the table that from then on, he wanted to be addressed as "Tom," which had technically been his name since

The critically acclaimed opera diva, **Maria Callas**, mistress of Aristotle Onassis, only briefly considered the role of Sissy Goforth, a dying, has-been music hall star spending her last days reconciling herself to her impending death in a villa by the sea.

Callas informed Tennessee, "Your script is too painful, and too close to home."

591

birth.

After drinks, the party was invited aboard the Burton/Taylor yacht.

"Even before we went aboard, while we were still onshore, at the bar, Tom spoke in a loud and powerful voice, very penetrating," Burton said. "He was incoherent, and it was somewhat embarrassing. Elizabeth told him to lower his voice a few times, since the Burtons attracted far too much attention as it was."

That evening aboard the yacht, moored next to one of Portofino's most prominent quays, would be the first of many disastrous nights associated with the Burtons. Those embarrassments continued regularly onto the island of Sardinia, where most of *Boom!* would be shot.

"Fortunately, our brood had already retired downstairs when the riffraff came aboard," Burton said. "And whereas Tom might have embarrassed us in the bar, Rachel was the supreme embarrassment once we climbed aboard."

Things started amicably aboard the *Kalizma*. Burton explained that the yacht had been purchased for $200,000, but that it had cost another $150,000 to refit it. Built in 1906, it had originally been commissioned by an eccentric Englishman who had installed an organ so that he could play Bach during storms at sea. At one point, Sir Winston Churchill was said to have sailed aboard it. The 120-foot motor ship had been used as a patrol boat during both World Wars. By the time Burton and Taylor acquired it, it cost $150,000 a year in upkeep costs.

Elizabeth invited Glavin, but not Tennessee, below for a view of her stateroom, where she explained that their designer, Arthur Barbosa, *[who had previously designed the Harrison's villa]*, had painted it the color of mustard. "I screamed when I saw it and immediately ordered that it be repainted canary yellow."

Tennessee noted that Glavin and Elizabeth were off alone together for a long time. It didn't help when Burton told Tennessee, "Maybe she's knocking off a quickie, if your boy is bisexual like me. With that miniskirt she's wearing, it would be convenient to mate."

Three hours later, the party dissolved into existential horror. As Tennessee recalled, "Roberts became drunk beyond belief," he said. "She lambasted Rex, telling him he couldn't satisfy a woman. She attacked his sex organ, claiming it was not big enough for the job, and that she might have to turn to Burton for the penetration she so desperately needed for sexual satisfaction."

Elizabeth and Burton, even Harrison himself, looked on helplessly. "Bill and I got up to leave after Rachel rolled around on the floor and began to masturbate her sloppy old Bassett hound," Tennessee said.

On the quay at Portofino, once again on *terra firma*, Tennessee and Glavin encountered a crowd of ragamuffin boys, shouting obscenities at Elizabeth on board.

Rachel Roberts...
Sex with a Bassett Hound

592

"For me, the scene evoked all those ravenous boys in the closing reel of *Suddenly Last Summer,*" Tennessee said. "Some of them had even taken out what Gore called 'their little pieces of okra,' and were shaking them at the yacht, yelling in Italian what they wanted to do to Elizabeth's snatch."

"Boom! Is So Atrocious, It's Perfect"

—*John Waters*

Beginning with *Cleopatra*, *Boom!* was the eighth film that the Burtons had made together. For their latest venture, they were paid one million dollars each.

But when Tennessee and Bill Glavin arrived on Sardinia for the first day of shooting, they found that Burton was unable to report to work. After forty-eight hours of heavy drinking, with no food intake, he'd lapsed into a coma. As he lay unconscious, Elizabeth had a specialist flow in from Rome. Five hours later, Burton regained consciousness, sitting up in bed and asking, "Where am I?"

The next day he was fine—"Ready and raring to go," he told the director, Joseph Losey.

Two days later, Burton noted in his diary, "Tennessee and Bill arrived. The former seemed to be tipsy. He is certainly not very prepossessing physically. I heard he tried to kill himself a few weeks ago, but was saved by Bill. There were no details."

Burton warned Tennessee about Losey. "So far, he is a bit of a crasher and a fusspot, interfering in every department. He'll probably want you to rewrite every line of dialogue."

Burton also told Tennessee, "My brother, Graham Jenkins, fancies himself a great critic. He read the film script. He claimed, 'There is no one to root for, that my character is just a male whore, and Flora Goforth is just a rich, self-indulgent bore.'"

"I've faced harsher critiques," Tennessee said."

Throughout the course of much of the filming, Elizabeth and Burton, along with their extended family, slept aboard the *Kalizma*, their yacht. After a night of drinking, Burton invited Tennessee to come aboard and have breakfast with him the following morning. When Tennessee arrived on deck, Dick Hanley, Elizabeth's secretary, led him down to the main stateroom. Hanley knocked on the door, and Burton called out for Tennessee to come in. Hanley opted not to follow him inside.

To Tennessee's astonishment, Burton was lying nude in the center of the bed he'd recently shared with Elizabeth. "He was masturbating," Tennessee later said. "I think this was done deliberately for my sake. I had not caught him accidentally. I don't think it was an attempt to seduce me, but knowing I was a homosexual, he decided to put on a little show for me. I understand that he often received well-wishers back stage at various theaters in the nude, so he was a bit of an exhibitionist."

"Excuse me," Tennessee said. "I'll come back."

"No! Stay!" Burton commanded, continuing to masturbate himself. "I'm almost there."

A few moments later, he erupted. Rising from the bed still half erect, he told Tennessee, "Sometimes when I didn't get any last night, I whack off in the morning."

"You are an impressive sight for my sad, sore eyes," Tennessee said.

Then Burton headed toward the bathroom for a shower, leaving the door open. "From the sound of things, he seemed to take a horse piss before getting into the shower. "I'm not a golden shower queen, so that offered little temptation for me."

Later that day, Tennessee met with Losey.

He told Tennessee that working with Elizabeth "is a journey on the road to absolute hellfire. She doesn't like her lines; she complains about her wardrobe. She says this film is causing her to suffer insomnia. She has struggled and fought with me right from the beginning. It took thirteen takes for the first scene alone. She kept fucking up her lines."

Later, during the director's assessment of Tennessee's condition, he didn't hold out much hope for him either. "He was a hell of a druggy mess and probably needed to be sent to rehab. Swimming, boozing, and sleeping it off seemed to be his main pastimes."

Elizabeth met privately with Tennessee for a very late lunch. She told him that she identified with much of the character of Flora Goforth—"The many marriages, the violent death of one of her husbands, the luxurious surroundings, the ostentatious display of wealth, a retinue of servants, physical back pain, and—through it all—an ever-lasting sense of personal loneliness."

"My favorite line," she told him, "is, 'If you have a world famous figure, why be selfish with it?'"

She said she also used her impressions of Vivien Leigh to help her develop her character on screen. "The declining health and eventual death of Vivien were always on my mind. She was a manic depressive slated for an early death after a destructive lifestyle, much of it a journey into madness."

She surprised him by telling him, "After forty movies, *Boom!* may be my farewell to films. I would be happy settling down as Mrs. Richard Burton. I've about had it. When you've reached the last rung of the ladder, there is nowhere to go but down. I don't want to be pushed off. I want to walk down with all the dignity I can summon—and not on crutches!"

"Creating a life off screen with Richard is far more interesting than playing someone's fantasy on the screen. I don't mean to insult your wonderful characters like Maggie the Cat, of course."

Up close, Tennessee witnessed Elizabeth's consumption of large amounts of both food and drink. "I begin with Bloody Marys after I brush my teeth in the morning. It's straight vodka throughout the day and champagne all night. My favorite foods include chocolate malted milkshakes, fried chicken with lots of mashed potatoes and gravy, large bowls of chili, plus caviar and *pâté de foie gras* at any time of the day or night."

"I tried to understand Elizabeth better," Tennessee said. "After repeated binges of heavy eating, she had to take off weight. She hated to diet. I'm not one to judge others, but I found it amazing that a woman like Elizabeth, celebrated everywhere in the world for her beauty, would eat and drink so much. I think at times she wanted to destroy Mother Nature's gift to herself. All her life, she'd been gaped at; men had lusted after her; women had envied her; the press had dissected her every move. Maybe she wanted to destroy the beauty that had made her the ongoing subject of such perverse scrutiny."

Before lunch was over, Elizabeth and Glavin had finished off two bottles of champagne. Tennessee kept noting their darting eyes, as they were clearly attracted to each other. He vowed to pay close attention.

Elizabeth introduced Tennessee to her brother, Howard Taylor, who was vacationing on Sardinia with his family. Losey had given him a small role in the film as a marine skipper. He told Tennessee that he was getting one thousand dollars for the cameo.

"No doubt, this will lead to a fabulous screen career for you," Tennessee assured him.

Then she told Tennessee that Noël Coward was scheduled to arrive on Sardinia later that day to settle in and prepare for his upcoming role as The Witch of Capri. "I'll set up a luncheon with you, Noël, and myself," she promised. "I'm afraid to invite Bill here because Noël would probably abduct him right away. Bill is his type."

Coward finally arrived on Sardinia, having been delayed by transportation problems. Burton was there to greet him. Both of them looked worse for wear, and both of them recorded their impressions of each other in their diaries. Coward asserted that, "Richard, of course, was sweet," but he hardly looked like the sexy, strikingly handsome youth Coward had first seduced when the actor was an eighteen-year-old cadet in 1943.

Conversely, Burton defined Coward as "looking very old and slightly sloshed. He proceeded to get more sloshed. He is almost completely bald, and the bags under his eyes made those eyes more Asiatic than hitherto. He called himself 'the oldest Chinese character actress in the world.'"

"When not due on the set, Noël and Elizabeth liked to deep-dish other actors." Tennessee said. "In one of my sessions with them, they both were aware that Noël had had sex with Burton long before Elizabeth got him. Between them, they discussed the dick sizes of their joint seductions, sometimes doubling up on the same actor. "The list was long, and my memory is bad. I recall some names, although I got all the measurements mixed up. John Gilbert, James Cagney (of all people); Louis Hayward, Cary Grant, Laurence Olivier, Tyrone Power, Ronald Reagan, President Kennedy, Errol Flynn, Eddie Fisher, David Niven, Montgomery Clift, Peter Lawford, Nicky Hilton, Frank Sinatra. Of course, Elizabeth knew that Noël had also seduced her previous husband, Michael Wilding, a bisexual."

The next day, Tennessee journeyed over to the Capo Cacchio Hotel, where

Coward was staying. Tennessee left a note for him at the desk. "Please feel completely free to alter any part of the dialogue you see fit—one playwright to another."

Actually, Coward disliked much of the dialogue, particularly one line: *"The Boss may be dying under the unsympathetic, insincere sympathy of the far-away stars."*

***

The filming of *Boom!* took place in Sardinia during the Red Brigade's terrorist scare.

[Organized in 1970, and based in Italy, the Red Brigade (Brigate Rosse) was a Marxist-Leninist paramilitary organization which claimed responsibility for several widely publicized bank robberies and assassinations, and attempts to destabilize Italy through acts of sabotage and kidnapping. Its mission involved the creation of a revolutionary government based on armed struggle, with the intention of pulling Italy out of NATO. Models for the Red Brigades included the Latin American urban guerrilla movements. After the mass arrests of their members in the late 1980s, the group became disorganized and fell apart.]

Elizabeth had already expressed her fear that one or more of her children might be kidnapped. She informed Tennessee that Lloyds of London had demanded $2.5 million for $15 million worth of life insurance during the filming in Sardinia. "In addition, I had to pay $2 million to have my jewelry insured while on island."

"Paste would have been cheaper, my dear," Tennessee suggested.

Ironically, although none of her children disappeared during their time in Sardinia, it was Burton who went missing during his sojourn there. Elizabeth called the police and an island-wide search was launched. By ten o'clock the following morning, the police located Burton standing atop a dining table, outdoors, reciting Shakespeare. The tavern associated with that table, a few paces away, was said to have been regularly patronized by a den of thieves.

Burton was orchestrating a competition for the tavern's largely illiterate patrons, none of whom had ever seen a play by Shakespeare. He offered the equivalent of $100—payable in Italian lire—to anyone in his audience who could name the particular Shakespeare play whose dialogue he was reciting. *[It was from* Titus Andronicus. *Whereas Laurence Olivier could have delivered the correct answer in a millisecond, none of the spectators that morning came even close to getting it right.]* Eventually, Burton was delivered back to Elizabeth in a police car.

During his disappearance, Losey had escorted Tennessee and Glavin on a tour of one of the key sets in the upcoming film, Flora Goforth's villa. Universal had spent $500,000 on the replication of a white marble palace-cum-mausoleum. Some of the travertine used in its construction had been pilfered centuries before from the ruins of the Colosseum in Rome.

In the immediate aftermath of Burton's return, he and Elizabeth had one of their knock-out, drag-down fights, ending in tempestuous love-making aboard their yacht.

***

One drunken night, Tennessee received the verbal lashings of a spectacularly intoxicated Burton, who appeared at the time, according to Tennessee, as demented. Burton recklessly, and falsely, accused Tennessee of "making a pass" at Chris Wilding *[one of the two boys Elizabeth had produced with Michael Wilding]* who was only eight years old at the time.

"You're nothing but a bloody, self-pitying pain in the ass," Burton charged. "You're depressed all the time. *STAY AWAY FROM MY CHILDREN!*"

The next morning, an angry Elizabeth confronted Burton after he rose from his drunken stupor with a hangover. "Luv, did you know last night you called Tennessee a child molester?"

"I would never do that, even if he were," Burton said. "I have no memory of that. Perhaps it was the Devil who lives inside me speaking, certainly not Sir Richard, who is forever gallant, a knight of the realm."

***

Tennessee had his most destructive fight with Glavin after he'd spent two hours alone with Elizabeth in her dressing room when Burton was away. "You obviously prefer to fuck her instead of me," he shouted at Glavin. "Not only that, but you've stolen my drugs and hypodermic needs."

[Whereas Tennessee may have been accurate about the seduction, he was wrong about his drugs, He had simply misplaced them.]

Tennessee remained on Sardinia long enough to witness the filming of one of the most dramatically campy scenes in *Boom!*: Flora Goforth's *[as played by Elizabeth]* rendezvous with "the Witch of Capri *[Noël Coward]*.

Elizabeth appeared in a Kabuki-style robe that weighed 42 pounds. It was festooned with 22,000 beads, each of them hand-stitched by seamstresses in Rome. She also wore an elaborate headdress and a 29.4 carat diamond, a gift from her late husband, Mike Todd, who had died in a plane crash over New Mexico.

As part of the logistics associated with the scene, the Witch, on film, had to be carried in a sedan chair across craggy, sun-blasted rocks by stout men for this treacherous *dîner-à-deux.* As a main course, Flora Goforth served him/her a monstrous baked black fish that repulsed him. On camera, "The Witch" *[Coward]* makes his distaste for "this monster from the sea" abundantly clear.

Tennessee watched the scene of Coward being carried around in the sedan chair, and pronounced it all "so very campy."

But when Losey demanded rewrites to the script, Tennessee knew he was in no condition to meet these requests. He was too heavily drugged and depressed. Without notifying Losey, Elizabeth, or Burton, he fled from Sardinia in ill health. Chartering a private plane at the nearest airport, he flew with Glavin to Rome. His intention involved an immediate return to New York for a "rejuvenation" of his drug supply, and for "urgently necessary" additional "treatments" from Dr. Feelgood.

***

As anticipated by some, when *Boom!* opened across America, it played to largely empty seats in movie houses. Universal suffered a loss of $7.1 million.

Hoping to lure the masses, it had advertised *Boom!* as a picture where the public could see the Burtons *"do things you've never seen before!"*

Burton biographer Michael Munn wrote: "*Boom!* proved that the public would no longer go and see Liz and Dick in just anything, and in effect, it brought to an end their reign as the supreme screen team of the 1960s."

Critic Judith Crist wrote: "Elizabeth Taylor is 20 years too young and 30 acting ones away from the role. Richard Burton looks more like a bank clerk on a campy holiday, kimono and all, than a poet."

In contrast, *The Village Voice* asserted, "Burton seems at first entrance utterly miscast as the morbid gigolo masquerading as the Angel of Death, but his final 'Booming' exit line caps what turns out to be the most brilliant performance of his career."

The Hollywood Reporter defined *Boom!* as "an ordeal in tedium." Critic Fergus Cashin stated that, *"Boom!* is an extravagant failure, a project weighed down with opulence." *Time* magazine charged that "*Boom!* displays the self-indulgent recklessness of a couple of rich amateurs hamming it up at a country club frolic, and with approximately the same results." *Life* magazine assaulted the Burtons citing the "tired, slack quality of their work that is, by now, a form of insult."

Burton himself had his own critique. "The film script was far too symbolic to attract a wide audience."

He told Losey, "Instead of Miss Tits and myself, you should have given the roles to Bette Davis and Robert Redford."

Tennessee delivered his own opinion of *Boom!,* one that would seriously alienate the Burtons: "Despite its miscasting, I feel that *Boom!* was an artistic success that eventually will be received with acclaim…It would have been received very differently if Hermione Baddeley, who did the first stage version on Broadway, performed on camera. If not Hermione, then perhaps Angela Lansbury or Sylvia Miles."

Chapter Forty-Two

In Cold Blood

Truman Falls in Love With a Mass Murderer

With Harper Lee—Two "Aliens From the Moon"— He Invades a Bleak Town in Western Kansas

"Reel life imitates real life in Truman Capote's bestseller *In Cold Blood*. **Richard Hickock** (*on the left*) and **Perry Smith** massacred four members of the Clutter family one bleak night in Western Kansas.

For the movie version of Capote's book, lookalike actor **Robert Blake** (*the left figure in the right-hand photo*) played Perry Smith, with **Scott Wilson** (*center*) interpreting the role of Richard Hickock. On the far right, **Capote** looks like a prisoner himself.

Even before he discovered "a cold-blooded murder case" in a Kansas farmhouse, Truman Capote was thinking seriously about non-fiction. Speaking to the press, he said, "I like the feeling that something is happening beyond and about me, and I can do nothing about it. I like having the truth be the truth so I can't change it."

Of course, being the inventive artist he was, he could never stick to so rigid a formula without taking "poetic license," as he did in his mega-bestseller, *In Cold Blood*.

"I couldn't sit down any more to write fiction," he said. "I felt there were chocolates in the next room, and I couldn't resist them. The chocolates were true life events."

"There were so many things I knew I could find out about," he said. "Suddenly, the newspapers all came alive, and I realized that I was in terrible trouble as a fiction writer."

One Monday morning, a hung-over Truman was reading *The New York Times.* On page 19, almost hidden, was a news story headlined: *WEALTHY FARMER; 3 OF FAMILY SLAIN.*

Four members of the all-American **Clutter family**, a few years before their annihilation.

Holcomb, Kan. Nov 15 (1959)(UPI)—A wealthy wheat farmer, his wife, and two young children were found shot to death in their home. They had been killed by shotgun blasts at close range after being bound and gagged. There were no signs of a struggle, and nothing had been stolen. The telephone lines had been cut.

Their farmhouse rose above the howling winds of a lonely plain. Word had spread through a Federal penitentiary that the Clutter family kept their doors unlocked at night.

A devout Christian and self-made man, Herbert Clutter employed nearly two dozen farmhands, depending on the season. He had four children—three girls and a boy. His older daughters, Beverly and Eveanna, had gotten married and moved out. Two children remained—Kenyon, 15, and Nancy, 16. Clutter's wife, Bonnie, was later described as a "basket case," suffering from clinical depression and various physical ailments.

Truman appeared the next day before William Shawn, the non-fiction editor of *The New Yorker,* and sold him on the idea of his going to Kansas, not to solve the murders, but to write about their effect on the small, remote community where fear prevailed. "Perhaps the murders will never be solved, but remain a lingering mystery to be talked about for years to come," Truman said.

Shawn liked the idea and gave Truman a green light on the project.

Truman's knowledge of Kansas was non-existent. "I knew the Deep South and the people who inhabit it," he told his friend, novelist Harper Lee, when he invited her to travel to Kansas with him. She would later make Truman jealous when she won the Pulitzer Prize for her novel, *To Kill a Mockingbird,* which had not been published by the time she set out with him for the bleakness of Western Kansas.

Shortly before Christmas in 1959, Truman and Harper, childhood friends and neighbors from their long-ago days in Monroeville, Alabama, boarded a train to Kansas. He carried with him food supplies stuffed into a footlocker. "I understand they eat nothing but cholesterol on the hoof," he said to Harper.

Their train pulled into Garden City, the seat of Finney County, just as dusk settled over the bleak little town. *[The massacre had occurred in the village of Holcomb, six miles west of Garden City.]* Truman recalled, "If I knew what was awaiting me, I would never have boarded the train. It is unwise for a man like myself to live outside New York, San Francisco, or Los Angeles."

A friend of his from childhood, novelist **Harper Lee**, accompanied Truman to Kansas, helping him break through to some of the local skeptics. Later, he'd be jealous of her spectacular success with *To Kill a Mockingbird*

In Garden City, in the foothills of the Great Plains, people were not initially impressed with Truman, viewing Harper and him as aliens just landed from the moon. Likewise, Truman was not impressed with the town. "The locals had never seen the likes of Truman with his high-pitched, squeaky voice, and his precise manners," Harper said. "Whenever he spoke to someone on the phone, he was often mistaken for a woman."

"When Harper and I arrived in Garden City, the natives were not dancing in the street to celebrate our arrival," Truman said. "My initial impression was that Garden City was something you flew over en route to California."

[Garden City, north of the Arkansas River, in the grain belt of Western Kansas, lay 65 miles from the Colorado state line. Some forty-six miles to the east was Dodge City, home of Bat Masterson and Wyatt Earp, who buried many an outlaw on Boot Hill. Founded in 1878, Garden City, with its large zoo, blossomed during the land rush that began in 1885, as horses, wagons, teams of oxen, and buggies navigated their way through the town's then-unpaved streets.

Traditionally, famous visitors to Garden City stayed at the Windsor Hotel. Dating from 1887 it called itself "the Waldorf of the Prairies," because of its luxury. Through its lobby had walked everyone from Lillian Russell to Buffalo Bill Cody. They had each been aboard the Santa Fe Railroad that passed through as part of its run between Chicago and Los Angeles.

Truman and Harper stayed at the Warren Hotel.]

After only a day, Truman concluded that Garden City was filled with "Sunday go-to-meetin' Christian zealots and right-wing Republicans of the neo-Nazi bent."

He encountered a town gripped with fear, the locals raiding the local hardware store for locks and bolts for their doors. Porch lights were kept on at night. Someone in the sheriff's department told Truman that if the killer were a local, and if he were still at large, Truman's own life, because of his investigation, might be in jeopardy at the hands of some psychopaths. "I know I'm putting my life on the line," he responded.

Truman and Harper called on Alvin Dewey, a tall, handsome man in his 40s, who was handling the massacre case for the Kansas Bureau of Investigation. Besieged by reporters, he was not impressed with Truman, who showed up in an overly large sheepskin coat that dragged the ground, a long, fairly narrow red scarf that cascaded to his ankles, a pill box hat in magenta, and a pair of Indian moccasins.

When Dewey asked for his press card, Truman told him he didn't have one, but that he'd go back to his hotel and show him his passport.

K.B.I.'s **Alvin Dewey** confronted Truman in his hotel room, where he was modeling his new pink *négligée*.

Truman was dismissed, but he didn't give up so easily. He showed up again and again over the course of the next few days, and amazingly, he impressed Dewey with the intensity of his determination. By then, Dewey had adjusted to his voice.

Actually, it was Harper who initially won Dewey over for Truman. "I made a smart move in taking her with me to Kansas," Truman said. "She's a gifted woman, courageous, and with a warmth that instantly kindles most people, however suspicious and sour."

After Maria Dewey met the odd couple and invited them to dinner, Truman finally won Dewey over.

Marie and Truman soon discovered that they each had roots in New Orleans, and both of them appreciated such dishes as okra-studded gumbo more than the usual steak-and-potatoes diet usually associated with Western Kansas.

After their first dinner together, Harper and Truman were invited frequently into the Dewey home. Truman thrilled them with stories of his encounters with and indiscreet gossip about such iconic women as Jackie Kennedy, Elizabeth Taylor, Audrey Hepburn, and Marilyn Monroe.

Harold Nye, an agent for the Kansas Board of Intelligence, remembered when Dewey introduced him to Truman in his hotel room. "He was wearing a new pink *négligée*, silk with lace, and he's strutting across the floor with his hands on his hips, telling us all about how he's going to write this book. Later, my straight-as-an-arrow wife accepted his invitation to go with him to Kansas City. He took us first to a lesbian bar, then to a gay male club, and, finally, to the Jewel Box to watch female impersonators."

In a follow-up story, a reporter for *Time* magazine appraised Truman's situation: "A diminutive, eccentric, and lisping presence in Midwest territory, whose citizens at first scarcely knew what to make of him, Capote commanded

602

the attention and ultimately the respect of everyone he approached, including the killers."

Truman began to pick up fascinating details about the case. From the local insurance office, he learned that on the morning of the massacre of his family, Herbert Clutter had taken out a $40,000 insurance policy with a double indemnity provision should he die of other than natural causes.

It was on December 30, 1959, while dining with the Deweys, that a phone call came in for Alvin. He was informed that two prime suspects in the Clutter murders, both of them men, had been arrested in Las Vegas and would be transported under heavy guard back to the Finney County Courthouse in Garden City. Their names were Richard ("Dick") Hickock and Perry Edward Smith.

Two Kisses Before Dying

Dick Hickock and Perry Smith were two ex-convicts on parole from the Kansas State Penitentiary. While in prison, they met Floyd Wells, who had once worked at the Clutter farm. He falsely informed Hickock and Smith that Clutter kept large amounts of cash stashed at his home, since he didn't trust banks. "The old shit is very, very rich," Wells claimed. "He's a sitting duck for a robbery. They don't even lock their doors at night."

Hickock lured Smith into the deal after they got out of prison. "It's a cinch, the perfect score," Hickock said. "We'll kill them, high-tail it to Mexico, and live high off the hog, happily ever after."

When the murderers were arraigned at the courthouse, Truman saw for the first time the two men who would play such a key role, not only in his personal life, but in his finances. In fact, he'd eventually make millions of dollars off the murders they committed—six million, to be exact.

Born in Kansas City in 1931, Hickock was about twenty-eight years old when Truman first trained "my hawk eye on him." He had blonde hair and stood less than six feet tall. A serious automobile accident in 1950 had left his face disfigured. Truman had a colorful way of describing his face as "halved like an apple, then put together a fraction off center."

A native of Kansas City, Hickock had been married twice and had fathered three sons. A former athlete in high school, he turned to petty crimes, including cashing bad checks. These crimes led him to prison, where he first met Smith and where they hatched a scheme to rob and murder.

A native of the now abandoned town of Hunt-

"I may have slashed throats, but actually, I'm a sensitive guy with feelings," **Perry Smith** told Truman.

ington, Nevada, Smith was the son of rodeo performers "Tex & Flo." He was of mixed Irish and Cherokee ancestry, and had raven black hair. He stood only one inch taller than Truman. He had nearly died in a motorcycle accident, which had left him permanently disabled, suffering leg pain.

Even into adulthood, he was a chronic bed wetter, which had led to severe punishment all his life, as he was transferred from orphanage to orphanage. In a Salvation Army orphanage, one caretaker was so furious at him that he attempted to drown the boy. In one Catholic orphanage, a sadistic nun rubbed a burning ointment on his small penis and stood by to watch him scream in pain. Another nun forced him into a tub of ice water and kept adding more ice until he caught pneumonia.

Joining the Army in 1948, he served in Korea, where his fights with locals and fellow soldiers led to stints in the stockade. After his discharge from the Army, a string of petty crimes eventually landed him in jail.

Actor **Robert Blake**, on the left side of this publicity poster, looked so much like Perry that Truman called him "a reincarnation of the killer."

As young adults, two of his siblings had committed suicide. A sister had jumped from her room in a San Francisco hotel, and a brother had shot his girlfriend after accusing her of adultery before committing suicide.

Truman carefully observed Smith in the courtroom, especially his "sad, droopy eyes. They just drew you into his tortured soul. He had a changeling's face. He could look at you with savagery one minute, then with almost adoration the next."

In the courtroom, Truman was no mere newspaper reporter, but went for precise details with the eye of a novelist. Observing the short, stumpy Smith, he described him as a "chunky, misshapen child-man with dwarfish legs. His tiny feet would have neatly fitted into a delicate lady's dancing slippers; when he stood up, he was not taller than a twelve-year-old child."

The arrest of Hickock and Smith greatly altered Truman's perception of his project. Before the telephone call came in from Las Vegas, Truman had more or less wrapped up his short story for *The New Yorker*. Now, he saw it as a larger tale, perhaps a non-fiction book.

On March 29, 1960, the jury in Garden City deliberated for only forty minutes before voting guilty. Judge Roland Tate pronounced the sentence that they should be executed. On the way out of the courtroom, Truman overheard Smith say to Hickock, "No chicken-hearted jurors, they!"

The execution was scheduled for May 13, 1960, when they were to be hanged at the Kansas State Penitentiary in Lansing. But there would be appeals and endless delays before the sentence was carried out.

In Lansing, Truman was granted unusual access to both men, with whom he was to develop intense personal relationships. At first, the warden was reluctant to let him in, but Truman bribed a highly placed official with $10,000.

Charles McAtee, former Director of Penal Institutions in Kansas, said, "Truman was a homosexual, and the warden at the prison thought the last thing in the world that he needed was to put up with a known homosexual visiting two guys on Death Row. He had enough problems with homosexuality inside the prison."

Harold Nye, the KBI agent who, with his wife, had been escorted by Truman to Kansas City for a tour of that city's gay night life, made the charge that Truman fell in love with Smith. "He spent hours and hours in Smith's cell. He bribed the guards for privacy. They were both homosexuals, and they had repeated sex in Smith's cell. That's what happened."

Right before facing the hangman, **Richard Hickock** whispered to Truman, "A lot of women are going to be disappointed."

As Smith—to an increasing degree—came to trust Truman, he confided very personal details. "I had assumed that Dick was 'the man.' But at the Clutter home, he chickened out before the actual shooting. I had to kill all four of them."

Smith said that he had to talk Hickock out of raping the Clutter's daughter, Nancy. "Dick has had a long history of raping young girls around the age of fourteen. He suggested that he could rape Nancy, and that I could rape Kenyon before we shot them."

"I told him I wouldn't," Smith said. "Sex was the last thing on my mind."

This confession matched what Hickock had claimed when the police had apprehended both of them in Las Vegas. "Perry did it!" Hickock had shouted at the police. "He killed all four of them!" After screaming that accusation, Hickock had fainted.

As Truman became more closely acquainted with Smith, he discovered that they had many similarities. Both of them had grown up in communities which had scorned them, and both of them had "booze hound" mothers and "fathers who fell in love with long distance." Foster homes and orphanages had led to shared self-assessments as "lost souls."

On their second afternoon together, Smith said, "I see that you brought your mistress *[a reference to Harper Lee]* to Kansas. I had taken you to be a homosexual."

"Harper is my friend, and I am a homosexual," Truman responded.

Smith then asked, "I guess you want to kiss me. Go ahead. The guard isn't looking."

"I thought you'd never ask," Truman said, later confessing this incident to his gay friends. "I even masturbated him that afternoon."

As time went by, Smith and Truman sometimes engaged in what was called "a lovers' quarrel." Smith would get angry at him, at one time accusing him of paying undue attention to Hickock. He'd call Truman either "Miss Piss Pot" or "Little Bastard."

Smith supplied him with details of how the murders were committed. "Clutter was tied up on the cold basement floor. I lifted him up and placed him on a mattress so he'd be more comfortable when I slit his throat. I thought he was a nice gentleman."

At one point, Smith said he didn't want to make Truman jealous, so he would not provide complete details about his relationship with Hickock. He did admit to having made nude drawings of Hickock, and Truman noticed that Hickock called Smith "honey."

Smith admitted that when he'd served in the Merchant Marines, many of his fellow servicemen had invited him to "roll over" at night.

He also shared his dreams with Truman. "I want to bill myself as Perry O'Parsons and sing and play my guitar in a cabaret."

Truman was surprised that Hickock had an amazing memory. He supplied so many minute details that it greatly helped Truman to enrich *In Cold Blood.*

Hickock later said, "If I had known Truman was a cocksucker in the beginning, I would have availed myself of his talent during our long interviews."

After extensive prison chats with both men, Truman boarded the train back to New York, having accumulated hundreds of pages of notes. As he told Harper Lee, "I think I have all of my book now, except for the final chapter—and that centers around the fate of both Dick and Perry. Of course, I already know their fate...I just need for the hangman to come for them."

In time, Truman became Smith and Hickock's only link to the free world. He recalled sitting for hours talking with them in their twilight existence, illuminated only by the eerie glow from a low-watt amber-colored lightbulb.

Truman was less intimate with Hickock, but yet was his only friend. When not visiting them in prison, Truman exchanged endless letters with both of them, and sent them magazines and books.

Denied exercise by the prison guards, both men began to age prematurely. They developed excruciating physical pain, especially Smith in his legs. Not that it mattered at this desperate point in his life, but Hickock became obsessed with his increasing baldness. "I'm ugly enough already without a bald head. When I get out of here, how am I going to attract any hot pussy with a bald head?"

During their final years, both Smith and Hickock began to feel that Truman, with all his powerful connections, would get them out of jail based on appeals to higher courts. In front of them, Truman had played up his long-standing friendship with John F. Kennedy.

"My god," Hickock said to Smith, "Truman is a good buddy of the President of the United States. If all else fails, Kennedy will pardon us. He has that right."

Of course, when they heard of Kennedy's assassination, they were bitterly disappointed.

Hickock wrote Truman of the "long, cold days and the desperate nights waiting to be hanged. I doubt if hell will have me. I'm feeling lower than whale manure."

On the fourth anniversary of his incarceration, Hickock wrote, "It feels more like forty years instead of four."

Before Kennedy's death, Smith had held out the hope that he would be freed and could come and live in New York with Truman "as your husband. You can introduce me to all your movie star friends like Elizabeth Taylor and Audrey Hepburn."

As early as 1962, in a letter to Bennett Cerf at Random House, Truman made it clear that he already knew that appeals of the killers' death sentences would hopelessly work their way through the State and Federal courts, with perhaps a final appeal to the U.S. Supreme Court. "It's no use, and both you and I know that, but I don't dare tell Dick and Perry that. They have too much hope."

The progression of events went as Truman had predicted. The last decision came down on January 18, 1965, when the Supreme Court of the United States refused to hear the appeal. "It is now certain that Dick and Perry will face the hangman," Truman wrote to Cerf from Verbier, Switzerland. "I'm very sad about it."

When he heard the news, Smith wrote to Truman, inviting him to "our necktie party."

To write In Cold Blood, Truman and his lover, Jack Dunphy, had escaped to their little condo in Verbier in the Swiss Alps. "Every page I write is painful," Truman confessed in letters to friends. "The material leaves me increasingly limp and numb—horrified, really."

Eventually, he perceived that Hickock had become relatively stoic about his upcoming death, handling it with relative resignation. In contrast, Smith began a hunger strike, eventually losing forty pounds. He'd told Truman, "Dick can wait for the rope, but I'm going to beat it."

The court had scheduled Smith and Hickock for the hangman's noose on April 14, 1965. They both wanted Truman to travel to Kansas for their final hours.

Truman's own life had come to something akin to an impasse. Months after months had dragged by, and he knew he couldn't write or publish the final chapter of In Cold Blood until both men had been hanged. In a final letter to Truman, Smith had written: "The date has been set for Dick and me to drop through the trap door."

Truman poured out his frustrations in a letter to Cecil Beaton. "I'm finishing the last pages of my book—I must be rid of it, regardless of what happens. I hardly give a fuck anymore what happens. My sanity is at stake—and that is no mere idle phrase. Oh, the hell with it. I shouldn't write such gloomy crap—even to someone as close to me as you."

Truman arrived in Kansas, but waited until the final hour to say farewell to Smith and Hickock. He spent two days vomiting and convulsing in a hotel before visiting them. "And yet," he said, "for the entire time I was throwing up and crying and carrying on, in another part of my mind, I was sitting and quite coolly writing the story."

He later admitted that he had great difficulty writing his "nonfiction novel's" final seven pages. He developed hand paralysis. "I finally used a typewriter—very awkward, as I had always written in longhand."

Hickock and Smith had been escorted under guard to a warehouse within the prison compound. Truman recalled his final moment with them as "the most devastating of my life."

"I first saw them in the holding room, where they were served their last meal—which needless to say, they didn't eat. They were strapped into these leather harnesses. I had to hold up cigarettes for them to smoke. They were trembling violently, not from fear but from being terribly nervous."

"Perry handed me a 100-page farewell letter. Dick kept talking right up to the end about his mother—he felt very sad about her—and some old girlfriends. Up to the end, he kept making jokes. Both of them had an extraordinary phosphorescence, so that they were practically glowing in the dark."

"Dick was the first to be summoned to his death," Truman said. "I looked into his desperate eyes, knowing that there was nothing I could do. In a soft voice, he said, 'I'm being sent to a better world than this ever was.' He kissed me goodbye before he was taken away by two guards. The kiss lingered on my lips. It was the kiss of death."

The farewell to Smith was especially painful for Truman.

Before his own departure, Smith said, "Maybe I had something to contribute, something." Then his voice wandered off. "It would be meaningless to apologize for what I did, even inappropriate. But I do apologize."

"He kissed me, a long, lingering kiss," Truman said. Then he said his final two words, but his eyes said so much more."

"*Adios, amigo.*"

And then he was gone," Truman said. "I cried for two and a half days afterward. I couldn't stop. It was convulsive."

It was Jack Dunphy who led Truman off Death Row. "Stop crying!" he shouted at Truman. "They're dead! You're alive!"

James M. Fox, Truman's editor at Random House, recalled, "I sat next to Truman on the plane ride back to new York. He held my hand and cried all the way. I remembered thinking how odd it must have seemed to passengers sitting nearby—those two grown men apparently holding hands and one of them sobbing. It was a long trip."

"Dick and Perry Had to Die So That My Book Can Live"

—Truman Capote

In April of 1965, Truman wrote to Cecil Beaton in Brooklyn. "Perry and Dick were executed. I was there because they wanted me to be. It was a terrible experience. Something I will never really get over."

In Cold Blood was first published in an unusual four-part serial in *The New Yorker* beginning on September 25, 1965. Random House released it in book form in January of 1966.

Most of the reviews were favorable, Conrad Knickerbocker defining it as a masterpiece in *The New York Times Book Review.* "It is agonizing, terrible, possessed, proof that the times, so surfeited with disasters, are still capable of tragedy."

Writing in the *New York Herald Tribune,* Maurice Dolbier claimed: "Capote has recorded this American tragedy in such depth and detail that one might imagine he had been given access to the book of the Recording Angel."

The celebrated social commentator and critic, Rebecca West, called Truman "an ant of genius who has crawled over the Kansas landscape in pursuit of his story."

Stanley Kauffman attacked the book in *The New Republic:* "It is ridiculous in judgment and debasing of all of us to call this book literature. Are we so bankrupt, so avid for novelty, that merely because he is a famous writer who produced an amplified magazine crime-feature, the result is automatically elevated to serious literature, just as Andy Warhol, by painting a soup-carton, has allegedly elevated it to art?"

Around the same time, Truman had defined Kauffman as a blood enemy after *The New York Times* published an article he had written entitled, "Homosexual Drama and Its Disguises."

Truman bristled at Kauffmann's analysis, interpreting it as an attack on homosexuals by questioning the ability of a gay playwright to create authentic heterosexual characters. In the ensuing decades, the article has occasionally been singled out as an illustration of the intolerance prevalent at the time. Kauffman was soon after replaced at *The New York Times* by the far more tolerant Walter Kerr.

A media blitz followed the publication of *In Cold Blood.* Truman appeared frequently on television, giving interviews, and he was featured on the covers of such magazines as *Newsweek.*

Naturally, there was a stampede to acquire the movie rights, which were being handled by the well-known agent, Irving (Swifty) Lazar.

At "21" in New York, Otto Preminger got into a fight with Lazar.

The temperamental director **Otto Preminger** *(left)* tangled with super agent **Swifty Lazar** *(right)* at the exclusive "21" over the film rights for *In Cold Blood.* Preminger ended up in the hospital, where fifty stitches closed the wound on his head.

609

The temperamental director accused the agent of reneging on a commitment to sell him the movie rights as a starring vehicle for Frank Sinatra, who had expressed an interest in playing Perry Smith.

The argument turned violent, and Lazar smashed a water glass against Preminger's bald head, seriously injuring him. Newspapers dubbed it "*L'Affaire 21,*" after Preminger was rushed to the hospital, where he received more than fifty stitches.

In Cold Blood made Truman more famous than he ever was, and it also brought him riches. But to many of his friends, it was the beginning of the end of him, and he began to descend into despair, soaked in booze and devoured by drugs.

"No one will ever know what *In Cold Blood* took out of me," he announced. "It scraped me right down to the marrow of my bones. It nearly killed me. I think, in a way, it *did* kill me. I just can't forget it, particularly the hangings at the end. *HORRIBLE!*"

Truman claimed that *In Cold Blood* was "100 percent true," and that was 100 percent wrong. There are many distortions, exaggerations, and inaccurate quotes. An investigative article in *Esquire* outlined the various exaggerations or distortions, and they were anthologized in Irving Malin's *Truman Capote's In Cold Blood: A Critical Handbook* (1968).

True crime writer Jack Olsen commented on fabrications that sleuths had discovered. "I recognized it as a work of art, but I know fakery when I see it," Olsen said. "Capote completely fabricated quotes and whole scenes. The book made something like six million dollars in 1960s money, and nobody wanted to discuss anything wrong with a moneymaker like that in the publishing business."

When Truman read Olsen's criticisms in *Esquire,* he claimed. "Jack Olsen is just jealous." Harper & Row had assigned Olsen the Clutter case as core material for a book, until it was discovered that Truman and Harper Lee had already been investigating it for six months.

Other critics immediately charged that Truman had changed the facts to suit the story, adding scenes that had never occurred, and re-creating dialogue that was not authentic.

The most painful attack on Truman was delivered by critic Kenneth Tynan, whom Truman had regarded as a friend.

After a reunion with Truman over dinner in New York back in 1960, Tynan claimed, "Capote regaled us with a dazzling account of the crime and his friendship with the criminals. I said they seemed obviously insane, and he agreed that they were 'nuts.' I asked him what will happen to the killers. 'They'll swing, I guess,' he told me."

Tynan also claimed that he later met with Truman during the spring of 1965, after the court had ruled to hang Smith and Hickock. "He hopped up and down with glee, clapping his hands, saying, 'I'm beside myself! Beside myself! Beside myself with joy!'"

Tynan also claimed that Truman could have saved Smith and Hickock from the gallows had he spent money hiring specialists to prove their insanity. "For the sake of millions of dollars in book sales, he let them hang. It seems to me that the blood in which the book is written is as cold as any in recent literature." Tynan concluded, "No piece of praise, however deathless, is worth a human life. It's sort of like letting the *Titanic* sink for literature's sake."

Stung by the criticism and the revelations, Truman shot back. He charged Tynan of "having the morals of a baboon and the guts of a butterfly."

But very privately, to Jack Dunphy one night, he confided that, "I wanted them to die so that my book could live."

In the aftermath of the publication of *In Cold Blood,* Truman was furious when literary prizes were awarded. He believed that he was "candidate *numero uno"* in line for both the Pulitzer Prize and the National Book Award.

He'd heard that *Newsweek's* Saul Maloff had been the judge who had nullified his chance of winning, asserting that *In Cold Blood* "was too commercial."

Truman responded with an scathing attack on Maloff's novel, *Happy Families.* "This novel is just what Frank Sinatra needs," he wrote. "Sinatra suffers from a bad case of insomnia, and this numbing little novel, an anthology of every *chichi* literary cliché, would tranquilize a kangaroo revved to the rafters on speed."

He was also outraged when Norman Mailer won the National Book Award for his *Armies of the Night,* a book about his participation in the protests against the Vietnam War. Truman claimed that Mailer's nonfiction book was "just a ripoff of my own literary style in *In Cold Blood."*

He also attacked prizes awarded to Bob Woodward and Carl Bernstein for *All the President's Men,* their Watergate exposé of the Nixon administration. "I created the literary format for them," he claimed. "Mailer, Woodward, and Bernstein got the prizes, and I got nothing. Here's my answer to the judges: 'Fuck you! All of you!'"

***

Finally, Columbia Pictures paid $500,000 for the movie rights to *In Cold Blood [released late in 1967],* a near record figure at the time. Having been impressed with *Cat on a Hot Tin Roof* and *The Blackboard Jungle,* Truman approved the studio's designation of Richard Brooks as director of the film adaptation.

Both Brooks and Truman opposed having the film shot in color, and both of them opposed the casting of Paul Newman as Hickock and Steve McQueen as Smith. Finally, Brooks won out, wrangled an agreement from the studio to shoot the film in stark black and white with two

Capote *(center)* stands with **Scott Wilson** *(left)* and **Robert Blake** *(right)* on that lonely Kansas road that led to the Clutter farm.

relative unknowns cast as the leads.

A Georgia native, actor Scott Wilson was cast as Hickock, with Robert Blake starring as Perry Wilson.

Wilson had made his screen debut that year in the role of a suspected murderer in the 1967 *In the Heat of the Night,* starring Sidney Poitier and Rod Steiger. Both Wilson and Blake, along with Truman, would appear on the cover of *Life* magazine on May 12, 1967, standing on a barren highway in the flatlands of Kansas.

When Truman was introduced to Blake and Wilson, he was stunned by how closely they resembled Hickock and Smith, especially Blake.

"The first time I saw Blake, I thought I'd seen a ghost of Perry sauntering in out of the sunshine, with his slippery hair and sleepy eyes. I couldn't accept the idea that this was someone pretending to be Perry—and not Perry himself. It was as if Perry had been resurrected, but was suffering from amnesia and remembered me not at all."

Ironically, Smith had told Truman that his all time favorite movie had been *The Treasure of the Sierra Madre* (1948)*,* starring Humphrey Bogart. As a child actor, Blake had been cast in that film as the little Mexican boy.

In another touch of irony, years later, Blake would be tried for the murder of his third wife, Bonny Lee Bakley, but would be acquitted. Subsequently, in a civil case brought by Bakley's three children, the verdict would go against Blake, and he'd be found guilty of her wrongful death and ordered to pay $30 million. In February of 2006, he'd file for bankruptcy.

Paul Stewart, a veteran *film noir* actor, was cast by Brooks to fulfill the role that Capote played in real life with the two murderers.

The film adaptation of *In Cold Blood* would be nominated for four Oscars, including Best Director.

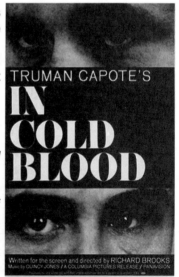

The eyes of two cold-blooded killers stare back from Truman's black-and-white film noir tale of ghastly murders.

***

Truman's researching and writing of *In Cold Blood* were depicted in the 2005 film *Capote,* starring Philip Seymour Hoffman, which won him an Oscar as Best Actor for his portrayal of Truman. A year later, *Infamous,* another film about Truman, starred Toby Jones. The book was also adapted for a 1996 TV miniseries, starring Anthony Edwards as Hickock, Eric Roberts as Smith, and Sam Neill as Dewey.

Harper Lee was portrayed by Catherine Keener in the film *Capote* (2005); and by Sandra Bullock in *Infamous* (2006).

Chapter Forty-Three

Myra Breckinridge
America's Foremost Literary Transsexual

"Don't Come Up and See Me Sometime"

— Mae West to Gore Vidal

Left photo: **Raquel Welch** as Myra Breckinridge decides to "pull down my bloomers" and show studio executives she's "the real thing. The boys might as well see what a real woman looks like," is Myra's boast. What they saw was not a real woman at all.

On the right are the assembled stars of the picture—*(left to right)* **John Huston** as Buck Loner; **Raquel** as Myra, **Mae West** as Leticia Van Allen, and **Rex Reed** as Myron Breckinridge, Myra's male counterpart.

The film was one of the most controversial ever turned out by a major film studio—20th Century Fox in this case. Because of its adult theme, it has rarely been shown on television, though in recent years, it was aired on the Fox Movie Channel.

When the film was released on DVD in 2004, minor changes were made to make the movie's ending more clear—that is, Myra never followed through with the conclusion of her sex change, so in essence, those studio chiefs were actually looking at Myra's dick.

Howard Austen, Gore Vidal's

longtime companion, once claimed that the inspiration for his controversial novel, *Myra Breckinridge,* actually came after Gore had sat through a 1949 movie, *Siren of Atlantis,* a frothy romance co-starring Maria Montez, the sultry actress from the Dominican Republic and her French husband-at-the-time, Jean-Pierre Aumont.

To Gore, the so-called "Queen of Technicolor" represented all that was campy and false about Golden Age Hollywood. His iconoclastic novel, published amid the social turmoil of 1968, was his attempt to satirize it, although his published attack on the motion picture industry was long in its gestation period.

Written in the form of a diary, the novel, according to Gore, was inspired by "the megalomania of the Anaïs Nin diaries."

In *Myra Breckinridge,* Gore's most outrageous fictional endeavor, he satirized such themes as transsexuality, deviant sexual practices, and feminism—each of them filtered through the lens of an aggressively campy sensibility.

His character of Myra was a re-creation of the ultimate Hollywood *femme fatale* from the Golden Age.

Gore Vidal was inspired by **Maria Montez** *(photo above)* and her screen image when he wrote his novel, *Myra Breckinridge.* Montez, born in the Dominican Republic, competed with Carmen Miranda as "The Queen of Cinematic Camp," forever associated with exotic Technicolor nonsense cranked out by Universal pictures in the 1940s.

Her acting was a joke, and her accent thick, but Montez had her devotees. She died of a heart attack at the age of 33.

Even though Myra is a fantasy invention of silicone and hormone injections, Gore claimed that her laugh is better than Carole Lombard's, she has more warmth than June Allyson, she's sweeter than Irene Dunne, she whispers better than Phyllis Thaxter, and her smile is more winning than Ann Sothern.

Shortly after Myra arrives in Hollywood, she imposes a legal claim on the land holdings of Buck Loner, a retired horse opera star. She cites her status as the widow of Buck's nephew, Myron Breckinridge, even though, in fact, "she" is Myron himself—his glamorous female incarnation in the aftermath of his sex-change operation.

"No One Would Ever Believe That I Was a Transsexual"

—*Elizabeth Taylor, on why she rejected the role of Myra*

With a sense of self-delusion, she declares that, "No man will ever possess Myra Breckinridge," insisting that it is she who will possess men in her "own good time and in ways convenient to my tyrannous lust."

She manifests that goal on the sexy, macho, and unwaveringly heterosexual Rusty Godowsky, who has already flaunted his manhood in front of her. After subjecting him to a series of sexual humiliations, she straps him to a table and triumphantly straddles him with a dildo.

"*I am a dish, and don't you forget it, you motherfuckers!*" Myra proclaims. Then she shares some of her Hollywood sexual fantasies with the readers of her diary, admitting that she maneuvered her way—in her incarnation as a woman—through a lesbian phase of her past, crushed between the heavy breasts of Lana Turner.

Myra goes on to announce that she abandoned that period of her life for the manly charms of James Craig, a dashing actor who, in the 1940s, was widely promoted as "the next Clark Gable."

"For years," the lush and beautiful Myra declares to her viewers and fans, "I practiced self-abuse, thinking of Craig's voice, those broad shoulders, those powerful thighs thrust between my own. No matter what condition James Craig is in today, decrepit or not, Myra Breckinridge is ready to give him a good time for old time's sake."

Sex icon **Raquel Welch,** cast in Gore Vidal's sexually confused *Myra Breckinridge.*

Welch didn't even rate a mention in the *Biographical Dictionary of Film,* but for a brief time, she was Hollywood's most visible sex symbol, a major-league, All-American box-office attraction except when she made that flop, *Myra Breckinridge.*

Mae West detested her. The feeling was mutual.

A subplot of *Myra Breckinridge* spins around the character of Letitia Van Allen, an aging but still sexually voracious talent scout who virtually invented the casting couch. As one of its workaday accessories, her office boasts a four-poster bed.

Myra meets Letitia and they become friends. Letitia confides that her studs provide her with "small attentions a girl like me cherishes, like a lighted cigarette stubbed out on my *derrière*, or a complete beating with his great thick heavy leather belt."

With some reluctance, and alert to the fear that a backlash might be imminent, Little, Brown Company published *Myra Breckinridge* in February of 1968.

Critiques included lavish praise from Christopher Isherwood and harsh attacks from William Buckley, Jr., who denounced Gore as a pornographer.

Critic Dennis Altman wrote: "*Myra Breckinridge* is part of a major cultural assault on the assumed norms of gender and sexuality, which swept the western world in the late 1960s and 1970s. It is tempting to argue that Vidal did more to subvert the dominant rules of sex and gender in *Myra* than is contained in a shelf of queer theory treatises."

Myra-How Did She Happen?

In 1968, shortly before the official publication date for the release of his novel, *Myra Breckinridge,* Gore Vidal sent a copy to director Joseph Losey. Gore felt that the controversial expatriate director would be ideal. A sexually sophisticated movie adaptation of the book seemed inevitable.

Losey had been blacklisted in Hollywood during the 1950s for having joined the Communist Party in 1946. Subsequently, he left the United States and moved to Europe, where he made the remainder of his films, mostly in England. Losey's previous so-called radical associations didn't frighten Gore at all, as his own left-wing views had often incited people who disagreed with him to label him as a communist.

In the late 1960s, Losey had formed a working relationship with playwright Harold Pinter, and had directed two films based on that writer's screenplays, including *The Servant* (1963) and *Accident* (1967). Both films had been lavishly honored, with awards from, among others, the British Academy Film Awards and the Grand Prix Special du Jury Award at the 1967 Cannes Film Festival. These movies examined the politics of sexuality and gender in the 1960s. Collectively, they seemed to make him the ideal candidate as director of an actress in a transgendered role.

Losey's response to Gore's proposal was immediate and enthusiastic. He'd not only read the novel twice, but had already developed strong ideas about how to cast it. He wanted Elizabeth Taylor to play Myra Breckinridge, and he thought Anne Bancroft would be ideal cast as Letitia Van Allen. He'd just seen her film, *The Graduate* (1967), and he thought he'd be perfect playing a sex-hungry film talent scout who liked to bed studs far more manly than Dustin Hoffman. After Losey managed to contact Bancroft by telephone, he learned that she, too, had read the novel and would be "delighted to sink my teeth into the role of Le*TIT*ia Van Allen."

Unable to reach Elizabeth Taylor on the phone, he wrote her a letter, dating it December 26, 1968, and addressing it to her chalet in Gstaad. With Richard Burton, she was staying in that fashionable Swiss resort over the holidays.

"I've been re-reading *Myra Breckinridge* by your friend, Gore Vidal, who served you so magnificently with the script he prepared for you for *Suddenly Last Summer*, where you gave a performance that should have won the Oscar. Done properly, *Myra Breckinridge* could make millions and neither of us need ever work again. You could afford not to work again, and I don't care—or, rather, we should put it the other way 'round. I could afford it (!) and *you* don't care."

When Elizabeth later encountered Gore at a Hollywood party, she said, "Under different circumstances, I might have considered it. But Losey's letter came at a very bad time for me. Of course, no one would have believed me as a trannie. But, what the hell, it would have been a lark. In that scene where I stand on a table and lower my lace panties to those guys, I would not have worn a sex-hider. With my back to the camera, I would have had great fun showing them the full Monty."

When she read Losey's letter, Elizabeth was behind schedule in the shooting of *The Only Game in Town,* a movie in which she was wrongly cast in a story about the romance of a chorus girl and a gambler, as played by Warren Beatty. After shooting in Paris, she would have to fly to Las Vegas for the final location sequences. This was the last film shot by director George Stevens, who had previously directed Montgomery Clift and her in *A Place in the Sun* (1951).

Overweight, especially for an actress playing a chorus girl, Elizabeth was also in constant pain because of her spine, and was taking a lot of painkillers. She was not only on pills, but consuming a lot of liquor. Burton often found her "incoherent and sloshed as a Cossack."

Burton later said, "I tried to get her to read Vidal's novel, but she wouldn't even finish reading the script for *The Only Game in Town.* I thought that if Losey directed it, I might put in a turn as Buck Loner, the part that eventually went to John Huston. I mean there was another problem. The ol' girl had just had her uterus removed."

Burton also said that although she didn't exactly tell Losey to "Fuck off," she "didn't give a rat's fart if she ever made another movie. But he didn't give up. That spring, he was asking both of us, or either of us, if we wanted to star in Edward Albee's *A Delicate Balance.* He got a firm NO for that offer as well."

When Gore Vidal was received by **Mae West,** the tarty, buxom, egomaniacal vaudevillian from yesteryear, she was, in his words, "Just a wee bit overdressed." She told him saucy, self-enchanted stories about her early days in Hollywood, including how Marlene Dietrich at Paramount tried to seduce her.

He was shocked when he discovered that Mae thought she was being cast in the film's title role as Myra, and not in a secondary part.

Before Gore left her apartment, Mae agreed to return to New York for the film's premiere after an absence of 20 years.

Placards hailing her as the "Queen of Sex—*Still*" greeted her as she stepped out of her limo in Manhattan, flanked by ten escorts and greeted by sixty patrolmen and six mounted police officers. Her diamond-and-ruby-laden hand waved to her hysterical fans. "I still know how to make an entrance," she whispered to her security guard.

The next morning, she was greeted with this headline: "*MAE WEST DOES PORNO!*"

***

After the release of the movie adaptation of his novel, *Myra Breckinridge,* Gore Vidal denounced the film as "an awful joke."

Trouble had begun with the casting of Mae West, who had last appeared on a movie screen in the box office disaster *The Heat's On,* released by Columbia Pictures during the dark days of war-torn 1943.

Although Gore had rejected an offer to write the screenplay of Breckinridge, he did accept an invitation to visit Mae at her residence in the Ravenswood Apartments (on North Rossmore Avenue) in Los Angeles.

The movie's producer, Robert Fryer, had called Mae to offer her a role in the film for $100,000. She mistakenly thought he was offering her the lead, and she was initially outraged that he wanted her to star in a movie for only $100,000.

The aging sex symbol of yesterday, **Mae West**, agreed to pose with the reigning sex queen of the 1970s, **Raquel Welch** *(right).*

"Fans call *Myra Breckinridge* the Mae West movie, not the Raquel Welch movie," Mae asserted. "My spiritual adviser told me to star in the movie, claiming that it was my destiny. In case you didn't see it, I played a talent agent who specializes in finding roles for oversexed leading men—but only after I've put them on my casting couch, which is actually a four-poster bed."

She told him that she would agree to a role in the movie only if she was given top billing, a free hand in rewriting her scenes, and $300,000.

At first, 20th Century hesitated, but they eventually agreed to her price. In response, she notified Fox executives that they had waited too long. She now demanded $350,000. Finally, they agreed to that, too, believing that the publicity of including her would be worth it at the box office.

***

The next time Elizabeth saw Gore, she told him that, out of curiosity, she'd gone to visit Mae West after she'd starred in *Myra Breckinridge.* Christopher Lawford, Peter Lawford's teenage son, had accompanied her.

"Mae wanted to know if Chris and I were having an affair," Elizabeth said. "She told me, 'We older gals need young stuff.'"

"The sex goddess of yesterday appeared in a curve-hugging silver gown and was practically held up by two bodybuilders. She did nothing but talk about herself and what a big star she still was. When she excused herself to 'go powder my muff,' I told Chris, 'Let's get the fuck out of here. Talk about the self-enchanted!'"

Gore relayed to Elizabeth the litany of his own (disastrous) experiences with Mae during the filming of *Myra Breckinridge.* "The wisest thing you ever did, Elizabeth, was to turn down the role."

When Gore had visited Mae, he recalled that she was dressed entirely in white, including her furs and diamonds. She blended in with her all-white apartment. "She was so heavily made up and so flamboyantly gowned that I had no idea exactly what was lurking behind all that artificial glamour," Gore recalled. "I feared a very old lady who had helped Lincoln draft the Emancipation Proclamation."

"Mae looked like a living refugee from the waxworks," he said. "No wonder Billy Wilder originally offered her the role of Norma Desmond in *Sunset Blvd.*"

"Beneath all that war paint, I sensed a tireless trouper from yesterday, a born entertainer who loved to perform, and a consummate publicity agent promoting only one product—herself, in all her faded glory."

Although she hadn't made a movie in twenty-three years, she wanted it clearly understood that she didn't want Fox to bill this picture as her comeback. "It's a return, not a comeback," she told him, parroting a line from *Sunset Blvd.*

"I'm still a star, one of the really big ones, right up there with Charlie Chaplin," she told him. "He was a little guy, but one with a big prick. I'm also a playwright. Speaking of playwrights, there are only three big ones—Tennessee Williams, Eugene O'Neill, and me."

"I can still undulate these old hips of mine, even if they date from the 19th Century," she told him. "I'm such a big name that I can carry the picture myself. They'll come to see me. Every birthday, I get so many phone calls from well-wishers that I practically shut down the phone lines with overload."

Before agreeing to participate in the project, she had definite requirements.

"First, I never play a character older than twenty-six," she told him. "Not only that, but I write my own lines, each guaranteed to get a laugh."

"When I went into her all-white bathroom to take a piss, I was shocked to see this large blowup, a frontal nude, of Jack Dempsey," Gore said. "She had a thing for boxers, especially if they were as black as Gorilla Jones, another one of her lovers."

["Gorilla" Jones (aka William Landon Jones (1906-1982), was an African-American, Memphis-born boxer and twice NBA Middleweight Boxing Champion of the World.]

"Earlier, she'd told me that when management had objected to her having black boxers come and go, she bought a large interest in the building and lifted the ban on Negroes."

Seated opposite her once again, Gore learned that she wanted to perform three or four musical numbers within the context of the upcoming movie. "She even sang a few lines from a song from one of her long-ago road shows. It was called 'Rub-a-Dub-Dub, Three Fags in a Tub.' I convinced her that that exact title might not be appropriate."

"After two of the most fascinating hours of my life, Mae announced that she had to retire for her afternoon beauty sleep so she would be in condition to rock 'n' roll around the clock till dawn breaks," Gore said.

"God, these young men of today are so demanding," Mae said. "They just can't get enough."

Gore kissed her diamond-laden hand and wished her luck with the movie.

He remembered her parting words to him: "Fox is sure lucky to get me in the picture. It'll increase sales of that novel of yours. I tried to read it but couldn't get through it. With me in the picture, it'll become a classic."

Some of her final words were filled with a certain nostalgia. "I never loved another person the way I loved myself, and I have no guilt about it. I'm in a class by myself. I have no regrets."

"How about you, Vidal?" she asked. "Did you ever love?"

"Only once in my entire life, and he was slaughtered by the Japs on the beaches of Iwo Jima."

***

Before the film's final cast was announced by 20th Century Fox, Candy Darling, the emerging superstar from the entourage of Andy Warhol, began to pursue Gore, even though he insisted with her that he had no say over casting. She didn't really believe him.

She was aggressively lobbying for the role of Myra. "Why get one of those Hollywood whores with a smelly vagina when you can cast a 'Trans woman' like me?" she asked. "I AM Myra Breckinridge. I understand her to my scarlet-painted toenails."

When she first came to call, Gore paid her a lot more attention, since he'd written a book (that was about to be adapted into a movie), about a transsexual.

Trannie **Candy Darling** (*both photos above*) tried to convince Gore Vidal and others that she—not Raquel—should play Myra Breckinridge on the screen. But to no avail.

Vidal, in retrospect, reconsidered, claiming "Candy might have given the movie the shot of testosterone it needed. The publicity alone would have been terrific."

She revealed to him that while she was growing up as James Lawrence Slattery (nicknamed Jimmy) in Queens (New York City), she had identified with Myra Breckinridge. Like the heroine of his novel, she was addicted to old movies.

She confided that she learned the mysteries of sex from a salesman (a child molester) in a local children's store.

Her mother confronted her one evening with rumors she'd heard that her son was a cross dresser. Jimmy went to his bedroom and emerged an hour later as "Hope Dahl," a name she later changed to Candy Darling. The name was chosen because of her love of sweets.

"I knew then that I couldn't stop Jimmy," her mother, Theresa Phelan, said. "He was too beautiful and talented. His beauty rivaled that of any girl I knew. I also knew that every red-blooded male in America would want my son in bed."

Gore, in time, heard all of Candy's stories, including details about some movie stars who had seduced her, including one who was the macho King of Hollywood at the time.

"I'm not going to name him, but movie buffs of the early 70s will know exactly who I mean."

Finally, Gore grew impatient, having by now heard all of Candy's revelations. He quit accepting her phone calls. She reacted by appearing on his doorstep several times late at night.

Finally, in exasperation, he threw open his door to confront her. "Fuck, Candy, let me get some sleep. If you want to play Myra, head over to Richard Zanuck's house and suck him off." Then he slammed the door in her face.

He never saw her again, but was saddened to learn of her death on March 21, 1974 of lymphoma. "She truly lived up to the motto of young people 'Live fast, die young, and leave a beautiful corpse.'"

***

At long last, the cast was announced by Fox, with Raquel Welch designated as the star who'd interpret the role of Myra. Mae West signed to play Letitia, but insisted that the character's name be changed to Leticia. "There's no way I'm going to play a character called Le*TI-Ti*a. Otherwise, the role was tailor made for me, that of a sexual predator talent scout who auditions only studs."

Director John Huston signed on for the role of Buck Loner after promising Fox that, "I won't try to take over as the director. Think of me as a piano player in a whorehouse."

Producers David Giler and Robert Fryer assembled a very talented cast, with

Competition for Raquel's status as a sex symbol did not really derive from the aging Mae West--by then an unwitting caricature of her former allure—but from a newcomer, **Farrah Fawcett** *(both photos above)*, cast as Mary Ann Pringle (Welch's lesbian lover) in Gore's film, *Myra Breckinridge*. Beginning in 1976, the Texas beauty went on to achieve international acclaim in the TV series *Charlie's Angels*.

She married Lee Majors in 1973, but was most famously involved in a love affair with Ryan O'Neal, when he wasn't otherwise banging Jacqueline Bisset, Joan Collins, Mia Farrow, Angelica Huston, Bianca Jagger, Ali McGraw, Liza Minnelli, Michelle Phillips, Linda Ronstadt, Diana Ross, Barbra Streisand, *et al.*

Roger Herren cast as Rusty Godowski, who is dildo-raped by Myra. The character of Rusty was described "as the last stronghold of masculinity in this Disneyland of perversion."

The movie critic, Rex Reed, was cast in a very brief cameo as Myron Breckinridge—that is, Myra "before she had it cut off."

Farrah Fawcett played Mary Ann Pringle, Rusty's girlfriend. Some very talented character actors filled out the bill, including Jim Backus as the Doctor; John Carradine as the Surgeon, Andy Devine as Coyote Bill, and Tom Selleck in an early role as "The Stud."

The surprise from Fox involved the hiring of the relatively unknown director, Michael Sarne, whose contract gave him total control over the expensive project. He did not set out to make "one of the fifty worst films of all time," but he succeeded in doing just that.

Sarne had previously directed a film, *Joanna* (1968), about a young country girl entangled in the murky morality of swinging London. Fox hired him as *Myra Breckinridge's* director, hoping to capture a youth market which had never before heard of Mae West.

A reporter asked Mae how she felt about the casting of Raquel Welch as Myra. "Who?" Mae asked. "Never heard of her." Consistently throughout the course of filming, Mae never called her by her name, but constantly referred to Raquel as "The Little Girl."

"What's her face has one or two little scenes in the movie—so I've been told," Mae said.

Mae was also asked if she'd heard rumors that both Gore Vidal and Rex Reed were homosexuals. "Gay lib?" she asked. "The gay boys? Looks like they're practically taking over. I think they invented the word 'gay' back in 1927 when I wrote a homosexual comedy called *Drag*. The gay boys have always adored me, and they're always imitating me. They know talent when they see it."

Mae was passionately opposed to the director's idea of defining the entire film as a fantasy. "It's like someone tells you a story and gets you all interested. Then they say, 'I woke up to find it was all a dream.' You want to smack 'em in the face!"

It was agreed that Mae would appear only in black-and-white outfits, her gowns designed by Edith Head. When Welch showed up for a photo shoot dressed in black, a feud was launched.

Behind Raquel's back, Mae was lobbying to have her replaced, even though she was the world's reigning sex symbol at the time. Mae wanted a homosex-

A male sex symbol of the 70s, **Tom Selleck** got his start as an actor playing "The Stud" in *Myra Breckinridge*. He later achieved incredible fame starring as the private investigator in the hit TV series *Magnum, P.I.* (1980-88).

When Mae West spotted him, she told Gore, "That's the kind of man I'd like to come up and see me sometime. Maybe I'll use him in one of my muscle-men shows. I like actors to wear a sheer male bikini when they show up for an audition so I can see what's up front. Steve Cochran made the grade but I had to reject Kirk Douglas years ago."

ual—"maybe like this Candy Darling that Gore Vidal was telling me about—cast as Myra instead of a biological woman. Only a homosexual can play the role."

Sarne informed Mae that in one sequence, she'd appear in front of a chorus line of African-American men, each of them dressed in white tie and tails. She issued a warning: "They must never touch me—because of all those rednecks in the South, you know."

When Gore heard that, he remarked, "In her private life, Mae never had any objection to being touched by a black man—that's touched, not fucked."

Raquel had her own views about Mae West, her casting, and the script itself.

"If you can buy the fact that a woman of 77 can send a 22-year-old stud to the hospital to recuperate after a night of sex, then you can buy anything in this picture."

At one point, Mae was introduced to Farrah Fawcett. "Oh, you play the lesbian lover of Myra Breckinridge," Mae said. "You certainly look the part. I guess you're quite familiar with mattresses."

[Mae's put-downs always contained a double entendre. She'd previously seen Fawcett advertising Beautyrest mattresses on TV.]

Sarne tossed out nearly all of Mae's quips, which seriously angered her. She later claimed "the movie would have been sure box office if they'd kept in my one-liners and some of my musical numbers."

[One of her memorable lines in Myra Breckinridge *is delivered when she auditions a row of good-looking men. One in particular strikes her fancy. "Cowboy," she asks. "How tall are you?"*

"I'm six feet, seven inches," he replies.

"Well, never mind the six feet—let's talk about the seven inches."

Gore read some of Mae's quips that she'd submitted for inclusion in the movie. "She must have gone down memory lane and opened an old stage trunk when these one-liners were first written. I think Theodore Roosevelt was in the White House. A typical sample would be, 'I don't expect too much from a man—just what he's got!'"]

In subsequent releases of *Myra Breckinridge*, some of which were heavily edited, some of the best scenes were cut, including when Rex Reed, as Myron, confronts the Surgeon, played by John Carradine. He's ready to un-

The director of *Myra Breckinridge* was the youthful and handsome British pop singer and later actor and director, **Michael Sarne**. Before the shoot was over, virtually every star on the set had turned against him.

In the beginning, Mae West had liked him. "I never could resist an English accent," she said, "especially if a good-lookin' Englishman is speakin' it."

Sarne claimed, "Raquel and Rex Reed didn't want Mae in the picture, and they launched a hate-fest against me."

dergo "the cruelest cut" in his attempt to transform himself into Myra.

"You realize that once we cut it off, it won't grow back?" Carradine warns Myron. "How about circumcision instead? It'll be cheaper."

Raquel and Mae, during a rare break in their frequent battles, agreed on only one point: Sarne should be fired and replaced with the gay director George Cukor. But finally, they decided that even Cukor wouldn't be able to save this picture.

***

When *Myra Breckinridge* opened in 1970, it was an immediate flop, and Fox soon withdrew it from circulation. It was one of two X-rated films that Fox released that year, the other being *Beyond the Valley of the Dolls.*

Movie critics at *Time* magazine pounced on it, asserting, "*Myra Breckinridge* is about as funny as a child molester. It is an insult to intelligence, an affront to sensibility, and an abomination to the eye."

Vincent Canby of *The New York Times* denounced filmmakers who go to "great lengths to try to be different and dirty. As for Mae West, she possesses a figure of a cinched-in penguin and a face made of pink-and-white plaster in which little holes have been left for her eyes and mouth."

Author Simon Louvish wrote: "The problem derives largely from the original material: Gore Vidal's mock-trashy vision of a morally and physically polluted America, drawn through the transsexual's eyes—and in particular, the subculture of Los Angeles, inhabited by a rogue's gallery of phonies and grotesques. George Cukor would have floundered as deeply as Michael Sarne, who survived the movie without being assassinated."

The film also attracted unwanted attention from Golden Age movie stars. From the Fox archives, footage of movies filmed in the 1930s had been inserted to punctuate the jokes, and as a spoof of the film's climatic dildo-rape scene. During the latter, images of Myra getting invasive with Rusty fade as footage from Shirley Temple's 1937 film *Heidi* appears on the screen. The 1937 clip showed Shirley (as Heidi) getting squirted with milk during her attempt to milk a stubborn goat. The symbolism of ejaculation in her face is quite clear.

Objections to the scene reached all the way to the White House. "Shirley's face, symbolically at least, is being sprayed with semen," claimed Richard Nixon, of all people.

For reasons known only to himself, Nixon had requested a screening of *Myra Breckinridge* at the White House. The morning after he saw it, he telephoned Richard Zanuck in Hollywood, asking him to remove the Shirley Temple footage from the context of the larger film, fuming, "Shirley is a staunch Republican and, as an ambassador *[to the United Nations in 1969; to Ghana in 1974; and to Czechoslovakia in 1989]* will represent the United States."

Loretta Young successfully sued to have old film footage of herself removed from the picture.

After the film's release, Gore picked up a copy of the *Los Angeles Times* to read a letter to the editor written by one J. Correll. "Mae West has become a tiresome old bore, forever talking about how wonderful she was—and she thinks she still is. At almost eighty, she's a gabby girl, but not the Mae West of forty years ago, when I was a fan of hers. She belongs to the past, and only the past, an old lady who thinks of herself as a sex symbol. It is sad and somewhat revolting."

Gore showed the letter to his breakfast companion, Howard Austen. "I couldn't have said it better myself."

The story may be apocryphal, but years later, Gore heard that Sarne was working as a waiter in a restaurant. "God does exist," he said.

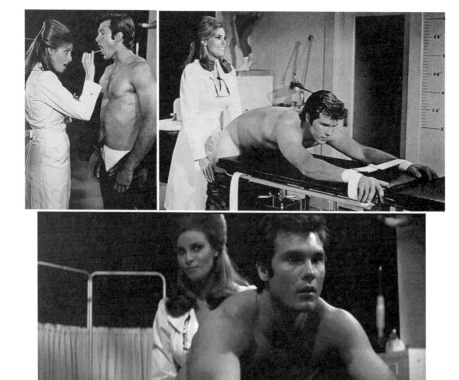

The most controversial scene in *Myra Breckinridge* was when Myra (**Welch**), disguised as a nurse, uses a dildo on (i.e. rapes) the school stud, Rusty Gadowsky. His role was interpreted by the handsome, muscular actor **Roger Herren**, who enjoyed his fifteen minutes of fame before fading into oblivion.

As Gore defined and phrased the scene in his novel, Myra encountered "the opening the size of a dime while the dildo was over two inches wide at the head and nearly a foot long. I pushed. The pink lips opened. The tip of the head entered and stopped as Rusty moaned that he could not take it—'It's just too big.' I plunged deeper. He cried out with pain. But I was inexorable. I pushed father even farther, triggering the prostate gland. He cried out, again, begging me to stop, but now I was a woman possessed, riding, riding, riding my sweating stallion into forbidden country, shouting with joy as I experienced my own sort of orgasm, oblivious to the staccato shrieks as I delved and spanned that innocent flesh. Oh, it was a holy moment!"

In spite of its initial reception, the film version of *Myra Breckinridge* has, since its release, become a cult classic.

Myra/Myron Trades Places with Cobra Woman

Despite the dismal reception of the movie, in 1974, based on the best-selling success of his 1968 novel, *Myra Breckinridge,* Gore, in 1974, released a sequel, *Myron,* which was published shortly after an anti-pornography crackdown by the U.S. Supreme Court. To show his contempt for specific members of the Court, Gore satirized their names by inserting them at unexpectedly salacious points within his manuscript. *[Example: "He thrust his enormous Rehnquist deep within her Whizzer White."]*

In the sequel, *Myron,* Gore went wild with the he/she fluidity. As literary critic Robert F. Kiernan encapsulated the novel, "Obscenities and recriminations shoot freely back and forth as the antagonists (Myra battling Myron) settle down to a stalemated war, and tweezered eyebrows, padded brassieres, and raw oysters become delightful beachheads in their battle for sexual supremacy. Myron threatens Myra that he will take male hormones and turn the Breckinridge body as hairy as a tarantula, and she threatens him that she will dance the tarantella in a Maidenform bra on his grave."

Maria Montez, the sultry Dominican star of such movies as *Cobra Woman* (1944), figures into the newer novel. One night, while watching *Siren of Babylon (Gore's satire of Montez's 1948 movie, Siren of Atlantis),* Myron/Myra is transported to a 1940s film set via his/her television set.

For the Myra aspect of the protagonist's character, this is a dream come true; for Myron, it's his worst nightmare. As he desperately tries to escape from the film set, he encounters Richard Nixon seeking a hideaway from the Watergate scandal.

Gore also used this novel to "send up" his critics. Its character of Whittaker Kaiser is clearly inspired by author Norman Mailer. From Kaiser's mouth emerges this declaration: "Look, every man wants to make it with another man, but the *real* man is the one who fights off his hideous weak fag self and takes one woman after another without the use of any contraceptives or pill or diaphragm or rubber, just the all-conquering sperm, because contraception of any kind is as bad as masturbation."

At the novel's climax, a former cowboy actor in the film, now a transsexual, has been elected as the Republican Governor of Arizona. The episode was an obvious spoof of Rex Bell, the former celluloid cowboy who became the Lieutenant Governor of Nevada who (unhappily) married the emotionally unstable silent screen vamp, Clara Bow.

Kiernan summed up the two *Breckinridge* novels: "They are preposterous, droll, and gaudily offensive—although altogether triumphant and altogether wonderful."

Chapter Forty-Four

The Black & White Ball

A Capote Caper Starring "The Five Hundred"

> "I've invited 500 guests and made 15,000 enemies"
>
> — Truman Capote

At the pinnacle of his success after the publication of *In Cold Blood,* **Truman Capote** decided to throw a costumed black-and-white ball "that will dazzle with its Oz-like splendor" at the Plaza Hotel *(photo above, right)* in Manhattan. Ostensibly, the shindig was in honor of a woman he hardly knew, **Katharine Graham** *(shown above left, with Truman),* the publisher of *The Washington Post,* and one of the most influential women in America at the time. Privately, Truman told designer Cecil Beaton, "Of course, the ball is really for *moi.*"

An invitation to the ball was highly coveted. Alice Roosevelt Longworth called it "the most exquisite of spectator sports." It was also called "a cultural happening that defined the 1960s."

With the success of *In Cold Blood,* Truman

Capote had joined the ranks of the nouveau riche, and he was ready to celebrate his good fortune.

He decided to throw a costume ball evoking the famous black-and-white scene supposedly set at the Ascot Races in *My Fair Lady,* whose sets and costumes had been designed by Cecil Beaton. Since Beaton was practically his best friend, Truman called him for advice. Beaton thought it was a bad idea.

He later told Noël Coward, "What is Truman trying to prove? The foolishness of spending so much time organizing such a party is something a younger man or a worthless woman indulges in if they have social ambitions."

Another friend, Leo Lerman, advised Truman, "You can't throw a ball in honor of yourself. Select one of your beautiful ladies—your 'swans,' as you call them—and toss the ball in her honor."

After thinking it over, Truman decided he'd make the swans jealous if he focused on just one of them, so he decided to designate Katharine Graham, the publisher of *The Washington Post* and *Newsweek,* as the event's guest of honor. He knew her only slightly, having been introduced to her by Babe Paley.

Remembering
Katharine
Graham
1917-2001

He'd heard that she'd been in the doldrums ever since her womanizing husband, Philip Graham, had committed suicide in 1963.

Truman called her, reaching her at her office in Washington, where she had just put down the phone after a dialogue with President Lyndon B. Johnson.

"I think you need cheering up, my dear, and I'm going to give you a ball at the Plaza Hotel in Manhattan."

"I was baffled," she later said. "I knew Truman, but not that well. I felt a little bit like Truman was going to give the ball anyway, and that I was just the major prop."

Truman is seen arriving at his party with **Katharine Graham**, his guest of honor. She was a veteran hostess herself, entertaining presidents, diplomats, and the power elite of Washington, D.C. An invitation to a party at her Georgetown mansion was as highly desirable as being "summoned" to the White House.

She confided to Truman, "In Washington, there is always a dilemma: Too much booze combined with conflicting ideologies can be lethal."

"The Parvenu Poodle of High Society Tries to Hide His Hound Dog Origins" —Gore Vidal

Truman made a wise choice in his selection of Graham as the party's honoree. With her media empire, she'd arguably become the most powerful woman in America. This was Truman's chance to introduce her to international society. Although she was familiar with the names and status of dozens of his guests, she had not met most of them personally.

Graham and Capote, in the short time they'd known each other, had confided secrets. She told him that nearly every senator or even a president who visited her office wanted to go to bed with her, including Lyndon Johnson. "It's not that they're attracted to a middle aged woman like me, but they like to get intimate with the seat of power."

A famous party giver and social arbiter, Babe Paley, wife of CBS's Executive Director William Paley, could be relied on for advice. Truman made repeated calls to her, explaining that he chose the black-and-white theme because he wanted his guests to provide the color. He was on the verge of ordering The Plaza to drape all the walls of their ballroom in red velvet. Instead, she advised that he decorate each table with flowers and with gold candelabra wound with smilax *[a thin-stemmed South African vine with glossy foliage that's popular as a floral decoration]* and bearing white candles.

To his amazement, Truman learned that the entire party would cost only $16,000 *[in 1966 currency],* and subsequently, he decided that he could afford it, having already made $2 million from *In Cold Blood,* with more to come.

As he told Paley, "To my Croesus-like friends such as you and Bill, or the Agnellis, that is not a lot of money. When you average it out over the six years I worked on the book, and take away a huge hunk for taxes, plus other fees, that's what any small Wall Street broker might have made over the same period."

"Working on *In Cold Blood* has scraped me right down to the marrow of my bones," he claimed.

He also discussed the guest list with her, deciding that the ballroom at the Plaza could accommodate only five hundred comfortably. He told Babe that he planned to make his costume ball the biggest *cause célèbre* since Ward McAllister in 1892 drew up the list of "The 400" *[i.e., the only people in New York "worthy of fitting into Mrs. Astor's Fifth Avenue ballroom."]*

Truman leaked news of his coming event—scheduled for November 28, 1966, the Monday after Thanksgiving—to the press.

As he made his rounds of the Manhattan watering holes, and as news spread of his ball, he was besieged with requests for invitations. "Am I going to be invited?" was a question he heard often.

He taunted these people. "Well, maybe you'll be invited." He paused. "But then again, maybe not."

He spent months revising his guest list, crossing off names and adding new ones. He consulted frequently with Cecil Beaton: "I'm going to have only a few Hollywood stars. I'm thinking of the times I was *fêted* on the West Coast during my last visit. Joan Crawford invited me to her home, but I don't think I'll invite her. I had lunch with Greta Garbo, and I will invite her. Marlene Dietrich prepared a supper for me, so I'll invite her. Oh, and Errol Flynn fucked me. But he's dead."

As it turned out, Dietrich was in Paris and cabled that she could not make it, and Garbo never responded to the invitation.

He decided to invite Carson McCullers, "against my better judgment." He really did not want her to come because of all her nasty comments about how he'd plagiarized her writing style. Nonetheless, he invited her anyway.

He had decided to leave Tallulah Bankhead off the list, because she was known for getting drunk and creating scenes. He'd heard stories about how, when she was younger in the 1920s and appearing on the stage in London's West End, she'd often attend parties in Mayfair, where she'd scandalously turn cartwheels wearing no bloomers.

When she found out she wasn't going to be invited, Tallulah called Truman six times, beseeching him to let her be a guest. "If you don't, I won't be able to show my face in this town again."

He finally acquiesced to her demands, although he said he'd have to call Carson McCullers and cancel her invitation to make room for Tallulah.

"Carson has got her heart set on coming," Truman said. "It'll break her heart."

"Well, *dahling,*" Tallulah answered. "All of us can't be Cinderella at the ball. The important thing is that I'll be there. Everyone there will know who Tallulah Bankhead is. Only a few people know who Carson McCullers is."

Impish Truman took a bit of glee in calling Carson to disinvite her. She was furious. An enraged Carson phoned Tennessee Williams and protested Truman's act of *triage.* "He was just a nobody, and I lent a helping hand. And this is his gratitude. In retaliation, I'm going to throw a party of my own and invite far more important guests. At the top of my list will be Miss Jackie Kennedy."

"Do you know Mrs. Kennedy?" Tennessee asked.

"I don't, but I know this: If I invite her, she'll come!"

In preparation for the event, Tru-

"Truman Capote," seen above putting on his mask for the ball, "is a small man of big dreams that turned into a nightmare." Or so proclaimed Gore Vidal, who did not get invited to the Plaza.

man called the catering department at The Plaza until he made a nuisance of himself. He ordered 450 bottles of Taittinger champagne as refreshments for his party. He also commissioned a supper menu *[scrambled eggs, sausages, biscuits, French pastries, spaghetti and meatballs, and the Plaza's famous high-cholesterol chicken hash with Hollandaise sauce]* for presentation at midnight.

Many wealthy people tried to buy their way in, some offering to donate $10,000 to charity, even if that "charity" were Truman himself, but he steadfastly refused. The beauty magnate, Charles Revson, owner of Revlon, even offered to provide very upscale door prizes and table favors in exchange for an invitation. As tempting as that offer was, Truman turned him down.

Even though an invitation to his ball had evolved into the most coveted in America, Truman was nonetheless stunned by the number of people who declined. Of course, he was inviting some of the most sought-after and busiest celebrities in America, many of whom had other commitments. He was "seriously pissed off" when Tennessee Williams turned him down. *[Actually, Tennessee might have attended, but Truman refused his request about bringing an escort, a young man he was dating at the time.]*

Although they had developed a reputation for attending parties almost anywhere, the Duke and Duchess of Windsor cabled their regrets.

Since the party was scheduled so close to the third anniversary of JFK's assassination in Dallas *[November 22, 1966]*, Jackie said no. So did her brothers-in-law, Bobby and Teddy.

In contrast, Lee Radziwill, Jackie's sister, accepted. At the time, Truman, in vain, was attempting to transform her into an actress.

With the country in upheaval over the Vietnam War, Robert McNamara, Secretary of State, told Truman, "It would be unseemly for me to be seen doing the Frug with our soldiers in Vietnam dying."

Filming Carson McCullers' *Reflections in a Golden Eye* at the time with Marlon Brando, Elizabeth Taylor refused the invitation. So did Richard Burton, as well as Audrey Hepburn and her husband, Mel Ferrer.

Ginger Rogers declined, sending Truman a note—"I don't go to parties."

Lena Horne was invited, although warned that an escort would not be allowed because of space considerations.

"*I DO NOT ATTEND PARTIES ALONE!*" she said, before slamming down the phone on Truman.

Mike Nichols claimed he was involved in a show; and Walter Cronkite was on assignment in England.

Truman by this time had forgiven Katherine Anne Porter for referring to him publicly as "The pimple on the face of American literature," and consequently, he invited her and she accepted. *[As it turned out, she became ill before the party and couldn't make it.]*

More rejections poured in, including from Governor Nelson Rockefeller, Robert Penn Warren, James Michener, Paul Mellon, Mary Martin, Samuel Goldwyn, Leonard Bernstein, and Harry Belafonte.

But for several weeks in a row, at least twenty requests a day came in, some of them almost demanding invitations. The word was out—if you didn't get invited, leave town. One didn't want to be seen in Manhattan on the night of the ball if you were not at The Plaza.

Truman had to hire extra secretarial help to deal with the mail.

The most skilled maskmakers in Europe and America were working overtime to create masks. Halsted, the designer, charged $600 for one of his "off the rack"

In addition to his celebrated guests, Truman invited what he defined as "the Kansas brigade" of females he'd met while researching *In Cold Blood*. In the beauty salon of *The Plaza (left to right)* **Margaret Masoner, Marie Dewey, Kay Wells,** and **Vi Tate** get ready for the big night.

masks—and often a lot more, depending on the concept and its design.

For his own mask, Truman strolled down to F.A.O. Schwartz, where he bought an ordinary black domino for 39¢. Later, he heard that one of his guests had commissioned a black velvet mask for $38,000. *[Inspired by* "Mephistopheles," *it was crafted to resemble acanthus leaves and adorned with marquise-shaped diamonds.]*

The most renowned hairstylists in Manhattan were booked for appointments during the crucial hours before the event. The most sought-after was Kenneth Battelle, the "Mr. Cool of Haute Coiffure." He "teased, tamed, and twisted" some of the most expensive female heads on the East Coast, adding hairpieces whenever he deemed it necessary.

Reflecting on the French Revolution, Leo Lerman joked, "The guest list, which includes such names as Henry Ford's, reads like an international list for the guillotine."

Before it began, Truman told Paley, "A hundred years from now, people will still be talking about my event. It will become part of my legend."

I've Renamed My Party "In Bad Blood."
The Enemies I've Made by Not Inviting Them!"

—Truman Capote

Although the weather was windy and rainy on the night of November 28, the international press and *paparazzi* converged outside The Plaza Hotel to photograph and call out questions for the parade of celebrity guests. As demanded, most of the men dressed in tuxedos, the women in black and/or white gowns or costumes. Extra security was added for the safeguarding of a vast fortune in furs and gemstones.

In advance, Truman had designated a phalanx of women designated as "hostesses" for groupings of between twelve and sixteen of his party guests, with the understanding that they'd supervise pre-party dinners at chic restaurants located near The Plaza. He not only designated these women as hostesses, but he specifically pre-designated the guests they were to entertain. *[Also, whereas he paid the dinner tabs of his hostesses, he did not volunteer to pay the dinner tabs of anyone else in their respective groups.]*

That evening, immediately prior to the debut of the party, which had been scheduled for 10pm, Truman with his guest of honor, Katharine Graham, shared drinks with William and Babe Paley, and then sequestered themselves alone within Graham's suite at The Plaza, where she'd arranged a private dinner for two *[caviar and roasted chicken]* catered by "21."

After their pre-ball dinner, they went downstairs to take their place at the door to greet their parade of 500 guests. Except for a slippage here and there, most of the gate crashers were turned away.

At ten o'clock, nobody had shown up. Graham expressed her fear that the ball would be a flop. But by 10:15pm, the first guests arrived to have their hands shaken and the air around their cheeks kissed.

By 10:30pm, a long and glamorous line had assembled at the entrance to the ballroom.

Outside, reporters shouted questions at the arriving guests. New York State Senator Jacob Javits arrived wearing a domino equivalent to something from a Hollywood Western. An effeminate young man, standing with three other similar young men, yelled out to Javits: "Here comes the Lone Ranger."

"Thank you, ladies," Javits responded.

Studio executive and movie producer Darryl Zanuck was asked by a reporter: "Are you someone important?"

"If you don't know, you shouldn't be here," the movie mogul snapped.

Although he slipped up here and

A masked vision in white, the indomitable **Tallulah Bankhead** arrived to attend Truman's ball. "Who does that girl think she is?" Tallulah had asked. "I had to call him five times and on bended nylon to practically beg him for an invitation. Frankly, I *made* his party."

there, Truman seemed to know each of his guests. When he didn't, he cleverly concealed it by pretending that the masks obscured everyone's features. He'd say, "Now who is this hiding behind the mask?"

The parade was dazzling, although, as to be expected, some guests outshone the others.

Oscar and Françoise de la Renta arrived, looking startling in soft, feathery headdresses inspired by the beaks of marabou. *[i.e., birds that resemble storks or ibises]*. On their heels, the social doyenne of New York City, Brooke Astor, wearing a white lace gown, looked as if she'd stepped out of a Goya painting.

Since the Black and White Ball had been inspired by Cecil Beaton's "Ascot scene" in *My Fair Lady* (1964), Truman expected Beaton to show up in a spectacular disguise. But to his disappointment, "He wore a simple Halloween mask tied with a little black bow at the top," Truman later lamented.

As an acknowledgement of the role he had played during Truman's research of the Clutter murder case, Truman invited Alvin Dewey of the Kansas Bureau of Investigation. As Norman Mailer later remarked, "Here he was, Alvin Dewey, the delegate from the Grain Belt, a real salt-of-the-earth guy surrounded by all these glamorous, bedecked pussies. I liked him."

Truman frequently referred to some of his closest women friends as "my beautiful swans." Each of them glided in from the rain outside, making spectacular entrances. His favorite, Babe Paley, poised in a dress of the sheerest white chiffon, looking dazzling. She wore an original by the Spanish fashion designer, Antonio Castillo, a sleeveless pillar of white zibeline faced in cardinal red. For some reason, perhaps fearing robbery, she opted to leave her jewelry in a safe at home, adorning herself instead with a simulated ruby-and-diamond paste necklace, also a creation of Castillo. She seemed to have adopted the Duchess of Windsor's advice: "You can never be too thin or too rich."

Lee Radziwill dazzled in a body-clinging gown of silver paillettes, a creation of Mila Schön, the Italian designer. Later in the evening, Radziwill would have a wardrobe misfortune on the dance floor, when beads from her gown came loose, and showered across the floor, creating a hazard for some of the other dancers.

Marella Agnelli joined the parade of *fashionistas*. Truman described her later as if she'd just stepped out of a portrait by Richard Avedon.

Jack Dunphy, Truman's longtime lover—by now mostly a companion—hated parties, but had nonetheless been ordered to attend. Although still friends, he and Truman were living in separate houses on Long Island. When Truman spotted him, he ushered him aside for a private reprimand: "That mask of yours is disgusting." Then he ordered Dunphy to take it off before he introduced him to Graham. Dunphy then infuriated Truman when he told Graham, "I don't usually attend these events. I leave it to Truman to brownnose high society."

Dunphy later said, "I'd never seen such ghettoizing, no group at the ball mixing with any other group. They seemed scared shitless of one another. When I asked Babe Paley to dance, this old Jew who sat next to her said, 'Don't go away now,' and he started clawing all over her. I did dance with Gloria Guinness. She told me, 'Jack, you cut a mean rug.' She was unaware that I used to be a professional dancer on Broadway."

The Kennedys had turned down Truman's invitation, with one exception, the clan's 76-year-old matriarch, Rose Kennedy. "She'd been attending balls since before the Civil War," Truman cattily remarked. "She wore a gown that she'd picked up in Paris wholesale. I introduced her to Brendan Gill, *[the editor of The New Yorker]*, who whirled her around the dance floor. As I noticed throughout the evening, she was constantly applying more makeup."

Truman had told Babe Paley that he didn't plan to invite President Lyndon and Lady Bird Johnson, "because I find all those Secret Service men too boring." However, he did invite the elder of the president's daughters, Lynda Bird Johnson, who arrived with a dozen masked Secret Service men. "I changed my mind when I saw one of them," Truman said. "He was gorgeous, looking like a blonde-haired version of Robert Wagner."

"Where is George Hamilton?" he asked Linda Byrd, who at the time was dating the perpetually suntanned actor. Her escort for the ball was Robert Stein, editor of *McCall's* magazine, for which Lynda Bird was working at the time.

When she passed by and was out of earshot, Truman told Graham: "George Hilton and another George, George Masters, have worked their magic on this former 'turd blossom' *[a Texas wildflower that grows in cow manure]* and transformed her into what the press now calls 'Lovely Lynda.'"

Truman also invited two more daughters of former presidents. One of them was Margaret Truman Daniel. *[She told Truman, "I wish the books I wrote about murders sold as well as yours."]*

The other was Alice Roosevelt Longworth, Theodore Roosevelt's daughter. For her, at least, the evening had a disastrous after-effect. During her time at Truman's party, her residence in Washington, D.C. was burglarized.

Douglas Fairbanks, Jr. showed up wearing a black executioner's hood, similar to the one Marie Antoinette faced at the guillotine. He told Truman, "I decided to come only after hearing that Dietrich wasn't going to be here. She's still angry at me for dumping her so long ago."

"Perhaps you'll find Candice Bergen enticing instead," Truman told him.

When the columnist Peter Hamill arrived, Truman chastised him. "You should have brought Jackie."

After having pleaded so long and so passionately for an invitation, Tallulah Bankhead showed up, a vision in white. Her all-white mask was one of the most stylish of the evening.

Later at the ball, Truman brought her together with her old nemesis, the playwright Lillian Hellman. Tallulah had starred on Broadway in one of Hellman's plays, *The Little Foxes.* Each of the women at various times had publicly referred to the other as "A dyke bitch."

But they embraced, Tallulah saying, "You know, Lillian, you and I should have a relationship like Bette Davis and Miriam Hopkins in *Old Acquaintance."*

Before the night was over, Tallulah picked up Jesse Levy, who became her paid escort, steward, handler, and secretary for a tumultuous period of several months.

When Lauren Bacall and choreographer Jerome Robbins took to the dance floor together, the other dancers made room for them. At one point, they did a fantastic jitterbug. In reference to one of their dances, Truman said, "I thought Fred and Ginger were out there on the floor."

Producer David Merrick noticed that Bacall and Frank Sinatra gave each other wide berth. Bacall apparently was still nursing a wound from the night Sinatra deserted her after discussions of marriage in the wake of the death of her first husband, Humphrey Bogart.

Sinatra had brought Mia Farrow, with her hair closely cropped from the movie she'd starred in, *Rosemary's Baby,* but didn't dance with her. So Farrow found younger dance partners, such as Christopher Cerf, the producer who at the time had recently graduated from college.

Earlier in the evening, after Truman had introduced her to the guest of honor, Farrow had asked Sinatra, "Who in the hell is Katharine Graham?"

Peter Duchin and his small band provided the dance music, occasionally playing numbers for the younger guests, including "Twist and Shout" and "Up and Down." Farrow found Duchin's music "intoxicating."

The waiter who had been assigned to Sinatra's table at The Plaza during Truman's party, Joe Evangelista, placed a bottle of Wild Turkey in front of the singer instead of a bottle of champagne.

Sinatra bored quickly and wanted to leave the party early. He invited everyone at his table to Jilly's, his favorite hangout. Truman spotted him leaving and tried to block his exit. "Please stay," Truman pleaded.

"We'll be back," Sinatra told him.

"No, you won't—you won't come back," Truman said. "I know you won't come back."

Truman was correct in his assessment. Farrow remembered that before the night was over, she and Sinatra, along with some cronies, ended up eating chow mein in some joint.

The scene stealer at the party was seventeen-year-old Penelope Tree. The *ingénue* appeared "half naked," dressed in a flowing black tunic and form-fitting tights designed by Betsey Johnson. Jean Harvey Vanderbilt defined her outfit as "stark, like a Halloween ballet costume." Claudette Colbert thought her black hip-hugger briefs could be mistaken for underwear, and that "this Penelope looks like a hooker at a stag party."

Cecil Beaton and Richard Avedon disagreed, finding Penelope mesmerizing. Her appearance at Truman's party on the arm of Ashton Hawkins launched her career as a cover girl on fashion magazines.

With her Vanderbilt hawkeye, Jean Harvey finally proclaimed that Truman's ball was "something out of the court of Louis XV and Madame de Pompadour. The guests promenaded around the room in all their finery, checking each other out, sometimes making bitchy remarks about another party once out of earshot."

Dawn was breaking over Manhattan as Truman bid his last guest goodbye. Katharine Graham and the "big names" had long ago left for various destinations.

Only eight waiters remained to remove the dishes and glasses. One in particular caught Truman's eye. He looked like a young Richard Harris.

Truman spoke to the young man and learned that he was from Limerick in Ireland.

As he later told Leo Lerman, "You know, I have this thing for Irish men. I asked the waiter if he'd like to earn a hundred dollars by spending time with me in my suite after he got off from work. The sweet boy eagerly accepted."

"I'd skipped dessert at my ball, since I was too busy telling everyone *adieu.* So my dessert was going to arrive at my suite, all six feet, two inches of him—and god knows how many more inches concealed."

Seventeen-year-old **Penelope Tree**, escorted to the ball by Ashton Hawkins, dazzled fellow party-goers when she removed her rain jacket to reveal a daring see-through black outfit designed by Betsey Johnson. Fashion arbiters such as Diana Vreeland were so impressed, they helped launch her career as a supermodel.

***

The next day, the party received massive coverage in the media. Truman exaggerated somewhat when he said, "No event got so much newsprint since the D-Day landings on the beaches of Normandy."

In *The New York Times,* Enid Nemy wrote: "The list of celebrities rolled off the assembly line like dolls, newly painted and freshly coiffed, packaged in silk, satin, and jewels addressed to Truman Capote, The Plaza Hotel."

Of course, any such massive event would have its detractors. Gianni Agnelli remarked, "If you want to attend an extravagant ball, get invited to the Beistegui Ball in Venice."

Peter Hamill sarcastically noted in his column, "There were some Negroes there, too."

Humorist Russell Baker said, "If Capote ruined a few lives among the uninvited, so much the better. You have to break a few egos to make an omelette."

Film director Joel Schumacher made an odd comparison, likening the ball to "the barbecue of the Wilkses at the beginning of *Gone With the Wind."*

Years later, Babe Paley would make a wry comment. "The ball was the last real time that Truman would be viewed as the fair-haired darling of the social set. In the years to come, it would be a downhill journey for him—in fact, he became *persona non grata* in society."

[She was referring to the rage he catalyzed through publication of the first chapters of his unfinished novel, Answered Prayers.*]*

In 1983, a year before he died, Truman spent his final months not writing his novel, but planning another black-and-white ball as a venue within a decaying palace in, of all places, Asunción, Paraguay.

His dress code focused on costumes inspired by the fashions of the local Spanish colonial aristocracy during the mid-19th century.

Horrified by the idea, his few remaining friends challenged him with, "No one is going to fly to Paraguay for a ball."

"They'll come," Truman said. "Just you wait and see. They'll come."

When Gore Vidal heard of this, he sneered at the idea that fashionable jet setters would fly to Asunción. "Capote will end up with all the remaining mass murderers of the dying days of the Third Reich. Some of these unrepentant old Nazis, on their last legs, are hiding out in Paraguay."

Truman's dream of a 19th-century Spanish colonial ball in faraway Paraguay, like so many other fervent hopes and visions, was meant to be in dream only.

This photograph of the revelers was snapped at midnight when the ball was in full swing. The cream of New York and international society was dancing on the floor of the Plaza Hotel that night.

Truman wanted his guests to wear black or white, or any combination thereof. "I prefer the people to provide the color."

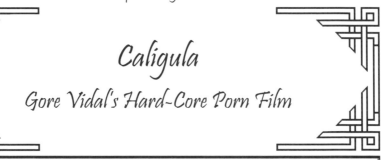

Chapter Forty-Five

Caligula

Gore Vidal's Hard-Core Porn Film

The 1979 film, *Caligula,* was an Italo-American erotic biography financed by *Penthouse* guru, Bob Guccione. With stars such as Peter O'Toole, Helen Mirren, John Gielgud, and Malcolm McDowell, it became the first major motion picture to feature both prominent stars and pornographic scenes. Even today, it remains the most infamous cult film ever made, and it is still banned in many countries around the world.

When it became clear that the film's boundaries went way beyond what he had contracted for, and that his scripts had been virtually ignored, Gore Vidal demanded to have his name removed from the title.

Gore Vidal became the original scriptwriter for

one of the most controversial movies of all time, the 1979 Italo-American erotic epic produced by Penthouse publisher Bob Guccione and Franco Rossellini. Originally entitled *Gore Vidal's Caligula,* it became the first hard-core porno film to cast A-list stars, although they didn't know at the beginning what they were getting into.

Malcolm McDowell, born in 1943 in the industrial city of Leeds, and the star of *A Clockwork Orange [released in 1971 and directed by Stanley Kubrick]*, was an unlikely choice for the role of Caligula, the ruler of the Roman Empire from 37 AD until he was butchered by his guards in 41 AD.

McDowell starred opposite Peter O'Toole as the syphilis-ridden, half-mad Emperor Tiberius. O'Toole looked like he'd been recently dug up after spending twenty years buried in a coffin.

Long before she played the Queen of England *[The Queen, directed by Stephen Frear and released in 2006]*, Helen Mirren was cast as the notorious courtesan, Caesonia *["the most promiscuous woman in Rome"]*, who married Caligula. Mirren appears in most of the movie's scenes dressed like a drag queen imitating a burlesque dancer.

Maintaining his dignity, John Gielgud played Nerva, a long-suffering friend of Tiberius, as if he were quoting Shakespeare.

His farewell to Tiberius (and to life itself) begins when he slits his wrists and submerges himself in a bath of hot water. Unaware of the sex scenes that Guccione would later insert into the context of the film, Gielgud, after seeing the final cut, announced to the press, "*Caligula* is my first porno movie."

Originally, Maria Schneider was cast as Drusilla, Caligula's sister and the love of his life. But when she learned the scope of her scenes, calling for nudity and sex acts, she

Penthouse founder and publisher, **Bob Guccione** ("the Caesar of sex magazine gurus"), believed in breaking taboos and outraging the so-called "guardians of taste." He made millions before drowning in a slough of bad investments, one of which involved financing the controversial pornographic epic, *Caligula.* Most movie houses refused to show it.

Guccione accumulated a vast fortune of $400 million, collecting art masterpieces and *Penthouse* pets, before losing it all.

Sir John Gielgud, cast in the stately role of Nerva, a loyal advisor to Caligula's dissipated great uncle, Tiberius, was about the only "class act" in the entire cast. He never regretted appearing in "my first porn movie."

Back in London, he told his friend, Noël Coward, "There were side benefits, at least a hundred Italian stallions working as extras."

Truman Capote Attends a Screening
"Just to See Malcolm McDowell Show the Full Monty"

retreated. That was perceived at the time as an unusual decision for the lesbian actress, since she had had no such inhibitions when stripping down for *Last Tango in Paris* opposite Marlon Brando in 1972. She was replaced in *Caligula* by Teresa Ann Savoy.

Gore developed his screenplay from Roberto Rossellini's conceived but never produced TV mini-series *Caligula*. One of the reasons for hiring Gore in the first place was that he'd been a scholar of ancient Rome.

Franco Rossellini, the nephew of Roberto Rossellini, had trouble obtaining financing, so Gore approached and solicited Bob Guccione, the founder of *Penthouse*. He agreed to put up the millions for this very expensive film, which demanded elaborate sets as a means of evoking the orgiastic heyday of Imperial Rome.

Shooting was to begin at the same studio in

Bob Guccione selected **Giovanni ("Tinto") Brass**, to helm his controversial *Caligula*. He'd been impressed with how daring Brass had been in his release of a 1976 film, *Salon Kitty,* which fused explicit sex scenes with historical drama.

Before *Caligula's* filming was over, Brass and Guccione were locked in a major battle. The director also ridiculed Gore Vidal's scripts.

In ancient Rome, courtesans of the Emperor Tiberius (Caligula's great uncle) occupy themselves in the pool when he was resting. When he opted to enter the water himself, he demanded that his "little fishes" go underwater to perform various sexual acts on his ravished, syphilitic body.

After murdering Tiberius and marrying the notorious courtesan, Caesonia, Caligula demanded that his armada of "little fishes" be recruited from the Empire's ranks of starving, nubile boys, aged 9 to 13.

Rome, (Cinecettà) where Richard Burton and Elizabeth Taylor had shot *Cleopatra* thirteen years earlier.

Guccione approached both John Huston and Lina Wertmüller to direct the epic, but each of them turned him down. A young Italian director, Tinto (Giovanni) Brass, was selected instead. Guccione had been impressed with his film, *Salon Kitty,* in which Brass had fused explicit sex scenes against a historical background.

[Salon Kitty was an erotic drama, among the prototypes of the "Nazisploitation" genre, set in an expensive brothel in Berlin. According to the plot, it was wiretapped and the whores were trained as spies for gathering data on various members of the Nazi heirarchy.]

Shooting of *Caligula* was scheduled to begin in Rome during the autumn of 1976. At first, Gore agreed to Guccione's request for the inclusion of sex and nudity, not realizing at the time that Guccione's vision meant hard-core porno.

Harmony prevailed in the beginning. Guccione referring to Gore as an immense talent and Gore telling the press, "Bob and I were made for each other."

Gore's relationship with Brass, however became toxic after Gore told *Time* magazine, "All directors are parasites just living off writers. All a director has to do is follow the directives of the author's screenplay."

Gore had turned in five different versions of his script, and Brass had detested all of them. In retaliation, Gore called Brass "Tinto Zinc" and denounced him as a megalomaniac. "In a perfect world," Gore said, "Brass would be washing windows in Venice."

After filming began, Roberto Rossellini sued Guccione and Gore for plagiarizing his material from the never finished TV series about Caligula. The suit, however, was eventually dropped.

In a surprise undercurrent of treachery, Brass turned to his star, McDowell, asking him to help with rewrites of the script. Gore, in his own words, "was seriously pissed off."

When word reached him that hard-core scenes were being filmed with Roman actors, and inserted into the context of the film, Gore demanded that Guccione remove his name from the film's titles. Consequently, *Gore Vidal's Caligula* was renamed as just *Caligula.*

Brass later told the press, "If I really get mad at Gore, I will publish the original script he turned over to me. It was laughable, it was so horrible."

Like *Cleopatra,* memories of which were still prevalent on the Cinecettà lot at the time, *Caligula* ran into costly delays in production. The costs of the lavish sets became outrageous, and there was

The English actor, **Malcolm McDowell**, played the title role as the depraved Emperor Caligula. His slightly startled look was defined by some critics as "emotionally greedy."

He was not ashamed to appear fully nude in the movie. Thanks to his striptease in *Caligula*, the star of Stanley Kubrick's *A Clockwork Orange* developed a whole new fan base.

a lot of graft and actual stealing by the Roman film crews. Guccione was outraged, and he and Brass feuded a lot.

Caligula ended up costing Guccione $25 million. He claimed that Brass shot enough film to make the original MGM *Ben-Hur* (1925) starring Ramon Novarro, about "fifty times over."

Brass and Guccione even fought over the actresses selected to appear in sex scenes as the wives of Roman Senators, whom Caligula had forced to become "harlots in the harem." The publisher claimed that Brass had hired, "fat, ugly, and wrinkled women, as opposed to my Penthouse pets I wanted cast."

Gore pocketed his $200,000 writer's fee and fled from the scene. "After *Myra Breckinridge,* I felt my reputation couldn't endure another sex scandal."

The most serious lawsuit Guccione faced was from actress Anneka Di Lorenzo, cast as Messalina. She sued him for sexual harassment, winning $60,000 in compensatory damages and $4 million in punitive damages. On an appeal, the punitive damages were determined by a judge as not recoverable, and the multi-million dollar award was invalidated.

Based partly on the delays and litigation, *Caligula* did not appear in theaters until late in 1979. Franco Rossellini, in the meantime, had taken advantage of the elaborate sets created for ancient Rome, and he'd made use of these backdrops by producing a film based on the life of *Messalina.* His movie actually made it into theaters before Guccione released *Caligula.*

Reviews of Caligula were harsh, Roger Ebert claiming "Caligula is sickening, utterly worthless, shameful trash. People with talent allowed themselves to participate in this vulgar travesty. Disgusted and unspeakably depressed, I walked out of the film after two hours of its 170-minute length."

Truman Capote, in New York, sat gleefully through the entire film. "I just had to see Gore's latest disaster."

Provocatively, he later asked a reporter working at the time for an underground gay

In one of the most artful of screen makeup jobs, **Peter O'Toole** played Caligula's great uncle, the half-mad syphilitic *débauché,* the Emperor Tiberius, who killed people for his own amusement.

In real life, as O'Toole grew older, battling alcoholism, he began to look more and more like Tiberius.

Helen Mirren was cast as the nymphomaniacal Caesonia, "the most promiscuous woman in Rome" and later, the wife of Caligula.

In later years, she was destined (brilliantly) to play more demure roles, including a 2006 portrayal of Queen Elizabeth *Segundo* in *The Queen.*

newspaper, "Do all Roman actors have such enormous cocks? Obviously, the casting director—lucky guy—auditioned them for reasons other than their thespian abilities."

"As a voyeur," Truman said, "I couldn't wait to see McDowell's dick in an outdoor nude scene shot in the rain. For me, seeing his Full Monty was the highlight of the movie, rivaled only by his beautiful ass on ample display."

Another critic made no comment on McDowell's penis, but wrote of his "emotionally greedy look, including elaborately made-up eyes gazing at the camera with all the loaded essence of charm, insolence, and trickery."

When Gore saw the final product for the first time, he sat through the entire picture aghast. Subsequently, he denounced it as "A joke of a movie, a hard-core disaster."

Guccione had hoped to make $100 million off *Caligula*, but it grossed only $24 million, a million dollars less than its production costs.

If a movie-goer wanted to see the full version of *Caligula,* he or she would have to have attended its original screening in New York in 1979.

Today, new generations of movie-goers will have to be satisfied with countless "butchered" versions of the film, including the 2007 three-disc special edition released by Image Entertainment. This edition, for example, left out some of Guccione's more explicit sex scenes, including a lesbian tryst and various sexual couplings during the Imperial Bordello sequence. One scene that was omitted involved Caligula ordering a newly married couple into his lavish bedchamber and raping each of them as part of their honeymoon ritual.

In 1982, Guccione's personal fortune of $400 million had defined him as one of the richest Americans, according to *Forbes* magazine. But at the time of his death in 2010, he was hovering close to bankruptcy because of a series of bad investments.

Chapter Forty-Six

Truman Takes a Swan Dive in
Answered Prayers

The Lapdog of Café Society Bites the Hands That Wined and Dined Him

Truman Capote's unfinished novel, ***Answered Prayers***, caused an uproar in café society, whose elite members read thinly disguised portraits of themselves. They were horrified. His beautiful elegant "swans," as he called them, swam away, never to return.

Truman even wrote an unflattering portrait of himself as P.L. Jones, a sleazy hustler with some vague dream of becoming a writer. He told his remaining friends, "I'm writing about the American dream and the dry rot thats lies just beneath the surface."

As he attempted to finish the novel, he experienced writer's block, which four psychiatrists could not remove from him. By the late 1970s and early 80s, his drinking and drug taking spiraled out of control. *Answered Prayers* existed only in his dreams, even though he told the world he was working every day to complete it.

Near the end of his life, Truman kept endlessly repeating the story of the night Cecil Beaton introduced him to the Queen Mother in London. "She said I was 'quite wonderful, so talented, so wise, so funny.' I think she also said 'genius.'"

First introduced to the gay bathhouses of
Manhattan by Gore Vidal, Truman Capote continued to visit them even after he became rich and famous. Surprisingly, he was almost never recognized along the dimly lit corridors.

Late one afternoon, clad in a towel, he wandered into the steam room, where he spotted a large, bald, and hefty man going down on a younger man who appeared to be in his 40s. Like a voyeur, Truman stood watching and waiting for the inevitable climax. When the fellator finished his task, he abruptly left.

As Truman would later tell his friends, "I faced a penis that might not have been the largest in the world, but was up there as a runner-up. Not only that, but it was the most perfect penis I had ever seen. Surely, Leonardo da Vinci had turned over his drawing of the perfect penis to God to add the final touches."

The recently fellated was a family man with a wife and four children, John O'Shea, who managed a small bank. Like Truman, he wanted to be a writer, and immediately thought that Truman might help him in his goal. He obviously wasn't attracted to Truman's pudgy, fifty-year-old body, but was willing to prostitute himself for a greater goal.

John O'Shea *(left)* was Truman's last lover. Here, spending the Christmas holidays of 1975 together on Long Island, is John's daughter, **Kerry** *(center)* with **Truman** *(right)*.

John used to say, "With my clothes on, I look like Charlie Middleclass, an average kind of Joe. With my clothes off, I can have virtually anybody I want."

He struck up a conversation, and he agreed to come by Truman's apartment the following afternoon after the bank shut down.

The next day, in Truman's apartment at the United Nations Plaza, John was not as alluring with his clothes on. He accurately labeled himself "Charlie Middleclass." He was a typical family man of 1973 who, as a devout Catholic, had a wife, Peg, and a 16-year-old son, Brian, along with a daughter Kathy, 15. There were also Kerry, age 12, and Chris, age 9. When he wasn't working at the bank, John was a track coach.

After two drinks, John asked Truman to direct him to the bathroom. Truman pointed the way. As John passed by his chair, he leaned over and kissed Truman's forehead.

He later recalled, "Boom, boom went the sound of my heart."

"Would you please stop that?" Truman scolded him. "In about fifteen years from now?"

Thus began the final turbulent love affair of Truman's life, launched at the expense of breaking up what had appeared to be a happy family.

Falling In Love Again: Truman Meets a Bad-Tempered Bank Manager with "The World's Most Perfect Penis."

From an author who had seduced John Garfield and Errol Flynn, John wasn't in that league when it came to looks. At the age of forty-five, he had "chocolate colored hair, heavy eyebrows, and average build, five feet, ten inches of height, and blue eyes to give Frank Sinatra competition," in Truman's estimation.

Beginning at twilight that dying afternoon, Truman found John "the best sex I've ever enjoyed, better than Jack Dunphy and the whole parade of men—David, Danny, Rick, Ralph, Peter, Steve, Paul, Dean, Mitch, Dan, Henry, Jimmy, Fred, Scott, and Jeff. Of course, far better than Errol Flynn, John Garfield, and Marlon Brando."

John was also an Irishman. "For some peculiar reason, I have always found that Irishmen make the best lovers," Truman said.

"John was too good to be true," Truman said. "I'm always suspicious of men who appear to be perfect."

The product of a violent family background, John, as Truman painfully learned, also had a violent temper when Truman did not do what he wanted. What John desired was to become Truman's business manager in charge of his deals and finances.

Finally, Truman agreed, after a night of heavy sex. He offered John $14,000 a year, which soon mushroomed to $30,000 with benefits, including traveling the world with Truman, leaving his family behind, although Truman provided for their needs out of his own pocket.

Brian O'Shea, John's teenage son, was surprised when he learned his father had taken up with Truman. He recalled watching Johnny Carson's *The Tonight Show* alongside his dad. When Truman had appeared on the screen, John had defined him as "a goddamn fag."

John and Truman went on what passed for a honeymoon in Europe, traveling as far as the Greek island of Spetsai, where they sunned themselves in the hot noonday sun, completely nude, with Aristotle Onassis and shipping magnate Stavros Niarchos.

Then it was off to dine with heiress Peggy Guggenheim in Venice before flying to Switzerland to spend time with Charlie and Oona Chaplin.

Back in Washington, Truman brought John to the home of publisher Katharine Graham. Reportedly, she was horrified at such a crude person. John was drinking heavily at the time. Under the influence of alcohol, he became belligerent.

Natalie Wood recalled the time Truman brought John to her home in California when she was married to Robert Wagner. "Everything this guy said was 'fuck that...or fuck this.' He was a monster."

John later recalled, "I was pampered, but in a prison with Truman as my jailer. I felt more and more castrated by him. He brought me sexual relief, but it was the equivalent of masturbation. We were drawn to each other, but I wouldn't exactly call it a love affair."

Both men continued to drink heavily and often got into fights with each other. At the home of Carol Matthau, wife of actor Walter Matthau, John even threw his drink in Truman's face.

To his gay friends, Truman lavished praise on John's sexual equipment. One night, at a Thanksgiving dinner at the home of Joanne Carson, former wife of TV host Johnny Carson, John got drunk and turned belligerent. At one point, he spit into the face of one of her guests.

Then he wandered off into the nearby study and fell asleep on the carpeted floor. One of the guests, a gay opportunist, slipped into the study and unzipped John's trousers, since he was slumbering deeply. He later told two of the other guests, both of them gay, "Capote didn't exaggerate. It's a whopper!"

During those turbulent years, Truman managed to write *Mojave,* a short story for *Esquire,* the first piece he'd published in eight years.

With John, he broke up, reunited, then broke up again. Truman admitted to friends, "John was poison to me, but we always got back together again. I must have developed a taste for arsenic."

When John bolted one time, Truman recruited some of his burly friends, ordering them to go after him and beat him to death. That never happened, but the two men did locate his apartment in Los Angeles. Instead of wreaking violence upon him directly, they set his car on fire.

John retaliated, finding out where Truman was staying at a motel in Malibu. He came to his room and, in his words, "beat the shit out of him." Truman was rushed to the hospital with a fractured rib, cracked fingers, and abrasions on his face, legs, and chest.

On another occasion, John and Truman agreed to meet in New Mexico for reconciliation, away from the homes of the rich and/or famous people he frequented. But during their time together, John kept slipping away to make phone calls out of earshot. Finally, he admitted that he'd fallen in love with Joanne Biel, a graduate student in philosophy at the University of Southern California. "At last I've found true love," John told Truman. "It's over between us."

"Let's call it the love affair that never was," Truman responded.

***

Months went by and Truman began to long for John again. He didn't know where he was, so he hired detectives to track him down. At the time, he was working on his final novel, *Answered Prayers.* When Random House began demanding to see some finished chapters, Truman didn't have them. He lied to his publisher, claiming that John O'Shea had stolen the rest of the manuscript. That was not true. There was no manuscript to steal.

Despite the many troubles they'd already experienced between them, Truman flew to Los Angeles, hoping for a final reconciliation with John, who met him at the airport. On the way to his hotel suite, they got into an argument.

Truman was drunk and heavily drugged and wanted to go to sleep immediately after entering the bedroom.

He later recalled, "I was not completely asleep. I was awake enough to see John going through my luggage, where he found $20,000 in one-thousand dollar bills in a manila envelope. He also went to my closet and took out my wallet from the jacket I'd worn on the plane. It contained $500. He removed only $300 of it, leaving me the final $200 for expenses. I heard the door softly shut before I drifted off. The man with the perfect penis was leaving my life forever. But even the perfect penis could no longer fulfill my needs or give me a reason to stay alive."

***

Truman believed that his final novel [*Answered Prayers*], would be his masterpiece if only he could write it. At a dinner with Marella Agnelli, he told her, "My novel will do for America what Proust did for France in *Remembrance of Things Past.*"

When Gore Vidal heard that, he claimed, "Capote has never read Proust."

Apparently, Truman wanted to replicate the disillusionment that overcomes the narrator in the final pages of the Proustian masterpiece set in *Belle Époque* Paris. For his novel's setting in the 1970s, Truman chose to expose "the beautiful people," especially the fashionable ladies he referred to as his swans.

The narrator of *Answered Prayers* is a seedy hustler, P.J. Jones, a dark *Doppelgänger* replica of Truman himself.

To a reporter from *People* magazine, Truman said, "My book is like a gun—there's the handle, the trigger, the barrel, and finally, the bullet headed for the heart. When that bullet is fired, it's going to come out with a speed and power like you've never seen before—*WHAM!*"

For years, he'd surrounded himself with what remained of café society. He fancied himself a reincarnation of his controversial late Victorian predecessor, Oscar Wilde, moving through society of the 1960s and 70s, dazzling ornamental trophy wives who included Slim Keith, heiress Gloria Vanderbilt, Gloria Guinness, and most definitely, the reigning *doyenne* of them all, Barbara Cushing Paley. Nicknamed "Babe," she was the spectacularly fashionable and deeply frustrated wife of William Paley, the head honcho at CBS.

William Paley, the chief honcho at CBS, is seen with his wife, the ever-fashionable **Babe Paley**, in Montego Bay, Jamaica. **Truman** *(right)* learned their darkest secrets, then exposed them in the early chapters of *Answered Prayers*. What he did not expose was his own dark secret: He was in love with Bill himself.

The darkest secrets of Truman's coterie of rich and stylish friends would be exposed with devastating detail within the gossipy pages of *Answered Prayers.*

He was especially harsh with Bill Paley's infidelities and cruel treatment of his wife. What wasn't widely known is that Truman harbored another reason for wanting to embarrass Bill. Every since he swam nude with him in the Paley's private pool in Jamaica, he'd harbored a crush on the CBS executive. When Bill brusquely refused Truman's request to "let me suck you off," Truman privately vowed revenge for the rejection.

Among Truman's many friends were two sisters, Lee Radziwill and Jacqueline Kennedy. He'd aggressively tried to coach Lee as an actress, successfully negotiating to get her contracts as the female lead in an onstage production of *The Philadelphia Story* and in a TV drama. *[It involved a 1968 remake of the classic Otto Preminger film,* Laura *(1944), which had starred Gene Tierney, JFK's former mistress, in the role of the mysterious Laura. Truman, with Thomas Phipps, co-authored the screenplay.]*

Truman is seen dancing with his favorite swan, **C.Z. Guest**, the only one of his elegant ladies who did not turn away from him after the publication of *Answered Prayers* in Esquire.

Of all his swans, Guest was the rebel, beginning when she'd rebelled against the Boston society into which she was born. She later worked in Manhattan as a show-girl and posed nude in Mexico for Diego Rivera.

But after her marriage to the super-wealthy Winston Guest, she settled down to help him spend his ancient trust funds. Her life became one of horses during the day and parties, often with Truman, at night.

Both Jackie and Lee joined the parade of the bitchy, barely disguised caricatures that Truman exposed to the world in print, revealing their lies, infidelities, indiscretions, abortions—"and all their other abominations," in his words.

In *Answered Prayers,* he gives Jackie the needle: "Very photogenic, but the effect is a little unrefined, exaggerated." Jackie, he wrote, did not strike him as being a bona fide woman, but rather "an artful female impersonator impersonating Mrs. Kennedy."

He wanted the world's two most famous sisters to join the ranks of what he defined as, "my exclusive gaggle of widows, rich wives, divorcées, and international riffraff—C.Z. Guest, Peggy Guggenheim, and Nedda Logan among others, and, of course, my dear Babe. I'm sorry to hear that Babe is dying of cancer, however."

When Gore heard of Truman's most recent *imbroglio*, he said, "Capote might call them swans, but I call these women fruit flies buzzing around the biggest fruit in America. Privately, these *grandes dames* call him 'Tiny Terror,' but find him amusing. Their husbands tolerate the five foot, three-inch faggot. He is their lapdog."

In November of 1975, a chapter of his projected novel, entitled "La Côte Basque 1965," appeared in that month's issue of *Esquire*. High society later compared it to the dropping of an atomic bomb. Many swans were at their hairdresser when the magazine was handed to them. "Read this!" was the frequent command. In lieu of that, swans—along with their allies and detractors—were urged to rush to the nearest newsstand to read "what this devilish little freak has written."

When Babe Paley read Truman's thinly disguised description of her in *Answered Prayers,* she said, "It was the most shocking *exposé* since Judas sold out Jesus Christ."

Perhaps as a face-saving device, Truman falsely claimed that, "I only hung out with the swans to learn their innermost, dirtiest secrets. Otherwise, these upper-crust dames with their interminable face-lifts bored me."

The most extreme reaction came from Ann Woodward, the socialite suspected of having murdered her husband in 1955, falsely claiming that she had mistaken him for an intruder. After reading a chapter containing Truman's revival of her sad story, she committed suicide.

[In 1985, another writer, Dominick Dunne, immortalized Woodward in his The Two Mrs. Grenvilles, *a roman à clef based on the sensational 1955 incident. It was made into a television movie in 1987. Directed by John Erman, it starred Ann-Margret, Elizabeth Ashley, Stephen Collins, Genevieve Allenbury, and in one of her last dramatic performances, Claudette Colbert.]*

Columnist Liz Smith wrote, "Never have you heard such gnashing of teeth, such cries of revenge, such shouts of betrayal, and screams of outrage."

The swans and the other ladies exposed vowed never to speak to Truman again, and refused his phone calls. To them, he was no longer a friend. Their various descriptions of him included phrases like: "a dirty little toad," or "a hideous fag." Some preferred to define him as "a rattlesnake," or "the monster."

Truman was stunned at his sudden fall from grace. "Who in the fuck did these empty-headed fools think they were talking to?" he asked the few friends who remained with him. "I'm a writer. All of them knew that. A good writer draws upon his own experiences. The swans have floated away from me, but I predict they'll come back because I'm the only person in their empty lives who can amuse them. Everybody else, especially their lovers and husbands, are so fucking boring."

Retreating from the glare of Manhattan, Truman fled to a safer haven in Bridgehampton on Long Island. Instead of swans, he frequently socialized with the resident literary set, including James Jones, John Knowles, and Kurt Vonnegut, who didn't give a damn if Truman had exposed café society or not. Truman was seen with members of both the *literati* and with "rough trade" *[hustlers]* at such watering holes as Bobby Van's or Mortimers.

"La Côte Basque 1965" was followed by two more libelous serializations in Esquire—"Unspoiled Monsters" (May, 1975); and "Kate McCloud" (December, 1976).

The titles of other potential chapters, perhaps never written, or if written, probably destroyed by Truman himself, had been pre-publicized with titles that included "A Severe Insult to the Brain," *[Truman's appellation for Los Angeles]*; "Yachts and Things," and "And Audry Wilder Sang." His most provocative title was "Father Flanagan's All Night Nigger Queen's Kosher Café." *[Only the titles, but not their corresponding texts, were discovered in the wake of his death.]*

Ironically, the original contract for *Answered Prayers* had been signed way back in January of 1966 for an advance of only $25,000. But after endless delays and missed deadlines over the years, Random House, in a reckless moment, had upped the ante in the early 1980s to a $1 million advance for a three-book contract that included *Answered Prayers.*

Sam Kashner wrote in the December, 2012 issue of *Vanity Fair:* "Truman Capote had unwittingly turned that gun he'd talked about on himself. Exposing the secrets of Manhattan's rich and powerful was nothing short of social suicide. Trying to write *Answered Prayers,* and its eventual fallout, destroyed him."

When the chapters of *Answered Prayers* were compiled and released at last in book form by New American Library in 1978, readers discovered an unfinished novel that contained only those chapters previously published in *Esquire.* During his final years, Truman had maintained the pretense that he was writing it, but he was too mired in alcohol and drugs to continue. Many critics compared him to Dylan Thomas, who in the 1950s was said to have drunk himself to death, mostly at the White Horse Tavern in New York City's Greenwich Village.

Upon publication, *The Chicago Tribune* referred to it as "The most talked about novel in publishing history." Less effusively, *Time* magazine claimed, "The author of *Breakfast at Tiffany's* is now lunching in Sodom, where the specialties include lightly fictionalized stories of lust, greed, envy, and homicide."

James M. Fox, Truman's editor at Random House, pondered various theories about the book's missing chapters. "The first and most obvious," he reportedly said, "was that they were never completed. Another theory was that they were stashed somewhere in a box, perhaps seized by an ex-lover for malice or profit. There was even a theory that they were placed in a bank somewhere—that is, a bank unknown. There's even a theory that he put them in a locker at the Greyhound Bus Depot in Los Angeles."

Fox also speculated that Truman did write the final chapters, but destroyed them in the early 1980s because they did not live up to his Proustian dream.

By 1984, the year Truman died, he'd been in and out of dry-out centers, though nothing at rehab seemed to work for him. His remaining friends thought he'd given up not only on *Answered Prayers,* but on life itself.

"Abandoned by his society friends, Truman was worn out," Joanne Carson said. "Really heartbroken."

"You've got to lie a little to tell the truth."

—*Truman Capote*

Chapter Forty-Seven

MEMORIAM

Literary Lions Deep in December

Tennessee Williams	Truman Capote	Gore Vidal
(1911-1983)	(1924-1984)	(1925-2012)

Three of the 20th century's most famous writers, each

a homosexual, formed part of a so-called "Pink Triangle" in letters. They might have claimed membership in the "Dead Poets' Society."

They were Tennessee Williams, Truman Capote, and Gore Vidal. Of the trio, only Gore lived to a ripe old age. At the time of their respective deaths, Tennessee was seventy-one; Truman fifty-nine; and Gore, eighty-six.

Of the three, Tennessee experienced the most bizarre death. (See below.) Some obituary writers noted a line that Blanche DuBois uttered in *A Streetcar Named Desire.* "You know what I shall die of? I shall die of eating an unwashed grape one day out of the ocean."

Both Truman and Tennessee had died before the world moved too deeply into the plague years. Gay artists died in droves from AIDS during the turbulent 1980s.

Although Tennessee continued to write until the year of his death, his "hits" were for the most part associated with the 1940s and 1950s, coming to an end in the early 1960s.

Truman only pretended to write in his later years. In contrast, Gore remained consistently productive until overcome with dementia.

TENNESSEE WILLIAMS

The Amethyst Light of Prima Sera

"How perilously do these fountains leap,
Whose reckless voyager along am I."

In a call to Maria St. Just, Tennessee remembered, "I once saw a movie with Glenn Ford, whom I never managed to seduce. It was called *The Return of October.* Well, October is here, and I've returned to Key West. I've been absent awhile, and even my cat and dog have wandered off to destinations unknown. How typical. Like all my so-called friends except for you."

Feeling depressed and alone in Key West, he flew to New York again, "Mostly, I was receiving obituary notices. It seemed that everyone I'd known and loved was dying."

> **Tennessee** confessed to Maria St. Just: "I had a bit of cosmetic surgery done on my eyes, but I am not satisfied with it. I think the surgeon was a sadist or homophobe, as I received no local anaesthetic, nothing, and it was the most physically excruciating experience of my life."

That November, he made his last public appearance at the YMHA on 92nd Street in Manhattan. When he walked on stage at Kaufman Hall, the audience, mostly young people, applauded wildly.

"I was expecting a rare evening in the theater," said student Richard Loomis. "But out staggered this poor, beaten-up relic of a human being on his last legs. I'd seen the movie versions of *The Glass Menagerie* and *A Streetcar Named Desire,* and I was impressed with his reputation, since I wanted to be a writer myself."

"I was shocked at how nervous Williams seemed to be," Loomis continued. "He read us this short story, which he defined as a work in progress. I don't remember much about it except that he used the words 'well hung' three times for his hero. The short story was called "The Donsinger Women and Their Handy Man Jack." Then he read some poems, including one called 'Old Men Go Mad at Night.'"

What's left is keeping hold of breath
And for cover never now a lover
Rests them warm…
Was that a board that creaked
As he took leave of us,
Or did he speak—
"I'm going to sleep, good night."

After reading that poem, he took off his glasses and confronted the audience. "My friends, that is the end. The curtain is going down on one Tennessee Williams."

After that, he walked off the stage. It took at least a minute, maybe more, before his ears were greeted with mild applause.

In 1981, **Tennessee** met with his beloved sister, the mentally impaired **Rose**, for a final time.

By December, he'd returned once again to Key West. Before flying out of New York, he'd met with Jacqueline Kennedy Onassis, who'd had a warning for him.

She suggested that he should sign a codicil to his will, entrusting his papers

"You couldn't ask for a sweeter or more benign monarch than Rose, or, in my opinion, one that's more of a lady. After all, high station in life is earned by the gallantry with which appalling experiences are survived with grace."

to Harvard University instead of to Sewanee, "The University of the South," a small *[1,600 student]* private, co-educational liberal arts college in Sewanee, Tennessee. The former First Lady advised him that she feared "the swarming locusts descending on America." She defined many of America's right wing political leaders as religious fanatics who prayed to God, thanking him for sending the AIDS virus to kill off gay men. Her fear was that at Sewanee, some of the executors, to whom Tennessee's work might represent heresy, might burn his papers and heavily censor his plays.

***

All calls to Tennessee's Duncan Street home in Key West had gone unanswered. Finally, neighbors contacted the police, thinking he might have been murdered. When the police arrived to investigate, they found the front door unlocked. They entered the house, discovering that it was empty except for one locked bedroom.

When they knocked on the door, no one answered. They forced the lock and entered the room to find a nude Tennessee, drunk and drugged, lying on the bed muttering incoherently.

In an ambulance, he was rushed to the hospital, where doctors found him totally dehydrated. His drug-filled system was flushed out, and after a few days' stay, he was released.

Back at Duncan Street, he slept there only one night before flying to New York the next day. He stayed at the home of Jane Smith, an actress and singer who had long been a loyal, supportive friend of his.

He felt well after some time with Smith, to the point that he was overcome "with a certain wanderlust."

To his remaining friends, he said, "I'm still Tom in *The Glass Menagerie: "The cities swept about me like dead leaves, leaves that were brightly colored but torn away from the branches. I would have stopped, but I was pursued by something."*

He began planning a return to Taormina on the eastern coast of Sicily, inviting his companion at the time, John Uecker, to accompany him. His sometimes secretary, however, had made other plans. "But I can probably find a suitable person to travel with you," he told Tennessee.

"I can no longer depend on the kindness of strangers," Tennessee responded. "I will go alone, like I used to back when I was called Tom, back when I followed in my father's footsteps, attempting to find in motion what was lost in space."

In Taormina, the staff at the San Domenico Palace Hotel *[a richly nostalgic historic monument whose core originated centuries ago as a cloister]* warmly welcomed Tennessee. Some of the older members recalled his first visit with them

Tennessee holds his beloved dog, **"Miss Sophia."** He was always partial to bulldogs.

At his last birthday party in 1982, he stumbled and nearly fell. He was rescued. "A short, dark young man grabbed hold of me. I turned to thank him, and it seemed that I was looking at Frank Merlo. He drove me home and stayed the night. He is pure Sicilian. He has the first real warmth, humanity, and tenderness in a man in these years since Frankie left us."

That night would be Tennessee's last romantic encounter.

when he was accompanied by his Sicilian lover, Frank Merlo. The hotel's aging manager told him, "You and Frankie looked so happy in those days."

"We did give that illusion," Tennessee responded. "The trouble with happiness is that it inevitably is followed by long periods of mourning over loss."

He was alone and depressed during his sojourn there. Acting on his own, the manager sent food and drink, which the maid, the following morning, would find uneaten.

One early evening, as a kind of *passeggiata [evening stroll]* along Taormina's Corso Umberto, Tennessee left his hotel room to wander over to his favorite bar, Caffè Wunderbar, a high-ceilinged gathering place opening onto the Piazza IX Aprile. Here he sat, looking out at the sea and the ominous

Mount Etna in the distance.

At that time of year, most of the tourists were gone, and a mean *sirocco* was blowing in from North Africa.

Many young Sicilian men were hustling and eager for a cash customer. Some of them solicited him at his café table, but he showed no interest in them, even though he had richly patronized them in his past.

Back at the hotel bar, the manager said that Truman Capote had visited, telling everyone that he was working feverishly on his novel, *Answered Prayers*.

"He fell in love with Taormina, and even purchased land here," the manager said. "For only $10,000, he bought Isola Bella, which is not an island, but land with a beach at the tip of a conical peninsula—small, ringed with sand, and absolutely beautiful. He told us he was going to build a villa there and invite all the beautiful people to visit Taormina. He and the landowner celebrated right in this bar. But the deal fell through. Truman's check was returned from a New York bank, marked 'insufficient funds.'"

Whenever he could, Tennessee flew to any city to see a major actress perform the role of Blanche DuBois in *A Streetcar Named Desire*. In 1974, in London, he gave Claire Bloom a kiss of approval for her brilliant interpretation of the role.

Later, he was asked about newspaper gossip suggesting that she might become "Mrs. Gore Vidal."

"That is about as likely to happen as I am to becoming Mr. Diana Barrymore...and she's DEAD!"

Before he left Taormina, Tennessee began work on a screenplay called *The Lingering Hour*, describing a forthcoming apocalypse of devastation and massive death.

"All the volcanoes in the world explode more or less at the same time, and there are earthquakes and destruction everywhere. Here in Sicily, there is Etna and the action is set in the main square, with people talking. The first earthquake happens in California. Hollywood disappears into the sea."

His title, *The Lingering Hour*, was his English-language equivalent of the Italian term *prima sera*, that time at dusk, right before the oncoming night. He described it in *The Roman Spring of Mrs. Stone*, as "the moment before the lamps go on, when the atmosphere has that exciting blue clarity of the nocturnal scenes in silent films, a color of water that holds a few drops of ink, the amethyst light of *prima sera*."

Tennessee cut short his trip and flew back to New York, ending his decades-long wandering on the Continent, specifically to his favorite country, Italy, and his favorite island, Sicily, home of Frank's ancestors.

In Manhattan, he checked into his final hotel stop at the Élysée. He passed his first evening in the Monkey Bar, where on some long ago night, he'd entertained Joan Crawford. She had appeared in a dress with large flowery prints, looking as if she'd just emerged from the set of *Mildred Pierce*.

The hotel had long been a hangout for artists and writers, including such old friends as Marlon Brando and Ava Gardner. He occupied the suite once rented to Tallulah Bankhead, who told him that John Barrymore had fucked her in the bed in which he now slept.

John Uecker moved back in with him, although reportedly he found Tennessee locked in his own world.

On the night of February 24, 1983, he retired to his bedroom after ordering a bottle of Bordeaux from room service. On his nightstand was an array of pills, including his favorite, special lavender capsules, which Truman Capote had long ago endorsed for him.

It was a night of drug ingestion, including doses of cocaine, consumed with wine.

When a maid entered his room the next morning, she found him dead. An autopsy was performed, and the examiner announced that the cap to a plastic container of barbiturates had lodged in his throat, choking him to death. According to the report, he had used it as a spoon to swallow two capsules loaded with Seconal. Apparently, he'd accidentally swallowed the cap.

The suggestion was that he had been so heavily drugged that his gag reflex had been suppressed.

Later, forensic detectives claimed that Tennessee had died of a drug overdose, not from choking. The autopsy report was later amended, stating that Tennessee died of acute Seconal intolerance. A friend, Scott Kenan, charged that "someone in the coroner's office invented the bottle cap scenario."

Dakin Williams flew to New York to claim the body. Contrary to his famous brother's wishes, Dakin arranged for the body to be shipped back to his native St. Louis, where Tennessee was interred in Calvary Cemetery, where his grave is visited today by tourists.

He had requested that he be buried at sea at approximately the same place where Hart Crane had committed suicide.

[On April 27, 1932, the American poet, Hart Crane, was sailing aboard the steamship Orizaba *en route from Mexico to New York. He had been beaten after making sexual advances toward a male crew member. Just before noon, he jumped overboard into the Gulf of Mexico. After his beating, he had been drinking heavily. He left no suicide note, but witnesses claim that his last words were, "Goodbye, everybody!" before throwing himself overboard. His body was never recovered from the shark-infested waters.]*

In the wake of Tennessee's death, various conspiracy theories have risen, some claiming that he was murdered, perhaps smothered to death under a pillow. Dakin himself was the first to promulgate such a charge, but no motive for murder was ever cited. Nor was any actual murderer ever fingered.

Hours after his death, Maria St. Just called Marlon Brando in Los Angeles. Brando told her, "By the time of Tennessee's death, he had been so close to it so many times psychologically, emotionally, and physically, it was probably just a shave-and-a-haircut to him. I always felt that Tennessee and I were compatriots. He told the truth as best as he perceived it, and never turned away from things that beset or frightened him. We are all diminished by his death."

After all his trials and tribulations, Tennessee, in a sense, wrote his own epitaph:

"I've had a wonderful and terrible life, and I wouldn't cry for myself. Would you?"

TRUMAN CAPOTE

After Many a Summer Dies the Swan Keeper

"Happiness leaves such slender records. It is the dark days that are so voluminously documented."

In September of 1980, Truman was in Los Angeles at the Beverly Wilshire Hotel, concluding negotiations for the film adaptation of his *Handcarved Coffins*.

[Handcarved Coffins was a well-written novella-length thriller about a series of bizarre murders that had taken place in Nebraska. It was subtitled "Nonfiction Account of an American Crime". For $300,000, he'd sold the film rights to Lester Persky who had produced such cinematic hits as Taxi Driver.]

Truman's traveling companion at the time was Rick Brown, a hillbilly from West Virginia whom Truman had met when he tended bar at a rough sailors' joint on Manhattan's West 45th Street near Broadway.

In Truman's upscale hotel suite, in the aftermath of a particularly excessive binge, Brown returned after an adventure of his own and found Truman lying nude in bed, steeped in his own waste.

Cocaine, which Truman praised for its "subtlety," remained his favorite drug. He carried his pills around in a purse from Tiffany's. They came in a rainbow of colors, but he preferred the lavender hue of Lotusate, a powerful sedative.

To friends, he announced, "Death comes in threes—first Marilyn, then Monty. Next: Yours truly."

The last picture of **Truman Capote**, one of the most photographed writers of all time, was taken on August 23, 1984, two days before his death. He's seen resting in the home of Joanne Carson in Los Angeles, with her beloved Doberman named "Cinnamon."

His health continued to deteriorate at an alarming rate. In August of 1981, he suffered a convulsive seizure and was rushed to Southampton Hospital on Long Island.

Back in Manhattan, on September 15, he was rushed to yet another hospital, generating a headline on the front page of the *New York Post*. A photographer snapped a picture of him strapped to a stretcher. Out of the hospital after a week, he resumed his heavy drinking.

Truman accurately predicted, "I will never live to celebrate my sixtieth birthday. I even know the city in which I will die—Los Angeles, not New York. Los Angeles is where all the locusts go to die."

As Truman neared the end, his longtime companion, Jack Dunphy, virtually deserted him. "He's dying right before my eyes. I don't plan to die with him. Even if I wanted to visit him, it would be in a hospital room. I get ill just going into a hospital."

His own doctor, Bertram Newman, told Dunphy, "Your friend is putting a gun to his mouth. I don't know when he's going to pull the trigger."

To all his critics, to all those who wanted to help him, Truman said, "It's my life, to live as I wish—or to die as I wish."

On July 1, 1983, he was arrested on a DWI in Bridgehampton on Long Island. He spent a night in the Southampton Town Jail, where he made the outrageous claim, "The inmates lined up to rape me. The same thing happened to Valentino when he was arrested."

The judge fined him $500 and sentenced him to a three-year probation.

In December of 1983. at a party for Liza Minnelli, he was virtually ignored. In the old days, he would have been surrounded by voyeurs who savored and thrilled to each outrageous tale after another.

He mourned the loss of "my armada of swans." Many of them, including Babe Paley, had died of cancer.

"Cecil Beaton is gone, even Tennessee," Truman said. "Tenn forgave me. Regrettably, Gore Vidal is still taking up space on this earth."

"My God, they've even closed Studio 54, where Andy Warhol and I spent so many wicked nights."

"I stayed up to watch 1984 come in, knowing it would be my last year on this dreadful cesspool called Earth. It began badly with two falls, both of which caused concussions, each rendering me almost incoherent for days."

In his last public appearances, **Truman Capote** disgraced himself. Here, in 1977, he had to be led off the stage when he became incoherent and started mumbling at a reading in Baltimore, Maryland.

Later, in 1983, he was photographed as he was carried comatose from his apartment in Manhattan. A picture of him on a stretcher made the tabloids in New York.

He had begun to hallucinate—in fact, medical scans revealed that his brain mass had perceptibly shrunk.

During his final days, Truman flew to Los Angeles to stay with his most steadfast and loyal friend, Joanne Carson, former wife of Johnny Carson. She and the TV talk show host had lived in elegant apartments at the United Nations Plaza, where Truman maintained a residence. Unlike his artful swans of yesterday, Joanne was more like a "lovely, lonely little wren," in Truman's words.

Before winging his way west, Truman had been rushed to Southampton Hospital. Doctors there had found him near death and put him in an oxygen tent.

Jack Dunphy was constantly nagging him to give up "booze and pills." When Truman got to Los Angeles, he told Joanne, "The time has come to say my farewell to Jack Dunphy."

In the twilight of his life, even though late at night he envisioned scene after scene spinning through his head, *Answered Prayers* was abandoned, albeit privately, without fanfare in the press or to any of his few remaining friends.

The morning of August 25, 1984, dawned bright and sunny over Los Angeles, City of Unfulfilled Dreams, with apartment after apartment inhabited by wannabee stars hoping to become a celebrity like Truman or, even better, like Marilyn Monroe or Paul Newman.

Joanne went to check on Truman, but he told her he wanted to rest some more, since he wasn't feeling well.

He begged her to stay with him. Until around noon, he talked incessantly, going over all the traumas of his life, some of them dating back to his childhood in Alabama.

Then he lay back on the pillow. Having told Joanne "the story of my life," he fell into a deep sleep.

His final words to her were, "Let me go, dear one."

He didn't want her to call paramedics, but she did. When they arrived, they pronounced him dead at 12:21pm.

Outside, the impossible traffic of Los Angeles moved on, but at a snail's pace.

Had he lived until late September of that year, Truman would have been sixty years old. The body of the dead author was cremated.

Over the coming years, Truman's ashes were stolen twice but recovered. Eventually, they were mixed with those of Jack Dunphy, who remained living until 1992. Their collective ashes were scattered to the winds at Crooked Pond, near his beloved home at Sagaponack on Long Island. The site is commemorated with a plaque affixed to a rock near the spot where their ashes, as they were tossed into the pond, were blown away by a terrific wind that descended unexpectedly from the north.

George Plimpton, editor of *The Paris Review,* wrote a kind of epitaph to Truman:

"He had the opportunity to observe first hand the crumbling-away, the loss of

morale and sense of consequence, the desperate and defiant secret lives, the hyperactive despair and ruinous lack of self-discipline of the monied class of our time: of being highly observant and intelligent witnesses to the decline of the West itself, spies in the house of Trimalchio."

GORE VIDAL

The Last Surviving Giant of American Literature's Golden Age

"I'm having one final drink of whiskey in the departure lounge of life. The plane to oblivion is about to fly away, destination unknown."

At the beginning of 1962, Howard Austen, Gore Vidal's longtime companion, checked into Memorial Hospital (now known as Sloan-Kettering Memorial Hospital) in Manhattan. A large growth had formed in his throat and was thought to be cancer of the thyroid.

Ironically, during his first visit to see his friend after his operation, Gore ran into Tennessee Williams in the hospital's corridor. The playwright was also visiting his longtime lover, Frank Merlo, who had lung cancer. Gore later claimed that Tennessee had proclaimed, "The bells will soon be tolling for me as well as for Frankie."

Fortunately, the growth was benign, and Austen recovered. But Frank died.

When Austen was released, and after his recuperation, he and Gore moved to Rome, taking an apartment on the Via Giulia overlooking the Tiber River. In time, they would move to a location further south, to Ravello, south of Naples, along the Amalfi Drive.

Most of their friends, including Claire Bloom and Susan Sarandon, reportedly speculated that Gore would be the first to die. But that was not the case.

In 1999—like Frank Merlo, whose death had preceded his—Austen was also diagnosed with

The saddest picture ever taken of **Gore Vidal** *(right)* was with **Howard Austen**, his life companion. They were resting on a bench at the Rock Creek Cemetery outside Washington, D.C.

They are overseeing their gravesites, which their remains would soon occupy.

lung cancer. Gore decided to leave his beloved "swallow's nest" in Ravello to secure better treatment for his companion in Los Angeles. He chartered a plane from Rome to fly them to Los Angeles, where he checked Austen into the Cedars-Sinai Hospital.

After receiving treatment, Austen was eventually discharged, but both men knew that death would occur soon. Austen's doctor told Gore, "I am almost certain the cancer will return. He will have to be checked regularly."

During the months ahead, Austen was said to have waged a focused battle to live, but did he? Friends noted that he smoked one cigarette after another. Sometimes he didn't finish one before lighting up again.

In 2003, as Austen complained of constant pain in his chest, Gore flew him once again to the Cedars-Sinai, where a radiogram revealed that he had lung cancer. An operation was called for at once.

Fearing he would never see Austen alive again, Gore said farewell, as he was wheeled into the operating room. He held Austen's hand.

His most loyal friend looked up at him. All he said was, "Gore, it's been great."

Once again, Austen survived the surgery and recovered enough to fly with Gore back to Italy. But his health deteriorated rapidly. Doctors in Rome discovered that the cancer had spread to his brain.

Sparing no expense, Gore once again chartered a plane to fly them back to Cedars-Sinai in Los Angeles for more tests, more radiation, more surgery.

An aging **Gore Vidal** is seen packing up to leave his beloved villa, La Rondinaia, in the little town of Ravello, high on a hill overlooking the resort-studded Amalfi Coast.

He sold La Rondinaia for $18 million, deciding to return to Los Angeles, scene of so many triumphs but also so many disappointments.

For a while, Austen was allowed to return to Gore's home in the Hollywood Hills, where the author hired male nurses for him.

Gore knew that Austen's imminent death was certain. For a final time, he was checked into the hospital. This time, as he was about to be wheeled into surgery, Austen said to Gore, "Kiss me."

Gore kissed him on the lips, later claiming, "We hadn't done that in fifty years."

Austen once again survived the surgery, but this time, in its aftermath, he recuperated in an oxygen tent in his hospital room. Gore noticed that as soon as the tent was removed, Austen asked for a cigarette. Gore realized that it didn't matter whether Austen smoked or not.

Austen began to hallucinate. He told Gore, "At the first light of day, the Angel of Death comes into my room, entering with the sun." When he could elucidate, he spoke of his failed dream to become a pop singer. "I could have become the next Frank Sinatra, or at least Perry Como."

On September 22, 2003, a nurse alerted Gore that Austen had stopped breathing. He rushed to his bedside. Gore later recalled that moment. "The optic nerve was still sending messages to his brain. I knew he could still see me. He'd died like the boy from the Bronx claiming, 'So this is the big fucking deal they call death that everybody carries on so much about.' He faded, but not before I looked one final time into his eyes, a beautiful gray, bright and attentive. We stared at each other one final time."

Months before, both Gore and Austen had purchased plots in Rock Creek Cemetery in Washington, D.C. Austen was buried there, next to a plot that awaited Gore. Ironically, it was near the grave of Jimmie Trimble, Gore's enduring passion from the 1930s.

***

In his villa at La Rondinaia in 1996, **Gore Vidal**—"long after the winds of September have come and gone"— writes his final chapters in his luxurious villa.

Friends recalled that after Austen's death, Gore began a long decline, suffering through years of depression as he lapsed into alcoholism. He was a diabetic and that

"I had a feeling that I was trapped inside Proust's last chapter, where all the characters meet again, each aged in the extreme."

no doubt shortened his life. In time, he developed dementia.

When he would be lucid, he was still interested in politics. By 2008, he'd switched his allegiance from Hillary Clinton to Barack Obama, although he feared that an assassin would mow him down the way it had his long ago friend, John F. Kennedy, in 1963.

Confined to a wheelchair, Gore often relived his feuds with Truman Capote. He even relived his long, drawn-out libel case against William Buckley, Jr. He feared that his old right-wing antagonist had accumulated documentation attesting that he'd had occasional sex with underaged boys. Gore had made several trips to Bangkok and had praised how submissive young Thai boys were.

In retaliation, Gore's attorneys had accumulated data about Buckley having had homosexual relationships when in college. If Buckley had ever publicized details about Gore's sexual interactions with underage boys, Gore planned to air his evidence against Buckley.

He had long ago been forced to sell his villa in Ravello. He told Sarandon, "I spent my final night there bathed in tears. I can't live there again. Too many memories of Howard."

During his final visit to the Cedars-Sinai, a nurse remembered Gore's conversation:

"In 1950, I went to see Gloria Swanson playing Norma Desmond in *Sunset Blvd.*," he said. "Did you see it?"

"Never heard of it," the young nurse responded. "I've also never heard of any actress by that name."

"Well, I am now Norma Desmond myself," he said. "She wanted a 'return' to pictures. She detested the word 'comeback.' Well, my Norma Desmond is not seeking a comeback. Nor a return. I'm going away, never to return."

As his weight dropped, he continued his prodigious consumption of single malt Scotch. He began to drink the moment he got up, and was often still drinking at midnight.

His final three years were the worst, as he ended up weighing only ninety pounds. He developed what his doctors defined as Wernicke-Korsakoff syndrome.

[Also known as wet brain, Korsakoff's psychosis, and/or alcoholic encephalopathy, Wernicke–Korsakoff syndrome (WKS) is characterized by ocular disturbances, changes in mental state, unsteady stance and gait, apathy, inability to concentrate, and a decrease in awareness of the patient's immediate circumstances.]

As a result of this affliction, he became confused and at times, hallucinated. Fluid built up inside him, and doctors had to "drain" him almost daily near the end. He also suffered from congestive heart failure.

***

Back from the hospital, at his shadowy home in the Hollywood Hills, Gore Vidal, American man of letters, died at 6:45 PDT on July 31, 2012. He was sitting up in his living room.

Newspapers and TV stations in Europe and America hailed his passing, the *London Daily Telegraph* defining him as "an icy iconoclast who delighted in chronicling what he perceived as the disintegration of civilisation around him."

His close family members, including half-sister, Nina Straight, and his loyal nephew, Burr Steers, were shocked to discover that he'd left his estate, worth nearly $40 million, with more millions to come in the future, to Harvard University.

He'd once told friends, "I was supposed to go to Harvard, but I didn't. Instead, at seventeen, I went into the Army. There was this thing called World War II, a little skirmish we were having with the Nazis and the Japs."

His remains were placed alongside those of Howard Austen in Washington, D.C.'s Rock Creek Cemetery.

He'd once said, "The epitaph on my tombstone should read: 'America, love it or loathe it, you can never leave it or lose it.'"

Late In Life World-Views of the Pink Triangle:
Streetcars Named "Elysium"

TENNESSEE WILLIAMS

"I believe I said I am a furtive cat, unowned,
unknown, a scavenging sort of blackish alley cat
distinguished by a curve of white upturned
at each side of its mouth, which makes it seem to grin
denial of its eyes.
The negative: unhomed.
It is too intricate for me to say.
I can't explain.
If I reached out my hand its bones would break.
If I should call you back and you should turn
It would be useless, no, I can't explain.
My smile is meaningless, our meetings burn
and homelessness is long and cooling rain.
Do you understand? I can't explain..."

TRUMAN CAPOTE

"My eyes are tired and sad, and I am growing weary day by day. The world has grown stale like a piece of week-old bread left in an abandoned kitchen. Sunshine and laughter have faded from the world. What wicked delights my lovers, my armada of swans, and my loved ones once provided. So many of them are now dead, and I must rush to join them, to get the party going again."

GORE VIDAL

"In my fantasy, I dream of going back ot Rome in that rented penthouse on top of the decaying 17th-century Palacio Origo where Howard Austen and I lived for some thirty years. I had never had a proper human scale village life anywhere on Earth until I settled there. Literature? Two blocks to our north, back of the Pantheon, Thomas Mann lived and wrote *Buddenbrooks*. Nearby, George Eliot stayed at the Minerva Hotel. Ariosto lived in Pantheon Square; Stendhal was also close by. In that apartment, I wrote *Myra Breckinridge* in one month, one spring, from new moon to new moon. But I'm too weak to return.

The question remains. On that upcoming dark and stormy day, as thunder is heard across the skies of Los Angeles, will there be any real sadness at my funeral?"

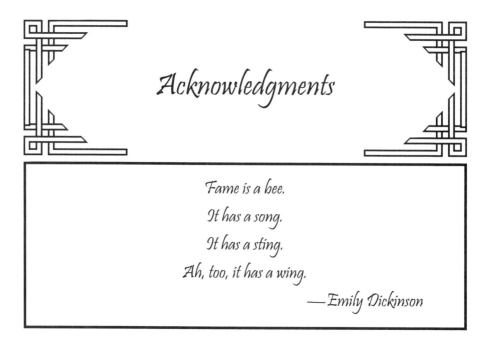

Acknowledgments

Fame is a bee.

It has a song.

It has a sting.

Ah, too, it has a wing.

—*Emily Dickinson*

Pink Triangle is dedicated to two exceptional men, **Frank Merlo** and **Stanley Mills Haggart**, both of whom I met one long ago winter's day in Key West, Florida, where I had been appointed as the young bureau chief of *The Miami Herald*.

Frank, in turn, introduced me to his longtime companion, Tennessee Williams. From that day, Frank and I bonded, and he invited me to virtually every party, premiere, or event revolving around Tennessee until Frank's early death.

When distinguished visitors came to Key West, Frank saw to it that I got to "hang out" with them in preparation for writing profiles on them. Guests flying in to confer with Tennessee in his heyday included some of the most flamboyant personalities in show biz—from Gloria Swanson to Marlon Brando, from Paul Newman to Geraldine Page.

In the early 1960s, after Frank and Tennessee separated, before Frank's death from lung cancer in a New York City hospital, he came to my home in Greenwich Village. There, he proposed that I write a memoir, with his help, about his experiences with Tennessee. Frank had been his companion during the most creative period of the playwright's life, an era when he created masterpieces which included *A Streetcar Named Desire* and *Cat on a Hot Tin Roof*.

Up until about a month before his death, Frank was still dictating his memoirs to me, but asked to stop the narrative when the topics addressed the collapse of his relationship with Tennessee. "I can't go on," he said weakly. "It's all too painful."

***

One of my first interviews in Key West was with a promising new playwright and novelist, **James Leo Herlihy**. He'd written a play, *Blue Denim,* on Broadway, and had just completed a nationwide tour of his latest play, *Crazy October,* starring Tallulah Bankhead and Joan Blondell, both of whom became friends of mine. Herlihy provided many insights for this book, years before he wrote his famous novel, *Midnight Cowboy,* which was filmed in 1969, winning an Oscar as Best Picture of the Year.

For years, Herlihy was my best friend. He introduced me to **Stanley Mills Haggart**, an author, art director for television commercials, and an awesome force in the arts and entertainment underground of Hollywood.

Stanley and his mother had arrived in Hollywood during its Silent Picture era, and got to know many of the players there, including both the friends and enemies of Greta Garbo, Charlie Chaplin, and later, Cary Grant and Randolph Scott. For years, he was a "leg man," and reporter, gathering secrets (many of which could not be printed back them) for Hedda Hopper's much-feared, widely syndicated newspaper column.

Until he died in 1980, I worked with Stanley in television advertising. In those days, movie stars shamelessly promoted commercial products, **Ronald Reagan** selling Arrow Shirts, **Eva Gabor** selling cigarettes, and **Joan Crawford** hawking Coca-Cola. *[Later, after she married Alfred Steele, Chairman of the Board at Pepsi, despite her preference for vodka, she switched soft drinks.]*

With Stanley, I created a series of travel guides to Europe that became known as the Frommer Guides, selling a few million copies.

Near the end of his life, Stanley had me ghost-write his memoirs, which eventually stretched out in a disorganized draft to five volumes, never submitted for publication. He'd known not only Tennessee, but Truman Capote and Gore Vidal. He'd become close friends of these writers in the immediate aftermath of World War II. He met them through a mutual friend, the diarist, **Anaïs Nin**. Although later, I got to know both Truman and Gore personally, for the purposes of this book I drew heavily on Stanley's revelations about Gore and Truman in the 1940s and 1950s.

Without the experiences of both Frank and Stanley, this book could not have been written—at least not with so much inside information into the writers' private lives.

I'm also deeply grateful to Key West resident and author **Donald Windham**, who had co-authored, with Tennessee, the play *You Touched Me!* in the early 1940s.

Three women in Tennessee's life offered invaluable information—**Marion Vaccaro, Maria St. Just**, and **Margaret Foresman**, the managing editor of *The Key West Citizen* before she came to live and work with me in New York.

Over the years, as I roamed the world doing research for Simon & Schuster, Prentice Hall, or any other entity then in control of the *Frommer Guides*, I encountered literally hundreds of people who had had some experience with Tennessee—everyone from movie stars, such as **Elizabeth Taylor** and **Richard Burton**, to hustlers and bartenders.

Countless others also had memories to share of Truman and Gore. Even if I couldn't use all their material, I did come across many revelations that made their way into this book. I can't mention all of those who contributed—some sources asked to remain anonymous—but my gratitude is extended.

There were, however, some people who were especially helpful because of their individual familiarity with one or even all three writers. I've singled them out for particular mention below:

Alvin Ailey (for his memories of *House of Flowers*); **Hermione Baddeley** (for her experience starring in *The Milk Train Doesn't Stop Here Anymore*); **Anne Bancroft** (a dear friend of long ago who shared her memories of both Broadway and Hollywood in the 1950s); **Tallulah Bankhead** (whose stories were always outrageous and fascinating); **Diana Barrymore** (a tragic, dear soul); **Barbara Baxley** (the female star of a film based on a novel I wrote and one of Tennessee's favorite actresses); **Anne Baxter** (for those long, soggy nights in Connecticut); **Ingrid Bergman** (who allowed me to visit her vacation home on an island in Sweden); **Lem Billings** (at the Garon/Brookes Literary Agency, JFK's best friend once discussed with me his hope of penning his memoirs); **Joan Blondell** (who was spontaneous and generous with her memories over extended periods in my home); **José Bolaños** (whom I first met in Puerto Vallarta); **Jane and Paul Bowles** (my friends when I lived in Tangier); **Marlon Brando** (who allowed me to show him "the hidden treasures" of Key West); **Montgomery Clift** (and especially his brother, **Brooks**); "Celebrity Seer" **John Cohan** (for his insider tips); **Noël Coward** (the information on this witty charmer came from **Greta Keller's** unpublished memoirs, which I ghost-authored); **Joan Crawford** (for our association during the period when she was promoting

Pepsi-Cola); **Candy Darling** (back when I was a frequent visitor to Andy Warhol's Factory); **Bette Davis** (who, to my knowledge, always spoke the truth, as devastating as it was); **Marlene Dietrich** (she told me only what she wanted to tell—and nothing else!); **Troy Donahue** (whom I met when the Hollywood parade had ended); **Tom Drake** (a gentle man ruined by Hollywood); **Mildred Dunnock** (a great actress and a great human being); **Jack Dunphy** (Truman was his favorite subject); **Carlos Fiore** (who knew most of Marlon Brando's secrets); **Frank Fontis**, Tennessee's Key West gardener and handyman, "a spy in the house of love"; actor **Robert Francis** (one of Gore's lovers who died before completing his life); **Ava Gardner** (my fellow Tarheel and a forever delight); **Tamara Geva** (a difficult friend, but a loyal one); my traveling companion in the Balearic Islands, **Dick Hanley** (for his memories of Elizabeth Taylor); **Gregory Hemingway** (for his remembrances of a brutal father); **William Inge** (my houseguest in Key West); **Christopher Isherwood** (who shared memories of all three writers, especially of Tennessee during his early days in Hollywood); my friend and neighbor **James Kirkwood** (who knew all three writers intimately); **Harold Lang** (for his relationship with Gore Vidal); **Guy Madison** (who, during our meetings in Thousand Oaks refused to let me ghost-write his memoirs—perhaps with good reason!); **Carson McCullers** (for her special, often provocative, insights into Tennessee and "that squeaky dwarf, Truman Capote"); **Anaïs Nin** (for her disapproving memories of Gore Vidal, and for the many times I was invited into her home in Greenwich Village); **Patrick O'Neal** (for his side of the story about the theatrical run of *Night of the Iguana);* **Anne Meacham** (for sharing details of those turbulent weeks she spent with Tennessee); and for my friend **Danny Stirrup** (for his shared memories of the early days, in the 1940s and 50s, of Tennessee and Frank Merlo's time together in Key West). I also owe a special debt of gratitude to the information relayed to me by Tennessee's long time literary agent, **Audrey Wood**. ("Marketing and coping with Tennessee was one bumpy ride," she said. "But what a thrilling experience it was.")

Most of all, I am grateful to my co-author, **Danforth Prince**, for the tireless months he spent reviewing mountains of data and researching the most minute details of what happened when. He's a marvelous young publisher and writer, a tireless researcher, who seems to know how to locate the "gold nuggets" in a field of stones.

Darwin Porter
January, 2014
New York City

Pink Triangle: Its Authors

DARWIN PORTER

As an intense and precocious nine-year-old, **Darwin Porter** began meeting movie stars, TV personalities, politicians, and singers through his vivacious and attractive mother, Hazel, a somewhat eccentric Southern girl who had lost her husband in World War II. Migrating from the depression-ravaged valleys of western North Carolina to Miami Beach during its most ebullient heyday, Hazel became a stylist, wardrobe mistress, and personal assistant to the vaudeville comedienne Sophie Tucker, the bawdy and irrepressible "Last of the Red Hot Mamas."

Virtually every show-biz celebrity who visited Miami Beach paid a call on "Miss Sophie," and Darwin as a pre-teen loosely and indulgently supervised by his mother, was regularly dazzled by the likes of Judy Garland, Dinah Shore, Veronica Lake, Linda Darnell, Martha Raye, and Ronald Reagan, who arrived to pay his respects to Miss Sophie with a young blonde starlet on the rise—Marilyn Monroe.

Hazel's work for Sophie Tucker did not preclude an active dating life: Her *beaux* included Richard Widmark, Victor Mature, Frank Sinatra (who "tipped" teenaged Darwin the then-astronomical sum of ten dollars for getting out of the way), and that alltime "second lead," Wendell Corey, when he wasn't emoting with Barbara Stanwyck and Joan Crawford.

As a late teenager, Darwin edited *The Miami Hurricane* at the University of Miami, where he interviewed Eleanor Roosevelt, Tab Hunter, Lucille Ball, and Adlai Stevenson. He also worked for Florida's then-Senator George Smathers, one of John F. Kennedy's best friends, establishing an ongoing pattern of picking up "Jack and Jackie" lore while still a student.

After graduation, as a journalist, he was commissioned with the opening of a bureau of *The Miami Herald* in Key West (Florida), where he took frequent morning walks with retired U.S. president Harry S Truman during his vacations in what had functioned as his "Winter White House." He also got to know, sometimes very well, various celebrities "slumming" their way through off-the-record holidays in the orbit of then-resident Tennessee Williams. Celebrities hanging out in the permissive arts environment of Key West during those days included Tallulah Bankhead, Cary Grant, Tony Curtis, the stepfather of Richard Burton, a gaggle of show-biz and publishing moguls, and the once-notorious stripper, Bettie Page.

For about a decade in New York, Darwin worked in television journalism and advertising with his long-time partner, the journalist, art director, and distinguished arts-industry socialite Stanley Mills Haggart. Jointly, they produced TV commercials starring such high-powered stars as Joan Crawford (then feverishly promoting Pepsi-Cola), Ronald Reagan (General Electric), and Debbie Reynolds (selling Singer Sewing Machines), along with such other entertainers as Louis Armstrong, Lena Horne, Arlene Dahl, and countless other show-biz personalities hawking commercial products.

During his youth, Stanley had flourished as an insider in early Hollywood as a "leg man" and source of information for Hedda Hopper, the fabled gossip columnist. When Stanley wasn't dishing newsy revelations with Hedda, he had worked as a Powers model; a romantic lead opposite Silent-era film star Mae Murray; the intimate companion of superstar Randolph Scott before Scott became emotionally involved with Cary Grant; and a man-about-town who archived gossip from everybody who mattered back when the movie colony was small, accessible, and confident that details about their tribal rites would absolutely never be reported in the press. Over the years, Stanley's vast cornucopia of inside Hollywood information was passed on to Darwin, who amplified it with copious interviews and research of his own.

After Stanley's death in 1980, Darwin inherited a treasure trove of memoirs, notes, and interviews detailing Stanley's early adventures in Hollywood, including in-depth recitations of scandals that even Hopper during her heyday was afraid to publish. Most legal and journalistic standards back then interpreted those oral histories as "unprintable." Times, of course, changed.

Beginning in the early 1960s, Darwin joined forces with the then-fledgling Arthur Frommer organization, playing a key role in researching and writing more than 50 titles and defining the style and values that later emerged as the world's leading travel accessories, The Frommer Guides, with particular emphasis on Europe, California, New England, and the Caribbean. Between the creation and updating of hundreds of editions of detailed travel guides to England, France, Italy, Spain, Portugal, Austria, Germany, California, and Switzerland, he continued to interview and discuss the triumphs, feuds, and frustrations of celebrities, many by then reclusive, whom he either sought out or encountered randomly as part of his extensive travels. Ava Gardner and Lana Turner were particularly insightful.

One day when Darwin lived in Tangier, he walked into an opium den to discover Marlene Dietrich sitting alone in a corner.

Darwin has also written several novels, including the best-selling cult classic *Butterflies in Heat* (which was later made into a film, *Tropic of Desire,* starring Eartha Kitt), *Venus* (inspired by the life of the fabled eroticist and diarist, Anaïs Nin), and *Midnight in Savannah,* a satirical overview of the sexual eccentricities of the Deep South inspired by Savannah's most notorious celebrity murder. He also transformed into literary format the details which he and Stanley Haggart had compiled about the relatively underpublicized scandals of the Silent Screen, releasing them in 2001 as *Hollywood's Silent Closet,* "an uncensored, underground history of Pre-Code Hollywood, loaded with facts and rumors from generations past." A few years later, he did the same for the country-western music industry when he issued *Rhinestone Country.*

Since then, Darwin has penned more than a dozen uncensored Hollywood biographies, many of them award-winners, on subjects who have included Marlon Brando; Merv Griffin; Katharine Hepburn; Howard Hughes; Humphrey Bogart; Michael Jackson; Paul Newman; Steve McQueen; Marilyn Monroe; Elizabeth Taylor; Frank Sinatra; John F. Kennedy; Vivien Leigh; Laurence Olivier; the well known porn star, Linda Lovelace; and all three of the fabulous Gabor sisters.

As a departure from his usual repertoire, Darwin also wrote the controversial *J. Edgar Hoover & Clyde Tolson: Investigating the Sexual Secrets of America's Most Famous Men and Women,* a book about celebrity, voyeurism, political and sexual repression, and blackmail within the highest circles of the U.S. government.

He has also co-authored, in league with Danforth Prince, four *Hollywood Babylon* anthologies, plus four separate volumes of film critiques, reviews, and commentary.

His biographies, over the years, have won more than 30 First Prize or runner-up awards at literary festivals in cities which include Boston, New York, Los Angeles, San Francisco, and Paris.

Darwin can be heard at regular intervals as a radio commentator (and occasionally on television), "dissing" celebrities, pop culture, politics, and scandal.

A resident of New York City, Darwin is currently at work on his latest biography: *Jacqueline Kennedy Onassis, A Life Beyond Her Wildest Dreams.*

DANFORTH PRINCE

The publisher and co-author of *Pink Triangle*, **Danforth Prince** is one of the "Young Turks" of the post-millennium, post-recession publishing industry. Today, he's president of Blood Moon Productions, a firm devoted to researching, salvaging, compiling, and marketing the oral histories of America's entertainment industry.

One of Prince's famous predecessors, the late Lyle Stuart (self-described as "the last publisher in America with guts") once defined Prince as "one of my natural successors." In 1956, that then-novice maverick launched himself with $8,000 he'd won in a libel judgment against gossip columnist Walter Winchell. It was Stuart who published Linda Lovelace's two authentic memoirs—*Ordeal* and *Out of Bondage.*

"I like to see someone following in my footsteps in the 21st Century," Stuart told Prince. "You publish scandalous biographies. I did, too. My books on J. Edgar Hoover, Jacqueline Kennedy Onassis, and Barbara Hutton stirred up the natives. You do, too."

Prince launched his career in journalism in the 1970s at the Paris Bureau of *The New York Times.* In the early '80s, he resigned to join Darwin Porter in researching, developing and publishing various titles within *The Frommer Guides*, jointly reviewing the travel scenes of more than 50 nations for Simon & Schuster. Authoritative and comprehensive, they were perceived as best-selling "travel bibles" for millions of readers, with recommendations and travel advice about the major nations of Western Europe, the Caribbean, Bermuda, The Bahamas, Georgia and the Carolinas, and California.

Prince, along with Porter, is also the co-author of several award-winning celebrity biographies, each configured as a title within Blood Moon's Babylon series. These have included *Hollywood Babylon—It's Back!; Hollywood Babylon Strikes Again; The Kennedys: All the Gossip Unfit to Print;* and *Frank Sinatra, The Boudoir Singer.* Prior to the publication of *Pink Triangle*, their most recent joint authorship venture was *Elizabeth Taylor: There Is Nothing Like a Dame.* Prince, with Porter, has also co-authored four separate volumes of film criticism.

674

Prince is the president and founder (in 1996) of the Georgia Literary Association, and of the Porter and Prince Corporation, founded in 1983, which has produced dozens of titles for both Prentice Hall and John Wiley & Sons. In 2011, he was named "Publisher of the Year" by a consortium of literary critics and marketers spearheaded by the J.M. Northern Media Group.

According to Prince, "Indeed, there are drudge aspects associated with any attempt to create a body of published work. But Blood Moon provides the luxurious illusion that a reader is a perpetual guest at some gossippy dinner party populated with brilliant but occasionally self-delusional figures from bygone eras of The American Experience. Blood Moon's success at salvaging, documenting, and articulating the (till now) orally transmitted histories of the Entertainment Industry, in ways that have never been seen before, is one of the most distinctive aspects of our backlist."

Publishing in collaboration with the National Book Network (www.NBN-Books.com), he has electronically documented some of the controversies associated with his stewardship of Blood Moon in more than 40 videotaped documentaries, book trailers, public speeches, and TV or radio interviews. Any of these can be watched, without charge, by performing a search for "Danforth Prince" on **YouTube.com**, checking him out on **Facebook** (either "Danforth Prince" or "Blood Moon Productions), on **Twitter** (#BloodyandLunar) or by clicking on **BloodMoonProductions.com**.

During the rare moments when he isn't writing, editing, neurosing about, or promoting Blood Moon, he works out at a New York City gym, rescues stray animals, talks to strangers, and regularly attends Episcopal Mass every Sunday.

INDEX

678

680

681

683

686

687

688

Meredith, Burgess 108, 252, 253
Merivale, Jack 526
Merlin, Oliver 400
Merlo, Frank 40, 98, 124, 128, 145, 151,
  155, 156, 189, 197-198, 199, 210, 221,
  224, 226, 227, 230, 233, 234, 235, 239,
  240, 241, 242, 270, 271, 280, 313, 315,
  320, 329, 333, 336, 338, 360, 370, 420,
  424, 451, 492, 514, 518, 523, 529, 531,
  533, 548, 549, 556, 583, 584, 585, 656,
  662
Merman, Ethel 292, 294
Merrick, David 323, 339, 340, 342, 343, 496,
  589, 636
Merrill, Gary 405, 413, 414, 415, 553, 555
Merrill, James 4
Merry Widow, The 549
Messel, Oliver 362, 363
Mexican Mural 87
MGM 121, 256, 389, 391, 427, 428, 435,
  467, 468, 469, 470, 474, 536, 539, 543
Miami Herald, The 40, 587
Miami-Dade Women's Detention Center 503
Michener, James 631
Midnight Cowboy 200, 442
Midsummer Night's Dream, A 83, 486
Mildred Pierce 341
Miles, Joana 123
Miles, Sylvia 243, 321, 559, 598
Milk Train Doesn't Stop Here Anymore, The
  238, 240, 321, 333, 336, 337, 338, 342,
  343, 516, 544, 578, 589
Miller, Arthur 129, 455, 484, 490, 491, 492,
  551
Miller, Jonathan 32
Milne, Tom 289
Milton, New York 38
Mineo, Sal 215, 238, 379, 380, 381, 383,
  392, 398, 474
Minnelli, Liza 49, 160, 660
Miracle of Morgan's Creek 408
Miriam 5
Mirren, Helen 640, 643
Misfits, The 492
Mishima, Yukio 461
Mitchell, Arthur 364
Mitchell, James 401
Mitchum, Robert 495
Miyako Hotel (Kyoto, Japan) 460
Moby Dick 233
Mogambo 230
Mohave 648
Mommie Dearest 28, 122
Monroe, Marilyn 126, 130, 320, 325, 423,
  432, 442, 448, 449, 454, 476, 477, 479,
  482, 484, 486, 489, 491, 493, 495, 498,
  508, 513, 515, 571, 587

Montagu, Judy 145
Montague, Edward 143
Montez, Maria 388, 614, 626
Montgomery, Elizabeth 398
Montgomery, Robert 35
Montparnasse Cemetery (Paris) 510
"Moon River" 496
Moore, Marianne 67
Moore, Mary Tyler 496
Moore, Roger 54
Moorehead, Agnes 398, 477
Morgan, Evan (2nd Viscount Tredegar) 215,
  216, 217
Morgan, Ted 310
Moriarty, Michael 123
Morley, Robert 86, 348, 350, 352
Morley, Sheridan 257
Moseley, Roy 269
Motion Picture Production Code 456
Moulin Rouge (1952) 347
Mr. Norris Changes Trains 49
Mrs. Miniver 469
Mulligan, Robert 286
Muni, Paul 206
Munn, Michael 598
Murder by Death 165, 166
Murder, Inc. 490
Murphy, Audie 285, 289
Murphy, George 413
Murray, Don 546
Murray, Mae 549
Murrow, Edward R. 391
Muses Are Heard, The 460
Mushy Callahan's Gym 313
Mussolini, Benito 140
Mutiny on the Bounty 464
My Fair Lady 628, 634
My Mother's Keeper 414
My Story 478
Myra Breckinridge 176, 354, 443, 578, 614,
  615, 616, 618, 623, 624, 626, 643
Myron 626
Nabokov, Vladimir 577
Nabuco, Carolina 418
Nacional Hotel (Havana) 500
Nader, George 394, 395
Naked and the Dead, The 2, 299
Naked Lunch 212, 297
Naked Men: Pioneering Nudes 1935-1955.
  60
Nathan, George Jean 114, 115
Nation, The 184
National Book Award 611
National Legion of Decency 100
National Republican Convention (1940) 223
National Velvet 581
Natwick, Mildred 359

691

694

697

698

BLOOD MOON PRODUCTIONS

Entertainment About How America Interprets Its Celebrities

Blood Moon Productions is a New York based publishing enterprise dedicated to researching, salvaging, and indexing the oral histories of America's entertainment industry.

Reorganized with its present name in 2004, Blood Moon originated in 1997 as the Georgia Literary Association, a vehicle for the promotion of obscure writers from America's Deep South. For many years, Blood Moon was a key player in the writing, research, and editorial functions of THE FROMMER GUIDES, the most respected name in travel publishing.

Blood Moon maintains a back list of at least 30 critically acclaimed biographies, film guides, and novels. Its titles are distributed by the National Book Network (www.NBNBooks.com), and through secondary wholesalers and online retailers everywhere.

Since 2004, Blood Moon has been awarded dozens of nationally recognized literary prizes. They've included both silver and bronze medals from the IPPY (Independent Publishers Assn.) Awards; four nominations and two Honorable Mentions for BOOK OF THE YEAR from Foreword Reviews; nominations from The Ben Franklin Awards; and Awards and Honorable Mentions from the New England, the Los Angeles, the Paris, the New York, and the San Francisco Book Festivals. Two of its titles have been Grand Prize Winners for Best Summer Reading, as defined by The Beach Book Awards, and in 2013, its triple-play overview of the Gabor sisters was designated as Biography of the Year by the Hollywood Book Festival.

For more about us, including access to a growing number of videotaped book trailers and public addresses, each accessible via **YouTube.com.** (Search for key words "Danforth Prince" or "Blood Moon Productions.")

Or click on **WWW.BLOODMOONPRODUCTIONS.COM;** visit our page on Facebook; subscribe to us on Twitter (#BloodyandLunar); or refer to the pages which immediately follow.

Thanks for your interest, best wishes, and happy reading.

Danforth Prince, President
Blood Moon Productions, Ltd.
January, 2014

INSIDE LINDA LOVELACE'S DEEP THROAT

DEGRADATION, PORNO CHIC, AND THE RISE OF FEMINISM

DARWIN PORTER

A Bronx-born brunette, the notorious Linda Lovelace was the starry-eyed Catholic daughter in the 1950s of a police officer who nicknamed her "Miss Holy Holy." Twenty years later, she became the most notorious actress of the 20th century.

She'd fallen in love with a tough ex-Marine, Chuck Traynor, and eventually married him, only to learn that she had become his meal ticket. He forced her at gunpoint into a role as a player within hardcore porn, including a 1971 bestiality film entitled *Dogarama.*

Her next film, shot for $20,000, was released in 1972 as *Deep Throat.* It became the largest grossing XXX-rated flick of all time, earning an estimated $750 million and still being screened all over the world. The fee she was paid was $1,200, which her husband confiscated. The sexy 70s went wild for the film. Porno chic was born, with Linda as its centerpiece.

Traynor, a sadist, pimped his wife to celebrities, charging them $2,000 per session, It became a status symbol to commission an "individualized" film clip of Linda performing her specialty. Clients included Elvis Presley, Frank Sinatra, Milton Berle, Desi Arnaz, Marlon Brando, William Holden, Peter Lawford, and Burt Lancaster. The Mafia had found its most lucrative business—pornography—since Prohibition.

After a decade of being assaulted, beaten, and humiliated, Linda, in 1980, underwent a "Born Again" transformation. She launched her own feminist anti-pornography movement, attracting such activists as Gloria Steinem, and scores of other sex industry professionals who refuted their earlier careers.

Critics claimed that Linda's *Deep Throat* changed America's sexual attitudes more than anything since the first Kinsey report in 1948, that she super-charged the feminist movement, and that to some degree, she re-defined the nation's views on obscenity.

The tragic saga of Linda Lovelace changed beliefs about entertainment, morality, and feminism in America. This book tells you what the movie doesn't.

Darwin Porter, author of more than a dozen critically acclaimed celebrity exposés of behind-the-scenes intrigue in the entertainment industry, was deeply involved in the Linda Lovelace saga as it unfolded in the 70s, interviewing many of the players, and raising money for the legal defense of the film's co-star, Harry Reems. In this book, he brings inside information and a never-before-published revelation on almost every page.

The Most Comprehensive Biography of an Adult Entertainment Star Ever Written
Softcover, 640 pages, 6"x9", with hundreds of photos. ISBN 978-1-936003-33-4

Darwin Porter's saga of power and corruption has a revelation on every page—cross dressing, gay parties, sexual indiscretions, hustlers for sale, alliances with the Mafia, and criminal activity by the nation's chief law enforcer.

It's all here, with chilling details about the abuse of power on the dark side of the American saga. But mostly it's the decades-long love story of America's two most powerful men who could tell presidents "how to skip rope." (Hoover's words.)

Winner of 2012 literary awards from the **Los Angeles** and the **Hollywood Book Festivals**

"EVERYONE'S DREDGING UP J. EDGAR HOOVER. Leonardo DiCaprio just immortalized him, and now comes Darwin Porter's paperback, *J. Edgar Hoover & Clyde Tolson: Investigating the Sexual Secrets of America's Most Famous Men and Women.*

It shovels Hoover's darkest secrets dragged kicking and screaming from the closet. It's filth on every VIP who's safely dead and some who are still above ground."

—**Cindy Adams, The New York Post**

"This book is important, because it destroys what's left of Hoover's reputation. Did you know he had intel on the bombing of Pearl Harbor, but he sat on it, making him more or less responsible for thousands of deaths? Or that he had almost nothing to do with the arrests or killings of any of the 1930s gangsters that he took credit for catching?

"A lot of people are angry with its author, Darwin Porter. They say that his outing of celebrities is just cheap gossip about dead people who can't defend themselves. I suppose it's because Porter is destroying carefully constructed myths that are comforting to most people. As gay men, we benefit the most from Porter's work, because we know that except for AIDS, the closet was the most terrible thing about the 20th century. If the closet never existed, neither would Hoover. The fact that he got away with such duplicity under eight presidents makes you think that every one of them was a complete fool for tolerating it."

—**Paul Bellini, FAB Magazine (Toronto)**

J. EDGAR HOOVER AND CLYDE TOLSON

Investigating the Sexual Secrets of America's Most Famous Men and Women
Darwin Porter
Temporarily sold out of hard copies, but available for E-Readers. ISBN 978-1-936003-25-9

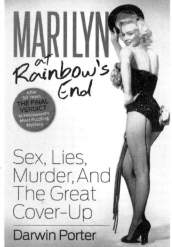

Damn You,
Scarlett O'Hara
The Private Lives of **Vivien Leigh**
and **Laurence Olivier**

by **Darwin Porter** and **Roy Moseley**

Scarlett O'Hara, in Love with Heathcliff, Together on the Road to Hell

Here, for the first time, is a biography that raises the curtain on the secret lives of **Lord Laurence Olivier**, often cited as the finest actor in the history of England, and **Vivien Leigh,** who immortalized herself with her Oscar-winning portrayals of Scarlett O'Hara in *Gone With the Wind,* and as Blanche DuBois in Tennessee Williams' *A Streetcar Named Desire.*

Dashing and "impossibly handsome," Laurence Olivier was pursued by the most dazzling luminaries, male and female, of the movie and theater worlds.

Lord Olivier's beautiful and brilliant but emotionally disturbed wife (Viv to her lovers) led a tumultuous off-the-record life whose paramours ranged from the A-list celebrities to men she selected randomly off the street. But none of the brilliant roles depicted by Lord and Lady Olivier, on stage or on screen, ever matched the power and drama of personal dramas which wavered between Wagnerian opera and Greek tragedy. *Damn You, Scarlett O'Hara* is the definitive and most revelatory portrait ever published of the most talented and tormented actor and actress of the 20th century.

Darwin Porter is the principal author of this seminal work.

Roy Moseley, this book's co-author, was an intimate friend of both Lord and Lady Olivier, maintaining a decades-long association with the famous couple, nurturing them through triumphs, emotional breakdowns, and streams of suppressed scandal. A resident of California who spent most of his life in England, Moseley has authored or co-authored biographies of Queen Elizabeth and Prince Philip, Rex Harrison, Cary Grant, Merle Oberon, Roger Moore, and Bette Davis.

"Damn You, Scarlett O'Hara can be a dazzling read, the prose unmannered and instantly digestible. The authors' ability to pile scandal atop scandal, seduction after seduction, can be impossible to resist."
—THE WASHINGTON TIMES

DAMN YOU, SCARLETT O'HARA
THE PRIVATE LIFES OF LAURENCE OLIVIER AND VIVIEN LEIGH

Darwin Porter and Roy Moseley

ISBN 978-1-936003-15-0   Hardcover, 708 pages, with about a hundred photos and hundreds of insights into the London Theatre, the role of the Oliviers in the politics of World War II, and the passion and fury of their life together as actors in Hollywood.
Also available for E-Readers

PAUL NEWMAN
THE MAN BEHIND THE BABY BLUES
HIS SECRET LIFE EXPOSED

Hardcover, 520 pages, with dozens of photos. ISBN 978-0-9786465-1-6

Also available for E-readers

Darwin Porter

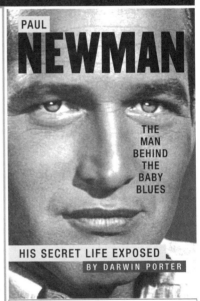

COMPLETELY UNVARNISHED, THIS IS THE MOST COURAGEOUS AND COMPELLING BIOGRAPHY OF THE ICONIC ACTOR EVER PUBLISHED.

Drawn from firsthand interviews with insiders who knew Paul Newman intimately, and compiled over a period of nearly a half-century, this is the world's most honest and most revelatory biography about Hollywood's pre-eminent male sex symbol, with dozens of potentially shocking revelations.

Whereas the situations it exposes were widely known within Hollywood's inner circles, they've never before been revealed to the general public.

If you're a fan of Newman (and who do you know who isn't) you really should look at this book. It's a respectful but candid cornucopia of once-concealed information about the sexual and emotional adventures of a workaday actor as he evolved into a major star.

"One wonders how he ever managed to avoid public scrutiny for so long."

THIS BOOK IS ABOUT A FAMOUS, FULL-TIME RESIDENT OF CONNECTICUT. SHORTLY AFTER NEWMAN'S DEATH IN 2009, IT WON AN HONORABLE MENTION FROM HIS NEIGHBORS AT THE NEW ENGLAND BOOK FESTIVAL

Paul Newman was a potent, desirable, and ambiguous sex symbol, a former sailor from Shaker Heights, Ohio, who parlayed his ambisexual charm and extraordinary good looks into one of the most successful careers in Hollywood.

It's all here, as recorded by celebrity chronicler Darwin Porter--the giddy heights and agonizing lows of a great American star, with revelations and insights never published in any other biography.

706

LOVE TRIANGLE
RONALD REAGAN, JANE WYMAN, & NANCY DAVIS
All the Gossip Unfit to Print / Available November 2014

Most of the world remembers Ronald Reagan and Nancy (Davis) Reagan as geriatric figures in the White House in the 1980s. And it remembers Jane Wyman as the fierce empress, Angela Channing, in the decade's hit TV series, *Falcon Crest*.

But long before that, two young wannabee stars, Ronald Reagan and Jane Wyman, had arrived in Hollywood as untested hopefuls. Separately, they stormed Warner Brothers, looking for movie stardom and love—and finding both beyond their wildest dreams. They were followed, in time, by Nancy Davis, who began her career posing for cheesecake in a failed attempt by the studio to turn her into a sex symbol.

In their memoirs, Ronald and Nancy (Jane didn't write one) paid scant attention to their "wild and wonderful years" in Hollywood. To provide that missing link in their lives, Blood Moon's *Love Triangle* explores in depth the trio's passions, furies, betrayals, loves won and lost, and the conflicts and rivalries they generated.

A liberal New Deal Democrat, Reagan quickly became a handsome leading man in "B" pictures and a "babe magnet." Reagan himself admitted he developed "Leading Lady-itis" even for stars he didn't appear with.

He launched a bevy of affairs with such glamorous icons as Lana Turner, Betty Grable and Susan Hayward, even a "too young" Elizabeth Taylor.

He eventually married Jane, but he was not faithful to her, enjoying back alley affairs with the likes of "The Oomph Girl," Ann Sheridan. Jane, too, had her affairs on the side, notably with Lew Ayres (Ginger Rogers' ex) while filming her Oscar-winning *Johnny Belinda*.

After dumping Reagan, Jane launched a series of affairs herself, battling Joan Crawford (for Hollywood's most studly and newsworthy attorney, Greg Bautzer); and Marilyn Monroe (for bandleader Fred Karger, marrying him, divorcing him, marrying him again, and finally divorcing him for good.)

Reagan's oldest son, Michael (adopted), later said, "If Nancy knew that one day she would be First Lady, she would have cleaned up her act." He was referring to her notorious days as a starlet in the late 1940s and early 50s, when the grapevine had it: "her phone number was passed around a lot." The list of her intimate involvements is long, including Clark Gable, whom she wanted to marry; Spencer Tracy; Yul Brynner; Frank Sinatra; Marlon Brando; Milton Berle; Peter Lawford; Robert Walker; et al.

Love Triangle, a proud and presidential addition to Blood Moon's Babylon series, digs deep into what these three young movie stars were up to decades before two of them took over the Free World.

LOVE TRIANGLE: RONALD REAGAN, JANE WYMAN, & NANCY DAVIS ALL THE GOSSIP UNFIT TO PRINT. Darwin Porter and Danforth Prince

A hot, scandalous paperback available in November, 2014. Biography/Entertainment 6" x 9" 520 pages with hundreds of photos ISBN 978-1-936003-41-9